Memory Systems and Pipelined Processors

Jones and Bartlett Books in Computer Science

Arthur J. Bernstein and Philip M. Lewis
Concurrency in Programming and Database Systems

Robert L. Causey
Logic, Sets, and Recursion

K. Mani Chandy and Stephen Taylor
An Introduction to Parallel Programming

Harvey G. Cragon
Memory Systems and Pipelined Processors

Michael J. Flynn
Computer Architecture: Pipelined and Parallel Processor Design

John Gregory and Don Redmond
Introduction to Numerical Analysis

James Hein
Discrete Structures, Logic, and Computability

E. Stewart Lee
Algorithms and Data Structures in Computer Engineering

Christopher H. Nevison, Daniel C. Hyde, G. Michael Schneider, and Paul T. Tymann, Editors
Laboratories for Parallel Computing

Charles Van Loan
An Introduction to Computational Science and Mathematics

Henry M. Walker
The Limits of Computing

3 Speculative operations, performed until a choice of path can be determined, will in most cases improve performance.

> Examples are found in late select caches, speculative execution of instructions while waiting for a branch to be resolved, and concurrent speculative address translation in a virtual memory system. Optimistic synchronization is another example of a speculative operation.

4 With concurrency and speculative operations, special control and record-keeping structures are required for undoing operations that are not continued and must be abandoned.

> Providing precise interrupts in a pipelined processor and undoing early state changes of unused speculatively executed instructions are examples.

Memory Systems
and Pipelined Processors

Harvey G. Cragon

The University of Texas at Austin

Jones and Bartlett Publishers

Sudbury, Massachusetts

Boston   London   Singapore

Editorial, Sales, and Customer Service Offices
Jones and Bartlett Publishers
One Exeter Plaza
Boston, MA 02116
1-800-832-0034
617-859-3900

Jones and Bartlett Publishers International
7 Melrose Terrace
London W6 7RL
England

Library of Congress Cataloging-in-Publication Data

Cragon, Harvey G.
    Memory systems and pipelined processors / Harvey G. Cragon.
        p.   cm.
    Includes bibliographical references and index.
    ISBN 0-86720-474-5
    1. Computers, Pipeline.   2. Computer storage devices.   I. Title.
QA76.5.C68   1995
004.25'6--dc20   95-22155
                                                                        CIP

Acquistions Editor: Carl Hesler
Production Editor: Anne S. Noonan
Manufacturing Buyer: Dana L. Cerrito
Editorial Production Service: Superscript Editorial Production Services
Typesetting: Scanway Graphics International
Printing and Binding: Braun-Brumfield
Cover Design: Beth Santos
Cover Printing: John P. Pow Company

Printed in the United States of America
99 98 97 96 95   10 9 8 7 6 5 4 3 2 1

Contents

Preface

Every difficulty slurred over will be a ghost to disturb your sleep.

— Chopin

The greatest difficulties lie where we are not looking for them.

— Johann Wolfgang von Goethe

The widespread demand for high-performance personal computers and workstations has stimulated a renaissance in computer design. VLSI permits many millions of transistors to be placed on a chip that will sell for a few hundred of dollars. The two forces of demand and low cost combine to stimulate innovative designers to revisit old schemes and devise new ones to satisfy the ever-increasing demands for more performance. The performance of microprocessors has increased at a compound rate of about 30 percent per year over the last decade. Positive feedback is supporting the demand for more performance; new software systems require more processor performance, while more processor performance permits more complex software systems. Many of the techniques discussed in this book had their birth in mainframe and supercomputer designs. However, with the success of the microprocessor, the architecture of large mainframe class computers is being brought into question.

This book describes and discusses the design details of high-speed memory systems and pipeline processors that underpin the modern microprocessor. I undertook the project of writing this book for several closely related reasons. First, I believed that there was a need for a graduate level course on the nitty-gritty details of computer system implementation and I could find no suitable text. A compendium of the implementation techniques used today by many designers has not been collected into one book. In addition, I wanted the experience, over a period of a few years, of collecting, reading, and interpreting the literature in this important field.

While reading the early literature on processor implementation, I found that the implementation techniques used by the pioneers are continually recycled into new designs. For example, queues, first used in some of the very early machines, are being used in processors such as the Pentium and PowerPC 601. Although this book is focused on uniprocessors, it is impossible to ignore the problems of coherency and synchronization, problems usually associated with parallel processors.

The material presented in this book is found in the open literature and in manufacturers' processor manuals. I have not used material that is unavailable to any student or researcher; however, the open literature contains much duplication and extraneous material that this book attempts to eliminate. On a discouraging note, much implementation detail of contemporary processors is not revealed by manufacturers without a nondisclosure agreement. Such an agreement is not possible when writing a textbook and thus there are unfortunate gaps. Because of competitive pressures, a manufacturer will disclose an overview of a processor in a conference followed later by various product manuals. The details of a processor unfold over a period of time after its introduction. For these reasons, some of the relevant details of a processor may be missing or incorrectly described in this book.

Because of the close tie between the memory and the processor and the commonality of a number of concepts, I believe that these two subjects should be treated together in one book. This text is intended for a one-semester graduate course for students who have either experience in processor and/or memory architecture or who have taken an undergraduate course in computer architecture or organization. The student should be conversant with the general ideas behind memory systems and pipelining. This book assembles the relevant information on memory systems and pipelined processors, and the references will lead a reader to the historical and contemporary literature on the topics discussed. This book examines the broad sweep of design issues and their historical precedence along with extensive references to specific topics. Care has been taken to reference the first mention of a topic so that students can gain an appreciation of the contributions made by the early researchers and understand the development patterns that lead to the systems of today. Unfortunately the search for a first reference to a given topic has not, in all cases, been successful.

Many advanced computer texts used in graduate courses cover a wide spectrum of topics in only medium depth. I have attempted to dig a small deep hole rather than a wide shallow one. Professionals in industry should find this text helpful as it presents an in-depth look at the many details of memory and pipelined processors that are not found in a single text.

Although the two topics of memory systems and pipelined processors are closely related, this text starts with memory systems based on the assumption that students have sufficient background in pipelined processors to appreciate the need for low latency and high bandwidth. Forward and backward references point to more detailed discussions of a topic that is being treated lightly.

This book addresses only a few of the design issues of multiprocessors. The student needs a firm understanding of uniprocessor design before multiprocessor design problems can be effectively addressed. Nevertheless, this book will, in several places, note the similarities between the problems of overlap in memory systems and pipeline processors and the problems with multiprocessors. Thus, the student, having been exposed to these problems in the uniprocessor domain, should be better able to understand and pursue research in multiprocessors.

Designers strive both to create processors that can execute programs in the shortest possible time and to achieve a balance between the speed of the processor and the available bandwidth and latency of the memory. This goal was important with the von Neumann architecture and is important today with the most recently announced RISC processors. Interleaved memory, hierarchical memory, and pipeline processors were first employed in high-performance supercomputers and mainframes. With the continued increase in circuit density available in VLSI devices, these memory systems and piplines have been used in microprocessors and are commonly integrated on the same chip. Thus, it is appropriate to combine in one book the salient design issues of memory and pipelines.

A recurring idea in this book concerns the abundant use of tags and control bits in the internal structure of the processor that are not a part of the instruction set architecture. In nonoverlapped processors most of the processor resources are explicitly controlled by the executing instructions. With overlap, additional resources are added to the processor that are not visible to the programmer. These resources, and the data they contain, are controlled by tags of various kinds [MALI89]. Tags perform a number of functions: They identify and route data, indicate validity, provide protection, and perform some control functions. These tags and control bits are usually not program accessible and contribute to the rich context of a process that must be managed, preserved, and, in some cases, carefully destroyed.

One of the goals of this book is to explain the techniques for managing the resources that are not visible to the program. Another goal of this book is to provide not only narrative descriptions of subjects but also analytical models and examples that can be used to make design tradeoffs. Published peformance results are compared to the models' results when it is possible.

The first section of this book covers memory systems. Chapter 1 addresses the two design goals of a memory system: low latency and high bandwidth. The approaches to providing these characteristics, hierarchical and interleaved memories, are briefly addressed. Chapter 2 starts the description of hierarchical memory by describing cache techniques and specific cache designs. Cache design issues, such as organization and performance, are described with illustrations of specific implemented cache. Chapter 3 addresses virtual memory, giving a rationale for virtual memory, organizations, and performance tradeoff issues. A number of references are made to operating systems; however, detailed discussions of operating systems are outside the scope of this book. Chapter 4 discusses the complementary issues of cache addressing with either real or virtual addresses and coherency maintenance in all memory spaces of a computer when input/output is involved. Chapter 5 completes the treatment of memory with a discussion of interleaved memory and disk systems. These two topics are important in the total memory hierarchy and virtual memory.

The second section of this book covers pipelined processors. Chapter 6 describes the general notions of pipelining with pipeline performance models. Partitioning, clock distribution, and atomic instructions are some of the issues discussed. Chapter 7 describes the issues involved in branching. A major detriment to pipeline performance is control transfers or branches. Branch strategies for pipelined proccssors and their performance models are discussed. Chapter 8 addresses the issues of dependencies, conflict detection, and resolution. Pipelined processors operate with a high degree of concurrency that leads to potential dependencies and conflicts. These problems require special design considerations in order to preserve the sequential model of computation. The chapter describes all of the techniques known to me for solving these problems. Chapter 9 describes the issues of exceptions and interrupts in pipelined processors. Solutions to the precise interrupt problem can hurt the performance of dependency resolution solutions. Thus, the design of these two facilities is closely integrated in real machines. However, for expository reasons, these two subjects are treated separately with references between the chapters.

Chapter 10 addresses the topics of superpipelined, superscalar, and very long instruction word processors. Performance models are presented to assist in the evaluation of design alternatives. Chapter 11 assembles many of the topics of pipelining found in vector processors. The rational for vector processors is discussed, along with performance models and benchmark performance of real machines.

As noted previously, this text combines both the historical and contemporary ideas on memory systems and pipelined processor implementation. Undoubtedly, I have missed some relevant information and some of the material has been misinterpreted. For those errors of omission and commission, I take full responsibility.

1

Memory Systems

1.0 Overview

There are many models that are used to evaluate the performance of a processor. One of the most insightful, the model for the time required to execute a task, is

task time = number of instructions executed × clocks per instruction (CPI) × clock period.

The number of instructions executed is usually a function of the instruction set design and is outside the scope of this book, but the second and third terms are the subject of this book. The design of the memory system and the pipeline processor have a direct bearing on the CPI that can be realized from a processor. As will be pointed out, there are CPI design considerations that affect the clock period; the CPI can be reduced at the expense of a longer clock and otherwise. The important metric is the product of these two terms, not their individual values. The interactions between the memory system and the processor will be evident as each of these major subfunctions is described.

The performance of a computer depends in large measure on the interface between the processor and memory. If this interface is not correct, a significant increase in CPI can result. The processor makes demands upon the memory for instructions and data, and this demand must be satisfied in order to realize the full potential of the processor. The following two quotes from [FLYN66] detail two parameters of the memory that are important.

Latency or latent period is the total time associated with the processing (from excitation to response) of a particular data unit at a phase in the computing process.

1

	SPARC Integer	SPARC Floating Point	MIPS Integer	MIPS Floating Point	IBM S/360	VAX	AVERAGE
Instruction	0.79	0.80	0.76	0.77	0.50	0.65	0.71
Data read	0.15	0.17	0.15	0.19	0.35	0.28	0.22
Data write	0.06	0.03	0.09	0.04	0.15	0.07	0.07

TABLE 1.1 Memory reference distribution.

Bandwidth is an expression of the time rate of occurrence. In particular, computational or execution bandwidth is the number of instructions processed per second, and storage bandwidth is the retrieval rate of operand and operation memory words (words/second).

The techniques used to provide low-latency and high-bandwidth memory for a processor depend heavily upon the nature of the references made to the memory by the processor. Table 1.1 shows the fraction of memory references classified as Instruction Fetch, Data Read, and Data Write for a number of processors. Notice that instruction fetches represent between 50% and 80% of all references. Data reads represent 15% to 35% of all references, while data writes represent less than 10% for all processors other than the IBM S/360.

The implication of these reference statistics is that the priorities of a memory system design are: first the instruction fetches, second the data reads, and last the data writes. The obvious solution to the problem of providing both low latency and high bandwidth is to use higher performance memory devices. However, the history of increasing the bandwidth of memory devices (circuits) over a ten-year period is not encouraging. Published data from the International Solid State Circuits Conference provide normalized information on the reduction of access times of dynamic RAMS and static RAMS shown in Figure 1.1.

Note that while clock periods have decreased by a factor of approximately 23 (a reduction of 27% per year over the last decade), SRAM cycle times have decreased by only a factor of 18 (a reduction of 25% per year) and DRAMS by a factor of 13 (a reduction of 23% per year). These data show that memory performance increases have not kept pace with reductions in processor clock periods.

One conclusion from the data of Figure 1.1 is that the required decrease in latency and the increase in memory bandwidth have come, and will continue to come, not from improved memory technology but from improved memory system design. Memory performance will probably continue to lag processor clock cycle-time improvements, and more processor concurrency will further increase the demand on memory. Thus

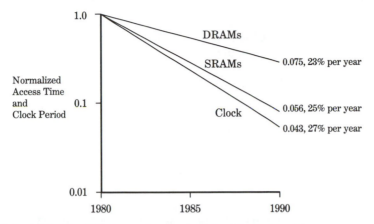

FIGURE 1.1   Memory and processor cycle-time improvements.

innovative memory architectures are mandatory if processor performance is to continue to increase.

The need for increased memory performance has occurred in a period
of significant memory cost decreases. Memory costs have been decreasing
dramatically since the early commercial computers. A 1-M byte of add-
on memory for IBM S/360 computers cost $1M in 1965! In 1994, a 1-M
byte of memory for a personal computer costs approximately $50; a
dramatic cost reduction of approximately 20,000-fold.

The relative cost relationship between fast and slow memory
components has remained relatively constant over this period and
can be expressed by Grosch's Law [GROS53]. This law is an empirical
observation that states "giving added economy only as the square root
of the increase in speed—that is, to do a calculation ten times as cheaply
you must do it one hundred times as fast." The converse has often been
stated as if you double the price of a computer or computer component,
the performance will increase by a factor of four. Grosch's law can be
confirmed by noting the relative cost and performance of SRAM and
DRAM chips. Note that Grosch's law, as posited, applies over time and
does not consider learning-curve effects. However, the law is frequently
applied to one time period as when looking at members of a computer
family.

The ideal memory for a computer would be one that removes the
memory bandwidth and latency constraints. Such a memory would have
zero access and cycle time (zero latency and infinite bandwidth), be of
infinite size, and have zero cost. Obviously, we will never have such an
ideal memory. Over three decades, designers have attempted to approach the zero latency of this ideal memory by the architectural path
of a memory hierarchy.

The following two sections introduce the issues of supplying low-

Latency Clocks per Instructions	Normalized Performance
0.0	1.00
0.2	0.83
0.4	0.71
0.6	0.62
0.8	0.55
1.0	0.50

Note: Basic CPI = 1.

TABLE 1.2   The effect of memory latency on processor performance.

latency and high-bandwidth memory. Chapters 2, 3, and 4 give details of low-latency memory in the forms of caches and virtual memory. Chapter 5 describes the techniques for providing high-bandwidth memory using interleaved low-bandwidth memory components.

1.1 Memory Latency

The issue of memory latency is quite important with regard to pipelined processors. Consider the effect of memory latency on VAX 11/780 performance. If this processor had a perfect memory, with a bandwidth of one clock per reference and no additional latency, an instruction execution would take approximately 9.5 clocks. Actual memory latency adds approximately 0.5 clocks, giving a CPI of approximately 10 clocks, which is an increase in the CPI of approximately 5%. However, with a pipelined processor that may have a CPI of 1.5 with a one cycle memory, 0.5 additional clocks (1 clock is accounted for in the basic CPI figure) represent a 33% increase in CPI. The reason latency is important is that when a memory request is made, the processor may be idle until that request is satisfied. Table 1.2 shows the impact of latency on the performance of a processor.

As expected, performance will decrease by 50% when the memory reference latency is equal to the processor performance without latency. Current memory technology is capable of satisfying memory bandwidth requirements for even the most powerful computers. But the satisfaction of latency is a major design problem. With increasingly faster processors, the memory performance bottleneck becomes even more pronounced.

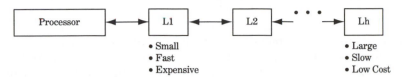

FIGURE 1.2   Hierarchical memory.

1.1.1 *Hierarchical Memory Systems*

Hierarchical memory uses a hierarchy of memory units, as shown in Figure 1.2, to satisfy the low-latency requirement of a memory system. Starting with the registers in the processor, the storage capacity in each level increases and the speed and the cost per bit decrease. For most references, the referenced item is found in a memory with low latency. Frequently referenced items are stored in high-speed, costly memory, and infrequently referenced items are stored in a low-speed, low-cost level. The weighted average latency is decreased by storing instructions and data in the level that is consistent with the frequency of the referenced item.

Interestingly, von Neumann [BURK46] noted in 1946 the requirement for a three-level memory hierarchy. The three levels are the processor internal registers, the main memory, and bulk storage on magnetic wire recorders. Hierarchical memory systems permit the designer to trade latency or access time against cost. The design goal is that the processor will see a memory that is only slightly slower than the fastest memory in the hierarchy.

This book does not directly address the processor registers, although they are a member of the hierarchy. The register-level design considerations are basically the concern of the instruction set designer. However, indirect effects on the performance of the memory hierarchy are found in such items as the memory bandwidth required to support context switching a very large register file.

Three terms that apply to all levels of the memory hierarchy are defined as follows.

The *hierarchical level* is usually denoted by an index beginning with 1 for the level nearest the processor and progressing upward. But, in relative terms, the "highest level" is the level closest to the processor and the "lowest level" is the slowest memory of the system. In the discussions to follow, the convention of the index 1 is used for the highest level, with indices $2 \cdots h$ denoting the lower levels.

Multilevel inclusion is the property that the contents of each level of the hierarchy h is always found at level $h + 1$ [LAM79], [BAER87].

Main memory is the largest random access memory in the system.

Early computers had four levels of memory: registers, main memory, disks or drums, and archival storage such as magnetic tape. For these computers, the main memory was magnetic core with rather long access and cycle times. Thus, the first introduction of another level in the hierarchy was a cache between the processor and the main memory. Further, these first caches were only instruction buffers that evolved to a unified cache holding both instructions and data.

Further evolution of the hierarchy consists of split caches for the private storage of instructions and data and, more recently, disk caches. With the advent of VLSI having more than one million transistors on a chip, the cache moved onto the processor chip and another level of caching was introduced between the on-chip cache and the main memory. Today, a memory system may consist of six levels: processor registers, on-chip cache(s), cache(s), main memory, disk cache, and disk.

Concurrent with the evolution of caching techniques, designers have been working on the management of the lower levels of the hierarchy. The programmer would, in general, like to see a single-level high-speed memory. This statement, however, is qualified because of the need to segregate various programs and data sets in the address space for file management and protection reasons. Nevertheless, the goal of the hierarchical memory is to provide the appearance of a large, fast single-level memory. The system, hardware and software, manages the memory system so that frequently referenced items will be found in the highest speed memory when needed.

Early systems employed *static* memory management; that is, the programmer determined the sequence of the required items and explicitly managed the memory hierarchy by overlays. A number of researchers, at Rice University, MIT, and Cambridge University [DENN70], were concurrently developing the ideas of virtual memory that provided for the automatic dynamic management of the memory hierarchy. Virtual memory gives the programmer the desired view of a flat memory, the size of which is equal to the processor's virtual address space. Even though the physical high-speed memory is much smaller than the virtual address space, the burden of managing overlays is removed from the programmer.

It is well known that a programmer can trade memory space for performance. For example, loops can be unrolled into a nonlooping program at the expense of a larger program. With virtual memory, the programmer must be aware that even though virtual address space is almost unlimited, as a larger address space is used, the memory system's performance will degrade. Thus, a programmer must use virtual memory system care. I note the fact of the increase in processor management of cache functions as discussed in Section 2.8.1. Thus, with some contemporary processors, we have gone almost full circle to static management of some of the memory hierarchy.

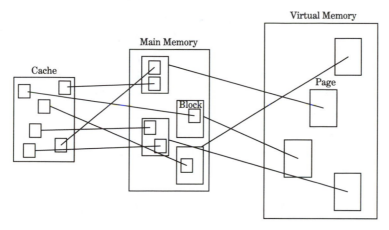

FIGURE 1.3 Hierarchical memory allocations.

A hierarchical memory allocates selected elements of a slow memory into a higher speed memory. Selected elements of this memory are then allocated in the next higher speed memory and so on. Figure 1.3 shows this process. Pages are taken from virtual memory space and allocated into main memory. Blocks from these pages are then allocated into the cache.

The hardware and software associated with a hierarchical memory must provide the following functions:

1. Detect a miss at the referenced level.
2. Identify the items to be vacated at the referenced level and perform the move to a lower (slower) level if required.
3. Map addresses between levels.
4. Read the new items from the lower (slower) level to the referenced level.
5. Complete the reference to the referenced level.

These functional requirements can be satisfied with hardware, software, or combinations of the two. I will describe the specifics of the design of these functions in Chapters 2 and 3.

1.1.2 *Memory Efficiency*

The access times of three levels of a hypothetical hierarchical memory are tabulated below. In addition, the ratios of access times are shown. Ratios are commonly used to normalize to the access time of the fastest member of the hierarchy.

Level	Access Time	Access Time Ratio
Cache	50 ns	1
Main Memory	200 ns	4
Disk	20 ms	100,000

These access times are the parameters of a two-level model for the effective access time at either the cache or main memory levels. Other models are described in Chapter 2.

$$\text{Effective Access Time } (t_{ea}) = t_h + P_{miss}(t_{h+1} - t_h)$$

where t_h is the access time of the highest level, t_{h+1} is the access time of the next level, and P_{miss} is the number of references to the cache that are not found in the cache divided by the number of references to the cache.

The effective access time model can be normalized to the access time of the highest level or cache as

$$t_{ea} = 1 + P_{miss} (R - 1) \quad \text{where } R = [t_{h+1}/t_h].$$

The value of R is the ratio of the access time of two levels that is rounded up to an integer because the memory cycle time is usually an integer multiple of the basic clock period. Furthermore, the cache cycle time is an integer multiple, frequently 1, of the clock period. The effective access time of the memory, as determined by this model, can be viewed as the weighted average memory latency—the average time required to satisfy a memory request.

Chapter 2 discusses in more detail the derivation of the t_{ea} model, with variations, and the values for P_{miss} in real systems. At this point, however, we will consider the efficiency of a hierarchical memory system. That is, the fraction of total time during which the memory is performing useful references when the total time is the useful time plus idle time when misses are being serviced:

$$\text{memory efficiency} = 100 \times \frac{1}{1 + P_{miss}(R - 1)} = \frac{100}{1 + P_{miss}(R - 1)}.$$

If $P_{miss} = 0$ or $R = 1$ or both, the referenced memory is said to be 100% efficient. That is, no undesirable latency due to a miss is associated with

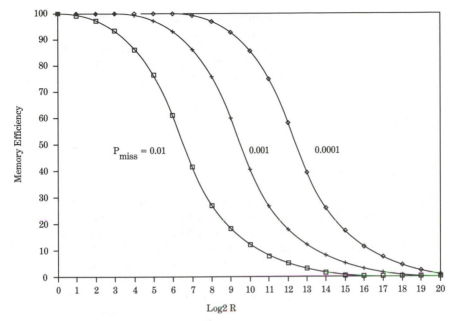

FIGURE 1.4 Hierarchical memory efficiency.

an access. Figure 1.4 shows a plot of memory efficiency for the locus of different values of P_{miss} as R is varied from 1 to 1,000,000. Note that for small values of R, the memory efficiency is approximately 100% regardless of the value of P_{miss}. Also, for large values of R, the memory efficiency is approximately 0% regardless of the value of P_{miss}.

Low values of memory efficiency are observed for large values of R, the domain of virtual memory level, and multiprogramming. A multiprogramming operating system will swap out the executing process for another process when a miss occurs at the referenced level. With large values of R, the management of the interface is performed by a combination of hardware and software because the time constraints are not overly demanding. At any design point, the efficiency of a memory can be improved by an equal percentage improvement in either P_{miss} or R. Practical considerations, however, limit these options. P_{miss}, in a virtual memory system, is limited by the workload, which is discussed in Chapter 3. Reducing the value of R is the only practical alternative under the condition when P_{miss} can be reduced no further.

Caches usually have small values of R and corresponding high values of efficiency. Thus, job swapping is precluded and requires that the management of the hierarchy is via hardware with a minimum of overhead. Because tasks are not swapped at the cache level, small P_{miss} values *and* small R values are design goals of cache systems. But as

Chapter 2 discusses, improvements in P_{miss} at the cache level are usually easier to obtain than improvements in R.

The concepts of managing the interface between different levels of the hierarchy are similar, if not identical. The major differences are in the implementation method, that is, the use of hardware or software or both; however, the terminology changes from level to level. The discussion of various types and levels of caches will precede the discussion of virtual memory.

1.2 Memory Bandwidth

Sufficient memory bandwidth is required to support the processing rate of the computer. Each instruction must be fetched, and an executing instruction may require one or more operands or may store a result or both. There must be a balance between the demand for and the availability of memory bandwidth. The memory/processor balance is illustrated in Figure 1.5, which plots the processing rate of a given processor/memory combination as the processor clock frequency is changed. Clock frequency is used as a surrogate for increased execution rate and thus memory bandwidth demand. The assumption is that the bandwidth of the memory system is fixed, as indicated by the arrow. At this point, the available memory bandwidth is reached and any further increase in the clock frequency will not yield a performance improvement.

The performance of a memory bound or limited processor can be increased by increasing the memory's available bandwidth. Alternatively, some architectures are devised to reduce the memory bandwidth

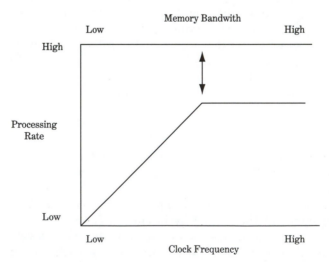

FIGURE 1.5 Processor/memory bandwidth.

requirement and, thereby, obtain increased performance with a limited bandwidth memory. Most CISC architectures are based on this approach. However, these architectures have been microprogrammed, and the bandwidth of the microstore can be included in the aggregate available bandwidth. Microprogram instruction sets are usually designed for high performance, and the bandwidth is not fully used. Thus, it is misleading to add merely the microprogram bandwidth to the instruction bandwidth of a CISC architecture and expect that bandwidth to equal the instruction bandwidth of a pipelined processor. Nevertheless, a well-designed processor memory is one with a close match between bandwidth demand and bandwidth availability. If the system is either processor bound or memory bound, inefficiencies result.

A well-known case of the negative effect of insufficient memory bandwidth is found in the Cray-1 and is discussed in Chapter 11. The Cray-1 had only one memory port, which resulted in a significant reduction of the processing rate for some problems. This defect was corrected in the Cray X-MP, which has three memory ports.

The bandwidth demand of CISC processors is illustrated by the demand of the VAX 11/780. This processor required, on average, 10 clocks of 250 ns (nanoseconds) to execute an instruction, or 2.5 µs. per instruction. Each instruction processed requires the fetching of an instruction and approximately 1.8 operands. Weicker [WEIC84] indicates that an average instruction is 3.8 bytes. With a four-byte operand, the average number of bytes referenced per instruction is

$$\text{bytes referenced per instruction} = \text{inst. bytes/inst.} + \text{operand bytes/inst.}$$
$$= 3.8 + 1.8 \times 4 = 11.$$

Thus, the bandwidth demand placed on the memory by the processor is approximately $11/2.5 \times 10^{-6} = 4.4$ million bytes per second.

On the other hand, a modern pipelined processor, as shown in Figure 1.6, must fetch an instruction every clock period and, for load and store instructions (approximately 30% of all instructions), there is a memory

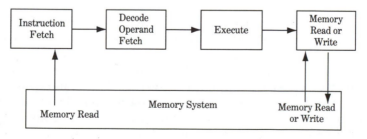

FIGURE 1.6 Pipelined processor.

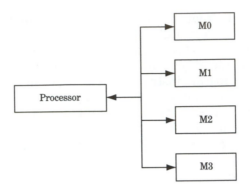

FIGURE 1.7   Interleaved memory.

reference of either a read or a write. With a clock period of, for example, 25 ns, and 1.3 four-byte references per clock, the memory must support approximately 52×10^6 references per second, or have the bandwidth of 200×10^6 bytes per second.

This back-of-the-envelope memory bandwidth analysis shows an increase in memory bandwidth demand by approximately a factor of 50 in the period from 1980 to 1990, an increase of approximately 48% per year. The modern pipelined microprocessor places a heavier demand on memory bandwidth that must be provided by innovative memory architectures and increased circuit speed.

Interleaved memory uses a number of low-speed and low-cost memory modules to achieve increased bandwidth by anticipating the distribution of accesses over all of the memory modules, as shown in Figure 1.7. That is, increased bandwidth can be obtained by accessing the memory modules in parallel. Chapter 5 discusses interleaved memory in detail.

Because the memory modules are accessed in parallel, the bandwidth (BW) of an interleaved memory approaches

$$BW(I) = \text{bandwidth of one module} \times \text{number of modules.}$$

In other words, two modules will have twice the bandwidth of one module because the two modules can be accessed in parallel and the referenced items, for reads or writes, are passed over the bus to/from the processor. With a high degree of interleaving, bandwidth can be increased to almost any desired value, keep in mind; however, that the latency of the first reference is still that of referencing the first module. Thus, interleaving does not solve the latency problem, only the problem of memory bandwidth. More realistic performance models are discussed in Chapter 5.

1.3 Queues

Queues have been used in the memory hierarchy beginning with the Stretch [BLOC59]. We find both fetch queues and write queues in many processors today. Fetch queues provide a technique for obtaining high bandwidth and low latency from an interleaved memory that has only high bandwidth such as early high-performance computers, the Stretch being an example. The Stretch processed variable length instructions thus presenting a varying demand (in bytes per clock) to the memory system. A queue is ideal for providing variable length instructions while hiding the latency of an interleaved memory.

The IBM 360/91 used fetch queues for instructions, target instructions, and data. The Intel ix86 family of processors as well as the VAX family have variable-length instructions and use instruction queues. Superscalar processors, which are described in Chapter 10, have the characteristic of variable-length instructions; the PowerPC 601 and the Intel Pentium are examples and use instruction fetch queues.

Instruction fetch queues continued to be used after the introduction of caches. The queue can hide, in many cases, the latency of the cache when there is a cache miss. Data queues require that there be a load prefetch capability in the processor. In general, instruction prefetch has been extensively studied but the study of data prefetch is relatively recent in the literature. The design and use of instruction and data fetch queues is described in Chapter 2. Write queues, which are also discussed in Chapter 2, have been used to hide the write time when a write to memory is required. By writing into a write queue, the processor can resume execution and the actual write (which may have a long latency) is hidden from the processor.

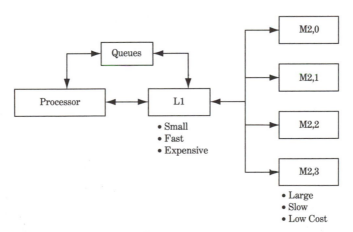

FIGURE 1.8 Memory system components.

1.4 Summary

As later chapters point out, the modern memory system combines queues with interleaved and hierarchical memories as shown in Figure 1.8. The cache, noted as M1, provides low-latency access to frequently used items while interleaved memory modules, noted as M2,n, are used to provide a high-bandwidth stream to the cache when an item is not found in the cache. Queues hide latency and smooth the flow of variable-length instructions.

In addition to the memories shown in Figure 1.8, interleaved disks can provide a high-bandwidth stream between the disk system and the main memory. The technology of interleaving disks (RAID) is discussed in Chapter 5.

2

Caches

2.0 Overview

The primary purpose of caches is to reduce the latency of references to memory. Ideally, the total latency should be one processor clock cycle for instruction reads or data reads or writes. The basic idea behind the design of all members of the memory hierarchy, including caches, is that the referenced addressable units (AU), instructions, and/or data will frequently be found in a high-speed memory. For any AU, a reference to a lower-speed memory will be required, which adds to the latency of the access.

Caches and related topics have been the subject of intense research for over thirty-five years. Cocke [COCK59] described a cache-like memory for the Stretch computer that is named a "virtual memory." This memory provided a form of lookahead and lookbehind for the data stream. Bloom [BLOO62] and Wilkes [WILK65] first described buffer memories that can be recognized as caches. The body of published material is immense and includes 403 citations in Smith's 1986 bibliography [SMIT86]. A comprehensive bibliography today would probably have in excess of 1,000 citations. For this reason, I am unable to cite every idea that has been posited concerning caches. Despite the large number of citations, however, I discuss a number of classifications and ideas in this text that may be outside the mainstream of current cache design practice.

Przybylski points out that "The entire cache design space is incredibly diverse" [PRZY90a]. He further states that "about 130 parameters are needed to fully specify a two-level cache system." This chapter catalogues the design space into taxonomies and provides analytic performance models to assist in making design tradeoffs.

The early literature referred to a cache as a *buffer* [GIBS67]. Over time, however, the name *cache*, first used by Conti et al. [CONT68], has become the preferred name. The various cache design issues addressed

15

in this chapter concern the reduction of delays that add to the basic—usually one cycle—latency of a cache.

Three major dimensions of cache design are discussed in this book, the first two of which are addressed in this chapter. They are

1. Organization or structure of the cache(s).
2. The set of rules that is followed when the cache is accessed and managed. These rules are known as the *policy*.
3. The cache address space. In Chapter 2, the address presented to a cache is viewed as just an address. The logical characteristic (real or virtual) of the cache address space is discussed in Chapter 4.

In addition to the organization component of cache design, the processor architecture and the program workload both contribute to the domain of cache design. These two additional components are outside the scope of this book and will only be briefly mentioned. The thrust of all innovations in cache design has been to design the cache so that the cache organization complements the characteristics of the address stream and increases the probability that a requested AU will be found in the cache. Recent research in compiler optimization for reordering the address stream to match a cache design is briefly discussed in Section 2.8.3.

Because of their importance to the operation of caches, I begin with a discussion of locality concepts, the three most frequently noted of which follow.

1. *Temporal locality*. Information recently referenced by a program is likely to be used again soon.
2. *Spatial locality*. Portions of the address space near the current locus of reference are likely to be referenced in the near future.
3. *Sequential locality*. A special case of spatial locality in which the address of the next reference will be the immediate successor of the present reference.

I believe that Gibson [GIBS67] was the first person to note these two distinct addressing patterns. Gibson points out that if references are purely random "any word is equally likely to be referenced by the CPU, variations of block size and replacement algorithms have no effect on the number of word references not found in the local store." These and other results [DENN70, DENN72] were produced through research on the virtual memory system and were later translated into cache concepts. Smith [SMIT82], however, was the first to use the terms "spatial" and "temporal" locality. Temporal locality is often referred to as "look backward." That is, an instruction sequence such as a loop will reuse instructions. Spatial locality is often referred to as "look forward." A program counteraccesses instructions in sequence. Thus, the next instruction will be fetched from a location adjacent to the present instruction and referenced next. Accessing a data vector also displays spatial locality even when the stride is greater than 1.

As caches have developed over the years, a rich and varied terminology has emerged. Various researchers and computer manufacturers have created new terms for identical concepts. Also, different terms are used at different levels of the hierarchy to identify identical concepts. I will try to point out the different terms by source in the following sections.

Caches are classified into the following four types according to their function or the nature of the information held in the cache.

1. An *instruction cache* holds only instructions. The design is optimized for the instruction stream only. Instruction buffers and instruction queues are sometimes used in place of instruction caches. Instruction caches are discussed in Section 2.3.
2. A *data cache* holds only the data stream. Data caches are discussed in Section 2.4.
3. A *unified cache* holds both instructions and data. The design is optimized for a mixed address stream. Unified caches are discussed in Section 2.5.
4. A *split cache* is a two-cache system, one for instructions and one for data. The two cache designs may be different for the two address streams. Split caches are forms of memory systems referred to as Harvard architectures [CRAG80] and are discussed in Section 2.6.

Processor designers face challenging problems in designing caches for VLSI processors. Usually there is a chip area budget for caches that should be used most effectively. Some design alternatives are

1. a large instruction cache,
2. the area split between an instruction cache and a data cache,
3. a large unified cache, and
4. a multilevel split cache.

Because each of the cache types may be designed for different address streams, their designs may be different. Therefore, the following sections of this book will examine each cache type individually.

Before proceeding, a comment on terminology is in order. The words *fetch* and *read* are generally synonymous. However, fetch is frequently used in the literature to refer to an *instruction fetch* while read refers to *data reads* and the method for handling a cache miss is sometimes referred to as the *fetch policy*. The vocabulary of this chapter is as follows.

Read, a read access is made by the processor to a cache for instructions or data.

Write, a write access is a processor write into the cache and/or main memory.

Fetch, a read access to memory to load a block into the cache.

Access, a generic reference to the cache or memory.

Caches can be classified by the interconnection topology; the selection and interconnection of the various cache components. A multilevel cache is one that has a first-level cache (either instruction, unified or split) and a second-level unified cache. The second-level cache is designed to accept the missed references from the first-level cache(s). Each of the two levels can be

N   Nil, not implemented;
I   Instruction cache, buffer or queue;
D   Data cache;
S   Split cache;
U   Unified cache.

Some reasonable, or known, two-level cache topologies are shown in Figure 2.1. A more complete description of various topologies is found in Section 2.6.

Historically, caches have been viewed as a pure implementation technique for improving performance that is transparent to the program. However, following this view, the program can misuse the cache with a performance penalty when there is no recognition of the presence or absence of a cache. This view of the cache has, of necessity, changed; software support for caches is now becoming the norm. There are things the program can or should explicitly do with the cache. For example, two of these actions are: (1) prefetch a cache block and (2) clear the cache to maintain coherency. These program actions are specific to individual architectures and are discussed in Section 2.8.1.

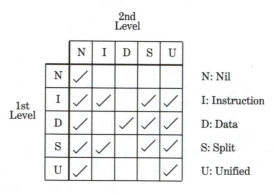

FIGURE 2.1 Common cache topologies.

The preceding discussion concerns caching of instructions and/or data. As I note in the following sections, caches for addresses play an important role in processor implementation. For example, speeding up virtual memory name translations with address caches is discussed in Chapter 3. Address caches used to improve branch performance are discussed in Chapter 7. In addition, the special cache designs needed to support superscalar processors are discussed in Chapter 10.

2.1 Cache Organization and Placement Policies

The mapping of addresses between the main memory and the cache is known as the *placement policy*. An address mapping is required because AUs taken from scattered main memory locations will be placed and accessed in a cache with a relatively small contiguous address space. The requirement for cache address mapping leads to the major design considerations of the cache, its organization and placement policy. These in turn are determinants of the P_{miss} (miss ratio) of a cache for a given workload. Two definitions of P_{miss} are in common use:

1. The number of references to the cache that are not found in the cache divided by the number of references to the cache. P_{miss} is the probability that a reference will miss in the cache. This definition of P_{miss} is used in this book.
2. The number of cache references not found in the cache divided by the number of instructions executed [KAPL73, ALEX86].

The first definition is used to evaluate the design of a cache alone, while the second definition allows the cache design to be evaluated per the instruction-level performance of the processor.

The main memory and cache are partitioned into equal-sized groupings of AUs, say for example, 16 bytes or 64 bytes [GIBS67]. The name *block* is used for these groupings even though other names, such as *fetch unit, line*, and *transfer size*, have wide usage. A memory address is composed of two fields, the *block name* and the *displacement*, within the block as shown in Figure 2.2.

The block size is the number of AUs transferred between the main memory and the cache. When the cache is accessed for either a read or a write, a mapping function is employed to locate the block holding the requested AU in the cache, if it is present. To accomplish this, a cache performs three major functions:

1. Translates the block name to a cache address.
2. Determines the presence or absence of the block containing the requested AU.
3. Provides the data storage component.

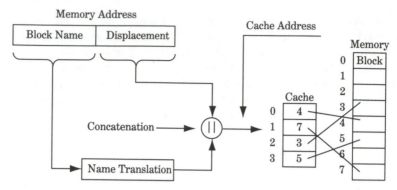

FIGURE 2.2   Memory partition into blocks.

Current practice is to integrate functions 1 and 3 into one structure that is referred to as a *late select* cache. When the functions are disjointed, the cache is referred to as an *early select* cache; these organizations are discussed in Section 2.1.2.

As previously noted, the placement policy is the cache organization, as shown in Figure 2.3. There is considerable diversity in the terminology of cache organization in the literature. The terminology used here is taken from [GIBS67] and the IBM S/360/85 [LIPT68], the first known commercial implementation of a cache.

The descriptions of the cache organization start with the smallest allocation.

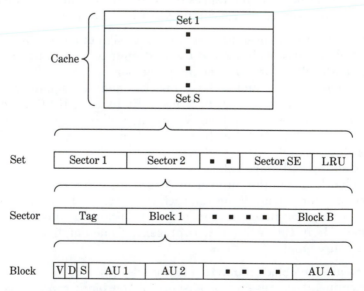

FIGURE 2.3   Cache organization.

An *addressable unit* (AU) is the unit addressed by the processor, a byte, word, or other unit.

A *block* contains A AUs with control bits (valid and dirty described in Section 2.1.3).

A *sector* contains B blocks plus a tag. The number of bits in a tag is a function of the size of the memory address and the parameters of the cache. A sector is also known as an *entry* [SMIT82].

A *set* contains SE sectors and, in some designs, LRU bits. SE is the degree of associativity.

A *cache* contains S sets. A set is a congruence class, to be described later.

As noted previously, the main memory is divided into blocks that are the unit of transfer between the main memory and the cache on a fetch operation. These units are also known as the *fetch unit* [PBZY90] or *transfer size*. The fetch unit is a multiple of the block size and is equal to or less than a sector size: $B \leq FU \leq SE$, with the most common fetch unit being a block. Depending upon the write policy, the write unit may be, and usually is, different from the fetch unit.

Note that each of the parameters (S, SE, B, A) are always integers and are usually even powers of two. This 4-tuple is used to denote the design of a cache and is similar to the 4-tuple of [PRZY90a] and the 3-tuple of [AGAR89]. The number of AUs in the cache, or cache capacity, is equal to the product of the values of the tuple; that is,

$$\text{number of AUs} = (S \times SE \times B \times A).$$

The original use of a block was reported by Gibson [GIBS67]. The grouping of blocks into sectors is used on the IBM S/360/85 to spread the cost of tag bits over a larger number of blocks. In later years, other terms were used to express the partitioning into sectors and blocks. These include *block frame and block* [HILL87] and *block and sub-block* [HILL84]. IBM recently introduced the term *page*, which refers to all of the sectors within a set [GROH90]. Table 2.1 provides a list of the synonyms of the terms used in this book.

Cache organization is illustrated with the following figures, which show the most common cache organizations. The first organization shown in Figure 2.4 is a canonical cache, which is used to illustrate the relationships between the various cache allocations; the organization is (8, 2, 2, 2). This example of the canonical cache has eight sets and two sectors; each sector has two blocks, and each block has two AUs.

The organization of the cache and the translation of the memory address to the cache address are tightly bound. As shown in Figure 2.5, the cache address is formed by allocating the memory address into fields.

Text	Przybylski [PRZY90]	Hill [HILL87]	Intel i486	PowerPC 601
block	sub-block	block	line	sector
sector	block	block frame	block	set
set	set	set	set	line
cache	cache	cache	cache	cache
fetch unit: block	fetch unit	sub-block	line	sector

TABLE 2.1 Cache organization terminology.

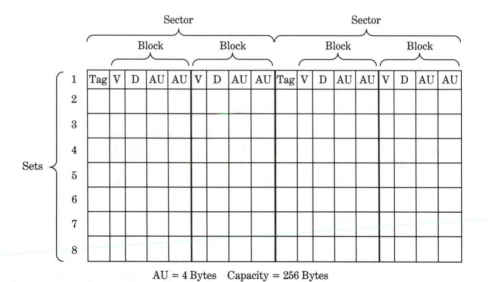

AU = 4 Bytes   Capacity = 256 Bytes

FIGURE 2.4 Canonical cache.

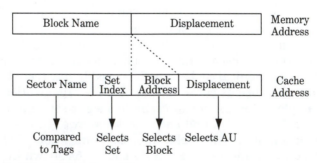

FIGURE 2.5 Cache address formation.

The memory address block name is allocated to:

1. the sector name, which is compared to the tags in sector(s) of the selected set,
2. the set index, which selects a set, and
3. a block address, which selects a block within a selected sector. As many caches have only one block per sector, this field can be of zero length.

The displacement is allocated to the displacement in the cache address.

This type of addressing is called *congruency mapping* [MATT70], which is defined as:

> Two integers are congruent to modulus m, if, after division by the modulus m, both have the same remainder r [GARN59].

Because the block name is divided into two fields, the set index and sector name, the set index is the remainder when the block name is divided by S, the number of sets in the cache. Thus, a block is divided into congruence classes. Stated another way, *a congruence class* consists of those AUs that have the same LSBs in their set index and different MSBs in their sector names. The remainders are found by division, that is, right shifting the block name, a trivial operation when base 2 design is followed. Note that memory is also divided into congruence classes as shown in Figure 2.2.

If there is only one block per sector, the block address field is of zero length. For these designs, is the proper name for this entity a sector or a block? This naming problem is resolved by using the term *sector-block*.

One cache design that has more than one block per sector, and hence a block address field, is the MC68030 instruction and data caches, which is illustrated in Figure 2.25. These caches are organized with four blocks per sector, requiring two block address bits. With a block of 4 bytes, or one word, no further subdivision by a displacement is required.

If there is only one set, that is, the organization has only one congruence class, there is no set index field. The block name from the memory address becomes the sector name of the cache as illustrated by the IBM S/360/85 shown in Figure 2.21. As described below, this organization is called an *associative cache*.

There are three classes of cache designs described below; the descriptions include the structure of the cache and the address field subdivisions.

1. An *associative cache* has one set and is organized as (1, *SE, B, A*). One can view an associative cache as having a tag comparison on each sector with no indexing into the cache. An example of this organization

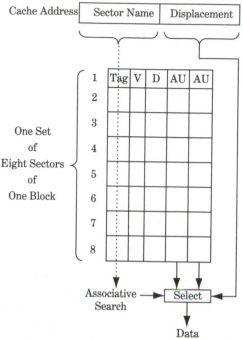

FIGURE 2.6 Associative cache.

for (1, 8, 1, 2) is shown in Figure 2.6. Mattson [MATT70] referred to the associative cache as *unconstrained* because any block from main memory can be placed in any sector in the cache. Conti [CONT69] named this organization *a fully associative buffer*; however, the term *full* or *fully* is not used in this text. However, if there is more than one block per sector, congruence mapping into the sector is required to identify the block, which was named a *sector buffer* by Conti.

Associative or unconstrained mapping does not require a set index in the address, because the tags are accessed by an associative search. In other words, the block name of the memory address and the values held in the tag field are the same. Thus, all blocks are in the same congruence class (the remainder is zero).

2. An *n-way set associative cache* is organized as (*S, n, B, A*) with $S \geq 2$. An example of an *n*-way set associative cache, organized as (4, 2, 1, 2), is shown in Figure 2.7. The associative cache shown in Figure 2.6 has been divided into four sets, reducing the number of comparison circuits from eight to two. The number of tag comparison circuits is equal to the value of SE and is the degree of set associativity of the cache. [MATT70] refers to the set associative cache as *partially constrained* because a block from main memory can only be placed in one

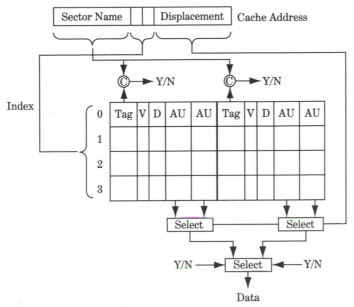

FIGURE 2.7 Two-way associative cache.

of the sectors of its equivalent set. Conti named this organization a *set associative buffer*.

Caches with *n*-way set associativity have always, to my knowledge, used an even power of two for *SE*: 1, 2, 4, ... Smith [SMIT78a] provides information on selecting the degree of associativity for both caches and main memory. A recent development, the Texas Instruments Super-scalar SPARC [WEIS92], has a 5-way set associative data cache. Having prime number associativity may tend to reduce set conflict misses. There seems to be no problem in addressing a set that has five sectors; the sector is selected by comparing the tag bits. There is no addressing modulo 5 required as is the case with prime number memory interleaving, which is discussed in Chapter 5.

3. A *direct cache* [BELL74] is organized as (*S*, 1, 1, *A*); an example of a direct cache organized as (8, 1, 1, 2) is shown in Figure 2.8. This direct cache is a further division of the 2-way set associative cache of Figure 2.7. With this cache, there are eight sets and only one comparison circuit; thus, it is 1-way set associative. Mattson [MATT70] referred to the direct cache as *fully constrained* because a block from main memory can only be placed in its equivalent set of one sector with one block. Conti named this direct cache organization a *direct mapped buffer*.

The following is a qualitative assessment of the effect on performance for each of the parameters of the cache organization. See Przybylski [PRZY90a] for a more complete set of "rules of thumb."

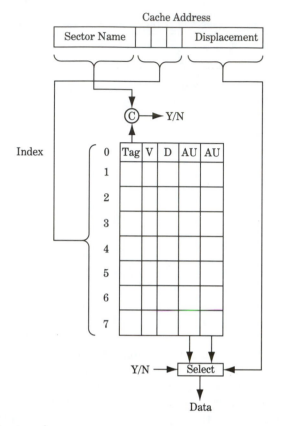

FIGURE 2.8 Direct cache.

Cache size is a first-order determinant of cache performance. As noted above, the size of the cache is the product of the terms of the 4-tuple. However, as cache size increases there can be a detrimental effect on the processor clock period. The dominant effect of cache size will be noted when P_{miss} data is examined.

The size of the AU is a function of the addressing method of the processor. In other words, the processor may do byte addressing or word addressing.

The number of AUs in a block influences the miss penalty by reducing the number of AUs that are either displaced or overwritten upon a miss. The transport time for a miss is a factor of the number of AUs in a block.

The number of blocks, B, in a sector is set to improve temporal locality of the cache by not requiring the replacement of a complete sector. Most contemporary caches, however, have $B = 1$.

The number of sectors, SE, is the degree of set associativity; it is also the number of tag comparators in the cache. Experimental data presented later in this chapter indicates that SE should be in the range of 4 to 16. As each sector has a tag that is compared to a portion of the address, the number of tag comparison circuits is equal to SE. The number of tag bits is also a function of SE, S, and the address space of memory. Hennessy [HENN90] provides a cache rule-of-thumb: "The miss rate of a direct-mapped cache of size X is about the same as a 2- to 4-way set associative cache of size $X/2$." Hill [HILL88] points out that higher levels of associativity tend to lengthen logic path delays and increase the clock period. Because of this, a cache with a higher P_{miss} can actually give the smallest t_{ea}.

The number of sets S is important if $S \neq 1$, that is, not an associative cache. Usually S is determined or selected to give the desired cache size after the other parameters are set.

2.1.1 *Set Index Allocation*

Figure 2.5 shows the set index field of the cache address positioned in the LSBs of the block name field of the memory address. Other options for the location of the set index field are illustrated in Figure 2.9. The examples shown are for a three-bit block name divided into two sets.

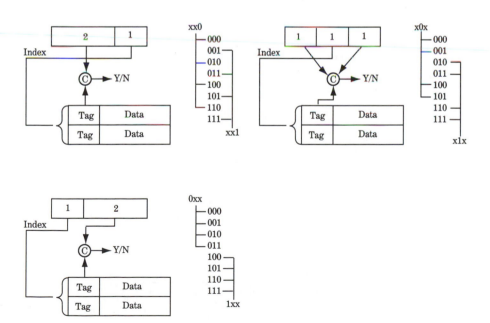

FIGURE 2.9   Set index bit positions.

The set index is one bit and can be positioned as shown in the figure. Also shown is a map of the addresses in the cache for each placement. The three illustrated options are:

1. With the one-bit set index in the LSB position, the sectors alternate in the cache sets, modulo the number of sectors in a set. This placement distributes the sectors uniformly across the cache addresses and gives congruent mapping.
2. If the one-bit set index is placed at the MSB position, the sectors are grouped together in such a way that, for this example, two adjacent sectors cannot be resident in the cache at the same time.
3. Placing the one-bit set index in the center of the address provides interdigitated groups of sectors.

The organization placing the set index field in the LSB position is the most common. As noted above, this organization places contiguous sectors into different sets of the cache, thereby reducing set conflict

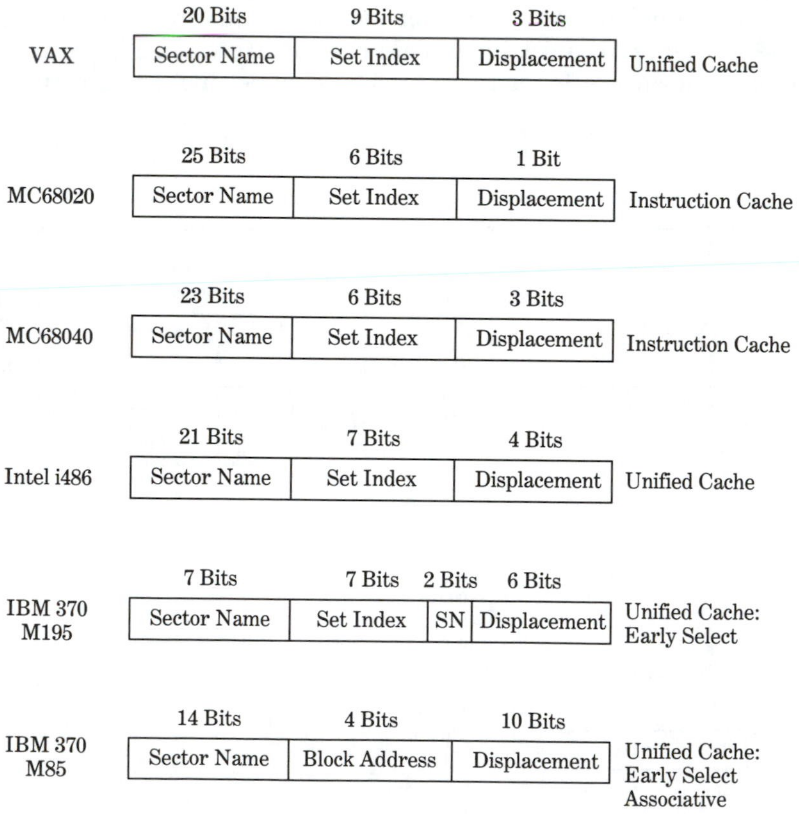

	20 Bits	9 Bits	3 Bits	
VAX	Sector Name	Set Index	Displacement	Unified Cache

	25 Bits	6 Bits	1 Bit	
MC68020	Sector Name	Set Index	Displacement	Instruction Cache

	23 Bits	6 Bits	3 Bits	
MC68040	Sector Name	Set Index	Displacement	Instruction Cache

	21 Bits	7 Bits	4 Bits	
Intel i486	Sector Name	Set Index	Displacement	Unified Cache

	7 Bits	7 Bits	2 Bits	6 Bits	
IBM 370 M195	Sector Name	Set Index	SN	Displacement	Unified Cache: Early Select

	14 Bits	4 Bits	10 Bits	
IBM 370 M85	Sector Name	Block Address	Displacement	Unified Cache: Early Select Associative

FIGURE 2.10 Cache address field examples.

misses. The author knows of no published research on the subject of how index placement affects P_{miss}.

Designers of cache systems have chosen to use a number of set index position schemes. Some of these options used in real systems are illustrated in Figure 2.10. These examples illustrate the diversity of index position design choices. Of particular interest is the IBM S/360/195. With this cache, the set index bits are central bits in the block name field of the address. The other illustrated designs differ primarily in the number of set index bits, not their placement.

2.1.2 *Late/Early Select Caches*

There are two methods for determining if a referenced AU is in the cache and, if present, accessing that AU.

1. *Early select.* With this selection method, the cache is organized with separate memories for tag/translation address and data memory and is known as early select because the determination of the presence of an AU in the cache is determined early in the cache cycle before the data memory is accessed. When a set is addressed, the tag/translation address memory is accessed and, if there is a valid tag comparison, the translated address is output. The translated address is then used as an index into a high-speed memory (cache) as shown in Figure 2.11. This method is used in the IBM S/360/85 [MATI77], which is discussed further in Section 2.5. Because of the mapping that is performed between the cache address and the cache data memory, early select caches are associative.

2. *Late select.* With this selection method, the cache is organized with a one-to-one correspondence between the sectors and the tags. Late select organizations are illustrated in Figures 2.6–2.8 and are further described in Figure 2.11. When a set is addressed, the tag and data are read in parallel; the tag is then compared with the sector name and, if valid, the data is gated out. This selection method is known as late select because the actual selection of the AU is late in the cache cycle after the data memory is accessed.

The cache address for an early select cache is formed by concatenating the base address found in the translation map with the displacement. Concatenation is used because of the use of congruence mapping. As discussed in Section 2.2.5, a cache write is implemented as a form of an early select cache. Early select is required because the determination of the presence of a block must be made before the write can proceed.

The time steps required for an early select cache are

1. Read the tag/translation-address memory.
2. Compare the tag(s) with the sector name (hit/miss).

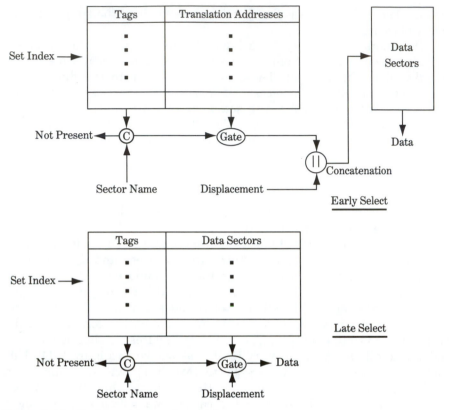

FIGURE 2.11 Early and late select caches.

3. Compose the address.
4. Read the data memory.

The time steps required for a late select cache are:

1. Read the tag and data memories.
2. Compare the tag(s) with the sector name (hit/miss).
3. Gate out the data.

The use of early select for the IBM S/360/85 cache is based upon the flexibility of an associative allocation and the technology available at the time. The data storage portion of the cache uses high-speed core memory technology that was inappropriate for the main memory due to its high cost. The tag memory, being small, could be implemented with registers and logic circuits. Because it is fast, the delay time through the tag memory is small compared to the time through the data storage memory. That is, times $1 + 2 + 3$ are small compared to time 4. Matick

[MATI77] states that the IBM S/360/85 cache requires three computer clocks to accomplish the four steps noted above.

All known contemporary caches are of the late select type. The use of late selection has come about because of the speed advantage and the introduction of cost-effective semiconductor memories that support the more homogeneous design of late select. However, as described in Chapter 3, virtual memory systems are early select.

A possible organization that combines the good points of early and late selects is the most recently used sector (MRUS) that keeps track of the last selected sector, giving a shorter logic path length than the late select path. This recently used sector, with its block, is conditionally read from the data section and presented to the processor. If the path through the tag memory indicates that the sector read is incorrect, the conditional read is aborted.

2.1.3 *Control Bits: Tags, Valid, Dirty, Shared, and LRU*

As shown in Figure 2.3, each sector has a tag containing the name of the stored sector. Each block has a number of control bits and a set can have LRU bits. The use of the tag bits was discussed in the previous section. The idea of sectors having multiple blocks in a sector stems from the desire to reduce bus traffic by the partial reading or writing of a sector and to reduce the number of tag bits needed for a cache of a given size.

The valid, dirty, and shared bits provide for control over a block that is resident in the cache. In general, all caches have valid bits, while dirty bits are used only with a write back cache and a shared bit is used with processors intended for multiprocessor applications.

Valid bits are used to indicate that the block contains valid information associated to its main memory address. The valid bit serves two functions. The first function is to indicate to the processor that the requested information is valid and not just a random collection of bits. For example, if a sector has multiple blocks, the tags can indicate the presence of the sector, but one or more of the blocks may not have been fetched. If a block that has not yet been fetched is addressed in this sector, the valid bit will indicate that the information contained should not be used. Usually valid bits are reset to zero when the contents of the cache are undefined as at the initial loading of a program into main memory.

A second use of the valid bit is described in Chapter 4. This use is associated with maintaining data coherency in the caches of multiprocessors. With one method of coherency maintenance, when noncoherence is

# Sectors	# Blocks	LRU Placement
$SE = 1$	$B = 1$	none required
$SE > 1$	$B = 1$	place in set
$SE = 1$	$B > 1$	place in sector
$SE > 1$	$B > 1$	place in sector or set

TABLE 2.2   LRU bits placement.

detected, the AU in the cache is invalidated and a future reference to that AU results in a cache miss.

Dirty bits (modified bits or *flags)* indicate the blocks that have been written into and subsequently modified by the processor. Dirty bits are not required for instruction caches or write through data caches. By using dirty bits on write back caches, the write back traffic on the bus can be reduced to only those blocks that have been modified by writes.

Shared bits are used in the management of a cache in a multiprocessor configuration. Data is shared between processors and, if cached, must be managed in order to maintain coherency. This subject is discussed in more detail in Chapter 4.

For a write back cache with a valid and dirty bit, a block can be in one of three of the four possible states: valid and clean, valid and dirty, and invalid. For this third state, the dirty bit is a don't care.

Least recently used (LRU) *bits* provide support for selecting a block for either replacement or overwrite. As shown in Figure 2.3, a set or a sector (if $SE = 1$) may have a field of bits devoted to managing the replacement policy of the cache. This field is called the least recently used (LRU) field, and its placement is a function of the organization of the cache as shown in Table 2.2.

When there is a capacity miss (which is discussed in Section 2.2.3), one of the blocks in the sector must be evicted if the cache is write back or overwritten if write through. The LRU bits provide the information to make this selection. Examples of the use of LRU replacement policy are illustrated with the caches of MC88200 (Figure 2.19) and the i486 (Figure 2.24).

2.1.4 *Nonblocking Caches*

Simple caches exhibit the characteristic that a read miss or a write will lockup or stall the cache until the request is serviced. A cache lockup prevents other requests from being serviced and places the processor into a wait state. Kroft [KROF81] first proposed a lockup-free instruction cache. This work has been extended with write buffers to provide lockup-free or nonblocking caches for both reads and writes.

Nonblocking Reads

There are a number of cases where a nonblocking read is beneficial to the processor performance. In these cases, there must be a pool of read requests that can be serviced out-of-order and effectively used by the processor. Software prefetching and processors that can support out-of-order execution are examples and are discussed elsewhere. Nonblocking can be useful for both instruction and data fetches.

Additional cache hardware is required to provide nonblocking capability. From [KROF81] this hardware is:

1. an unresolved miss information/status holding register (MSHR) for each miss that will be handled concurrently or is pending;
2. one n-way comparator, in which n is the number of MSHR registers, for registering hits n data in transit from main memory;
3. an input stack to hold the total number of received data words possibly outstanding;
4. MSHR status update and collecting networks; and
5. the appropriate control unit enhancement to accommodate 1 through 4.

From this list of hardware additions it can be seen that providing a single nonblocking read is relatively inexpensive; however, providing the ability to queue up a number of reads can become unworkable. Also, the additional hardware will inevitably add gate delays that will give a slower cache and a longer hit time. The only known nonblocking caches can queue only one nonblocked read.

Nonblocking Writes

A cache can be prevented from being placed in a wait state on a write by means of a write buffer or write queue. A buffer or queue permits writes to occur without wait states until the queue is full. The first known, to the author, example of a write buffer is the *store data buffer* (SDB) of the IBM S/360/91 [TOMA67] that held three double-precision floating point values. Store operations placed the result into the SDB and forwarded the result to destination registers as described in Chapter 8.

There are two types of write buffers: (1) for write through caches and (2) for write back caches. The Intel i486, an example of write through, has a four-level write buffer queue feeding the main memory. This write queue eliminates, in most cases, stalls of the processor on consecutive writes as measurements on the i486 show that the average number of pending writes is 3 [CRAW90]. This type of write buffer must be addressable, usually by some form of associative search, for resolving true dependencies. The IBM S/360/91 [ANDE67], for example, can buffer three writes that have pending true dependencies (discussed further in Chapter 8). A programming style that is rich in procedure calls necessitates pushing a number of parameters on the stack that results in a number of consecutive store instructions. Thus a write buffer can significantly improve procedure call performance.

The IBM RS/6000, an example of a cache with a write back policy, has write buffers named *store back buffers* (SBB). Because the data cache is write back, all writes occur via the cache. When a block is evicted from the cache, the SBB takes a 128-byte block from the cache in one clock cycle and transfers the block to the main memory over the memory bus in 8 clock cycles [IBM90a]. The write buffers of the PowerPC 601, an architectural derivative of the RS/6000, illustrate how snooping (described in Chapter 4) is incorporated into the write operation.

2.2 Read Policies and Performance Models

The purpose of a cache is to provide a low-latency memory for the processor. Thus, a designer is interested in having some method of evaluating the efficacy of a design in matching the characteristics of an anticipated address stream. The following sections describe basic performance models and the cache design parameters of the models. It is helpful in modeling the operation and performance of caches to consider the following three cycles or states of operation noted by [MATI89].

1. The Read Access Cycle or State.
2. The Write Access Cycle or State.
3. The Reload Cycle, Penalty, or State (called *transport time* in this book).

The most commonly used measure of cache performance is its effective access time. The effective access time (t_{ea}) for a read is the weighted average access time of the AUs found in the cache and the AUs found in memory.

$$t_{ea} = (1\text{-}P_{miss}) \times \text{cache access time} + P_{miss} \times \text{transport time.}$$

Transport time is the time required to access an AU that is not found in the cache. Other terms for transport time are *miss delay, miss penalty, cache miss penalty,* and *reload time.* Transport time is discussed further in Section 2.2.1.

There are four read policies that can be modeled with variations of this simple cache performance model. These models are based on (1) the time at which the access is made to the main memory and (2) whether or not the AU fetched from the main memory is passed to the processor in parallel with the cache or if a second reference to the cache is required. These variables are

Main memory reference.

Sequential. Memory reference is made after the miss is detected.

Concurrent. Memory reference is made in parallel with the reference to the cache.

Fetch method.

Simple fetch. AU is stored in cache, and a second cache reference is required.

Forward. AU is stored in the cache and forwarded to the processor.

Timing diagrams of these four cases are shown in Figure 2.12, where the cache cycle time is normalized to 1 and the transport time is mea-

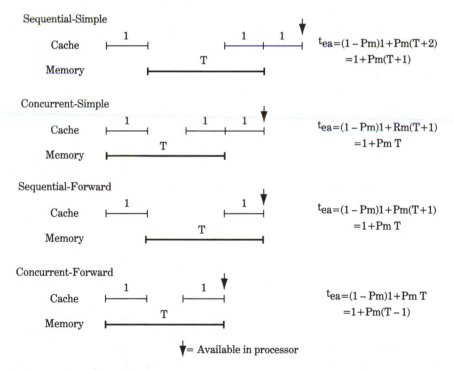

FIGURE 2.12   Four cache models.

sured in cache cycles. Consider the *sequential-simple* fetch design; a reference to the system accesses the cache first. If the requested AU is found, the effective access time is the normalized cache access time of 1. If the AU is not found, the main memory is accessed and the requested AU(s) are stored in the cache in T cycles. The cache is then accessed again taking another cache cycle time. The down arrow indicates when the AU is available in the processor. The assumption is made that the cache access time is equal to the cache cycle time.

The *concurrent-simple* fetch design accesses both the cache and the main memory at the start of the access cycle. This design has the accessed AU available in the processor one clock earlier than the sequential-simple design when there is a cache miss. The operation of the other two designs can be followed from Figure 2.12. The forwarding designs pass the referenced AU to the processor in parallel with writing it into the cache.

The t_{ea} models of the weighted average access times for the cache and the main memory clearly indicate the added latency that is a result of a cache miss. The *concurrent-forward* design gives the best performance—that is, the smallest t_{ea}—because the two memories are accessed concurrently and the transfer from the main memory is forwarded to the processor. However, this performance advantage is at the expense of a main memory cycle and a bus request for every cache access, which for some systems is an unacceptable load on the main memory bus. Thus, all known cache systems employ the *sequential-forward* design. A version of these models was first used by Lee [LEE69]. In addition to the effective access time, t_{ea}, there are two other metrics that are used for measuring the effectiveness of a cache design.

The *bus traffic ratio* is the ratio of bus traffic with a cache to the bus traffic without a cache [HILL84]. It should be noted that this metric can be greater than 1 in some cases. This situation occurs when the bus traffic servicing misses exceeds the bus traffic reductions due to hits in the cache. Bus traffic is discussed further in Section 2.2.4.

The inverse of the first metric is known as the *bus traffic reduction factor* (BTRF) [ALEX86].

Caches with more than one block per sector have interesting read hit and miss properties. A hit requires that the tag matches and that the addressed block is valid. A miss can occur if there is not a tag match or if a tag matches but the addressed block is not valid. On a cache miss because of the failure to match on a tag, a sector is selected by an LRU strategy and all 16 of the tag bits are reset. The selected sector tag is updated, and the sector in the data memory is then filled on a block-by-block basis as required by each subsequent reference that misses. For the second case, if there is a match on a tag but the requested block is not valid, that block is fetched and the valid bit is set. The write policy for this organization is discussed in Section 2.2.5.

2.2.1 *Transport Time*

A *transport time* model describes the time required to respond to a cache miss. Transport time, measured in either clocks or in time, is a function of the method of accessing main memory and transferring a block to/from the cache. The transport time model is based on the interleaved memory configuration as shown in Figure 2.13. For interleaved memory systems, including bus systems, the model for the transport time is composed of the following parameters:

T transport time.
a latency in clocks required to access the first AU of the block.
b number of clocks required to produce each subsequent AU of the block.
A number of AUs in a block.
Wd width of the path to the cache in AUs and the number of AUs per memory word.

From these parameters, the transport time required to transfer a

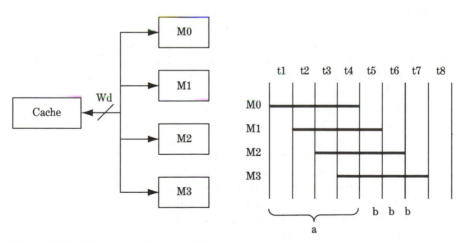

FIGURE 2.13   Transport time model.

block between the main memory and the cache is

$$T = a + b\left(\frac{A}{Wd} - 1\right).$$

This transport time model is typical of interleaved memories that supply blocks to the cache. An example is found in the IBM S/360/85, which has $a = 4$, $b = 1$, $A = 32$, and $Wd = 8$. The clock period is 80 ns. Thus, transport time is 7 clocks or 560 ns.

The transport time model will be used in a modified form in later sections when write policies are described, because some fetch and write policies require that a block must be moved from the cache to main memory (*evicted*) before the desired block is moved from the main memory to the cache. For those cases, T is multiplied by $(2 - P_c)$, where P_c is the probability that a block is clean, that is, the block has not been modified.

Because the transfers to/from the main memory and the cache are by way of the bus, another important performance model concerns the *bus traffic*, which is defined as

bus traffic = bytes per second across the cache–main memory bus
= requests/inst. × inst./clock × clock freq.
× block size × P_{miss} .

This model assumes that there is one bus transaction for each cache miss—a correct assumption for read misses but not for write misses. Nevertheless, the model gives some indication of the bandwidth required of a bus. For example, a processor with requests/inst. = 2, inst./clock = 0.66, clock freq. = 10 MHz, block size = 16 bytes, and $P_{miss} = 0.05$ will consume 10.66 million bytes per second of bus capacity. This model will be modified in the following sections to accommodate the write policy employed for the cache.

VLSI technology makes possible large caches with small values or P_{miss}. Thus, a designer is quite concerned with reducing the transport time without the complications of interleaving. When interleaving is not used, the transport time is simply the number of memory cycles (in time or clocks) required to transfer the block. Today, semiconductor manufacturers are producing DRAMS with organizations that support the efficient transfer of a block to a cache. These organizations, discussed further in Section 5.1.6, are known as *nibble mode, word (page) mode,* and static *column mode* devices.

In the late 1980s, VLSI implementation of caches became practical and changed the long-held assumption of independence of cache cycle time and transport time. Transport times have been reduced to a few clocks (2–5), and processor clock periods are a few tens of nanoseconds. Jouppi disputes this assertion, however, and says that transport times are lengthening [JOUP90].

2.2.2 *Cache Miss Characteristics*

Traditionally, the three major cache parameters (cache access time, P_{miss} and T) have been viewed as orthogonal. That is, one parameter can be changed independently of the other two. There is evidence that this orthogonal view is no longer correct. For example, a larger cache may provide a lower P_{miss} but will have a longer access time. And, as T is an integer multiple of the cache access time, there can be an increase in T. The issue of cache design becomes one of minimizing the effective access time of the cache as the three parameters are varied. This design approach is the subject of current research by [HILL88, HILL87, PRZY88, PRZY90, JOUP90].

There are a number of conditions, both transient and steady state, under which misses occur in a cache. From the discussion to follow on the various causes for misses, a cache designer should be cautious about accepting only one value of cache miss. P_{miss} can vary widely due to the instantaneous state of the processor and the nature of the program that is in execution.

Transient misses occur due to initial loads, context switches, and operating system calls. Two types of transient miss conditions have been noted by [AGAR88].

Cold start misses arise because the program starts executing with an empty cache, the same as compulsory misses.

Warm start misses arise after a context switch that has evicted a portion of the cache's contents.

A warm start miss is also known as the *cache reload transient* [THIE87]. Thiebaut and Stone studied cache transients and developed an analytical model to measure its influence on cache performance.

The steady-state misses are those that occur after the transients have subsided. These misses are classified by [HILL87].

Compulsory misses arise from references to previously unreferenced blocks. The compulsory P_{miss} is equal to the P_{miss} of an infinite cache.

Capacity misses arise because the cache is finite. Space must be provided in the cache for the referenced AUs.

Set conflict misses arise because of too many references to the AUs in the same set or congruence class. Space must be provided for the referenced AU.

A classification of factors that cause cache misses is given by Agar-wal et al. [AGAR89] and reviewed here.

Startup effects are the same as cold start misses and compulsory misses.

Nonstationary behavior of the cache is caused by the slow change of a program's working set over time.

Intrinsic interference is the same as set conflict misses.

Extrinsic interference involves the invalidation of cache locations of one program by another program in a multiprogramming system.

The transient behavior of cache misses was studied by Voldman and Hoevel [VOLD81]. They proved information on miss spectrum for instructions and data as well as intermiss distances. Their results clearly show the effect of the change in locality resulting from a context switch on the cache P_{miss}. Additional information is given in [VOLD83] that shows the fractal nature of the change in locality.

The cache performance models discussed previously and shown in Figure 2.12 use some form of weighted average P_{miss}. However, with capacity misses and set conflict misses, transport time may increase to $2T$ to accommodate the time needed to write a block and then access a block. For a write back cache (discussed in Section 2.2.5), the fetch policy requires that a dirty block is written into the main memory for a capacity or set conflict miss. This write is not required for a write through policy.

The sequential-forward model will be modified to account for the need to evict or write a dirty block to the main memory before the missed block is fetched. Clean data blocks do not have to be evicted even on a capacity or set conflict miss. This model applies only to data references under the assumption that instruction fetches do not need to evict a block; instead, the fetched block can overwrite a cache block.

$$t_{\mathrm{ea}} = (1 - P_{\mathrm{miss}}) \times 1 + P_{\mathrm{miss}}(P_c(T + 1) + (1 - P_c)(2T + 1)$$
$$= 1 + P_{\mathrm{miss}}T(2 - P_c)$$

where P_c is the probability that the block is clean (not dirty).

The effect of various forms of miss is illustrated by considering the performance model for a sequential-forward, write back cache. This model, which accommodates the block writes that occur with capacity and set conflict misses, is

$$t_{\mathrm{ea}} = 1 + P_{\mathrm{miss}}T$$
$$= 1 + P_{\mathrm{mcomp}}T + (P_{\mathrm{mcap}} + P_{\mathrm{mset}})T(2 - P_c)$$

where

$$P_{mcomp} = \text{probability of a compulsory miss,}$$
$$P_{mcap} = \text{probability of a capacity miss,}$$
$$P_{mset} = \text{probability of a set conflict miss,}$$
$$1 = P_{mcomp} + P_{mcap} + P_{mset}.$$

This model includes the effect that, for a write back cache, a compulsory miss requires only one transport time while capacity and set conflict misses require two transport times if the block is dirty in the slot that must be available for allocating the fetched block.

2.2.3 *Sources of Miss and Hit Data*

A cache designer has a number of sources for P_{miss} data. The first, and most abundant, source of general data is published data by [SMIT82], [SMIT87], and [HILL84]. In addition, [HILL87] also reports miss data for the three classes of steady-state misses noted above. Transient miss data is provided by [STRE83] and [THIE87]. Miss data for the SPEC benchmarks suit executing on a number of processors was published by Gee et al. [GEE91].

Davidson [DAVI87] studied cache misses on the basic and two modified versions of the VAX instruction set. A number of benchmarks are simulated, and the results indicate that for relatively small caches (8K to 32 Kbytes) there can be as much as a 60% difference in P_{miss} for the same program. For large caches (64 Kbytes), the influence of code density disappears as the cache can hold the complete working set. These results indicate that code density can be a significant design consideration for on-chip caches that are of limited size. The point should be made that P_{miss} is not independent of the underlying processor architecture. That is, the instruction set and resulting code density can be a significant determinant of P_{miss}. For a given size of cache, the higher the code density, the lower the P_{miss}. While instruction set design is outside the scope of this book, I suggest consulting the research of [MITC86] and [STEE89] in addition to [DAVI87].

Miss data for operating systems and multiprogramming workloads is provided by [AGAR88]. This data is collected by trace-driven simulation for various configurations of caches with various workloads and measurements on actual caches when executing benchmarks.

Mogul and Borg [MOGU91] reported on the effects of context switches on the performance of a cache. Their results are important because of the increased context switch rate that results from program execution under highly modularized operating systems. They simulated three caches: a level-one instruction cache, a level-one data cache, and a level-two unified cache. Their results show that the cost of a context switch can be in the tens of thousands of cycles due to the reduction in cache performance or the increase in memory latency.

The empirically derived formulas by [HIGB90] are another source of miss data source. These formulas are the product of curve fitting to trace-driven simulation data. Higbie also gave formulas for evaluating the average access time of a cache as a function of its organization. These formulas are useful for making first-order performance approximations of a cache design before expensive simulations are conducted. The discussions of each of the cache types in Sections 2.3 to 2.6 include identification of the published P_{miss} data for the various cache types.

In conclusion, P_{miss} data is usually obtained by simulating a cache, testing it with an address trace, and recording the P_{miss} results. Special methods of performing cache simulations have been effective in significantly reducing the simulation time for a large number of cache designs [HILL87, MATT70]. Some new microprocessors, such as the Intel Pentium, have counters on the chip that can log cache misses permitting in situ and at-speed miss data collection.

2.2.4 *Fetch Policies*

In addition to the organizational aspects of cache design, there is the issue of the *fetch policy* that can influence the effectiveness of a cache by changing P_{miss}. It is stated as the algorithm for determining (1) the conditions that trigger a fetch from the main memory into the cache, (2) the order of moving AUs from the main memory to the cache, and (3) when the CPU can resume processing after a cache miss. Fetch policy is also called *fetch strategy* [PRZY90].

The policies discussed in this section are used for both instruction and data caches. However, most instruction caches only have need for a fetch policy, since writes into an instruction cache are usually not allowed. Recall, from Table 1.1, that approximately 90% of all memory references are reads and 10% writes. Our primary attention is devoted, therefore, to reducing fetch time even at the expense of write time.

Before fetch policies are discussed, a historical note is in order. The first caches were quite small by modern standards. Because the caches were small, capacity misses are large and "fine tuning" of the cache organization and fetch policy was employed to improve P_{miss} as much as possible. For example, Gibson [GIBS67] examined the impact of block size in a small cache.

However, as the absolute size of the cache has increased and with the use of two-level caches, fine tuning of block size and fetch policies are no longer the dominant considerations they once were. The use of direct caches with $SE = 1$ and $B =$ one word, as found in the MIPS R2000, indicates current thinking in cache design. Also, Przybylski's [PRZY90] simulations indicate that "fine tuning" of the fetch policy can yield only marginal improvements in cache performance. Nevertheless, it is important to consider all aspects of fetch policy design as some of the issues remain relevant.

Conditions for a Fetch from Main Memory

This section briefly discusses the three common conditions for initiating a fetch from the main memory to the cache. The first two conditions apply equally to instruction and data references to split or unified caches.

Fetch on miss. This condition is the common case of accessing a block from the main memory into the cache only on a cache miss, sometimes known as *demand fetching*. For caches having more than one AU per block, prefetching occurs because more than the missed AU is fetched.

Software prefetching. With software prefetching, a block is fetched under program control or automatically before an AU is needed. When software prefetching is used to preload a conventional cache, it is anticipated that there will be a decrease in P_{miss} for the program. Software prefetching with a performance model is described in Section 2.8.1.

Software prefetching is a much studied but, as yet, little implemented idea. The reason for this is discussed in Section 2.8.1, where a performance model for software prefetching is developed and its performance is evaluated. Special cases of software prefetching can be found, such as instruction buffering, where prefetching is effective.

Hardware prefetching. A special form of prefetching is hardware driven and is used for instruction and data stream prefetching into queues (described in Section 2.3.2) and prefetching of branch target instructions (described in Chapter 6). A special case of hardware prefetching is *instruction prefetching*, which is defined as: "Instruction words ahead of the one currently being decoded are fetched from the main memory before the instruction decoding unit requests them" [GROH82]. This definition is general enough to cover prefetching into queues as well as into pipeline stages.

Ordering Main Memory to Cache Moves

For cache having more than one AU per block, the effective access time, t_{ea}, can be improved by the use of an efficient fetch policy. There are three known design options for handling multi-AU block on a fetch. These options assume that a cache read miss can occur on any address within the block, including the first address. Recall that the block is the unit of transfer between the main memory and the cache. Timing dia-

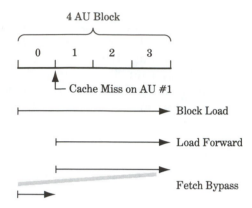

FIGURE 2.14   Load policies.

grams of the following three options are shown in Figure 2.14, illustrated
with a miss occurring on the access of AU#1 of a four-AU block.

1. *Block load.* The complete block is loaded starting with the first AU
   in the block [HILL84].
2. *Load forward.* The AUs forward of the miss and within the block are
   loaded. The AUs behind the miss are not loaded. This option is also
   named *loading partial blocks on miss* [HILL87]. Note that valid bits
   are needed for each AU and the valid bits of only the loaded AUs are
   set. With a valid bit, a miss can occur either because of a tag that
   does not compare or a valid bit in a block that is not set.
3. *Fetch bypass.* The block is loaded starting with the missed AU; then
   the AUs behind the missed block are loaded [SMIT87]. Fetch bypass
   is also known as a *wraparound load.* This option is employed on the
   IBM S/360/85 [LIPT68]. Unfortunately, the term *fetch bypass* has
   another usage with the IBM RS/6000; see Section 2.4.2.

For systems that have a bus with a high level of utilization, selecting a load policy that reduces bus usage may be beneficial. Note that for
options 1 and 3 the complete block is always loaded into the cache.
Option 2 loads only a partial block, thereby reducing the bus traffic ratio,
usually at the later expense of an increased P_{miss}. The higher P_{miss} may
then increase the bus traffic, for no net average reduction. Hill [HILL84]
performed simulations that suggest that the load forward policy reduces
the bus traffic ratio in the range of 10% to 20% at the cost of an increase
in P_{miss} of less than 10%. The net effect of these changes is negligible
and is probably not worth the complication of the load forward design.

There are further complications with a fetch policy. For example,
what happens with a sequential-forward or concurrent-forward policy if
there is another cache miss while the block, or partial block, from the

previous miss is still being loaded into the cache? There are two options for handling this situation [PRZY90].

1. For a nonblocking cache, hold the second miss until the first block load is completed. This strategy is called *nbdwf*.
2. The block load from the first miss is aborted and the second is started. This strategy is called *adwf*.

The temporal clustering of cache misses for a particular cache design and workload is a major factor in selecting an option; [PRZY90] provides some insight. As the block size increases, the temporal clustering decreases. However, the decrease is not significant for relatively small blocks, leading to the conclusion that the simple *nbdwf* option is the best choice.

Resumption of Processing

The processor can resume processing when the requested AU is available. There are two variations of each of the three load policies that concern how the missed AU is passed to the processor. These two policies are introduced in Section 2.2 and shown in Figure 2.12.

1. *Simple fetch.* The block is loaded into the cache, with any of the three policies above, and the reference to the cache is reinitiated.
2. *Forward.* As the block is being loaded into the cache, the missed AU is passed to the processor that resumes processing while the balance of the block is filled. This policy is named *out-of-order fetch* [HENN90], *continuation*, or *early restart* [PRZY90].

In general, the forward policy reduces the number of cycles required to service completely a cache miss and resume processing. However, this policy is more difficult to implement than the simple policy and may not be worth the cost for systems with small P_{miss} and relatively short transport time. And, as noted above, there can be cache misses because of the early restart of processing.

With a nonblocking cache (discussed in Section 2.1.4) and a pool or queue of reads, the processor can resume processing immediately after the miss service is initiated. Thus, the simple fetch policy may be satisfactory.

2.2.5 *Write Policies*

Section 2.2.4 discussed fetches from the main memory to the cache. When there is a data write from the processor, the cache must have a policy for handling a number of situations. Consider first a write to a sector or block that may or may not be in the cache. An *early select* strategy must be used because the cache must be checked for a hit or miss before the write is initiated. What this means is that writes are accomplished by a read–test–modify–write protocol. A *late select* policy, if one could be devised, would cause an invalid write that would incorrectly change the value of an AU in the cache.

Instruction caches are, in general, read-only and do not require a write policy. For data writes, policies for all cases of hits and misses and writing into the cache and main memory are needed.

Write Hit

After the early select process determines that the write will hit in the cache (that is, the tags match), the write must update both the cache and the main memory. For write hits there are three strategies.

1. *Write through (store through)*. For this policy, the AU is written into the cache and into the main memory. For performance enhancement, a write buffer can be employed to hold the AU before it is written to the main memory. The write buffer permits the processor to continue while the write to the main memory is pending.

Write through has a number of characteristics that must be accommodated. (1) There can be a coherency problem because the value of the AU in the cache can be different from the value in the main memory while the AU is in the buffer. (2) The write through policy requires that every write to a location causes a memory bus transaction. And, (3) as there can be a sequence of writes to a particular location, there will be more bus activity than with the write back policy.

2. *Write back (copy back, store in, nonstore through, swapping)*. For the write back policy, the AU is written into the cache and the dirty bit is set if it has not already been set. At some future time when the sector or block must be evicted from the cache for a read miss, only the dirty block(s) must be written to the main memory. Dirty bits would not be required if the full sector was always moved to the main memory on a miss. However, writing a full sector imposes a significant performance penalty because of unnecessary moves. With dirty bit control, only the last write to a location is updated into the main memory, which results in lower bus activity than with the write through policy.

A read miss may require the eviction of a block if the block is dirty. Thus, the selection of a write back policy can impact the transport time required to service a future read miss. There is a coherency problem with the write back policy because the value of the AU is different in the cache and the main memory until the write back is accomplished. Coherency is discussed in Chapter 11.

3. *Write once*. This policy treats the first write as write through and then reverts to write back for all subsequent writes to the same block.

Write once reduces the need for invalidations or updates for maintaining coherency, which is a problem with multiprocessor systems, while reducing the bus traffic found with a pure write through policy.

Write Miss

The first-level design options for write misses (that is, the tags do not match) concerns whether on not the block into which the write will occur is allocated (fetched from the main memory) or not allocated. The second-level design options are *write through* and *write back* as with write hits. The allocation design options are as follows.

Write-allocate can be used by either the write through or write back policies and treats a write miss similarly to a read miss. The sector or block that is the target of the write is fetched into the cache. One of the replacement policies described in Section 2.2.6 must be observed. After the block is fetched, either write through or write back policy can be followed.

No-write-allocate (write around, write direct) is used only with the write through policy. With this policy, the write is made directly to the main memory or to the main memory via a buffer as in the write through policy.

Writes into Write Through Caches

Write through caches with multiple AUs per block have an advantage with writing [HENN90]. If there is a hit (tag match) the write to the cache, and to the main memory, can proceed regardless of the state of the valid bit. However, if there is not a tag match, the AU can be written, the tag updated, the valid bit set, the other valid bits in the block reset, and the AU written into the main memory. The reason this works is that there is a valid image of the block in the main memory for the block that does not hit.

Write Policy Taxonomy

With two policy options for a write hit (not considering the write once policy) and three policy options for a write miss, there are six possible write designs, as shown in Table 2.3.

Four combinations of policies are the most used and are indicated by designs A, B, C, and D. Note that options B and D use allocate, and the P_{miss} of future reads may be reduced because a requested AU may now be present in the cache. On the other hand, a future read may have a higher P_{miss} due to the eviction of a block that will be needed at that time. There is no published research on this issue known to the author. Cases A and C require that the block is fetched with read misses only

Design	Write Hit	Write Miss
A	Write through	No write-allocate, write through
B	Write through	Write-allocate, write through
	Write through	Write-allocate, write back
C	Write back	No write-allocate, write through
	Write back	Write-allocate, write through
D	Write back	Write-allocate, write back

TABLE 2.3   Write policy taxonomy.

since write misses do not cause a block to be fetched from the main memory.

With the four designs, there is another design option. This option is the inclusion of a write buffer or queue discussed in Section 2.1.4. All known contemporary cache designs use a write buffer. Recall that the write buffer used with a write through cache (designs A and B) buffers processors writes while a write back cache (designs C and D) uses a write buffer with the eviction of a block.

Write Policy Performance Models

Simple models are developed to assess the performance of the four cache designs. There are two performance issues that are a consequence of the selected write policy: (1) the effective write time of the cache, and (2) the bus traffic. These issues are discussed separately later in this section.

Simple flow charts for the four write designs are shown in Figure 2.15. The models are for a unified cache and assume the following.

1. All hits take one clock to read from the cache.
2. The transport time of a block to/from the main memory is T bus cycles and the ordering is block load.
3. For misses where a dirty block is moved from the cache to the main memory before the block is fetched, the transport time is $2T$ bus cycles.
4. All writes are buffered and take 1 cycle; the write buffer is never full.
5. Write to the main memory of a single AU requires w cycles on the bus.
6. Dirty bits are set in parallel with the cache and/or the main memory buffer write.

Cache Access Time Models

For the four cache designs A–D described previously and illustrated in the flow charts, Table 2.4 describes the write time in cycles. Because of

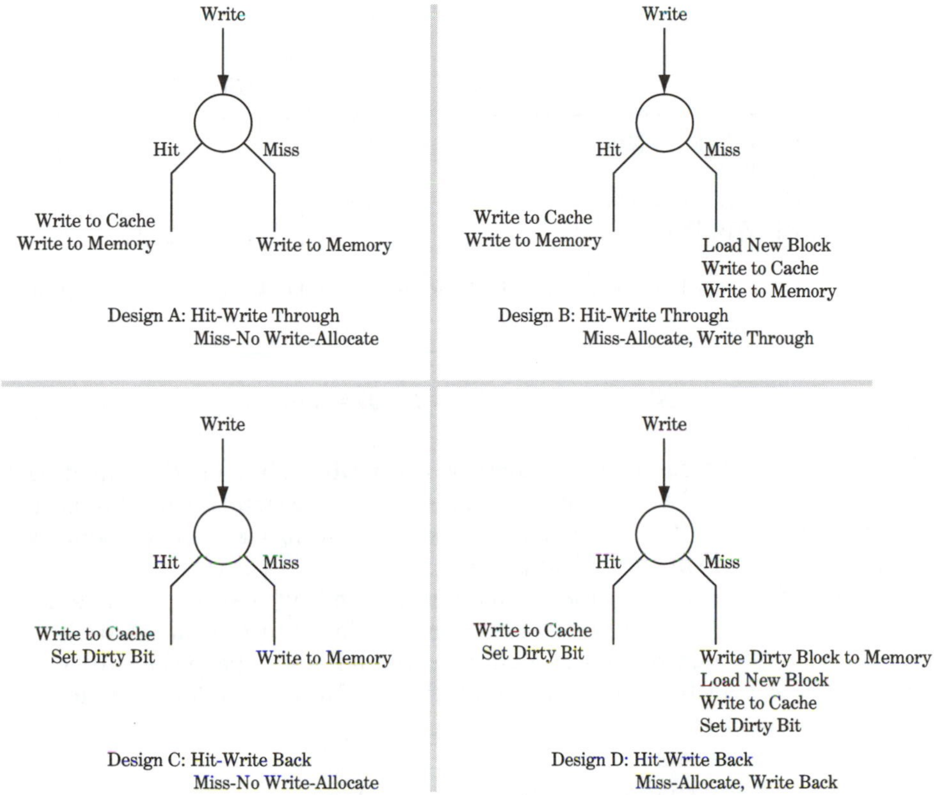

FIGURE 2.15 Write design flow charts.

the use of write buffers, all writes take one cycle. All actual writes to memory are overlapped and do not delay the processor.

Note that while the hit events for designs C and D set the dirty bits, no eviction transport time is charged because the transport time is accounted for on a subsequent read that requires that the block be evicted. The effective write time t_w is the same for all cache designs and is based on the effective use of write buffers to hide all transport times

Design	Write Hit	Write Miss	Examples
A Hit-WT, Miss-NWA	1	1	i486, MC68040*
B Hit-WT, Miss-A, WT	1	1	MC68030*
C Hit-WB, Miss-NWA	1	1	
D Hit-WB, Miss-A, WB	1	1	MC68040*

*Depending upon the mode.

TABLE 2.4 Cache write cycles.

Write Design	Read		Write	
	Hit	Miss	Hit	Miss
A Hit-WT, Miss-NWA	1	$1 + T$	1	1
B Hit-WT, Miss-A, WT	1	$1 + T$	1	1
C Hit-WB, Miss-NWA	1	$1 + T(2 - P_c)$	1	1
D Hit-WB, Miss-A, WB	1	$1 + T(2 - P_c)$	1	1

P_c is the probability that a block is clean; that is, the block has not been modified.

TABLE 2.5   Memory access cycles.

$$t_w(A) = t_w(B) = t_w(C) = t_w(D) = 1 \text{ cycle.}$$

We now consider the overall effect of the write policy on the effective cache access time by modeling the effective cache access time for both reads and writes. The read policy is sequential-forward. The memory access cycles are shown in Table 2.5.

The effective access time for both reads and writes can be modeled by forming the weighted average of the clocks required for reads and writes. A unified cache is assumed even though split caches can also be evaluated by selecting the proper parameters. New terms for these models are defined as

P_r Probability that a memory access is a read
P_{mr} Probability that a read access misses
P_w Probability that a memory access is a write
P_{mw} Probability that a write access misses

$$P_r + P_w = 1.$$

Designs A and B provide the same effective cache access time; designs C and D also have the same effective access times

$$t_{ea}(A) = t_{ea}(B) = P_r(1 + P_{mr}T) + P_w,$$
$$t_{ea}(C) = t_{ea}(D) = P_r(1 + P_{mr}T(2 - P_c)) + P_w.$$

Bus Utilization

The effective access time of the cache is not the only performance measure that should be considered. Each of the four designs presents a different traffic density or bus utilization. High bus utilization can be a significant problem in a shared memory multiprocessor because of contention on the bus from a number of processors. A write back policy is expected to result in lower bus utilization. The models to follow show the number of clock cycles that each reference to the cache will generate; bus activity is measured as

BCR = the weighted average number of bus clock
cycles per memory reference.

If a split cache is evaluated, BCR will be the sum of the BCRs for each of the two caches. The model of bus utilization makes the assumption that the cache is always active; that is, the processor is completely overlapped with cache access time. Thus, the bus utilization fraction is

bus utilization (BU) = BCR/t_{ea} (A, B, C, or D).

The transport time model determines the time to move a block between the cache and the main memory. For write through and no-write-allocate caches only a single AU, not a block, is usually written to the main memory and a bus and the main memory usually handle single AU writes differently than a block write. While write buffers hide a single AU write time from the processor, the number of writes is a factor in determining bus traffic. Therefore, a parameter is needed to quantify single AU writes to the main memory; specifically it is defined as w, the number of clocks required to write an AU to the main memory and is usually less than T because a single AU is written to the main memory over the bus rather than a complete block.

Table 2.6 shows the contribution made to BCR for each of the four events and each of the four designs. These models are derived from the flow charts of Figure 2.15 and Tables 2.4 and 2.5. The models are the same with and without buffers because a buffer can only delay, but not eliminate, bus activity.

Write Design	Read		Write	
	Hit	Miss	Hit	Miss
A Hit-WT, Miss-NWA	0	T	w	w
B Hit-WT, Miss-A, WT	0	T	w	$T(2 - P_c) + w$
C Hit-WB, Miss-NWA	0	$T(2 - P_c)$	0	w
D Hit-WB, Miss-A, WB	0	$T(2 - P_c)$	0	$T(2 - P_c)$

TABLE 2.6 Bus clock cycles, BCR.

The BCRs for each of the four designs are

$$BCR(A) = P_r P_{mr} T + P_w w,$$
$$BCR(B) = P_r P_{mr} T + P_w (w + P_{mw} T(2 - P_c)),$$
$$BCR(C) = P_r P_{mr} T(2 - P_c) + P_w P_{mw} w,$$
$$BCR(D) = T(2 - P_c)(P_r P_{mr} + P_w P_{mw}).$$

For evictions, transport time can be reduced for a cache that has more than one AU per block if dirty bits are given to each AU. These dirty bits can reduce the bus traffic to w clock cycles for each AU transported, not T cycles for the complete block. Needless to say, instruction caches do not require dirty bits because there will be no writes for systems that prohibit self-modifying code.

Write Policy Performance Impact

The models developed in the previous section will now be used to evaluate the four cache designs for access time and bus utilization. The parameters of the bus design are from Figure 2.13 plus the word write time: a is the bus latency, b is the transfer rate, and w is the write time. The following assumptions are made on the workload and bus parameters.

$$
\begin{aligned}
P_r &= 0.9, & a &= 2, \\
P_{mr} &= 0.1, & b &= 1, \\
P_w &= 0.1, & A &= 16, \\
P_{mw} &= 0.15, & Wd &= 4, \\
P_c &= 0.9, & w &= 2.
\end{aligned}
$$

By applying the models developed in the previous section, we obtain values for t_{ea}, BCR, and BU as shown in Table 2.7 for the four designs. First, the value of T is determined as

$$T = 2 + 1\left(\frac{16}{4} - 1\right) = 5 \text{ clocks.}$$

These results indicate that, as expected, designs A and B have the

Write Design	t_{ea}	BCR	BU
A Hit-WT, Miss-NWA	1.45	0.65	0.45
B Hit-WT, Miss-A, WT	1.45	0.73	0.50
C Hit-WB, Miss-NWA	1.49	0.52	0.35
D Hit-WB, Miss-A, WB	1.49	0.57	0.38

TABLE 2.7   Cache design model results, clocks.

best performance and the highest bus utilization. These results compare favorably to simulation results of the cache for the i486 described by [GROC89]. The i486 has a unified cache that is write through on hit and write direct on miss (design A). Their simulated results show BU in the range of 0.38 to 0.55 for a suit of five benchmarks with the same bus design.

Simulations were also performed to assess the impact of changing the bus parameters for design A. The bus transport time parameters a, b, and w are varied; Wd is 4 and A is 16. For each of the bus configurations the execution clocks are normalized to a bus with $a = 0$ and $w = 0$. The simulations provided a count of the number of execution clocks with different bus configurations; the results are compared to the models in Table 2.8. The simulation-measured number of execution clocks as the bus parameters is changed. As a surrogate for processor performance, the model for t_{ea} is used also to normalize $a = 0$ and $w = 0$.

The model results compare favorably with the simulation results, that is, ±8%. The bus designs with the greatest difference are the 2-2-2 and 4-1-4. One reason for the differences is that the simulation measured the effect of processor execution clocks rather than just the cache clocks. In an actual system the processor and cache are not completely overlapped, and the cache is the idle part of the time. For example, the processor may have to wait on a write to the buffer to update in the main memory; this is a delay that is in the simulator but not in the model. Nevertheless, the models do indicate the effect of the bus design on the performance of a cache. The values of a and b are more important than w.

[GROC89] also performed a simulation that evaluates the bus utilization for four bus designs with both write through and write back policies. The columns of Table 2.9 labeled SIM are the simulation results, while the columns labeled MOD are the model results. The workload

Bus Designs (a b w)	Normalized Execution Clocks	Normalized t_{ea}
2 1 2	1.17	1.14
3 1 2	1.21	1.21
4 1 2	1.26	1.28
2 1 3	1.21	1.14
2 2 2	1.28	1.38
4 1 4	1.38	1.28

TABLE 2.8 Simulation and model results comparison.

Bus Design	Write Through		Write Back	
a b w	SIM	MOD	SIM	MOD
2 1 2	0.40	0.45	0.27	0.35
4 1 3	0.53	0.57	0.35	0.44
6 2 4	0.68	0.71	0.48	0.57

TABLE 2.9   Bus utilization.

and cache design parameters are the same as used in the examples above; only the bus parameters are varied.

The modeled values of bus utilization are quite close to those found by simulation, validating somewhat the analytic models. The model results are, in all cases, conservative, showing greater utilization that is indicated by simulation. As would be expected, a slow bus exhibits higher utilization for both write through and write back designs.

2.2.6 *Replacement Policy*

When there is a read miss or a write-allocate, it may be necessary to evict a block from the cache to the main memory to make room for the block that is to be fetched.

Replacement policy determines the block or sector to be evicted; hence, it is only needed for write back data or unified caches as write through data caches and instruction caches can have a block overwritten as the main memory is consistent with the cache. The cache organizations and their constraints, also noted in Section 2.1, on a replacement policy are as follows.

Direct caches (S, 1, 1, A) offer no eviction alternatives. There is only one block into which the new block can be placed.

Even though *direct caches (S, 1, B, A)* may have more than one block per sector, a selection of blocks is not required as the sectors and blocks are uniquely addressed.

Set associative caches (S, SE, 1, A), (S, SE, B, A) have more than one sector within a set and each sector may have more than one block. Thus the replacement choice is one of selecting the sector and/or block based on a use factor.

The fetched block can replace any block of an *associative cache (1, SE, 1, A)*. The selection techniques for identifying a sector or block are the same as for the set associative cache. The set chosen for eviction is determined by a use factor.

For the caches with replacement policies based on a use factor, there are a number of methods that can be used to select the sector or block for eviction. These methods have been extensively discussed by [PUZA85] and others and were first investigated in the context of virtual memory; much of the relevant literature is found in that area. The primary concern when selecting a method is to reduce the bus traffic that will result if a sector or block is moved to the main memory only to be needed again in a short time. In other words, attempts are made to identify temporal locality and only move a sector or block that will not (one hopes) be needed in the near future. These selection methods are briefly discussed below for blocks or sectors; the term *block* will be used for this discussion.

The block to be evicted can be selected by a *random choice*. A random choice can be made in a number of ways, including sampling a pseudorandom number generator, such as the low-order bits of the real time clock, in order to obtain the designator of the block to be evicted.

The block can be selected based upon the criteria of *least recently used* (LRU). The LRU policy is based on the idea that the least recently used block is least likely to be used in the future. Implementation of this method requires that an activity file be maintained for each block; the activity file is probed to find the block to evict.

The LRU strategy has the unfortunate property that a block can be evicted just before it is requested again. The reason that this untimely eviction can happen is that cache misses do not have a uniform distribution within the address space but can be clustered. The blocks associated with these clusters stand a good chance of being evicted from the cache just when they are needed. Pomerene et al. [POME84, STON93] described a technique that anticipates premature eviction and creates a *shadow directory* that assists in improving the replacement policy of LRU.

With the *first in first out* (FIFO) method, the block that has been in the cache the longest is assumed to be the least likely to be needed again and can be evicted. The FIFO method requires a queue for each sector or set. As a block is referenced, its name is placed on the top of the queue. When a miss occurs, the block name on the bottom of the queue is selected for eviction. Large caches require a large number of queues, which can result in a slower cache.

The LRU and FIFO policies become quite complicated to implement for set associative caches with multiple block sectors. Simulations and performance measurements of real systems indicate that the simple random policy is usually adequate for most cases. On the other hand, processors such as the MC88100 and i486 have caches with modified LRU policies that are discussed in Sections 2.4 and 2.6.

2.2.7 *Block Size Considerations*

The design issue of block size was mentioned in previous sections. Two consequences of block size selection are important: (1) block size effect on P_{miss} and (2) block size effect on transport time. These two effects combine to make block size a significant determinant of small cache performance and were studied extensively by Smith [SMIT87].

The effect of block size on P_{miss} is considered first. For increasing block size, P_{miss} will decrease because of spatial locality. In effect, prefetching larger blocks of information decreases future misses. On the other hand, as the size of the block becomes large with respect to the size of the cache, P_{miss} will begin to increase. This increase in P_{miss} occurs because the capacity of the cache is divided into a smaller number of uniquely AUs. This leads to dominance of capacity misses as a result of information loaded into the cache that is never used and is given the name *memory pollution* [SMIT78].

Smith [SMIT87] gave data on P_{miss} as a function of block and cache sizes for unified, instruction and data caches; an excerpt of this data is shown in Table 2.10. The excerpted Smith data shows that P_{miss} decreases monotonically with an increase in block size. However, for very small caches (the data is not shown in this table) there is a block size that gives a minimum P_{miss}. Since large caches dominate today's designs, small caches are of little practical interest.

The second consideration of block size selection is the impact on miss transport time (discussed in Section 2.2.1) as well as the resulting impact on the weighted average cache access time. Recall that for the sequential-forward cache

$$t_{\text{ea}} = 1 + P_{\text{miss}}T \text{ and } T = a + b(\tfrac{A}{Wd} - 1), t_{\text{ea}} = 1 + P_{miss}(a + b(\tfrac{A}{Wd} - 1)).$$

Cache Size	Block Size (bytes)					
Unified cache	4	8	16	32	64	128
2048 bytes	0.405	0.258	0.170	0.124	0.098	0.093
8192 bytes	0.232	0.135	0.080	0.050	0.033	0.025
32768 bytes	0.124	0.070	0.040	0.024	0.014	0.009
Instruction cache						
2048 bytes	0.391	0.234	0.150	0.098	0.068	0.057
8192 bytes	0.172	0.100	0.060	0.037	0.230	0.016
32768 bytes	0.091	0.052	0.030	0.017	0.010	0.007
Data cache						
2048 bytes	0.256	0.169	0.120	0.094	0.083	0.089
8192 bytes	0.214	0.129	0.080	0.053	0.039	0.032
32768 bytes	0.108	0.065	0.040	0.025	0.017	0.012

TABLE 2.10 P_{miss} as a function of cache size and block size.

Cache Type-Size	Block Size (bytes)					
Unified cache	4	8	16	32	64	128
2048 bytes	160	110	100	105	112	200
8192 bytes	75	50	35	30	30	32
32768 bytes	50	32	24	20	18	21

TABLE 2.11 Nanoseconds/memory reference.

Smith [SMIT87] provided results of simulations that show the effect on t_{ea} as the cache and block sizes are varied and for various values of a and b. Table 2.11 shows an excerpt of results for a unified cache with $a = 360$ ns and $b = 15$ ns.

These results clearly show, due to the interaction between P_{miss} and transport time, that there is a clear minimum in the time for a memory reference as the block size is varied. For the small cache of 2 Kbytes, the minimum occurs with a block size of 16 bytes. For the larger 32-Kbyte cache, the minimum moves out to 64 bytes. However, for the larger caches, the minimum is very shallow, which indicates considerable latitude in block size selection. This data suggests that larger block sizes will be more common with the larger cache sizes of today. For example, the RS/6000 64-Kbyte data cache has a 128-byte block.

Hill and Smith [HILL84] reported on the effect of sector and block sizes on the bus traffic ratio. They pointed out that an instruction miss can fetch more instructions than will be used by the processor. Thus, it is possible to have a bus traffic ratio that is greater than one. Caches with a one-word block ($A = 1$) and an AU equal to the instruction word length will always have a bus traffic ratio of one or less for instruction caches.

As previously noted, the bus traffic ratio may be a major design concern for shared memory multiprocessors that have a multiplicity of caches on one bus to the main memory. As the bus traffic is proportional to the product of P_{miss} and the transport time, the bus traffic ratio can increase with block size. The reason for this is that, as the block size increases, the transport time may increase faster than P_{miss} decreases due to the larger block size. For this and other reasons, processors intended for multiprocessor use may have sets with one sector of one block of one word [STEN90]. The penalty of an increased P_{miss} is viewed as acceptable so as not to saturate the bus.

2.2.8 *Bus Design Considerations*

In previous discussions, there have been a number of references to the bus that connects the cache to the main memory. A complete discussion of buses is not possible in this book; however, a few comments are still needed. See [LEVY78, BORR81, VAND89, WARD90] for more details. An excellent collection of papers on various buses is found in [DIGI90]. The engineering aspects of bus design are carefully described in [DELC86].

Computers of the 1950s and 1960s had their major functional modules interconnected by ad hoc connection paths. The designers of the PDP-5 [BELL78] introduced the concept of the bus, which provided for modular interconnection of the functional modules by a standard interface known as a *BUS*.

There are two basic low-level control methods with buses: synchronous and asynchronous. Examples of both types can be found in systems and standards. For example, the *Futurebus* (IEEE896) is asynchronous and the *NuBus* (IEEE1196) is synchronous. Another low-level architectural feature is whether or not the addresses are multiplexed with the data blocks on the bus. Because the receiving device must decode addresses before the data can be accepted or generated, it is natural that address/data multiplexing be used. However, multiplexing adds timing and control complexity to the bus to accommodate saving conductor paths. Examples of these two methods are found in the *Futurebus*, which is multiplexed, and the *VMEBus*, which is not multiplexed.

Regardless of the control method, there are two performance parameters of interest in relation to cache–main memory interconnections. These are the latency and transfer rate, in other words, the components of the transport time model. Unlike the multiplicity of ad hoc buses used on the early computers, a single interconnection bus must be time shared among the various requesters and bus designers strive to provide the smallest latency and the highest bandwidth possible between the sources and sinks. A bus transfer consists of the following steps:

1. Arbitration for bus mastership.
2. Transmission of the address.
3. Receipt of the address, decoding, and acknowledgment.
4. Transfer of data.

The first three steps constitute the latency of the transaction while step 4 gives the transfer rate. The total time of the transaction is the sum of the latency and the data transfer time. Because the latency is usually larger than the transfer time of a single AU, block transfers are employed if at all possible. The bandwidth of a bus is derived from the transport time model of Figure 2.13.

$$\text{Bandwidth} = \frac{A}{\text{latency} + \text{transfer time}}.$$

It follows from the above that the maximum bandwidth of a bus has an upper limit of A/transfer time that is achieved only when the block becomes very large and the latency is totally prorated. However, as was discussed earlier, a typical block size is only 4 to 64 AUs. Thus, low latency is a prime requirement for a good bus.

A number of manufacturer-supported buses have been developed over the years. A brief, and incomplete, list includes:

Manufacturer	Bus Names
DEC	*Unibus*
	VAX SBI
IBM	AT Bus
	Micro Channel
Intel	Multibus
Motorola	VMEBus, IEEE P1014/d1.2
Texas Instruments, MIT	NuBus
Several	Futurebus, IEEE

As processors and memories have become faster, bus technology has not kept pace. System designers are therefore reverting back to the techniques of the 1950s and 1960s and employing special dedicated buses that do not need the generality of the buses discussed above.

An example of a dedicated bus is found in the Compaq *Deskpro* 386/20 [VANN88]. An IBM AT compatible bus interconnects the main memory to the DMAs. A special 32-bit bus connects the cache to the main memory. With a dedicated bus, the design is specific to the task of transferring blocks between the main memory and cache. The number of loads on the bus is fixed as are the physical distances involved. Thus, the latency can be minimized and the bandwidth improved. A dedicated graphics bus is common today with high-performance personal computers.

Borrill [BORR81] has classified the various levels and use of buses. By his taxonomy, a dedicated bus is known as a component-level bus and named *Level* 0. The bus connecting the main memory to DMAs is named *Level* 1 and is more commonly known as the *backplane bus*.

The bus between a cache and the main memory is usually optimized for fetching a block. However, a nontrivial fraction of bus transactions are writes of a single AU that result from the use of a write through policy. Recall from Table 1.1 that reads represent, on average, 93% of memory references while writes represent 7%. If a unified cache has a P_{miss} of 0.05 for reads and all writes are sent by the bus to the memory (as with a write through policy), then writes constitute approximately

60% of the bus transactions. With the i486, for example, writes on the bus constitute 70% of the bus transactions [CRAW90].

The IEEE Futurebus has been adopted by a number of manufacturers for new processors such as the Intel Pentium and the PowerPC 601. This bus, in conjunction with the MESI cache coherency protocol [GALL91], supports multiprocessors and is discussed in Section 4.2.5.

Another newcomer in the field of buses is the RAMBUS [WILS92]. The bus structure is integrated into the DRAM and can provide rapid block transfer. The DRAMS operate in a mode similar to the nibble mode described in Section 5.1.6. Advertised performance values for byte transfers are $a = 48$ ns, $b = 2$ ns. The proponents of these devices suggest that by sufficiently reducing the transport time between the main memory and the cache, the need for second-level caches is eliminated.

Bus latency and bandwidth are being recognized as limiting factors in the performance of processors for some workloads. This limit is discussed in Chapter 11 with regard to the CRAY-1 and CRAY X-MP memory buses. The commonly used SPEC benchmarks, except for one case, are processor bound and do not hit the bus limit to performance. However, as contemporary microprocessors tend toward the execution of programs with poor locality, the bus performance limit will become critical.

2.3 Instruction Buffering Schemes

Because the major source of memory references is instruction reads, computer designers first applied hardware assistance to instruction latency reduction and increased instruction bandwidth. This section discusses instruction *buffering schemes* that are represented by three very distinct techniques: *instruction buffers*, *instruction queues*, and *instruction caches* [KURI91]. These three buffering schemes are designed specifically to support instruction reads, and their organization and policies are based on the particular characteristics of instruction addressing patterns.

By employing an instruction buffering scheme, two paths to the main memory are provided: the instruction path and the data path. The effect can be a substantial improvement in performance for processors that require high-memory bandwidth. Therefore, if, for any reason, only one buffering scheme can be implemented, it should generally be as an instruction buffer, which can provide another path to the main memory.

Instructions are read, except for branches, from adjacent memory locations giving a high degree of spatial locality. Also, scientific programs are characterized by an extensive use of loops that provide a high degree of temporal locality. In the sections to follow, buffers, queues, and caches that support one or both of these locality characteristics will be described. The three instruction buffering schemes to be discussed are:

1. *instruction buffers* that catch and hold previously used instructions for reuse, providing look behind;
2. *instruction queues* for prefetching instructions, providing look ahead;
3. *instruction caches*, providing both look ahead and look behind.

Instruction buffer schemes are unique in that only a fetch policy is required; the processor does not write into the instruction buffer, queue, or cache. Thus, instruction buffering schemes do not have the complications of supporting writes. However, for systems executing self-modifying code, a unified cache is usually employed in conjunction with branch instructions that flush the instruction prefetch in the hierarchy so that modified instructions can be written directly into the cache without a coherency problem. The Intel Pentium caches, to be described later, are exceptions to this generalization.

Another form of an instruction buffer scheme is known as a *branch target cache* (BTC), sometimes known as a *target instruction buffer*, that stores the stream of an instruction path that may be taken. BTCs are discussed in Chapter 7.

2.3.1 *Instruction Buffers*

The CDC 6600 is a scientific supercomputer that uses instruction buffering. This computer, designed by Seymour Cray in the early 1960s, has an instruction buffer that supports temporal locality [THOR70]. The use of a buffer that can hold a loop eliminates further references to the main memory for instructions. The loop is loaded into the buffer on the first instance of fetching an instruction in the loop; thus, this type of instruction buffer is referred to as a *loop catcher*.

The buffer is a push-down-stack-like structure, called an *instruction stack* by CDC, to save instructions for reuse. New instructions are fetched, placed in execution, and pushed on the top of the stack. When the program counter reads the next instruction, the address is compared with the addresses of instructions available in the buffer by an associative search. If the instruction is in the buffer, it is read from the stack; if it is not in the stack, it is fetched from the main memory. When the buffer is full, additional fetches from the main memory will cause the buffer to overflow and, hence, some of the instructions to be lost. Note that an associative cache with a FIFO replacement policy is functionally equivalent to the CDC 6600 instruction buffer.

The instruction buffer consists of eight 60-bit registers that are able to hold sixteen 30-bit instructions or thirty-two 15-bit instructions or combinations of the two. Thus, a large fraction of loops found in scientific programs can be made resident in the stack, thus eliminating subsequent fetches from the main memory. The access time to the stack is one clock (100 ns) while a fetch from the main memory requires a minimum of 4 clock cycles; in some cases the latency is larger because of the time required to access the interleaved core memory.

The Cray-1 and subsequent Cray processors employ similar instruction buffers. The major difference is found in the size of the buffer, which has been increased to 256 16-bit instructions. The buffer is interleaved four ways so that concurrent fetches into the buffer from the main memory and instruction reads by the processor can be sustained. The interleaving matches the interleaving of the main memory, which results in a fetch rate of four 16-bit instructions per clock.

2.3.2 *Instruction Queues*

An instruction queue solves many of the problems associated with supplying an instruction stream without delays in two ways.

1. An instruction prefetch queue can hide the memory system latency by prefetching instructions. The latency can be either the latency of an interleaved memory or the delay latency caused by a cache miss. If enough instructions can be queued up, the delay of a cache miss is hidden as the processor can continue to fetch instructions from the queue. Two contemporary examples of this use of instruction queues are found in the Intel Pentium and the PowerPC 601. In the case of the Pentium, there are two queues—one stores the in-line instruction stream and the other stores the target instruction stream, as described in Chapter 7.

2. Some instruction queues provide read latencies of one clock for many variable-length instructions or multiple instructions when the queue is not empty. A smooth flow of variable-length instructions can be supplied to the decoder, making the instruction fetch into the decoder a single-clock event for most instructions. Otherwise, instruction fetches are multiple-clock operations without the prefetch queue. For RISC processors with fixed-length instructions, this type of queue and instruction prefetching is not required.

Instruction queues work because of spatial locality of instruction streams while temporal locality is usually not supported. Instruction queues are found in two topologies, as shown in Figure 2.16. One topology uses an instruction queue between the processor and an interleaved memory, while the other topology has a cache between the queue and the interleaved memory. As will be discussed later, the management policies and performance models of these two topologies are different.

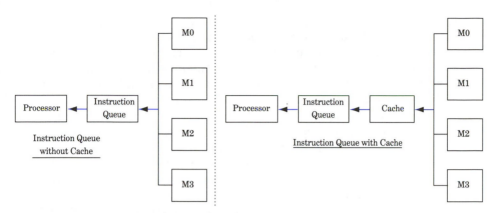

FIGURE 2.16   Instruction queue topologies.

An instruction queue that smoothes the flow of variable-length instructions has interesting properties. Instructions fill the queue in sequential order at the top. At the bottom of the queue, there is logic that permits a variable number of bytes, or instructions, to be extracted broadside from the queue. Up to a design limit, four bytes for example, instructions with one, two, three, or four bytes can be extracted in one clock and passed to the processor. The span of the extraction logic is controlled by the instruction fetch stage and may require a partial decode of an instruction byte to determine the number of subsequent bytes to extract.

The IBM 7030 Stretch is the first known use of an instruction queue. This computer was developed for The Lawrence Livermore Laboratory starting in 1956 [BLOC59]. This processor has a 64-bit bus to an interleaved memory and instruction lengths of 32 and 64 bits. The queue holds four 32-bit instructions. Sixty 4-bits (two 32-bit instructions) are fetched in one bus cycle into the queue. When the first instruction is read from the queue by the processor, a reference is made to the main memory to fetch another 64 bits. The queue supplies one instruction, single or double length, in one cycle. In the absence of branches, the instruction processing rate of the processor is exceeded by the fetch bandwidth and there are no delays for instruction fetches.

The IBM S/360/91 extended the use of an instruction queue while continuing the ability to smooth variable-length instruction issue to the execution units. The instruction queue is 8 deep with each level having words of 64 bits, holding approximately 16 instructions [ANDE67]. The instruction queue can be placed in "loop mode," which halts prefetching and locks in loops to provide "look behind" supporting temporal locality.

The main memory of this processor consists of interleaved memory modules, which will be discussed in Chapter 4.

The VAX 11/780 has an instruction prefetch queue, which is named an *instruction prefetch buffer* [LEON87]. The maximum length of a VAX instruction is 50 bytes; however, the weighted average VAX instruction length is 3.8 bytes; 96% are 3 bytes or less and 98% are 8 bytes or less [FITE90]. The instruction queue holds 8 bytes; thus, the queue can hold approximately two instructions when it is full, and instructions are removed from the queue 1 byte at a time. When there is space for a 4-byte block load from the cache, the prefetch is triggered and the block is loaded broadside into the queue. This flow of instructions continues until a branch is encountered.

The VAX 9000 expanded the instruction queue of the VAX 11/780 to 25 bytes [MURR90], a queue that holds approximately six 3-byte instructions. More importantly, the decoder can read up to 4 bytes (the op-code and three specifiers) in one clock from the queue by conditionally decoding the next instruction.

An interesting case study on the use of instruction queues is found in the ix86 family. The first member of this family, the i8086, employed a queue (named a buffer by Intel) of 6 bytes. This depth was selected by simulation and by considerations of the chip area required for the queue [MCKI79]. The i186 and i286 retained the 6-byte queue but added a second queue that holds three decoded instructions, and the fetch path to the main memory was extended to 16 bits.

The size of the ix86 processor queues has increased with the evolution of this processor family. The i386 has a similar instruction prefetch mechanism. However, the prefetch is 4 bytes rather than 2, and the queue is 8 bytes rather than 6. Simulation results [GROC89] show that the instruction queue of the i386 had $P_{miss} = 0.05$ while the i486, described later in this chapter, has $P_{miss} = 0.03$. The meaning of P_{miss} in a queue is that the requested AU is not in the queue and that a reference to a lower level in the memory system is required. In other words, the prefetch queue has not been able to keep up with the flow of instructions into the processor.

The i486 employs instruction prefetching into a 32-byte queue from a unified on-chip cache [CRAW90]. This queue is required because instruction can vary in length between 1 and 15 bytes, with an average length of 3 bytes. The first stage of the pipeline prefetches instructions into one of two 16-byte queues. Three bytes are read in parallel from the queue into the first decoder stage of the pipeline; the prefetch stage and its queues operate independently from the balance of the pipeline. With this system, a large number of the simple instructions can be decoded at a rate of one per clock even though they are of variable length.

The average input and output data rates from the queues are equal, but the queue is required to smooth out the flow due to the variable-length instructions if one instruction per clock is to be fetched. To achieve this smoothing effect, the i486 path between the on-chip cache and the instruction queue provides approximately 9 times the required instruction bandwidth. This path transfers 16 bytes in one clock into the queue. The i486 CPI is approximately 1.75, and each instruction is approximately 3 bytes. Thus, instruction fetching from the queue consumes $3/1.75 = 1.7$ bytes per clock, giving a bandwidth multiplier of $16/1.7 = 9.4$. Because the input is driven by a prefetch type request, in the steady state, the average input bandwidth to the queue is equal to the consuming bandwidth of the instruction processor.

The PowerPC 601 [MOTO93] instruction queue holds up to eight instructions prefetched from tl ̄ ̇ ̄-line instruction stream. The Power PC 601 is a superscalar processor, which will be discussed in Chapter 10, and can issue up to three instructions in one clock. The queue control attempts to keep the queue full at all times by fetches from the on-chip unified cache. When there is a cache miss, the main memory access will occur only if the top five entries are empty. This strategy delays main memory references until a useful number of instructions, that is a block of 16 bytes, is needed, thus reducing the number of bus access cycles.

Simple models for two systems using interleaved memory without a cache are developed in the following paragraphs. The two systems are for double buffers and a single queue that has concurrent loads and stores.

Double Buffer Model

A simple model for the size of a double buffer instruction queue that is serviced from an interleaved memory, without a cache, is developed here. Three parameters are of interest in an instruction queue:

1. the rate at which the lower level of the memory hierarchy can fill the queue,
2. the rate at which the processor consumes instructions,
3. the size of the queue.

If the queue is too small or the fill rate is too low, the inherent processing rate of the processor cannot be sustained. A simple match of the steady-state bandwidths may indicate that a queue is not needed. However, the real problem is not the steady-state rate at which the queue is filled but, for an interleaved memory, the transport time required to fill the queue or, for a cache system, the time to fill the queue if there is a cache miss.

For the model, the queue is assumed to be a double buffer, as with

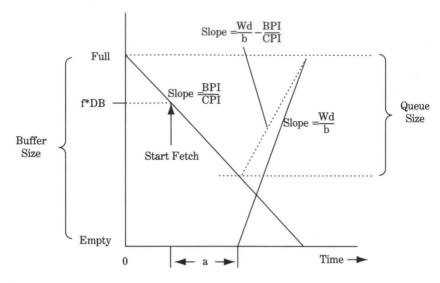

FIGURE 2.17 Queue fetch model.

the Pentium. One buffer is supplying instructions while the other buffer is being filled from the memory. As shown in Figure 2.17, one buffer is assumed to be full at t_0 ($DB = 1$) and the processor is extracting instructions at the rate:

$$\text{extraction rate} = \frac{\text{bytes per instruction}}{\text{clocks per instruction}} = \frac{\text{BPI}}{\text{CPI}}.$$

When the queue has been depleted to a point $f \times DB$ (f is a design parameter), an access to the interleaved memory begins. The second buffer must be filled from the interleaved memory before the first buffer is emptied by the processor. After a delay of a, the second buffer fills at the rate Wd/b; these variables are taken from the transport time model.

From the geometry of Figure 2.17, the following time equality (the time to fill the second buffer must equal the time to empty the first buffer after the fill starts) must hold:

$$a + \frac{b \times DB}{Wd} = \frac{f \times DB \times CPI}{BPI}.$$

And, solving for *DB*,

$$DB = a \left/ \left(\frac{f \times CPI}{BPI} - \frac{b}{Wd} \right) \right..$$

For an example of estimating the size of the buffers, assume the following:

$$a = 8, \qquad b = 1, \qquad Wd = 8, \qquad CPI = 1.25, \qquad BPI = 3, \qquad f = 0.85.$$

Using these system parameters, each of the buffers should be 34.9 bytes. This result agrees with the actual design of the Pentium, which has a double buffer of 32 bytes each. If the first buffer is emptied before the second buffer is full, the processor must stall, an effect that has been called a queue miss.

Queue Model

While a double buffer is easier to control, it requires more bits than is required for a true queue as a queue will fill as it empties. As shown in Figure 2.17, the queue issues a request after the processor has depleted the queue to f and starts to refill after the latency a at the net rate shown in the dotted line (the difference between the fill and extraction rates of the interleaved memory). The queue must only be large enough to be empty when the fill begins, and the fill rate must be greater than the empty rate. A model for the size of a queue can be found from the geometry of Figure 2.17 as

$$Q = a \bigg/ \left[\frac{f \times CPI}{BPI} - 1 \bigg/ \left(\frac{Wd}{b} - \frac{BPI}{CPI} \right) \right].$$

For an example of estimating the size of a queue, the approximate parameters of the IBM S/360/195 are

$$a = 8, \qquad b = 1, \qquad Wd = 8, \qquad CPI = 1.55, \qquad BPI = 4, \qquad f = 0.9.$$

Using these parameters, the model shows a queue size of 61.9 bytes compared to the actual IBM S/360/195 queue that has 64 bytes. Thus, the model gives a reasonable estimate for the size of an instruction queue. This model can be extended to assess the sensitivity of the processor performance as the queue size is varied (recall the discussion about the simulations performed on the i8086).

Table 2.12 gives a summary of instruction queue designs. The queue depth, queue width, memory data path, and whether or not instructions are decoded in the queue are noted. A desirable property is to decode and identify branch instructions in the queue so that branch delays can be reduced (a feature discussed in Chapter 7).

Processor	Queue Depth	Queue Width	Cache/Mem Path Width (Wd)	Decoded Instruction Queue
IBM 7030 (Stretch)	2	4 bytes	4 bytes	No
IBM S/360/91	8	8 bytes	8 bytes	Yes
VAX 11/780	8	1 byte	1–4 bytes	No
i086	3	2 bytes	2 bytes	No
i386	8	2 bytes	4 bytes	Yes
i486	16	2 bytes	4 bytes	Yes
Pentium	1	64 bytes*	32 bytes	No
PowerPC 601	8	4 bytes	32 bytes	Yes

*Double buffers, 32 bytes each.

TABLE 2.12   Processor prefetch queues.

2.3.3 *Instruction Caches*

Since the early 1980s, instruction caches have received accelerated research interest, because VLSI technology provides sufficient chip area for the inclusion of an instruction cache on the chip with the processor. The organization of an instruction cache must now comprehend not only P_{miss} but also the efficiency of layout in order to minimize the chip area devoted to the instruction cache. Also, timing considerations are different with on-chip caches due to the elimination of delays between the processor chip(s) and the cache chip(s).

Instruction caches for VLSI implementation were first discussed by [KATE84] while a separate cache chip was proposed for the RISC II processor [PATT83]. Hill and Smith [HILL84] extended the evaluation by considering on-chip instruction caches. Small instruction caches have given way to larger, more general split caches due to the ability to include relatively large caches on a processor chip.

The RISC research group at Berkeley [PATT83] considered a number of alternative cache designs and issues such as fault tolerance, remote program counters, and Huffman coding of instructions. A cache chip was proposed that is organized as (64, 1, 1, 4). These chips could be configured as either direct or set associative organizations. Simulation results indicate that the set associative configuration provides a slightly better P_{miss}. Each block has a fault tolerant bit that could be used to disable a block precluding its use if an AU is faulty.

Hill and Smith [HILL84] reported on their research into instruction caches for the PDP-11, Z8000, VAX-11, and IBM S/370 architectures. The term *minimum cache* is used to identify a cross between an instruction buffer and a cache. A minimum cache is a buffer that can, unlike pure buffers, recognize branch addresses. The authors use a descriptor that is different than the one introduced in this chapter to describe their caches. They use the 2-tuple (bx, sx) where bx is the number of bytes in the sector (block) and sx is the number of bytes in the block.

Agarwal et al. [AGAR87] investigated alternative organizations for the instruction cache of the MIPS-X processor. In their paper, three cache organizations are analyzed:

1. a set associative cache that uses approximately half of the available space for tag bits; this organization is named a "c cache";
2. an associative cache that is named a "buffer";
3. a set associative cache that reduces the area used for tag bits from that of 1; this organization is named a "hybrid buffer."

Each of these cache variants is evaluated; the block size is varied and P_{miss} data obtained. Trial layouts are also made to assess the chip area required for implementation.

Another instruction cache design is described by Hill [HILL87] for the Berkeley SPUR single-chip microprocessor. The issues and tradeoffs of instruction caches and target instruction buffers (TIB) are examined. TIBs are discussed in Chapter 6; the discussion in this section will deal with the instruction cache only. Hill's research is noteworthy in that circuit implementation issues are considered as well as the more conventional P_{miss} data for the various configurations. As the clock periods decrease, small design details can, if improperly implemented, reduce performance more than changes in cache organization.

The instruction cache for SPUR would, of necessity, be relatively small and have a relatively high P_{miss}. Hill believed that cold starts and multiprogramming effects would be small relative to the naturally high P_{miss}. Thus, multiprograms with cold starts are not directly simulated. However, as a surrogate for real programs, multiprogramming effects are modeled by evicting all of the blocks in the cache after every 30,000 references. Three mutually exclusive policy modes are implemented for the SPUR instruction cache: (1) disabled, (2) enabled without prefetching, and (3) enabled with prefetching. Prefetching in this case refers to fetching the next AU from a miss. The policy modes are program-selectable in order to permit a closer match of the program to the cache policy.

2.3.4 *Published Instruction Cache Hit Data*

In this section we discuss published P_{hit} data for instruction caches. Smith and Goodman [SMIT83] published early results directed to the design of instruction caches based upon a Markov model for the behavior of instruction references. Smith and Goodman considered three replacement algorithms—Random, LRU, and FIFO—for direct-mapped and set associative caches. The Markov models gave qualitative indicators concerning the replacement method and the cache organization. Their model results are also compared to experimental results of three benchmarks written in C, running on a VAX -11 under UNIX.

The conclusions from their experimental results are that the replacement method affects the value of P_{hit} in the second or third decimal place. For this reason, a designer may opt for the simpler design. The second conclusion is that for a given block size, $A = 16$ bytes in this case; P_{miss} for a cache of a given size is not influenced by the number of sets and the number of sectors.

Table 2 of the Smith and Goodman study provides the results that are reproduced in Table 2.13 for caches organized as $(S, SE, 1, 16)$. The figure displays the P_{hit} for the evaluated combinations of S and SE. 45-deg lines from lower left to upper right are lines of equal cache size; these caches also have approximately equal P_{hit}. For example, the design $S = 1$ and $SE = 512$ has the same capacity (8 Kbytes) as the cache with $S = 512$ and $SE = 1$, given that the block sizes are equal. Furthermore, these caches have the same P_{hit} of 0.998. Likewise, other cache designs that are on a diagonal have approximately the same value of P_{hit}.

A conclusion that can be drawn from this data is that the effectiveness of an instruction cache, as measured by P_{hit}, is primarily based upon its size—all other factors are of second-order importance. A further

No. of Sec./Set	Number of Sets									
	1	2	4	8	16	32	64	128	256	512
1			.699	.727	.779	.829	.905	.959	.990	.998
2		.697	.731	.777	.838	.915	.980	.996	.998	
4	.700	.726	.768	.839	.921	.989	.998	.998		
8	.727									
16	.768									
32	.816									
64	.901									
128	.944									
256	.998									
512	.998									

Block size is 16 bytes.

TABLE 2.13   Smith instruction cache P_{hit} data.

observation, for the benchmarks used, is that there is a practical maximum size of an instruction cache. That is, increases in P_{hit} will be relatively small as the size of the cache is increased. When all of a program can be stored in a cache, there is little reason to increase the cache size further. An increase in instruction cache size may even be counterproductive as its cycle time may increase as well.

However, this conclusion can be seriously in error because the benchmarks are quite simple and the study only investigated the effect of capacity and compulsory misses, not the effect of context switching. These effects can significantly change the view of instruction cache size on P_{hit} [THIE87].

Recent research into the effect of instruction cache size and organization $(S, SE, 1, 16)$ on P_{hit} rates used large caches and the SPEC benchmarks [GEE91, GEE93]. These results are published as P_{miss} but are shown, in excerpted form, as P_{hit} in Table 2.14. The values of P_{hit} shown are with a composite workload of floating point and integer programs. Notice that as the cache becomes larger, the influence of organization on P_{hit} is as muted as with the smaller instruction caches shown in Table 2.13. For example, a cache with $S = 4K$ and direct access has $P_{hit} = 0.997$, while the same size cache organized as $SE = 512K$ and $S = 8$ has $P_{hit} = 0.9993$. The difference is probably insignificant for practical purposes.

It is interesting to consider the effect of doubling an instruction cache size using the data of Table 2.14. For example, if the initial organization has $S = 128$ and $SE = 2$, the P_{hit} is 0.976. Doubling the size by doubling the number of sets or the degree of set associativity gives approximately the same P_{hit} (0.983 and 0.984). The design choice then is based on the availability of set index bits in the address and implementation difficulty as the resulting P_{hit} will be approximately the same.

No. of Sec./Set	Number of Sets						
	64	128	256	512	1K	2K	4K
1	.949	.961	.969	.98	.988	.993	.997
2	.966	.976	.983	.99	.992	.997	.9998
4	.977	.984	.991	.992	.999	.9998	.9999
8	.984	.991	.992	.9993	.9998	1.0	1.0

Block size is 16 bytes.

TABLE 2.14 Instruction cache P_{hit}, SPEC benchmarks, overall.

2.3.5 *Contemporary Instruction Caches*

There are few examples of contemporary instruction caches that are not used in conjunction with a data cache. The reason for this is that the rapid increase in circuit density has permitted the inclusion of a split cache on the chip; small on-chip instruction caches were quickly made obsolete by split on-chip caches. For some contemporary processors, the instruction and data caches are identical in organization so as to reduce the design task.

One example of a solo instruction cache is found in the Motorola MC68020. The MC68020 is designed with a small instruction cache so as to reduce the number of instruction fetches from the main memory [MACG84]. With an instruction cache, accesses of instructions and data can overlap when there is an instruction hit on the cache. The chip area was limited, and the area that was available could best be used as an instruction cache.

The MC68020 cache is a direct cache organized as (64, 1, 1, 2) [MOTO90b]. The instruction AU of the MC680x0 processor is 32 bits, 4 bytes, and each sector-block contains two of these AUs. The policy of the cache can be selected from a number of options under program control that is exercised by 4 bits in the Cache Control Register. Bit 0 enables/disables the cache. Bit 1 freezes the cache so that valid data cannot be evicted. Bit 2, named the Clear Entry bit, permits the location in the address to be invalidated. Finally, bit 3 clears the cache of all data and tags. The requirement for these programmable policy functions is discussed in Section 2.8.1.

An example of a unique instruction cache that works with a data cache is found in the IBM RS/6000. This instruction cache has special properties that are needed to support superscalar operation and is described in Chapter 11. I note that the Motorola MC88110 superscalar processor uses almost symmetrical instruction and data caches [DIEF92]. The difference being that the data cache has snoop tags that the instruction cache does not need. Snoopy controllers are discussed in Chapter 4.

2.4 Data Caches

Data caches are provided, usually in combination with an instruction buffer, queue, or cache, to reduce the latency of data fetches. Unlike instruction caches, data caches must support writes as well as reads. As shown in Table 1.1, approximately 29% of all memory references are data reads and approximately 7% of all references are data writes. However, writes to a data cache constitute approximately 25% of all data cache references while reads are 75% of all data cache references. Thus, improving reads is more important than improving writes. The design issues of data caches concern organization and the method of supporting write operations (discussed in Section 2.2.6).

2.4.1 *Published Data Cache Miss Data*

Data-addressing patterns have poorer temporal and spatial locality than instruction-addressing patterns. Unlike instruction and unified caches, until recently, there has been little published P_{miss} data for data caches. Table 2.15 shows the P_{miss} data for data caches excerpted from [GEE91, GEE93] for SPEC benchmarks. The combined floating point and integer (called overall) P_{miss} values are shown for an organization (S, SE, 1, 16).

The information in Table 2.15 shows a significant increase in P_{miss} for direct caches as compared to other organizations of the same size. For all other organizations, the value of P_{miss} is only sensitive to cache size. Note the tradeoff derived from doubling the size of a data cache. For a small cache ($S = 64$, $SE = 1$) it is better to double the number of sectors rather than the number of sets, if possible. However, for a large cache, there is no significant difference in P_{miss} for the two options if the original cache design is not direct ($SE = 1$). These observations are similar to those made about instruction caches.

			Number of Sets				
No. of Sec./Set	64	128	256	512	1K	2K	4K
1	.255	.216	.170	.114	.087	.069	.057
2	.188	.155	.104	.074	.059	.048	.039
4	.134	.098	.071	.058	.047	.038	.028
8	.091	.069	.057	.047	.038	.028	.017

Block size is 16 bytes.

TABLE 2.15 Data cache P_{miss}, SPEC benchmarks, overall.

2.4.2 *Contemporary Data Caches*

Data caches, used in split cache topologies, are becoming common with contemporary processors. In this section, a representative sample of data cache designs are described. In some cases the data cache organization is the same as the instruction cache and, in other cases, different.

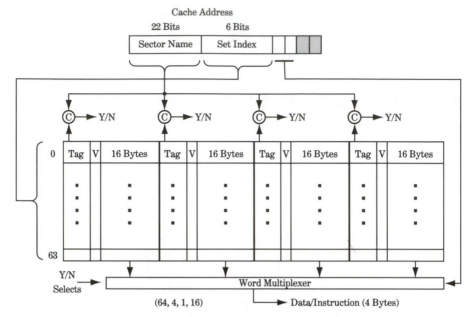

FIGURE 2.18   Motorola 68040 data and instruction cache.

MC68040 Data Cache

The designers of the MC68040 chose to have a symmetrical cache
[MOTO89]; that is, the instruction and data caches are identical. Each
cache is 4 Kbytes, organized as (64, 4, 1, 16) [MOTO89] and shown in
Figure 2.18. This cache has 22 tag bits per sector, various control bits,
and a 16-byte block. Two bits of the address select one of four words in
the sector-block that is passed to the processor.

We speculate that the reason behind the design decision to use the
same organization for the data and instruction caches is that the design
effort is less costly due to reduced the design cycle time and design cost
of the processor. The P_{miss} data of Table 2.14 and Table 2.15 for SPEC
benchmarks indicate that, for two 4-Kbyte caches, identical organizations
provide reasonable P_{miss} for both caches. Tweaking the organizations
would be of little benefit.

The split caches of the MC68040 communicate to the memory system
over a common bus that serves cache misses. A second-level cache is
not anticipated because of the relatively large size of the on-chip caches
and the resulting low P_{miss}.

For caches with one block per sector (sector-block), a replacement
policy is needed to select a sector-block for eviction for a data cache, or
overwriting for an instruction cache, when all of the tag comparisons

indicate occupied sector-blocks. Such a replacement policy is illustrated with the MC68040 data cache. The replacement policy follows two steps.

1. Locate the first invalid sector-block and replace it.

2. If step #1 does not succeed, a pseudorandom algorithm selects one of the valid sectors (blocks) and replaces that sector. There is a 2-bit count that is incremented once for each half-sector access; this counter provides the pseudorandom pointer to the sector to be replaced.

Motorola MC88100 Data Cache

The Motorola MC88100 architecture specifies two paths to the main memory—one path for instructions and another for data. In support of this memory organization, the MC88200 provides two caches of equal size and organization. Note that this is a chip separate from the processor chip and that instruction and data references pass from the processor to this chip. The two caches can be addressed with either virtual or real addresses. The block diagram is shown in Figure 2.19 [MOTO90a].

This cache organization is (256, 4, 1, 16) with the usual tag bits for

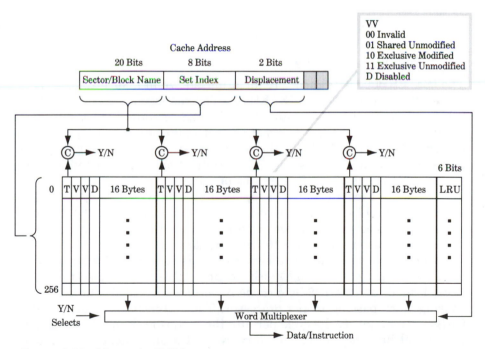

FIGURE 2.19   Motorola 88200 cache.

each sector-block. In addition, there are two V bits and a D bit that have the coding shown in the figure. These bits are used to manage the cache and preserve coherency in a multiprocessor configuration (discussed further in Chapter 4). In addition, each set has six bits that maintain an LRU status of the four sectors within each set. These bits support an LRU replacement policy for the cache. Upon a miss, if one or more of the valid bits are not set, that sector-block is used for the new sector. However, if all of the valid bits are set, the LRU mechanism selects the sector-block to be written back if in the write back mode or to be over-written if it is in the write through mode.

As the cache is filled, the six pseudorandom bits, numbered L0 through L5, are set as follows.

Sector-block1 is *more recently used than* Sector-block0, Set L0.
Sector-block2 is *more recently used than* Sector-block0, Set L1.
Sector-block2 is *more recently used than* Sector-block1, Set L2.
Sector-block3 is *more recently used than* Sector-block0, Set L3.
Sector-block3 is *more recently used than* Sector-block1, Set L4.
Sector-block3 is *more recently used than* Sector-block2, Set L5.

Identification of the LRU sector-block can be made by examination of these six bits. It can be shown, for example, that for the LRU bits 111001 (L5–L0) sector-block3 is the most recently used and is the candidate for replacement.

IBM RS/6000 Data Cache

The IBM RS/6000 data cache organization, shown in Figure 2.20, is (128, 4, 1, 128) with 64 Kbytes [BAKO90]. The management policy is late select, allocate, write back (store in). The 128 sets are divided into four groups of 32 sets; the five LSBs of the set index access the four groups in parallel. The two MSBs of the set index are provided after they are translated via the TLB (discussed in Chapter 4 and Fig. 4.5) and provide a late select of one of the four groups of sets.

The write back strategy is supported by 128-byte *store back buffers* (SBB). When a block is to be written to the main memory, all 128 bytes of the sector-block are transferred in parallel to the SBB and then sent to the main memory in eight, 16-byte chunks.

When a reload of a cache sector-block is required, the strategy is *fetch bypassed (load through)* (see Section 2.2.4) with the sector-block being loaded into the 128-byte *cache reload buffers* (CRB) and the miss causing word passing to the processor. The sector-block resides in the CRBs until an idle cache cycle permits the sector-block to be transferred in parallel into the cache. The duty cycle of a data cache is less than that of an instruction cache; as a result, idle cycles will occur. If a read

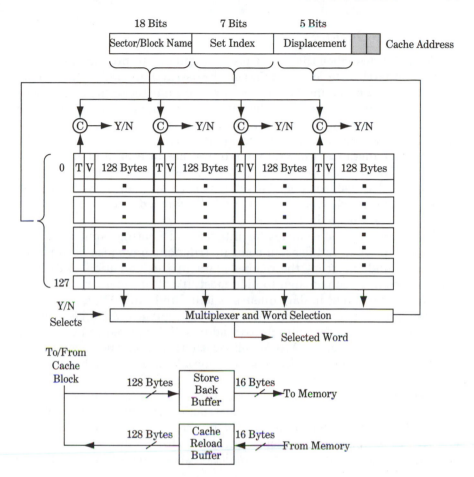

FIGURE 2.20   IBM RS/6000 data cache.

reference is made to this sector-block before it is transferred into the cache, the fetch is satisfied from the CRB. This action precludes the cache being locked out from other references during the time the new block is waiting for an idle cache cycle. Nonblocking loads are possible because the CRB is disjoint from the cache.

There is only one CRB; therefore, if a second cache miss occurs before the CRB has been transferred, the second miss is not served until the first load is complete. The CRB acts like a one sector-block cache with tags that permits reads from it. It appears from [MATI89] that a write miss uses an allocate strategy on the CRB. The sector-block is fetched into the CRB, modified, moved into the SBB, and then written back to the main memory.

2.4.3 *Data Queues*

Section 2.3.2 describes the use of prefetch queues to provide a constant instruction fetch rate for variable-length instructions and to hide memory latency and cache miss transport time. Similar techniques have been used for data fetches as well. The same two problems are present with data fetches, namely, variable-length data types and the desire to hide memory latency and cache miss transport time.

The first instance, known to me, of the use of a data queue is with the IBM S/360/91 [AND67]. When an instruction that requires a memory reference is decoded, the effective address is computed, the read request is sent to the interleaved memory, and the fetched data is sent to one of two of the six-deep data queue.

There are separate queues for integer and floating point data. The predecoded integer and floating point instructions have also been placed on queues and intercept the queued data in the execution units. The data queues are deep enough to hide most, if not all, memory latencies.

Renewed interest in data queues is found in [EICK93], a paper that reports on recent research on the use of data queues. A major problem with data queues is that an effective address is required to access data to be placed in the queue. With pipelines, there can be true dependencies on the effective address, leading to a problem. As with branches, a prediction of the effective address must be used that may prove to be incorrect. For example, one prediction strategy is to use the same effective address used the last time the instruction was executed. However, this predicted effective address may be incorrect, and the prefetch is not effective and unnecessarily loads the bus with traffic. The [EICK93] paper describes effective address prediction strategies and assesses their effectiveness.

2.5 Unified Caches

A unified cache holds both instructions and data and is a manifestation of the von Neumann architecture. It provides a single port to the main memory, via the cache, for both instruction and data references. The organization of a unified cache is selected to best match the address sequences of combined instruction and data reads and must support data write operations.

Early research and design of caches focused on unified caches as seen in the work of [BLOO62, LIPT68, LEE69]. During this early period, processors were either hard-wired or microprogrammed with little overlap in execution. Thus, instruction and data reads did not usually contend for access to the cache. Without instruction and data contention, the single access port toe unified cache is satisfactory. This is not the case with pipelined processors. An early processor that could have contention is the UNIVAC LARC, an experimental pipelined processor that could simultaneously fetch both instructions and data [ECKE59]. However, the use of a large general-purpose register file reduced the number of contentions.

Bloom et al. [BLOO62] described the first cache when studying design alternatives for a high-performance computer. The cache organization is (1, 16, 1, 1). Each sector-block of the cache contained the tag, valid bits, and one computer word of data. This cache is named a *look aside buffer*, a term later associated with virtual memory. Replacement of a sector-block is on an LRU basis and determined by the charge on a capacitor associated with each sector-block. Other early work on caches was performed by Project MAC, sponsored by ARPA (a.k.a. DARPA).

The IBM S/360/85 is the first known commercial implementation of a cache in a large-scale computer [LIPT68]. Subsequent to the implementation of the IBM S/360/85, unified caches have become pervasive and are employed in many computers. Only with realizable, practical VLSI technology have unified caches given way to split caches, which are discussed further in Section 2.6. In many contemporary designs a unified cache is the second level to a first-level split cache or used with systems having a first-level instruction buffer or queue.

The IBM S/360/85 cache is used as an example of an early select cache and is shown in Figure 2.21 [MATI77] and organized as (1, 16, 16, 64). The sector name in the cache address field is associatively searched against the tag bit fields. If the sector is resident in the cache, the 4-bit sector base address is gated out and concatenated with the block index and displacement fields to form a 14-bit data memory address.

Each of the 1024-byte sectors is divided into sixteen, 64-byte blocks. Each of the 256 blocks has a valid bit that is collected into a validity bit register, which is a special register that is addressed by the block index concatenated with the translated set base address. Because the data memory is implemented with core, integration of the valid bits would have been difficult. A cache miss fetches one block of 64 bytes, and the write policy is write through on hit and no-write-allocation miss.

Another early unified cache that used the early select method is the IBM S/360/195. This cache is organized as (128, 4, 1, 64) [MATI77] and is shown in Figure 2.22.

The set index selects one of 128 sets having four sectors containing the sector base address for accessing the data memory. Note that the seven set index bits are displaced to the left and there are nine tag bits. The reason this displacement is carried out is to make each of the 128 sets match the 8-Kbyte page size of the virtual memory. However, this cache organization is not a pure congruent system because of this arrangement of address bits. This cache is early select and has a

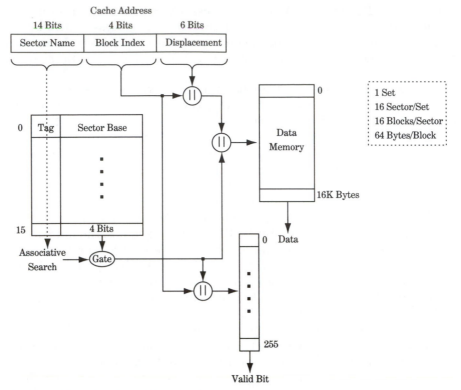

FIGURE 2.21   IBM S/360/85 unified cache.

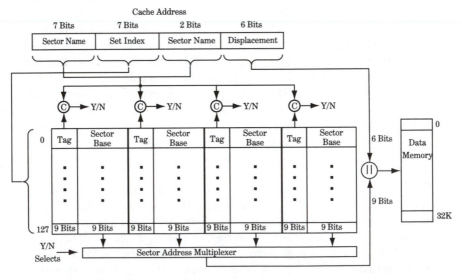

FIGURE 2.22   IBM S/360/195 unified cache.

three-level write buffer providing nonblocking write operations. The write buffer is associatively searched to resolve true dependencies on memory (discussed in Chapter 8).

The PowerPC 601 uses an on-chip unified cache. This cache supplies data to the register file and instructions to the instruction queue. The cache is organized as (64, 8, 2, 64) for 32 Kbytes [MOTO93].

2.5.1 *Published Performance Data*

Most early published data on P_{miss} is on unified caches (see [GIBS67, LIPT68, LEE69, MEAD70, KAPL73, BELL74, SMIT82, GOOD83]. Some of these papers report on cache performance, while in other papers P_{miss} data is reported for various cache organizations and workloads. The published unified cache data has usually been secured by trace-driven simulation, and the results are usually reported for varying cache size, varying block size, varying degree of associativity, etc.

Smith [SMIT87] published P_{miss} data from an investigation into cache and block size variations that segregated the P_{miss} data for unified, instruction and data caches. The P_{miss} data is presented as *design target miss ratios* (DTMR) "to provide for the computer system designer a set of numbers that he or she can use to estimate the performance impact of certain design choices." Smith's data, however, has some problems. The only organization parameters changed are cache size and block size. The other organization parameters are not reported in the paper; however, it is assumed that the organization is (S, 1, B, Byte). One of the interesting aspects of the experimental unified cache P_{miss} data of [MEAD70] is that it is reasonably close to the design target miss ratios of [SMIT87].

Research of [GEE93] provides information on unified cache P_{miss} for various organizations when executing the SPEC benchmarks. Table 2.16

No. of	Number of Sets						
Sec./Set	64	128	256	512	1K	2K	4K
1	.151	.114	.086	.056	.039	.029	.020
2	.092	.069	.047	.031	.023	.016	.011
4	.062	.044	.029	.022	.015	.010	.007
8	.041	.028	.021	.015	.010	.008	.005

Block size is 16 bytes.

TABLE 2.16 Unified cache P_{miss}, SPEC benchmarks, overall.

shows excerpted P_{miss} for the benchmarks, a combination of floating point and integer, and a block size of 16 bytes.

A unified cache, as with instruction and data caches, shows that the size of the cache is paramount and the organization is of secondary importance. For example, an 8-K cache, organized as (64, 8, 16, 1), has a P_{miss} of 0.041 while the organization (512, 1, 16, 1) has a P_{miss} of 0.056. On the other hand, for cache design where the number of sets is constrained for some reason (discussed in Chapter 4), doubling the size of the cache by increasing the number of sectors can cause a significant decrease in P_{miss}. For example, an organization (256, 2, 16, 1) has $P_{\text{miss}} = $ 0.047 while (256, 4, 16, 1) has $P_{\text{miss}} = 0.029$.

2.5.2 *Contemporary Unified Caches*

Many contemporary first-level caches are designed for VLSI implementation of new processors and new operating systems. For a number of reasons these caches are split as discussed in Section 2.5. All known new processors are implemented as pipelines that place heavy demands on the memory system. Because of this factor, some form of first-level split caches or multilevel caches is the design of choice today. The exception to the universal use of split caches is the IBM RS/6000 Model 220, which has a unified cache purely because of a marketing consideration; this processor model is targeted for a low-cost, low-performance market.

However, with split on-chip caches, a second-level unified cache is the norm. For example, the VAX 9000 has a first-level instruction cache followed by a second-level unified cache. The i486 has a second-level unified cache and an instruction queue. These caches are discussed in Section 2.6.

2.6 Split and Multilevel Caches

I can find no historical evidence of separate data and instruction caches before the mid-1980s. During the generation typified by IBM S/360 and VAX architectures, the caches were generally unified. It is only since microprocessor pipelining that the possibility of making concurrent references to instructions and data and with VLSI technology that designers have considered split and multilevel caches.

The major reason for using split caches is to provide a second path to memory from the processor. With pipelined processors, an instruction fetch and a data read/write can occur on the same clock, creating a structural hazard if there is only a unified cache. Two caches eliminate this hazard and permit concurrent references. Early use of two paths to memory were called *"Harvard Architectures"* [CRAG80]. Structural hazards are discussed further in Chapter 8. However, a split cache has problems with self-modifying code because a specific instruction could have two values—one in the instruction cache and another value in the data cache.

Another reason for the use of split caches is that P_{miss} is different for instructions and data. A look at the data from Tables 2.12, 2.13, 2.14, and 2.15 shows that significant differences between instruction P_{miss}, data P_{miss}, and unified P_{miss} can exist for caches of equal size. For example, a 16-Kbyte cache organized as (512, 2, 1, 16) will have instruction $P_{\text{miss}} = 0.01$, data $P_{\text{miss}} = 0.104$, and unified $P_{\text{miss}} = 0.047$ for the overall SPEC benchmarks. With these differences, the possibility exists that the design of the three caches of a two-level cache system can be customized. There is a significant problem with split caches if self-modifying code is used, resulting in coherency problems between the two caches. A modified instruction in the data cache may be referenced in the instruction cache—a problem that must be managed either by software or hardware means.

Most of the early research on hierarchical memory systems recognized that there would be a continuum of levels [MATT70, MEAD70] and not just the processor/cache/memory levels. With practical VLSI and pipeline implementations, interest in multilevel caches has revived. Przybylski [PRZY90] discussed two reasons for renewed interest. First, all of the information presented previously shows that the P_{miss} of a cache is not significantly improved if the cache size is increased beyond 64 Kbytes. Thus, ever larger caches are ineffective. Second, transport time can be reduced with a second-level cache, which reduces the number of cycles of a first-level cache miss. The reason for this is basically that the clock period for determining transfer time between the first- and second-level caches is much shorter than that between a single-level cache and the main memory.

Baer [BAER87] reports that the only system, as of 1987, to have a multilevel cache is the Facom M-3825. The first-level cache is organized as (64, 16, 1, 64) 64-Kbytes write through, while the second level is organized as (1024, 4, 1, 64) 256 Kbytes write back. Note that contemporary multilevel cache systems usually employ a very large second-level cache. The reason for this is that with VLSI memory devices, the second-level cache can be made large enough to hold a complete working set, thereby significantly reducing bus traffic to the main memory.

As shown in Figure 2.1, there are a number of topological configurations of cache systems that cannot be simply classified. This section will describe some configurations that have been employed. A partial listing of processors and their topologies is given in Table 2.17. Examples of the cache designs are described in the paragraphs below.

First Level	Second Level	Examples
I-Queue	Unified	i386, AM29000
I-Queue	Unified, off-chip	i486, PowerPC 601
I + D Unified		
I-Cache	Unified, off-chip	MC68030, MC68040
D-Cache		MC88200, RS/6000
I-Queue	Unified	VAX 9000
I-Cache		
I-Queue	Unified, off-chip	Intel Pentium
D-Cache		

TABLE 2.17   Processor cache topologies.

First level,   I-Queue;
Second level,   Unified Cache;
Example,   i386

The i386 processor is implemented with limited chip area with space for only an instruction queue. The supply of instructions to the queue and the supply of data are provided by an off-chip unified cache [ELAY85]; the organization is shown in Figure 2.23.

As previously discussed in Section 2.3.2, the on-chip instruction queue is used to smooth out the flow of variable-length instructions to the processor and hide cache misses. The off-chip unified cache organization and size are the responsibilities of the system designer for this processor. However, a suggested cache design is given by Intel in

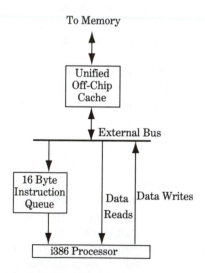

FIGURE 2.23   i386 cache and instruction queue.

[INTE86] along with an application note on the design of caches in general [SHIR86].

One of the major considerations that led to the selection of a unified cache is that the i386 had to execute old versions of MS-DOS that have self-modifying code. This consideration dictated a unified cache, external to the processor, for the i386. Intel also provides a cache component (part number 82396SX) for use with the i386. This cache organization is (256, 4, 1, 16) using a pseudo-LRU replacement algorithm and is the precursor to the i486 on-chip data cache, which is discussed below. Shires [SHIR86] provides hit ratio and performance ratios of various i386 unified cache organizations, executing an anticipated workload. This data indicates the dominant effect of cache size rather than organization as noted in previous sections.

First level,   I-Queue;
Second level,   Unified Cache;
Example,   AMD 29000

AMD moved away from split caches for the AM29000 family. Software portability problems, in addition to complex bus issues, led to a return to a single bus access to the main memory. There is a four-word instruction queue (called a prefetch buffer by AMD) and a very large (192-word) register file that provide cache-like characteristics. A single bus services requests to memory that may be partitioned into instruction and data regions [AMD90].

First level,   I-Queue + Unified;
Second level,   Unified Cache;
Example,   i486

The designers of the Intel i486, [FU89, CRAW90], needed to support two memory accesses (instruction and data) per clock period. The instruction length is 1 byte to 15 bytes and the data word is 1 byte to 8 bytes. Thus the cache bandwidth needs to be in the range of 2–23 bytes per clock. In addition, the designers had a chip budget of 8 Kbytes in which to provide an on-chip cache.

As with the i386 cache, a unified cache is needed to support old MS-DOS and OS/2 systems that did not have "cache flush" instructions that evict the complete cache. These instructions are generally needed to support cache consistency. See Section 2.8.1 for more details.

The organization of the i486 cache is (128, 4, 1, 16) [INTE92]. To provide the ability to read instructions and read/write data simultaneously, the i486 has an instruction queue, as shown in Figure 2.24 and described in Section 2.3.2. The size of the cache and the number of sets are directly related to the size of the page (4 Kbytes) used in the virtual

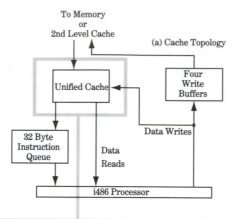

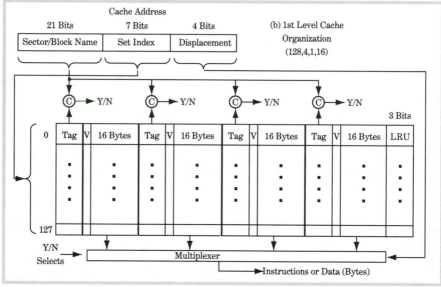

FIGURE 2.24   Intel 486 cache.

memory. By matching these dimensions, one-half of the cache (two sector-blocks from all of the sets) is equal to one page. This organization permits a cache access and an access to the TLB to be made in parallel (an issue that is discussed in Chapter 4).

Each of the 128 sets has four sector-blocks with tags and valid bits. Because the write policy is write through, dirty bits are not required. However, each set has three bits (B2, B1, B0) for maintaining a pseudo-random LRU status of the sector-blocks within each set. These bits are set/reset as the cache is filled and sector-blocks are modified as shown in Table 2.18.

Sector-Block Used	B2	B1	B0
S0	X	1	1
S1	X	0	1
S2	1	X	0
S3	0	X	0

TABLE 2.18   i486 cache LRU bits.

If all of the valid bits are "set," a sector is selected for replacement using the LRU bits that have recorded the use patterns of the sectors. Selection is simply the decoding of the B bits. For example, [0X0] identifies S3 as the LRU sector-block, and it should be overwritten; write back is not required since the write policy is write through.

A complete discussion of the design tradeoffs of the i486 cache is found in [GROC89]. The i486 cache design was tested by trace-driven simulation and gave a $P_{miss} = 0.08$ versus the $P_{miss} = 0.044$ shown in Table 2.16 for the same organization executing the SPEC benchmarks. These simulations showed that with a fast bus, the write through policy is only slightly faster than a write back policy. As the bus slows down, the write through cache slows down more than the write back and the bus utilization increases more for the write through cache. However, a write through cache is simpler to implement and was selected for the i486. With a write through policy, the bus can be expected to be utilized approximately 68% of the time, making shared memory multiprocessor configurations difficult to implement.

The instruction queue prefetches instructions via a 16-byte-wide bus from the unified cache in one clock into the prefetch queues. Thus, one block, which is four average-length instructions, is fetched into the queue in one clock. Instructions are then read from the queue into the processor.

It is interesting to note that, because the cache is on the same chip as the processor, the 16-byte bus between the cache and the prefetch queues poses minimum wiring problems as would be the case if such a wide bus is required to traverse chip boundaries.

First level,   I-Queue + D-Cache;
Second level,   Unified Cache;
Example,   MC68030

The Motorola MC68030 has on-chip split instruction and data caches. Due to the limited chip area, these caches are only 256 bytes each. Because these caches are small, an effective application of this processor demands an off-chip second-level unified cache. Figure 2.25 illustrates the cache topology and the identical instruction and data caches.

The instruction and data caches are organized identically as (16, 1,

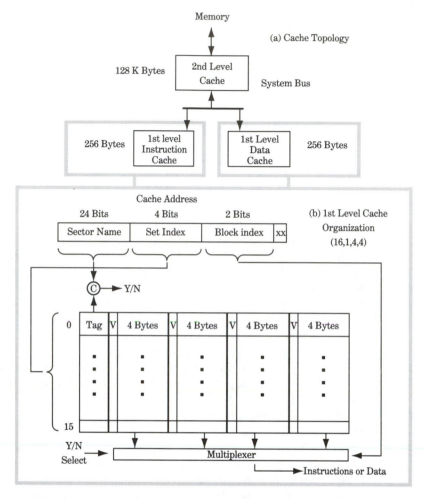

FIGURE 2.25   Motorola 68030 instruction and data caches.

4, 4); the set index of four bits selects one of the 16 sets. If the set is present, the two block index bits select one of the four 4-byte words in the block; each block has a valid bit. The data cache uses a write through policy on a write hit. The data cache policy on a write miss is program-selectable for either write-allocate write back or no-write-allocate write through. As with all instruction caches, there is no write policy for the instruction cache. Furthermore, as self-modifying code is not supported, the instruction read process does not have to check the data cache for an instruction that has been modified.

First level,   I-Queue + D-Cache;
Second level,   Unified Cache;
Example,   DEC Alpha

The DEC Alpha processor, introduced in 1992, has a split cache on-chip and a second-level cache off-chip. The data cache has a capacity of 8 Kbytes, write through, direct mapped, and write-allocate. The data cache is byte addressable and the organization is (256, 1, 1, 32). The instruction cache has a capacity of 8 Kbytes, is also direct mapped with a 32-byte block, and is organized (256, 1, 1, 32). Both caches are addressed with the real addresses. The second-level cache, named the B-Cache, is unified, and the design is the system designer's responsibility.

First level,   I-Queue + I-Cache;
Second level,   Unified Cache;
Example,   VAX 9000

The VAX 9000 [FITE90] has a multilevel cache consisting of a first-level instruction cache of 8 Kbytes and a second-level unified cache of 128 Kbytes as shown in Figure 2.26. There is no first-level data cache; data transfers directly to and from the register file and the second-level cache. The variable-length instructions are issued from a 25-byte instruction queue.

The instruction cache organization is (256, 1, 2, 16) and is addressed with virtual addresses to reduce latency and simplify the design. The cache address has a one-bit (B) block address and a one-bit (D) displacement address. As the cache AU is eight bytes, the three LSBs of the address are not used. A miss can load either one or two blocks as there is a valid bit per block. There are two sets of 256 valid bits (one for each sector-block); these bits are not integrated into the cache array (similar to the IBM S/360/85 cache).

The second-level unified cache is organized as (1024, 2, 1, 64) and is also addressed with virtual addresses. This cache is 2-way set associative and uses a FIFO block replacement scheme. It is believed that a write back policy is used in conjunction with a write queue.

First level,   I-Queue + I-Cache + D-Cache;
Second level,   Unified Cache;
Example,   Intel Pentium

The recently announced Intel Pentium employs a split cache, unlike previous members of the ix86 family. The very large number of transistors available to the designers allowed them to solve the self-modifying code problem. The instruction read path is, starting at the processor, via a decoded instruction queue, an instruction queue, an instruction cache,

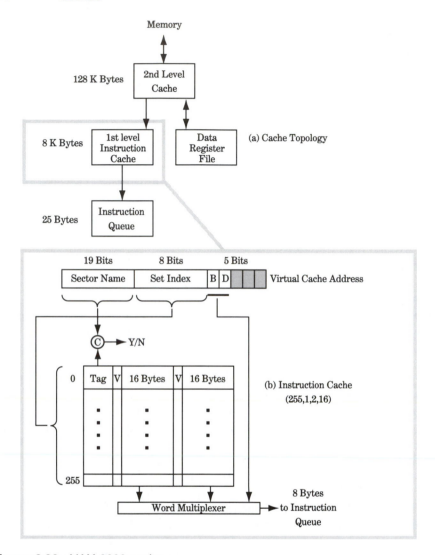

FIGURE 2.26   VAX 9000 cache.

a unified cache, and the main memory. The data read path is via a data cache, unified cache, and the main memory.

As discussed previously, the Intel ix86 family of microprocessors have employed unified caches because of the problem of self-modifying code. This design philosophy has changed with the Pentium processor [INTE93, CRAW92, GWEN92, SLAT92]. There are two on-chip caches, an 8-Kbyte instruction cache and an 8-Kbyte data cache, and both are organized as (128, 2, 8, 4). The transfer path between the caches and the main memory is via a 64-bit bus. Logic is included to test for true dependencies in the data cache to determine if instructions have been modified. Dependency management is discussed in Chapter 8.

The instruction queue can supply up to three instructions in one clock, while the data cache can supply two 32-bit words to the register file. The data cache has a unique interleaved organization that supplies operands to the superscalar pipelines (this design is described in Section 10.2.2).

2.7 Multilevel Caches

The idea at work with a multilevel cache is that a small and fast first-level cache is used and that the second-level cache can (1) reduce the transport time to the first-level cache and (2) reduce the bus loading. With the proper interplay of these ideas, the cache system performance will be improved. Reduction in transport time is advantageous because on-chip caches were initially small with a resulting high P_{miss}. Because the weighted time to reference an AU not in the cache is the product of P_{miss} and transport time, these two parameters are kept in balance with a second-level cache. (Another form of multilevel cache, *disk cache*, is discussed in Section 4.2.4.) Bus-loading reduction is important for multiprocessor systems where a number of processors must communicate over one bus to the main memory.

A simple two-level unified cache system is shown in Figure 2.27. This system has caches L1 and L2 between the processor and the main memory. The access time of L1 is t_1, the transport times for the second-level cache and the main memory are t_2 and t_3, respectively; and P_{miss1} and P_{miss2} are the *local* P_{miss} for the two caches. *Local* P_{miss} is the number of misses in a specific cache divided by the number of references to that cache.

The effective access time, as seen by the processor, for the simple two-level cache system using the sequential-forward model and local P_{miss} values is

$$t_{\text{ea}}(\text{two levels}) = t_1 + P_{\text{miss1}} \times t_2 + P_{\text{miss1}} \times P_{\text{miss2}} \times t_3 .$$

The performance of a two-level cache can be compared to a one-level

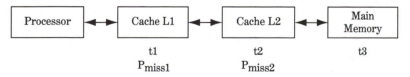

FIGURE 2.27 Two-level cache.

cache under the assumption that the P_{miss} of a single-level cache is the same as the P_{miss} of the first-level cache C1. The speedup is

$$S = \frac{t_{\text{ea}}(\text{one level})}{t_{\text{ea}}(\text{two levels})} = \frac{t_1 + t_{\text{ea}} P_{\text{miss}} t_3}{t_1 + P_{\text{miss}1} t_2 + P_{\text{miss}1} P_{\text{miss}2} t_3}.$$

For example, assume the parameters

t_1	1,
t_2	4,
t_3	10,
$P_{\text{miss}1}$	0.05,
$P_{\text{miss}2}$	0.02.

Using these parameters, the speedup of the two-level cache over the single-level cache is $S = 1.5/1.21 = 1.24$. In other words, adding this second-level cache provides a reduction of approximately 20% in effective access time. Note that P_{miss} for different levels are not independent. Changing the design of one level will, in many caches, influence the P_{miss} of another level. In the context of multilevel caches, two other definitions are of interest:

Global P_{miss} is the number of misses in a cache or memory in the system divided by the total number of references to the memory system from the processor.

Global P_{hit} is the number of references satisfied in a cache or memory in the system divided by the total number of references to the memory system from the processor. The sum of all global P_{hit} values of a system is 1.

For an example of global P_{miss} values and global P_{hit} values, consider the following. If local $P_{\text{miss}1} = 0.1$ and local $P_{\text{miss}2} = 0.05$, then the *global miss ratio* for level two is $0.1 \times 0.05 = 0.005$. A more useful global metric is the global hit ratio. In this example, 90% of all references are satisfied in the first-level cache, 9.5% in the second-level cache, and 0.5% in the main memory.

The complexity of selecting an organization and policy for a one-level cache is compounded in the case of a two-level cache. The number of points in the design space is approximately the square of the number of design points of a one-level cache. For example, what is the policy when there is a miss on one of the caches? And, what is the policy when there is a miss on both of the caches. J.-L. Baer [BAER87] provides a discussion on these design problems.

To illustrate the complexity of a policy for a two-level cache, consider that the four write policy designs discussed in Section 2.2.6 will expand

	L1	L2	ACTION
READ	Hit	X	read L1 → processor
*	Miss	Hit	Reload L2 → L1, read L1 → processor
	Miss	Miss	Reload Mem → L2, L2 → 1, read L1 → Processor
WRITE	Hit	Hit	Write processor → L1 → L2
*	Hit	Miss	Allocate to L2, write processor → L1 → L2
*	Miss	Hit	Write processor → L2
	Miss	Miss	Allocate to L2, write processor → L2

*Does not provide multilevel inclusion.

TABLE 2.19 Multilevel cache policies.

to sixteen possible designs for a two-level cache. Not all of these designs are reasonable. One example that illustrates a particular selection of write strategies is found in the policy described in [BAER 87] and in Table 2.19. The write policies of the two caches are

Level 1: (hit) Write Through, (miss) No Write-allocate (Design A);
Level 2: (hit) Write Back, (miss) Write-allocate (Design C).

With this multilevel cache if, for example, there is a miss on L1 and a hit on L2, the block in L1 is replaced by the block in L2 and the new ALU is read into the processor. The actions in the table are viewed as logically sequential; however, a parallel implementation is possible. In other words, the new block of this example can be placed in L1 and forwarded to the processor.

For a single-level cache, the assumption is made that resident blocks in the cache must be found in the main memory. In other words, all blocks in the cache are *included* in the main memory. The cache system cannot have a valid block that is not represented in the main memory; the values may not be the same due to the delay waiting for a write back. With the addition of another cache level, *multilevel inclusion* (MLI), which means that the contents of a cache at level $l + 1$ is a superset of the contents of its cache at level l (MATT70, LAM79, BAER87]), may not exist unless explicitly enforced.

The lack of MLI is illustrated by an example. Consider a block that has been moved to the L2 and L1 caches due to misses at both levels. A subsequent reference to the L2 cache (from I/O, say) may, due to a set conflict miss, evict that block. Now the block exists only in the L1 cache and in the main memory, not in the L2 cache. In this case, multilevel inclusion is not provided. When there is a multiprocessor with a cache for each processor, MLI is more difficult to achieve.

Note in the example of Table 2.19 that this cache design does not provide MLI. For the read cases, as there can be an L1 hit and L2 miss, L2 is not a superset of L1. Likewise, as there can be a write with a miss on L1 and a hit on L2 and a hit on L1 with a miss on L2, L2 is not a superset of L1. Baer states that the first-level cache must be write through if multilevel inclusion properties are to be maintained.

There is also the issue of addresses presented to the various cache levels. The question of whether a cache should be addressed with real or virtual addresses will be discussed in Chapter 4. With a multilevel cache the issue is even more difficult. In fact, [WANG89] argues that the first-level cache should be addressed with virtual and the second-level with real addresses, an organization named *V-R caching*.

2.7.1 *Published Performance Data*

Przybylski [PRZY88] provides a wealth of information on the design and optimization of multilevel cache. Data on the effect of a second-level cache on bus utilization and increases in system performance are found in [GOLB92] for i486 processors. Bus utilization reduction is compared to an i486DX processor without a second-level cache. Two bus configurations are evaluated, namely, a slow bus that has a one clock hit and a four clock miss time and a fast bus with a one clock hit and a four clock miss time. The second-level cache is set at 128 Kbytes, 256 Kbytes, and 512 Kbytes. Excerpted bus utilization data are shown in Table 2.20. Note that a large second-level cache reduces the bus utilization to a negligible amount.

The performance improvement with a second-level cache was also measured and normalized to a 25-MHz i486 without a second-level cache. A 50 MHz without a second-level cache was evaluated to show the performance improvement obtainable with raw processor performance, and then this system was measured with a 256-Kbyte second-level cache.

Second-level Cache	Slow Bus	Fast Bus
None	88%	68%
128 Kbytes	19%	11%
256 Kbytes	15%	6%
512 Kbytes	5%	4%

TABLE 2.20   i486 bus utilization with a two-level cache.

	Benchmarks		
System	ispec	fspec	spec
25-MHz i486 (none)	1	1	1
50-MHz i486 (none)	1.61	1.62	1.61
50-MHz i486 (256 Kbytes)	2.09	2.1	2.1

TABLE 2.21 i486 performance improvement with a second-level cache.

The results of measurement while executing three SPEC benchmarks are excerpted in Table 2.21.

The interesting results here are that while doubling the clock rate of the processor gives a speedup of 1.6, adding a second-level cache gives an additional speedup of 1.3. This result compares favorably with the results of the speedup model developed earlier.

2.8 Other Cache Considerations

In addition to the design issues of organization, policies, and performance, there are other issues that influence the design and efficacy of caches. Some of these issues are control of the cache by the processor, transport time reduction techniques, compiler optimization, and pipelined caches.

2.8.1 *Processor Control*

Caches have historically been viewed as transparent to the user or processor. That is, the cache provides lower latency reads and writes than can be provided by the main memory, and the executing program should not be aware of the presence of a cache. This view of a transparent cache is no longer valid, and it has been found that there are situations that require direct processor control of the cache. A cache that has processor control is known as a *software visible cache*.

Bakoglu discusses the requirements for software visible caches [BAKO90].

> Software visible caches have two implications: The first is that any program that uses data references to create instructions (for example, loaders, debuggers, and simulators) must explicitly force these instructions from the data cache into the instruction cache. Additionally, to perform input or output operations on the processor main

memory, device driver code must properly flush the necessary lines from the caches before the I/O operation can begin.

There are two types of processor control exercised over the cache. These are:

1. establishing the cache operation mode,
2. dynamic pre-emption of normal cache functions.

Establishing Cache Operation Mode

As has been discussed previously, a processor may be used in an application that may favor a particular cache operation mode. For example, where bus loading is a factor, a write back mode is desired because the write through mode can load the bus with unnecessary traffic. However (as discussed in Chapter 4), data coherency maintenance may be desired, suggesting a write through cache. Consequently, a cache with an operational mode set by the designer is less desirable than a cache that can be set to a particular mode by the user of the system. The operating mode of a cache is usually established by a mode control register that is loaded by the processor. Thus, a move instruction is executed in order to change or modify the operation mode of the cache.

An example of processor control of a cache mode is found in the MC68040 [MOTO89]. Four modes can be specified.

1. *Noncacheable mode.* For various reasons, it is desirable to prevent some AUs from being cached. One example of this need is found in a multiprocessor system that has multiple caches. A noncacheable mode can be set by the processor to prevent some shared variables from being cached.

If all shared variables are cached, a coherency problem can exist that can be solved by not caching. The processor can thus specify that the following references are not to be cached. Reads, and writes that miss, do not allocate but access the main memory. Noncached writes that hit a resident cached block cause the valid bit to be reset, and the block, if dirty, is written to the main memory before the write access is made to the main memory.

2. *Cacheable, write through mode.* In addition, for cached operation, the processor can specify the write policy to be write through. Write through is handled as a no-write-allocate policy.

3. *Cacheable, copyback (write back) mode.* For the cacheable write back mode, write hits update the cache and set the dirty bits. A write miss is handled by allocation.

4. *Special access.* The last mode is special access. Read or write accesses that miss the cache do not allocate but read or write to/from

the main memory. Read or write hits are handled by a mode specifier in the access address.

Another example of processor control over caches is found in the MC68030 [MOTO87]. The on-chip data cache can be set for either allocate or no-write-allocate on a write miss.

Pre-emption of Cache Functions

Recall that the purpose of a cache is to reduce the latency of reads and writes. Depending upon the operation mode, when a read or write instruction is executed, various control bits are set or reset and blocks are moved to/from the main memory. All of these actions can be viewed as *side effects* of the LOAD and STORE instructions as they hit or miss the cache. For particular situations it is desirable to pre-empt these side effects and execute instructions that explicitly cause the side effects. Pre-emptive fetches and evictions of the cache are desirable instructions for synchronizing the memory in a multiprocessor configuration.

Some processors, such as the PowerPC 601 [MOTO93], have the ability to evict the cache contents or invalidate the cache. There are four cache instructions: data cache block store (*dcbst*), data cache block flush (*dcbf*), data cache block set to zero (*dcbz*), and instruction cache block invalidate (*icbi*). If the cache organization is write through, flushing is done by an instruction that turns off all of the valid bits. For write back caches, flushing must move the modified contents of the cache to the main memory. The net effect of complete eviction is that subsequent cache operations are similar to a cold start and all references are misses.

Multiprogramming a virtual memory system with a virtual cache and a write back policy requires the facility to evict dirty blocks (an issue discussed in Chapter 3). A write through cache requires only a valid bit, and complete or partial eviction is not required. The software prefetching cited and discussed in Section 2.8.2 is another example of processor control over the operation of a cache.

2.8.2 *Transport Time Hiding or Reduction Methods*

Hiding or reducing the transport time between the main memory and the cache is a major avenue for improving cache and processor performance. Multilevel caches (discussed in Section 2.6) are one method used to reduce transport time while instruction queues (discussed in Section 2.3.2) and data queues (discussed in Section 2.4.3) can hide transport time. Other available techniques include hardware-controlled prefetching, software prefetching, and special-purpose caches. These techniques are discussed in the following sections.

Hardware Controlled Prefetching

Various techniques have been use to prefetch instructions and data under hardware control. By this we mean that prefetch mechanisms are wired into the processor and perform their function without software interaction.

Instruction Prefetch

Smith [SMIT78] presented early research on the benefits of prefetching instructions from disk to memory and memory to cache. His results indicate that prefetching is only effective for small fetch units such as 32-byte to 64-byte blocks and is not effective for pages of approximately 1 Kbyte to 2 Kbytes. His results also show that prefetching can be effective in increasing CPU speed by 10% to 25% when prefetching is used at the memory–cache level.

Smith [SMIT82] provides a description of the issues involved in prefetching either instructions or data and notes three prefetch strategies.

1. *Always prefetch*. For every access to AU_i, a prefetch to AU_{i+1} is initiated.
2. *Tagged prefetch*. When a block is referenced for the first time, the next block is prefetched.
3. *Prefetch on misses*. This prefetch type implies that the block is greater than one AU.

One form of instruction prefetching is found in processors that have instruction queues; prefetching is initiated by monitoring the content of the queue. When there is a vacancy in the queue that can be filled by a reference to memory, a prefetch cycle is initiated (this operation is described in Section 2.3.2).

Another form of hardware-controlled instruction prefetch is found in systems that prefetch a branch instruction's target stream in tandem with continued fetching of the in-line instruction stream. These systems are described in Chapter 7.

Data Prefetching

Hardware data prefetching has usually been accomplished in register file architectures with a delayed load strategy. Useful instructions are interposed between the load instruction and the instruction that will use the loaded AU (a strategy discussed in Chapter 8). Another form of data prefetching is found in processors such as the IBM S/360/91 [ANDE67] that decodes load instructions in the instruction fetch queue and begins the load before the instruction is released to the execution unit. Data returned from the memory are stored in a queue that joins the execution pipeline at the proper point. Memory delays are hidden by the queue.

A significant problem with data prefetch is that the effective address is sometimes not known until after some registers have been adjusted; this is a true dependency on addresses and is called an *address generation interlock* (AGI). R. J. Eickemeyer [EICK93] suggests ways for predicting the effective address and gives measured data to show the effectiveness of data prefetching.

Software Prefetching

When a referenced AU is not found in a cache, a cache miss results and the missed AU is fetched along with a number of AUs in contiguous memory locations (the block). Some programs have addressing patterns that are highly predictable, such as signal processing and graphics. Under these situations, why not have an instruction that will prefetch a block into the cache rather than wait on a miss? Prefetching of instructions or data into caches that are nonblocking is an interesting concept. *Software prefetching* [CALL91] is a program-initiated, nonblocking load of a cache block in anticipation of need.

Prefetching into a nonblocking cache will not halt execution as does a normal cache miss because the executing program is not in immediate need of the instruction or data AU. Recall that when a normal miss occurs, the processor must wait until the miss has been serviced. If a prefetch command is issued well in advance of the need for the AU, there will not be a miss when the AU is read during the normal instruction execution cycle.

An example of a data-prefetching instruction is the PowerPC 601 [MOTO93]. The instruction Data Cache Block Touch (dcbt) loads a block into the cache. In other words, this is a load instruction that loads a block into the cache rather than loading an AU into the register file.

Simulation results of [CALL91] indicate that approximately 33% of all software data prefetches are useful in that they accurately anticipate a future reference to the prefetched block. With this level of success, the number of cache misses is reduced because the data has already been prefetched. However, the reduction in P_{miss} is not without cost. The use of a prefetch instruction increases the number of instructions that must be executed, hence adding to the length of the program. If the cache is blocking, all prefetches steal cycles from the cache and ineffective prefetches degrade the available performance of the cache.

A performance model is developed to investigate the effectiveness of software prefetching. Consider a unified blocking cache of the sequential-forward type. The model is based upon the parameters

F_f = fraction of normal instructions that are preceded by a prefetch instruction,

P_{eff} = probability that a prefetch has been effective and a future miss does not occur,

P_{miss} = probability that a memory reference misses in the cache for the program without prefetching,

L = number of clocks the cache is blocked due to a prefetch,

T = transport time.

There are eight possible events, with each event having a delay. The effective access time of the cache will be 1 + weighted average delay. These events and delays are shown in Table 2.22.

The event 0 1 0 is a normal cache access with a miss and a delay of $1 + T$ cycles. For the case 1 1 0, there has been an ineffective prefetch: the delay is $1 + L + T$ because the executing instruction misses the cache requiring the normal delay of T cycles and L cycles to be lost due to the blockage of the cache during the prefetch. Notice that when a prefetch instruction is executed ($F_f = 1$), the cache loses a cycle for the instruction fetch plus the number of cycles to transfer the block T. From the event probabilities, the effective cache cycle time is

$$t_{ea}(\text{PF}) = 1 + P_{miss}(T(1 - P_{eff}) - P_{eff}) + F_f(1 + L).$$

The effective cache cycle model is optimistic, as a prefetched block may evict a block already in the cache because of a capacity or set conflict. For the cases when unnecessary eviction happens, the delay would be two transport times. Prefetching may increase the P_{miss} of the executing program because a prefetched block may evict a block in the cache that

Events			Delay	Comments
F_f	P_{miss}	P_{eff}		
0	0	0	0	
0	0	1	0	
0	1	0	$1 + T$	Previous prefetch not effective
0	1	1	0	
1	0	0	$1 + L$	Cache blocked for L cycles
1	0	1	$1 + L$	Cache blocked for L cycles
1	1	0	$1 + L + 1 + T$	Cache blocked for L cycles
1	1	1	$1 + L$	Cache blocked for L cycles

$F_f = 0$ means no prefetching.

TABLE 2.22   Software prefetching delays.

may need to be fetched again. The eviction problem decreases as the degree of associativity of the cache increases. The speedup of using software prefetching is found by dividing $1 + P_{\mathrm{miss}}\, T$ by $t_{\mathrm{ac}}(\mathrm{PF})$.

$$\mathrm{Speedup} = \frac{1 + P_{\mathrm{miss}}T}{1 + P_{\mathrm{miss}}(T(1 - P_{\mathrm{eff}}) - P_{\mathrm{eff}}) + F_f(1 + L)}.$$

Break-even points for software prefetching compared to not prefetching are found by equating $t_{\mathrm{ac}}(\mathrm{PF}) = 1 + P_{\mathrm{miss}}\, T$ and solving for P_{eff}, F_f, and T according to the equations

$$P_{\mathrm{eff}} = \frac{F_f(1 + L)}{P_{\mathrm{miss}}(1 + T)},$$

$$F_f = \frac{P_{\mathrm{eff}}P_{\mathrm{miss}}(T + 1)}{1 + L},$$

$$T = \frac{F_f(1 + L)}{P_{\mathrm{eff}}P_{\mathrm{miss}}} - 1.$$

For example, for a system with $P_{\mathrm{eff}} = 0.3$, $P_{\mathrm{miss}} = 0.1$, $T = 3$, $L = 2$, and $P_{\mathrm{eff}} = 0.3$, no more than 4% of the instructions of the original program can have an associated prefetch instruction or prefetching will lose performance.

For a system with nonblocking caches $L = 0$, assuming that the cache can queue up an unlimited number of requests. For $P_{\mathrm{eff}} = 0.3$, $P_{\mathrm{miss}} = 0.1$, and $F_f = 0.1$, the break-even value of T is 9. Thus, for systems with T greater than 10, software prefetching may be beneficial with a nonblocking cache. With a blocking cache with $L = 3$, T must be larger than 40 in order to improve the performance with prefetching.

The speedup and break-even models indicate a major concern: Software prefetching is unlikely to improve the performance for most systems with blocking caches and small values of T. In fact, the likelihood is that performance will be lost.

A significant contributor to reduced speedup is the overhead associated with increasing the program length with prefetching, that is, the factor F_f. D. Callahan et al. [CALL91] report that if $F_f \approx 0.28$, prefetching is unlikely to reduce the time of program execution. There are situations that may significantly reduce F_f and favor the use of software prefetching. Superscalar processors with nonblocking caches (described in Chapter 10) that issue more than one instruction per clock may be the best candidates for prefetching because the prefetch instruction can be introduced into an instruction slot that would otherwise be unused. As a result, for many programs, there is no increase in program length (that is, $F_f = 0$) due to the prefetch instructions. And, with a nonblocking cache, the cycles are not lost while waiting for the fetch of a block from the main memory.

Another situation concerns disk caches. Notice that the value of T plays an important part of the possible speedup; cache systems with small values of T, in general, do not benefit. However, due to the difficulty of providing low values of T, software prefetching may be helpful when high values of T are necessary. Moreover, for disk systems with very high values of T, software prefetching is frequently employed. Some operating systems (as discussed in Chapter 3), can fetch instructions and data into main memory from the disk before they are needed.

[CALL91] discusses the various considerations of software prefetching. These considerations include the time interval between the prefetch and the actual need (known as *prefetch distance*), the influence of block size, the need to abort prefetches already in the cache, and the additional load placed on the bus. Prefetch distance must be large enough so that the prefetched data is in the cache before the explicit reference is made to the data. On the other hand, if the prefetch distance is too large, cache residency time increases and the effective size of the cache is reduced. Long residency can also increase bus traffic because prefetched data may not be used due to a change of program flow. This research reports that the cache hit ratio for a suit of six benchmarks improved from an average 72.7% to 99.4% with prefetching.

A. J. Smith [SMIT78] gives a detailed description of the cache of the Amdahl 470V/6 and the IBM S/360/168–3 along with implementation suggestions for prefetching. He projects that the inclusion of prefetching could improve system performance by 10% to 25%. The machine studied required 7 to 8 clocks per instruction and had transport time cost of 12 to 15 cycles. These results may not be representative of pipeline microprocessors with an instruction execution rate of approximately 1 clock per instruction. For pipelined processors, the effect of cache delays is far more damaging and small improvements in P_{miss} can have a significant positive performance impact if the other factors do not overshadow the P_{miss} improvement.

The DEC Alpha architecture provides a data prefetch instruction, named *FETCH*, that moves an aligned 512-byte block from a low level of the hierarchy to a higher level. Specific implementations of the Alpha architecture may or may not provide this instruction and, if provided, the block moved may be smaller or larger than 512 bytes. The order of prefetching within the block is unpredictable. The break-even models developed above clearly show that software prefetching is only useful for systems that have long transport times. This conclusion is confirmed by the DEC Alpha handbook, which indicates that prefetching is useful for transport times on the order of 100 cycles, that latencies on the order of 10 cycles will not be helped, and that code scheduling is suggested for these small latencies. I assume that these comments on the Alpha are based on a nonblocking data cache. One would not expect to improve system performance with software prefetching without including a nonblocking cache.

The MC88100 has a mechanism named *instruction prefetching* [MOTO90]. However, this mechanism is not software prefetching as described above but Motorola's way of describing the pipeline that contains two stages for instruction fetching, a common approach in pipelined processors. With a two-stage instruction fetch pipeline, two program counter stages are required. These are named the *fetch instruction pointer* and the *next instruction pointer*. The requirement for these registers is described in Chapter 8.

Special-Purpose Caches

Recall from Section 2.1.4 that nonblocking caches permit read operations to proceed out of order without blocking. Another approach to nonblocking is to provide two caches, similar to double buffering, that eliminate the structural hazard of a single blocking cache. Klaiber and Levy [KLAI91] proposed a dual cache scheme that improves the chances of useful speedup. With this scheme, a blocking cache that is blocked during a block prefetch is augmented with a buffer that is used for storing the prefetched blocks. Subsequent reads to the cache search both cache and the buffer in parallel. Figure 2.28 shows a block diagram of this cache scheme.

A prefetch request is queued up to the memory that then places the requested block into the prefetch buffer. The fetch queue issues a fetch

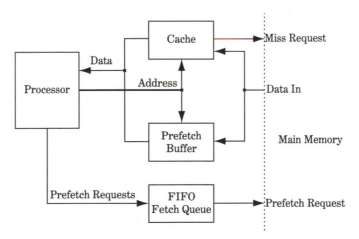

FIGURE 2.28   Klaiber-Levy cache.

request only if a miss from the cache will not be blocked. A read request checks both the cache and the prefetch buffer and takes an instruction or data from the one that hits.

With the prefetch buffer, there is no blocking of the main cache during the prefetch. The model for this cache is found by setting L in the $t_{ac}(\text{PF})$ model to 0. The speedup becomes

$$\text{Speedup}(K - L) = (1 + P_{\text{miss}}T)/(1 + P_{\text{miss}}T(1 - P_{\text{eff}}) + F_f) .$$

Simulations using the Livermore Loops by Klaiber indicate that a memory speedup of 3 to 8 is achievable using this cache. For the model above and using the values $P_{\text{miss}} = 0.05$, $T = 13$, $P_{\text{eff}} = 0.9$, and $F_f = 0.05$, a speedup of 5.84 is predicted. This model prediction compares favorably to the speedup of 6.5 obtained from Klaiber's simulation.

Jouppi [JOUP90] proposes three augmented cache schemes that give the advantage of a small transport time. The idea behind the Jouppi extension is primarily the reduction of delays due to conflict misses. M. D. Hill [HILL87] shows that approximately 25% of all misses are conflict misses with a unified direct cache. If these 25% of the misses could have a transport time of one cycle rather than the normal 4- to 10-cycle transport time, then a significant improvement in cache performance is obtained. The idea is to cache the miss path from the main cache. Then the auxiliary cache is addressed in parallel with the normal direct cache. Jouppi's three schemes are illustrated in Figure 2.29.

1. *Miss cache.* A small, 2- to 5-word, associative cache is loaded with the AU from a miss in parallel with the AU being loaded into the direct cache. The two caches are accessed in parallel. If the block is subsequently evicted from the main direct cache, a one-cycle latency brings the missed AU into the cache as well as the processor. Miss caches are more effective for a data cache than for an instruction cache because data references are more random than instruction references.

2. *Victim cache.* A small, associative cache is loaded with the block that is evicted from the main cache due to a conflict miss. A future reference may find the evicted block in the victim cache; a one-cycle latency will bring the evicted AU into the processor. Jouppi claims that a victim cache will always outperform a miss cache.

3. *Stream buffer.* A small FIFO queue that can be associatively addressed in parallel with the main cache is provided. The stream buffer prefetches the addresses following the missed address of main cache. All references check the tags of both the main cache and the stream buffer and read the one that hits. Stream buffers reduce compulsory misses as well as capacity misses. Multiple-path stream buffers are also proposed.

The use of victim caches or stream buffers of 5 to 16 words reduces the apparent P_{miss} of a first-level direct cache by a factor of two to

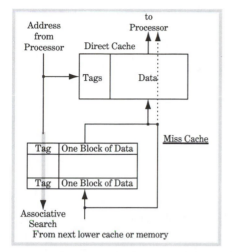

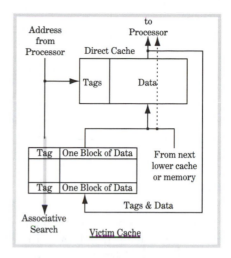

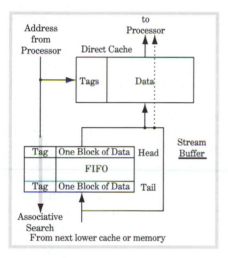

FIGURE 2.29 Jouppi caches.

three depending upon the executing program [JOUP90]. For a pipelined processor with CPI = 1, a performance improvement of 15% to 25% is realized with a modest hardware investment.

Schauser et al. [SCHA91] describe a special instruction cache named a "stall cache." This cache is associated with processors having a single bus to the main memory. With a single cache, the designer has options such as (1) an instruction buffer, queue, or cache, and (2) an on-chip split cache. The stall cache is another design option for this problem. With this option, a split cache is off-chip and the stall cache is on-chip, as shown in Figure 2.30.

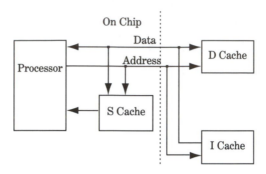

FIGURE 2.30 Stall cache.

The instruction stream is usually fetched over the bus from the instruction cache. If a data read occurs at the same time as the instruction read, the instruction is taken from the stall cache. A miss on the stall cache is filled from the instruction cache. Consequently, the instruction path is similar to a two-level cache. Table 2.23 shows the events and actions for the stall cache.

For example, if there is a data read or write cycle and no instruction cycle, the read or write is from/to the D Cache. The stall cache is a restricted instruction cache, similar to a branch target cache (discussed in Chapter 7).

A simulation of the stall cache shows that the performance of the stall cache approaches the pure split cache with two buses. Equal performance requires an on-chip instruction cache that is 1.5 to 2 times larger than the stall cache. This evaluation assumes that the latency of an off-chip cache is the same as an on-chip cache (an assumption that may not be reasonable). Thus, the benefits of this scheme are to reduce the chip area needed for an instruction and/or split cache while retaining the single bus between the processor and the main memory. For example, if

External Bus Cycles		Instruction in Stall Cache?	Action
Inst.	Data		
Yes	No	X	Read I Cache
No	Yes	X	Read D Cache
Yes	Yes	Yes	Read I from S Cache and D from D Cache
Yes	Yes	No	Read D Cache and add cycle to fetch instruction block into S Cache and processor

TABLE 2.23 Stall cache events and actions.

a split cache requires 30% of the chip area, equally divided between the instruction and data caches, the chip area can be reduced by 20% if there is a 1.5 factor of instruction cache area reduction.

2.8.3 *Compiler Optimization*

The organization and policies of caches are selected to match the design to the expected address sequences of instruction and/or data. The measures of success are the reduction of effective access time, reduction of P_{miss}, and the reduction in the bus traffic.

Another approach to achieving the desired goals stated above is to use the compiler to reorder the instruction and data sequences so that, for a given cache design, the desired goal of reducing P_{miss} can be achieved [HWU89, MCFA89]. The compiler attempts to maximize the temporal and spatial localities and minimize mapping conflicts.

The results of this research into compiler optimization show that, with compiler optimization, a direct cache compares favorably with a set associative cache of equal size. McFarling [MCFA 89] studied instruction caches only. His results show that compiler optimization can be as effective as increasing the cache size threefold. And, "Optimized programs on a direct mapped cache have lower miss ratios than unoptimized programs on set associative caches of the same size."

With the complexity of n-way set associative caches, the use of optimization should be exploited. In addition, the logic path of a direct cache is slightly shorter than that of an n-way set associative cache, thereby reducing the basic hit time of the cache.

2.8.4 *Pipelined Caches*

The assumption has been made in this chapter that the cache access time with a hit is a one clock cycle per operation. With the increasing demand for cache bandwidth, pipelining the cache is becoming an important design option. While pipelining is discussed in Chapters 6 to 9, the idea behind cache pipelining for performance reasons is briefly discussed here.

An early implementation of a pipelined cache is found on the Xerox Dorado [CLAR81]. This cache is an early select design that lends itself to pipelining, as shown in Figure 2.11. The first pipeline stage accesses the tag memory with the translation addresses and performs the tag check. The second stage accesses the data memory. The Dorado cache could support one cache reference per cycle, as long as there are no cache misses.

Recall, however, that modern caches are late select and can also be

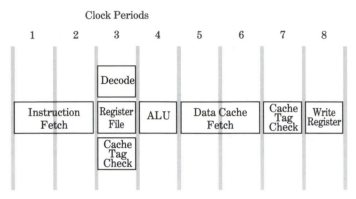

FIGURE 2.31   R4000 pipelined cache.

pipelined into at least two stages: Stage (1) reading the cache and the tags and Stage (2) comparing the tags with the address. Because reading the data and tag memories is a longer operation than the tag check and selection operation, the two stage times allocated to these two steps are not balanced. With pipelining, the first stage can be decomposed into two stages, giving a three-stage pipeline with reasonable balance between the stage times. Note that an interstage register is not required between the stages (a form of maximum rate pipelines to be discussed in Chapter 6). Thus, reading the cache can be a three-pipeline stage operation, as illustrated by the MIPS R4000 [MIRA92] and shown in Figure 2.31.

With the MIPS R4000, an instruction is decoded and the register files are read in parallel with tag checking. Thus, decoding and register file reads are conditional and can be abandoned if the tags check fails because of an instruction cache miss. An incorrect tag check will abort the instruction before it is issued to the ALU. However, tag checking of a write to the register file that results from a LOAD instruction is performed in serial. The reason for serial checking is that an incorrect conditional write would require extensive buffering and load true dependencies can be resolved with short circuiting. These issues are discussed further in Chapter 7.

3

Virtual Memory

3.0 Overview

Virtual memory has evolved in response to a number of factors. First, the address space of early processors was closely matched to the size of the *real memory* (main memory) and, for many reasons, was found to be inadequate. Second, software schemes that enabled the operating system to manage the transfer of information from bulk storage were developed. Third, virtual memory helped to overcome the performance penalty generated by these software memory management schemes.

The organization, or structure, of the virtual memory system results from matching the data structures employed by programmers. Program (code and data) modularity has been an accepted practice for many decades to facilitate independent development and checkout of software. Modules can be viewed as a hierarchy, and the allocation system should facilitate the modular view. A common data structure for representing modules is the tree, as shown in Figure 3.1, that reflects the hierarchical nature of many commonly occurring data structures. Files are referenced from the Root Directory via interior nodes or subdirectories. The files for early versions of UNIX were variable-length segments.

It is informative to survey the evolution of software memory management systems that preceded virtual memory. Figure 3.2(a) shows that the early *simple batch monitors* provided a single contiguous memory partition for a single user. When the user program is changed—due perhaps to the termination of a job—the active user partition is written out to disk and a new job is read in. The major drawback with this system is the overhead incurred in swapping and the inefficient use of processor and memory resources.

These early batch monitor systems were also called *roll-in/roll-out* because of the way jobs are moved from disk to the main memory. Upon the first instance of the job being moved to the main memory, real addresses are assigned that are used in subsequent references. This

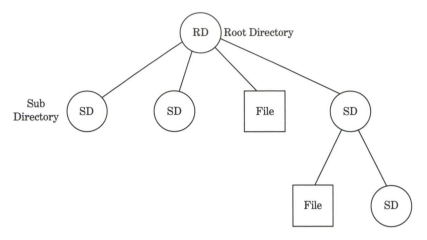

FIGURE 3.1 Data structure.

presents the problem that a new job may not be loadable from disk, even though there is available memory space, because the particular required address space is occupied.

The efficiency problems of the batch monitor are addressed in software-managed memory systems by *partitioned allocations*, as shown in Figure 3.2(b). Given that real memory is large enough to hold a number of partitions, each partition is allocated its own address space in real memory. The monitor then manages these partitions, assigning space, adjusting addresses, and swapping partitions in and out. As jobs are completed, space in memory is vacated and the monitor attempts to load another partition. The problem with this system is primarily that memory becomes fragmented and is used inefficiently.

Figure 3.2(b) shows a 30-K job (Job 5) waiting to be allocated. Even after Jobs 1 and 4 are complete (the assumed completion sequence) Job 5 cannot be allocated, even though 35K of memory space are available. Only after Job 2 is completed does space in memory become available for allocation of Job 5. Fragmentation clearly results in the inefficient use of memory.

Early research into solutions for the problem of fragmentation led to the identification of two types of fragmentation in a virtual memory system [RAND68, RAND69].

External fragmentation is caused in real memory when the allocation system does not relocate used space to free up unused space for allocation to a new task. Thus, the real address space becomes fragmented into groups of unusable spaces. (This fragmentation is the situation described above.)

Internal fragmentation occurs when the average space required for

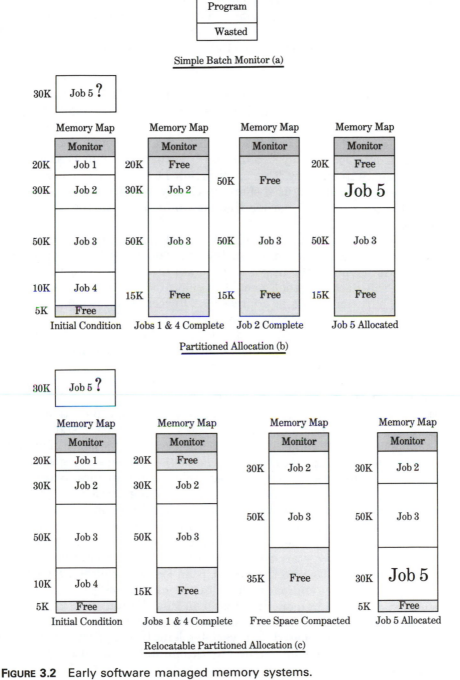

FIGURE 3.2 Early software managed memory systems.

111

an allocation is slightly larger than a page, which is a fixed-length allocation unit. Thus an extra page must be allocated, which wastes real memory space. Note that external and internal fragmentation were first applied in relation to the allocation of files on a disk. The meaning of these terms has been somewhat altered since they were applied to virtual memory systems. (This form of fragmentation is described later.)

External Fragmentation was solved by means of a *relocatable partitioned allocation*, which is illustrated in Figure 3.3(c). Relocatable partitioned allocation means that as jobs are terminated, the operating system compacts the remaining partitions so that free space is made available to waiting jobs. Note that after Jobs 1 and 4 are completed, the operating system moves Jobs 2 and 3 so that all free space is compacted into one address space in memory. This space is now large enough to allocate Job 5. Not only is memory used more efficiently by this process, Job 5 is available for execution earlier than it would be with the partitioned allocation system.

Relocation introduces an addressing problem, however. When partitions are moved, all addresses in the program must be changed. This problem is solved by the use of a *relocation register*, which points to the start of the partition that had been allocated under the assumption that the partition starts at address 0. All accesses to memory have the relocation register's contents added to the address. Relocation registers do not eliminate the need to actually move the partition, but they do minimize the addressing problems. Relocatable partitioned allocations go a long way to solve the external fragmentation problem but can introduce significant overhead because of the need to move the partitions around in memory.

Paged allocation extends relocatable partitioned allocations into a more generalized technique. Instead of a relocation register for each partition, paged allocation uses a relocation register for pages of approximately 4 Kbytes (size varies across systems). In some early systems the operating system managed these page relocation registers. Because the partitions are subdivided into pages, each having a relocation register, it is unnecessary to move pages as with relocatable partitions. A partition is broken into pages and placed into available page locations in the address space of real memory. The program can still be written under the assumption of a start address of 0 because the relocation registers change each address into the correct page location address. Paged allocation is the basic approach found in *demand paged virtual memory*, which is described in more detail later in this chapter.

Segmented allocation involves relocatable partitions of variable length and may be viewed as a variable-length page that supports the program's view of the data structure. Segmentation facilitates the sharing of programs and data.

The problems of software support of the above-mentioned memory management schemes have led researchers to see if the processor itself could make these tasks transparent to the executing program, in other words, the development of *virtual memory*. The first description of a virtual memory applied to the Atlas computer [KILB62], a design motivated by the desire for a large linear address space that hid the memory management tasks from the programmer. Another early experimental paged system was implemented at Berkeley [LAMP66]. The IBM S/370 family, first delivered in 1970, extended the IBM S/360 family to paged virtual memory capability. Cocke [COCK59] described the "virtual memory" of Stretch; however, this scheme is in reality an early form of cache.

A "pure" segmented system (pure means that a complete segment is fetched at one time from disk) was first implemented in the late 1950s on the experimental Rice University computer. The Burroughs B5000, first delivered in 1965, was the first large-scale commercial implementation of virtual memory and used segmentation [LEVY84]. In England, ICL implemented a segmentation machine in the early 1960s [ILIF68].

For almost three decades, research activity has produced hundreds of research papers and reports. An authoritative early work on virtual memories is by Denning [DENN70], a paper that explains most of the tradeoffs in the design of a virtual memory system. [PARM72] is another review paper, describing work at IBM, with an annotated bibliography. This paper looks not only at virtual memory but virtual machine concepts as well. [DONO72] reflects the MIT Project MAC view of memory management and virtual memory.

3.1 Virtual Memory Concepts

The term *virtual memory* has been used to denote a computer with a large linear address space that hides memory management tasks, discussed above, from the programmer. Virtual memory can be implemented with pure software or combinations of hardware and software. The following sections describe the use of hardware support to remove from the operating system some of the requirements that are necessary to manage the details of allocation. For the ensuing discussion, I define the following terms.

Symbolic name is the set of all names used by the programmer.

Effective address is the address generated by the processor and may, in some cases, be extended into a virtual address.

Virtual address is the machine equivalent of a symbolic name.

Real address (physical address) is the set of all addresses in the real memory.

Virtual memory system translates a user's virtual addresses into real memory addresses.

Allocation is the process of reserving storage locations.

Page is an allocation of fixed-length aggregations of addressable units.

Demand paging is a virtual memory system that moves pages to real memory as needed rather than prior to need.

Paging is the process or moving pages back and forth between real and auxiliary memory.

Segment is an allocation of variable-length aggregations of addressable units.

Paged segmentation is a virtual memory system that uses segments composed of integer pages, not addressable units.

There are differences in vocabulary for virtual memory concepts used by different researchers and manufacturers. For example, the address presented to the virtual memory system is known as either *virtual address, logical address*, or *linear address*. Another example is found in the names for the address presented to real memory: *real address, main memory address*, or *physical address*.

The most common and serious error in computer design has been to design an address range that is too small [BELL76]. It seems that few processor designs can outlive this flaw without a significant extension to the address range. An extension of the address range has been accompanied by a transition to virtual memory, a move that is typified by the DEC transition from the PDP-11 to the VAX 11/780 and the IBM transition from S/360 to S/370. Dennis [DENN65] pointed out the rationale behind the need for a large virtual address space.

1. A computation should have the use of a name space sufficiently large so that all information it references may be assigned unique names and such that reallocation of information within its name space is never necessary.
2. Data objects of a computation should be expandable without requiring a reallocation of name space.
3. Information referenced in common by several computations should have the same name for all computations that reference it.
4. A protection mechanism should operate in name space to permit access to information by a computation only in an authorized manner.

These requirements established the direction of virtual memory development. Research into techniques for the manipulation of symbolically addressed files with software was the precursor for virtual memory. This research established most of the concepts now embodied in virtual memory. As noted in [DENN70] four research objectives were: (1) program modularity, (2) varying data structures, (3) protection, and (4) sharing. The virtual memory systems discussed in this chapter deal with the way in which systems can be implemented in hardware and software to provide these functions.

When a program with symbolic names is compiled, two address translations are performed. First, the symbolic names are translated into virtual addresses that are used by the processor to address the virtual memory. Second, the operating system allocates the program and data to the disk system providing addresses such as drive, head, track, and record (discussed further in Section 3.5.9). The translations are

Compiler/Operating system translations.

Symbolic names-*translated to*-Virtual addresses,
Symbolic names-*translated to*-Disk addresses.

For a system with a cache, a program reference to memory may require three run time translations. The address translations, called Maps by [MATI77], are

Run Time translations.

Virtual addresses $\Rightarrow$ MAP 1 $\Rightarrow$ Cache addresses,
Virtual addresses $\Rightarrow$ MAP 2 $\Rightarrow$ Real memory addresses,
Virtual addresses $\Rightarrow$ MAP 3 $\Rightarrow$ Disk addresses.

MAP 2 and MAP 3 are the major subjects of this chapter. Translation to a cache address, MAP 1, is discussed in Chapter 4. Caches (discussed in Chapter 2) are used to improve the performance of the memory system by reducing the latency of the main memory as seen by the processor. Virtual memory, on the other hand, reduces the capacity limitations of small real memories by bringing the disk system into the address space of the processor. In early systems, the capacity gap is managed by programming with overlays. That is, the programmer divided the program and data into modules and scheduled their movement from the disk to memory. A virtual memory automatically manages this operation and presents a "one-level" memory to the user.

In addition to, and perhaps more important than, the one-level memory concept, virtual memory implementations have evolved to support useful data structures and programming methods. A multi-user system will have a number of active programs with requirements for sharing and protection that can be satisfied by virtual memory. Multiprogramming systems (*multitasking*) also require the same sharing and protection capabilities. In addition, programmers want to be able to develop and test individual programs that would not interact with other programs. These issues all stimulated the development of virtual memory concepts. There are three ways that virtual memory can be provided.

1. The processor can perform virtual memory functions completely in an interpretative mode. The speed penalty, as great as a factor of 100, may result when using interpretative virtual memory.

116   *Virtual Memory*

2. The compiler/loader can perform the virtual memory functions by relocating all addresses prior to execution (discussed in Section 3.0).
3. There can be hardware support for some of the virtual memory functions that overcome many of the performance penalties of pure interpretative mode. Combined hardware/software virtual memory is the predominate technique and is described in the sections that follow.

The implementation concepts of virtual memory and caches are similar. The differences are in the selection of the design parameters and the use of software rather than the hardware implementations of caches. Because the speed ratio between the real memory and the disk is quite large—100,000 to 1 or greater, there is abundant time for the use of software-implemented policies when there is a miss in the main memory; see Figure 1.7. Another difference between virtual memory and a cache is the terminology. Virtual memory and caches were developed almost concurrently, but they are described by different researchers using different terminology.

The basic idea behind virtual memory is that main memory is a cache for the disk just as the cache, discussed in Chapter 2, gives the illusio.. ˜f a fast main memory. Thus, the discussion of virtual memory will address the same two issues that are addressed with caches:

1. organization and structure of the memory hierarchy (discussed in Section 3.2),
2. set of rules to follow when main memory is accessed (discussed in Section 3.5).

As with caches, the translation of address spaces is directly related to the organization of the virtual memory system. The process of converting the processor effective address into the real memory address is performed in two steps, as shown in Figure 3.3.

The first step, sometimes called *mapping*, takes the processor effective address and extends it into the virtual address (discussed in Section 3.2.1). Some processors, however, use the term *segmentation* for this first step; examples are found with IBM RS/6000 and Intel x86. Some processors, by virtue of their long processor effective address, do not extend to a longer virtual address.

The second step, also shown in Figure 3.3, translates the virtual

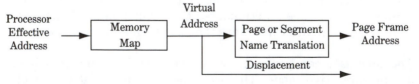

FIGURE 3.3   Address conversions.

page name into the *page frame address* (PFA) or segment name into a base register value to be combined with the untranslated displacement into the real memory address; a step is called *name* or *address transla-tion*. Early systems, such as the IBM 7040, used the processor effective address as the memory real address. In these cases, the mappings are identities. Some contemporary systems have, as part of their virtual memory management hardware, an identity name translation path for accessing special system areas in memory such as name translation tables.

Virtual memory is similar to caches because the major functions to be provided are the same. In addition, they are early select because of the process of performing the name translation. These functions are

1. to detect the presence or absence of the referenced AU in real memory;
2. if the AU is present, to translate the virtual address into the real address and access the real memory;
3. if the AU is absent, to determine if a page or segment must be evicted from real memory as well as select the page or segment to be evicted;
4. to evict the page or segment and bring in the new page or segment;
5. to update all translation tables and reinitiate the access.

These functions are tightly interwoven into the design of what is now known as the *Memory Management Unit* (MMU). The discussion of virtual memory starts, in Section 3.2, by describing the methods that extend the effective address into the virtual address. The method by which the page or segment name is translated is discussed in Section 3.3. A major consideration in the design of a virtual memory is the reduction of the time to make the above-mentioned translations. The other virtual memory functions are discussed in Section 3.4.

3.2 Memory Mapping

Most early computers and microprocessors suffered from limited address space. Examples include the PDP-8 with 12 bits of address and the i8088 with 16 bits of address. Short addresses limit the amount of random access memory that can be attached, and a number of techniques have been employed to extend the address range of processors. A complete survey of these techniques can be found in [POPP77]. Invariably, these extension techniques produced a granularity in addressing that com-plicated the programming.

3.2.1 *Creating Large Virtual Addresses*

This section discusses the problem of creating a virtual address for systems where the processor space or effective address is less than the desired virtual space. The page or segment name portion of the large virtual address is then translated into the real memory address. The inadequacy of a 32-bit virtual address has been recognized for three decades and extensions have been applied to 32-bit addresses. For example, the IBM S/370/168 (circa 1965) had a 3-bit extension of a user ID that extended the virtual address. The creation of large virtual addresses is more commonly viewed as creating a set of large segments that are of a fixed maximum length and can overlap. For this reason, the mapping function is frequently referred to as *segmentation*.

In general, extensions are found in a map that is indexed by a small number of bits in the effective address or indexed by implication. The steps used to extend the effective address are usually accomplished in one level of mapping.

3.2.2 *One-Level Map Address Extension*

The first use of maps to extend an address is found in short word-length minicomputers of the 1970s. For these machines, the virtual address is too short to address the desired real memory directly. Thus, a map is used to extend the virtual address [POPP77]. An example of this technique is found in the Z800 memory system, as shown in Figure 3.4.

Z800. This processor generated a 16-bit effective address. The 4 MSBs are used as an index into a 16-entry table containing control

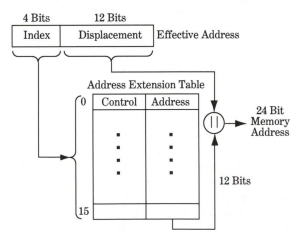

FIGURE 3.4   Z800 address extension.

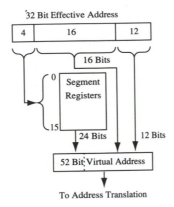

FIGURE 3.5   RS/6000 MAP.

bits, for access control, and a 12-bit address extension. The address and displacement are concatenated to provide a 24-bit memory address.

RS/6000. This processor takes a similar approach to generating a long virtual address from its 32-bit effective address. The virtual memory system of this processor is directly related to that of the IBM 801 [CHAN88, OEHL90]. With this processor, the effective address is 32 bits and is mapped into a virtual address of 52 bits. Figure 3.5 shows the mapping of the processor effective address into the virtual address.

The four most significant bits of the effective address are an index used to select one of sixteen segment registers that store 24-bit segment identification numbers (SID) or addresses. These 24 bits are concatenated to the 16 virtual page indices, which creates a 40-bit virtual page name. These 40 bits are concatenated with the 12-bit displacement, creating the 52-bit virtual address. The address extension mapping provides 16 active segments of 2^{28} bytes, or 256 Mbytes, at any one time. The total number of segments in virtual memory space is 2^{24}. During a memory reference, the 40-bit virtual page name is translated into a real address as discussed in Sections 3.3 and 3.4.

HP Precision Architecture. The HP Precision Architecture [MAHO86, FOTL87] generates a 32-bit effective address. The two MSBs index into a four-entry map that contains 0-, 16-, or 32-bit extensions (depending upon the processor model). These extension bits are concatenated with the remaining 30 bits of the effective address to produce a 30-, 46- or 62-bit virtual address. The page is 2 Kbytes; thus there are 2^{19}, 2^{35}, or 2^{51} virtual pages.

Motorola MC68040. This processor extends its 32-bit effective address by implication indexing one of two 23-bit registers and concatenating it with the effective address. There is one register for user and

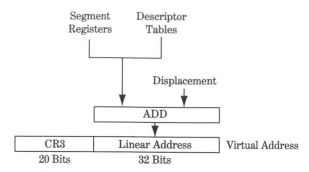

FIGURE 3.6   i386, i486, and Pentium register based address extension.

one for supervisor mode. The result of this operation is a 55-bit virtual address. With a page of 8 Kbytes, there are 2^{42} virtual pages. The contents of these extension registers are called *root pointers* because they point to the root directory in the virtual memory space.

3.2.3 *Register Extensions*

The i386, i486, and Pentium extend their 32-bit segmented address (the generation of this address is described in Section 3.3.3) by 20 bits to form a 52-bit virtual address as shown in Figure 3.6. This extension is taken from CR3, one of four control registers (CR0–CR3) in the processor, that is loaded by the program using move instructions. The extension is called the *page director base register*, which is sometimes called the *root pointer* because it points to the root directory in the page tables.

3.2.4 *Summary*

Many processors extend their effective address as discussed above. Extension is used, in some cases, to extend the address space in conjunction with providing support for paged segmentation. Table 3.1 lists the number of extension bits and the number of virtual pages that can be addressed. In all cases, except for the IBM S/370/168, the effective address is extended from 32 bits.

The extension registers are loaded under program control and, in some designs, provide segmentlike virtual address on top of a paged system. In these cases, the management of the segments is a pure software function. Paged segmentation is discussed in Section 3.3.3.

Processor	Extension Bits	Page Size	No. Virtual Pages
RS/6000	20	4 Kbytes	2^{40}
MC68030,40	23	8 Kbytes	2^{42}
MC88200	20	4 Kbytes	2^{40}
i386 and i486	20	4 Kbytes	2^{40}
HP Precision	0,16, or 32	2 Kbytes	2^{19}, 2^{35}, or 2^{51}
MIPS R2000	6	4 Kbytes	2^{26}
IBM S/370/168	3	2 Kbytes	2^{15}

TABLE 3.1   Effective address extensions.

3.3 Virtual Memory Organizations

A basic function performed in a virtual memory system is the translation of virtual addresses to real addresses. A number of methods for performing the name translation function have been used in virtual memory systems, and a taxonomy of these methods is shown in Figure 3.7. The taxonomy shows the three major types of virtual memory—paged, segmented, and paged-segmented—and the translation methods used for each. The sections to follow discuss the translation.

Two design features are common to paged and paged-segmented virtual memory organizations: (1) congruence page mapping, and (2) early selection (see Figure 2.11). Within these two design features, the translation of a virtual address into the real memory address is performed by accessing *tables* that contain preloaded translation information, which is an operating system function. Segmented systems that

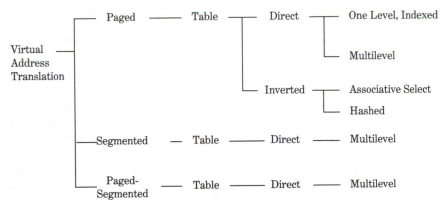

FIGURE 3.7   Virtual memory and translation taxonomy.

also use a translation table for name translation are early select but are not congruence mapped.

The use of early select techniques in virtual memory systems is based on the following consideration. The real memory, unlike a cache, is quite large. Thus, the number of tag bits needed for a late select real memory presents a significant cost problem as the implementation of the tag memory could best be accomplished in the memory technology itself. Early selection requires a number of memory cycles for name translation but, like most references, would be served by the cache; very few references require this slow translation process. Some of the terminology, expanded from earlier definitions, used with virtual memories include the following.

A *page* is a length allocation of bytes that is transferred to/from the real memory and the disk, similar to a block in the cache. Pages are congruence mapped. Consequently, pages do not overlap within the virtual memory address space.

A *segment* is a variable-length allocation or page. However, there is usually a limit to the size of a segment. The segment is addressed from a base register, and segments can overlap partially or fully. Segments are not congruence mapped and can overlap.

A page and segment can be defined by the Cartesian product of fixed- or variable-length and overlap or nonoverlap as

Fixed length, nonoverlap   Page
Fixed length, overlap   Segment
Variable length, overlap   True segment
Variable length, nonoverlap   Not defined

A *page frame* (*page slot*) is a page-sized space in real memory that can hold a page.

A *page fault* occurs when a requested AU is missing from the real memory; similar to a cache miss.

The *page fault ratio* is the ratio of unsuccessful accesses of real memory to total accesses of real memory.

A *demand paging system* is a hardware implementation of virtual memory.

The taxonomy presented in Figure 3.7 is based upon the structure of the translation mechanism. Moore [MOOR91] provides other taxonomies. One of his taxonomies is based upon the granularity of the data structure: word, page, segment, and page-segment; while a second taxonomy is based upon the allocation and management methods: manual static, manual dynamic, compiler, linker/loader, and automatic dynamic.

Another consideration in the organization of the name translation system is the inclusion of control bits. These bits are required for maintaining the context of the translation system [MALI90] and are in addition to the pointer or address bits found in the translation table entries. The following sections discuss the control bits for each of the virtual memory organizations and describe the methods for performing name translation. Note that most systems also provide direct untranslated paths, or identity translations, used by the system software and the operating system.

The reader should keep in mind the changes in name translation techniques that have occurred over time. Early systems with small effective or virtual address spaces and small virtual memory used hardware-based translation tables that are fast and implementable with the available technology at reasonable cost. As the size of the address space and virtual memory increased, these tables were placed in memory at a significant cost in increased access time. To overcome this problem, small hardware-based translation systems called a translation lookaside buffer are used so that a large fraction of the translations are made in fast hardware. The translation lookaside buffer is identical to the early hardware-based translation systems. Today's virtual memory systems are an amalgam of the early hardware-based translation combined with memory resident translation tables.

3.3.1 *Page Allocation Systems*

For page allocation systems, the following translation of the virtual address into the real memory address is taken from [DENN76]:

$$\text{virtual address} \Rightarrow (n, d) \Rightarrow (f(n), d) \Rightarrow f(b) \; \emptyset \; d = \text{real address}$$

where n is the page name; d is the displacement within the page; $\emptyset$ denotes the concatenation; (n, d) = [virtual address/s] or virtual address mod s, [ ] denotes the quotient of dividing the virtual address range by s, which is a trivial step when s is an even power of two; and s is the size of the page.

This translation process describes congruence mapping. That is, the virtual address is de-allocated into the pair (page name, displacement). The page name is translated with function f, and the result is concatenated with d to give the real memory address. Note that the displacement is NOT translated. Because virtual memory systems are early select, the mapping is associative and any page can be placed in any page frame of real memory. Each of these methods of table-based page name translation, as shown in the taxonomy of Figure 3.7, are discussed in the following paragraphs.

A major virtue of a paged system is that upon a page fault, it is only necessary to find space in real memory for a fixed-size page as the address translation process is congruence mapped and associative. This policy, however, does lead to some waste of real memory space because a segment of the data structure is not always an exact number of pages. This waste is known as internal fragmentation, which was previously defined.

Table Translation

Translation of the page name of a virtual address into a real address is accomplished by the use of tables, called *page tables* or *maps*, that contain the translation information. There are three types of table-based translators.

Direct page table. A direct translation table has one entry for every page in virtual memory and is accessed by one or more indexing steps (discussed in Section 3.3.1).

Inverted page table. An inverted translation table has an entry for every page that is resident in real memory and is accessed by some form of associative or hashed index search [CHAN88].

Cache-like page table. A number of structures are used that take advantage of the temporal locality of addresses and use smaller tables than inverted translation tables. These tables that hold the translation information for a subset of the pages in real memory are generally called *translation lookaside buffers* and are discussed in Section 3.4.

Direct table translation is sometimes known as *forward-mapped translation*, and inverted translation is sometimes known as *reverse-mapped translation* [HUCK93]. Note that the word *direct* has a different meaning when used to describe cache organizations. There are variations in translation systems based on page, block, instruction, and data name translations. These variations will be discussed in the following sections.

Direct Page Table Translation

A direct page translation table has *one table entry for each virtual page*. The page table is direct mapped and addressed by an index of the virtual page address that is the name of the virtual page [BAER80, WILK68]. With a large virtual address space, the direct page table can get quite large because of the large number of virtual pages. The variations discussed later address this issue.

The direct page tables discussed in this section may be viewed as a data structure, held in memory and manipulated by the processor's program. However, in the interest of decreasing the time required to perform a page name translation, hardware tables and other hardware assists can be provided. For example, the traverse of the tables is called table-walking and, in some processors, is implemented in microcode.

One-Level Direct Page Tables

A one-level indexed direct page table is also known as a *linear map*. For processors with a small virtual address space, these tables have been implemented completely in hardware. A direct page table is illustrated in Figure 3.8. This example assumes a virtual memory of eight pages and a real memory of four page frames. The page table is indexed by the page name from the virtual address and has eight entries, each of which consists of a present bit plus the frame address. A page can be placed in any page frame; thus the translation is associative.

The state of the system shown in Figure 3.8 is: page 4 is resident in page frame 0, page 7 is in page frame 1, page 3 is in page frame 2, and page 5 is in page frame 3 of the real memory. If a reference is made to, say, page 7, the present bit (= 1) indicates that the page is resident and the page frame address is selected, concatenated with the displacement from the virtual address, and indexes into the real memory. This method of generating the real address is recognized as early select.

A page name that indexes the table and finds the present bit a zero causes a page fault. With a page fault, a real memory page frame must be selected to receive the new page based upon criteria discussed in

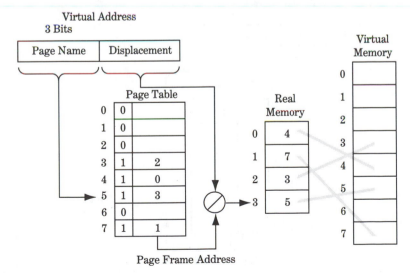

FIGURE 3.8 One-level indexed direct page table.

Section 3.5.2. If there is a vacant page frame, the requested page can be loaded into that frame and the present and address fields are updated. If there is no vacant page frame, a page frame must be selected based on some use criteria. If the page in the selected page frame is dirty, it must be written out to the disk before the new page is read in. After the page is loaded, the page frame address and the present bit are adjusted to indicate the presence of this new page in the real memory. No known implementations of a direct page table use a dirty bit to indicate a modified value in a page frame. The assumption is made that all page frames are dirty and must be evicted if selected. Page frames holding only nonmodifiable code would not need to be evicted, and a dirty bit could be of some value for these situations.

One of the first time-sharing virtual memory machines used direct translation [MEND66]. This machine, the Xerox Sigma 7, was developed by Scientific Data Systems based upon research performed at U.C. Berkeley. The processor effective address is not extended because it is relatively long (17 bits) for its day. The Sigma 7 had 256 virtual pages of 512 32-bit words, as shown in Figure 3.9. Real memory can have up to 256 page frames installed.

As Figure 3.9 illustrates, an 8-bit page name indexes into one of 256 page table locations containing a present bit and the 8-bit translated page frame address. Each page table entry also has protection bits, not shown, for memory access and write protection.

An advantage of one-level direct translation of a virtual address is its simplicity and a relatively short latency if the page table is in hard-

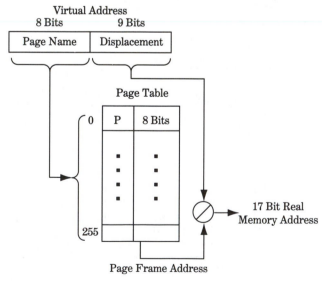

FIGURE 3.9 Sigma 7 page name translation.

ware registers. On the other hand, as the number of pages in the virtual memory gets very large, the size of the table increases to the point that there may be more bits in the table than in real memory. For example, assume a virtual address of 32 bits (address to the byte), a page size of 1 Kbytes, and real memory of 1 Mbytes. The number of entries in the page table is

$$\text{number of entries} = 2^{32}/2^{10} = 2^{22}.$$

The number of page frame address bits in each entry of the page table is $\text{Log}_2\ 1024 = 10$ bits. For this example, the page table has more than five times the number of bits as the real memory (5.5 Mbytes versus 1 Mbytes). As the virtual address size increases, the size problem with a one-level page table increases as well.

It is possible to store a one-level direct page table in virtual memory space that is itself paged. The table described above would occupy approximately 0.1% of the virtual address space. In other words, the real memory acts as a cache for the page table, greatly reducing the real memory space required to hold the page table. An example of this technique is found in the VAX 11/780 page table organization. Three base registers hold base addresses for three page tables that are indexed by the sum of a value in a base register and the virtual page name [STRE78]. Not only can portions of the page tables be paged, but portions of the page tables can be in the cache. In other words, the table structure is treated as any other data structure insofar as allocation to the memory hierarchy is concerned. This one-level page table is supported by a translation lookaside buffer (discussed in Section 3.4).

Multilevel Direct Table Translation

Multilevel direct tables, sometimes known as *hierarchical tables*, have a consistent relationship to the structure of the program and data as illustrated in Figure 3.10. The multilevel tables are arranged in a tree structure that contains two or more levels of partial direct page tables [ARDE66]. The first level is generally associated with the root node of processes that are resident in real memory, while the second and third or fourth levels provide the name translation for the individual process segments. With this structure, some degree of protection between processes is provided. The advantages of the multilevel page table technique over the single-level indexed direct technique have been discussed in [FURH87] and include

1. more sophisticated protection,
2. accommodation of a larger address space,
3. page and segment sharing between processes.

Protection is discussed in Section 3.5.7. The second issue of the accommodation of a larger address space is addressed in the following paragraphs and is a major benefit of the structure of multilevel translation tables.

Recall that direct page tables have one entry per virtual page and can become quite large with large virtual addresses. Because pages have locality, it is possible to restructure a one-level page table into a hierarchy (multiple levels) and page the active portions of the page table into real memory. In other words, the active portions of the page table are "cached" in the main memory so that accesses to the disk are not required to perform page fault detection and page name translation. While caching does not save table bits—in fact, it requires more bits—only the first-level root and the active levels, including the leaf levels, need to be in real memory at any time. Note that the leaf-level tables are usually referred to as the *page tables*. As will be shown, multilevel page tables permit the dedication of a relatively small portion of real memory to the "caching" of the active portions of the page tables.

A one-level indexed page table can be restructured into a multilevel page table of any number of levels, as illustrated in Figure 3.10. The structures of one-, two-, and three-level systems are illustrated. The page name is N bits (the displacement field of the virtual address is ignored for simplicity), and the number of page frames in real memory is 2^P. The one-level page table has 2^N words—each having p bits of page frame address that index into the real memory. These p bits are concatenated with the displacement, as shown in Figure 3.8. Control and present bits are in addition to the P address bits and are not shown or counted.

For this model development, a two-level page table divides the page name into two equal parts. The root directory table, the first level, has $2^{N/2}$ entries of $N/2$ bits each. The first-level table is indexed by the most significant half of the page name bits. There are now $2^{N/2}$ second-level page tables, each with P bits. The second-level table is selected by the address bits in the first-level table and indexed by the least significant half bits of the page name.

Note that there are more bits in the two-level system than in the one-level system. The leaf tables, in sum, have the same number of bits as the one-level system. The root-level bits are added to the leaf-level bits to give the total number of bits in the set of tables.

A three-level system is formed by dividing the one-level page table into $2^{2N/3}$ leaf tables, each have $2^{N/3}$ entries with P bits. A second level consists of $2^{N/3}$ tables of $2^{N/3}$ entries having $2^{N/3}$ bits. The root level has $2^{N/3}$ entries of $N/2$ bits each. The three-level system also has more bits than the one level due to the addition of the root- and first-level to the third-level bits.

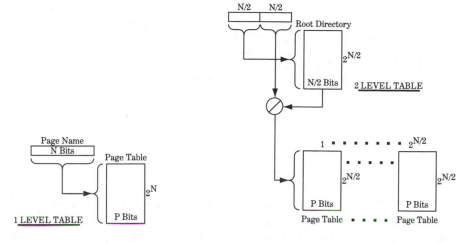

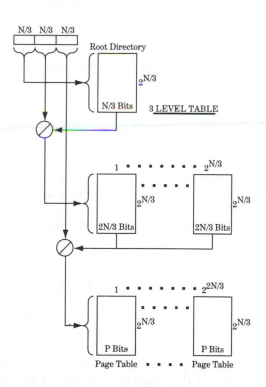

FIGURE 3.10   Multilevel page tables.

 # Tables / Levels

Map Level	1	2	3	4
1	1	1	1	1
2		$2^{N/2}$	$2^{N/3}$	$2^{N/4}$
3			$2^{2N/3}$	$2^{N/2}$
4				$2^{3N/4}$

 # Entries / Table

Map Level	1	2	3	4
1	2^N	$2^{N/2}$	$2^{N/3}$	$2^{N/4}$
2		$2^{N/2}$	$2^{N/3}$	$2^{N/4}$
3			$2^{N/3}$	$2^{N/4}$
4				$2^{N/4}$

 # Bits / Entry

Map Level	1	2	3	4
1	P	N/2	N/3	N/4
2		P	2N/3	2N/4
3			P	3N/4
4				P

FIGURE 3.11   Multilevel table parameters.

Figure 3.11 shows the number of tables per level, the number of entries per table, and the number of bits per entry for one-, two-, three-, and four-level multilevel page tables. These parameters are based on page name lengths with factors of 2, 3, and 4. With real systems it is not always possible to factor the page name and the number of bits shown in Figure 3.11 will not apply exactly.

As shown in Figure 3.11, a one-level page table has 2^N entries of p bits. A three-level page table, for example, has $1 + 2^{N/3} + 2^{2N/3}$ tables, and each table has $2^{N/3}$ entries. The first-level page table has $N/3$ bits; the second level has $2^{N/3}$ bits; and the third level, leaf, page tables have p bits. The total number of bits in an l-level page table is given by the formula [HABA93]

$$\text{total bits} = 2^{N/l}\left[\left(\sum_{x=0}^{l-2} 2^{xN/l}(x+1)\frac{N}{l}\right) + 2^{(l-1)N/l}p\right]$$

where l is the number of levels.

Matick [MATI77] gives the following formula for the number of levels of a multilevel page table that is set by the page size, the number of virtual pages, and the number of AUs required for an entry in the page tables.

$$\text{number of levels} = \left[\frac{\text{no. of V.PageNameAddressBits}}{\text{no. of PageAddressBits} - \lg_2 \dfrac{\text{no. of AUs}}{\text{Entry}}}\right]$$

As the number of AUs per entry increases, fewer entries can be held in a given size page and the number of levels of the page table must increase. While each leaf table is small, the total storage of all the leaf tables is the same as for a one-level direct translation system. The number of entries is 2^N, as shown in Figures 3.10 and 3.11, a fact to be noted when multilevel page table systems are discussed.

What has been accomplished by subdividing a one-level page table into multiple levels? Each of the leaf tables has become relatively small. Subdividing is similar to block size selection in cache design. Smaller leaf tables will have a shorter transfer time from disk to the main memory but will also have a higher "miss ratio." Because portions of the page table are "cached" in real memory, there can be misses on the access of the page table itself. A page table miss is detected by a valid bit in the page table entry at each level except the leaf level.

The benefit of multilevel table translation is that large virtual address spaces can have translation tables that occupy a relatively small portion of real memory because only the active page table entries are resident. As a result, the miss ratio on the page tables, after the load transient, can be quite small. With portions of the multilevel page tables located in real memory, special provisions must be taken to prevent undue performance degradation when accessing these tables. Each level of the page table takes at least one memory reference to access the table itself, thereby increasing the latency of the page name translation process. Reasonably fast techniques, called *table walking*, for searching these tables are needed and are discussed in Section 3.5.5.

Multilevel Page Table Control Bits

The control bits required in a multilevel page table differ depending upon the level in the hierarchy. A one-level system or the leaf tables of a multilevel table has control bits required to manage the access to the page in memory, while the non-leaf tables have bits to manage the translation tables. Examples of the control bits used are

Leaf Table.

Modified or *dirty bit* indicates that one AU in the page has been written into and that the page must be written back into the virtual memory space if the page frame is to be vacated.

Referenced bit indicates that an AU has been referenced. This bit is required to support replacement algorithms.

Protection bits are required to ensure that the access method is correct—as is the case, for example, of Read Only, Read/Write, and Execute Only. Also, the access can be verified with protection bits for protected accesses such as User, System, or Operating System. These issues are discussed in Section 3.5.7.

Leaf and Nonleaf tables.

Valid bit or *present bit* indicates that the table entry is valid and/or that the referenced page is in real memory.

Valid or present bits are used differently in different levels of multi-level page tables. Some systems, notably the i386, i486, and the Pentium, view the valid bits uniformly. That is, an invalid entry at any level signifies that the page is not in real memory. When an invalid bit is encountered in the translation process, a page fault interrupt is generated. Other systems, such as the MC68040, have a nonuniform treatment. The valid or present bits of the nonleaf tables indicate whether or not the reference to the next level translation table is valid. The bit in the leaf table indicates whether or not the referenced page is resident in real memory.

Example Systems

Intel i386 and i486. An example of a two-level multilevel table is taken from the i386 and i486 [ELAY85] and is shown in Figure 3.12. Note that the 32-bit processor address is known by Intel as the *linear address*. The linear address is expanded to 52 bits by concatenating the 20 MSBs of processor register CR3. The virtual address is divided into three fields: two fields from the virtual page name and the displacement. The 30 bits formed from CR3 and the directory field index into the first-level page table, called the *page directory*. The second level produces the page frame address for the real memory access.

Note that the leaf nodes, page tables, have 1K pages of 1K entries. This page table design is clearly not a complete direct translation table system. If it were complete, with 2^{40} virtual pages, four levels of translation would be required and the total number of leaf entries would be 2^{40}, not the implemented 2^{20} Also, because there can be only 2^{10} unique

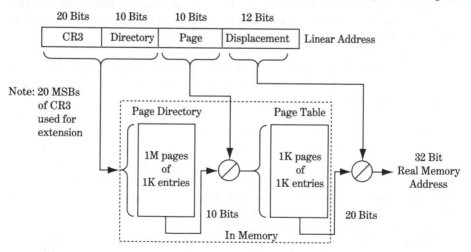

FIGURE 3.12   Two-level page table (i386, i486).

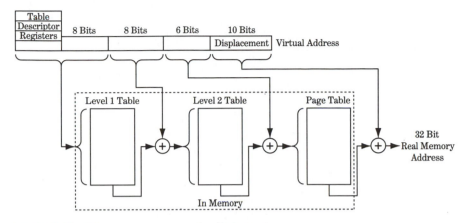

FIGURE 3.13 Three-level page table (Z80,000).

instances of page frame addresses in the page directory of 2^{30} entries, address aliasing is possible. The design compromise made between a full or partial implementation is based, it is believed, on the desire to reduce the translation time via the page tables.

Zilog Z80,000. An example of a three-level page table system is found in the obsolete Z80,000, as shown in Figure 3.13 [FURH87]. The 32-bit virtual address is divided into a 10-bit displacement and a 22-bit page name address and is extended with bits from one of the four table descriptor registers that are addressed by two bits in the processor status word. The page name address is divided nonsymmetrically with an 8-bit index into the first level, an 8-bit index into the second level, and a 6-bit index into the third level.

Note that the Z80,000 page name translation system adds the index from the virtual address to the base from a table. The consequence of this is that entries in the page tables can overlap, providing for sharing but a more complicated software management system. Because of the use of addition, this system could be classified as paged-segmented; however, it is referred to in the literature as a pure paged system. The design details of this mapping system are not available, making it impossible to determine the size of the tables and other design details.

MC68851. The Motorola 68851 MMU is a stand-alone device intended for use with the MC68020 microprocessor [MILE 90]. This device is unique in that the structure is highly programmable or configurable by the user. The following structural parameters are available:

Page size	256 bytes to 32 Kbytes,
Number of levels	1 to 5.

An unusual feature found in the M68851 is the capability of storing

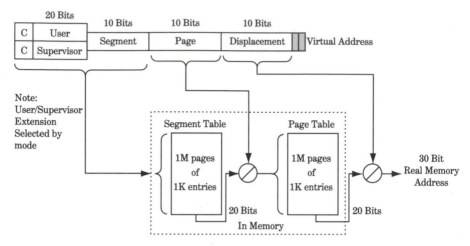

FIGURE 3.14   MC88200 table structure.

a pointer in the leaf tables that point not to the page in real memory but to another leaf table. This feature supports sharing of real pages but can significantly increase the number of references to memory that are required before a page fault is detected. I believe that there is a time-out feature to stop endless looping around indirect addresses.

MC88200. It is interesting to note that Motorola eliminated the programmability of the MC68851 in the MMU of the MC88200 [MOTO90a]. The table structure of the MC88200 is shown in Figure 3.14. This device supports a fixed page size of 4 Kbytes. The 32-bit effective address is extended by 20 bits using two registers found in the MMU that are loaded by the processor. Depending upon the mode of operation, the user of supervisor extension is concatenated to the effective address, providing a 52-bit virtual address. There are two levels of translation. The first level, called the segment table, has 2^{30} entries of 20 bits that are concatenated with the 10-bit page field that address the page table. Motorola calls their system a segmented system; segmentation is provided by software that determines the values to be used in the extension registers. The balance of the system is a hardware-paged system.

As with the i386, i486 page name translation systems, the MC88200 is a partial implementation of a direct map. There are 2^{30} entries in the page table rather than 2^{40} as required for a full implementation. The number of entries is greater than that of the i386, i486, thus requiring fewer allocations of translation information to the page table.

Control Bits

The use of control bits in a multilevel page table system is illustrated with the MC88200, which has an extensive control bit repertoire to provide flexible support of differing operating systems. The first level of control bits is contained in the two *area descriptors* that are selected by mode to extend the processor effective address, as shown in Figure 3.14. These bits, noted as *C* in the figure, consist of

WT	Write Through: controls the write policy of the cache;
G	Global: controls the scope of snoopy coherency measures (Chapter 5);
CI	Cache Inhibit: inhibits caching of local instructions;
TE	Translation Enable: if not set, no page name translation.

The first-level table, known as the *segment table*, has entries called *segment descriptors*, with the following control bits:

WT	Write Through;
G	Global;
CI	Cache Inhibit;
SP	Supervisor Protection: controls translation of supervisor;
WP	Write Protect: controls write protection;
V	Valid: if not valid, translation fault (table not present).

The second level, known as the *page table*, has entries called *page descriptors*, with the following control bits:

WT	Write Through;
G	Global;
CI	Cache Inhibit;
SP	Supervisor Protection;
WP	Write Protect;
V	Valid (Page is valid);
M	Modified: indicates that the page has been modified;
U	Used: indicates that a page has been accessed.

Note that some of the levels have control bits for the same function. An example is the WT, Write Through bit. These bits are ORed together, and if any one is set the resulting action is taken based on this test of the control bits.

Inverted Page Table Translation

Direct multilevel table translation has served well for processors with virtual addresses limited to 32 bits. With virtual address extensions, partial page table implementations have been required. In the early 1980s designers at IBM contemplated very large virtual addresses and determined that a different translation method would be required. For a system with a 1-Kbyte page and a 52-bit virtual address, the leaf nodes would require approximately 6×2^{42} bytes. Systems that followed this study are the IBM System 38 with a virtual address of 48 bits [HOUD80, HOUD81] and the IBM RS/6000 with a 52-bit virtual address [OEHL90]. A direct page table for a large virtual address would not only be very large but also sparsely populated and inefficient. The inverted page translation systems described in this section are both small and densely populated.

To reduce the size of the translation table, an inverted page table that contains *only the virtual pages that are currently resident in real memory* can be used [CHAN88] to translate long virtual addresses. An inverted page table can provide a substantial reduction in the size of the page tables and reduce the number of memory accesses required for a page name translation. The page name can be translated into the real address by either an associative search of the translation table, an *n*-wise set associative search, or by hashing into a linked list. Current design practice does not use *n*-wise set associative searching, thus associative search and hashing are discussed in the following paragraphs.

All known contemporary implementations of inverted page table virtual memory have been designed by either IBM, Hewlett-Packard, or the IBM/Motorola/Apple group (Sumerset). These systems will be described in the following sections.

Inverted Associative Page Table Search

An inverted *associative page table* (APT) has one entry for each of the pages in real memory. This page table is accessed by an associative search from the page name in the virtual address. As with all known virtual memory systems, an APT system is early select and congruent mapped.

The Atlas [KILB62, MATI77] is an example of an inverted APT. This memory system has a page size of 512 words, a virtual address of 2048 pages, and a real memory of 32 pages (16K words). A block diagram of the map is shown in Figure 3.15. The dotted arrow with A at its head signifies an associative search. The page table contains the page frame address and the page name of the pages in real memory, called *tags*. A page name is the key for an associative search of the tags. Note the one-to-one correspondence in the number of entries in the page table and the number of page frames in real memory.

A hit on the tags produces a 5-bit page frame address that is concatenated with the 9-bit displacement from the virtual address. The resulting 14-bit address is presented to the real memory. If the addressed page is not in real memory and therefore not in the page table, a miss occurs and the page is fetched from a drum memory in virtual address space.

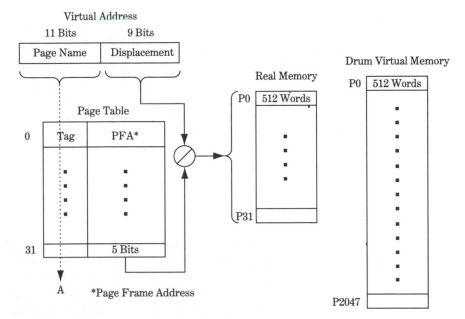

FIGURE 3.15   Atlas page name translation.

The drum address is found by sequentially searching a table holding the 11-bit virtual page number and the corresponding drum address (a process described in Section 3.5.9).

The designers of Atlas considered using a direct table method with the table in real memory. However, this form of translation requires that at least one real memory reference must be processed to see if there is a page fault and to generate the real memory address. This design would make every reference to real memory cost (at a minimum) two memory cycles. The APT method provides a faster associative search of a hardware table, adding only a small increment of time to the real memory access latency. Because it is faster, the associative method is superior and is used on the Atlas even though there was a significant circuit cost for the associative translation table.

For very large virtual addresses and large real memory, the size of an inverted APT is too large and costly for consideration. The small virtual address of the Atlas will never be used again. However, the APT is used in systems in the form of translation lookaside buffers (discussed in Section 3.4).

APT Control Bits

Systems using APT control the page name translation process by an associative search mechanism and require no control bits. Recall that there is one table entry for each real page frame. The entries in the inverted page table contain the page base address in real memory and the page name. If there is a hit on the search, the translation is complete. If there is a miss, then there is a page fault.

Protection bits should be required with the APT as with the other page name translation systems. However, as protection was not a requirement for APT systems that were implemented, such as the Atlas, there are no examples to cite of protection bits. Protection bits are used in TLBs (described in Section 3.4), which are similar to APTs. For example, valid bits are required to indicate the presence of valid translation information in the page table.

Hashed Inverted Page Table Search

The inverted translation scheme of the Atlas is costly to implement if the size of the real memory and the virtual address become very large. This is now the case with many virtual memory systems. Hashing is the translation technique of choice today for IBM systems with large virtual addresses. The index into an inverted page table is found by hashing the page name (the displacement bits are not hashed). The hash number is then used as an index into the page table, which provides the page frame address. This technique is properly known as *key transformation* [PRIC71]. The key transformation technique reduces the large number of virtual page addresses into one of a number of noncongruent classes in which the real page addresses are linked together.

Hashed access into large address spaces or data structures was developed in the 1960s for access to symbol tables and the like [JOHN61, MORR68]. These techniques were then applied to the accessing of large files and have been, since the late 1970s, applied to virtual memory page name translation. A good hash transformation is one that "spreads the calculated address (sometimes known as hash addresses) uniformly across the available addresses" [MORR68]. The design of hashing functions is beyond the scope of this book, however, a tutorial on hashing can be found in [LEWI88].

It is possible to have a one level translation table that is accessed by hashing the virtual page name as illustrated in Figure 3.16. This method for translating virtual addresses into real memory addresses divides the virtual address into the page name field and the displacement field. The page name field is hashed for an index that accesses the page frame table. The table contains entries for all of the pages that are resident in real memory—an inverted translation system. The page frame table entry carries the page name *tag* and the page frame address of the page in real memory. When the page table is accessed the tag is compared to the page name and, if the comparison is true, the page frame address is gated out and concatenated with the displacement to

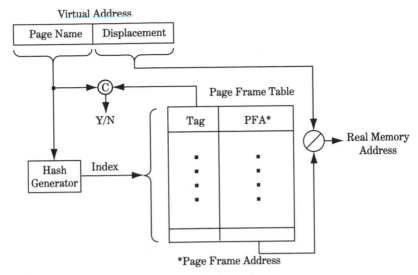

FIGURE 3.16   Hashed page name translation.

form the real memory address. If the comparison is false, the addressed page is not in real memory and a page fault is signaled.

A problem with this simple hashed translation is that two or more virtual addresses can hash into the same value, creating a collision into the same page frame table entry. These collisions increase the page name translation fault rate, significantly increasing the average page name translation time. A number of techniques for managing collisions and reducing their performance impact have been developed and implemented in real systems [MORR68]; a list of these techniques is given in Table 3.2 with examples noted. These examples will be described in the following paragraphs.

One-Level Large Page Frame Table

HP Precision Architecture. A system that uses a one-level page frame is the Hewlett-Packard Precision Architecture as shown in Figure 3.17

Technique	Example
One-level large page frame table	HP Precision Architecture
One-level linked list	None
Two-level linked list	IBM S/38–RS/6000
One-level sequentially indexed list	PowerPC 601
One-level disjoint collision table	Proposed [HUCK93]
n-way set associative	IBM S/360/168 TLB

TABLE 3.2   Collision handling techniques.

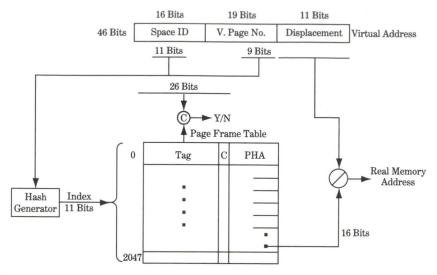

FIGURE 3.17   HP PA page name translation.

[MAHO86, LEE89]. This system depends on reducing the probability of a collision by implementing a large page frame table. Because the translation time through this system is quite fast, a translation lookaside buffer is not used. However, Hewlett-Packard describes this system as a translation lookaside buffer without another table structure for handling TLB misses.

The virtual address is composed of an 11-bit displacement, a virtual page number (either 19, 35, or 51 bits), and a 16-bit space ID. Nine bits of the virtual page number and 11 bits of the space ID are hashed into an 11-bit index. This index references a one-level, direct page frame table, called a translation lookaside buffer by HP. An entry contains a 26-bit tag that is compared to 26 bits in the virtual page name. The table produces a 16-bit page frame address that is concatenated with the 11-bit page displacement. A collision (no match on the tag but with a true valid bit) requires a full virtual software page name translation.

One-Level Linked List Page Frame Table

The approach to collision management discussed in this section is commonly used today because it provides a good balance between speed and cost. A one level system that mitigates the problem of hashing into the same page table entry by using a linked list is shown in Figure 3.18. Each entry of the *page frame table* (the name used in the IBM RS/6000) contains three fields: a page name tag, a page frame address, and a link field (*chain*). When a page is loaded into a page frame in real memory,

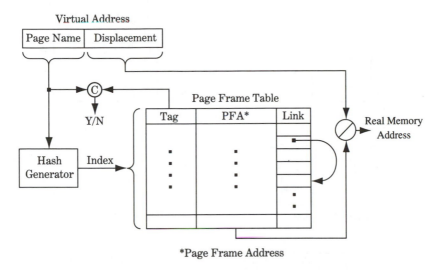

Virtual Address

Page Frame Address

FIGURE 3.18 One-level hash accessed inverted page table.

its page name and the page frame address are placed into the page frame table.

A virtual memory page name translation is performed by hashing the page name to an index into the page frame table. The page name field of the addressed entry is compared to the page name of the virtual address. If they are the same, the correct page frame address is concatenated with the displacement to give the real memory address. If the page name is not the same, a hash collision has occurred and the link pointer accesses another entry, and so on, until there is a match on the tags or a terminator symbol is encountered in the last entry. If the last entry has been accessed without a match on the page names, the referenced page is not in real memory and a page fault results.

A one-level hash accessed translation suffers from a significant problem. For some update cases, the entries in the page frame table must be moved to make room for the allocation of a new entry in the page frame table. Moving entries in the page frame table consumes time and reduces the overall performance of the system. Allocation in a one-level system is illustrated in Figure 3.19, which shows the states of the page frame table before and after allocation. Before allocation we see three linked lists of page translation information. Note that the page names *A* and *B* both hash into "1", the page name *D* hashes into "8", and the page names *P*, *Q*, and *R* hash into "17". In this example, the page frame table entries have been allocated into consecutive locations following the hash address and are linked via the link fields. A valid bit is needed in each entry to identify the page frame table entries that are allocated or vacant.

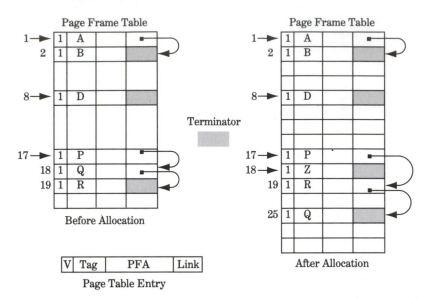

Figure 3.19 Allocation with a one-level hash accessed inverted page table.

Consider what happens if a new page is allocated and its page name "Z" hashes to the value "18". The entry "18" in the page frame table is already occupied by *Q* and must be moved in order to vacate location "18". This can be accomplished by moving the *Q* entry into location "25" and adjusting the link pointers. A vacant entry is found by scanning the PFT until a "0" is found, signifying a vacant table entry that can be allocated.

If there is a second allocation of a page with a page name that hashes into "18", its translation information is allocated to a vacant page frame table entry and appended to the linked list that starts with "18". Another situation exists for a new allocation hashed to an unused entry in the page frame table (the valid bit is 0). For this case, the tag and address information are allocated and the link field is loaded with the terminator symbol. This is a simple case, and no entry movement is required.

Two-Level Linked List Page Frame Table

A solution to the problem of page frame table movement is to introduce another level in the translation process that, in effect, provides an indirect pointer to the translation information in the page frame table. With a level of indirection, allocating new entries to the page frame table does not require that other entries be moved. This first-level table, named a *scatter index table* in the early literature, is known as a *hash index table* in the IBM System 38, a *hash table* in the IBM 801, and a

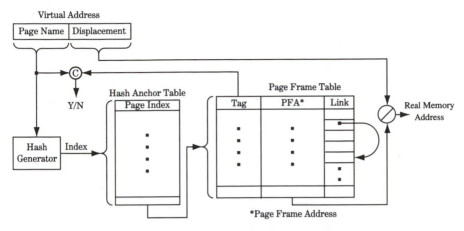

FIGURE 3.20   Two-level hash accessed inverted page table.

hash anchor table with the IBM RT PC and RS/6000, which is the term used in this text.

A two-level system is shown in Figure 3.20 [JOHN61, MORR68]. With this system, the page name is hashed for an index into the hash anchor table, which contains an index into the page frame table. The page frame table contains the page name (that is compared to the virtual address page name), the page frame address, and a link. The page frame address is concatenated with the displacement to form the real memory address.

The allocation example in Figure 3.18 used for the one-level system is illustrated in Figure 3.21 with the before and after cases shown. Here, the hash anchor table contains a pointer into the page frame table. For this example, the linked list *A*, *B* is located starting at location 100 of the page frame table, *D* is located at 200, and the linked list *P*, *Q*, *R* starts at 300. A memory reference to pages *P*, *Q*, or *R*, for example, hashes into address "17" and the pointer 300 is found that indexes to location 300 of the page frame table. The proper page frame address is found by comparing the tags to the virtual page name and traversing the linked list if necessary.

When page "*Z*" is allocated, location "18" in the hash anchor table is vacant and the page frame table entry is placed in a vacant location, 250 for example, of the page frame table. No movement of page frame table entries is required to effect the allocation of the new page. If a page is allocated with a page name that hashes into an already used hash anchor table address, the allocation can be to any vacant location in the page frame table. It is only necessary to append the entry to the linked list. The more successful the hashing function is in providing a uniform

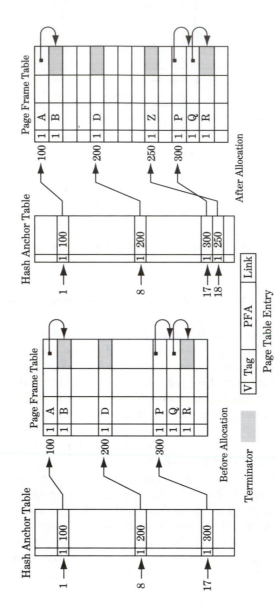

FIGURE 3.21 Allocation with a two-level hash accessed inverted page table.

distribution of transformed keys, the more balanced will be the length of the linked lists.

How many entries should there be in the page frame table and the hash anchor table? First consider the page frame table. Because an inverted page translation system has one entry for each page frame of real memory, the minimum number of entries is the number of real page frames. A large page frame table will have more vacant positions, reducing the length of the linked lists and the time required to find a page frame address.

The size of the hash anchor table is determined by the desired performance. A large hash anchor table has a larger hashed address, reducing the frequency of collisions in the page frame table. Johnson [JOHN61] determined that the average number of probes (reference attempts) into the page frame table is a function of the size of the page frame table and the hash anchor table:

$$P \approx 1 + \frac{\text{no. of entries in page frame table}}{2 \times \text{no. of entries in hash anchor table}}$$

where P is the average number of probes into the page frame table to translate a page name.

For example, if the hash anchor table has the same number of entries as the page frame table, 1.5 probes are required, on average, into the page frame table plus the access of the hash anchor table to translate a page name. If the hash anchor table has only 10% of the entries of the page frame table, six probes are required on average. An explanation of this model is found in the following consideration. If there is only one entry in the hash anchor table, every page name hashes into the same entry and all of the entries of the page frame table are linked together in one linked list. In this situation, the average number of probes approaches half the number of entries in the page frame table. This behavior is as expected from the time required to search a linked list sequentially. On the other hand, if the hash access table is very large, there are no collisions and each entry in the page frame table is unique (not linked). In this case only one probe is required.

Four IBM systems (S/38, 801, PC RT, and RS/6000) use a two-level hash access technique and are discussed in the following paragraphs.

IBM S/38. The virtual memory of the S/38 resulted from research at IBM in the late 1960s and early 1970s on the so-called Future System, which was abandoned due to lack of compatibility with S/370 [LEVY84]. The S/38 virtualized a segmentation system on top of the hardware-paged system [HOUD79, HOUD81]. The S/38 has a 48-bit virtual

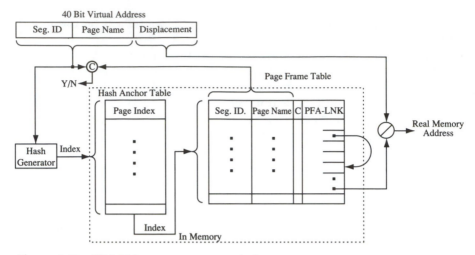

FIGURE 3.22   IBM 801 page name translation.

address, with a 512-byte page. The 39-bit virtual page name is hashed by logical XORing three fields (two of which are bit reversed) in the virtual page name in order to generate a 7-bit index into the hash anchor table. A page frame table index that indexes into the 128-entry page frame table is produced, and the entries in the page frame table are linked together with pointers. Approximately 2.5 memory accesses are required to translate a page name in the page frame table; the total translation time is 3.5 accesses.

IBM 801. The inverted page table system of the S/38 evolved into the virtual memory system of the experimental IBM 801; its page name translation tables are shown in Figure 3.22 [CHAN88]. The IBM 801 generates a 32-bit effective address that is expanded to a 40-bit virtual address using a map that is similar to that adopted by the RS/6000 shown in Figure 3.5. Page name translation is via a hash anchor table and a page frame table stored in real main memory. Unfortunately the published literature does not give the sizes of the three fields of the virtual address.

The IBM 801 design combined the page frame address and link into one field of the page frame table. This field is noted in Figure 3.22 as the PFA-LNK field and is large enough to address any page frame in real memory (at the page level) or to address the next entry in the page frame table [CHAN88]. The operation of this combined field is described below.

A page name extended with a segment ID is hashed for an index into the hash anchor table, which then provides an index into the page frame table. If there is not a match on the page name, the link field indexes into another entry. If there is a match, the link field is the page frame address in real memory and is concatenated with the displacement field from the virtual address. In other words, the link field is multiplied by 2 to the power of the displacement bits (left shifted the number of bits of the displacement). When there is not a match, the link field has its MSBs set to zero and the resulting value becomes the index into the page frame table. This process assumes that the page tables are allocated in the low address page frames of real memory.

Both the hash anchor table and the page frame table are stored in real memory. Therefore, a translation requires a minimum of two memory accesses to translate a page name. The size of the hash anchor table and page frame table are set when the system is generated depending upon the amount of installed real memory in the system. The hash anchor table can be set to be either equal to or twice the size of the page frame table.

IBM PC RT. The IBM PC RT also stores both the hash anchor table and the page frame table in memory [SIMP86, HEST86], as shown in Figure 3.23. The 32-bit effective address is expanded to a 40-bit virtual address by means of a 16-entry segment register. The page size can be set at either 2 Kbytes or 4 Kbytes, leaving either 28 or 29 bits that are hashed by an XOR operation for an index into the hash anchor table.

Experience with the IBM RT PC [CHAN88] shows that 2.5 storage accesses, or 1.5 probes to the page frame table, are required per page name translation. From this result we would assume that the hash anchor table has the same number of entries as the page frame table—a conclusion based on the Johnson [JOHN61] model. As with the IBM 801, setting the size of these tables is done when the system is generated.

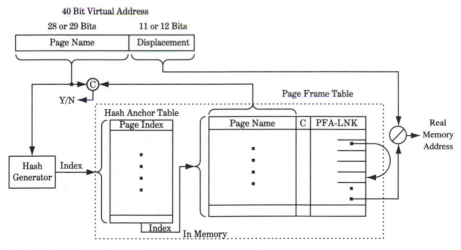

FIGURE 3.23 IBM PC RT page name translation.

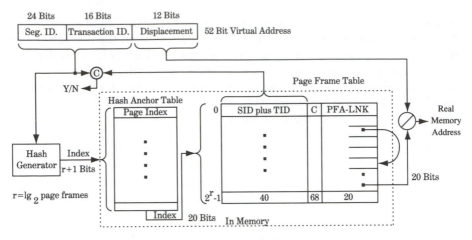

FIGURE 3.24   IBM RS/6000 page name translation.

IBM RS/6000. The IBM RS/6000 continues the approach started with the IBM Future System development [IBM90]. Because the RS/6000 is a recently introduced computer, its virtual memory system is described in more detail than the other IBM systems described above. The RS/6000 can be viewed as a paged-segmented system with the segments defined by the address map of Figure 3.5; the balance of the system is pure paged. A block diagram of the RS/6000 page name translation is shown in Figure 3.24.

The 52-bit virtual address is divided into three fields: a 24-bit segment ID, a 16-bit transaction page ID, and a 12-bit byte displacement [IBM90]. The hash generator XORs the 24-bit SID and the 16-bit TID extended with zeros to 24 bits. The low-order $r + 1$ bits of the result index the hash anchor table.

The size of the hash anchor table is set to be twice the number of real pages installed on the system, while the number of entries in the page frame table is set equal to the number of pages in installed real memory, which can reach a maximum of 2^{20} pages. These table size selections are made by the operating system.

Each entry in the page frame table consists of 16 bytes (4 words). A 20-bit link field (PFA-LNK) links to the next entry if the comparison fails. If the comparison succeeds, the link value of the entry point to the succeeding comparison is the page frame address and is concatenated with the 12-bit displacement, providing a 32-bit real memory address. In other words, on a hit the link field is multiplied by 2^{12}, while on a miss the link is used as the address into the page frame table in the low addresses of real memory.

		S/38	801	PC-RT	RS/6000
Names	Level 1	Hash Index Table	Hash Table	Hash Anchor Table	Hash Anchor Table
	Level 2	Page Directory Table	Page Table	Inverted Page Table	Page Frame Table
Sizes	Level 1	128		r	2^{r+1} up to 2^{21}
	Level 2	64		r	2^r up to 2^{20}
No. of Real Memory Page Frames					up to 2^{20}
Page Size		512 bytes		2 K or 4 Kbytes	4 Kbytes
Virtual Address		48 bits		40 bits	52 bits
Max Real Memory Size				2^{22} bytes	2^{32} bytes

Note. $r = \lg_2$ (Number of page frames in real memory).

TABLE 3.3 IBM hash accessed inverted page tables.

A linked list presents the danger of an infinite translation loop due to a programming error. That is, the links can create a circular list and, if there is no hit on tag comparisons, the translation can run forever. To prevent this from happening, a maximum of 127 probes are permitted before a search is declared a failure. The number of probes for the other systems described above is not known.

The IBM systems have evolved over a period of time. In order to illustrate this evolution, Table 3.3 contains a summary of the relevant parameters of the IBM systems discussed above.

As noted previously, the hash anchor tables and page frame tables are too large to be stored in fast hardware registers. Consequently, it is necessary to enhance the performance of these systems by using a translation lookaside buffer [HOUD81, CHAN88, OEHL90]. After a page miss, the requested page is loaded into the real memory. In addition, the TLB, the hash anchor table, and page frame tables are updated. A subsequent reference to this page will find the page name translation information in the TLB. However, later references may find that an address cannot be translated in the TLB and recourse to the translation tables is required. After this translation, the TLB is updated. TLBs are described in Section 3.4 and memory allocation is discussed in Section 3.5.2.

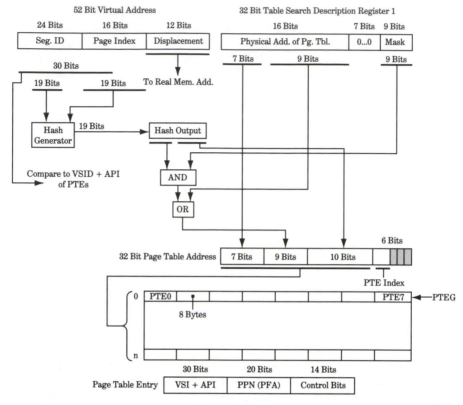

FIGURE 3.25   PowerPC 601 page name translation.

One-Level Sequential Indexed Page Frame Table

PowerPC 601. The PowerPC 601 uses a hash-indexed inverted page name translation that resolves collisions by sequentially searching the page table entries. A simplified description of this system is given and illustrated in Figure 3.25; the terminology of [MOTO93] is used.

The virtual address is formed by a map that is similar to that of the RS/6000 shown in Figure 3.5. This 52-bit address is used in conjunction with a 32-bit register called the table search description register 1. A 19-bit hash index is formed by taking the XOR of the 19 LSBs of the segment ID and the 16-bit page index, zero extended to 19 bits. The 9-bit mask of the TSDR1 is ANDed with the 9 MSBs of the hash output; the result is ORed with 9 LSBs of the physical address field of the TSDR1. These fields are concatenated to form the 32-bit page table address.

The page table is organized as a collection of the 64-bit (8 bytes) page table entries. The page table address indexes into a *page table entry*

Total Main Memory	Memory for Page Tables	Number of PTEGs	Number of PTEs
8 Mbytes	64 Kbytes	1 K	8 K
128 Mbytes	1 Mbytes	16 K	128 K
4 Gbytes	32 Mbytes	512 K	4 M

TABLE 3.4 PowerPC 601 page table size recommendation.

group (PTEG) consisting of eight PTEs. The VSI + API bits of PTE0 are compared to 30 bits of the virtual address. If there is a miss, the low-order bits of the page table address are incremented by 8, to give a new PTE, and the tag of PTE1 is compared. This process continues until all eight PTEs have been tested. If there is still no hit, a second hash function is applied and the page table is again accessed. An excerpt of the recommended size of the page table is given in Table 3.4.

As with other table translation systems, the PowerPC 601 uses a translation lookaside buffer (described in Section 3.4).

One-Level Linked List Into a Disjoint Collision Table

J. Huck et al. [HUCK93] describes an inverted name translation system that combines a one-level system with the combined page frame address and link field of the IBM systems. This system is shown in Figure 3.26 and is called by the author a *hashed page translation table*. The first allocated entry to a hashed index is placed in the page frame table, and subsequent allocations are placed in the disjoint collision resolution table.

The page name is hashed, providing an index into the page frame table. A collision is followed by the link accessing another entry in a disjoint address space called the *collision resolution table* that cannot be accessed by a hashed index. Thus when new page information is allocated, its entry can go into (1) the page frame table if vacant or (2) any vacant slot in the collision reservation table. The entries in the collision resolution table are organized as a linked list. The advantages of this system are that noncolliding translations require only one memory reference and that the need to move entries in the page frame table is eliminated with disjoint link entry storage. As with all hashed access systems, increasing the size of the table will reduce the probability of a collision.

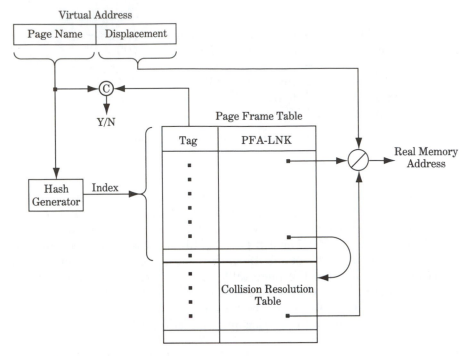

FIGURE 3.26 Hashed page translation tables.

Control Bits

This section uses the IBM RS/6000 design to illustrate the control bits used in these systems. The hash anchor table has only one control bit, a valid bit that is used to indicate whether or not there is a valid pointer into the page frame table. If valid, the translation proceeds; if not, then a page fault results because an inverted page table has entries for all resident pages. In addition, there are various control and protection bits.

i	Invalid		l	Lock Type
f	Reference		w	Grant Write Lock
c	Change		r	Grant Read Lock
p	Protection keys (4 bits)		a	Allow Read
b	Lock Bit for cache lines			

Other bits provide a transaction ID, and there are a number of reserved bits. Note that the RS/6000 treats valid bits nonuniformly across the hash anchor table and the page frame table. The valid bit of the hash anchor table signifies that the entry is vacant and can be allocated to a new translation. The valid bit in the page frame table signifies the presence of the requested page in real memory, assuming a hit on the page name comparison.

3.3.2 *Segmented Systems*

Segmented systems have a variable-length allocation unit known as a *segment* that should not be confused with the fixed-length virtual address extensions shown in Table 3.1. Segment name translation can be accomplished with both one-level and multilevel systems. A one-level system is described first. The operating system sets the length of a segment under the constraint that the sum of all active segments must be no greater than the available real memory.

This discussion on segmented systems is brief because of the many problems associated with these systems. No segmented systems have been designed since the first early machines; paged-segmented systems have replaced them. Interactive programming systems such as Lotus 1-2-3 virtualize a rudimentary form of segmentation to provide interactive allocation and de-allocation of segments.

The motivation for segmentation is that the size of each allocation unit can be set to reduce internal fragmentation. With fixed size pages, some fraction of a page frame (on average, 1/2 page) will be wasted when allocating variable-length records, an issue extensively studied by Wolman [WOLM65]. Because real memory was very expensive, wasted memory was a cost that was difficult to justify and segmentation minimized this undesirable cost. However, as will be discussed, segmentation introduces a number of undesirable problems that must be solved.

The address translation process for a segmented system consists of the steps [DENN76]

$$\text{virtual address} \Rightarrow (n, d) \Rightarrow (f(b), d) \Rightarrow f(b) + d = \text{real address}.$$

That is, the virtual address is first de-allocated into the pair (segment name (n), displacement (d)). The segment name portion is translated by a function f, and the result is added to the displacement. Recall that for paged systems, the translated page name and displacement are concatenated because the allocation unit is fixed at some binary multiple.

The design of the processor, by selecting a displacement field length, sets the maximum length of a segment. Any allocated segment must be equal to or less than this length. Thus, the *segment length* (SL) field of the segment table will be the same length as the virtual address displacement field. When a segment is accessed, the contents of the displacement and segment length fields are compared and the access is valid if $(d) \leq (\text{SL})$.

Figure 3.27 shows a one-level segment translation table that is recognized as a direct map with an entry for every virtual segment. Because $f(n)$ is not constrained, segmented systems are not congruence mapped. That is, segments can be of variable length with the maximum length

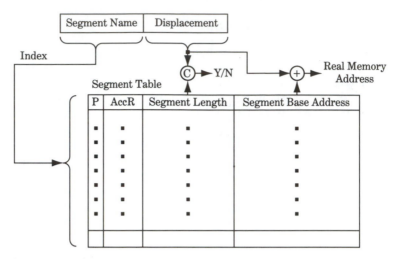

FIGURE 3.27 One-level segment table.

set by the displacement d. Variable-length segments lead to the requirement that there must be a way of specifying the length in the segment
table.

Segment table entries have at least the following fields:

1. present bit, similar to the present bit of a one-level direct page table,
2. access rights or control bits,
3. segment length,
4. segment base address.

The segment name indexes into the segment table. If the present bit
is set, the access rights are proper, and the segment length is equal to
or greater than the displacement value, then the segment base address
is added to the displacement providing the real memory address. Note
that because the segment base address is added to the displacement,
segments can overlap, unlike paged systems. If the present bit is not
set, a missing segment fault is indicated that requires a segment fetch
from virtual memory. When a segment is allocated to real memory, its
length is placed in the segment length field of the segment table. If the
segment length is less than the displacement value or if the access rights
do not check, an error signal is generated and the name translation
process will not continue.

There are a number of serious problems with segmentation. For
example, it can be more difficult to find a place in real memory to allocate
a requested segment. This allocation problem exists because of the need
to find a contiguous space in real memory that is large enough for

the new segment, a problem similar to Relocatable Partitioned Memory described in Figure 3.2.

Another problem with segmented systems is *external fragmentation*, previously defined. As segments of various sizes are moved in and out of real memory, open or unused spaces appear in real memory and the available space becomes fragmented. It becomes difficult, if not impossible, to find a contiguous space for a new segment even though there is ample, but fragmented, space in real memory. From time to time the operating system must compress or compact the allocated spaces to open up contiguous space for new segments. Note that as the allocated space is exactly the space needed, there is no internal fragmentation as with a paged system, one of the benefits of a segmented system. Section 3.5.2 discusses the allocation of segments.

I am only aware of one system that is implemented with a one-level segment table, the Rice University Computer [LEVY84]. This processor, implemented in the early 1950s, had a virtual address that specified a maximum 32-K word segment (a 15-bit displacement field). The experimental purpose of this computer was to evaluate capabilities addressing objects in conjunction with a segmented virtual memory.

Control Bits

The use of the present bit was noted above. The access rights bits provide for various levels of protection. For example, read-only data segments and read/write segments can be indicated in the access rights field. Other information such as lexical level and the data type of the segment can also be indicated.

Multilevel Segmentation Systems

A multilevel segmented system uses the first-level table to select subsequent translations for each of the active processes as shown in Figure 3.28. Note that the first level is indexed by the MSBs of the segment name and organized like a paged system with the first level similar to the map shown in Figure 3.5. The second level is identical to that shown in Figure 3.27.

The LSBs of the segment name and the table address are concatenated to form the segment table address, thus segment overlap is prevented. Said another way, there are 2^B nonoverlapping segment tables of $2^{\text{Table Address}}$ entries. I know of no actual system that is implemented with multilevel segment tables. Concurrent with the realization of the problems with pure segmentation, paged segmentation became the implementation method of choice and is discussed in the following section.

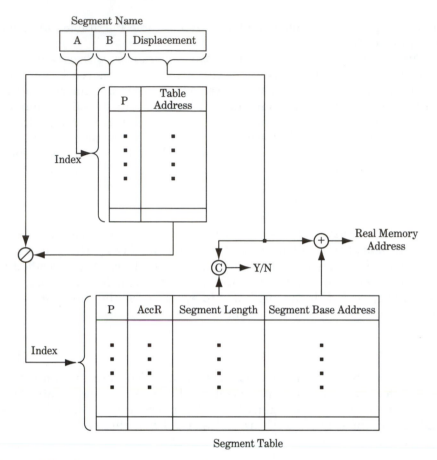

FIGURE 3.28 Two-level segment table.

3.3.3 *Paged Segmentation*

As noted previously, there are a number of problems with segmentation systems that have hampered their use. One significant problem involves finding space for a new segment in real memory. This allocation problem is difficult, and external fragmentation can significantly reduce the effectiveness of real memory. If compaction is used, there can be a serious reduction in performance. Another significant problem is that a TLB, described in Section 3.5, has to be allocated at the word or byte level; this process makes the TLB quite large, slow, and expensive. Researchers have recognized that if the allocation unit is a page of, say, 1 Kbyte, a compromise system combining the characteristics of a segment system with a paged system could be designed. In other words, a segment is not a variable number of AUs but is a variable number of pages.

The tradeoffs that favor a paged-segmented system over a pure segmented system concern accepting internal fragmentation for no external fragmentation, the simplicity of allocating a page as compared to a variable-length segment, and the performance improvement due to simpler allocation.

The organization of a paged-segmentation system is shown in Figure 3.29. This system has two levels; the first level establishes the segments of pages while the second level is a one-level page system. Note that the second level could translate page names by any one of the techniques discussed above. This translation can be associatively searched, one-level or multilevel page tables or translation information could be hash addressed. The example shown, however, is a one-level page translation system.

The virtual address is divided into three fields: segment name, page name, and displacement. The segment name may be concatenated with a user ID number, forming an index into the segment table. The register holding the user ID is also known as *segment table origin register*. A length field in the segment table is compared with the virtual page name

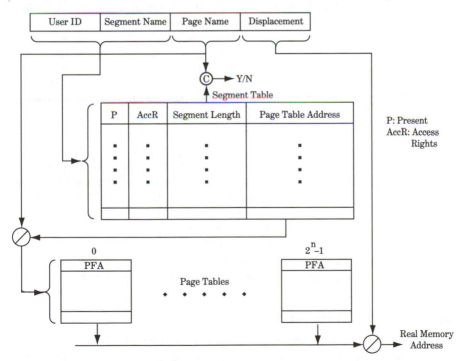

FIGURE 3.29 Paged segmentation.

field to verify that the length of the segment, in increments of pages, is proper. In other words, the page name is a displacement into a segment. The page table address, from the segment table, is concatenated to the page name field to index into the page tables. The selected page frame address is concatenated with the displacement field to give the real memory address. A present bit indicates whether or not an entry in the segment table has its corresponding page table in real memory. Access rights bits provide for protection and control.

Only multilevel paged-segmentation systems are possible; one-level systems cannot be implemented. This is because, as shown in Figure 3.29, at least one level is required for the segmentation table and another for the page tables. As with the other systems discussed earlier, all of the page tables do not need to be resident in real memory at once, only the active tables. If an access is made to a segment or page table that is not in memory, it can be assumed that the page is not in memory and the operating system must fetch the page(s) and update the segment/ age tables. The Multics system paged the segment table, leading to complications discussed below.

The paged-segmented system overcomes many of the problems of a pure segmented system. The unit of allocation of a segmented system is a word or byte, while the unit of allocation of a paged system is a page. Because of this difference, the segment system can now operate as a demand paged system that shifts the problem of finding space to the page system. Also, the problem of external fragmentation and space compaction found in pure segmented systems are eliminated. However, because the pages of a segment are not placed in contiguous locations of real memory, locality for caching may be degraded; the same effect is found with a paged system that does not consider locality during a page swap.

For the above reasons, many of the high-performance microprocessor memory management units now support both paged and paged-segmented operation [MILE90]. The operating system can manage a virtual segment table on top of a pure paged system. The page tables are stored in memory, loaded and modified by the operating system, and may be paged themselves. See [MOTO87] for the details of a system. With such a system, no special hardware is needed to support the segment table as a paged-segmented system can be implemented in software on a hardware-paged system. Thus the two systems are isomorphic.

Segment Table Support

Because of the complicated organization of segment tables, interpretive segmentation has been found to be out of the question for performance reasons. Therefore, hardware support is mandatory if a reasonable level

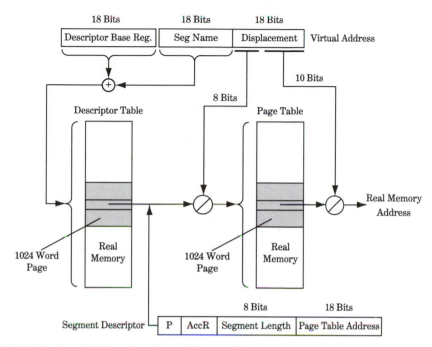

FIGURE 3.30 Multics name translation tables.

of performance is to be achieved. One of the earliest segmentation systems is Multics, which was developed at MIT in conjunction with General Electric. A GE 635 computer was modified to support paged segmentation becoming the GE 645. Multics system [SCHR71, ORGA72] used a multilevel paged-segmentation system completely implemented in software, augmented with a TLB. Figure 3.30 shows a simplified view of the Multics segment name translation system.

The processor produces a 36-bit effective address, the page size is 1K Words, and a segment can have up to 256 pages or 256K Words. The effective address is augmented with an 18-bit program loaded *descriptor base register* that points to the beginning of a segment in the descriptor table allocation of real memory that contains *segment descriptors*. Note that the segment descriptors are themselves paged.

A segment descriptor contains a segment length field of 8 bits, a page table address of 18 bits, and various control bits. The segment length field is compared, by the processor, to the eight MSBs of the displacement to verify that a displacement is within the allocated segment. The page table address is concatenated with the eight MSBs of the displacement to form the address into the page table, also in real memory and paged. The entries in the page table contain the page frame address that is concatenated with the ten LSBs of the displacement to form the real memory address.

This system required two memory accesses to perform a name translation, a rather slow process as the processor did not have a cache. As will be described in Section 3.4, the GE 645 also used a translation lookaside buffer to cache the most recently used segment descriptors.

Due to the poor performance of a segmented system that is virtualized in real memory, two forms of hardware supported segment tables have evolved. One system supports segment length checking, while the other does not. Examples of these two types are given in this section.

Hardware Support with Segment Length Checking

An example of hardware support for the segment table of paged segmentation is found in the Intel i386, i486, and Pentium microprocessors shown in Figure 3.31, which is an extension of Figure 3.6. The i386 member of the x86 family had significant changes to the memory management system that have carried over into all subsequent members of the family. While there are differences between these later processors, they are sufficiently similar that only one description is given. The terminology used is that of the i486 and Pentium, which is different from the terminology of the i386. The segmentation system evolved from steps taken to extend the address space of the ix86 family of processors. Evolution of the mapping structure design was constrained by the requirement for upward compatibility for MS-DOS and applications software. A break in this capability occurred with the i386 with its effective address extended to 32 bits compared to the 16 bits of previous members of the family [MORS80].

There are two paths for obtaining a segment base address value; one path uses active descriptors stored in segment registers, the other path uses descriptors found in descriptor tables in memory. The six active descriptors, found in the *invisible part* of the segment registers, are indexed by implication with each memory reference in parallel with the selectors in the *visible part* of the segment registers; this is essentially a zero time access. The descriptors (both in the segment registers and descriptor tables) have a 32-bit segment base address field, a 20-bit segment limit field, and 12 control bits. One of the control bits is a valid bit, indicating that the descriptor information contained is valid. If the entry is valid, segment base address value selection is performed via the descriptor table and the memory resident translation tables are bypassed. The linear address is formed by adding the segment base address to the displacement field from the instruction.

In addition to various access checks based on the control bits, the

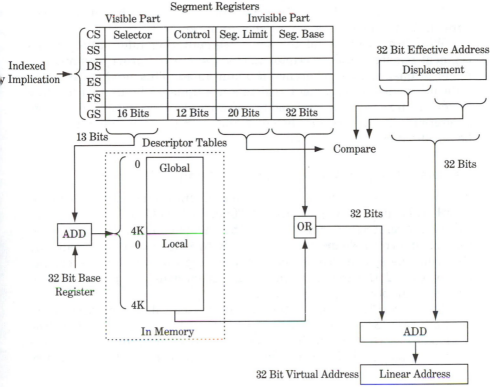

FIGURE 3.31   i386, i486, and Pentium segmentation support.

segment length is also checked. A bit in the control field determines if the comparison is between the 20 MSBs or the 20 LSBs of the displacement: if the MSBs, the segment length is measured in pages as a page is 4 Kbytes; if the LSBs, the segment length is measured in bytes. Thus the segment size is either $2^{20} - 1$ pages or bytes.

If the segmentation information in the segment registers is not valid, segment base address values are obtained via memory-based descriptor tables indexed by one of six, 16-bit selector registers, called *visible selectors*. These selectors are indexed by implication in parallel with the hidden descriptors. The 13 MSBs of the indexed selector register are used, after being added to a 32-bit base register value, as an address into memory to access a descriptor table entry; each descriptor is eight bytes. These tables are in two halves: the *global* table and the *local* table. The field allocation to the entries of the descriptor tables is identical to the hidden descriptors. The same access checks and segment limit checks are made before a memory access can proceed. The segment base and displacement are added to form the linear address that will be the address for the paged system, as shown in Figure 3.12.

With two instances of the same segmentation information in the segment registers and descriptor tables, the normal provisions must be made to ensure that coherency is maintained. This problem is made difficult because the segment registers are updated by hardware while the descriptor tables are updated by software. Thus, software can change a descriptor in memory and the descriptor in the segment registers must be invalidated.

Hardware Support Without Segment Length Checking

A number of systems provide hardware segment tables without segment length checking. Examples are RS/6000, PowerPC 601, and the HP Precision Architecture. For example, the RS/6000 map of segment registers, as shown in Figure 3.5, is loaded with values that are created by the operating system. The function of assuring that valid displacements do not exceed the segment length and generating the page table addresses is an operating system task.

The PowerPC 601, one of the examples of paged segmentation without hardware for segment length checking, is shown in Figure 3.25. The page index is 16 bits, which constrains the segment size to be no more than 2^{16}-1 pages. With a page size of 4 Kbytes, a segment is 26 Mbytes.

3.4 Translation Lookaside Buffers

The translation of a virtual page name into the page frame address via memory resident tables can take a significant number of memory cycles. To hide the translation time, a page table system (direct or inverted) is usually augmented with a cache of active page frame addresses. This type of cache is usually known as a *translation lookaside buffer* (TLB), a name used by IBM. Motorola uses the term *address translation cache* (ATC); DEC uses the term *translation buffer* (TB); and Intel uses the term *page translation cache* (PTC). The Multics system employed the first known instance of a TLB [SCHR71].

Translating page names and block names, as shown in Figure 3.32, is usually performed in a hierarchy of translation systems, much as a memory reference is processed in a hierarchical memory. This figure illustrates the number of translation maps possible, not the tables for any particular processor. Usually, all of the TLBs are accessed in parallel and the first valid translation is used to form the real memory address. If translation fails in the TLBs, the page tables, either direct or inverted, are then accessed before a page fault is declared. As will be discussed when the MC88200 TLBs are described, one level of this hierarchy may

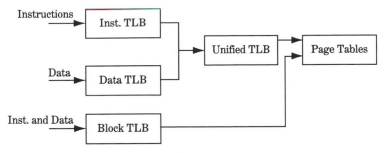

FIGURE 3.32   Canonical name translation hierarchy.

be implemented for both page and block name translation. Also, portions of the page tables may be resident in the processor's cache, further improving the name translation time.

Multilevel TLBs have many of the design problems of multilevel caches and hierarchical memories. There are design issues of information allocation, coherency, particularly when the processor is used in a multiprocessor configuration, and multilevel inclusion. There is no need for read and write policies as with a cache, but there are issues dealing with invalidating the contents of TLBs.

The reduction in name translation latency with a TLB is similar to that of a data or instruction cache. There is some probability that the page frame address will not be found in the TLB; as a result, the name translation time is the weighted average of the time to translate in the TLBs or in the page tables. On a TLB miss, the delay in access time is the two or more memory cycles for accessing the page tables plus the table walking time (discussed in Section 3.5.5). Note that there can be two reasons for a TLB miss. First, if the referenced page is not in real memory, there will be a miss in the translation tables. Second, a miss occurs when the page is in real memory and its translation tables are correct but the translation information is not in the TLB. It is this second form of TLB miss that is most often noted in the literature.

A TLB holds the translated addresses of pages that are also resident in the page tables. Most access checks have been made and do not require verification when translating a virtual page or segment name in a TLB. Because the name translation process can be hierarchical, the treatment of multilevel inclusion is a design issue.

The PowerPC 601 has three levels of translation: the Instruction TLB (ITLB), Unified TLB (UTLB), and the hash-accessed inverted page tables. For this system, multilevel inclusion is maintained with the following policy. Allocation of translation information to the page tables is a software process that follows a page fault. Allocation to the ITLB and UTLB is performed by hardware following a page fault that brings

Operation	ITLB	UTLB	Page Table
Add entry	Add on most recent translation (MRT), set valid bit.	Add on most recent translation (MRT), set valid bit.	The page table is locked, the entry added with a move instruction, then the table is unlocked, all under program control.
Replace entry	Replace if a new entry is translated and there is no vacant slot. MRT bits select entry to be replaced.	Replace if a new entry is translated and there is no vacant slot. MRT bits select the slot within the sector if there is a set conflict.	An entry is: locked, invalidated, flushed, updated, marked valid and unlocked, all under program control.
Delete entry	Valid bit is reset explicitly by the execution of tibie instruction or as a side effect of some other instructions.	Valid bit is reset explicitly by the execution of the tibie instruction or as a side effect of some other instructions.	All entries have their valid bits reset when there is a context switch.

TABLE 3.5 PowerPC 601 maintaining translation multilevel inclusion.

a new page into the real memory. At any time, entries that are in the ITLB are in the UTLB and the page tables and entries in the UTLB are in the page tables but not necessarily in the ITLB.

The management policy of the three tables, ITLB, UTLB, and the page tables, is shown in Table 3.5. Three cases must be comprehended to assure multilevel inclusion: adding a new entry, modifying an old entry, and deleting an old entry. Note that the two TLBs are managed by hardware, while the page table is managed by software. Also note the synchronization operations that are required to lock and unlock the page tables.

3.4.1 *TLB Organization*

The organization of a canonical TLB is shown in Figure 3.33. Note that this figure is similar to Figure 2.4 and differs only in that page table entries (PTEs) with page frame addresses are stored rather than data and only a valid bit is required. If a page is evicted to the disk, the entry in the TLB can become invalid and is modified by the operating system or microcode. A TLB, being a cache of translation information, can be organized for access as: (1) associative search, (2) *n*-way set associative search, and (3) hash accessed.

Note that the size of a TLB is sometimes described by its *length* or *size*, not the number of sets. With associative TLBs, the size is described in *entries*, not sectors as with caches. A TLB operates on the principle of temporal page locality; when a page is loaded into real memory, the page tables and TLB are updated. Because of page locality, caching addresses can be quite effective in reducing the latency of name translation and the access of real memory. Simulations and measurements show that TLBs have a hit ratio in the range of 90% [SATY81]. The hit ratio

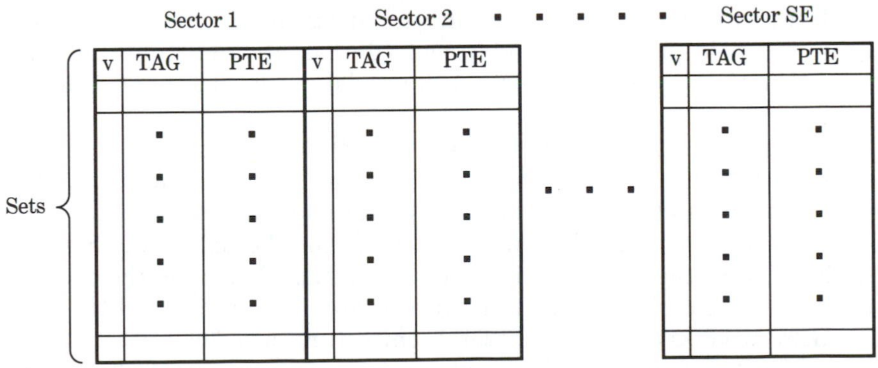

FIGURE 3.33 Canonical TLB.

of a TLB is, as with other caches, a function of its size. D. W. Clark et al. [CLAR85] and M. D. Hill [HILL87] provide data on TLB hit ratios.

In general, TLBs are invisible to the program as they are loaded under hardware control and serve to speedup the name translation process. However, TLBs must usually be invalidated when there are changes to the page tables such as will occur when a page table change occurs that will violate coherency. There must be a replacement policy for the *n*-way set associative TLB, and the same policies described in the section on caches apply here. For example, the policies may be MRU, LRU, Random, Clock, and others [BAER80].

Associative Searched TLBs

Associative searched TLBs have a number of positive features. One feature is that, for small TLBs, the latency of translating a name is quite small. Another feature is the ease of expandability. As there is only one set, the number of sectors in the TLB can be increased without architectural change. And, the number of sectors need not be an even power of two. This feature eases implementation of TLBs on a chip. For these reasons, most contemporary microprocessors use associative searched TLBs. Examples are discussed in the following paragraphs.

MC68451. An example of an associatively searched TLB, called an *address register translation table*, is the Motorola MC68451, shown in part in Figure 3.34 [MOTO83]. This rather strange device was designed for use with the MC68000 to support paged segmentation. Providing virtual page and segmentation support for functions such as segment length checking and table management is a pure software function.

The virtual 23-bit word address is divided into a segment name and displacement fields. The segment name is the key for an associative access of the page directory, reading out a page frame address, mask, and control bits. The mask selects the MSBs of the page address and the LSBs of the segment name concatenating them with the 7-bit displacement field to form the 23-bit real address. By adjusting the mask, the size of the segment varies for 128 words (mask all 1s) to 65K words (mask all 0s).

Wakerly [WAKE89] states that the MC68451 was not successful because of its limitations, which are believed to be the limited virtual address space and too much flexibility. For this and other reasons, the MC68451 was not used by early customers for the MC68000. Sun and Apollo crafted their own MMU, which are modeled after the memory mapping system of the Atlas Computer (described in Figure 3.15).

IBM RS/6000. This processor architecture specification calls for a unified TLB, but specific implementations may have separate ITLBs and DTLBs [IBM90]. One such implementation has a split TLB. The DTLB

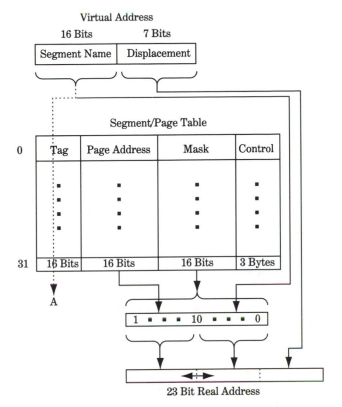

FIGURE 3.34 Associative register name translation.

is organized as (64, 2, 1, PTE) and is late select. However, the ITLB of this processor is believed to be associatively searched as shown in Figure 3.35. The 40-bit page name is used as the key to search the ITLB associatively; the number of sectors is not revealed in the literature. A hit on a translation provides a 20-bit page frame address that is concatenated with the 12-bit displacement of the virtual address. If the translation is successful, the reference to real memory is initiated. If not successful, the reference address is translated in the translation tables resident in either the cache or real memory.

Note the similarity between this TLB design and the Atlas name translation system depicted in Figure 3.15. The major differences between the two are the design parameters, not the organization.

MC88200. The MC88200 that supports several Motorola processors (88100, 68030) has two UTLBs, one for user programs with 4-Kbyte pages and one for system programs with 512-Kbyte blocks [MOTO90a]. Note that Motorola calls TLBs *address translation caches*. Both of the TLBs are unified, translating the page and block names of both instruc-

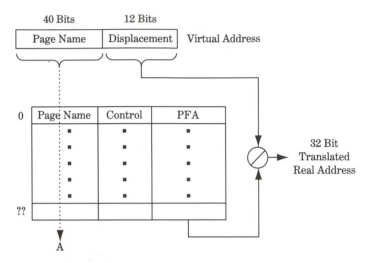

FIGURE 3.35   RS/6000 ITLB.

tions and data. Block diagrams for these TLBs are shown in Figure 3.31, and note should be taken again of the similarity between these TLBs and the Atlas name translation system.

The block TLB contains high-use translation information that is cached at the block level, thereby reducing TLB misses. Operating systems occupy the same address space, for instructions and data, over long periods of time. Thus, having a large page, called a *block,* can significantly reduce the number of block name translation misses and page misses. Note that these blocks are not the same as cache blocks.

The block TLB has 10 sectors that are associatively searched on the 13-bit block name and is organized as (1, 10, 1, PFA). On a hit, the 13-bit page frame address is concatenated with the 17-bit block displacement to give a 30-bit real memory address. Two of the 10 sectors are hardwired to provide an identity mapping in the upper 1M bytes of real memory for supervisor space.

User programs have higher paging activity, and the page TLB reduces external and internal fragmentation that would occur if the page is the same size as the block. The page TLB, also shown in Figure 3.36, has 56 sectors that are associatively searched on the 20-bit page name from the virtual address. The organization is (1, 56, 1, PFA). The 20-bit page name is associatively compared to the 56 page name tags of the resident pages. Upon a hit, the 20-bit page frame address is concatenated with the 10-bit page displacement to give a 30-bit real memory address. The page TLB is managed by the operating system with entries being evicted on a FIFO basis; a new entry pushes out the oldest entry.

A page name translation is conditionally and concurrently attempted

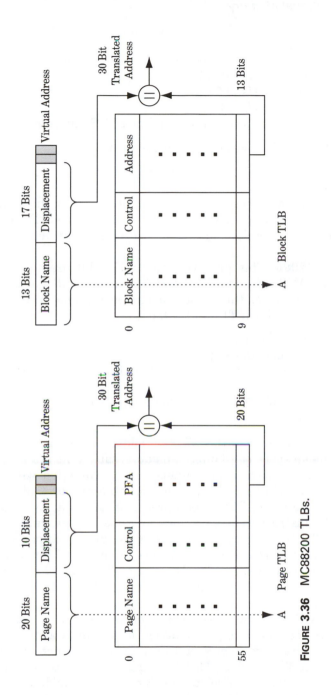

Figure 3.36 MC88200 TLBs.

169

PTLB	BTLB	Action
Hit	Hit	Use BTLB
Hit	Miss	Use PTLB
Miss	Hit	Use BTLB
Miss	Miss	Table search, update PTLB and retry translation

Note. The BTLB is loaded by the operating system.

TABLE 3.6   MC88200 TLB management.

in both TLBs. If an access misses on *both* of the TLBs, the name translation is made via the page tables previously described. Table 3.6 shows the action taken for the four possible events when accessing the two TLBs.

MIPS R2000. This processor has a TLB integrated onto the processor chip [MIPS87]. The TLB has 64 entries and is accessed by an associative search on the 20-bit virtual page name. The page size is fixed at 4 Kbytes. Each TLB entry has the fields:

20 bits: virtual page name;
20 bits: page frame address;
 6 bits: PID number that must match the PID value in a processor register;
 4 bits: Control bits: Read Only, Non-Cacheable, Valid and Global;
14 bits: unused.

The page name from the effective address plus the PID value gives a virtual name space of 26 bits. The addressable unit is a 4-byte (32-bit) word. The 20-bit page frame number is concatenated with the 10-bit displacement, giving a 30-bit real memory address or 4 Gbytes.

DEC Alpha. The DEC Alpha processor has split, associative TLBs: one for the instruction page names and one for the data page names [DIGI92]. The virtual memory of the Alpha system is paged with variable page sizes. The I-Stream TLB has 12 sectors, 8 for 8-Kbyte pages and 4 for 4-Mbyte pages. The D-Stream TLB has 32 sectors, each of which can be used to translate to 8-Kbyte, 64-Kbyte, 512-Kbyte, or 4-Mbyte pages.

PowerPC 601. The PowerPC 601 has a small first-level instruction TLB (ITLB) for translating instruction page names and a unified TLB (UTLB) for data page names and instruction page names that miss in the ITLB [MOTO93]. The ITLB is searched associatively and has four sectors. The 20-bit page name of the 32-bit effective address is the search key. A hit provides a 20-bit page frame address that is concatenated with the 12-bit displacement to give the real memory address. Note that the extension to the virtual address is not part of the search key.

If the instruction page name translation fails in the ITLB, the translation is attempted in the UTLB organized as (256, 2, 1, PFA). If this translation fails, page name translation is then performed via the tables described in Section 3.3.1.

In addition to the ITLB and UTLB, the processor can also translate block names in a small TLB, called *block-address translation registers* (BATR). These registers are organized as (1, 4, 1, PFA). The BATR holds four block name translated base addresses. The size of the blocks is a programmable parameter and can be in the range of 18 Kbytes doubling to 8 Mbytes.

VAX 11/780. The VAX 11/780 has a small first-level instruction TLB, called an *instruction translation buffer*. This ITLB has only one sector organized as (1, 1, 1, PFA). In other words, the last translated page name is held in the ITLB and is concatenated to the displacement for every instruction read. Thus instruction page name translation is a zero time process. If an instruction fetch crosses the boundary of the page (the page name changes), the new page name is translated in a second-level unified page table.

n-Way Set Associative TLBs

A number of TLBs are implemented with *n*-way set associative organizations in which the page name is congruence mapped for translation. To accomplish this, the page name is allocated to a set index field and an unnamed field that is compared to the tags of an accessed set. Some of the TLBs that use this organization are discussed below.

i386, i486, and Pentium. These processors support paged segmentation, and virtual page names are translated via a multilevel page tables system as shown in Figure 3.12. A TLB organized as (8, 4, 1, PFA) is implemented as a unified TLB on the i386, as shown in Figure 3.37. This same design is also used as a unified TLB on the i486. With the Pentium, two copies of the same TLB are used as split TLB without a unified TLB.

The page name is allocated into two fields: an 8-bit index into the TLB and a 12-bit field that is compared to the TLB tags. If there is a true comparison on one of the four sectors, the 20-bit page frame address is concatenated with the 12-bit page displacement to form the real memory address. If there is a miss in the TLB, the address is translated via the multilevel page tables.

Note that the TLB provides name translation of the 20-bit page name and not the extended virtual address; the 20-bit extension is not translated. The consequence of this restriction is that only translated page names for one root directory at a time are in the TLB. As a result,

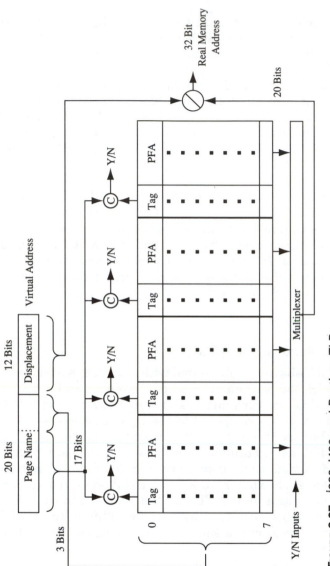

FIGURE 3.37 i386, i486, and Pentium TLBs.

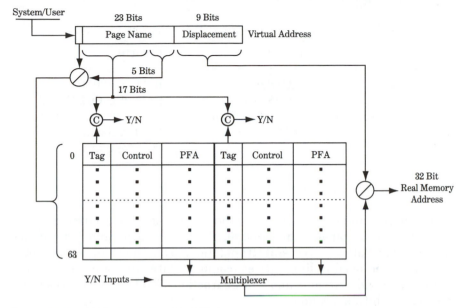

FIGURE 3.38 VAX 11/780 unified TLB.

aliases are possible. To prevent aliases, any change of the root directory by the executing program requires a reload of the TLB.

VAX 11/780. The VAX 11/780 has a unified TLB that translates the page names of data references and misses in the ITLB [SATY81] and [HAMA90]. A block diagram of the unified TLB is shown in Figure 3.38. The 32-bit virtual address is divided into a 9-bit page displacement field and a 23-bit page name field. The five LSBs of the page name are concatenated with the MSB to form a 6-bit index into the 2-way set associative TLB organized as (64, 2, 1, PFA). An interesting feature of this TLB is that the MSB of the page name (system/user bit) is used as the MSB of the index to select between two halves of the TLB. This guarantees that the system and user both have full access to 1/2 of the TLB and 1/2 of virtual memory space.

PowerPC 601. The PowerPC 601 has a first-level TLB and a unified (UTLB) that translates instruction page names that failed to translate in the ITLB and data page names. This TLB is organized as (256, 2, 1, PFA).

Hash-Accessed TLBs

IBM S/370/168. This system has a unified TLB translating both instruction and data references. The 14-bit page name is hashed to create a 6-bit index into the TLB that is organized as (64, 2, 1, PFA), an unusual organization [MATI77]. By making the TLB 2-way set associative, two

TLB Access Method	Page Table Access Method	
	Direct	Inverted
Associative	MC88200, MC88110	IBM RS/6000 PowerPC 601 (Inst.)
n-Way set associative	i386, i486, Pentium	PowerPC 601 (Unified)
Hashed	IBM S/370/168	HP Precision (only one in the system)

TABLE 3.7　Name translation methods.

virtual page names can hash into the same page table entry and yet produce a valid translation. Remember that approximately two probes are required for a successful translation. This level of redundancy eliminates the need to link entries (common with full name translation in hash accessed systems), and a large fraction of collisions can be accommodated with this design.

HP Precision Architecture. This processor does not have a TLB to speedup the name translation process. The hashed access page translation (Figure 3.24) is as fast as a TLB, thus one is not used.

Summary of TLB Organizations

The selection of the TLB organization by a designer is sometimes constrained by the design of the translation tables. Table 3.7 shows the TLB design and the table translation method for a number of processors.

3.4.2 *TLB Miss Ratio Data*

Satyanarayanan and Bhandarker [SATY81] performed a miss ratio evaluation of TLB size, degree of associativity, sensitivity to context switching, and replacement algorithms. The tests are conducted by means of a simulator and FORTRAN programs for the VAX product family. The evaluation was performed to set the design parameters prior to the construction of a processor. A clear interval is used as a surrogate for context switching. By periodically clearing the TLB, the effect of clearing based on a context switch can be evaluated. The authors of this evaluation characterize TLB performance as

$$\text{TLB miss ratio} = \frac{\text{no. of main memory references to page table}}{\text{explicit virtual memory reference}}$$

No. of Sectors per Set	No. of Sets			
	32	64	128	256
1	97	47	22	8
2	25	9	3	2
4	7	2	1.5	1

Number of page table references $\times 10^3$ for 5.5×10^6 explicit references.

TABLE 3.8   VAX TLB miss ratios.

Explicit virtual memory references are those references generated by the program. In addition, there are *implicit* references to memory that are generated by the translation process itself. The number of implicit references is influenced by the organization of the translation tables themselves, such as the number of levels. One of the performance results of the VAX study is shown in Table 3.8. The data indicates the reduction in page table references as the size and organization of the TLB are changed.

As with other figures that show P_{miss} data for cache, the diagonals of this figure are for TLBs of equal size. The total number of explicit references to the memory system is 5.5×10^6, and the number of references that miss the TLB are shown. Thus, for this table, small numbers represent an improvement in the number of page names translated in the fast TLB. This data indicates a clear preference for a large TLB and for higher degrees of associativity and a smaller number of sets. Higher degrees of associativity reduce the occurrence of set conflicts. Thus the preference is for associative TLBs in many processors that are implemented in VLSI technology where the increase in tag bits is not a significant cost problem.

Another source of TLB miss data is [WOOD86]. Five benchmarks are executed on six processors. Four of the processors are of the VAX family (512-byte page) and two are IBM S/370 or Amdahl compatibles (4-Kbyte page); excerpted results of the tests for TLB miss ratios, expressed in percentages, are shown in Table 3.9.

This information is quite interesting in that while the size and organization of the TLB are important, the size of the page is even more important. A larger page will result in a lower miss ratio for TLBs of equal size. This result confirms the use of a page TLB, as with the MC88200 and the PowerPC 601, for the operating system. This data also confirms the advantage of associative TLBs.

Saavedra and Smith [SAAV93] measured TLB miss ratios on a number of commercial processors for six SPEC benchmarks. Table 3.10

No. of Sectors per Set	No. of Sets		
	128	256	512
1 (VAX, 512 Kbytes)	3.68		0.639
2 (VAX, 512 Kbytes)	1.78		0.324
2 (IBM S/370, 4 Kbyte)	0.097	0.023	0.014

LISZT Benchmark.

TABLE 3.9 TLB miss ratios (%).

Processor	No. of Sets	Sectors per Set	Page Size	Miss Ratio (%)
DECstation 3100	64	64	4096 Bytes	2.42
DECstation 5400	64	64	4096 Bytes	2.42
DECstation 5500	64	64	4096 Bytes	2.42
MIPS R/2000	64	64	4096 Bytes	2.42
VAX9000	1024	2	8192 Bytes	0
RS/6000 530	128	2	4096 Bytes	1.31
HP 9000/720	64	64	8192 Bytes	1.30

TABLE 3.10 TLB percentage miss ratios for SPEC Benchmarks.

shows an excerpt of their results; the average TLB miss ratio is given for the six benchmarks.

This data also indicates the primacy of page size in determining TLB miss ratios. A large page, or the granularity of the TLB, significantly reduces the miss ratio.

We can speculate that the arguments advanced by Hill and others on the advantage of direct caches will apply to TLBs as well. The arguments (discussed in Chapter 2) suggest that a direct cache, with its shorter logic path but with a higher miss ratio, may be the most effective design for reducing TLB translation time. [HILL86] also provides TLB miss ratio data for a number of processors and three benchmarks.

As discussed in Chapter 5, TLB translation time is of significant importance for caches that are addressed with translated real addresses. However, for some cache organizations, the TLB must be only fast enough to match the access time of the cache. Thus, higher degrees of set associativity, with lower miss ratios, may be quite satisfactory.

TLB Size, Sectors	Normalized No. of Instructions Executed	TLB Miss Ratio
0	1.0	1.0
4	2.3	0.106
8	2.6	0.029
16	2.8	0.0125

Note. LRU algorithm.

TABLE 3.11   GE-645 Multics performance.

3.4.3 *TLB Impact on Virtual Memory Performance*

There is little published information on the performance of a virtual memory system as the various parameters (for example, page size, TLB size and organization, and main memory size) are varied. The little data that does exist is some material on performance: the papers on Multics [SHEM66, SCHR71] and the VAX 11/780 [CLAR85].

Schroeder [SCHR71] reports on the performance of a virtual memory system as the TLB size is varied. The system is the GE-645; the operating system is Multics, which is a paged-segmented system. The page size is 1K words or 4.5 Kbytes. The system was evaluated with associative TLBs having 0, 4, 8, and 16 entries. The time for a TLB search is between 200 and 600 ns, while the main memory is 1.2 us—a ratio of 2:6 to one. This ratio is probably valid today under the assumption the tables are cached. Table 3.11 shows the normalized number of instructions executed per unit of time. This metric is a relatively good measure of the TLB's effectiveness; the larger the number, the more effective is the TLB. Table 3.11 also shows the TLB miss ratios as the size is varied.

These data indicate that an associative TLB with 8 sectors is probably large enough, nor do these data support the large TLBs found in modern memory systems; the reason being that the GE-645 is a microprogrammed machine that takes many clocks to execute an instruction, unlike modern pipelined processors with CPIs of 1–2. Thus, with modern pipelined processors, name translation delays have a greater impact on overall performance. Additional information on the impact of TLBs on performance is found in [SHEM66].

3.4.4 *Instruction Support for TLBs*

TLBs are generally considered to be invisible to the program, as with early caches, and serve only to reduce the time of name translation.

Unfortunately, this simple view is not completely correct. Recall the use of processor instructions for enforcing MLI, described in Table 3.5. Two classes of instructions are required. First, some of the TLB registers must be loaded explicitly under program control; second, the TLB must be invalidated in order to maintain coherency. The complexity of invalidation is illustrated by the PowerPC 601 *translation lookaside buffer invalidate entry* (*tibie*) instruction, which is used for MLI control.

A name translation of the page name of the *tibie* instruction (a supervisor-level instruction) is attempted. If there is a hit on the TLB, the TLB entry is invalidated by setting the valid bit to zero. A TLB invalidate is also broadcast on the system bus so that coherency can be maintained across the system.

With a multiprocessor system, the broadcast *tibie* must be in a critical section controlled by software locking so that only one *tibie* can be issued at a time. Resynchronization is established by issuing a *sync* instruction after every *tibie* at the end of the critical section. When a processor receives a broadcast *tibie* instruction, it halts the execution of new load, store, cache control, and *tibie* instructions; waits for the completion of all memory operations; and then invalidates both sectors in the user TLB.

3.5 Virtual Memory Accessing Rules

This section discusses the rules that are followed when a virtual memory system is accessed for reads and writes. The effect of a cache on this process is ignored; however, the combination of a cache with virtual memory is addressed in Chapter 4. The reader should note that all of the design ideas and much of the published performance data on virtual memory systems are from an earlier time when small memory was the rule. Today, with significantly larger memories, these designs may no longer be appropriate. Caution should therefore be exercised in the use of specific design data.

3.5.1 *Read Accesses*

The various policies that govern the actions when a paged virtual memory is accessed are discussed in this section. The various design issues involved are described here with illustrations taken from an actual virtual memory system. The basic steps in performing a read access into a virtual memory system consist of the following.

1. Determine if a referenced page is in real memory; detect for a page fault.

2. On a hit (the referenced page is determined to be in real memory)

translate the virtual page name to the page frame address and fetch the AU into the processor.

3. On a miss (the referenced page is determined to be absent from real memory):

(a) Determine if a page must be evicted because of a capacity miss; identify the page to move; evict the page to the disk. This policy is known as the *replacement policy*.

(b) Depending upon the organization of the virtual memory, a determination of the page frame to receive the loaded page may need to be made. Fetch the page from the disk into the real memory and adjust the tags and valid bits in the name translation tables. This policy is known as the *placement rule*. Translating the virtual address to the disk address is discussed in Section 3.5.9.

(c) Complete the read of the AU into the real memory.

Note that if the system is multitasking, a new task may be swapped in during this process. There are commonly three successful name translation paths through a virtual memory with a TLB and a cache; the fourth path is the page miss path. These paths are shown in Table 3.12.

Path 1. The page frame address is found in the TLB.

Path 2. The page frame address is not in the TLB but is found in the page tables that have been placed in the cache. After the reference, the TLB is updated with page name translation information for use by a future reference.

Path 3. The page frame address is found by table walking in real memory. After the reference, the cache and the TLB are updated with page name translation information.

Path 4. The translation misses on the TLB, cache, and tables in memory. This is a page fault path and requires the allocation of the missed page into real memory. All translation tables are updated.

The three successful cases above are for the name translation only. The assumption is made that a name translation miss on a page that is resident in real memory is not permitted. For Path 4, the total failure

Path	Page Name Translation Path Hit/Miss		
	TLB	Cache	Memory
1	Hit	X	X
2	Miss	Hit	X
3	Miss	Miss	Hit
4	Miss	Miss	Miss

TABLE 3.12 Name translation paths.

of name translation indicates that the page is not in real memory and results in a page fault.

3.5.2 *Allocation*

This section discusses the issues of allocating new pages or segments into real memory following a page fault—a problem that can be different from late select cache allocation. Recall that congruence-mapped, n-way set associative (including direct) late select caches dictate the sector into which a new allocation must be placed. Only the block within the sector is open to choice. Associative caches, on the other hand, can allocate into any segment with the choice based on one of the replacement policies discussed in Chapter 2.

Virtual memory page or segmentation organization is early select, which is an associative accessing process. Therefore, allocation of pages to real memory is a matter of (1) finding a vacant location and (2) if a vacant location cannot be found, creating a vacant space using one of the policies discussed in Section 2.1.7. In addition to the allocation problems associated with finding space for a page frame or a segment, the name translation information must be allocated to the name translation tables as well. The problem here is quite similar to the allocation problems of caches, noted above. The organization of the translation tables dictates the allocation of name translation information.

The techniques for performing allocation in virtual memory systems have their historical roots in the problems of allocating files to disks, discussed in many texts on operating systems. Also, because allocation is highly dynamic and interactive in LISP systems, research in these systems has made significant contributions. Even interactive programming environments such as Lotus 1-2-3 must have solutions to the requirement for dynamic allocation and de-allocation of segments.

Page Allocation

The procedure for allocating pages to page frames is the same regardless of the name translation method. That is, either direct or inverted mapping systems use the same procedure. The operating system maintains a *free page frame list* (a linked list of vacant page frames in real memory) that contains the starting addresses of all unallocated pages. The list can be maintained as a linked list or a LIFO stack. Upon a page fault, the free page frame list is searched; if there is a free page frame, it is allocated. Recall that because a paged virtual memory is early select, congruence mapped, and associative, any free page frame can be allocated. If a page frame is not available, a replacement policy is then invoked.

There can be additional policies imposed by the operating system on page allocation from the free list. For example, should there be reserved page frames for the operating system and the user? If the system is multiprogrammed, should there be page frames reserved for each of the resident programs? These issues are beyond the scope of this book but are treated in books on operating systems.

The hardware must support reading and writing the free page frame list. Thus linked list or stack manipulation is needed. Most processors designed today provide for stack manipulation, which is the implementation of choice. Processors that have been optimized for list or LISP processing use linked lists for the free page frame list. The size of the free page frame list is not excessive, as there must be, at most, one entry for each real memory page. For a system with a 4-Kbyte page and 16 Mbytes of real memory the free page frame list has only 4K entries. If an entry is 4 bytes, 4 pages are occupied by the free page frame list, approximately 0.1% of the total real memory space.

The question of whether or not the free page frame list itself is paged or locked into an unpaged region of real memory is addressed in Section 3.5.4. Recall that most virtual memory systems today provide for an identity page name translation for operating system access to memory. In addition, some systems provide block name translation facilities to enhance the management of the operating system in virtual memory space. A block composed of a number of pages eliminates much of the paging that could occur if only pages are implemented.

Segment Allocation

For the discussions to follow, it is helpful to remember that space in memory, either page frames or space for segments, can be in one of three states.

1. *Free*. The space is vacant and available for allocation.
2. *Allocated*. The space is occupied by a valid segment, either clean or dirty.
3. *Garbage*. The space is occupied by a segment that has been deallocated.

Segmented systems pose additional, and significant, allocation problems to those of paged systems. There must be a way to locate a contiguous region of free space in real memory that is equal to or larger than the segment to be allocated. This requirement means that a *free space list* (called spaces because they are not yet allocated to segments) must contain not only the starting address of free space but the length of each space as well. Note that the size of a free space list is not bounded, as is a free page frame list, because in the limit, every space can be one addressable unit and the free space list would occupy all of real memory! Segments can overlap for sharing, thereby creating further allocation problems. Allocation for nonoverlapping segments follows three steps.

1. Find a free space that is large enough to receive the allocated segment.
2. If step 1 fails, determine if there is enough total free space in real memory. If there is, compact enough available free space to create a space for the segment to be allocated.
3. If steps 1 and 2 fail, find an allocated segment that is large enough and can be evicted based on criteria discussed in Chapter 2.

Step 1. This step is similar to page allocation. A *free space list* is maintained that lists the starting addresses and length of all free space. A number of algorithms have been proposed [KNEE68, DENN70] for segment allocation from the free space list. A detailed discussion of these algorithms is outside the scope of this book; nevertheless, four algorithms are

1. *First-fit*. Search the free space list, and find the first space into which the segment will fit regardless of the efficiency of space use. Place any unallocated portion of this space on the free space list.
2. *Best-fit*. Search the complete free space list, and find the free space that gives the most efficient use of space. Place any unallocated portion of this space on the free space list.
3. *Worst-fit*. Search the complete free space list, and find the free space segment that gives the least efficient use of space. Place any unallocated portion of this space on the free space list.
4. *Buddy*. Free space is initially divided into groups having even power of two AUs as with pages. When a page is allocated one of three allocations is made: (i) half the group with the other half placed on the free space list; (ii) the full group; or (iii) two groups, four groups, etc. This requires that all free space groups and allocated segments must be even power of two in length.

Knuth [KNUT68] reports on simulations that show that the first-fit policy gives the best results, defined to be that allocations continue longer before Step 1 fails and a garbage collection pass is required.

Step 2. When a new segment is to be allocated the total free space may be sufficient to hold a segment but the space may not be contiguous, which is a condition required for segmentation. A full discussion of the many techniques for compacting fragmented free space and de-allocated space, generally known as *garbage collection*, is outside the scope of this book. However, I want to provide a brief discussion of the issues involved. A comprehensive survey of garbage collection techniques can

Memory Allocations

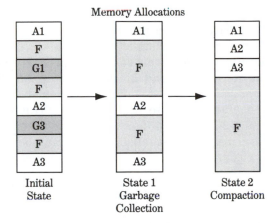

A: Allocated, F: Free, G: Garbage.

FIGURE 3.39 Garbage collection.

be found in [COHE81]. Note that not all algorithms for managing free space are known as "garbage collectors."

One of many types of compacting garbage collection systems is illustrated by the example shown in Figure 3.39. In the initial state the map of memory shows areas that are of the three states noted above: free, allocated, and garbage. The state of each area is denoted by means of a tag in either the space lists or by two control bits that impart *coloring* to the three states.

The initial state of the memory is shown and consists of three allocated spaces, three free spaces, and two garbage spaces. The first step, to State 1, in the garbage collection process searches out the garbage spaces and turns them into free space by placing these spaces on the free space list. The tag bits are also changed as required, and no movement in memory takes place. The second step moves both the allocated and free spaces into two compact regions of real memory. Thus all of free space is in one compact space and is available for allocation.

Step 3. If garbage collection and compaction do not yield a space that is large enough for allocating the new segment, an already allocated segment must be evicted. The algorithms for making the selection for eviction are based on (1) selection of a segment of appropriate size, (2) the usage criteria, and (3) the choice of a modified or nonmodified segment (clean or dirty).

If a modified segment is chosen for eviction, it must be copied back onto the disk. The free space thus made available is placed on the free space list and allocation Step 1 is initiated. In the chosen segment is not modified, it is only necessary to place the segment on the free space list and proceed with allocation Step 2.

From the above brief discussion of segment allocation it is clear that considerable operating system overhead is required. Hardware assist for this process consists of stack and block move support. The amount of overhead is proportional to the size of the segment being allocated and the state of the memory prior to the allocation. This overhead can be observed in Lotus 1-2-3 by the difference in time taken to return to the READY state after allocating small and large numbers of cells by, for example, a COPY command.

3.5.3 *Write Access*

Write accesses proceed just like read accesses. This is because virtual memory systems are early select and the presence or absence of a page or segment is determined before real memory is accessed.

If the write access is a hit, the write is made to the AU in real memory and the page table dirty bit, if used, is set. A dirty bit is used in conjunction with the valid bit to manage the de-allocation and allocation of pages or segments in real memory. Unlike caches, there are no known implementations of the equivalent of a write through strategy for a virtual memory system, because the time to write a single AU to the disk is quite large and would block the disk from other activity. Write buffers would not eliminate this problem. Thus, all virtual memory systems use a write back strategy.

If the write access is a miss, the missed page is allocated into real memory and the write operation is performed again. There are no known no-write-allocate strategies, like those of caches, with virtual memory systems. The reason for this is the same as for not using a write through strategy: the very long transport time makes writing a single AU to disk unjustifiable.

3.5.4 *Location of Tables*

The first virtual memory machine, the Atlas shown in Figure 3.15, had its page table in an associatively searched hardware register file. As the size of the virtual address space has increased, larger tables have been required and placed in real memory.

One might ask if the tables in real memory are addressed in real memory space or virtual space? To my knowledge, (except for Multics) the tables are never placed in just any virtual space but in dedicated pages (identity name translations) of virtual memory space. If the page tables are paged, there can be a deadlock in paging as one name translation is forced to wait on another name translation that is waiting on the first, and so on. Thus, access to page tables is mapped by identity and the time for name translation via a page table tree is eliminated. The RS/6000 accesses its table in real addresses without the identity translation step [IBM90].

In addition to storing the page tables in real memory (or an identity translation), if the system has a data cache the page tables may be cached as well. Caching of page tables can further reduce the name translation time, as is described in the model found in Section 3.6. There is no known published data on cache P_{miss} when storing page tables. It may well be that a page table cache could be a useful variation of caches. On the other hand, any chip area needed for this cache may be more usefully devoted to larger TLBs.

Section 3.4 discusses the Motorola MC88200 [MOTO90a], which provides a dual TLB facility. A separate TLB known as the *block address translation cache* (BATC) translates the virtual address into a pointer into a 512-Kbyte block of real memory. Management of the BATC is under program control as there is no recourse to a multilevel translation table if there is a TLB miss. With a miss, the operating system is invoked to perform all of the management functions and is supported by some special instructions for loading the BATC.

3.5.5 *Table Walking Methods*

The MC68040 multilevel direct page tables are stored in real memory, as shown in Figure 3.40. If a successful name translation cannot be accomplished in the TLB, the address is translated with the memory resident tables. The various address fields and control bits of the table entries are allocated into groups of the AUs. The use of real memory for page tables leads to the requirement that the tables must be traversed by fetching and decoding the entries of each valid level of the hierarchy, a function called *table walking*.

Early systems such as the GE-645 Multics [DENN72, ORGA72, MATI80] and at least one contemporary system, the MIPS R2000/R4000 [MIPS87], perform table walking with a program using the normal instruction set of the processor. For these systems, referencing each level of the page table requires a sequence of instructions such as

1. Load page entry.
2. Select valid bit.
3. Branch to 8 on not valid.
4. Select pointer field.
5. Extract Index value from address.
6. Concatenate to form memory address.

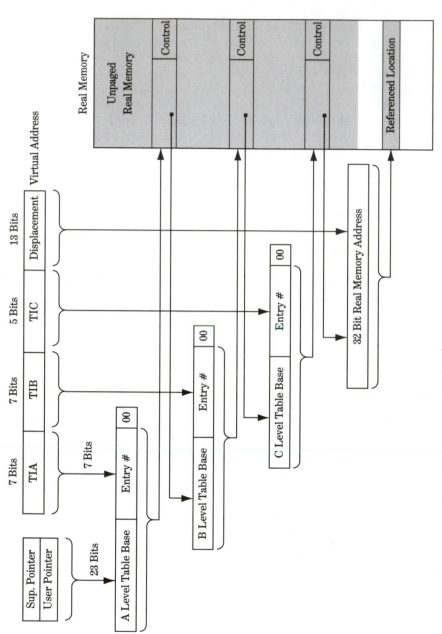

FIGURE 3.40 MC68040 multilevel page table storage.

186

7. Leaf node? no, branch to 1; yes branch to 9.
8. Fault exit.
9. Continue.

Each level of the page table will have an overhead of approximately eight instructions. A three-level system has an overhead of approximately 24 instructions or 30 memory cycles for each memory reference that is not translated in the TLB. The actual time required for a translation is a function of whether or not the page tables are cached and whether or not there is an instruction cache that may be holding the short program. Also, if the program is paged and the page is not "locked in" there could even be page faults during a table walk.

This software approach is still possible, but many modern memory management units have special logic that performs these functions. The logic is known as *table walking hardware,* and it significantly reduces the time required to access the page tables. Motorola calls this operation *translation table searching,* a function implemented in microcode.

The page table walking overhead burden is reduced by incorporating a state machine controller that implements the table walking function; an example of this controller is found in the MC88200 Memory Management Unit. Using hardware table walking eliminates most of the memory cycles and the possibility of cache misses and page faults. The net result is that the time required to translate is approximately one memory cycle per level of translation.

Inverted page tables, such as those used in the RS/6000, use a form of table walking in their linked list structure. For these systems, the control of searching down the list is vested totally in hardware. There are no known systems that are software-based. The reduction in weighted average name translation time with hardware over software table walking is dramatic and is modeled for the VAX 11/780 in Section 3.6.

3.5.6 *Instruction Set Support for Virtual Memory*

As I noted previously, a major portion of the work (but not the time) associated with servicing a page or segment fault is performed by the processor. Instruction set support is found in the three general areas of (1) table walking, (2) table management, and (3) interrupt support. For multitasking systems, the time to execute a table walk is important if it cannot be overlapped with other processing. For single-user virtual memory systems, the table walk time is small with respect to the disk time and can usually be ignored.

Table Walking Support

Table walking with software requires instruction set support to execute the algorithm noted above. The instruction set should include the usual field extraction, logical operations, and testing instructions found in general purpose instruction sets. In general, no additional instructions are required. Table walking code can be provided as a subroutine that is called when there is a miss on the TLB.

If page faults are frequent, a special subroutine call/return, designed for this purpose only, can eliminate most of the overhead for this rather special subroutine. It may also be helpful if the subroutine is locked into the cache to eliminate instruction cache misses.

Table Management Support

Table management support is required due to the large number of tables that must be loaded and stored under program control. The extension register(s) portion of the virtual address are loaded by the operating system with special load instructions. Special load instructions are also necessary for the segment registers for those systems that use this method for extending the effective address.

The IBM RS/6000 is one example of the special load instructions. There are a number of hardware registers collectively named *storage control registers*. First, there are 16 *segment registers* (SR); the most significant bit of each signifies if the segment is an I/O or processing (normal) segment. Another register is the *transaction ID register* (TID); this register contains a 16-bit segment identification number. Two other registers are named the *storage description registers* (SDR0 and SDR1). Special instructions are provided to load all of these registers. Note that these registers are never modified by a translation or a side effect of a translation; however, they can be modified as the result of a page fault. Thus, a store instruction must also be provided to store these tables for a context switch. Loads and stores are accomplished with move to sri (*mtsri*) and move from sri (*mfsri*) instructions that are moves between the special registers and the general purpose registers.

An inverted hash access system has other tables, the hash anchor table and page tables, that must be loaded and stored under program control. These tables are located in real memory, and the usual instructions that manipulate memory locations serve to load and store these tables. TLBs and other cachelike translation tables must be loaded and stored as well. The need to store the tables is a consequence of the fact that these tables can be modified between context switches.

Page Fault Interrupt Support

An executing program references memory with name translations via the TLB and the page tables assuming that the referenced pages are in real memory. If the page is not in real memory, the present bit in the translation system will trigger an interrupt, an action known as a *page fault* or *memory exception trap*. When there is a page fault, there are a number of tasks that must be accomplished. The following list is for a uniprogramming environment. Multiprogramming or multitasking requires other steps and is outside the scope of this book.

1. Trap the operating system.
2. Save the user and process state.
3. Write out a "dirty page" if necessary (virtual memory uses write back).
4. Allocate the new page to real memory.
5. Translate the virtual address to a disk file address.
6. Issue a read to the file system.
7. Read page into the allocated location.
8. Update translation tables and TLB.
9. Restore user and process state.
10. Resume processing.

The actual time required to execute these steps is not as great as the length of the list would suggest. For example, assume eight of the steps (not counting the transport times of steps 3 and 7) require an average of 1,000 instructions and each instruction requires 50 ns. The total time to service a page fault interrupt is 0.4 ms, a trivial part of the one or two 20-ms to 30-ms disk latencies.

3.5.7 *Memory Access Control*

This section discusses two issues: *protection* and *proper access*. Protection has to do with assuring that a reference to memory is authorized. Proper access has to do with the correctness of the access, as in not attempting to execute a floating point datum as an instruction. The issues of protection of objects or abstract data types and system access security are outside the scope of this book, and references to these subjects can be found in most books on operating systems.

Protection

Early research into the implementation of multiuser time sharing systems pointed to the need to protect programs and data from unauthorized access [DENN65, GRAH65, WILK68, GRAH72]. For reasons of

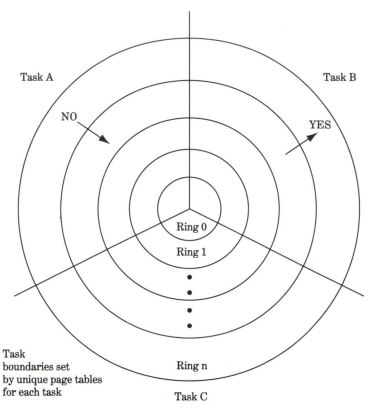

FIGURE 3.41   Rings of protection.

efficiency, however, it is desirable to permit sharing between users of programs and some data, a desiderata that introduced the need for protection. Graham [GRAH72] lists seven levels of protection for multiuser time sharing systems; each level requires additional hardware support for their implementation. The requirement for sharing and protection is just as important in processors that execute a number of tasks (multiprogramming or multitasking) that share resources.

The view of protection we have today has its roots in the MIT Project MAC and Multics. Graham [GRAH65] published the idea of *rings of protection,* which is shown in Figure 3.41. Briefly stated, Graham's idea is that a "process executing in ring i has no access whatever to any segment in ring j, where $j < i$." This view of protection leads immediately to the requirement that somewhere in the name translation system there must be a tag to denote the level of protection. Because control bits are somewhat limited in the page table entries, there is a limit to the number of rings of protection.

For paged virtual memory systems, protection is exerted at the page level, or at the block level if block translation is employed. Examples of the use of control bits that provide protection can be found in a number of processors. The i386, i486, and Pentium devote two bits in the descriptor tables, which provide four levels of protection. These levels are: kernel, system services, custom extensions, and application. Two protection bits are also used in the page frame table entry of the RS/6000. In the most general implementation of rings of protection, if control is being transferred to a ring other than the current one, an interrupt occurs and the operating system is invoked to perform the proper housekeeping tasks.

Proper Access

Protecting memory from an improper access is the second issue of access control. One task should not be able to interfere with another task without mutual agreement. Four possible ways [SITE80] of providing memory protection are

1. bounds registers,
2. memory keys,
3. translation table keys,
4. distinct addresses spaces.

These four protection methods are discussed individually below. It should be noted, however, that combinations of the four methods are implemented in some specific computers.

Bounds registers were first used in nonvirtual memory machines. Bounds registers provide two pointers: one to an upper address limit, the other to a lower address limit. Bounds can also be specified with a starting address and length. If a reference is found to be outside these bounds, an error interrupt is signaled. The bounds registers are loaded and stored by the operating systems using privileged instructions.

For a system that will have a number of tasks resident in memory at one time, there may be a number of bounds register pairs, one for each task. The register pairs are addressed by a pointer that is set when a task is switched in. The use of bounds registers assumes that a task, program, and/or data, is allocated within a contiguous address space. Bounds registers permit sharing between tasks of an address space by identifying overlapping spaces by the bounds registers. Bounds registers, however, present restrictions with, for example, a single word containing a semaphore that is accessed by a number of tasks. The semaphore would have to be in the highest address of one task and in the lowest address in a second task. Access by three tasks is difficult.

For paged systems, protection is at the page or block level and for segmented systems at the segment level. For example, the segment length field of a segment table operates in the fashion of a bounds register. An example of this is the block translation system of the PowerPC 601 that has a block partition of memory that is similar to a segment. A block name is presented to the block TLB and is checked for being within the starting address and the length of the block. Block length is encoded with six bits, rather than having an upper address, in the BAT registers discussed previously. The length of the block is a binary progression: 128 Kbytes, 256 Kbytes, 512 Kbytes, ... , 8 Mbytes, an encoding designed to facilitate length checking [MOTO93].

Memory keys specify the type of access that is permitted to a memory location, page, or segment. Typical access types are: Unlimited, Read Only, Execute Only, and/or a task I.D. The executing program key is usually found in the processor status register that, in combination with the type of access, is compared to the "lock" associated with the memory and found in the name translation system. If the key matches the lock, the requested access is performed. There is usually a "skeleton key" that can be used by the operating system to access all of memory regardless of the key associated with each of the keyed memory spaces.

The memory keys are usually contained in the name translation maps and/or the TLB. Thus, an improper access is terminated before the read or write is actually performed. Memory keys permit access to noncontiguous page frames in real memory, unlike bounds registers. Sharing is more difficult, however, as sharing is at the block level. Shared variables may need to be relocated with a context switch increasing context switch overhead. If different accesses are legal for different tasks, the protection fields in the TLB must be changed when tasks are switched.

The PowerPC 601 illustrates the use of memory keys. The supervisor mode has the keyed accesses of read/write and read only, while the user mode has the keyed accesses of no access, read only, and read/write. The operating system can block user programs from accesses by evoking the no access key. This description is not complete; additional information can be found in [MOTO93].

Translation table keys provide protection by having an access table for each task. These tables, one for each task, contain the legal access methods for each page of real memory and permit different legal accesses for different tasks with a minimum of overhead. As there are multiple tables, only a switch of a pointer is needed to select the table for the new task. Images of the keys are found in the page tables and are checked along with the check of the virtual address tag.

Distinct address spaces can be used to provide protection by assuring that different tasks do not share the same virtual address space. This protection is accomplished by making the task name a part of the virtual address. With the task name in the most significant bits, there can be no overlap between addresses in different tasks. One example of a distinct address space system is found in the ix86 processors that have segment registers associated with each type of access, for example, code and stack.

3.5.8 *Choice of Page Size*

This section addresses four tradeoffs in determining page size.

1. Reducing internal fragmentation.
2. Reducing disk/memory transfer time.
3. Matching the page size to the levels of the name translation tables.
4. Reducing the miss ratio.

Internal fragmentation was introduced in Section 3.1. When a page size is selected, there is a waste of usable memory space. First, because the allocation block is not an exact multiple of the page size, internal fragmentation occurs. Internal fragmentation is reduced with small pages because the wasted space is limited to a fraction of a smaller page. Second, when a program and its data is allocated to real memory, space must be provided for the page table entry of the allocated page. Page table space is not available for the program and data; it is pure overhead space. As the page size decreases, more pages must be allocated and the space used for page table entries increases. Thus, what page size will balance these two counterforces and minimize the loss of memory? Early work on this design problem, and the model derived below, is found in [WOLM65], who attributes the first version of the model to J. B. Kruskal. This model determines an optimum page size to minimize wasted real memory.

Assume that the number of AUs that must be allocated for a program (instructions and data) is n; the page size is p; and a AUs are required for each page table entry. A di.cct one-level page table, in memory, is assumed. Thus, the use of main memory by page tables and internal fragmentation represents a loss of real memory to the user.

Memory loss = loss due to internal fragmentation + loss for allocating a page table entry,

$$\text{Loss due to internal fragmentation} = \frac{p}{2},$$

$$\text{Loss for allocating a page table entry} \approx \frac{an}{p},$$

$$\text{Memory loss} = C = \frac{p}{2} + \frac{an}{p}.$$

The derivative of C with respect to p is taken and set to zero as

$$p_{\text{opt}} = \sqrt{2an}.$$

This model shows that in order to minimize the loss of real memory due to internal fragmentation and page table entries, large pages are best for large programs and data sets that are becoming more common. However, with lower cost memory resulting in larger real memory, internal fragmentation is not viewed to be the problem it was three decades ago.

As described in Section 3.3.1, today, page tables are allocated into pages themselves, making this model incorrect as the first allocation requires a full page. With the internal fragment loss of one-half page and with page tables allocated to pages that lose one-half page, the total loss is one page and is invariant with page size or the number of allocations. Thus, the size of a page is more-or-less not an issue as far as real memory loss is concerned.

Reducing disk/memory transfer time is the second tradeoff option for determining page size. Pages transported between the disk and real memory incur a significant overhead due to the long access time of the disk. The time per byte transferred is reduced as the page size is increased. As with the discussion of block size for caches found in Chapter 2, if the page size is very large, the transfer time per byte approaches the data transfer time with the access time overhead totally prorated. Note, however, that page sizes today are far from this limit. The larger main memories of modern computers and the reduction in disk access and transfer time, discussed in Chapter 5, tend to drive the page size upward.

Matching the page size to the levels of the name translation tables is a determining factor. The choice of page size can determine the number of levels in a direct multilevel page table. This issue is discussed in Section 3.3.1. Larger page sizes require fewer levels for name translation.

Reducing the TLB miss ratio is another consideration in the selection of a page size. The larger the page size, the smaller the TLB miss ratio and the smaller can be the TLB. This is the reason for the use of two TLBs for two different page sizes in a number of processors such as the MC88200 as described in Section 3.3. Larger page sizes led to smaller TLBs, which is an important consideration in some designs. A large page has another virtue because a cache can be placed in virtual memory space. That is, the displacement in the virtual address addresses the cache while the virtual name translation is being performed. This cache architecture is discussed in Chapter 4.

From the above discussion, it can be seen that page size selection is a tradeoff process to achieve a balance between transport time, internal fragmentation, and name translation time. It is interesting to note that the flexibility in page size provided by the Motorola 6851 has been largely abandoned by designers for a fixed page size. However, the IBM RS/6000 gives a choice of two page sizes while the Digital Alpha provides page sizes of 8 Kbytes, 64 Kbytes, 512 Kbytes, and 4 Mbytes. The evolution of virtual memory systems has arrived at the consensus of a 4-Kbyte page size. The page sizes of some contemporary processors are given below.

VAX	512 bytes
IBM S/370	4096 bytes
RS/6000	4096 bytes
PowerPC 601	4096 bytes
i486	4096 bytes
Pentium	4096 bytes
MC88200	4096 bytes
MC88100	4096 bytes
R2000	4096 bytes
SPARC	8192 bytes

3.5.9 *Addressing the Disk*

This section discusses the way that the disk address is found when a new page is allocated following a page fault. Recall from Section 3.1 that the required name translation is referred to as using Map 3. This name translation problem is similar to the issues discussed in the preceding sections, which deal with translating virtual names to page frame addresses. Here we need to translate a virtual name to the disk addresses of a page, a process that requires a table(s) to hold translation information. Note that as with virtual memory, only page names need translating as the disk is never addressed at a lower level.

There are two ways of providing translation tables. First, the disk page address is contained in the page table entry [TANN84]. With this approach, the leaf page table entry would contain not only a field for the page frame address of the page in real memory but also a field that contains the address of the page on the disk. These disk address fields

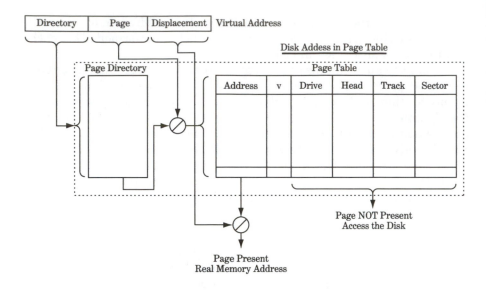

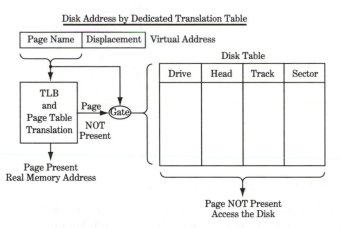

FIGURE 3.42   Disk translation table placement.

would have information on drive, head, track, record, and the like, which
as Figure 3.42 indicates, is a relatively large number of bits.

A variation of this technique is found in the i386, i486, and Pentium
[INTE90]. Because multilevel tables are direct with an entry for each
page in virtual memory, the page table entries can be either the translation address or the disk address (MAP 2 or MAP 3). Only one map is
valid at a time; the valid bits indicate which address is stored. When
there is a page fault, the disk address is used to access the disk and is
then replaced with the page frame address and the various control bits.

Neither version of the technique of placing disk address information in the page tables is suitable for inverted page table name translation. The reason is that an inverted page table contains only the name translation information of pages resident in real memory. Thus, another technique for disk address translation is needed.

This second technique, also shown in Figure 3.42, starts anew, upon a page fault, with the virtual address that caused the page fault, and translates that address via a dedicated translation table (MAP 3). With this method, the same number of bits are required to address the disk, but they are managed in a separate table. The translation of the virtual address into the disk address can be via direct multilevel translation or the file management system of the operating system.

3.6 Virtual Memory Performance Issues and Models

There are two major performance issues with virtual memory systems: name translation time and page fault time. The time to service a page fault has been discussed previously; thus this section deals only with name translation time. A rather old annotated bibliography of virtual memory performance measurements is found in [PARM72].

Name translation time is the weighted average time needed to translate a name and is added to the access time of main memory for systems without a cache and is added to cache access time for real address caches, as with the VAX 11/780 discussed in Chapter 4. Name translation by accessing tables can be a lengthy process, and multilevel translation tables create a significant performance problem. Each virtual memory reference requires one or more real memory references to access the tables, and if page table walking hardware is not provided, a number of instructions must be executed by the processor to interpret the contents of each page table entry.

A simple model for the time required to make a name translation is given below. This model is based on the unified TLB design of the VAX 11/780 [SATY81, CLAR83, EMER84, CLAR85]. The steps of translating an address are

1. Search the TLB and use the page frame address on a hit.
2. If the TLB search fails, the address is translated with cached page table information. On a translation hit, the translation information is placed in the TLB and the name translation is restarted in the TLB. Note that while a normal cache access requires a translated address, microcode has untranslated access to the cache for name translation purposes.
3. If the cache translation fails, the name is translated with page table

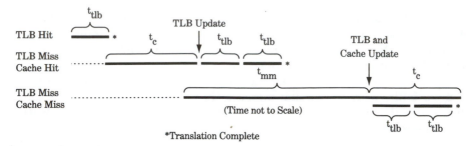

FIGURE 3.43 Name translation time.

information found in real memory. The translated information is placed in the cache and, in parallel, the TLB. The name translation is restarted in the TLB. Note that microcode table walking is provided for untranslated access to the page tables in real memory.

The VAX 11/780 memory performs name translation on data accesses and instruction accesses that miss the small instruction TLB. A timing diagram of the name translation process is shown in Figure 3.43.

The weighted average translation time (WATT) for a successful translation is

$$\text{WATT} = f_t \times t_{tlb} + f_c(t_c + 3t_{tlb}) + f_m(t_c + 3t_{tlb} + t_{mm})$$

where

f_t = fraction translated in TLB,
f_c = fraction translated in cache,
f_m = fraction translated in memory,
t_{tlb} = time for a TLB translation or update,
t_c = time for translation in the cache and a cache cycle (read or write),
t_{mm} = time for a translation in main memory.

The following assumptions are made:

$$2t_{tlb} \ll t_{mm}, \qquad f_t + f_c + f_m = 1.$$

Note that the fraction of translations performed at each level are equivalent to global hit ratios of multilevel caches. Clark [CLAR85] provides values for the parameters for this model derived from simulation. These parameters are

$$f_t = 0.97, \qquad f_c = 0.012, \qquad f_m = 0.018,$$
$$t_{tlb} = 1 \text{ clock}, \qquad t_c = 6 \text{ clocks}, \qquad t_{mm} = 18 \text{ clocks}.$$

Using these parameters in the model gives a weighted average name translation time of 1.56 clocks. For the VAX 11/780, the average number of clocks per instruction, without TLB miss delays, is approximately 10. This time includes the one clock for translating the data addresses through the TLB. Thus, for the parameters above, 0.56 clocks must be added to the 10 clocks of the basic execution time. TLB misses, therefore, add approximately 6% to the total execution time. This result compares favorably to the measured results of [CLAR85] of 5.1% to 8.0%, for various benchmarks. From the same parameters, 19.8 clocks are spent for each miss on the TLB. This result also compares favorably to the measured results of 21.0 to 22.1 clocks [CLAR85].

A name translation time of 1.56 clocks is a reasonable penalty for a processor that spends 10 clocks per instruction. For pipelined processors, however, discussed in Chapters 6 to 10, the clocks per instruction is approximately 1.5 (without translation delays). If there is an additional 0.64 clocks for name translation, the total execution time will be increased by approximately 30%. This is a major reason why real addressed caches are not used in most pipelined processors (described in Chapter 4).

Another issue can be addressed with this model. What is the performance benefit of hardware table walking? Assume that t_{mm} is 48 clocks rather than 18 with table walking. The weighted average translation time is 3.08 clocks rather than 1.56. The performance impact on the VAX 11/78 would be approximately 20% rather than 6%, a clear performance advantage for a processor with a cache addressed with real addresses.

3.6.1 *Published Page Fault Ratio Data*

This section discusses the identified published page fault ratios; unfortunately, little current information has been found. Rather old information on page fault ratios, as a function of page and real memory size (expressed as number of allocated pages), is provided by [CHU74] and excerpted in Table 3.13. Note that this data was taken in the era of small memory on the Sigma 7 and may not be representative of contemporary systems.

The presentation of this data is similar to other tables displaying miss ratio data. Diagonals from lower left to upper right are equal real memory sizes. This data shows very interesting properties. First, and this is to be expected, for any page size, as the size of real memory is increased permitting more pages to be allocated, the page fault ratio becomes constant at the value required to page in/out the working set. Once a working set is in memory, no further paging is required until the working set is paged out to the disk. When the memory is large, a larger

Memory Partition in Pages	Page Size in 24-Bit Words			
	64	128	256	512
8				.0018
16			.0012	.0002
32		.0012	.00002	.00001
64	.0012	.000035	.00002	
128	.00007	.000035		
256	.00007			

Note. FORTRAN compilation, LRU replacement.

TABLE 3.13   Page fault ratios.

page size will give a smaller page fault ratio because fewer page faults are required to page in the working set. Loading and storing the working set presents a minimum page fault ratio regardless of the page size, thus larger pages will reduce the page fault ratio.

Another interesting observation is that for a fixed memory size, the page size should also be as large as possible. For example, with a partition of 256 pages and a page size of 64 words, the fault ratio is 0.00007, while with a partition of 32 pages and a page size of 512 words, the fault ratio is 0.00001.

4

Memory Addressing and I/O Coherency

4.0 Overview

The issues addressed in this chapter are frequently viewed as related to multiprocessors. However, contemporary uniprocessors with caches, virtual memory, and concurrent input/output data transfers have the same characteristics and problems that must be solved. This chapter addresses these issues in the uniprocessor context.

In the 1970s, before virtual memory systems gained acceptance, processor designers debated the advantages and disadvantages of the type of address generated by the processor; should this address be real or virtual? Morris and Ibbett present the arguments in [MOOR79]. With the almost universal acceptance of virtual memory, however, the issues now become the nature of the address presented to the cache and the address domain of the I/O system. This chapter considers two issues: (1) the addresses presented to the cache and I/O in a virtual memory system, and (2) coherency (also known as consistency) maintenance between the various spaces in a computer and its memory. These issues are present in even rather simple systems and become quite complex with larger multiprocessors.

Virtual memory computers must cope with the coexistence of virtual and real addresses in the system. Problems arise from two sources: multiple virtual addresses and replicated memory spaces. Examples are

Multiple virtual addresses
- Concurrent processors, such as I/O and the main processor
- Multiple processes;

Replicated spaces

- Two processes accessing the same value but in two locations
- A value can be in the cache and main memory

For systems with multiple virtual addresses and replicated spaces, there are four cases of relationships, which are noted below couched in terms of *virtual address* and *real address*.

Case I. Multiple instances of the *same virtual address—same real address*. A normal and correct access results when the same virtual address issued from any process accesses the same real address or entity.

Case II. *different virtual addresses—different real addresses*. This situation is normal and presents no problems in the correct execution of a program.

Case III. *different virtual addresses—same real address*. This situation is called a *synonym* or *alias* and is illustrated by

Program 1, Virtual Address $A \rightarrow z$;
Program 2, Virtual Address $B \rightarrow z$.

Synonyms are viewed as either a virtue or a vice by different system designers. For example, the Multics system depends on synonyms for sharing and has a system call to provide a synonym for a given name [ORGA72]. The CMU system MACH also depends on synonyms. On the other hand, the prevention of synonyms is important to other systems. A discussion of the unique problems of synonyms in real address caches is found in [WHEE92].

Case IV. Multiple instances of the *same virtual address—different real addresses*. This situation has the potential for a *coherency problem* if the values in the different real addresses are different. For example,

Program 1, Name $A \rightarrow x$;
Program 2, Name $A \rightarrow y$.

If the values in x and y are different, the values are not coherent. Note that addresses x and y may be in the same physical memory, such as a cache, or in multiple physical memories, such as multiple caches. One solution to this problem is to include the process name in the virtual address thereby creating unique names for the variables, converting a Case IV into a Case II. This solution requires a longer virtual address and more tag bits but is consistent with the view of large virtual addresses, a technique used with the IBM S/38 [DAHL80] and AS/400. There are other solutions to ensuring coherency that are discussed in later sections in terms of cache coherency.

4.1 Cache Addressing, Virtual or Real

Chapter 2, on caches, takes the simple view that an address is presented to the cache. Chapter 3 introduced the concept of virtual and real addresses. This section discusses the relationships between virtual addresses and real address as applied to caches. Recall that a cache is used to reduce the latency of a memory system while a virtual memory system introduces a name translation step that can add latency to the memory system. It would seem, therefore, that caches and virtual memories are at odds with each other. The primary design problem addressed in this section is balancing synonym and coherency control with cache performance and cache size. Note that nonvirtual memory systems do not have the problems discussed in this section as all addresses are real.

Before proceeding further, I give a brief review of addresses that are present in a system. Figure 4.1 shows seven address forms of interest: virtual address, effective address, real address, cache address, TLB address, BTB/BTC address, and I/O address. A virtual address has a page name field that may be divided into two or more subfields for addressing translation tables and a displacement field. A real address has a page frame address, which is the translated page name, and a displacement field. The cache address consists of a sector name, field that may or may not align with the boundaries in a real address or a virtual address, a set index field, a block address field, and a displacement field. Note that in the discussion to follow, the term sector is used even if there is only one block per sector. Finally, the address used by the TLB, BTB or BTC, and the I/O system for reading and writing memory will be either real or virtual and have fields allocated by the details of the specific designs.

Are real or virtual addresses presented to the cache and what are the consequences of one or the other? The issue is more complicated than

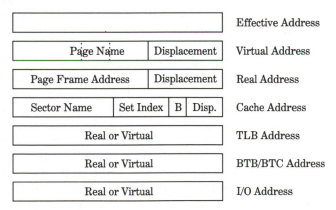

FIGURE 4.1 System address.

Set Index	Sector Name	Cache Name
Real	Real	Real address cache
Real	Virtual	No known implementation or name
Virtual	Real	Pipelined real address cache
Virtual	Virtual	Virtual address cache
Untranslated displacement		Restricted virtual cache

TABLE 4.1   Cache addressing options.

suggested by the simple choice of real or virtual addresses. Recall from Chapter 2 that a cache is addressed via two paths: the set index path and the sector name that is compared with the tag. These two paths can be either virtual or real, leading to four design options as shown in Table 4.1. The taxonomy of Table 4.1 is similar to that of [WU93].

The following sections will discuss these four design options. The real/virtual design is not considered.

4.1.1 *Real Address Caches*

Figure 4.2 shows the organization of a cache that is in real address space. The page name of the virtual address is translated via the TLB and page tables and then concatenated with the displacement. This process forms the real address, as shown. Fields of the real address are delineated to form the address into the cache: the sector name, the set index, block address if used, and the displacement. As the cache can be organized in any of the ways discussed in Chapter 2, the fields shown are for illustration only.

The sector name portion of the real address is stored in the cache tags and is compared to the sector name field. If a hit occurs, the data found in the cache is valid and is sent to the processor. If the comparison fails, a cache miss occurs, the memory is referenced with the real address, and the cache is updated.

A major benefit of a real address cache is that synonyms are not a problem. Two or more different virtual addresses cannot translate to the same real address location in either real memory or the cache. Another virtue of this organization is that there is no limit to the size of the cache. As many bits as desired can be selected from the real address for the cache address. The designer does not have to resort to extending the degree of associativity to increase the size of the cache. The only constraints on cache size is the total number of bits in the real address.

The most significant problem with a real address cache is its performance. With a cache in real address space, the virtual address must be translated before the cache can be accessed. The time to perform the

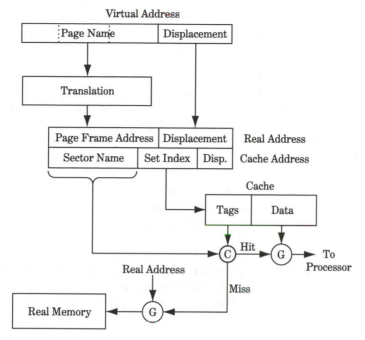

FIGURE 4.2　Real address cache.

page name translation via the TLB and/or page tables is added to the cache's access time. Since the TLB and the cache are usually constructed from the same technology, the cache's access time can be more than doubled. Recall from Chapter 3 that a typical address translation time can be 1.5 cycles. These cycles add directly to the cache access time. For processors such as the VAX 11/780 that have a CPI of 10 cycles, this overhead is not a significant loss of performance. The effective access time of a real address cache is

$$\text{Eff. } t_{\text{ea}} = (\text{WATT} + t_{\text{ea}})$$

where WATT = weighted average translation time.

However, note that because of unlimited cache address space, a large cache can be used, and the P_{miss} of the real address cache may be significantly lower than the P_{miss} of a virtual address cache. Reducing the P_{miss} of the cache may overcome some of the performance loss due to the serial name translation.

The cache addressing of the VAX 11/780 is a good example of a real address cache, as shown in Figure 4.3. The 30-bit virtual address is divided into a byte displacement field and a virtual page name field. The page name is translated via a TLB and page tables, which gives

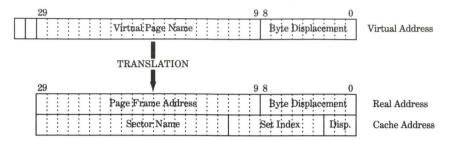

FIGURE 4.3   VAX 11/780 cache address generation.

the real page frame address concatenated with the untranslated displacement. The real address is partitioned into a sector name, set index, and displacement fields that constitute the cache address [LEVY80, LEON87].

The VAX 11/780 has a rapid address translation of an instruction page name (described in Chapter 3). Thus, for instruction fetches, the WATT delay is quite small. The benefits of a real cache (lack of synonyms and unlimited size) are realized at a small performance cost for a processor with a large CPI.

4.1.2 *Pipelined Real Caches*

From the above discussions, we see that a pure real address cache can have a significant performance problem. A form of cache that has the benefit of no synonyms of a real address cache and very small access latency has been called a *pipelined cache* [STON93] and is called a *pipelined real cache* in this book. As Figure 4.4 shows, the displacement field of the virtual address accesses the cache. In parallel with the cache access, a virtual page name is translated into a page frame address, a portion of which is compared to the page frame address that is stored in the cache's tag field. If the tags compare, the data is gated out of the cache to the processor. Otherwise, the real address accesses the main memory to fetch a new block into the cache. This cache organization permits the cache access and the translation operations to proceed in parallel.

The price paid for low latency and lack of synonyms is that the size of the cache is limited. The size limitation is bounded by *"the page size is larger than the cache size divided by the associativity"* [AGAR84]. For example, a byte displacement field of 10 bits and a set associativity of 4 limits the cache size to 4 Kbytes or AUs. While the logic paths via the cache and address translation are roughly equivalent, strict pipelining with latches may be required because a TLB miss can lengthen the translation time.

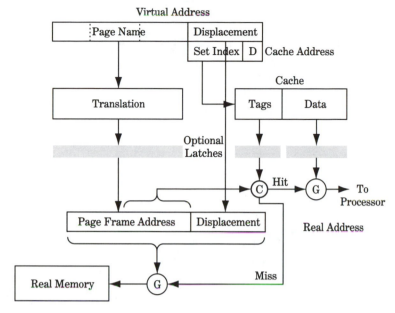

FIGURE 4.4 Pipelined real address cache.

If a constant stream of addresses is presented to a pipelined real address cache, this cache scheme will run very close to the pipeline rate of one cache access per clock. The effective clock period, however, will be determined by the maximum of the delays through the address translation path or the cache access time. The effective cache access time is

$$\text{Eff. } t_{ea} = \text{Max}[\text{WATT}, t_{ea}].$$

It may be unnecessary to use strict pipelining with latches; a technique called *maximum rate pipelining* does not use latches and is discussed in Chapter 6. The result of the address translation and the cache's output should arrive at the compare circuit at approximately the same time and then can gate out the data on a valid compare. Provisions must be made for long translations on a TLB miss.

Designers of the IBM S/360 pioneered the use of the pipelined real cache [MATI77]. The IBM 3090 has continued this cache design [TUCK86] as have cache designs in other processors. Figure 4.5 shows the pipelined real address cache address formulation for the IBM S/370/168, the Intel i486, and the IBM RS/6000.

The IBM S/360/168 cache is early select; the displacement provides the set index and displacement into a table of cache address information. The real sector names are found by translating the page name with the user ID via hash tables and comparing it with the real sector name tags

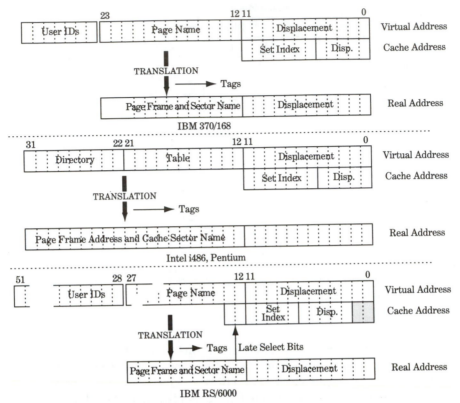

FIGURE 4.5 IBM 370/168, Intel i486, and Pentium, IBM RS/6000 cache address generation.

in the cache address cache. The output of the table is concatenated with the 5-bit displacement field to form the cache address itself.

The Intel i486 also uses the pipelined real cache organization. Although I am unfamiliar with implementation details of the i486, I believe that it does not have latches. The i486 cache is late select. The set index and displacement select the data from the cache sector that was identified by the translated directory and table names. For the i486, with a page size of 4 Kbytes and a 4-way set associative cache, a maximum cache size is 16 Kbytes.

The RS/6000 cache is another variation of the pipelined real cache. The 12-bit virtual address displacement accesses four 16-Kbyte caches in parallel as shown in Figure 2.20. Each of these four caches has 32 sets, 4 sectors with one block, and 128 bytes per sector. After the virtual page name and ID are translated, the two LSBs provide a late select of one of the four caches. Documentation on the RS/6000 indicates that latches are used to delineate the stages of this pipeline.

The PowerPC 601 changed the cache mapping of the RS/6000 by dropping the translated late select scheme. The 12-bit displacement is divided into a 6-bit set index and a 6-bit displacement; the cache is 8-way set associative. The 20 bits of the translated virtual page name are compared with the eight tags of the selected set. The organization of the cache is (64, 8, 1, 64) for a 32-Kbyte cache, half the size of the RS/6000 cache.

4.1.3 *Virtual Address Cache*

A solution to the performance problem with real address caches is the elimination of the translation latency by addressing the cache with virtual addresses, as shown in Figure 4.6. With this cache scheme, the virtual address is allocated into fields for accessing the cache. These fields are the usual ones: sector name, set index, and displacement. This scheme allows full flexibility in selecting these fields so that a cache of any size can be addressed. In parallel with the cache access, the page name is translated and concatenated with the displacement to form the real memory address.

Because page name translation is required only on a cache miss, the effective access time of this organization in the absence of cache misses

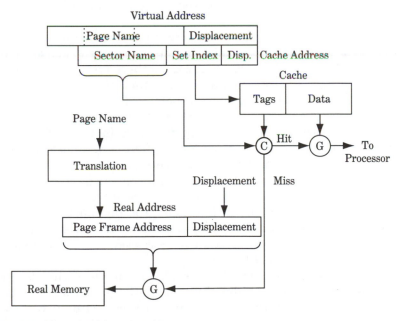

FIGURE 4.6 Virtual address cache.

is merely the access time of the cache.

$$\text{Eff. } t_{ea} = t_{ea}.$$

Synonyms are a major problem with a virtual address cache that does not use the entire page name for the sector name because two virtual names can refer to the same address in the cache. Figure 4.6 illustrates this problem in that not all of the page name is used as the sector name. A cache hit signifies that the AU has been stored in the cache under the page name that is currently being used and the AU is loaded into the processor. However, what happens if there is another access with a different page name that has the same LSBs and displacement but differs only in its MSBs? This access will use the same sector name and find the same AU in the cache.

What is to be done? A solution is to ensure that different MSBs of the page name are not used if a synonym will be a problem. M.D. Hill [HILL86] points out that most context switches call for a change of virtual address space. Thus there must be a guarantee against two processes using the same symbolic addresses that would permit the new process to read valid but incorrect data from the cache. One solution is to provide the capability to flush the cache on a context switch. Another solution is to extend the sector name to the length of the full virtual address. This is very expensive as the cache tags must be extended as well.

Another problem occurs if the operating system permits synonyms. If there is a cache miss, the miss is not conclusive evidence that the referenced AU is not in the cache; it can be there under a different page name. If the miss is processed, a new instance of the same variable is placed in the cache, which produces a potential coherency problem.

To prevent two instances of the value, there must be a search of all the real addresses of all the sets and sectors in the cache to see if the requested value is resident under a different virtual address. This procedure requires performing an inverse mapping of the cache sector name (that is, finding its real address) and comparing it to the inverse mappings of all the blocks in the cache. If this search of real addresses finds that the value is really in the cache, the tag must be adjusted so that the access can proceed without processing the miss. If the search fails, there is a true cache miss that is processed in the knowledge that a coherency problem is not being created.

The process of searching for a synonym in the cache can be accomplished in hardware; the Intel i860XP provides an example [INTE92a]. This processor has split instruction and data caches that both have support to prevent synonyms from becoming coherency prob-

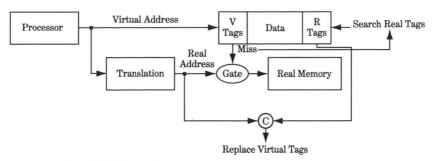

FIGURE 4.7   Intel i860XP caches.

lems. The caches are organized as (128, 4, 1, 32), and each sector has both virtual and real tags, as shown in Figure 4.7.

The cache is accessed with the index and sector name taken from the virtual address. If the tag matches, the cache access is normal for both a read or write. However, if the tag does not match, there is a potential miss, and a search is made of the real tags by comparing them with the now-available real address. If there is no match on the real sector name, there is a true miss and a bus cycle to the memory is initiated with the translated (real) address. Table 4.2 shows the action taken for four cases of read-write and hit-miss on the search of the real tags.

It can be seen that this system permits synonyms and ensures that there cannot be duplicate entries in the cache that can cause coherency problems.

The virtual address cache address fields of the i860 and SPUR processor [HILL86] are shown in Figure 4.8. The i860 has a very large virtual page, 2^{22} bytes, and an unextended virtual address that is consistent with the intended purpose of this processor. The caches are organized as (128, 4, 1, 32), and they carry a long (20 bits) tag.

Access	Real Tag Hit	Real Tag Miss
Read	Use entry and replace virtual tag with virtual page name that caused the miss	Place block returned from memory into cache and update both the virtual and real tags
Write	Write to block and replace virtual tag with the virtual page name that caused the miss	Use no-allocate policy and write direct to memory

TABLE 4.2   i860 synonym processing.

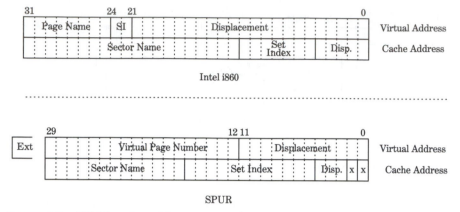

FIGURE 4.8   SPUR cache address generation.

The SPUR cache is organized as (4096, 32, 1) for 128 Kbytes and is word addressed. There are 13 tag bits with each sector along with a valid bit; the cache uses the write through policy. The two MSBs of the virtual address index into a table to select a virtual address extension of eight bits, giving a 38-bit global virtual address. This global virtual address is translated via tables if there is a cache miss.

D. Roberts et al. [ROBE90] and C. E. Wu [WU93] discuss the MIPS R6000 processors that use virtual first-level caches for instruction and data. However, the second-level cache is indexed by a translated real address while its tags are virtual. This hybrid scheme uses the second-level cache to help resolve synonyms and reduce the size of the on-chip TLB.

4.1.4 *Restricted Virtual Caches*

Restricted virtual caches are special cases of virtual caches. This organization combines the positive features of a virtual cache and a pipelined real cache. As shown in Figure 4.9, the cache set index plus displacement are constrained to be no longer than the displacement field of the virtual address. A portion of the full page name becomes the sector name of the cache address and is compared to the tags. A cache miss uses the translated virtual address to access the memory.

The advantage of this cache organization is performance because a page name translation is not required before the cache is accessed and pipeline delays of the pipelined real cache are eliminated. The problem, however, of synonyms remains and, as with pipelined real caches, the cache size is limited to the address span of the displacement (page size) times the degree of associativity. The size of the cache, once the page size is fixed, can be increased only by increasing the degree of associativity.

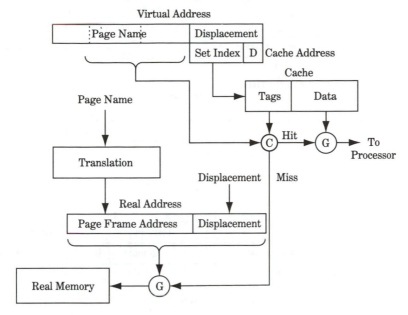

FIGURE 4.9 Restricted virtual cache.

Two examples of restricted virtual caches are the MC68030 and MC68040. Figure 4.10 shows the address generation for these two designs. These two caches are both on-chip and are accessed in parallel with the TLB. If a cache miss occurs, the off-chip memory is addressed by the real already-translated address.

The caches of the MC68040 use a smaller portion of the virtual address displacement for the set index and displacement. The MC68040 has a larger page—4 Kbytes or 8 Kbytes—than does the MC68030, and the full displacement field is not used for generating the cache address. The 6-bit set index is taken from the page displacement field of the virtual address. Each set consists of four words, each selected by the 2-bit displacement field. Note that the number of sets or the number of words in a set, or both, can be increased by a factor of 8 for future expansion.

4.1.5 *Summary*

Table 4.3 summarizes the characteristics of the four cache design options. There is no clear advantage to any one of these designs, as illustrated by the fact that all are used in contemporary processors. Note again that there are no known implementations of a cache with a real index and virtual tags.

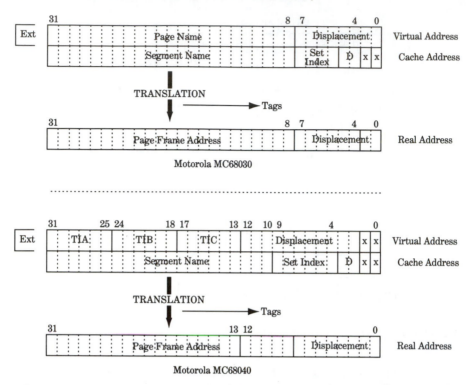

FIGURE 4.10   MC68030 and MC68040 restricted virtual caches.

Cache Type	Synonym Problem	Coherency Problem	Performance	Cache Address Size	Example System
Real	No	Yes	Translation delay	Unlimited	VAX 11/780
Pipelined real	No	Yes	Pipeline	Limited by degree of associativity	i486 PowerPC 601
Virtual	Yes	No	No delays	Unlimited	i860 SPUR
Restricted virtual	Yes	No	No delays	Limited by degree of associativity	MC68040

TABLE 4.3   Cache characteristics.

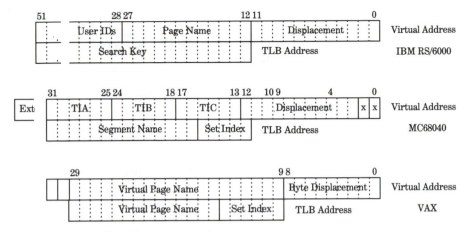

FIGURE 4.11   TLB address generation.

C.E. Wu [WU93] performed extensive simulations for evaluating the performance of these cache addressing options, cache organizations, and replacement policies. They conclude that pipelined real cache or the restricted virtual cache using MRU replacement provides the best choice for high-performance computers. These results are confirmed by the number of processors that use this cache today.

4.1.6 *TLB Addressing*

Translation Lookaside Buffers (TLB) are cache-like buffers that contain pretranslated page names. The purpose of a TLB is to reduce the latency of a page name translation when a reference to main memory is required. Because a TLB translates only the page name, the displacement field of a virtual address is usually (there are exceptions) not a component of the TLB address. Three examples of TLB addressing are shown in Figure 4.11.

The IBM RS/6000 has an associative TLB as shown in Figure 3.35. The 40-bit extended page name is used as the key to search the tag field of the TLB. The MC68040 has a 4-way set associative TLB with 16 sets. The set index and segment name are extracted directly from the virtual address. The VAX TLB has 32 sets and is 2-way set associative.

4.2 I/O System Addressing Design Issues

Section 4.1 discussed the issue of cache and TLB addressing with either real or virtual addresses. The same issue is present with the I/O system;

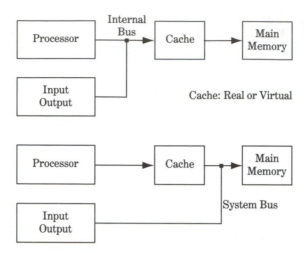

FIGURE 4.12   Data transfer paths.

should the I/O system be in real or virtual address space? The address-ing issue is usually only a consideration for the case when an I/O process is writing into the system main memory and ultimately the I/O system must provide real addresses for storing data in the memory. As will be discussed in this section, designers must consider certain performance and coherency problems with I/O systems.

Before discussing I/O addressing, I will discuss the issue of routing data between the I/O processor and the memory. Figure. 4.12 shows two ways of routing data: (1) I/O via the cache and (2) I/O via the system bus to main memory.

Placement of the I/O transfer path impacts two areas: performance and coherency. The performance issue here is that if the I/O data path is via the cache, valuable cache cycles can be stolen from the processor. If the processors have a multiple cycle CPI (such as the Amdahl 470/v6), this is not a significant problem. But, with the I/O data path via the system bus to memory, bus cycles can be stolen that, with heavy bus loading, can impact the time for servicing a cache miss. Recall from Chapter 2 that bus utilization with a single processor can be approxi-mately 50%.

With modern pipelined processors that can generate two cache ac-cesses per clock, loading the bus seems to be a less serious problem than loading the cache. Data caches, however, are not as loaded as instruction caches and warrant investigation for data cache routing. In addition, contemporary microprocessors with on-chip caches transfer via the sys-tem bus—a practical consideration based on the need to minimize pin count. Only older processors without on-chip caches transfer via the internal bus and cache. Given these considerations, the design of choice today is to route via the system bus to memory. For systems that route the I/O data via the system bus, the issue of the logical consistency or coherency becomes a significant design consideration which is discussed in the following sections.

4.2.1 *Cache Coherency*

The literature discusses the concept of coherency, discussed briefly in Section 4.0, in terms of shared-variable cache coherency for shared memory multiprocessors [CENS78, STEN90]. As pointed out, however, in [LEON87, GROC89, CRAW90], coherency problems can exist in uniprocessors with a concurrent I/O. Knuth [KNUT66] and Dijkstra [DIJK71] provide seminal references to the general issues of coherency. The following is an informal definition of a coherent system:

> A memory system is coherent if the value returned on a LOAD instruction is always the value given by the latest STORE instruction with the same address [CENS78].

van de Goor [VAND89] states that this definition is too weak to cover multiple-access problems found in multiprocessors or even processors with I/O channels. van de Goor's definition covers the case of a Read-Modify-Write operation that is sometimes used for synchronization, as in a Test and Set instruction (discussed in Section 6.7).

> A memory scheme is coherent if the value, returned on a LOAD instruction, is always the value of the latest STORE instruction to the same address; and a multiple-access operation has to be executed atomically—that is, excluding any other operation to the same address.

Based upon his definition, van de Goor gives two conditions that must be met to achieve coherency.

1. There is a single path to every AU.
2. There is a single copy of every AU.

Clearly both of these conditions can never be met in any reasonable computer system. The one path consideration is usually achieved, in part, for memory if the system contains only one memory bus. Dijkstra [DIJK71] states the requirement in another way, with regard to mutual exclusion, when he says: "The switch granting access to store on word basis provides a built in mutual exclusion." Having only a single copy of every AU is difficult for systems with caches, register files, TLBs, and other such resources where an AU can reside in more than one space at a time.

Ensuring coherency and resolving true dependencies are closely related issues. Coherency relates to *values*, while true dependencies relate to *spaces* (discussed in Chapter 8). However, since values are bound to spaces during execution, the solutions to both problems revolve around managing spaces.

The potential for the lack of coherency in a shared memory multiprocessor with private caches is well documented. However, the potential coherency problems associated with an I/O process that reads and writes in memory concurrently with processor reads and writes are not covered as well. Consider the following operations and the related problem spaces.

Cache write through. As discussed in Chapter 2, if the memory system has a write buffer, the value in the buffer can be different from the value in the memory. Thus, reads from the cache must be checked against the value in the buffer.

Cache write back. This operation mode can only have a coherency problem if another processor (such as autonomous I/O systems) references the memory before the write-back has been accomplished.

A lack of coherency arises from the following situation: An AU has been fetched into the cache, loaded into the processor's register files, modified, and stored from the processor into the cache with a write-through policy. During the time from when the AU is modified in the processor to when the store into the main memory is completed, the AU is incoherent. That is, a read reference to the same main memory address by an I/O processor during this time will not produce the most current value of the AU. A write-back policy increases the time of incoherency.

Designers use four basic methods to maintain cache coherency for either a multiprocessor with multiple caches or a uniprocessor with a cache and concurrent I/O systems.

Method 1. *Noncached shared-variables.* Shared-variables are prohibited from being cached. Thus, all references to shared-variables must be served from the main memory. This method is sometimes called *static coherency protection.*

The VAX 8800 and the i486 are two examples of processors that use Method 1 to ensure that coherency problems do not occur with I/O operations. A buffer area in memory, addressed with real addresses, is reserved for I/O, and interlocks are provided to ensure that information in the buffer is not placed in the cache until the I/O operation is completed. These processors reserve 64-Kbyte buffers for I/O. When the I/O transfers are in the assigned buffer spaces, the system inhibits the detection of possible false alarm coherency problems, as they cannot occur. Note that this method depends on the software to ensure that coherency problems do not occur.

Method 2. *One space for shared-variables.* Shared variables are cached in only one cache. This cache may be a dedicated cache or may be one of the multiple caches in the system.

This method requires that I/O be via the internal bus to/from the cache. The only known example of the use of this method is found in the Amdahl 470/v6. The performance penalty is too great for this method to be used with today's processors.

Method 3. *Write invalidate.* This method requires that a write to a shared-variable result in the invalidation of all other instances of that variable. Two forms of invalidation have been used: total invalidation of the cache and selective invalidation of the invalid AU [CASE78].

Method 4. *Write update (write broadcast).* This method requires that a write to a shared-variable be broadcast to all other instances of that variable, which are then updated.

Site [SITE80] generalizes Methods 3 and 4 by giving the design principle involved whenever buffers of any type (for example, caches, register files, and TLBs) are used to improve a processor's performance. This principle is: "If a datum is copied and the copy is to match the original at all times, then all changes to the original must cause the copy to be immediately updated or invalidated."

For both Methods 3 and 4, all caches must have the ability to detect a write from another processor to a variable currently resident and either invalidate that entry or update it. For the uniprocessor case with only one cache and one I/O port, the bus activity is observed to detect a write from the I/O port to the memory that should either invalidate or update the cache, a process called *bus snooping*. With the VAX, this action is called *watching the bus* [LEON87].

Methods 3 and 4 for maintaining cache coherency result in significant overhead to the memory system. If a write results in an update, all of the caches must halt and perform the update cycle even if the AU in the cache will not be later referenced. On the other hand, an invalidation strategy requires that the valid bits be turned off in all of the caches, causing a cache miss if the AU is later referenced. Weber [WEBE89] presents a study on invalidation patterns that shows 0.3 to 3.0 invalidations per shared-variable write for systems with 4 to 16 processors. Note that this data will not apply to the uniprocessor I/O coherency problem, which is the subject of this book, and no published data is known to exist.

If the caches are multilevel, the system must contain a method of identifying all of the caches that require invalidation or updating. The complexity of this task is reduced if multilevel inclusion is enforced.

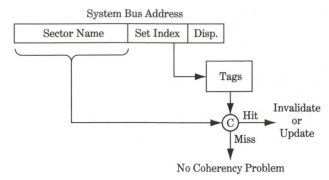

FIGURE 4.13   Snoopy controller.

4.2.2 *Snoopy Controllers*

As noted above, the problem of coherency exists in a uniprocessor with a cache and an I/O system with or without virtual memory capabilities. I/O reads-and-writes over the system bus have a policy that depends on the types of addresses used by the cache and the I/O system. The situations that will have a coherency problem can be detected by means of a *Snoopy Controller*, as shown in Figure 4.13.

When there is a write-to-memory by the I/O processor, a test must be performed to see if the address is present in the cache, indicating a possible cache coherency problem. With a snoopy controller, the system bus accesses a copy of the cache tags, or the tags themselves, with the set index and compares the accessed tag with the sector name. In general the snoopy controller is accessed by every bus. If there is a hit on the tags, the sector is resident in the cache and must be either invalidated or updated. If there is a miss, there is no coherency problem.

The snoopy controller function requires access to cache tags, a capability that can be provided in one of three ways. The design selection is based on cost and performance criteria.

Shared tags. One set of tags is shared between the users (I/O and processor) with the potential of a structural hazard. Concurrent accesses to the tags will result in a loss of performance, but sharing eliminates any tag coherency problem.

The least costly method for providing a snoopy controller is for the I/O processor to steal a cache cycle, access the cache tags themselves via the index field, and compare the tags with the sector name. This method eliminates the cost of duplicating the cache tags but has the problem of reducing the system's performance due to cache cycle stealing. As a point of interest, if one directory of tags for the system exists as compared to a directory of each cache's tags, the system is called *directory based*.

Replicated tags. There is one set of tags for each user. There will be no structural hazards, but coherency of tag information itself must be maintained.

A data coherency check is made by accessing memories containing replicated cache tags that can be accessed in parallel with cache cycles. Each of the tag memories for each of the sets must be replicated. Obviously, the tag memory of the snoopy controller must contain an exact image of the cache tag memories in order for the tags to be coherent. Thus, when a change is made to the cache's content that modifies a tag field, this change must be reflected in all the snoopy controller's tags.

With a replicated snoopy tag memory, the tag memories must be as large as the total tag memory of the cache. For a high degree of associativity, this can be a significant burden on the snoopy memory, another reason for the preference of direct caches in contemporary processors. The IBM S/370/195 reduces the cost of its snoopy controller by snooping only the tags of one cache sector by the replacement policy, thus restricting I/O operations to the snooped cache sector.

Shared tags with multiports. Concurrent access can be performed without a loss in performance and without the tag concurrency problem.

The third approach to snoopy capability is to make the processor's cache tag memory multiported. This approach gives the performance of replicated tag memories at a relatively small cost. This approach also eliminates the tag memory coherency problem as there is only one copy of tag information. The Intel Pentium and the PowerPC 601 processors provide examples of multiported snoopy cache tag memory.

For the i486 and MC88200, snooping is used only for multiprocessor systems, not for I/O. For these processors, duplication of tags is an unacceptable cost over the tags of the on-chip data caches. Writes to memory should be infrequent for small multiprocessors and the snooping function using the cache tags themselves eliminates the problem of tag coherency with replicated tags. The Intel i486 and the MC88200 use invalidation with the consequence that a subsequent reference to the invalidated location by the processor will cause a cache miss. For processors with on-chip caches, invalidation is the preferred design when the processors are used in a multiprocessor configuration. The processor detecting the conflict broadcasts an invalidation signal to all the other processors.

I/O Snoopy Operation

The snoopy controller must detect four cases that are the combinations of Read or Write of memory and the addressed sector being cached or not cached. Each of these four cases calls for a different action, as summarized in Table 4.4. The snoopy controller must detect the presence

Operation	Sector in Cache?	
	Yes	No
Write to memory	Invalidate or update cache and write to memory	Write to memory
Read from memory	Write through cache: Read from memory Write back cache: Read from cache and write back	Read from memory

TABLE 4.4   I/O cache coherency.

of the sector in the cache, comprehend the type of I/O operation, and command the proper action.

The first case consists of an I/O write to memory and a sector that is not cached. In this case, no coherency problem exists and the write can proceed without a problem. The second case is an I/O write to memory and a sector that is cached. There are two basic design options: (1) write to memory and invalidate the sector in the cache, or (2) write to memory and update the sector in the cache.

The third case occurs when there is an I/O read from memory of a sector that is not in the cache. In this case, the read proceeds with the danger of a future coherency problem. Finally, the fourth case occurs when there is an I/O read from memory and a sector that is in the cache. If the cache is write through, the read is made from memory. If the cache is write back, the read is made from the cache. These policies ensure that the most current value is sent to the I/O system.

There are a number of papers describing the performance of various snoopy cache systems when used in multiprocessors [ARCH86] and [EGGE89]. To my knowledge, however, no similar published data exists on the performance for the uniprocessor case with I/O operations.

4.2.3 *DMA I/O Configurations*

With the above background, I turn to the design options for virtual memory systems with caches and concurrent DMA I/O, that is, the design options for addressing the cache and the type of address used by the DMA I/O system. The term DMA I/O is used here to signify not only DMA but programmable channel controllers as found in systems such as the S/360. Table 4.5 shows the four design options for real/virtual cache and real/virtual DMA I/O addressing. In the discussions to follow on these four design options, attention in the figures is focused on the addresses. The data routing for each of these cases is via the

Design Options	Cache	DMA I/O
1	Real	Real
2	Real	Virtual
3	Virtual	Real
4	Virtual	Virtual

TABLE 4.5 Cache and DMA I/O addressing.

system bus as shown in Figure 4.12. For expository purposes, Figures 4.14 to 4.17 show the snoopy controller with replicated tags.

Design Option 1, *real cache—real DMA I/O*. The cache is accessed with real addresses, as shown in Figure 4.14, and the DMA I/O processor writes into the memory with real addresses. A coherency problem can result if a DMA I/O port is writing into a cache sector of memory that is resident in the cache. If a DMA I/O-write is allowed to proceed, an incoherent situation can result between the memory and the cache. The bus snooper, indicated by *S*, observes all addresses passing across the bus and the addresses are compared to tags in the cache that are represented in the snoopy controller. If a match is found, the cache is directed to invalidate or update the sector in the cache.

Design Option 2, *real cache—virtual DMA I/O*. The cache is accessed with real addresses, as shown in Figure 4.15, while the DMA I/O processor uses virtual addresses. The virtual DMA I/O system addresses must be translated to give real memory addresses. This translation can be accomplished either by time sharing or multiporting one address translation system or by duplicating the address translation system. Time sharing one translation system may create a performance problem, while duplication has a cost and a coherency penalty because the duplicate tags must also be coherent.

Design Option 3, *virtual cache—real DMA I/O*. A virtual cache with

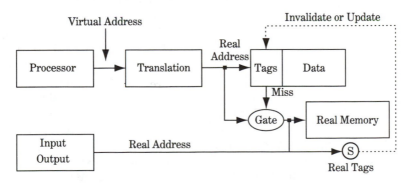

FIGURE 4.14 Real cache—real DMA I/O.

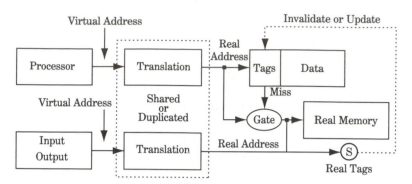

FIGURE 4.15 Real cache—virtual DMA I/O.

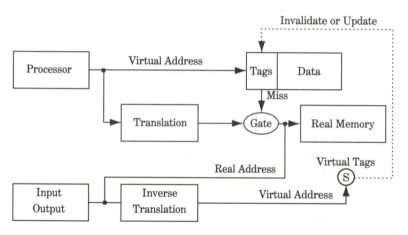

FIGURE 4.16 Virtual cache—real DMA I/O.

a real DMA I/O system presents a major design problem. Figure 4.16 shows this configuration. The cache is addressed with virtual addresses and the DMA I/O processor reads or writes into memory with real addresses that, in themselves, require no translation. A coherency problem, however, can exist if a sector is in the cache from the real address space being used by the DMA I/O. This problem is detected by performing an inverse address translation (real addresses to virtual addresses) that is applied to the tags of the snoopy controller. The cache sector is either invalidated or updated depending upon the detection of a coherency problem. The inverse translation system is usually called an *inverse translator* or a *reverse translation buffer*.

Design Option 4, *virtual cache—virtual DMA I/O*. Figure 4.17 illustrates this design in which both the cache and the DMA I/O processor use virtual addresses. Thus, the DMA I/O processor virtual addresses must be translated into real addresses for accessing memory. The ad-

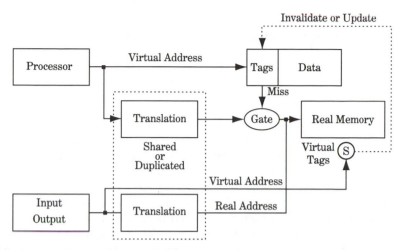

FIGURE 4.17 Virtual cache—virtual DMA I/O.

dress translation can be by a shared or replicated translation facility. Because the address translation system for the processor is used only on cache misses, it seems reasonable to share the translation facility. A shared system should have a minimum performance penalty plus the elimination of translation table coherency problems.

4.2.4 *Processor Control Over Snoopy Controllers*

For a number of reasons, the processor needs to be able to exert control over the snoopy controller. This is particlarly true for designs where the snoopy controller time shares the cache tags between the processor and DMA I/O. As discussed in Chapter 5, DMA I/O data transfer activity can be relatively high, in the range of one to eight bytes per instruction executed. Thus, there is the potential for a cache access conflict every eight or so instructions—a significant performance hit due to locking out the cache from the processor. For these systems, it is desirable to have the capability of inhibiting snooping to improve performance. Furthermore, for systems that have program control over the data cache for write through or write back, the snoopy controller must respond properly for invalidation or update on a snoopy hit, as noted in Table 4.4.

From the above discussion, the basic cache effective access time model from Chapter 2 can be modified, as follows, to comprehend shared snoopy accesses of the data cache tags. The tag snoop by the processor is accounted for in the normalized access time of the cache as

$$t_{ea} = 1 + P_{miss}T + P_{sn} \times t_{sn}$$

where P_{sn} is the probability of a snoopy cache access concurrent with a normal cache access and t_{sn} denotes the time to snoop the cache, usually one cache cycle or 1. The net effect of shared snoopy cache access is to lengthen the effective cache access time, in the absence of a miss, from 1 cycle to $1 + P_{sn}$ cycles. High DMA I/O activity ($P_{sn} \to 1$) can result in a significant performance penalty. For cases where snoopy activity is this high, the snoopy tag memory should be replicated or multiported.

For systems with write through caches, all DMA I/O reads from memory can be accomplished without accessing the cache, as shown in Table 4.4. Only DMA I/O writes to memory need to access the cache. This policy has the potential for reducing the need to access the cache by approximately 50% and provides an argument in favor of write-through caches. If the cache, in the example above, is write through, the effective access time would be approximately 1.13 rather than the 1.27 with a write-back cache.

The MC68040 provides an example of a snoopy controller under control of the processor [MOTO89]. Within the status word there are two control bits (SC1, SC0) for the snoopy controller interpreted as shown in Table 4.6.

The MC68040 shares the cache tags with the snoopy controller. Thus there are two access paths and priority must be established for access; snooping has priority over data accesses from the processor. Also, the MC68040 snoopy controller provides functions to support multiprocessors that exceed the requirements of DMA I/O data transfers only. Interested readers should see [MOTO89] for additional details.

The PowerPC 601 shares the on-chip data cache tags with the snooping function. To reduce the cycle stealing from bus snoops, explicit control

Control		Requested Snoopy Operation	
SC1	SC0	Read Access	Write Access
0	0	Inhibit	Inhibit
0	1	Read from cache	Update cache, write mem.
1	0	Read from memory	Invalidate cache, write mem.
1	1	Reserved, inhibit	Reserved, inhibit

TABLE 4.6   MC68040 snoopy control.

must be asserted by the bus. There are two bus signals, TS' (transfer start) and GBL' (Global, and I/O signal), that must be simultaneously asserted to qualify a snoop operation. When a snoop is initiated and there is a hit on the tags, the processor emits signals to the bus that are used by other processors. Motorola [MOTO93] provides details on the behavior of loads for different bus operations and cache sector states. Similar information is provided for stores as well.

4.3 Other Considerations

This section will briefly discuss three other considerations with I/O systems: memory-mapped I/O, the MESI cache coherency protocol, and snooping on write queues. Some of these issues are relevant to multiprocessor systems and are only briefly discussed.

4.3.1 *Memory-Mapped I/O*

A number of processors augment the DMA I/O systems described above with memory-mapped I/O. This form of I/O reserves a region of the processor's address space for I/O control and data registers. Transfers to and from I/O can then be accomplished with the normal load and store instructions of the processor. The advantage of this form of I/O is low latency; the disadvantages are the loss of some address space, the use of program space to explicitly perform I/O, and complications to the bus so that the addresses can be recognized.

With memory-mapped I/O, the virtual addresses created by the processor must be translated into real addresses before they can be placed on the bus. Thus, the TLB will be called upon to hold an entry for I/O. The protection afforded in the TLB is available for I/O as well as normal data movement due to page faults. A significant design consideration is whether or not to cache the address space reserved for I/O. Write-back caches are unacceptable because of the long delay that can occur with an output operation.

The PowerPC 601 uses a bit in its segment registers (discussed in Chapter 3) to identify when an address is to memory or to a reserved space for memory-mapped I/O [MOTO93]. Likewise, the Pentium uses memory-mapped I/O while providing direct I/O instructions.

4.3.2 *Cache Coherency Protocols*

The previous discussion on the response of a cache to a snoopy hit assumes a simple model of cache behavior; the block is either valid or invalid [DUBO88]. This is an appropriate model for a simple write-through cache in a uniprocessor because a sector can be in only one of two states.

As discussed previously, when the snoopy controller finds that a write to memory by the I/O will invalidate the contents of the cache, the cache sector can be either invalidated or updated depending upon the protocol selected by the designer.

With multiprocessors, the write-through protocol creates bus traffic that can be detrimental to the performance of the system, leading to the use of the write-back protocol. With a multiplicity of caches, the problem ᵒf coherency must be addressed, and a number of protocols have been investigated for this purpose. Some of these are: Write-Once protocol with four states, the Synapse protocol with three states, Berkeley protocol with four states, the Illinois protocol with four states, the Firefly protocol with three states, and the Dragon protocol with four states. These protocols are described by Archibald and Baer [ARCH86].

In the early 1980s, a working committee of IEEE started drafting a standard protocol that would be used with the IEEE Futurebus [GALL91] and a write-back protocol. The result of this early work is a five-state protocol called MOESI for Modified, Owned, Exclusive, Shared, or Invalid. Table 4.7 shows the state of the three sector control bits—valid, dirty, and shared—along with the five state names of the MOESI protocol. Note that if the sector is invalid, the clean and shared bits are don't cares.

The five-state protocol would be very expensive to implement for on-chip caches. Motorola's Greiner noted that the owned state could be eliminated if the modified and shared states were made illegal at the same time [GALL91]. This results in the MESI protocol that has been adopted as an IEEE standard and is considerably less costly to implement [IEEE90].

A sequence of events that must be taken for a read or write for each of the four states (eight events) is specified in the standard. The design of a cache consistency protocol is tied closely to the design of the bus

Sector Control Bits

Valid	Dirty	Shared	MOESI	MESI
Valid	Clean	Shared	Shared	Shared
Valid	Clean	Not shared	Exclusive	Exclusive
Valid	Dirty	Shared	Owned	Not permitted
Valid	Dirty	Not shared	Modified	Modified
Invalid	X	X	Invalid	Invalid

TABLE 4.7 Cache sector coherency control.

because signals must be transmitted over the bus to inform the other processors about what is happening. Thus, there must be signal lines on the bus to permit a cache to signal to other processors a code, indicating the state of the cache sector and the transition that is being made.

The MESI protocol is used with the unified caches of the PowerPC 601 [MOTO93] and the internal data cache and external unified cache of the Pentium [INTE93, INTE93a]. The Pentium on-chip instruction cache implements only the invalid, shared portion of the protocol as the instruction cache is read only and does not have to contend with data.

4.3.3 *Snooping on Write Queues*

As discussed in Chapter 2, processor writes update the cache before the block is written back to memory over the bus. This action presents the potential for a coherency problem, and the PowerPC 601 is an example of how coherency is maintained [MOTO93]. The write queue (buffer) holds a dirty block (eight words or 32 bytes) that is being written out to memory as a result of a cache miss. Each entry of the write queue carries the virtual address for the write along with the block of data. A bus action from an I/O operation that is to be snooped on the processor is presented as a key to the addresses that are associatively searched. If there is a hit on a write queue element, the block is first loaded into memory before it is used as an update to the cache of the snooping master.

If the source of the snoop signal is a DMA I/O read operation, the transfer to memory is accomplished before the read. If the DMA I/O operation is a write, the DMA I/O write to memory is completed and the contents of the write queue are erased.

Configuration	DMA I/O via System Bus
Real cache—real DMA I/O	VAX*, IBM 370
Real cache—virtual DMA I/O	
Pipelined real cache—real DMA I/O	i386, i486, Pentium
Pipelined real cache—virtual DMA I/O	IBM RS/6000, PowerPC 601
Virtual cache—real DMA I/O	i860*
Virtual cache—virtual DMA I/O	SPARC II
Restricted virtual cache—real DMA I/O	
Restricted virtual cache—virtual DMA I/O	MC68030, MC68040
* Not snooped, software controls coherency.	

TABLE **4.8** Example cache—DMA I/O configurations.

4.3.4 *Summary*

Consider the four methods of cache access, discussed previously, combined with the two variations of DMA I/O system addressing, real and
virtual, giving eight possible system configurations. Table 4.8 shows
these configurations and identifies known computers for each.

Six of the eight organizations are represented by actual implementations. I can only speculate on the reason for the omission of the real
cache—virtual DMA I/O and restricted virtual cache—real DMA I/O.

5

Interleaved Memory and Disk Systems

5.0 Overview

This chapter discusses two important subjects, interleaved memory and disk systems, that are usually given only minor attention. Interleaved memory, which is used to provide high bandwidth, was of great importance prior to the advent of practical high-speed memories for caches. Currently, innovative architectures of modern DRAMS and various forms of interleaving are receiving design and research attention. Disk technology has had a remarkable life since the first commercial disks in 1956, the IBM 350 RAMAC. Disks have survived all predictions that the technology could go no further; indeed, cost and performance of disks have continued to improve.

5.1 Interleaved Memory

Interleaved memories provide high-memory bandwidth by distributing the read or write accesses over a number of memory modules, which is a form of parallelism. The array disk to be described in Section 5.2.3 is another instance of memory interleaving. Early research into interleaving was concurrent with and a "back up" to hierarchical memory research. In the late 1950s and 1960s no one was sure if cache technology development would be successful.

The first known reference to interleaving is found in a description of the IBM Stretch [BLOC59]: "The memories themselves are interleaved so that the first two memories have their address distributed modulo 2 and the other four are interleaved modulo 4."

A later reference to the IBM S/360 [FAGG64] points out that: "When accesses are made to sequential storage addresses, the storage units operate in an interleaved fashion."

Pirtle [PIRT67] observes: "... the addresses are distributed over an n module memory so that address 0 is in $m(0)$, address 1 is in $m(1)$ and, in general, address X is in $m(i)$ where $i \equiv X$ modulo n."

We can see from these statements that there are two uses of the word *interleaved*. One use concerns the *units* or *modules*. Interleaved modules subdivide the module cycle time into clock periods that establish the streaming rate of the memory system. The degree of module interleaving is m and is formally defined as the number of requests that can be issued by the processor in one memory module cycle [BURN70]. Note that the clock period of the memory and the bus system are related as $m = t_m/t_c$ where t_m denotes the memory cycle time and t_c the bus or processor clock time. The other use of the term interleaving concerns *addresses*. Interleaving addresses across modules establishes the sequence of module access for a stream of requests. The degree of address interleaving is n, which is defined as the number of memory modules over which the addresses are interleaved [BURN70].

In this chapter, memory systems are described for $1 < m \leq n$. With many systems, the two degrees of interleaving are equal; that is, $m = n$. However, with some systems, such as those found with supercomputers, the degree of address interleaving is greater than the degree of module interleaving; that is, $m < n$, which is called *superinterleaving* and is discussed in Section 5.1.3.

Interleaving presents two questions of interest to researchers. First, can interleaved memories provide enhanced bandwidth to supply instruction and data streams to a processor? And second, what are the design parameters of an interleaved memory that supports vector reads and writes of supercomputers? With the success of caches, the first research objective has almost disappeared as an interesting topic. The second research topic is still an area of active research and is discussed in more detail in Section 5.1.3. Note that the IBM RT uses a noncache interleaved memory system [ROWL86] to provided instruction and data bandwidth.

The requirement for accessing vectors comes from two sources. The first source is found in the main memory references of supercomputers. Scientific programs frequently access arrays of data stored in memory as vectors. The second source is found in the interface between a cache and the main memory. A block of AUs are transferred between these two memories; this block is a vector of length 4 to 16 and is discussed in Chapter 2.

Interleaved memories are ideal for providing high bandwidth access to a long vector of data (either read or write). An interleaved memory requires two addresses: the address of the module and the address of

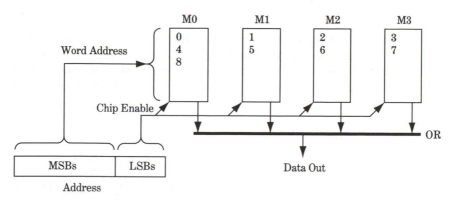

FIGURE 5.1   Four-way interleaved memory.

the word within the module. Low-order interleaving generates these two addresses by dividing the memory address by the address interleaving degree n: the quotient is the word address presented to each module and the reminder selects the module. This division by an integer power of two is a trivial operation for designs having a degree of interleaving that is an integer power of two.

Consider a memory of total size 2^s, with $m = n = 4$, as shown in Figure 5.1. The four modules are addressed by the two LSBs of the address, and the word within the addressed module is selected by the high-order bits. This process is called *low-order interleaving*.

Addressable units are stored in the modules according to the sequence

Module	Addresses
0	$0, 4, \ldots, 2^s - m + 0$
1	$1, 5, \ldots, 2^s - m + 1$
2	$2, 6, \ldots, 2^s - m + 2$
3	$3, 7, \ldots, 2^s - m + 3$

A major disadvantage of low-order interleaving is the difficulty of expanding the installed memory. If the installed memory is to be expanded by a factor of 2, for example, how is this to be done? Should the degree of interleaving be increased by 2, or should the module size be increased by a factor of 2? Increasing the interleaving factor requires a major hardware modification. Increasing the size of each of the modules is a rather straightforward task. However, both expansion methods become completely intractable if the expansion is something other than an integer power of 2.

Another form of interleaving is called *high-order interleaving*, in which the quotient selects the module and the remainder selects the word within the module. High-order interleaving does not enhance the bandwidth of the system over the bandwidth of a single memory module but instead provides for easy memory expansion. High-order interleaving also permits the easy intermixing of different memory technology such as a combination of RAM and ROM in a small dedicated controller.

5.1.1 *Performance Models*

Performance models for various types of accessing patterns were developed during early research on interleaved memories. The following paragraphs will briefly describe the models of Flores [FLOR64], Hellerman [HELL67], and Burnett and Coffman [BURN70]. These models were created to assist designers evaluate the performance impact of various interleaved memories with different workloads.

There are three useful metrics for measuring and evaluating the performance of an interleaved memory. These are

1. Speedup, S = ratio of the bandwidth of an interleaved memory to the bandwidth of a single module.

2. Acceptance ratio, AR = steady-state ratio of accepted memory requests to total memory requests [CHEU86], $0 \le AR \le 1$. AR is an indicator of how effectively the memory design sustainable bandwidth is being used.

3. Mean acceptance ratio, MAR = acceptance ratio that prorates the latency of accessing the first module over all of the AUs accessed [CHEU86]; $0 \le MAR \le 1$.

Instruction and Data Streams

The models for estimating the performance of an interleaved memory are of three forms: (1) instruction references, (2) data references, and (3) combined references. The addressing patterns of these three streams are quite different and require different performance models. Note that the problems or conflicts associated with interleaved memory systems are special cases of *structural dependencies* (discussed in Chapter 8).

Flores [FLOR64] modeled the situation where a processor and I/O channels are contending for access to an interleaved memory. He modeled the time that a request must wait, waiting time, as a function of the degree of interleaving, the ratio of I/O time to processor time, and the fraction of time that the memory is busy. For an equal ratio of I/O time and as the memory busy time approaches one, the model gives the expected result that the speedup (ratio of waiting time of an interleaved memory to a single module memory) is equal to m, the number of interleaved modules.

The next published model is by Hellerman [HELL67]. This model can be used to predict the performance of an interleaved memory when operands are being fetched. Hellerman assumed an equal probability of access to each module for the first fetch, followed by fetches to sequentially addressed modules until the Kth reference, as

$$S = \sum_{K=1}^{m} \frac{(m-1)! \, K^2}{(m-k)! \, m^K}$$

where K denotes the length of a sequence of reads ending in a nonsequential access. With an approximate solution

$$S = m^{0.56} \approx \sqrt{m} \quad \text{for } 1 \le m \le 45.$$

The implication of Hellerman's model is that if four memory modules are interleaved, the effective bandwidth is approximately twice the bandwidth of one module for the data streams of a typical general purpose computer.

Coffman and Burnett [COFF68] developed performance models for instruction, data, and combined streams. Their performance model for interleaved memories supplying an instruction stream is

$$\text{instruction speedup} = \frac{1 - (1 - \lambda)^m}{\lambda}$$

where λ, the probability that an instruction is a taken branch, is equal to $1/K$. For example, consider a program stream with $\lambda = 0.2$ and $m = 8$. The speedup over a single memory module is 4.16, while Hellerman's model suggests a speedup of 2.82 for a random data reference stream, which is not a surprising result. The Hellerman model should have poorer spatial locality than an instruction stream, hence a smaller speedup.

A data stream model is developed by Burnett and Coffman [BURN70] and described in [BAER80]. This model, called the α–β model, estimates speedup for a data request stream. The assumption is made that the first module is selected at random and that for each subsequent request there is a stationary probability $1 - \lambda$ that the next module in sequence is accessed on the next request. Any one of the other modules is accessed with equal probability $\beta = (1 - \lambda)/(m - 1)$. This model, without a closed form solution, is solved numerically. This solution convincingly shows the advantage memories where $n > m$.

Models such as the α–β model are no longer useful to designers because most computers buffer instructions, and the data references are for vectors with a stride of one. Models that have stride as a parameter are discussed in the following sections.

Vector Data Streams

Interleaved memory has been recognized as an ideal organization for providing high bandwidth for long vectors of reads or writes. Vector access of memory has a characterization parameter, *stride*, that is not present with the models above.

Stride is the difference between addresses of successive references. The addresses, starting at 0, for various strides are

$$
\begin{array}{ll}
\text{Stride} = 1 & 0,1,2,3,\ldots, \\
\text{Stride} = 2 & 0,2,4,6,\ldots, \\
\text{Stride} = 3 & 0,3,6,9,\ldots.
\end{array}
$$

A basic performance model assumes that a vector of consecutive AUs (stride = 1) is fetched from an interleaved memory. For a stride of one (illustrated in Fig. 2.12), the time per AU is equal to

$$ t_{AU} = \frac{t_m}{t_c}\left(1 + \frac{m-1}{K}\right). $$

The speedup of the interleaved memory is

$$ \text{speedup} = S = \frac{m}{1 + (m-1)/K}. $$

The time per AU model assumes that the first reference is to a module that is nonbusy. Subsequent references are to non-busy modules as guaranteed by the degree of interleaving and stride. Table 5.1 shows the performance limits of vector data streams on an interleaved memory over a single module memory.

From the speedup limit we can see that the speedup of an in-

	Vector Length K	
	1	∞
t_{AU}	t_m	t_m/m
Speedup	1	m

TABLE 5.1 Vector performance limits.

terleaved memory accessing a vector that has a stride of 1 is in the range $1 \leq S \leq m$.

The acceptance ratio and mean acceptance ratio indicate how well the memory system supports the demands placed upon it. For $AR = 1$, all requests are being serviced without delay. For $MAR = 1$, the vector length must be very long, $K \to \infty$, or the effective startup overhead must be reduced by concurrency.

5.1.2 *Reducing the Effect of Strides $\neq$ 1*

The models presented above show, for strides of 1, the influence that the degree of interleaving has on performance. As the models will show, strides other than 1 reduce the performance of an interleaved memory. For this reason, there is a body of research directed to decoupling the effect of stride and leaving only the degree of interleaving in the performance models. Most of the reported research was performed in the 1960s; however, there is renewed interest in this line of research today.

When low-order interleaved memories were applied to pipelined and array computers, performance problems were discovered. For example, if a matrix is stored by row in an interleaved memory and is read by column, the read AR may not be the same as the write AR. Instead of the addresses smoothly progressing from module to module as with the writes, there can be conflicts in the modules when the array is read. Figure 5.2 illustrates an example of this problem. In this example, a 4×4 matrix is stored by column in a 4-way interleaved memory. That is, successive AUs of each column are placed in different memory modules with a stride of 1. If the matrix is then read by row, each AU of a row is read from the same module with a stride of 4 resulting in $S = 1$ and $AR = 0.25$. The first row (1,1 1,2 1,3 and 1,4) is contained within memory module 0 and can be read no faster than the cycle time of one module.

The reduction in potential speedup when accessing this matrix can be generally attributed to conflicts resulting from the interactions of stride values and degree of interleaving. Reducing conflicts with interleaved memories has been a research topic for over two decades

$$
\begin{bmatrix}
1,1 & 1,2 & 1,3 & 1,4 \\
2,1 & 2,2 & 2,3 & 2,4 \\
3,1 & 3,2 & 3,3 & 3,4 \\
4,1 & 4,2 & 4,3 & 4,4
\end{bmatrix}
$$

M0	M1	M2	M3
1,1	2,1	3,1	4,1
1,2	2,2	3,2	4,2
1,3	2,3	3,3	4,3
1,4	2,4	3,4	4,4

FIGURE 5.2   Matrix stored in interleaved memory.

Stride	S	AR
1	4	1
2	2	0.5
3	4	1
4	1	0.25
5	4	1

TABLE 5.2 Speedup and AR for various strides, $m = 4$.

[BUDN71, HARP91, RAU91]. Access conflicts can result in a significant performance decrease with vector processors when, for example, the output of one vector operation is stored by row and the next operation needs to read the matrix by column.

Conflictfree access is possible only if the stride is not a factor or a multiple of the degree of interleaving, except for a stride of 1. In the example above, the stride is 4 when reading by column and the degree of interleaving is also 4. A stride of 3 would be accessed with no degradation. Table 5.2 shows the acceptance ratio of a 4-way interleaved memory for various strides.

For strides of 1, 3, and 5, $AR = 1$ while for a stride of 4, $AR = 0.25$ because all of the references are to the same module. Several approaches have been proposed and used to solve the stride-induced conflict problem for interleaved memories having $m = n$. These approaches are discussed below.

1. Skewed addressing;
2. Dynamic skewed addressing;
3. Pseudorandom skewed addressing;
4. Prime number interleaving;
5. *Superinterleaving*, $m < n$ (discussed in Section 5.1.3).

Skewed Addressing

Skewed addressing maps an address into the modules in such a way as to reduce the conflicts [BUDN71]. An example of skewed storage is shown in Figure 5.3, which shows the 4×4 matrix mapped into skewed storage. If the matrix is stored by row, the AUs of row 1 are stored in M0, M1, M2, M3. However, the second row is skewed one memory module, beginning with M1 and wrapping around to M0. The second row is stored with an additional skew of 1 and the third with an additional skew of 1 and so on. Note that the word addresses from the high-order bits are unchanged from the nonskewed case. However, the low-order bits of the address must be mapped into the module selection bits.

$$\begin{bmatrix} 1,1 & 1,2 & 1,3 & 1,4 \\ 2,1 & 2,2 & 2,3 & 2,4 \\ 3,1 & 3,2 & 3,3 & 3,4 \\ 4,1 & 4,2 & 4,3 & 4,4 \end{bmatrix}$$

M0	M1	M2	M3
1,1	1,2	1,3	1,4
2,4	2,1	2,2	2,3
3,3	3,4	3,1	3,2
4,2	4,3	4,4	4,1

FIGURE 5.3   Skewed address interleaving.

The full speedup, $S = m$ and $AR = 1$, can now be obtained with either row or column accessing. Observe that there are strides that will interfere with the degree of interleaving and reduce S. For example, if one of the diagonals of the matrix is read, the AUs 2,2 and 3,3 are both found in M0 while 2,2 and 4,4 are both in M2, which results in $S = 2$ and $AR = 0.5$. The other diagonal finds all AUs in M3, resulting in $S = 1$ and $AR = 0.25$. Skewed storage requires that a skew factor be built into the hardware and used by all accesses. This poses a design problem for selecting the skew factor that will give the best performance over the anticipated workload.

Table 5.3 shows the addresses that needed to read the third column of the matrix with both normal and skewed (skew = 1) interleaving. The word address is the high-order bits, while the module address is the low-order bits. To read a column, the stride is four; for normal interleaving, the module address is unchanged as the word address is incremented. With skewed addressing, the word address increases as with normal addressing while the module address is formed by adding the skew factor to the current module address modulo the degree of interleaving. That is, add the skew factor to the module address but do not propagate a carry into the word address. The normal interleaved case works the

Interleaving Method			
Normal		Skewed	
Word	Module	Word	Module
00	10	00	10
01	10	01	11
10	10	10	00
11	10	11	01

TABLE 5.3   Skewed address interleaving.

same way: the skew of zero is added to the module address, keeping the module address unchanged.

An interesting application of skewed storage is found in [MATI 89]. This study describes the design of a cache that uses multiple chips, requiring skewed storage. With this design, reading words from the cache into the processor and loading a block from memory into the cache will not have stride conflicts.

Dynamic Skewed Addressing

Unlike the skew scheme discussed above, dynamic skewed addressing selects a skew for the anticipated access pattern of the data that is currently active [HARP91]. This technique assumes that the compiler can determine the skew that is added to the remainder of the address. The addition is done dynamically and can be implemented for a relatively low hardware cost.

In order for dynamic skewed storage to work properly, there must be some way to bind the skew value that is used for a write to a subsequent read of the same data. In other words, a read must have access to the corresponding write skew.

Pseudorandom Skewed Addressing

Rau [RAU91] points out that any scheme for reducing conflicts that depends upon a fixed skew mapping of any type is suspect because there are some address patterns that will conflict. As an alternative, he describes and evaluates pseudorandom skewing of addresses.

Two schemes for providing pseudorandom skewing are discussed. First, the module address is XORd with a key generated with a pseudorandom generator; and second, the module address is XORd with a polynomial whose coefficients are in the Galois Field. As with dynamic skewed addressing, the skew factor must be stored by a write and be available for future read operations.

Prime Number Interleaving

Recall that conflicts will occur if, and only if, the stride is a factor or a multiple of the degree of interleaving. Thus, by selecting m to be prime, the number of strides that can produce conflicts is significantly reduced. For example, if $m = 5$, then $AR = 1$ for all strides except $5, 10, 15, \ldots$. For many problems the stride is an even power of two, thus these strides can be process conflictfree.

The first known proposal for prime number interleaving in the literature is found in [BUDN71]. I believe that prime number interleaving was used on some early drum computers to assist in minimum latency scheduling. The Burroughs Scientific Processor used prime number interleaving with $m = 17$ [LAWR82].

Yang [YANG93] describes a cache for vector processors with a prime number of sets rather than an even power of two. The cache is late select with the sets interleaved to achieve a high streaming rate. With prime sets, the addressing patterns of various strides is broken up, permitting the cache to stream without interference. Recall from Chapter 2 that a variation of the SPARC has a prime number of sectors [WEIS92].

The problem with prime number interleaving is that the address, as with all interleaved memory systems, must be divided by the prime number degree of interleaving. The quotient is the high-order word address into the modules while the remainder is the module select address. Division by an even power of two is much simpler than division by a prime number. However, it is possible with available VLSI technology to perform the division, so prime number interleaving may become a viable alternative. The Yang design is based on interleaving with a Mersenne prime number of the set $(3, 7, 15, \ldots, (2^c - 1))$, thus facilitating the generation of the cache address.

5.1.3 *Superinterleaving*

Another technique for reducing the effect of stride on speedup and AR of an interleaved memory is to provide more memory modules than the address degree of interleaving, that is, $m < n$; this method is called *superinterleaving*. Recall that for any m, the clock rate of the system is the memory module cycle time divided by m. By implementing a memory with $m < n$, the number of strides that will produce a conflict in a module is reduced.

Computers such as the CDC6600 have addresses interleaved over more memory modules than the module degree of interleaving; $m < n$. This technique is also used in the Cray-1 and other computers of the Cray family. For the CDC 6600, the memory module cycle time is 1,600 ns, the system clock is 100 ns, and there are 32 memory modules giving $m = 16$ and $n = 32$ [THOR70]. The Cray-1 has 16 50 ns modules with $m = 4$, $n = 16$, and a clock period of 12.5 ns.

Figure 5.4 illustrates, by example, the benefit of superinterleaving. For this example, the addresses are interleaved eight ways ($n = 8$) while the modules are interleaved four ways ($m = 4$). Recall that m is set by the clock period of the processor and the cycle time of the memory modules. Eight cases are shown as the stride is varied from 1 to 8. A form of reservation table is used to illustrate the operation of this memory; reservation tables will be described in greater detail in Chapter 6. A

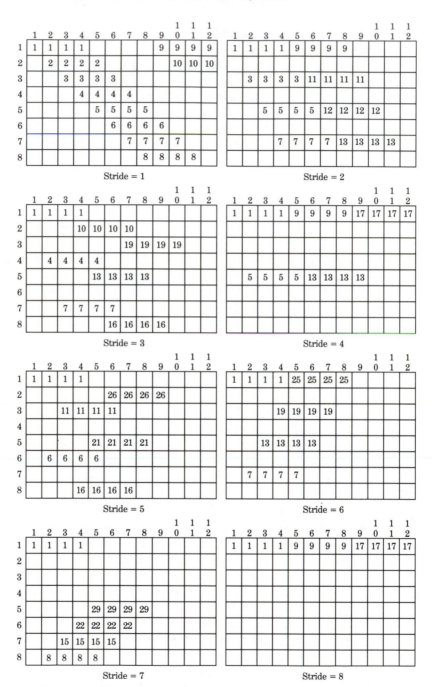

FIGURE 5.4 Superinterleaving example, *m* = 4, *n* = 8.

Stride	S	AR	Memory Utilization
1	4	1	0.5
2	4	1	0.5
3	4	1	0.5
4	2	0.5	0.25
5	4	1	0.5
6	4	1	0.5
7	4	1	0.5
8	1	0.25	0.125

TABLE 5.4   Superinterleaving performance, $m = 4$, $n = 8$.

reservation table is a display of space (the memory modules) on the vertical axis and time (in clocks periods) shown on the horizontal axis.

For the first case with a stride of one, the addresses are applied to modules 1, 2, 3, ..., 8, 9, 10, ... Each module is busy for four clocks, indicated by the address number in the table. Because $m = 4$, each module is busy for four clocks when it is cycled. For this case, $AR = 1$.

Considers a stride of 3. The modules addressed are 1, 4, 7, ..., 2, 5, ... The memory can sustain one reference per clock, $AR = 1$, after the initial 3 clocks of latency. Note that $AR = 1$ is obtained because each of the modules is used half of the time. In other words, there is a 2X overdesign in bandwidth that is devoted to ensuring that $AR = 1$ is sustainable.

Drawing from the information presented in Figure 5.4, Table 5.4 tabulates S, AR, and memory utilization for the different strides. For strides except four and eight, this memory has $S = 1$ and $AR = 1$. Interference resulting from a stride of four reduces to $S = 2$ and $AR = 0.5$, while a stride of eight will have $S = 4$ and $AR = 0.25$ — a performance that is no better than a single module because all of the references are to one memory module.

The reservation tables clearly show how excess latent bandwidth is used to improve the performance for different strides. Except for the cases where the stride is a factor or multiple of n; the utilization of the memory modules is

$$\text{utilization} = \frac{\text{used bandwidth}}{\text{available bandwidth}} = \frac{AR \times m}{n}.$$

With this example of superinterleaving, if the strides are uniformly distributed, the weighted average AR is 0.84 as compared to the $m = n = 4$ case shown in Table 5.1 with a weighted average AR of 0.68.

Processor	Memory Words per Clock	Bus Words per Clock	Memory Utilization; $AR = 1$
Cray-1	$16/4 = 4$	1	0.25
Cray X-MP	$32/4 = 8$	3	0.375

TABLE 5.5 Cray memory system designs.

The Cray-1 memory is superinterleaved and has one port between the memory and its internal registers. The memory is organized $m = 4$, $n = 16$. This means that approximately 75% (12/16) of the latent bandwidth of the memory is wasted to reduce stride conflicts. The Cray X-MP extends the address interleaving to $n = 32$, which provides eightfold bandwidth over the capacity of one port [CHEN84]. With this overcapacity, three ports (two input and one output) to/from the internal registers can sustain continuous transfers for many strides. However, the Cray X-MP memory must support multiprocessors plus an I/O port per processor that reduces the bandwidth available for any one processor. The memory of these two processors is described in Table 5.5.

The memory words per clock indicates the maximum bandwidth of the memory. Bus words per clock represents the number of buses, and the maximum memory utilization is for $AR = 1$ and includes the effect of the number of memory ports.

Memories with one port to the processor and a relatively small interleaving factor, as is the case of the Cray-1, are relatively simple to implement. When the address interleaving is increased along with an increase in the number of ports to memory, the complexity of the interleaving schemes becomes costly to implement. The memory system of the TI ASC, for example, had eight memory modules ($m = n = 8$) and eight user ports, requiring two racks of equipment for the crossbar switch [CRAG89] (which is a very expensive system component).

Two of the major changes from the Cray-1 to the Cray X-MP are an increase in the number of memory modules from 16 to 32, and an increase in the number of ports from one to four (two read, one write, one I/O). The memory module cycle time is 36 ns, and with $n = 32$ the potential streaming rate out of the memory system is one word every 1.125 ns. Given the complexity of a full 32×4 crossbar switch, some hierarchical interconnection or multiplexing system is called for, as shown in Figure 5.5.

The 32 memory modules are grouped into four sections of eight modules each. The modules of a section pass data via eight *lines* (8 to 1 multiplexer-demultiplexer) that are then selected by a 4×4 crossbar switch. With this interconnection scheme, the potential bandwidth of the

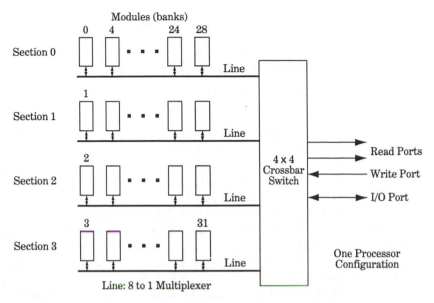

FIGURE 5.5 Cray X-MP-2, one processor, memory organization.

memory is reduced from 32 possible memory references per clock to 4 memory references per clock because of the constrictions imposed by the four lines. With four ports active, there is no excess bandwidth to mitigate the effects of conflicts. Note that for each processor in the system the four lines and the crossbar switch are replicated.

The crossbar switch of Figure 5.5 is assumed to be conflictfree for all accesses from all ports. However, conflicts exist with the Cray X-MP-2 memory in addition to the stride conflicts of the Cray-1. The conflicts are:

1. Module (bank) conflict due to access from one port—a *stride conflict*;
2. Module (bank) conflict due to access of an idle module by two or more ports—a *simultaneous bank conflict*;
3. Line conflict due to access by two or more ports—a *section conflict*.

The effects of these three types of conflicts have been extensively studied [CHEU84, CHEU86, OED85, WEIS92, CALA88, CALA88a]. Cheung and Smith [CHEU84] used reservation table analysis of memory conflicts to evaluate *MAR* values; excerpted results are shown in Table 5.6. Their reservation tables include memory banks and lines as resources. In all of the cases evaluated, stride is set to 1. Their results indicate that *MAR*s of 0.8 or better are achievable with the Cray X-MP-2 memory.

Conditions	*MAR*
Two-vector stream	0.975
Three-vector stream	0.80

TABLE 5.6   Cray X-MP-2 memory conflicts.

The line conflict problem of the Cray X-MP-2 suggested an improvement for the Cray X-MP-4. This improvement *renumbers* the memory modules, which is a technique similar to skewed storage described in Section 5.1.2. The address interleaving (module numbering) scheme for these two processors is shown in Table 5.7 for the first 32 references, starting with 0. For example, for the X-MP-2, address 13 is found in Bank 3, Module S1. With renumbering, the X-MP-4 address 13 is found in Bank 1, Module S3.

Cheu [CHEU86] shows that the renumbering scheme of the X-MP-4 improves the *MAR* over that of the X-MP-2. Specifically, this reassignment changes *MAR* from 0.929 to 1.0, an improvement of approximately 7%.

Note that the number of interleaved addresses per line, called

Cray X-MP-2

	Bank							
	0	1	2	3	4	5	6	7
Section 0	0	4	8	12	16	20	24	28
Section 1	1	5	9	**13**	17	21	25	29
Section 2	2	6	10	14	18	22	26	30
Section 3	3	7	11	15	19	23	27	31

Cray X-MP-4

	Bank							
	0	1	2	3	4	5	6	7
Section 0	0	1	2	3	16	17	18	19
Section 1	4	5	6	7	20	21	22	23
Section 2	8	9	10	11	24	25	26	27
Section 3	12	13	14	15	28	29	30	31

TABLE 5.7   Cray X-MP-2 and X-MP-4 address interleaving.

Number of Sections (*NS*)

NBPS	2	4	8	16
1	0.5	0.25	0.125	
2	1.5	0.75	0.38	
4	3.5	1.75	0.88	
8	7.5	3.75	1.88	0.94
16	15.5	7.75	3.87	1.93

TABLE 5.8 Cray X-MP memory latency
(clocks).

number of banks per section (*NBPS*), can be 1 (X-MP-2), 2, 4 (as shown above), or 8. Another parameter is the *number of sections* (*NS*). The selection of *NBPS* for a given *NS* can have a pronounced effect on the performance of the memory system. However, improving *MAR* by module renumbering works at the expense of increasing the latency (sometimes called *startup delays*) while transient conflicts are resolved. Simulation results on the latency for various *NBPS* and *NS* from [CALA88] are given in Table 5.8 for a two-port system.

The change in interleaving for the Cray X-MP-4 results in an additional 1.25 clocks of latency. Similar results for a three-port access show that the Cray X-MP-2 has a delay of 0.67 clocks and that the Cray X-MP-4 has a delay of 5.11 clocks. Latency is reduced as the number of sections increases. This is not a surprising result because if the number of sections is equal to the number of modules, then a full crossbar switch is specified. For one section, all memory modules are connected by one line or a multiplexer offering the maximum potential for conflict from references from another port.

The memory designer must face the issue of balancing *MAR* and latency. As discussed in Chapter 11, for short vectors latency should be minimized while for long vectors *MAR* should be minimized. Additional recent research on the issue of high-performance interleaved memory for vector processors is found in [CHEN91] and [HARP91].

An interesting comparison of the memory configurations for various members of the Cray X-MP family is shown in Table 5.9.

The data in this table is extracted from [THOM86] and shows the number of memory modules in **bold** and the number of modules per port in *italics*. For example, a four-processor configuration with 8 Mwords of memory has 32 memory modules. The number of modules/port is based on three ports per processor; the I/O port is ignored. For example, the four-processor system with 64 memory modules has 12 ports and 5.33 modules per port.

	Memory Modules No. of Processors			Modules/Port No. of Processors		
Memory Size	1	2	4	1	2	4
16 Mwords		**32**	**64**		*5.33*	*5.33*
8 Mwords	**32**	**32**	**32**	*10.6*	*5.33*	*2.66*
4 Mwords	**16**	**16**		*4.33*	*2.66*	
2 Mwords	**16**	**16**		*4.33*	*2.66*	
1 Mwords	**16**			*4.33*		

TABLE 5.9   Cray X-MP memory modules and modules/port.

With $n = 4$, the observation can be made that some models of this processor do not have enough memory modules to support the number of ports. Any module/port value less than 4 is marginal in memory bandwidth and may suffer performance degradation for some benchmarks. The X-MP-4 with 8 Mwords of memory can be a marginal performer.

5.1.4 *Interleaving for Multiport Access*

Memory module interleaving is also used to permit concurrent access to a memory when two or more addresses are not to the same module. This capability is a feature of the Cray memories described in Section 5.1.3. However, a simpler system is used in the Intel Pentium for its data cache [ALPE93]. This processor is a superscalar implementation (discussed in Chapter 10) that has the need to perform two cache transactions in one clock period. This memory system is discussed in this chapter because the technique is applicable to multi-access memories in general, not just to caches for superscalar processors.

The basic idea is that with addresses interleaved across m modules ($m = n$), accesses to adjacent address will not conflict and can be processed in parallel. Only when there is a module conflict will one of the requests be deferred. A simplified block diagram of the Pentium data cache is shown in Figure 5.6. This cache has 8 modules, $m = n = 8$, with each module organized 256×4 bytes. The total cache capacity is 8 Kbytes.

Two addresses can be presented at the same time to the cache. If the addresses are not the same, the two addressed memory banks are cycled and the two AUs are gated out through the multiplexers. If there is a conflict, the U access has priority and the V access stalls for one cycle. The designers of the Pentium considered a dual-port cache as well

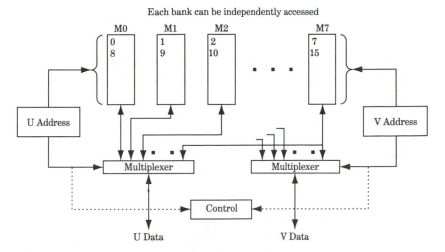

FIGURE 5.6 Pentium interleaved data cache.

as this interleaved cache and selected this design based on its smaller area and reduced complexity for handling data dependencies. This cache is discussed further in Section 10.2.2.

5.1.5 *Cache-Memory Transfers*

The use of interleaved memory as a technique for reducing the transport time of a block to/from a cache is discussed in Section 2.2.1 and Figure 2.13. Because a block is a vector with a stride of one, an efficient transfer is achieved. For example, the IBM S/360/85 has a 4-way interleaved core memory, each module having a word length of 16 bytes and cycle time of 1.04 µs. The processor and cache have a cycle of 80 ns. The interleaving is specifically designed to transfer a 64-byte block. After the first module cycle is initiated, the second module read starts 80 ns later, then the third, then the fourth. The first 16 bytes of the block are transferred at the end of the access portion of the cycle, and each of the other 16 bytes comes 80 ns later. For this design, $a = 1.04$ ns and $b = 80$ ns. Note that the parameters a and b are defined in Chapter 2 in terms of clocks, not time.

The performance effect of block size and interleaving is modeled in [SMIT87]. The length of the block can have a critical impact on the cache performance if the cache is blocked during a block load. However, if one of the methods of load forward or fetch bypass is used, this performance penalty can be reduced.

5.1.6 *Nibble, Page, and Static Column Mode Drams*

This section briefly describes memory chips that achieve an efficient transfer similar to that possible with interleaving. Nibble-mode DRAMS supply four bits in one cycle. A page-mode DRAM accesses the array and holds the accessed row in a buffer that is then accessed by the row (low-order bits) address. The size of the buffer is the square root of the number of bits in the chip. For example, a 1 M-bit device will have a 1024-bit buffer, which provides a possible block size of 128 bytes. The static column mode is similar to the page-mode DRAM and provides a faster transfer of bits after accessing the row.

The Texas Instruments TMS44C256 DRAM serves as an example of a nibble-mode device, shown in Figure 5.7. The TMS44C256 is organized 256 Kbits × 4 bits (1 M-bit DRAM). Internally it consists of 4, 256-Kbit arrays as shown in Figure 5.6. This device is supplied in three speed ranges; this example uses the highest speed one.

A read cycle is initiated with the presentation of the address (18 bits), and each of the four arrays are read. As shown in the cut-out, each array is organized 512 × 512 bits. Nine bits select a word in each array, and the output bit is selected by the other nine bits. The read cycle places 512 bits in each of four buffers for a total of 2 Kbits. These bits are gated into the output, either as a 4-bit nibble or, if in the page mode, up to 512 nibbles in sequence.

The performance model for the nibble, page, and static column devices is the same as that of interleaved memory. That is, there is a time a required to fetch the first AU and then a time b to fetch each of the successive AUs. The total transport time increases monotonically with the block size unless another fetch is required to start the cycle over again. For the TMS44C256, the read and write cycle time is 150 ns and the read or write page mode is 50 ns. The parameters for computing the transport time are $a = 150$ ns and $b = 50$ ns.

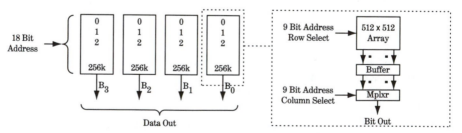

FIGURE 5.7   DRAM organization.

5.1.7 *Wide-Word Interleaved Modules*

Another method for increasing the bandwidth of a memory is to increase the width, in bits, of a memory module to a multiple of the addressable unit (2X, 4X, ...). In addition, a number of these modules can be module interleaved for even greater bandwidth.

Consider a memory module with a width of two AUs and with four of these modules interleaved as shown in Figure 5.8. The matrix of Figure 5.2 is stored in this memory as shown. The high-order address bits select the word in each of the modules; the low-order address bits select the module and the left-hand or right-hand word of the addressed module.

If the matrix is accessed by row, the maximum bandwidth is obtained because the stride is one. Under these conditions, the speedup is $S = m \times W$; where W = number of AUs per memory word = 2, $S = 4 \times 2 = 8$.

On the other hand, there can be addressing patterns that will reference only one module. Under these conditions, $S = 1$. Thus we see that $1 \le S \le (m \times W)$.

Experience has shown that wide-word interleaving yields a speedup that is similar to module interleaving. Expressing this relationship in the terms of Hellerman's model for random data addressing patterns, the effect of interleaving is $\sqrt{m}$ and the effect of having a wide-word is $\sqrt{W}$. Furthermore, the effect of these to enhancement steps is multiplicative; $S = \sqrt{(m \times W)}$.

It is interesting to note that von Neumann [BURK46] proposed wide-word interleaving as a memory organization. The memory is discussed in Chapter 2 in terms of being a queue. In the simple example given in

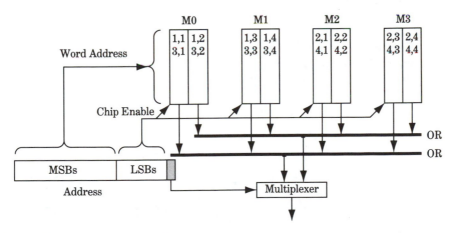

FIGURE 5.8 Wide-word interleaving.

Chapter 2, three memory cycles are required to read five instructions. A memory that is only 20 bits wide would require five memory cycles. Thus, the speedup is 5/3 or 1.666, which is rather close to $\sqrt{1 \times 2} = 1.414$. The simple model and example give speedup predictions that are reasonably close to each other.

The most compelling reason for wide-word memories today is to reduce the cache miss transport time. Wide-word memories complement wide busses, reducing the number of clocks required to transfer a block to/from a cache. Recall from section 2.2.1 that the memory modules of the IBM S/360/85 are eight bytes wide. Thus only four clocks are needed to transport a 32-byte block from the memory to the cache.

5.2 Disk Systems

The input/output of a computer has always been a bottleneck in system performance. During the early years, punched cards were the primary I/O media, followed later by magnetic tape. With the advent of the first commercial disk in 1956, cards have disappeared and magnetic tape has become archival media. The IBM 350 RAMAC, introduced in 1956, had a capacity of 40 Mbits (not bytes!) on 100 surfaces with an access time of 0.5 seconds [MATI 77]. Access to the RAMAC is random when compared to magnetic tape, and the name RAMAC is taken from Random Access Memory with the then-common suffix AC. Even though magnetic drums were used for mass storage and virtual memory as early as 1948, they were severely limited in capacity and the RAMAC type disk was a welcome replacement.

A disk is organized in a hierarchy of data storage areas described in Figure 5.9. The basic storage unit is the *sector*, which contains 32 Kbytes to 4 Kbytes. A sector is the unit of transfer between the disk and main memory and is usually the page in a virtual memory system. A track consists of 4 Ksectors to 8 Ksectors, and there are 30 to 2,000 tracks on a surface. Note that the disk sector and cache sector are not the same thing. The tracks are accessed with Read/Write (R/W) heads on an arm

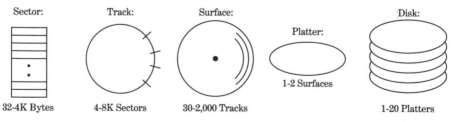

| Sector: | Track: | Surface: | | Disk: |

32-4K Bytes   4-8K Sectors   30-2,000 Tracks   1-20 Platters

Platter: 1-2 Surfaces

FIGURE 5.9   Disk storage hierarchy.

positioned over a track by an actuator. Each platter has one or two surfaces, and 1 to 20 surfaces make a disk unit. Needless to say, these hierarchy numbers change with time, generally increasing, and are only a guide to the relative dimensions.

Another component of disk organization concerns the relationship between the arms with their R/W heads and the tracks; each surface has at least one arm with its R/W head. Disk systems with more than one arm (either more than one arm for one surface or more than one surface each with one arm) can have either independent arm movement (independent actuators) or the arms can be ganged together in groups. The tracks under a ganged group of heads are known as a *cylinder*, a term taken from drum technology. A cylinder consists of the tracks that are under the heads at one time. Note that for a system with independent arm movement, cylinders can be virtualized by positioning the arms over the tracks of a cylinder.

The discussion above highlights heads that have the combined function of read and write. However, disk technology is moving in the direction of independent read and write heads. The reason for this is that recording and reading are no longer complementary with the higher areal densities and purpose-designed heads are required as well as accompanying arms and positioning circuits.

Two examples of disk organization hierarchy are shown in Table 5.10: the Cray DD-49 disk unit, as reported in [KATZ89], and the EX-2, 5-1/4″ floppy reported by [SARG86]. The first is a high-capacity disk for a supercomputer. These parameters reflect formatted disks.

Disk surface areal density (bits/inch × tracks/inch) has increased at a rate of 26% per year since 1971, and these increases have translated almost directly into cost reduction. However, even with improvements in both latency and transfer rate of the early disks as compared to magnetic tape, disk systems remain a limiting factor in computer system performance because of their mechanical characteristics that limit lat-

	Cray EX-1	Cray EX-2 (floppy)
Bytes/Sector	42	512
Sectors/Track	4096	15
Tracks/Surface	443	80
Surfaces/Platter	2	2
Platters/Disk	8	1
Total Capacity	1.2 Gbytes	1.2 Mbytes

TABLE 5.10 Example disk parameters.

ency reductions. In this chapter several issues concerning disk systems are addressed, including disk latency, bandwidth requirements, performance, cost projections, interleaved disks (RAID), and disk caches.

5.2.1 *Disk Requirements*

There is very little solid information published on the question of the disk bandwidth and storage requirements based upon workloads that can serve as a design guide [GOLD87]. The usual design approach is to assume that all of the disk parameters are inadequate to the task and the designer should provide the needed capacity and then just provide the best performance possible with the selected disks. In fact, most of the research in the use of disks has been directed toward this second step: overcoming the inadequacies of the disks. For example, [MILL91] reports on measurements of I/O activity made on a Cray Y-MP 8/832 when executing scientific benchmarks. Unfortunately, most of the data is referenced to CPU time and are therefore of limited use for design guidance.

Five parameters are commonly used to characterize a disk system.

1. Capacity. Bytes of storage (formatted).
2. Bandwidth. Bytes transferred/unit of time.
3. Service rate. Number of service requests satisfied/unit of time.
4. Response time. Time between the start and completion of an event.
5. Cost. $/Mbyte.

The reader should keep in mind that the requirements for disk systems are different for mainframes and single-user computers. In the former case, capacity and service rate are of prime importance; for the latter, response time is of prime importance. These differences are discussed in the following paragraphs.

Capacity

A study by Goldstein [GOLD87] indicates, for mainframe computers, that the average disk storage capacity is 3.7 Gbytes per MIPS; see Figure 5.10. The plot shows the capacity per MIPS from a customer survey taken in 1985. This data is for large mainframe applications and does not reflect the requirements of work stations and other single-user computer systems. However, servers should have approximately the same disk capacity per MIPS as mainframes.

Other data from Goldstein's study, reflected in Table 5.11, shows that the capacity index has remained relatively constant at 3.7 Gbytes/MIPS since 1980.

The capacity of the hard disk of a typical personal computer has

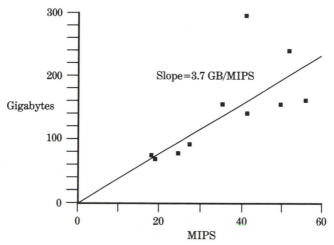

FIGURE 5.10   Mainframe disk capacity versus MIPS.

Year	GB/MIPS
1972	1.5
1974	2.0
1976	2.6
1978	3.5
1980	3.7
1982	3.6
1983	3.7

TABLE 5.11   Mainframe disk capacity versus year of survey.

grown from 5 Mbytes in 1988 to 250 Mbytes in 1994, which is an absolute capacity growth rate of 32% per year. A typical PC of 1980 and 1994 both have approximately 5 Mbytes per MIPS; installed hard disk capacity is tracking the increase in processing rate. Note, however, that the PC ratio of 5 Mbytes per MIPS is 1/740 that of the Goldstein mainframe ratio noted above. We can see from this information that there can be a major difference in ratio of disk capacity to MIPS depending upon the particular use and application of the computer.

Bandwidth

One of the famous computer design "laws" is the Amdahl Law, also called the CASE/AMDAHL law [HENN90, AKEL91], that states that a balanced system should provide a bit of I/O transfer for every instruc-

Problem Type	Bits Transferred per Instruction Executed
Scientific	1
Commercial	2
Interactive	4–8

TABLE 5.12 I/O bandwidth requirements.

tion executed. However, I cannot find a reference to this law in the published literature attributable to either Amdahl or Case. I can only conclude that this law is a rule-of-thumb in the computer art with no recognized reference to an author. A balanced system is one in which all of the queue depths are stable and are approximately equal to one and one component is not significantly limiting the performance of the system.

The definition of bandwidth in Chapter 2 is changed when referring to Amdahl's law in that the normalizing function is an executed instruction rather than time. Taken at its face value, Amdahl's law means that a processor executing at the rate of 10 MIPS will require an average I/O transfer of 10 million bits (1.25 Mbytes) per second. And, because the transfers would be in bursts, the peak transfer rate will be much higher.

Another view of the bandwidth requirement is given by Matick [MATI77] and shown in Table 5.12. The data shown is a composite view of data published by other researchers in 1970 and 1971 and is quite old.

Notice that for scientific processing, one bit is transferred for each instruction executed, which is the same value cited as Amdahl's Law. However, for interactive processing, the I/O requirement is 4 to 8 times more demanding, and transaction processing should have approximately the same requirement. As interactive and transaction processing increase in importance, the need to provide high I/O bandwidth is an important design problem.

A small amount of contemporary data exists on this issue. An I/O demand of 0.73 bits per instruction has been reported for a VAX 8800 executing a mix of batch, system, and interactive tasks [CLAR88]. For a scientific program, an atmospheric simulation model on a Cray-2, 0.32 bytes per instruction are required [CATL92].

Data presented in [KATZ89] shows that the bandwidth of a single-disk system is in the range of 0.3–3.0 Mbytes per second. Based upon one bit per instruction, these disks are capable of supporting approximately 1 MIPS of interactive processing. Thus, a single disk is inadequate for high-performance processors in most programming environments.

Current research concerns techniques for improving disk system bandwidth by spreading the data over a number of disks, or disk array. An early survey of disk array research is found in [KATZ89]. A simple example of the disk array technique is to consider that 32 disks are used to store data. If the basic disk bandwidth per disk is 2 Mbytes per second, the aggregate bandwidth is 64 Mbytes per second. The technique of arraying disks is similar to interleaving memory modules discussed previously. Some of the major design issues with disk arrays are data layout, buffering, reliability, and error recovery (discussed further in Section 5.2.3). The first known example of a commercial disk array can be found in the Connection Machine Data Vault [KATZ89].

Latency

The deficiency in disk bandwidth or transfer rate is usually masked by the very long latency of a disk access. Latency of a disk consists of two components: (1) seek time and (2) rotational latency. Seek time is the time needed to position the head under the desired track and consists of the arm start time, traverse time, and stop time. Complex hardware mechanisms have been designed to reduce seek time and improve the positioning accuracy of the head. Nevertheless, seek time can be in the range of 2 ms to 10 ms depending upon the number of tracks to be crossed.

In addition to hardware approaches to reducing seek time, arm scheduling algorithms can be employed to reduce effective seek time. Effective seek time reduction can be achieved by taking requests off the queue such that the request for a close track is served before a request for a distant one. For heavily loaded systems that have a large number of requests in the queue, arm scheduling works well. However, arm scheduling does not always improve seek time. For example, systems that are balanced with regards to processing and I/O should have an average queue depth of less than one; consequently, arm scheduling becomes ineffective [KIM 87]. Also, arm scheduling is of little benefit to single-user systems unless there are background batch jobs executing that will fill the request queue.

Rotational latency is the time required for the desired sector to reach the R/W head and is set by the rotational speed of the disk. Rotational latency is, on average, one half of the disk's rotation time. Many disks rotate at 3,600 RPM, giving an average rotational latency of 8.3 ms.

One approach to improving the rotational latency of a disk is *rotational positioning sensing* (RPS). One use of RPS is to schedule disk transfers of the queue based on serving the first sector that will be under the heads, which is similar to arm scheduling. Another use of RPS is to improve the utilization of the disk channels. With RPS, after the access command is presented to the disk, the channel is disconnected and made available for another access. Then the position of the disk is sensed and as the desired sector approaches the head the channel is reconnected. RPS is discussed further in Section 5.2.2.

Ng points out that there is a potential problem with RPS when used to improve channel utilization [NG91]. Because of the great difference between latency and data transfer time, large systems disconnect the channel after a request has been made to the disk for an access. Therefore, the channel is free to transfer data to/from another disk. However, there is a possibility that the channel is still connected to the other disk and cannot be restored to the disk that released it. When this happens, an RPS*miss* occurs, requiring another complete rotation before the request can be serviced. The latency of an RPS*miss* can be greater that the seek time. Ng discusses four methods by which the problem with RPS*miss* can be reduced. These include three forms of data redundancy and a dual actuator approach.

The dual actuator approach has a heritage in the paging drums of the 1960s, which had two heads per track and zero seek time because each track had a head and the average rotational latency was cut in half to approximately 4 ms. Data redundancy is also used on paging drums with only one head per track; redundant data is placed 180 degrees apart. Thus, one copy is always within a half rotation of the head. Another trick for eliminating rotational latency is to have the sector size equal a full rotation of the drum. The sector is transferred into a random access memory; consequently, the transfer could start at any point in the sector. Paging drums are no longer used because of the availability of low-cost RAM used as either main memory or as a disk cache.

The total latency (seek plus rotation) for one actuator of a mainframe class disk has decreased from approximately 30 ms in 1985 to approximately 15 ms in 1990—a reduction rate of 13% per year. Even if the rate of decrease in total latency continues to the year 2000, the latency will still be approximately 4 ms—the same as that obtained with paging drums.

In addition to arm scheduling and RPS, the use of buffers or disk caches has significantly improved the latency of disks where either (1) software prefetching is effective or (2) the pages demonstrate temporal locality. A hypothetical system, circa 1965, is shown at the top of Figure 5.11. This system transfers I/O directly into and out of main memory. Using the Matick data of 1 million bits per 1 million instructions for scientific programs and assuming that the sector size is 8 Kbits, the sector accesses per million instructions is

$$\text{accesses/million inst.} = \frac{1 \times 10^6}{8} \times 10^3 = 125.$$

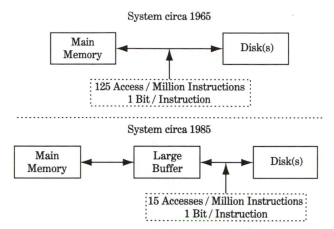

System circa 1965

System circa 1985

FIGURE 5.11 Disk requirements reduced with disk buffers.

The systems of the 1960s had small buffers that only smoothed the flow of data between the main memory and the disk. However, as the buffers increased in size, the "miss rate" on these buffers decreased and the traffic on the bus between the buffer and the disk decreased. The transition is now underway to convert the buffers into hardware-managed "disk caches." The benefits of buffers can be found in Goldstein's data from a 1985 survey, which shows 15 disk accesses per second are required for each MIPS or 15 accesses/million instructions; see the bottom of Figure 5.11. The 1985 system has a buffer between the main memory and the disk that operates similar to a cache and has a P_{miss} estimated to be $15/125 = 0.12$.

Note that the number of bits of real-disk I/O and the number of real-disk accesses per instruction is reduced by the use of buffers only to the extent that files have temporal locality. The buffers decouple many of the disk accesses and transfers from the physical disk by servicing them in the buffer, hence reducing the number of real-disk accesses/instruction by a factor of eight over this twenty-year period. This reduction is 11% each year, which is close to the 10% reported by Goldstein for the period 1980–1985.

Because of increasing instruction processing rates, ever higher access rates and I/O bandwidth are required. Table 5.13 shows projections of bytes/instruction, bytes/second, and accesses/second for the disk system (that is, buffer accesses of the disk). This projection is based on an increase in MIPS of 30% per year and a decrease in I/O bytes per instruction of 10% per year resulting from buffering. By the year 2000, the disk must be capable of 6 Mbytes/sec and 225 accesses/sec.

The developments in disk arrays will ensure that the bandwidth requirements are achieved. However, research into short latency disks

Disk, After Buffering

Year	MIPS	Bytes/Inst.	Bytes/Second	Accesses/Sec.
1985	5	0.10	500,000	15
1990	20	0.06	1,200,000	36
2000	300	0.02	6,000,000	225

TABLE 5.13 Disk bandwidth requirement projection.

has not yet indicated a way to achieve the goal shown in the table. As with caches and virtual memory, buffers must still be loaded with the working set and, this time, may be a major determinant in the response time of a system, regardless of the use of a buffer. Long response time or disk latency is particularly detrimental to single-user workstations and PCs.

Service Rate

Service rate (also called *throughput* and *bandwidth*) is defined as "the amount of work completed in a specific interval of time" [DONO72]. There are two views of service rate: The theoretical maximum service rate of a system and the actual service rate of a system that is receiving work requests. The latter is always less than the former. Factors such as the number of disk channels and load on the CPU play significant roles in setting the service rate of a disk system.

The combination of latency, bandwidth, and scheduling produce a service rate measure of the disk in terms of transactions/second. The first commercial disks, circa 1965, could perform approximately 3 accesses per second. Referring again to the data of [KATZ89], for the disks listed, the maximum service rate is in the range of 0.8 to 50.0 I/Os per second per actuator, not counting queue time.

Analytic modeling techniques have been developed that permit designers to evaluate trial designs and to assess tentative system changes to improve performance. Buzen developed a canonical model of a processor system [BUZE71, DENN78] that is used to evaluate processor and disk configurations and the level of multiprogramming. The issues discussed in the next paragraphs concern how the mean service rate varies as the system parameters are changed.

The Buzen model, as shown in Figure 5.12, is called the *central server model*. The central server model has one CPU and m I/O devices with service rates m_i. As a task completes processing, it is put into one of the I/O queues or exits and is replaced by an identical task that is placed on the CPU queue. The probabilities of these paths are given by

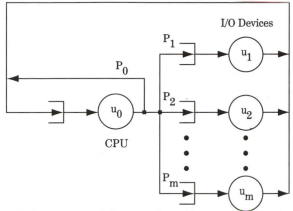

FIGURE 5.12   Central server model.

P_m. After an I/O event, the job is placed on the CPU queue. The I/O devices are assumed to be disks, drums, or a combination of the two. The response time solution to this model is found by recursively evaluating the response as the degree of multiprogramming is increased from 1 to 2 and so on. In addition to response time, the utilization of each of the I/O devices and the CPU can be determined.

Allen [ALLE80] provides an example of the use of the central server model for a system with a CPU and two I/O devices. The service rates and transition probabilities are

$$\mu_0 = 100/\text{sec}, \quad P_0 = 0.1;$$
$$\mu_1 = 25/\text{sec}, \quad P_1 = 0.2;$$
$$\mu_2 = 40/\text{sec}, \quad P_2 = 0.7.$$

The level of multiprogramming is set to 4. A proposed change is to replace I/O device #2 with a faster device; what are the original and the improved service rates? The results from the Buzen Central Server model are shown in Figure 5.13. By doubling the service rate of the disk #2 from 40 to 80 I/Os per second, the service rate of the system increases from 5.17 to 7.43 tasks per second — an increase of 43%. Other system changes can be investigated, such as a faster processor and/or increasing the performance of the slowest I/O device. Note that the asymptotic service rate of this system, with I/O devices that are infinitely fast, is 10 tasks per second as 10 passes through the CPU are required to complete a task. With these very fast disks, the system becomes CPU bound.

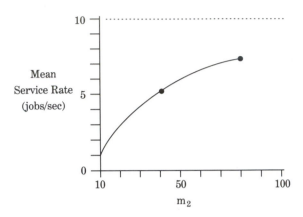

FIGURE 5.13   Service rate, mean jobs per second.

Analysis of systems performing conventional file-based I/O clearly indicates the detrimental effect of slow disk systems on total system performance. Reddy and Banerjee [REDD89] examined various alternative configurations of multiple disks and evaluated their performance for various scientific workloads. Akella and Siewiorek [AKEL91] survey various performance models. They measure the performance of VAX processors in relation to the measured performance of their models.

Response Time

Response time (also called *latency*) is the time between the start and completion of an event. The techniques of queuing theory are useful in evaluating response time for certain classes of systems. A thorough discussion of queuing theory is outside the scope of this book. However, I want to discuss a simple model; interested readers can consult [JAIN92].

For transaction processing and batch systems, response time is an important service parameter. While the system owner is interested in service rate and system utilization, users want rapid response time. A large transaction system may process thousands of transactions per second, and each transaction may require tens of disk accesses. Thus, the service rate of the disk system is an important parameter in satisfying a response time specification.

An open system queue model can provide an estimate of the response time of a transaction-processing system. The model assumes that there is an infinite pool of requesters and that when a request is serviced, the requester leaves the system. The arrival rates and service rates have Poision distribution. Transaction-processing systems, as well as grocery checkout and airline service counters, can be analyzed by this model.

The mean time in the system is

$$t_q = \frac{1}{\mu - \lambda}$$

where t_q denotes the mean time in the system, that is, queue time + service time; μ is the mean service rate; and λ is the mean arrival rate.

Two observations can be made about this model. If the arrival rate approaches zero, the mean time in the system is $1/\mu$, and if the mean arrival rate approaches the mean service rate, the mean time in the system approaches infinity. Both of these results can be observed in real life situations.

We can apply this model to the system described in the discussion on service rate, that is, a system with $\mu = 5.17$ tasks per second. If tasks are arriving at $\lambda = 2$ requests per second, the mean time in the system for a task is 0.315 seconds. A task is in the queue for 0.122 seconds and is processed for 0.193 seconds. With the infinitely fast disks, μ becomes 10 and the mean time in the system increases to 0.125 seconds. With this model, a system designer can trade off system cost with customer response time.

Note that the open system model can give misleading results if not properly applied. The assumption of an infinite source of requesters and no return to the input is not valid for many systems. For example, a system with a number of terminals must be modeled by a closed system model. Denning [DENN78] provide an excellent treatment of closed system models.

Disk Cost Projections

The areal density of disk recording increased from 0.002 Mbits/in^2 in 1957 to 10 Mbits/in^2 in 1980—an increase of approximately 43% per year [HARK81] that continues today. The cost of disk storage is shown in Figure 5.14, using data taken from IBM prices to the user that do not reflect the cost for PC related disks today. The slope of the curve is indicative of the reductions in price that have resulted from the stimulus of cost reductions of PC disks. Note that the figure uses dollars of the year. As inflation has been approximately 5% per year over the period 1965–1990, the reductions in disk price in constant dollars have been an astounding 25% per year. Note that 1 Mbyte of Model 2311 disk cost $3,300 in 1964. By 1993, the user price of the IBM 9377 disk array is $6.64 per Mbyte. There is little reason to doubt that similar cost reductions will continue at approximately the same rate over the next 10 years.

The lowest cost per Mbyte in the 1990s is found in disks used in

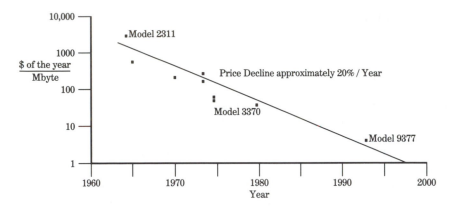

FIGURE 5.14   Disk cost history.

personal computers; high-volume applications costs are one-third to one-half those shown in Figure 5.14. Replacement disk systems for PCs cost approximately 50¢ per Mbyte in 1995. The major reason for this difference in cost, I believe, is that the cost learning curve that has been at work in the semiconductor industry is at work in the disk industry as well. Another reason for this difference is that high-volume PCs are sold with overhead and profit margins significantly lower than those found with mainframe computers.

Summary of Disk Projections

Goldstein's [GOLD87] survey, for moderate to large commercial MVS installations, shows that disk system response time in 1980 was in the range of 40 to 60 ms; an average of 46 ms is used in his studies. One survey shows response time averaged 30 ms — a decrease of 9% per year. It is projected that the trend to shorter response times will continue. Goldstein believes that a reduction of 13% per year in average response time will be required by systems and is possible to be obtained.

Goldstein combined his projections of 1987 and made a forecast of the performance of an "average installation" using a 30% per year growth rate in the installed MIPS. His projections are shown in Table 5.14.

The reduction in response time for the systems of 1990 and 1995 is predicated on caching. These caches are assumed to have a hit ratio of approximately 0.9. For any of the years, the installed disk capacity is in excess of a single drive and requires an aggregation of disk drives. The 510 Gbytes of 1990 requires 68 IBM 3380 units. Large computer installations often speak of their disk "farms" in terms of "acres of disks."

	1985	1990	1995
Installed MIPS	35	130	483
Gbytes of Disk	130	510	2092
Accesses/Sec (λ)	525	1387	3078
Response Time (t_q)	30 ms	15 ms	4.9 ms
Disk Access Time	34 ms	22 ms	22 ms
Acc/Sec/Gbyte	4.1	2.7	1.8

TABLE 5.14   Average installation disk system projections.

An approach to the design of arrays of small disks is discussed in Section 5.2.3.

5.2.2 *Disks in File I/O and Virtual Memory*

Up to this point, disks have been discussed in terms of a peripheral device. There are two ways that disks are connected to the processor and memory: (1) a file I/O system in which files of variable length are transferred or (2) as the lowest level in a virtual memory system in which pages are transferred. This section briefly discusses the issues of these two uses of disks.

The earliest computer systems used magnetic tape mass storage organized as files, usually of variable length. These files were transferred to/from the main memory under an operating system that managed files. With the advent of disk storage in the mid 1960s, the concept of a variable-length file was difficult to incorporate into operating systems. Because disks are physically divided into a hierarchy (sector, track, and surface), the sector is a natural addressable unit and is the unit of transfer between the tape, disk, and main memory; the sector is similar to a page in a virtual memory system. The operating system allocates a file to a set of consecutive sectors on the disk, hence wasting a portion of the last sector.

Files were user-defined collections of sectors that were managed in much the same way that pages are managed in real memory in a virtual memory system. The system must allocate space for new files on the disk, manage free space, and collect the garbage when blocks are de-allocated. The subject of allocation and de-allocation is discussed in Chapter 3, and reference to a book on operating systems is suggested for further details.

The most widely used operating system today, MS-DOS, is, as its name implies, a disk operating system. The user creates files that are managed, with considerable user intervention, by the operating system.

It is quite likely that disk file operating systems will continue to be used for many years. In fact, as discussed in Chapter 3, the disk file operating system is used in some virtual memory systems to map the virtual address to the disk when a page fault occurs.

The first virtual memory system, Atlas, used a drum for low-level memory backed up with tape. Drum technology was rapidly replaced by disks as they became available. With a virtual memory system, the concept of a file can, in theory, disappear into the very large virtual address space. That is, as every addressable unit is within the scope of the address space, no files are required. The IBM System/38 is an example of a fileless system. The elimination of a conventional file system leads to all sorts of problems that are outside the scope of this book; however, I want to mention a few.

One problem with a fileless system is the naming of virtual pages. In a system with a very long virtual address, a page name is assigned when a page is allocated and that name is never used again. The S/38 has a 55-bit virtual page name, and if 1 million names are assigned every second, over 1,000 years would elapse before the pool of names is exhausted.

Programming systems such as LISP assume a large name space. These systems and multiprocessor configurations of large name space machines present the problem of managing names. For example, how are new names assigned and how does one program that is calling a procedure with a name find the location of that name in the system? A distributed database known as the *namespace database* is used with a network of LISP machines to solve the problem of a very large name space [BROM87].

Another problem with a pure virtual memory system is backup and recovery. With a file-based I/O system, files can be periodically archived on magnetic tape or other removable media. If the system should fail, the system is restored from the backup material. With a virtual memory system, how does one back up an address space of 2^{64}, as is the case with the S/38? Furthermore, how is garbage collection (discussed in Chapter 3) performed on a very large virtual address space?

The problems of virtual memory described above lead to the design of systems that employ their disks in a hybrid configuration. That is, virtual memory demands that paged systems are implemented on top of conventional disk I/O. An example of this hybrid trend is found in the IBM RS/6000 and the various interactive systems implemented on top of MS-DOS, such as Windows and Lotus 1-2-3. I believe that these hybrid systems will be the implementation of choice for many years. There are just too many problems with fileless pure virtual memory system implementation for them to be viable.

Interconnection Topology

I now consider the issue of the connection between the processor and the disk(s). Figure 5.15 shows three typical disk system organizations [KIM86]. A single-disk system is shown in Figure 5.15(a); disk requests arrive at a rate λ, pass through the channel, and are serviced by the disk. The disk must have a service rate greater than λ, otherwise the queue in the processor will overflow. The model described above for the open system queue model applies, approximately, to this system.

Figure 5.15(b) shows a multiple-disk system with a single channel and multiple queues in the processor. By scheduling requests to the disks, the requests can be evenly distributed across the disks in a fashion similar to interleaved memory modules. Because the disks all share a single channel, rotational positioning sensing (RPS) is required to inform the queues when a request can be released to a particular disk. RPS sensing permits seek, latency, and RPS misses to be overlapped.

Figure 5.15(c) shows a system where more than one disk shares a channel, that is, a common system configuration. There is a queue in the processor for each disk, and disk requests are taken off the queues as each disk completes its current transaction. Disk requests arrive at the rate λ and are placed in the proper queues. Experience has shown that in a multiple-disk configuration there is a concentration of requests to a few of the disks, which is a distribution of requests known as *skew* [KIM86]. Reported skews for an eight-disk system are 0.388, 0.225, 0.153, 0.12, 0.068, 0.054, 0.01, and 0.001 for each of the eight disks (the conditions or operating system are unknown but are believed to be a data base machine). Thus the requests serviced by each disk are λ Skew(i). If the requests to the disks are balanced, the skew for each disk would be 0.125 for the eight-disk system. Three of the disks are overused and five are underused, leading to a diminution of potential response time of the system. Models show that a system with balanced skews gives the lowest weighted average response, as would be expected.

Shortest Access Time First Scheduling

A form of scheduling that was used prior to RPS with disks is *shortest access time first scheduling* (SATF), which was used with paging drum storage in early multiprogrammed systems [DENN67]. This scheduling technique is now routinely used in disk systems. A typical paging drum performed reads and writes, bit-parallel, with one R/W head per track; there is no head positioning time, and the tracks are divided into sectors of 1,024 bits. For a 32-bit word and with 32 R/W heads, each sector has 4 Kbytes.

Each sector has a queue, as shown in Figure 5.16, and the sectors

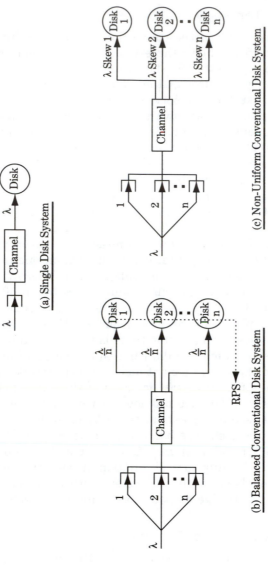

FIGURE 5.15 Disk system organizations.

(a) Single Disk System

(b) Balanced Conventional Disk System

(c) Non-Uniform Conventional Disk System

268

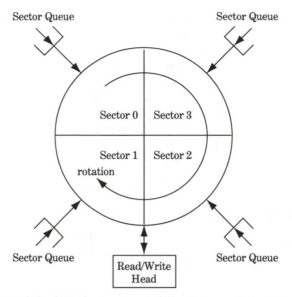

FIGURE 5.16 SATF scheduling.

rotate under the R/W heads in order $(1, 2, \ldots, n, 1, 2, \ldots)$. When, for example, sector 2 rotates to the point that the head could read or write from/to that sector, a request would be taken from the #2 queue and serviced. For a fully loaded system that has requests in all the queues, the drum would be continuously reading or writing, thereby achieving its maximum utilization.

A simple drum or disk without SATF scheduling has an average rotational latency equal to half the rotation time or an average service rate of two requests per revolution or a latency of one half-rotation. With SATF scheduling, the rotational latency is reduced because sectors are served as soon as possible but not necessarily in the order received by the drum system [FULL75]. Fuller and Baskett, whose work is modified by Pohm [POHM81], give an approximate service rate model of a paging drum using SATF scheduling:

$$\mu_{\mathrm{d}} = \frac{s}{t_r}\left[1 - e^{\frac{-(J_d+1)}{s+1}}\right]$$

where μ_d is the paging drum service rate; s is the number of sectors; t_r is the rotation time of the drum; and J_d is the mean number of requests in the disk queues, $1 \le J_d \le 10$.

J_d	Service Rate	Utilization
1	106	0.110
2	155	0.161
3	201	0.210
4	244	0.254
5	286	0.298
6	324	0.337
7	361	0.375

TABLE 5.15   Paging drum service rate and utilization.

The utilization of the disk is

$$\text{utilization} = 1 - e^{-\frac{(J_d+1)}{(s+1)}}.$$

An example of the results obtained from this paging drum model for $t_r = 0.0166$ seconds (3600 RPM) and $s = 16$ is shown in Table 5.15. The number of requests in the queues, J_d, is varied from one to seven.

As the load increases, the service rate increases from 106 transactions per second to 361 transactions per second—a 3× increase in service rate. Note that the simple model for one queue is $2/0.0166 = 120$ transactions per second, which approximately agrees with the Fuller model results for $J_d = 1$. The utilization of the paging drum also increases by a factor of three from 0.110 to 0.375. For very large values of J_d, the service rate approaches $s/t_r \approx 16/0.0166 \approx 960$, and the utilization approaches 1.

As noted previously, SATF scheduling only improves the service rate if there is a full queue of requests to be serviced. SATF scheduling does nothing to reduce the latency or increase the service rate for an interactive single-user system that has only a small mean number of requests in the disk queue, say, 0 or 1. SATF scheduling can be used on moving head disks if there is more than one request in the queue for the current track or cylinder. Note that sector scheduling is similar to the balanced system of Figure 5.15(b), where each R/W head is equivalent to a disk.

Multiprogrammed Systems

Large mainframe computers or servers are generally multiprogrammed systems for which the processing rate is usually more important than latency or response time. The first, known to me, multiprogramming system is the Burroughs B5000. It was built in 1960 and was also the first commercial virtual memory system with pure segmentation [LEVI84]. A restricted form of multiprogramming is found today in systems that support foreground/background processing. The UNIX operating system is an example because its foreground process is usually interactive while its background is batch.

The basic idea of multiprogramming is that when an executing program must wait for an I/O operation, the CPU switches to another program that is resident in main memory. Another form of multiprogramming switch is based on a fixed elapsed time, say every 100 ms. The purpose of multiprogramming is to increase the utilization of the system. The number of resident programs is known as the *level* (*degree*) *of multiprogramming*.

Increased CPU utilization is not without cost. To be effective, there is processor overhead not required for a uniprogramming system such as context switching and queue management. In addition, there must be sufficient real memory to hold the additional programs and their data. Also there must be enough I/O channels (either real or shared) to support the concurrent I/O transactions generated by the resident programs.

Consider the issue of the real memory required to support multiprogramming. With a virtual memory system, memory capacity does not, at first, seem to be a problem. With a very long virtual address, each resident program has an almost unlimited memory space. However, as the real memory is finite, programs are competing for the limited real memory space and excessive paging may result. This causes another program to be switched into execution, which in its turn causes more paging until the system fails due to thrashing or lockout. Multiprogramming will not work unless there is enough real memory to support the degree of multiprogramming.

The capacity of the I/O system is also an issue. The executing program calls for an I/O operation, the next program is switched in, and it calls for an I/O operation and so on. Thus there must be sufficient I/O channels and bandwidth to support the degree of multiprogramming if 100% CPU utilization is to be achieved. Some smart I/O channels start the disk access for a read, disconnect while waiting for the disk latency, and can process another access. Nevertheless, the number of disks and channels (real or virtual) must be equal to the degree of multiprogramming and the accesses must be distributed over these disks; otherwise the queues will build up in front of one or more of the disks and further delay the access. The foreground/background type of multiprogramming may not suffer from the problem of large queues and blocking because the foreground may be inactive due to the user's thinking or otherwise not using the processor. There are a number of techniques for scheduling the swapping of jobs that are outside the scope of this book. Reference to most books on operating systems will find a description of these techniques.

5.2.3 *Disk Arrays*

Disk arrays are receiving extensive attention from both university and industrial researchers. This attention results from the desire to overcome some of the aforementioned deficiencies of disks (cost, bandwidth, latency).

> A *disk array* is a grouping of a number of physical disks that makes these appear to applications as a single logical disk (paraphrased from [KATZ89]).

Various researchers [PATT88, HENN90] have observed that the cost learning curve has overtaken the law of scale with disk technology. In other words, the cost reductions due to vastly greater manufacturing volume produce a lower cost per bit than the reduction in cost due to the design and manufacturing of large scale disks.

In addition to potential cost advantages, disk arrays can provide, in some situations, a reduction in latency and an increase in bandwidth. If disk requests are interleaved across a number of disks in a balanced organization, a significant reduction in response time is possible if there are a number of active disk I/O requests. Also, because there are more than one active R/W head, the bandwidth is increased and the transport time can be reduced. Thus, proposals have been made to configure large-capacity disk systems from arrays of relatively small disk modules. If the overhead of interconnection can be controlled, an array system will have a lower cost than a single-disk system.

Consider the problem of designing a 100-MIPS computer installation requiring 3.7×10^9 bytes per MIPS. If this installation is served by IBM 3380 class disks having 7.5×10^9 byte capacity, approximately 50 disks are required. On the other hand, if an array of 300×10^6 byte modules are used, approximately 1,250 disks are required. Thus, disk array design must comprehend arraying large numbers of disks to support mainframe computers.

Arrays of disks will also have a higher transfer bandwidth because of the number of R/W heads that can be active at one time. The bandwidth increase is a function of the design approach, to be discussed below. It should go without saying that as the bandwidth of the disks is increased with arrays of disks that the bandwidth of the channel must also increase. In all of the discussions to follow it is assumed that channel bandwidth is not a limiting factor.

There are a number of instances of arraylike operation with conventional drums and disks. Special purpose drums that provide equal bandwidth for access of a matrix [CRAG68] and operating systems that use more than one disk channel are found on supercomputers such as SCOPE OS [JOHN84]. Thus the current thinking on disk arrays builds upon these early efforts. A recent product announcement from IBM is for the IBM 9337 Disk Array Subsystem [IBM 92], which offers up to seven 3.5-inch disk drives. One model uses 542-Mbyte disks while the other uses 970-Mbyte disks. The implementation is RAID-5, which is discussed later in this section.

Disk Array Taxonomy

There are a number of design options for a disk array that are described in a taxonomy with three dimensions shown in Figure 5.17. These dimensions are (1) the *degree of interleaving*, which concerns the layout of the sectors on the disks; (2) the rotation of the disks, which can be synchronous or asynchronous; and (3) R/W heads, which can be positioned either independently or as a group. This disk array taxonomy is based on [KATZ89].

There are three possible design cases of rotation and arm movement (shown in Figure 5.17) that are discussed later. There is no known implementation of a synchronous disk with independent arm movement. Two definitions from [KATZ89] apply to disk arrays.

Stripe unit (SU) is the unit of data interleaving, that is, the amount of data that is placed on one disk before data is placed on the next disk. The stripe unit may be as small as one byte [KIM86] and as large as a disk sector. In terms of interleaved memory discussed in Section 5.1, a stripe unit is an addressable unit.

Data stripe (DS) is a sequence of logically consecutive stripe units.

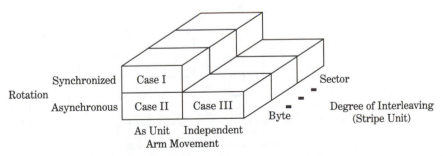

FIGURE 5.17 Disk array design options.

A logical I/O request to a disk array corresponds to a data stripe. In terms of an interleaved memory (discussed earlier), a data stripe is a vector of AUs with a stride of 1.

Degree of interleaving (m) is equal to the number of disks in the system over which the stripe unit is stored. This term is equivalent to the interleaving factor, m (discussed in Section 5.1 in reference to interleaved memory modules).

Degree of Interleaving

The degree of interleaving depends on the number of disks in the array and the size of the stripe unit. In other words, at any one time a number of R/W heads can be active depending on the number of disks in the array. The stripe unit can be, for example, a byte, word, quadword, or sector. The selection of the stripe unit size is a tradeoff between the number of disks in the array, the size of the data stripe and whether it is of fixed or variable length.

Figure 5.18 shows, for expository purposes, a disk array system with four disks, with one track per disk, and with four 1-Kbyte segments per track. The stripe unit is a sector. There are obviously more tracks, but only one track per disk is active at the time in this example.

Assume that a data stripe or file consisting of five stripe units, or five sectors, is to be written to the disk array. There are four possible assignments of these five sectors to the four disks; this assignment is similar to skewed interleaving of memory modules. The time required

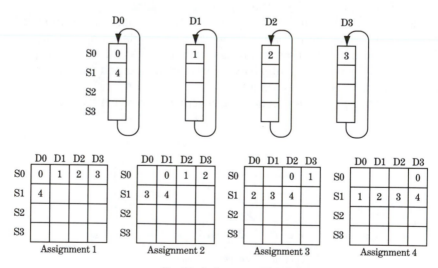

Possible Assignments of Five Sectors

FIGURE 5.18   Disk array layout.

to write these five segments is the latency of the disks (rotation, head position) plus the time to transfer two segments rather than the time to transfer five segments if all of the segments are on one track of one disk. Note that the four disks are assumed to be accessed in parallel. Another assumption is that the disks are rotating synchronously, that is, the same sectors of all disks are under the R/W head at the same time. The other case (to be discussed later) is for asynchronous rotation.

Case I. Synchronous Disk With As-Unit Arm Movement

The synchronous disk organization, as shown in Figure 5.19, is an organization similar to the single-disk system of Figure 5.14(a). Fiducial marks are provided to the drive controller in order to maintain synchrony and to identify the beginning of the first sector, similar to RPS. The m heads are reading or writing in parallel, and the same sector is under the R/W heads of each disk at the same time. The access delays of head positioning and rotation are in parallel. The channel issues a request and, when the correct sector appears under the R/W heads, the request is honored. Kim [KIM86] named this system organization *synchronous disk interleaving* and assumes that the stripe unit is a byte—an assumption that is not a requirement for this organization.

The number of segment read/write times is

$$\text{segment times} = \left\lceil \frac{\text{data stripe size}}{\text{stripe unit size} \times \text{sector size} \times \text{number of disks}(m)} \right\rceil$$

For example, if a data stripe is 16 Kbytes, a stripe unit is 1 Byte, the sector size is 1 Kbyte, and $m = 4$, the data stripe can be transferred in four sector times as compared to sixteen sector times if disk interleaving is not used.

A conversion buffer is required to format a data stripe into the serial

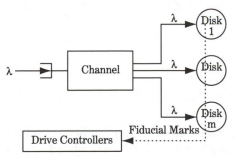

FIGURE 5.19 Synchronous disk organization.

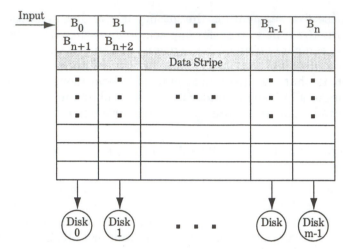

Figure 5.20 Conversion buffer.

streams required for each disk, as shown in Figure 5.20. This buffer design assumes that the incoming data stripe is serial by byte and the stripe unit is a byte. After the buffer is loaded horizontally, the buffer is then unloaded vertically into the disk units [KIM86].

There are a number of implementation problems with synchronous disks. The paramount one is providing synchronization of the disk spindles themselves. Kim [KIM86] discusses the problems of using synchronous motors driven from a common clock with feedback control (the fiducial marks noted in Figure 5.19). Another problem is coping with sectors that go bad after the disk array is placed in service. Reliability and failures are discussed later in this section.

Kim provides extensive model results on performance parameters such as service time, peak transfer rates, queuing delays, disk utilization, and weighted average response time. The effect of block (data stripe) size on response time and service rate is also evaluated [KIM86]. Chen and Patterson [CHEN90] have also investigated the impact of the size of the stripe unit on the service rate of this organization. The most significant parameter is the degree of concurrency of the input requests to the disk system.

Case II. Asynchronous Disk With As-Unit Arm Movement

An asynchronous disk organization is shown in Figure 5.21. With this system, after the data stripe has been loaded into a conversion buffer, the access operations (head positioning) of the disks are initiated and

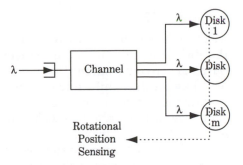

FIGURE 5.21 Asynchronous disk organization.

RPS informs the channel when each sector of each disk is available to receive its allocated stripe units. This system organization has the major advantage of not requiring synchronization of the spindles and the disadvantage of potentially lower performance due to the lack of concurrency in the read/write operations between the disks.

The conversion buffer of Figure 5.20 is modified so that the stripe units are read or written to/from the sectors of the disk at the correct time. This system organization has been named *asynchronous disk interleaving* by M. Y. Kim et al. [KIM87] and *disk striping* by [SALE86].

Case III. Asynchronous Disk With Independent Arm Movement

This system organization not only has asynchronous disk rotation but each arm of each disk can be independently positioned. This system organization appears to provide the greatest possibility for concurrency and therefore should improve the disk system's performance. This system organization is also the most consistent with the concept of an array of independent disk modules as would be created by racking up a multiplicity of PC disk modules.

Kim and Tantawi [KIM87] modeled this system configuration, and they point out that the effective rotational latency approaches that of the disk having the longest latency for a data stripe. That is, the expected seek plus rotational latency is greater than that expected of a synchronous system with unit arm movement. This result is intuitive in that the complete data stripe cannot be transferred until the last stripe units are transferred. Another variant of this system organization is named *declustering* under the assumption that the stripe unit is a sector [LIVN87].

Data Redundancy and MTBF

A direct consequence of the use of a disk array is the danger of reducing the reliability of the disk system, that is, decreasing the *mean time between failure* (MTBF). A conventional multiple-disk system, as shown in Figure 5.12(b), will have a disk failure from time to time, with the consequence that a portion of the stored data is lost. When the disks are arrayed as described above, a failure of one disk can corrupt all of the stored data because the data is interleaved.

In general, the MTBF of a disk array system is lower than that of a single unified disk. The reason is that disk units have roughly equal MTBFs. For example, the IBM 3380, a large mainframe disk, has an MTBF of 52,000 hours while the Conner CP3100, a smaller PC class disk, has an MTBF of 30,000 hours [KATZ89].

Katz illustrates the MTBF problem by comparing the MTBF of the IBM 3380 to an array of CP3100 disks that have the same storage capacity. Equal capacity, not considering redundancy, is achieved with 75 of the CP3100 disks that have an MTBF of 16.6 days. The single IBM 3380 has an MTBF of 2,166 days. The design of an array of disk modules must anticipate a high failure rate and the corruption of all or part of the stored data. Thus, an important and vital consideration in disk array design is providing a high level of data reliability in the face of poor hardware reliability or low MTBF.

The goal of schemes to cope with the low MTBF of disk arrays is to "fail soft," that is, operation continues while a repair is made. Fail soft schemes all depend upon some form of redundancy. A simple example is the use of error correcting codes in memory or communications systems. The design issue thus becomes one of choosing the best form of redundancy. There is an extensive body of knowledge on the use of redundancy for error detection and correction to give fail soft operation [SIEW82].

Kim [KIM86] proposed expanding the conversion buffer of Figure 5.20 to include horizontal *error correcting codes* (ECC). Check words are stored in an added disk along with vertical end-of-block check bytes. The described form of *X-Y* check bits has been used extensively in magnetic tape drives for many decades [MATI77]. With EBCDIC encoding, there is a parity bit for each byte (giving nine tracks) and a longitudinal parity byte recorded at the end of the record.

Patterson et al. have created a taxonomy of six disk array configurations that can be used to achieve data reliability or fail soft operation [PATT88, KATZ 89]. The term RAID (redundant array of inexpensive disks) is used to describe these systems briefly discussed in the following paragraphs. The six RAID configurations are shown in Figures 5.22 and 5.23.

RAID 1. Basically this reliability technique is simple redundancy — a traditional approach to the reliability of any disk system, arrayed or not. RAID 1 is also known as *mirrored disks* and *shadowing*. All reads

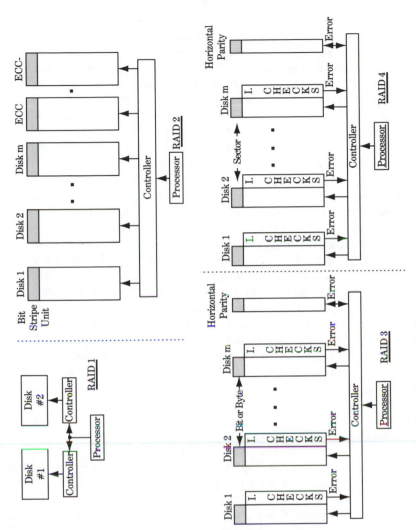

Figure 5.22 RAID 1 to RAID 4 designs.

279

and writes go to/from two identical disks, and the read and write bandwidth is not compromised. However, the cost is 2 times that of a nonredundant system. Errors are detected by comparing the results of both reads. If the comparison fails, the operating system must intervene to determine the correct data, which is a fundamental problem with duplicate redundancy. This organization may give a marginal performance increase if a read operation selects the disk unit that has the shortest latency using RPS information from both disks.

RAID 2. The data stripe is interleaved bitwise across a number of disks as shown in Figure 5.22. The redundancy is provided by horizontal ECC bits stored in separate disks. The use of ECC across a wide memory word has been used in computers using semiconductor memories for several decades. ECC identifies not only that an error has been made but the location of the bit(s) that are in error. The number of bits, thus ECC disks, required to detect two errors and correct one error (DEDSEC) must satisfy the relationship $2^c \geq d + c + 1$ where c is the number of check bits and d is the number of data bits [HAMM50]. A discussion of the number of required ECC bits is outside the scope of this book, but there are many good references. However, the degree of redundancy required for this scheme is $O(\log_2 m)$. For example, if the data stripe is applied across eight disks, four disks are needed to store the DEDSEC bits. The DEDSEC bits must themselves be interleaved because of the potential for a failure in one of the redundant disks. Simple parity for detecting but not correcting an error can be accomplished with one redundant disk.

Because a fraction of a data stripe will reside in a sector and the data in the sectors of all disks participate in the generation of the ECC bits, writes must be conducted as Read-Modify-Write operations, which reduce the bandwidth of the system. Read-Modify-Write operations are required for any memory where the memory word is larger than the addressable unit.

RAID 3. This method, as shown in Figure 5.22, of providing data correction in the face of a disk failure is a simplification of RAID 2. The stripe unit is a bit or byte. Because there is significant data checking provided on each of the disk drives, it is not necessary to have full ECC capability as with RAID2, simple parity will suffice. The redundant disk contains simple parity that is used to identify and correct the bit(s) in the disk that has failed or produced an error. The failed disk is identified by the internal checking hardware in each of the disks.

For example, assume a byte is interleaved across eight disks with even parity in the parity disk, as shown in Table 5.16. If disk 4 fails, the value of the bit is unknown: it could be a one or zero. The fact that the disk has failed is known, and the parity bit is 1 while there is an

Disk

	1	2	3	4	5	6	7	8	P
Normal	1	0	1	1	1	0	0	1	1
Disk 4 fails	1	0	1	x	1	0	0	1	0
Restored	1	0	1	1	1	0	0	1	1

TABLE 5.16 RAID 3 example.

even number of remaining good bits. From this information, the true value of 1 can be reconstructed.

The RAID 3 scheme requires Read-Modify-Write operations to compute the parity bit. However, the incremental hardware cost is small as the degree of redundancy is fixed at one disk module for any degree of disk interleaving.

RAID 4. This redundancy method is a modification of RAID 3 in that the stripe unit is a sector rather than a bit or byte. However, RAID 4 does not interleave across the disks, thus there is no improvement in transfer rate for a single stripe unit compared to a single disk. Some of this performance loss can be recovered with independent head movement that permits more then one read/write to be in process at once. For writes to the disk, the Read-Modify-Write operation is still required. Parity is provided at the byte level in the parity disk, and internal checking of each disk unit is used to identify the location of the data failure.

RAID 5. This redundant disk array system, shown in Figure 5.23, distributes the contents of the parity disk of RAID 3 or RAID 4 across all of the disks. The internal checking of RAID 3 and RAID 4 is not shown. A fraction of all of the disks is used to store parity bits rather than a separate disk; the amount of storage is the same even though a parity disk is not used. There are two failure modes that can be handled. First, a disk can fail that does not contain the parity of the accessed data stripe, this case is identical to RAID 3 or 4. For example, for the stripe unit identified •, if disk 1 fails, the data can be recovered because parity is not lost. Second, if the disk that fails contains the parity of the accessed data stripe, the correct data can still be recovered since only the parity bit is unknown. For example, if disk m fails the identified stripe unit can be recovered. As noted previously, the IBM 9337 is a RAID 5 system.

RAID 6. This disk array system extends the two-dimensional organization (one dimension of disks and one dimension of sector) of RAID 5

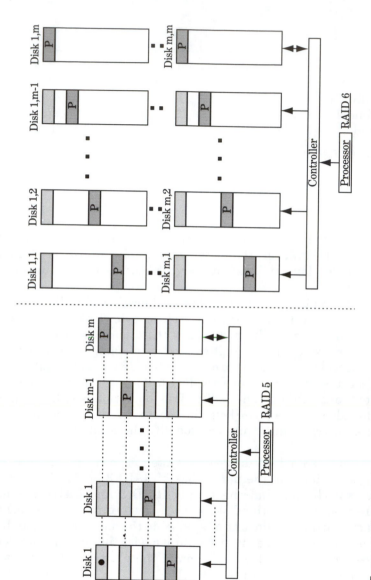

FIGURE 5.23 RAID 5 and RAID 6 designs.

to the three-dimensional (two dimensions of disks and one dimension of sectors). Each disk now contains both row and column parity plus the parity in the segments. Thus, RAID 6, due to its two-dimensional redundancy, can sustain two disk failures and still function. The RAID 6 redundant system checks the data in the column and does not depend on the internal checking hardware. Multidimensional disk arrays and their redundancy codes are discussed in [GIBS89].

5.2.4 *Disk Caches*

The very long latency of disks leads to significant delays for servicing page faults and requests for I/O. As with caches that effectively reduce the latency of main memory, a method for reducing the effect of disk latency is via use of the disk cache. Discussion in Section 5.2.1 shows how the use of software buffers has reduced the number of actual accesses to the disk. The question addressed in this section is whether or not a hardware-managed cache would be effective in reducing latency while transparent to the operating system.

I have no knowledge of specific disk cache implementations, thus I will speculate on their organization. A disk cache would probably be organized early select, direct access. The disk cache sector would probably be a disk track composed of a number of disk sectors that would be the disk cache blocks. The reason for this organization is that the transfer of a track from the disk to the cache sector would not have rotational latency because the read can start at any point of the track and can be mapped into the random access cache sector. A transfer from the cache that evicts a sector to the disk can also start at any point in the track since the source is a random access memory. A track size segment has been used with some paging drums to eliminate rotation latency.

A major design issue is where to place the disk cache in the processor-disk path. Figure 5.24 shows the typical topology for connecting disks to a processor. There can be a multiplicity of channels, a multiplicity of storage controllers, and a multiplicity of string controllers, each connected to a multiplicity of disk units.

The options for placing a disk cache are: (1) main memory, (2) channels, (3) storage controllers, (4) string controllers, or (5) at each of the disks. As the location of the caches is moved toward the processor, more disk accesses are handled by the cache and the utilization of the cache increases. For example, when placed at the main memory, all disk references pass through the cache. If placed at one of the disks, only the accesses to that disk are handled. Because of disk skew, it can be argued that the disk cache should be placed at the disk that has the heaviest

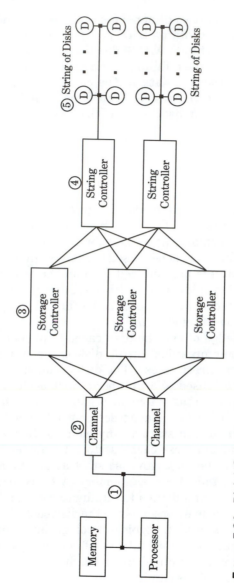

FIGURE 5.24 Disk I/O cache placement options.

load. However, Smith [SMIT85] showed that skew is dynamic and changes from disk to disk over time. One placement, therefore, may be far from ideal for a varying workload on the system. A cache would then be required for all disks. For disk manufacturers, incorporating the cache into the disk permits the manufacturer to sell the cache as well as the disk. However, this is not necessarily the best for overall system cost and/or performance. As discussed below, for a case where there is a fixed amount of memory available for a cache, the memory should be placed at the processor.

Smith's paper on disk caches gives miss ratio data derived from trace data on an IBM S/360/91, 370/165, 370/168s and an Amdahl 470V/6 [SMIT85]. The trace data is then used to evaluate disk cache miss rates for various cache sizes, organizations, and locations in the system. Of the five possible locations for caches shown in Figure 5.24, three locations are evaluated. The results of the simulation are shown in Table 5.17.

Global. One cache at the main memory (location 1).
Controller. Multiple caches, one with each I/O Channel (location 2).
Device. Multiple caches, one with each disk (location 5).

The results of these simulations indicate that for the evaluated disk caches sizes, the best miss ratio is obtained with global disk caches. However, as would be expected, there can be significant variations in the miss ratios for different workloads. Ousterhout [OUST85] reports that for measurements on VAX with a 2-Mbyte disk cache, only 17.7% of all requests are actually served by the disk. Goldstein [GOLD87] uses a miss ratio of 0.1 to justify the use of disk caches in the future—a figure

Total Cache Capacity (Mbytes)	Crocker Bank Business Data Processing			SLAC Scientific Calculations		
	Global	Controller	Device	Global	Controller	Device
1	0.316	0.475	0.610	0.330	0.601	0.630
2	0.259	0.365	0.450	0.226	0.414	0.496
4	0.225	0.275	0.330	0.146	0.326	0.370
8	0.197	0.233	0.266	0.099	0.227	0.271
16	0.172	0.203	0.224	0.070	0.136	0.174
32	0.150	0.177	0.199	0.050	0.085	0.109
64	0.139	0.155	0.175	0.033	0.061	0.071

Note. The total cache capacity is evenly distributed over the controllers or devices.

TABLE 5.17 Disk cache miss ratios.

that is consistent with this data. Therefore, it seems that a miss ratio in the range of 0.1 constitutes a reasonable estimate for design purposes.

There are a number of system issues concerning disk caches. In general, these are the same issues addressed in Chapter 2 on multilevel caches. A disk cache should be write back because of the disk latency, and multilevel inclusion should be enforced. In addition, there are operating system issues such as operating system control of the disk cache and error recovery. Additional issues are problems in coherency and reliability with the disk cache operating in write-back mode. Most of these design issues are discussed at length in [SMIT85]. It is interesting to note that the software-controlled disk cache of MS-DOS places such considerations under user control.

Smith presents an interesting discussion on alternatives to disk caches. Today, with large main memories and large buffers, the disk cache may not be the most effective method of reducing disk accesses. Alternatives discussed by Smith include large cache block sizes that benefit from spatial locality, larger main memory to reduce the need to page temporary files, solid state drums and disks, using the virtual memory system to map the disk address space into the program address space, and others. If a designer has a fixed additional memory, how should this memory be allocated; should it be used as a disk cache, more main memory, or as program managed buffers? The conclusion seems to be that system simplification issues are more important than performance issues in answering this design question.

While not a disk cache, an extended memory as a paging device (solid state drum) has been used with a number of supercomputers. These devices have been very effective in reducing the time required for page-out and page-in when a task is swapped out in a multiprogramming environment.

6

Pipelined Processors

6.0 Overview

The design process of early computers began with the instruction set and progressed to implementation. While instruction set design and implementation were not completely disjoint, they were reasonably so. Once an instruction set was designed, with some forethought of its implementation, the specified functions were hardwired into a controller. The controller could be a decoded counter or a tapped delay line that produced the timing pulses to enable the transfer gates.

Wilkes [WILK53] wrote the seminal paper on microprogramming in which he suggested that there is a better implementation technique for sequential machines than hardwiring. He suggested that the instruction set of a processor could be interpreted by another processor. Thus, the program of the second processor is the controller for the first program. The name given to this technique is *microprogramming*.

The technology of the 1950s did not permit the use of microprogramming because Read Only Memory (ROM), in the form of diodes, was just too expensive. A single germanium diode sold for as much a $10 in 1953! However, with time, the cost of ROM for microprogram stores decreased to the point that the IBM S/360 family was designed, with a very complex instruction set, for microprogram implementation. This family of processors used a number of ROM technologies to store the microprogram, except for the very high performance members of the family that are hardwire controlled.

Microprogramming technology provided a convenient way to exploit concurrency or function overlap because a long micro-instruction permitted a number of transfer paths to be enabled simultaneously. However, the programming task required to accomplish this was, and still is, daunting because identifying concurrency is a manual task and is subject to procedural error. Microprogramming gave the instruction set designer almost unlimited freedom, which supported the design of the so-called

287

CISC architectures. These early processors followed the serial execution model.

A *serial execution model* processor is one in which a program counter sequences through instructions one by one, finishing one instruction before starting the next (paraphrased from [HWU87]).

Most of the parallelism controlled by the microprogram was within the execution of a single instruction. However, there are exceptions to the serial execution model where portions of two instructions are performed together. For example, instruction $i + 1$ could be fetched while instruction i is completing. Recall that the von Neumann architecture fetched two instructions at once. Nevertheless, if for some reason the flow of control is changed, no state has been changed and the execution continued to follow the serial execution model.

Pipelines do not follow the serial execution model. At any one time only one portion of a given instruction is being processed in the pipeline. However, other portions of a number of different instructions are being simultaneously processed. This major and fundamental characteristic of pipelines—that is, the concurrent execution of portions of a number of instructions—leads to most of the pipeline design problems. Pipelining formalizes the identification of parallelism and replaced the asynchronous interface between functions with synchronizing clock pulses. A task is broken up into its constituent parts, and a special purpose hardware function is developed for each part. If the workload is a long vector, the vector AUs can be streamed down the pipeline, producing one result per clock.

A *pipeline* is "a structure that consists of a sequence of stages through which a computation flows with the property that new operations can be initiated at the start of the pipeline while other operations are in progress through the pipeline" [STON93].

The IBM 7094 (1963) is an example of an early overlapped architecture and is the successor to the nonoverlapped IBM 704 (1956). The 7094 had three functional units that could be operated concurrently: the instruction fetch unit, the decode and data fetch, and the execution unit [CHEN80]. Additional concurrency is provided by fetching two instructions (as with the von Neumann architecture) and two operands at once. Complex interlocks controlled the execution of an instruction because the three functional units operated asynchronously. Another example of overlap is found later in the Intel 8086. The designers considered a number of overlap schemes selected to enhance the performance of this processor. The issue was to provide reasonable performance with a reasonable die size [MCKE79]. The selection of overlap options and their resulting performance is described in Section 6.4.

During World War II, code-breaking computers were developed at Benchly Park by Allen Turing. This work was followed in the early 1960s, at the National Security Agency, with the development of special-purpose computers for breaking codes and ciphers using pipelined processors. Researchers at the National Security Agency with assistance from their contractors, IBM and UNIVAC, played a significant role in the development of pipelining techniques in general and of circuit techniques for pipelining in particular.

Concurrent with the development of microprogramming and simple overlapped processors, researchers were investigating methods for speeding up frequently used functions and algorithms by using attached processors [ESTR60]. Many of these special purpose processors were directed toward various forms of signal processing and seismic data processing. FFT processors and the more general convolver processors were produced [TEX65]. The special purpose processors have evolved to the coprocessors-processors (attached processors) used with many microprocessors today. In the main, attached processors only addressed the problem of high-speed execution of arithmetic operations. The main processor handled other functions such as instruction fetching and processing. Vector processors (discussed in Chapter 11) are direct descendants of the pipelined convolver boxes of the 1960s.

In 1955 the UNIVAC Corporation and IBM began designing a new generation of general scientific computers for the Lawrence Livermore Laboratory. These machines were conceived to push the state-of-the-art in architecture and achieve a greater performance increase than could be obtained from faster circuit and memory technology alone.

The UNIVAC machine, named LARC, was delivered in 1959. This processor used a four-stage pipeline that is clocked from a common source [ECKE59] and is the precursor of the technique of pipelining as practiced today. The IBM Stretch, delivered in 1961, design goal was an increase of $100\times$ in performance with a memory speed increase of $6\times$ and a logic speed increase of $10\times$ [BLOC59, BUCH62, ROSE69]. These numbers indicate that a concurrency level of 10 to 15 would be required to meet the design goals. The Stretch architecture explored several ad hoc concurrency techniques and used a number of functional stages operating asynchronously. By means of interlocks between these stages, work is passed down the pipeline as completed.

The LARC and Stretch are important precursor supercomputers, but they were not commercial successes and were followed by the first generation of pipelined supercomputers. These supercomputers are pipelined for instruction processing as well as execution. The dates of first installation of these machines are:

CDC 6600	1964	[MATI80]
IBM S/360/91	1967	[CASE78]
CDC 7600	1969	[MATI80]
TI ASC	1972	[CRAG89]
CDC STAR 100	1974	[RIGA84]
Cray 1	1976	[MATI80]

Two early pseudo-pipelined processors deserve notice: the VAX 11/78 and the Intel 8008. The VAX-11/780 employed a three-stage pipeline [EMER84] that is reminiscent of the Stretch pipeline. That is, each of the three stages is an autonomous processor that executes its own microcode instruction stream to perform the function of the stage. Interlocking between the stages controls the flow of an instruction down the pipeline.

Microprocessor design has followed the path of the supercomputers. The first microprocessors, the Intel and Texas Instruments 8008 [NOYC81], are hardwired processors. As the 8008 evolved, its serial execution model was replaced by pipelining: The i486 is pipelined with five stages, for example [FU89, CRAW90, INTE90]. Processors such as the IBM S/360 are initially microprogrammed sequential machines, but contemporary models are implemented as pipelines. Researchers at IBM have published many of the "tricks" of pipelining a CISC architecture in the form of patents and in the IBM Technical Disclosure Bulletin. Pipelining is now such an accepted implementation approach that all new architectures after 1985, such as the MIPS, SPARC, PowerPC, and others, are based on pipelining as a first consideration followed by the design of an instruction set that is amenable to pipeline execution—a procedure that is the reverse of that used for the early computers. The Intel Pentium represents an architecture that was not intended for pipelining but is now being pipelined—a significant challenge.

6.1 Pipeline Performance Models

The first performance models for pipelines were developed by Cotton [COTT65]; he investigated the tradeoffs between gate delay, latch delay, pipeline length, and, significantly, the issue of clock skew and latch setup time. Clock skew plagues pipeline designers with problems of clock distribution even today.

Davidson [DAVI71] formulated a graphical representation of the temporal behavior of pipelines named *reservation tables*. Similar graphical representations of the space–time relationship of pipelines, which

Time →

		1	2	3	4	5	6	7	8
S	1	I1	I2	I3	I4				
T	2		I1	I2	I3	I4			
A									
G	3			I1	I2	I3	I4		
E	4				I1	I2	I3	I4	

FIGURE 6.1 Reservation table by stage.

evolved from Gantt charts, are described by [CHEN71]. Tables of this type in their original and modified form serve today to help explain pipeline operation.

A reservation table is shown in Figure 6.1. Time steps, in clocks, are shown on the horizontal axis, and the pipeline stages are shown on the vertical axis. The vertical lines between time steps signify the clock pulses. This reservation table illustrates a pipeline of four stages and a four-instruction sequence: I1 to I4. The first result, I1, can be clocked out of the pipeline at the end of t_4 and the last result at the end of t_7. The instruction sequence, for this example, is broken with instruction 4 and cannot be resumed until time 8, after the pipeline is emptied, which is referred to as *flushing*. This form of reservation table is similar to the presentation of a logic analyzer with a probe on each of the pipeline stages.

A common variation of the reservation table is to show time on the horizontal axis and the sequence of instructions on the vertical axis. The same pipeline and workload illustrated in Figure 6.1 are shown in Figure 6.2.

Note that for both of these reservation tables, at t_3 for example, instructions I1, I2, and I3 are active in stages S3, S2, and S1, respectively. An objection to this form of reservation table is that it expands in two dimensions as the number of instructions increases; the first form

Time →

	1	2	3	4	5	6	7	8	9
Inst. 1	S1	S2	S3	S4					
Inst. 2		S1	S2	S3	S4				
Inst. 3			S1	S2	S3	S4			
Inst. 4				S1	S2	S3	S4		

FIGURE 6.2 Reservation table by instruction.

expands in only one dimension. It is a matter of choice as to which form of reservation table best conveys the desired information. However, both forms are frequently used in reference manuals of microprocessors, while the first form is used exclusively in this book.

A processor pipeline can be viewed as a single entity. However, many early pipelines are decomposed into two major functions:

1. Instruction Processor Unit (IPU),
2. Execution Unit(s) (EU).

This subdivision is useful in explaining the operation of a pipeline. For example, low-density circuit technology often requires a functional partition into physical cabinets. In some cases, the instruction processor was in one cabinet and the execution unit resided in another. The interconnections between the two cabinets had to be a pipeline stage that provided no logic function. This technique is beginning to be used again for communication between chips.

The performance models developed below consider the pipeline as a unit; the division into IPU and EU is not made. The unit of time in these models is a clock period, and the unit of work is an instruction. Note that only one instruction can be issued in one clock period. Processor implementations that can issue more than one instruction in a clock period are discussed in Chapter 10.

The simplest possible scheduling strategy is assumed for this model. That is, a break in the flow of instructions causes the pipeline to stall, introducing delays, until the last instruction in the sequence exits the pipeline; this strategy is illustrated in Figure 6.1. Other scheduling and strategies are discussed in Chapters 7 and 8.

For this model, known as the *pipeline model*, the number of clocks required to process a sequence of k instructions is

$$\begin{aligned} \text{number of clocks} &= \text{clocks for the first result to exit} \\ &\quad + \text{length of a run of instructions} - 1 \\ &= n + k - 1 \end{aligned}$$

where n is the number of pipeline stages and k is the length of an instructionsequence ending in a taken branch. And the clocks per instruction (CPI) is

$$\text{CPI} = \frac{n + k - 1}{k} = 1 + \frac{n - 1}{k}.$$

As $k \rightarrow 1$, $\text{CPI} \rightarrow n$ and as $k \rightarrow \infty$, $\text{CPI} \rightarrow 1$. In other words, $1 \leq \text{CPI} \leq n$.

For the limit of $\text{CPI} = 1$, all of the overhead (delays) needed to fill the pipeline have been prorated over the large number of executed instructions. For the limit of CPI $= n$, there is only one instruction and it must be clocked down all of the pipeline stages.

For a serial execution model implementation, n clocks would be required to execute a single instruction. That is, using a time-shared common block of logic, the instructions make n passes through the logic to complete the execution of an instruction. Note that the number of passes is the same as the number of pipeline stages. If the clock period for both the serial execution model processor and the pipeline implementations is the same, the speedup of a pipelined implementation over a sequential model implementation is

$$S = \frac{\text{serial execution model time (in clocks)}}{\text{pipeline time (in clocks)}}$$

$$= \frac{nk}{n + k - 1}.$$

As $k \to \infty$, $S \to n$.

These limits tell us that for pipelines to be effective, the length (k) of the stream of AUs processed must be as long as possible. However, there can be an n-fold increase in the hardware of the pipeline over the simple serial execution model. The major goal of a processor pipeline design is to reduce the value of CPI by increasing the apparent value of k. Methods for achieving large values of k are the subject of Chapters 6 to 8.

When the stream of instructions is broken, a pipeline delay, *stall* or *break*, is said to have occurred that produces *bubbles in the pipeline*. For example, Figure 6.1 has a delay of four clocks. These delays will reduce the performance by increasing CPI to a value greater than 1. The model for CPI has two terms: the steady-state term, which indicates that the pipeline will produce one result every clock, and the delay term, which indicates the increase in clocks due to delays:

$$\text{CPI} = \text{steady state} + \text{delays} = 1 + \text{delays}.$$

Pipeline delays occur for three major reasons.

1. *Control.* Change of flow control caused by branches (Chapter 7), interrupts (Chapter 9), traps (Chapter 9), and exceptions (Chapter 9).

2. *Data* dependencies (Chapter 8), particularly true dependencies, anti dependencies, and output dependencies.

3. *Structural* delays, pertaining to logic resources (Chapter 8) and memory delays (Chapters 2, 3, 4, and 5).

Note that the delays added to the steady-state CPI = 1 are the probabilities that a delay will occur (such as a taken branch) times the delay that results with the event (such as the taken branch delay). The magnitude of the delay is of primary concern to the processor designer and is discussed in the noted chapters. The probability that an event will occur is partially a function of the instruction set architecture and the workload, subjects not directly addressed in this book.

6.2 Pipeline Design Considerations

Selecting the number of pipeline stages is a significant design problem because of the following considerations. For a given logic path, the greater the subdivisions into stages, the shorter the logic path per stage, the faster the clock, and, since performance has been stated in CPI, the faster the execution of a program. Also, recall that the speedup of a pipelined processor compared to a serial execution model processor is the number of pipeline stages, as $k \to \infty$. However, as the length of the pipeline increases, the delays due to flushing the pipeline increase because very large k is not realistic. Thus there is an optimum number of pipeline stages.

The logic path is the number of levels of logic required if the processor executed an instruction in one clock, typically in excess of 100 gates levels or delays. Figure 6.3 shows a one-stage pipeline with L logic levels between two registers clocked from the same source. If the pipeline is subdivided into two stages, each stage of logic has $L/2$ of the gate level, and so on.

In addition to the logic path, each stage of the pipeline requires a fixed time for clock skew and latch setup. If the subdivision of the logic path into stages is overdone (that is, it has too many stages), the clock skew and latch setup time will dominate the clock period determination. The design question is: What is the optimum number of pipeline stages? Larson and Davidson [LARS73] formulated the first known model that relates the processing rate to clock skew, the value of k, and the number

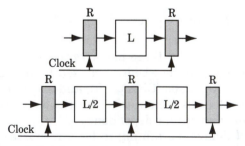

FIGURE 6.3 Pipeline subdivision of stages.

of pipeline stages. They showed that as the number of stages increases, performance increases until a maximum is reached, at which point performance starts decreasing. Consider a simple pipeline with delays due only to program control, as shown in Figure 6.1. More complex control flow situations are discussed in Chapter 7.

The number of clocks to process a simple sequence is

$$\text{number of clocks} = n + k - 1.$$

The clock period is

$$\text{clock period} = \frac{L}{n} + t$$

where L is the logic path length in gate delays, t is the clock skew plus latch setup in gate delays, and n is the number of pipeline stages.

$$\text{processing time} = \text{number of clocks} \times \text{clock period}$$

$$= (n + k - 1)\left(\frac{L}{n} + t\right) \quad \text{(in gate delays).}$$

The first derivative of the processing time with respect to n is set to zero and solved for the optimum number of pipeline stages, n_{opt} as

$$n_{opt} = \sqrt{\frac{L(k-1)}{t}};$$

for large values of k,

$$n_{opt} = \sqrt{\frac{Lk}{t}}.$$

As an example, consider a pipeline with $L = 128$, $t = 2$ and 4 and an instruction sequence of $k = 4$. Figure 6.3 shows a plot of the processing time, in gate delays, for this workload as n is varied between 1 and 128. For $t = 2$, there is a minimum processing time for values of n between 8 and 16. For $t = 4$ the minimum occurs around $n = 8$. Solving the equation for n_{opt} shows that $n_{opt} = 13.86$ and 9.8 for the two cases of t. As the number of stages in a pipeline must be an integer, n could be either 13 or 14 for $t = 2$ and $n = 10$ for $t = 4$. This example illustrates

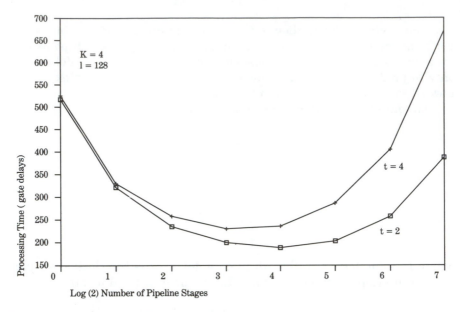

FIGURE 6.4 Pipeline performance.

the performance increase that can be achieved by reducing t as much as possible.

The optimum length of the pipeline is the length that provides the minimum execution time for a sequence of length k. Note, from Figure 6.4, that if clock skew and setup time are not controlled, the optimum length of the pipeline can change significantly. Furthermore, because a longer pipeline gives a higher speedup over a serial execution model processor, the minimization of t is a paramount design issue.

Clock skew plus latch setup is normalized to gate delays and is in the order of 2 to 3. It can, however, go to 10 in some extreme designs. VLSI technology has not eliminated the problem of clock skew; while the clock distribution paths are on the chip, the gates are faster and the problem remains. As an example of the lengths taken to balance clock delay and control skew, consider the clock distribution scheme of the DEC Alpha microprocessor shown in Figure 6.5. The clock is generated by a common generator and distributed over equal-length paths to each of the clocked registers. Note that the total delay from the clock pulse generator is not important, only the skew at each of the destinations. A similar scheme is described by Cotton [COTT65] and used with the TI ASC [CRAG89]. Recent research on clock distribution to nonuniform destinations is reported by Kahng et al. [KAHN90].

Early pipeline computers had pipeline lengths of 12 to 15 stages primarily because of the use of core memory and relatively slow,

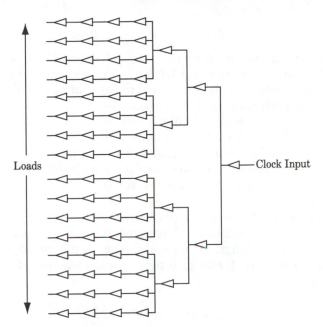

FIGURE 6.5 DEC Alpha clock distribution.

low-density logic such as used with the IBM S/360/91. Modern microprocessors such as MIPS and SPARC, however, have 4 to 6 pipeline stages.
The reduction in pipeline length is an attempt to reduce, for example, the
branch delays discussed in Chapter 7. Superpipelining (to be discussed in
Chapter 9) explores the possibility that pipelines have become too short
and the clock period too long—a continuing research topic. A model for
optimum pipeline length can be developed that attaches a cost of the
latches required when the logic path is partitioned into stages. The cost
can be in terms of chip area and power.

The latch or flip flop setup time is included in parameter t used
above. A discussion of the design of latches for pipelines is outside the
scope of this book. However, a few comments are in order. There is the
potential for race conditions in a pipeline with two solutions. First, JK
flip flops are, in effect, dual-rank latches, which triggered at different
times can be used to eliminate race conditions. The second solution for
this problem is the use of balanced logic paths and fast latches. The Earl
latch, for ECL, is an example of such a latch and is described by Kogge
[KOGG81].

VLSI CMOS implementations of pipelines registers have the same
problems of setup time, clock skew, and clock distribution as with bipolar
circuits. A thorough discussion of these problems along with various flip-
flop designs for pipelines can be found in [WEST93].

6.3 Other Pipeline Performance Models

Kunkel and Smith modeled the optimal pipeline length by considering a number of factors in one model [KUNK86]. Their paper looks at not only circuit design considerations, such as clocking, but also at dependencies that limit the performance of pipelines. However, I believe that they look only at the execution pipelines, not at the total pipeline, which includes the IPU, as branch delays are not considered. Their results show that the number of useful gate delays per pipeline segment is in the range 6 to 8. These results are consistent with the results discussed above only if there is buffering between the IPU and EU that eliminates branch delays.

Another approach to pipeline performance modeling is found in work of Dubey and Flynn [DUBE90]. Their model considers the utilization of the pipeline, not the length of an instruction sequence. Pipeline utilization varies from 0 to 1 and is roughly equivalent to 1/CPI. Pipeline utilization is defined as

$$u = u_{\max} - rs^2 - vs$$

where $u_{\max}$ denotes the upper limit on utilization, independent of pipeline length, cache misses, page faults and the like; s the stages in the pipeline; r the dependency delays; and v an experimentally derived coefficient.

If this model is used to evaluate only the pipeline (for example, without cache misses), $u_{\max}$ is equal to 1. Note that the dependency delays (I believe this includes branch delays as well) reduce utilization by the square of the pipeline length. Dubey and Flynn compare their model to the simulation results of [KUNK86] and find agreement. The conclusion of their modeling is that the optimum pipeline length is in the range of 6 to 8 stages and is limited by clock skew and dependencies, which is the same result as given by the other models.

[LANG79] gives another approach to pipeline modeling. The authors of this paper have used queuing theory to model the performance of a pipeline that has a multiplicity of execution units. As described in Chapter 8, various delays can build up in the processor, and these delays can be viewed as queues. This model gives results that are within ±10% of measured performance for two benchmarks on three computers: the Cray-1 and two configurations of the TI ASC. A Markov chain form of modeling is reported by [HSIE85]. This modeling method allows a close examination of the benchmark parameters and their relationship to the pipeline parameters.

Emma and Davidson [EMMA87] investigated the optimum length of pipelines under the constraints of branch and dependency delays.

They examined a number of execution traces and noted the interference between branches and dependencies that preclude accurate analytical models that treat these two delays as orthogonal.

For this model, the pipeline is divided into two sections: setup and execute (equivalent to the IPU and EU discussed previously). The total length of the pipeline determines branch delays while only the execute section determines dependency delays. Thus there is interest in the ratio of the lengths of these two function pipelines.

Let

I = number of stages in the setup pipeline,
E = number of stages in the execution pipeline,
$R = E/I$,
$n = E + I$.

It follows that $n = I(R + 1)$.

Based upon their workload models Emma and Davidson found that $I_{\mathrm{opt}} = \sqrt{0.33L/t}$. Thus, the optimum length of the pipeline is

$$n_{\mathrm{opt}} \approx (1 + R)\sqrt{\frac{0.33L}{t}}.$$

This model suggests that for a given technology that sets the value of t, R should be as large as possible. That is, the execution units should be long compared to the setup stage. For integers, this ratio is difficult to achieve unlike floating point execution units. For an example where $R = 1.5$, L $= 128$, and $t = 2$, the optimum pipeline length is 11.48, which in this case means either 11 or 12 stages. The performance curve is rather flat at the maximum, so the choice is not critical. For an 11-stage pipeline, $S = 4$ and $E = 7$ would be a reasonable distribution of stages for floating point execution.

I conclude this section on pipeline modeling with the mention of a modeling technique briefly described by Kain [KAIN89] and expanded by Guo [GUO89] and Unwalla [UNWA94]. This modeling method views the stages of a pipeline as a binary state vector. That is, various stages are active (= 1) and others are inactive (= 0), and the maximum number of pipeline states for an n-stage pipeline is $\leq 2^n$. Some of the states are usually not reachable, such as the state of all 0's. These states are then viewed as a Markov chain and the transition probabilities are determined based upon such considerations as branching probabilities, memory delays, and true dependencies.

When the states and transition probabilities are determined from the analysis of instruction flow, it is a relatively simple matter to compute the *average instruction execution rate* (AIER), which is the inverse of the CPI. This modeling technique should be effective for short pipelines, but for a long pipeline the number of states can become quite large and determining the transition probabilities is difficult.

6.3.1 *Pipeline Efficiency*

Early researchers who considered pipeline designs were concerned with how efficiently the hardware was used. This concern is understandable due the very high cost of logic in the 1960s and 1970s. Today with low-cost logic, the CPI of the pipeline is of greater concern. Nevertheless, efficiency considerations are of historical interest.

The issue of efficiency poses the question: How does the space × time product of a pipelined processor compare to an implementation using the serial execution model? The space × time, $ST(s)$, product of a serial execution model processor is

$$ST(s) = \text{space} \times \text{time} = (1 \times n)k = nk.$$

That is, the processor logic space is equivalent to one pipeline stage, processing one instruction takes n passes through this logic, and there are k instructions processed. The space × time product of a pipelined processor, $ST(p)$, is the number of stages times the number of clocks.

$$ST(p) = \text{space} \times \text{time} = n(n + k - 1).$$

The ratio of these two space × time products gives the relative efficiency

$$\frac{ST(s)}{ST(p)} = \frac{nk}{n(n + k - 1)} = \frac{k}{n + k - 1} = \frac{1}{1 + (n - 1)/k}.$$

Only as $k \to \infty$ does the space × time product of the pipelined processor approach that of the serial processor. This is one reason that pipelining was reserved by designers for high-performance computers, which were not too cost-sensitive. As can be seen from this model, the efficiency of the pipeline is very sensitive to the value of k, as would be expected. For $k = 1$, the efficiency is $1/n$. And, as $k \to \infty$, the efficiency $\to 1$. This efficiency consideration is also not of great concern today because the cost of logic has decreased and current design emphases is focused on performance rather than pipeline efficiency. However, attention to low-power processors may revive interest in other optimizations.

6.4 Pipeline Partitioning

In order for a processor to be pipelined, it is necessary for the designer to partition the logic path into pipeline stages. Kogge [KOGG81] lists the conditions for partitioning a function into the subfunctions of pipeline stages.

1. Evaluation of the basic function is equivalent to some sequential evaluation of the subfunctions.
2. The inputs for one subfunction come totally from outputs of previous subfunctions in the evaluation sequence.
3. Other than the exchange of inputs and outputs, there are no inter-relationships between subfunctions.
4. Hardware may be developed to execute each subfunction.
5. The times required for these hardware units to perform their individual evaluations are usually equal.

Condition 5 places a burden on the designer for partitioning and grouping of sequential functions into one stage. In some pipelines, operands are fetched from the registers in the decode stage. Other designs may better meet condition 5 if the register fetch occurred in the execute stage. The clock period must be set to be greater than the longest time interval, requiring careful balancing of stage partitioning to minimize the clock period.

An interesting, but dated, example of partitioning possibilities is found in the design of the Intel 8086 [MCKE79, MCKE92]. The four designs considered were not pipelines but what might more properly be called overlap design options. Nevertheless, these designs do serve as an example of the partitioning used in an overlapped design and they are informative for pipeline partitioning. Four partitions were considered and evaluated by simulation. The chip area and yield for each of these partitions was determined and a selection made based on performance and chip cost.

Four steps are required to interpret an 8086 instruction, and each of these steps requires a number of clock cycles. An estimate of the number of clock cycles per step is

Instruction fetch	4 clock cycles,
Instruction decode	2 clock cycles,
Effective address + memory	7 clock cycles,
Execute and write back	3 clock cycles.

Reservation tables are shown for the four designs in Figure 6.6. The assumed workload consists of three instructions, one of which requires a memory reference for data. From the reservation tables, the number

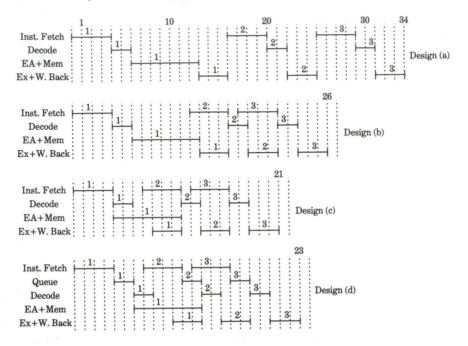

FIGURE 6.6   Intel 8080 partition alternatives.

of clocks required for the three-instruction sequence executing on the four designs is determined.

Design (a) is a pure serial execution model processor with no overlap and requires 34 clock cycles for the three instructions; CPI = 11.33. Design (b) overlaps the instruction fetch of the second and third instructions; a simple form of overlap that provides a CPI of 8.66 or speedup of 1.31 over design (a). The third design, (c), increases the degree of overlap and provides a CPI of 7 or a speedup of 1.62 over design (a). Design (d) introduces a queue into the system with an en queue time of 2 clocks. With this queue, additional overlap is provided for all instructions after the first one, providing a CPI of 7.66 or a speedup of 1.48 over design (a).

The relative performance, normalized to design (a), of the four designs, as predicted by the reservation table models and the simulation, is shown in Table 6.1.

These results illustrate how simple reservation table models can be used to evaluate design alternatives. However, the assumptions made for these models lead me to believe that good fortune is as responsible for the close agreement with the simulation results as good modeling. The exact details of the designs are unclear in the published results, and a number of assumptions had to be made to create the models. Not

| | Speedup | |
Design	Model	Simulation
(a)	1.00	1.00
(b)	1.31	1.35
(c)	1.62	1.65
(d)	1.48	1.50

TABLE 6.1 8080 design alternatives.

included in this discussion are the issues of implementation cost in terms of chip area and yield; these issues are discussed in [MCKE79]. Design (d) was selected for the 8086 because it provided the best balance of performance and cost.

Another technique for speeding up a processor is named *maximum-rate pipelining* (also known as *wave pipelining*). This technique was first described by Cotton [COTT69] and has been the subject of intermittent research since then. This technique permits each stage to process at a rate set by the gate delays without intermediate pipeline storage. As shown in Figure 6.7, storage is provided only at the input and output of the pipeline, and all of the logic path lengths must be balanced between the input and output registers.

A model is developed to evaluate the performance improvement that is possible using this technique over a conventional pipeline. The time $T(mr)$, in gate delays, to process a sequence k is

$$T(mr) = \text{clock period} \times \text{number of clocks}.$$

The clock period is determined by delays through the gates as

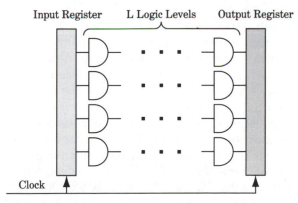

FIGURE 6.7 Maximum-rate pipeline.

"waves" of signals are sent down through logic. The separation of waves is determined by the Nyquest period of the gates and is equal to twice the gate delay. Thus, the clock period in gate delays is

$$\text{clock period} = (2 + t) \text{ gate delays.}$$

The number of clocks, in this clock period, to process k operations is

$$\text{number of clocks} = \frac{L}{2} + k - 1.$$

The $L/2$ term is the number of clocks for the first operation followed by $k - 1$ clocks. Thus, the time to process the sequence k is

$$T(mr) = \frac{2 + t}{L/2 + k - 1}.$$

The speedup of a maximum-rate pipeline over a conventional pipeline is

$$S = \frac{(n + k - 1)(L/n + 1)}{(L/2 + k - 1)(2 + t)};$$

as $k \to \infty$

$$S = \frac{L/n + t}{2 + t}.$$

An example of the speedup available with maximum-rate pipelining over normal pipelining assumes that $L = 128$, $n = 8$, and $k = 4$. The clock skew and setup time for the normal pipeline is $t = 2$. For these values, speedup is $S = 0.73$. In other words, the maximum-rate pipeline is slower than the normal pipeline for $k = 4$. The question can be asked as to what value of k will give performance parity. By setting $T(mr)$ equal to the time for the normal pipeline and solving for k, we find that, for the system of this example, equal performance is obtained when $k = 6.7$.

The maximum-rate pipeline technique has not been widely exploited, but it has the potential for significant performance gains over conventional pipelines for large values of K. Extensive design aids are required to balance the logic paths [KLAS92]. The MIPS R4000 caches use a form or maximum-rate pipelining and are discussed in Section 2.8.4. Further discussion of maximum-rate pipelining is outside the scope of this book, however, Kogge [KOGG81] offers an excellent summary of the design technique and practical implementation problems.

6.5 Contemporary Pipelined Microprocessors

Contemporary microprocessors such as MIPS, SPARC, PowerPC 601, and others have relatively short pipelines. An example of such a pipeline with five stages is shown in Figure 6.8.

The functions performed by each stage of this pipeline are described in Table 6.2. Note that one stage, the execute stage, performs two integer functions: the ALU operation and computing the memory effective address. In some designs, the ALU is duplicated to remove this structural hazard as discussed in Chapter 8.

As noted in Section 2.8.4, caches are now being pipelined, which increases the number of stages in the processor. For example, the instruction fetch stage may become two or three stages as will the memory read or write stage. Thus a pipeline of 8 to 10 stages can result. Long pipelines having a minimum clock period have been named "Superpipelining" and are discussed in Chapter 10.

When an instruction is in the decode stage of a pipeline, a decision must be made if the instruction can be issued to the execution stage. If there are data dependencies the instruction cannot issue. The design

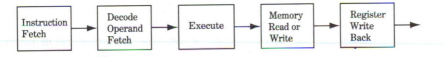

FIGURE 6.8 Short pipeline.

Pipeline State	Function
Instruction fetch	Fetches the instruction from cache
Decode	Decodes the instruction and fetches the operands from registers
Execute	Performs the ALU operation and sets condition codes if used. Computes the effective address for a memory reference
Memory Read or Write	Completes a data reference to the cache for either a load or store
Write Back to Register	Writes the result of an ALU operation or Load into the destination register

TABLE 6.2 Pipeline functions.

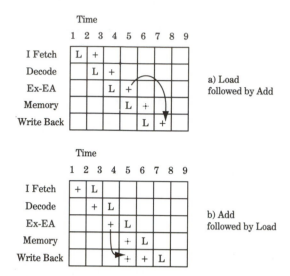

FIGURE 6.9 Pipeline stage scheduling.

considerations of instruction issue are discussed in Chapter 8 and are deferred to that chapter.

Another consideration with pipelines is the question of scheduling past or around unused pipeline stages. Consider two classes of instructions: Loads or Stores and Register-ALU-Register. Load or Store instructions use all five of the pipeline stages while the Add instruction uses only four of the stages as shown in Figure 6.9.

The case of a Load followed by an Add is shown in (a). The Load instruction uses all five of the stages, while the Add instruction passes through the memory stage without any performed operation. However, if the scheduling is greedy, both the Load and the Add would attempt to use the Write Back stage at the same time; t6. For the case of an Add followed by a Load, shown in (b), a greedy schedule for the Add could have been used without a structural hazard. However, there is no gain in processing rate if this is done.

For most pipelines, scheduling past unused pipeline stages is not done. The steady-state CPI of the pipeline is set by the instruction issue rate, and scheduling past unused pipeline stages does not increase the CPI. In the absence of interrupts and branches, the number of instructions issued is equal to the number completed. Thus, the completion rate and the issue rate are the same.

6.6 Exclusion or Synchronization Instructions

Processors that are multiprogrammed, have concurrent I/O, or are used in a multiprocessor system need the ability to access shared variables in such a way that the program execution is logically correct. This requirement leads to the notions of a critical section and an atomic instruction.

A *critical section is* "a section of a program that can be executed by at most one process at a time" [STO93].

An *atomic instruction meets two criteria*: "(1) it proceeds to completion in an operation that cannot be interrupted, and (2) other process cannot access its operands or its result until it is finished" [BARO92].

The capability to implement critical sections requires some form of programmed interlock that will assure *exclusivity* or *mutual exclusion*. Interlocks are provided with semaphores and some way of ensuring sequential access to the semaphore from the multitude of users. The instructions that access the semaphores are referred to as *synchronization instructions*. A full discussion of all the issues of mutual exclusion and synchronization is outside the scope of this book; however, some of the issues are addressed that relate to processor implementation.

One method of providing exclusion is to associate with each shared item of data or data structure a control variable called a semaphore [DIJK68], a nonnegative integer, s (in some cases only 0 or 1 for a binary semaphore), that is the subject of two operators:

P(semaphore): Test unit $s > 0$ and then execute $s \leftarrow s - 1$;
V(semaphore): Execute $s \leftarrow s + 1$.

The semaphore can be either a "general semaphore" (SG) or a "binary semaphore" (SB) and can be the basis for ensuring mutual exclusion and synchronization. For either type, the semaphore is stored in a memory location that is shared by the processes or processors that must cooperate.

To implement the $P(s)$ operator for a SG properly a compound operation consisting of a conditional test, a read, a modification, and a write is required that is noninterruptable or atomic. The $V(s)$ operator has to perform an atomic read, modify, and write operation on a SG.

With binary semaphores, the implementation of the $P(s)$ operator is greatly simplified because "the test and increment operations can be deferred as long as the read and write operations are atomic" [DIJK68]. This approach to providing $P(s)$ leads to the *Test-and-Set* (Figure 6.10) instruction that is followed by a branch. This name is unfortunate as no test, in the sense of a test for a branch, is made as part of the instruction.

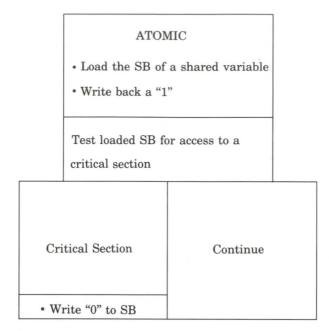

FIGURE 6.10 Test-a-Set instruction.

The synchronization primitives require three steps, the first two of which are atomic.

The new value written back is simply a **one**. If the SB semaphore is already a one, no change occurs. Because the load and write are atomic, the processor and its memory must support read-modify-write operations atomically. With atomic Test-and-Set, the $V(s)$ becomes a simple write of a **0** to the SB; normally writes are atomic.

The following discussion of synchronization instructions with binary semaphores considers two classes of processor implementation:

1. Processors with compound instructions that address memory,
2. Load/Store pipelined processors with instructions that do not directly address memory.

Dijkstra [DIJK65] shows that if a processor satisfies the serial execution model, providing mutual exclusion does not require special instructions because the normal instructions are atomic. For this reason, serial mode processors had little difficulty providing atomic $P(s)$ and $V(s)$ operators; instructions are noninterruptable and lock the bus during all of the steps needed to perform the instruction. With the bus locked, another processor cannot gain access to the semaphore during instruction execution, regardless of the number of clocks required. With concurrency in pipelined processors, this observation concerning serial execution model processors is primarily of historical interest.

6.6.1 *Processors That Address Memory*

Many processors designed in the 1950s and 1960s are now called CISC architectures. These processor have instructions that address memory and, in some cases, perform read-modify-write operation on memory locations. Some of these processors have byte AUs while others can address to the bit. With these facilities, implementing binary semaphores is a reasonably easy task.

However, the requirement for being atomic required that the bus be locked out from other users while a processor is executing a synchronization instruction. Two methods for accomplishing bus locking are used: (1) the bus is implicitly locked as a side effect of the synchronization instruction, and (2) the bus is explicitly locked by executing a lock instruction. An example of implicit locking is the IBM S/360, while explicit locking is used in the Intel ix86 family.

For the following discussion, assume that the binary semaphore (SB) has the following states defined:

1: The semaphore is already in use and is not available to a requester.
0: The semaphore is available to synchronize a requester's process.

IBM S/360. The IBM S/360 architecture was designed with a rich instruction set to be implemented by microprogramming. The Test-and-Set instruction, to be described below, was proposed during the development of the S/360 in 1963 [BLAA 86]. Because operational instructions address memory at the byte level, an entire byte is allocated for a binary semaphore; the left-hand bit is used and the other bits are don't cares. It is easier to implement a binary semaphore when the entire addressable unit is the semaphore; a read-modify write operation is not required, only a read-write. Atomic action is provided by implicitly locking the bus as a side effect. Memory is serialized before the byte is fetched and again after the modified byte is stored, adding time to the synchronization process.

The Test-and-Set (TS) instruction reads the addressed byte, copies the left-hand bit into the condition code, and writes all ones to the addressed byte. A following instruction tests the condition code to determine if the critical section can be entered; the truth table of the Test-and-Set instruction is shown in Table 6.3. $SB(t)$ is the state of the semaphore at time t while $SB(t + 1)$ and $CC(t + 1)$ are the states of the semaphore and condition code at time $t + 1$.

If $CC = 1$, the critical section is not entered; the process waits, or

	$SB(t)$	$SB(t+1)$	$CC(t+1)$	Action
TS	0	1	0	Requester can enter critical section that may include the manipulation of a general semaphore
	1	1	1	Requester cannot enter critical section

TABLE 6.3   IBM S/360 Test-and-Set instruction.

spin locks, and tries TS again until $CC = 0$. When the critical section is finished, the processor performs a store immediate operation that resets the semaphore to zero, an instruction that is inherently atomic. Note that the IBM S/370 has other synchronizing instructions that provided more capability than the simple TS instruction [IBM76].

Pentium. The Intel Pentium instruction set architecture is based on the ix86 family and has instructions that address memory locations to the bit. The synchronization instructions, first used on the i386, are Bit-Test-Set, Bit-Test-Reset, and Bit-Test-and-Complement [INTE86a, INTE92]. Bit addressability required a true read-modify-write capability to be implemented as part of the instruction set because SB bits are embedded in bytes. So that only one processor at a time can have access to the memory location holding the binary semaphore, a process explicitly locks the bus, making the next instruction implicitly atomic.

The *LOCK* instruction places a "true" signal on the processor lock pin. Hardware, external to the processor, detects the lock signal and gives the processor exclusive access to memory, holding the bus locked for the *next instruction* only. The next instruction executed (BTS, BTR or BTC, and others) is now implicitly atomic. The lock process guarantees that the semaphore cannot be modified during synchronization by another processor nor can these instructions be interrupted.

The Bit-Test-and-Set copies the value of the semaphore into the carry flag (CF) and stores a 1 into the semaphore. The process then tests the value in CF, and only if it is a 0 will the process enter a critical section; the semaphore is available before the critical section obtained control. If the semaphore had been a 1, it is set to a 1 and the test will show that $CF = 1$ because the critical section is with another process; this operation is shown as a truth table in Table 6.4. The column $SB(t)$ is the state of the semaphore before the atomic instruction, while $SB(t+1)$ and $CF(t+1)$ are states after the atomic instruction.

A process releases control over the semaphore by executing a BTR instruction. This instruction writes a 0 into the addressed binary semaphore to release it. Because the SB is embedded in a byte, a read-modify-write-operation is required that necessitates the use of a preamble LOCK

	$SB(t)$	$SB(t+1)$	$CF(t+1)$	Action
BTS	0	1	0	Requester can enter critical section that may include the manipulation of a general semaphore
	1	1	1	Requester cannot enter critical section
BTR	0	0	x	No action is taken (not expected to happen)
	1	0	x	Process exits critical section

TABLE 6.4   BTR and BTS instructions.

instruction. If the semaphore is in the 0 state, the semaphore remains a 0. Note that these two instructions, BTS and BTR, are symmetric so that the binary semaphore assignment is not fixed.

For these processors, and others of their class, any program appears to be able to reset or clear a semaphore. However, as a reset instruction can only be at the end of a critical section and a particular critical section can only be in execution in one place at a time, this event should not happen. If it does happen, a programming error has occurred.

A significant problem with the synchronization scheme used with these processors is that the bus will be locked for a number of cycles, thereby reducing the available bus bandwidth. As high-bus availability is important to multiprocessors, synchronization with bus locking becomes increasingly unattractive as the number of processors increases. Access to memory by the other processors is blocked during synchronization. Even if another processor is trying to access a variable that is not shared, it can find the bus locked.

There are a number of design questions with these systems such as whether or not semaphores are in virtual or real memory space and whether or not they are cached. If in virtual memory space, the time of bus lockout can be as long as the time to service a page fault. If semaphores can be cached, multilevel inclusion and coherency between the various caches must also be enforced. Enforcing these policies increases the time that the bus is locked, further increasing the bus utilization by the synchronizing processor to the detriment of other processors.

6.6.2 *Load/Store Processors*

Some of the early pipelined RISC processors ignored the need to provide semaphores, the MIPS and RS/6000 being examples. A Load/Store processor cannot easily implement atomic test-and-set instructions but need another solution to provide exclusion and synchronization. The problems posed by these processors are:

1. Load/store RISC architectures do not, by definition, have operational instructions that operate directly on memory locations nor support compound operations such as read-modify-write. Buses and main memory support reads or writes but do not support read-modify-write transactions.
2. Pipelined processors have a number of instructions in simultaneous execution, making it possible to have two or more synchronizing instructions in simultaneous execution on one processor.

The use of the bus lock instruction strategy is impractical for these processors. A synchronization sequence would call for a sequence such as: (1) lock the memory, (2) flush the pipeline, (3) load the semaphore into the register file, (4) perform the test-and-conditional modify operation, (5) store the semaphore back into memory, (6) unlock the memory, and (7) resume normal processing. This sequence of operations can block the memory bus for a considerable period of time, many tens or hundreds of clock cycles.

A solution to the problem of providing synchronization with these processors is found in a technique called *optimistic synchronization* [JENS87]. This scheme was first used as a synchronization method for data bases [ULLM82]. Recall that the predicted instruction stream of a branch is conditionally processed until the branch is resolved and the commitment can be made or the instructions abandoned. Commitment is defined in Chapter 9.

Optimistic synchronization works in a similar way. The process starts the synchronization process that is conditional up to the time that it is committed in a one clock operation. At the end of the synchronization process, the commitment is made unless another process has already committed a synchronization of the semaphore. The ideas behind optimistic synchronization are:

1. A process performs all of the steps of synchronization, using a general semaphore, conditionally up to the last step when it may be committed.
2. Each processor has a single *reserved* bit (R) that is set, optimistically, when a synchronization is attempted. The effective address of the SB is saved and associated with the R-bit. This address is snooped, and the bit will be reset by any other processor in the system that attempts a synchronization.
3. The synchronization is committed when the modification to the semaphore is completed *and* the R-bit has not been reset by another

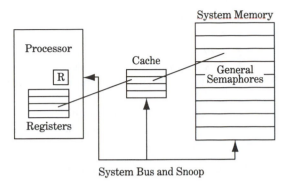

FIGURE 6.11 Optimistic synchronization.

processor. Thus, only one processor at a time can commit a modified semaphore.

4. The semaphores are assumed to be in the processor's cache and are coherent.
5. Two or more attempts to commit on the same clock are resolved by priority logic in the memory system.

A simplified block diagram of this system is shown in Figure 6.10. General semaphores (SG) are allocated to an AU in memory space and are addressed by the synchronization instruction's effective address. These semaphores may be in the cache or will be loaded into the cache on a cache miss. A *reservation flag* (R) is allocated to each processor and is part of the processor's implemented state. The R-flag is set as a side effect of the instruction that loads the semaphore into the register. The caches and flags will be snooped by all processors in the system.

The synchronization process consists of the following steps. Only if the processor's R-flag is one will the synchronization be committed.

- Load (SG) into processor register and set R to one.
- Test (SG).
- Modify (SG).
- If $R = 1$, Write modified (SG) to memory, snoop and modify all caches and reset all other R-bits in the system.

This solution to the problem of providing exclusion and synchronization is used on pipelined RISC processors, such as the PowerPC 601 and the DEC Alpha. This technique significantly reduces bus blocking because the load and store instructions use the bus as any other load and store instruction. In addition to significantly reducing bus blocking, a major benefit of this approach is that it directly supports higher order synchronization methods such as Fetch-and-No-Op, Fetch-and-Store, Fetch-and-Add, and Compare-and-Swap.

	$R(t)$	$R(t+1)$	Operation
lwarx	0	1	$rD \leftarrow SG, R \leftarrow 1$
	1	1	Abnormal but error free
stwcx	0	0	Synchronization cannot be committed, reset EQ but to zero
	1	0	$SG \leftarrow rS$ commit synchronization, snoop and modify the caches and R-bits of all other processors

TABLE 6.5 PowerPC 601 synchronization instructions.

PowerPC 601. This processor is a pipelined load/store architecture. The synchronization problem is solved by the optimistic technique [MOTO93]. Two instructions are used for synchronization: lwarx and stwcx. The lwarx instruction loads the semaphore and sets R, while the stwcx instruction conditionally stores the modified semaphore and commits the synchronization. The instructions are illustrated in Table 6.5; the formulation of the effective address is not shown. $R(t)$ is the state of the R-flag before the instruction, while $R(t + 1)$ is the state after the instruction.

As there is only one execution stage in the pipeline and the lwarx and stwcx instructions can be executed in one clock, another lwarx or stwcx instruction in the pipeline would not execute during its current trip down the pipeline nor as long as the R-bit is set. The conditional store of the stwcx instruction can be performed in one clock. After the stwcx instruction is conditionally executed, a branch instruction can test the condition code, found in CR0, to determine if the store was successful, and then the synchronization is completed.

An example of the use of lwarx and stwcx is the Test-Test-and-Set operation performed by the following program fragment. The general semaphore is interpreted to be in one of two states: $= 0$ and ≈ 0. If the semaphore is equal to 0, the semaphore is available for synchronization. In this example, it is assumed that the address of the word to be tested is in GPR3, the new value (nonzero) is in GPR4, and the old value is returned in GPR5 [MOTO93]. Note that this procedure is incorrectly called the Test-and-Set procedure in the reference and loops until synchronization is achieved.

```
loop    lwarx    r5,0,r3      # load SB into r5 and reserve
        cmpwi    r5,0         # if SB = 0, set CC
        bne      CR0, loop    # try again if SB not equal to 0
        stwcx    r4,0,r3      # try to store non zero
        bne      CR0, loop    # try again if lost reservation
exit                          # enter critical section
```

	$R(t)$	$R(t+1)$	Operation
LDx_L	0	1	$Ra \leftarrow Sd$, record the translated virtual address in a per-processor location
	1	1	Abnormal, but errorfree
STx_C	0	0	Synchronization has been lost, loop
	1	0	$SG \leftarrow Ra$, snoop all caches, modify and clear all system R-bits

TABLE 6.6 DEC Alpha synchronization instructions.

DEC Alpha. This processor uses a system that is almost identical to the PowerPC 601 in that it uses the optimistic synchronization technique [DIGI92a]. The instructions are described in Table 6.6.

As with the PowerPC 601, the effective address is loaded into a register on an LDx_L instruction that is the base address of the protected memory region. It is not known if this register is stored on a context switch.

6.6.3 *Synchronization Summary*

The paragraphs above have discussed a number of synchronization methods that are summarized in Table 6.7. The steps contained within a box must be executed atomically. The table shows the $P(S)$ operation, the implicit and explicit Test-and-Set operations, and Optimistic Synchronization of Test-and-Set.

The important item of interest in this table is the elimination of atomic compound instructions by the use of optimistic synchronization. This method is ideally suited to the constraints of pipelined load/store

$P(S)$	Test-and-Set, Implicit IBM S/370		Test-and-Set, Explicit Pentium		Optimistic PowerPc, DEC Alpha	
Load (S)	Load (SB), $CC \leftarrow 1$		Lock Bus		Load (SB), $R \leftarrow 1$	
Test (S)	Store $SB \leftarrow 1$ Test CC		Load (SB), $CC \leftarrow 1$ Store $SB \leftarrow 1$		Test SB $SB \approx 0$	$SB = 0$
$S > 0$ $S \leq 0$	$CC = 1$	$CC = 0$	$CC = 1$	$CC = 0$	Conditional	$R \leftarrow 0$
$S \leftarrow S - 1$ Loop	Critical Section	Loop	Critical Section	Loop	store	Loop
Critical Section					Critical Section	

TABLE 6.7 Synchronization instructions.

architectures. However, the caches must be coherent, and the R-flags must be snooped. There is also a problem called *false sharing* in the cache when a semaphore is embedded in a cache block having nonshared values. This, and other problems, can lead to a high rate of snooping invalidations or modifications to the cache.

The technique used by the PowerPc 601 and the DEC Alpha provides effective atomic management of semaphores for exerting exclusion, in the context of Load/Store RISC architectures. The effect of concurrent instructions in the pipeline is overcome because each of the synchronizing instructions execute in one clock. There is a substantial reduction in the number of bus cycles used in this approach over that of the S/360 and Pentium because the memory location that holds the semaphore is blocked for only one clock when the semaphore is in the cache; the bus is not locked for a number of clocks. Even if there is a cache miss when the semaphore is loaded, the bus is not locked during the transport time, as with any other data cache miss.

Optimistic synchronization scales well; a large number of processors can perform synchronization in their L1 caches on different semaphores. Also, a number of processors can execute the same critical section at once because only one will actually commit and invalidate all others. Flexibility is provided in that any other synchronization primitive can be synthesized. In addition, the cache coherency hardware required for multiprocessors is used to maintain the coherency of the semaphores. However, there must be snoop hardware on the R-bits. Finally, optimistic synchronization matches the complexity of pipelines, providing an elegant solution to synchronization.

7

Branching

7.0 Overview

Delays in a pipeline that result from the execution of branch instructions contribute to significant performance degradation. This chapter discusses some of the branching strategies that are designed to reduce this performance loss. A modeling technique is used to provide a first-order estimate to the performance of a strategy for a given pipeline and workload. A more complete discussion of these issues can be found in [CRAG92]. The special treatment of branching in superscalar processors is discussed in Chapter 10.

Two types of branch instruction architectures are used by computer designers. The first branch instruction type consists of an orthogonal pair of instructions; the first instruction sets condition codes, the second instruction tests the condition codes, and either takes the branch or continues to execute in-line instructions. Condition codes can be set either explicitly or implicitly as side effects of other instructions. The condition codes are nonvolatile and need not be tested in the immediately following instruction. This type of branch is called CC for Condition Code.

The second branch instruction type uses one nonorthogonal instruction that makes a test, assesses the outcome of the test, and either takes or does not take the branch. Condition codes are volatile and cannot be tested by a subsequent instruction. This type of branch is called TB for Test and Branch.

Research continues to explore the advantages and disadvantages of these two types of branches [CMEL91], and both types are employed in modern microprocessors. For example, the MIPS uses a TB strategy, while the SPARC and IBM RS/6000 use CC strategies. Branching strategies can be classified into the following taxonomy:

1. pipeline freeze strategies,
2. prediction strategies,

3. instruction reordering strategies,
4. fetch multiple paths strategies,
5. condition code strategies.

7.1 Modeling Technique

This section describes a modeling technique that comprehends three design considerations: the architecture of the pipeline, the workload, and the design of the branch strategy. The architecture of the pipeline is modeled by means of a reservation table, which is described in Chapter 6, Figure 6.1. Generality for the models is provided by identifying three participating pipeline stages.

Stage s is the stage at which the outcome of the branch is *known* or *resolved*. This is the stage in which condition codes are set for CC instructions or that TB instructions execute.

Stage s' is the stage at which the effective address of the branch target is computed or is known.

Stage s'' is the stage at which the instruction is decoded.

A particular pipeline may decode instructions and compute the effective address in the same stage, that is, $s'' = s'$. The Berkeley RISK I pipeline of two stages, for example, has $s = s' = s'' = 2$ [PAT83].

Workload parameters describe the dynamic characteristics of the executing instruction stream in relation to branching. Initially two parameters are introduced; other parameters are introduced later as required.

P_b denotes the probability that an executed instruction is a branch. This parameter comprehends both unconditional and conditional branches. P_b is a dynamic measure.

P_{bt} denotes the probability that an executed branch is taken.

These parameters combine the effects of conditional and unconditional branches that have three possible events: an unconditional taken branch, a conditional taken branch, and a conditional not-taken branch. Performance models that comprehend the three events can be derived. However, it is not always possible to find published data on unconditional branches that permit this distinction. Thus P_{bt} comprehends both unconditional branches and taken conditional branches. An important definition is the basic block.

A *basic block* is "an instruction sequence terminated by an instruction that might change the PC" [DERO87]. It follows that a basic block is equal to $1/P_b$.

The parameter k was introduced in Chapter 6 as the length of an instruction sequence ending in a taken branch; thus, $k = 1/(P_b P_{bt})$. There are a number of published sources for values of P_b and P_{bt} [LEE84, DERO86, CMEL91]. Values from these sources are used later in this chapter to illustrate the performance of the various strategies. For most programs, P_b is usually in the range of 0.2 to 0.4 and P_{bt} is usually in the range 0.6 to 0.8. A basic block length is in the range of 2.5 to 5 instructions while k is in the range of 3 to 8 instructions.

The pipeline performance model that comprehends branching delays is

$$CPI = 1 + P_b \times WABD$$

where WABD is the weighted average branch delay of the workload executing on the pipeline. Predicting the performance of a branch strategy requires that the WABD be known. This is done by modeling the delays for each event of the executing program as discussed in the following sections.

7.2 Pipeline Freeze Strategies

The simplest possible branching strategy for a pipelined processor is as follows: When a branch is detected at stage s'', stop fetching instructions until the branch is resolved at stage s. This action is referred to as *freezing the pipeline*.

This strategy is illustrated in Figure 7.1. The WABD for this strategy is determined from the two reservation tables, one for the not-taken case ($P_{bt} = 0$) and the other for the taken case ($P_{bt} = 1$). The branch instruction is indicated by **B**, the following in-line instruction by **i**, and the target instruction by **T**. Note that $s'' - 1$ in-line instructions will be fetched after the branch is decoded. The effective address, computed in stage s', is saved in a temporary register until the outcome of the branch is known at stage s.

For the case when the branch is not-taken, $P_{bt} = 0$, at $t4$, the outcome of the branch is known and fetching of in-line instructions resumes. The delay is

$$Delay = s - 1 - (s'' - 1) = s - s''.$$

For the case when the branch is taken, $P_{bt} = 1$, the effective branch target address is placed in the program counter to fetch the sequence of

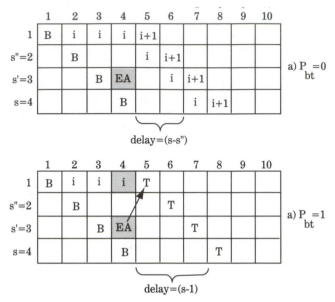

FIGURE 7.1 Pipeline freeze at decode (©IEEE [CRAG92]).

target instructions at $t5$. The delay is

$$\text{Delay} = s - 1.$$

Combining the taken and the not-taken delays gives the WABD as

$$\text{WABD} = P_{bt}(s - 1) + (1 - P_{bt})(s - s'')$$
$$= s - s'' + P_{bt}(s'' - 1).$$

Note that when the branch is resolved, for the taken case, the in-line instruction **i** and, for the not-taken case, the target address value in the buffer register are abandoned; this action is indicated by shading. It then follows that

$$\text{CPI} = 1 + P_b[n - s'' + P_{bt}(s'' - 1)].$$

For an example of the performance of this strategy, consider the pipeline for which $s = 4$, $s'' = 2$ and the workload is $P_b = 0.3$, $P_{bt} = 0.6$.

$$\text{CPI} = 1 + 0.3[4 - 2 + 0.6(2 - 1)] = 1.78.$$

This pipeline has been degraded by 78% because of branching delays. It should not be surprising that the strategies described in the following sections are designed to surpass the performance of this rather simple strategy.

Abandoned instructions present significant problems to the design of a pipelined processor. If an instruction has generated side effects and is abandoned, these side effects must be undone. Side effects are changes to either the state of the machine or the program that are not the primary purpose of an instruction. The pre-auto-increment addressing mode of the VAX instruction set is a good example of a side effect. The problem with abandonment is discussed in Chapter 8.

For the pipeline freeze strategy, the only side effect that has occurred is that the program counter has been incremented to fetch the in-line instruction **i**. This side effect is automatically undone when the target address is loaded into the program counter when the branch is resolved.

7.3 Prediction Strategies

Prediction strategies fall into three classes: static, semistatic, and dynamic. These strategies are discussed in this and the following sections. Before discussing these strategies, I need to descrive the general issues and performance models of branch prediction.

The event probabilities of a branch instruction can be described in a Karnaugh map, as shown in Figure 7.2. The prediction can be to *take* or *not to take* the branch while the actual outcome can be either *taken* or *not-taken*. The subscript indicates the prediction and actual event. The sum of the first column is P_{bt} and the sum of the diagonal ($P_{t/t} + P_{nt/nt}$) is the accuracy of prediction A_p. The fraction of branches that are predicted to be taken is F_{pt}.

Each of the four events corresponds to a delay, also shown in Figure 7.2 [LEE84]. These delays are functions of the branch strategy and the pipeline implementation. The WABD for any prediction strategy is the

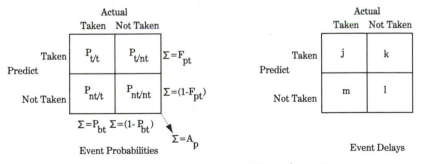

FIGURE 7.2 Prediction events and delays (©IEEE [CRAG92]).

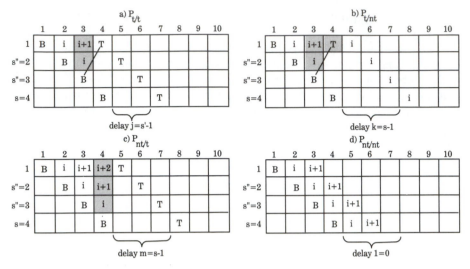

FIGURE 7.3 Prediction method A (©IEEE [CRAG92]).

dot product of the event and delay Karnaugh maps as

$$\text{WABD} = (jP_{t/t}) + (kP_{t/nt}) + (lP_{nt/nt}) + (mP_{nt/t}).$$

Two prediction methods have been identified and called prediction method A and prediction method B. The first of these is shown in Figure 7.3. The symbol **B** is the branch instruction. The symbols $i, i + 1, i + 2, \ldots$ are the in-line instructions following the branch. The symbol **T** is the target instruction. Cross-hatched instructions are instructions that are abandoned and side effects, if any, are undone.

For the $P_{t/t}$ case, when the target address is known the target is fetched and the partially processed in-line instructions are abandoned. Thus, delay j is $s' - 1$. If, after predicting a taken branch, the branch is not-taken ($P_{t/nt}$), the fetched target instruction is abandoned and the first in-line instruction is re-fetched. If s is much larger than s', there can be a number of target instructions fetched that would need to be abandoned. The delay for this case is $s - 1$. The delays of the other two cases are similarly evaluated as: delay $m = s - 1$ and delay $l = 0$.

The WABD for this strategy is

$$\text{WABD(A)} = P_{t/t}(s' - 1) + (P_{t/nt} + P_{nt/t})(s - 1)$$
$$= P_{t/t}(s' - 1) + (1 - A_p)(s - 1)$$

and

$$\text{CPI(A)} = 1 + P_b[P_{t/t}(s' - 1) + (1 - A_p)(s - 1)].$$

It is necessary to devise some approximations for the event probabilities because it is difficult, if not impossible, to determine the value of F_{pt} required to solve explicitly for the four event probabilities. For special cases, such as looping, $F_{pt} = 1$ because all branches are predicted to be taken. The event probabilities are approximated based upon knowing A_p and P_{bt}. The following assumption is made:

$$P_{t/t} = A_p P_{bt}.$$

Then it follows that

$$P_{nt/t} = P_{bt}(1 - A_p),$$
$$P_{t/nt} = (1 - A_p)(1 - P_{bt}),$$
$$P_{nt/nt} = A_p(1 - P_{bt}).$$

The approximate model for CPI(A)(app) is found by substituting the approximations for the exact event probabilities as

$$\text{CPI(A)(app)} = 1 + P_b[A_p P_{bt}(s' - 1) + (1 - A_p)(s - 1)].$$

The second prediction method is shown in Figure 7.4. With this strategy, the in-line instructions are not abandoned until the branch is resolved at $t4$.

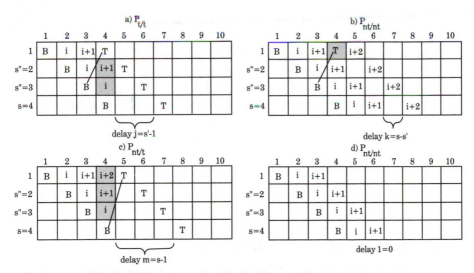

FIGURE 7.4 Prediction method B (©IEEE [CRAG92]).

Using this prediction method, the WABD can be written as

$$\text{WABD(B)} = P_{t/t}(s' - 1) + P_{t/nt}(s - s') + \text{P}_{nt/t}(s - 1)$$

and

$$\text{CPI(B)} = 1 + P_b[P_{t/t}(s' - 1) + P_{t/nt}(s - s') + P_{nt/t}(s - 1)].$$

The approximate model is

$$\begin{aligned}
\text{CPI(B)(app)} &= 1 + P_b[A_p P_{bt}(s' - 1) + (1 - A_p)(1 - P_{bt})(s - s') \\
&\quad + P_{pt}(1 - A_p)(s - 1)] \\
&= 1 + P_b[(1 - A_p)(s - s') + P_{bt}(s' - 1)].
\end{aligned}$$

It is informative to examine the theoretical performance of these two prediction methods under the assumption of $A_p = 1$. Techniques for driving to $A_p = 1$ are discussed in this chapter. For $A_p = 1$

$$\begin{aligned}
P_{nt/t} &= P_{t/nt} = 0, \\
P_{t/t} &= P_{bt}, \\
P_{nt/nt} &= 1 - P_{bt}
\end{aligned}$$

and

$$\begin{aligned}
\text{CPI(A)} &= 1 + P_b[P_{bt}(s' - 1)], \\
\text{CPI(B)} &= 1 + P_b[P_{bt}(s' - 1)].
\end{aligned}$$

The result here is interesting. Reducing WABD with prediction strategies depends on two major considerations. First, a good prediction strategy is needed to drive the prediction accuracy to 1; second, the location of stage s' is the primary architectural determinant of branch performance. Stage s' should be as early in the pipeline as possible. For example, if $s' = 1$, the branch delay can be zero. Some of the dynamic prediction strategies (discussed in Section 7.3.3) are designed to achieve the goal of improving A_p. Strategies for reducing s' are described as well. Frequently branch implementations integrate both prediction and reduction of s' into the same mechanism.

7.3.1 *Static Prediction Strategies*

The first prediction strategies discussed are static; that is, the prediction direction (take or not-take) is wired into the processor and cannot be changed. The WABD for these strategies can be derived directly from the models of the two general prediction strategies described above and in Figures 7.3 and 7.4.

Consider a static prediction strategy based on the prediction method A, which is shown in Figure 7.3. There are two versions of this strategy: (1) predict that all branches will be taken (predict take), and (2) predict that all branches will not be taken (predict not-take).

For the predict take strategy, two of the event probabilities are equal to zero:

$$P_{nt/t} = 0, \qquad P_{nt/nt} = 0.$$

Thus,

$$P_{t/t} = P_{bt}, \qquad P_{t/nt} = 1 - P_{bt}$$

and

$$\text{WABD} = P_{bt}(s' - 1) + (1 - P_{bt})(s - 1),$$
$$\text{CPI} = 1 + P_b[\, s - 1 - P_{bt}(s - s')].$$

Using this method, the CPI models can be written for the four versions of the static prediction strategy as

Predict take, method A	$\text{CPI} = 1 + P_b[\, s - 1\ - P_{bt}(s - s')],$
Predict not-take, method A	$\text{CPI} = 1 + P_b[P_{bt}(s - 1)],$
Predict take, method B	$\text{CPI} = 1 + P_b[s - s' + P_{bt}(2s' - s - 1)],$
Predict not-take, method B	$\text{CPI} = 1 + P_b[P_{bt}(s - 1)].$

The performance of these four strategies can be evaluated using the pipeline and workload parameters used in the example of Section 7.2 with the additional assumption $s' = 3$. The CPIs for these strategies are

Predict take, method A	$\text{CPI} = 1.72,$
Predict not-take, method A	$\text{CPI} = 1.54,$
Predict take, method B	$\text{CPI} = 1.48,$
Predict not-take, method B	$\text{CPI} = 1.54.$

We can see that the best performance is provided by the predict take, method B strategy. This is because more instructions are conditionally processed (also called *speculative execution*) up to the time that the branch is resolved. However, these instructions may present side-effect problems that will require time, in terms of a longer clock period, to undo. If this is the case, the performance advantage may not be as significant as indicated in the performance models.

With a CPI of 1.48, this strategy has a 16% performance advantage over the simpler freeze strategy, which has a CPI of 1.78. Note that even though most branches are taken, the predict not-take strategies give relatively good performance. The predict take, method A performance is marginally better than the simpler freeze strategy.

7.3.2 *Semistatic Prediction Strategies*

Static prediction strategies have the prediction of take or not-take wired into the processor by the designer and cannot be changed. With semistatic prediction, the programmer has the option of selecting the branch prediction direction for each instance of a branch instruction.

For a semistatic prediction strategy, a bit is provided in each branch instruction that is set to one or zero depending upon the anticipated direction of the branch when it is executed. This bit cannot be changed during the execution of the program, assuming that self-modifying code is not permitted. The bit has been called the *take/don't take bit* (TDTB) by Dietzel and McLellan [DIET87]. Models for semistatic prediction strategies can now be derived for strategies based on prediction method A and prediction method B.

The four WABD models that are derived from the two prediction models in Section 7.2 and their approximations are

Strategy	WABD
TDTB/A	$P_{t/t}(s' - 1) + (P_{t/nt} + P_{nt/t})(s - 1)$
TDTB/A(app)	$A_p P_{bt}(s' - 1) + (1 - A_p)(s - 1)$
TDTB/B	$P_{t/t}(s' - 1) + P_{t/nt}(s - s') + P_{nt/t}(s - 1)$
TDTB/B(app)	$(1 - A_p)(s - s') + P_{bt}(s' - 1)$

Note that as $A_p \to 1$, due to the knowledge of either the programmer or the compiler, these strategies are the same as the models for theoretical perfect prediction described earlier. That is, WABD $= P_{bt}(s' - 1)$.

The PowerPC 601 uses a take/don't take bit in the instruction and calls this strategy *static branch prediction* [MOTO93]. This processor does not have early state changes, and in the case of a miss-predicted branch, the conditionally executed instructions are abandoned.

7.3.3 *Dynamic Prediction Strategies*

This section describes the two functions required to achieve a branch strategy with a small WABD: good prediction and a reduced s'. These two functions are accomplished in separate structures or, in some cases, the functions are tightly integrated into one structure.

Instead of wiring in the prediction strategy or having the prediction made by a bit in the instruction, it is possible to have dynamic prediction that follows the executing program. These strategies depend on predicting the outcome of the branch instruction currently being processed. In other words, as a branch instruction is decoded at s'', some information is associated with that instruction from which a prediction is made. Figure 7.5 shows a taxonomy of dynamic branch prediction strategies and is followed by a brief discussion of their elements. The entry in each block refers to a full description and performance model found in [CRAG92].

The issues of prediction concern where in the pipeline the prediction is made and the information on which the prediction is made. Three major classes of strategies are indicated by the right-hand columns of the figure. One class of strategy consists of strategies that predict the branch direction based upon information available at the decode stage. The second class uses a cache to store target addresses with various prediction methods for reducing s'. The third class uses a cache to store target instructions with various prediction methods that also reduce s'.

The rows of the figure signify the other division of the taxonomy, that is, the various methods by which the prediction is made. In the discussion below, the strategies are discussed by column. The X's in Figure 7.5 signify strategies that are not feasible.

			Decode Stage	Instruction Fetch Stage	
				Store Target Address	Store Target Instruction
Current Instruction	History	Update	Predict on History of Outcomes	Predict on History of Outcomes	Predict on History of Outcomes
		Last	Predict on Last Outcome	Predict on Last Outcome	Predict on Last Outcome
	Uniform History		Predict on Uniform History	Predict on Uniform History	Predict on Uniform History
	Nonuniform History		Predict on Nonuniform History	Predict on Nonuniform History	Predict on Nonuniform History
	Characteristic	Branch Direction	Predict on Branch Direction	Predict on Branch Direction	X
		Branch Magnitude	Predict on Branch Magnitude	Predict on Branch Magnitude	X
		Op-Code	Predict on Op-Code	X	X

FIGURE 7.5 Dynamic branch prediction strategies (©IEEE [CRAG92]).

Prediction at the Decode Stage

The first column lists the strategies that use information available at the pipeline decode stage s''. Even though the prediction can be made at stage s'', the target instruction cannot be fetched until the effective address is known at stage s'. Consequently, these strategies strive only to achieve accurate prediction, not to reduce the WABD by reducing s'. For the current instruction, the prediction can be made based on the history of that instruction or the characteristic of that instruction. These prediction methods are described below.

History: Update

The first row of the taxonomy describes strategies that predict at the decode stage based upon the branch history of the instruction being decoded. This strategy requires that a history log or record be associated with each branch instruction. This log can be a field in the instruction format or appended to an instruction when it is fetched into the instruction cache on a miss. When appended to the cache, the log is similar in nature to other appended information used in a cache such as valid bits, dirty bits, and activity information for implementing a replacement strategy. As the instruction is decoded, the history value stored in the log is tested and the branch is predicted to be taken or not-taken. When the instruction executes, this log is updated in the cache.

The log can be an up/down counter that is incremented or decremented as the outcome of the branch instruction is known. The value of the log determines the prediction direction. As a cache cycle may be required to update the log for every branch instruction, an additional cycle is added to the WABD. The CPI for strategies using this prediction method is

$$CPI = 1 + P_b[WABD + 1].$$

The value of WABD is that found from the model for the selected prediction strategy using the anticipated value of A_p. The update cycle may be hidden in some cache designs by using a special write buffer. However, hiding may be difficult because instruction cache is usually accessed every cycle. Because this update occurs after the outcome of the branch is known, another execution of the same branch instruction before the update may predict based on a stale history record.

History: Last

This strategy is the same as the history update strategy except that the log is only one bit that is set or reset based upon the outcome of the branch. By using only one bit, it is only necessary to change the bit if the prediction is wrong. The CPI for strategies using this form of prediction is

$$\text{CPI} = 1 + P_b[\text{WABD} + 1 - A_p].$$

The update cycle is required only on an incorrect prediction. Prediction with only one bit of history will have a poorer A_p than prediction with more bits, and the effectiveness of a one-bit predictor is discussed in the next paragraphs. However, the reduction in update cycles may still make this a superior strategy.

Uniform History

Lee and Smith [LEE84] measured the distribution of consecutive executions of specific branch instructions; excerpted data from one benchmark (IBM CPL) is shown in Table 7.1. Branch prediction is made using this uniform history by maintaining a log of the outcome of each instance of branch instructions. These logs are allocated in the blocks of the instruction cache. The logs consist of the outcomes of the b most recent branches. The prediction of the $b + 1$ branch direction is made from this log.

For example, if the last four branches are NTTN (read the history from left to right), the next instruction is predicted to be TAKEN. This

Branch History	Event Probability	Branch History	Event Probability
NNNNN	0.275	TNNNN	0.011
NNNNT	0.008	TNNNT	0.002
NNNTN	0.008	TNNTN	0.003
NNNTT	0.003	TNNTT	0.001
NNTNN	0.008	TNTNN	0.007
NNTNT	0.002	TNTNT	0.016
NNTTN	0.002	TNTTN	0.002
NNTTT	0.003	TNTTT	0.014
NTNNN	0.012	TTNNN	0.002
NTNNT	0.003	TTNNT	0.001
NTNTN	0.027	TTNTN	0.002
NTNTT	0.009	TTNTT	0.008
NTTNN	0.001	TTTNN	0.002
NTTNT	0.002	TTTNT	0.008
NTTTN	0.002	TTTTN	0.008
NTTTT	0.014	TTTTT	0.534

TABLE 7.1   Branch history distributions for IBM CPL benchmark.

is because probability of the sequence NTTNT (0.002 for IBM CPL) is greater than the sequence NTTNN (0.001 for IBM CPL).

A strategy that considers only the direction of the preceding instance of the branch instruction can be quite effective. That is, the prediction is made based on the direction taken of the last execution of a particular instruction. The event probabilities for this scheme, taken from Table 7.1, are

$$NN\text{-}0.309, \quad NT\text{-}0.07,$$
$$TT\text{-}0.565, \quad TN\text{-}0.056.$$

Thus, if the next branch is predicted to be in the direction of the last branch (the NN and TT events), $A_p = 0.874$. This simple strategy gives excellent results and is the history: last strategy discussed above. This prediction strategy is easily implemented with a single bit associated with the branch instruction in the cache. This bit will need to be modified only when the prediction was incorrect—about 15% of the time. Note that if the prediction logic is set based upon one benchmark, then the execution of other programs may not give the same A_p.

Nonuniform History

Lee and Smith [LEE84] describe three nonuniform history prediction strategies that are made by a state machine associated with each instance of a branch instruction with transitions based upon an accumulated branch history derived from executing benchmarks. The state transition diagrams for one of the strategies are shown in Figure 7.6. The state names are the last two branch directions and the T or N below the name is the prediction. For example, the upper left-hand state

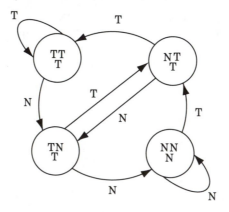

FIGURE 7.6   Branch prediction state diagram (©IEEE [LEE84]).

indicates that the last two branches have been taken and the prediction is made to take the next branch.

If the branch is actually taken, the state transition goes back to the same state. If the branch is not-taken, the transition is to the TN state, which will then predict a taken branch. When this prediction strategy is applied to the IBM CPL program, $A_p = 0.933$, while for the IBM BUS program, $A_p = 0.965$. Lee et al. [LEE84] describe other nonuniform strategies, one of which is used in the $s - 1$ processor. These nonuniform history prediction strategies show A_p in the range of 0.802 to 0.978, which is not significantly different from that achieved with a one-bit history.

Characteristic: Branch Direction

The direction of the branch being decoded can be used as a predictor. For example, loops usually branch backward with respect to the program counter; consequently backward branches are most likely taken. Forward going branches usually are not-taken. For an absolute branch, the branch address is compared to the program counter to find the direction. For most cases, the branch displacement field in the instruction can be used without modification. However, If the branch address is sign and magnitude, the prediction may not be possible until after the effective address is determined as stage s'. In this case, the sign bit gives the branch direction. The comparisons may require a longer clock because of the additional logic paths in the effective address stage s'.

Characteristic: Branch Magnitude

The distance of the branch has been observed to be a relatively good predictor of whether or not the branch will be taken. A short branch is usually taken while a long one is usually not-taken. Looping is an example of a short branch. For both absolute and signed branch addresses, the value of the branch effective address must be compared to a threshold value. A simple way of doing this is to set the threshold to an even power of two and simply test for leading zeros in the effective address. However, it may be necessary to wait until the effective address is determined at stage s'.

Characteristic: Op-Code

Lee [LEE84] shows that specific branch instructions exhibit a propensity to be either taken or not-taken. For example, an unconditional branch is always taken. Thus a prediction strategy can be based upon the op-code being decoded. Based on statistical evidence, such as Lee's, the designer could decide the threshold for prediction. For example, if a particular branch instruction has shown on a number of benchmarks that $P_{bt} = 0.6$, a prediction of taken can be wired in.

This strategy can be used with either prediction method A or B. Because no update cycle is required, a poorer A_p may give a satisfactory reduction in branch delays. As this is a static strategy that is dynamically interpreted, a compiler that did not know of the strategy could generate code that gives poor performance.

Store Target Address

Recall that as $A_p \to 1$, the value of s' is the major determining factor of the WABD. This section describes strategies in the second column of Figure 7.5, that is, strategies that reduce s' by storing the precomputed target addresses in a cache called a *branch target buffer* (BTB). This does not eliminate the need to compute the branch address in stage s' as the cached target address may be incorrect. History information is also stored in the BTB, and the type of history is identified by the rows of the taxonomy. This cache is shown in Figure 7.7.

When an instruction address is presented to the instruction cache, the same address accesses the branch target buffer that can be organized as fully associative or as any degree of set associative. If that branch instruction has been recently executed, the address of the target should be in the BTB along with the historical information of that branch. Depending on the history information and the prediction strategy, the instruction cache may be accessed to fetch the target stream into the decode stage. Note that the size of the BTB is finite and that old information must be evicted by a replacement strategy.

The performance model for this strategy must comprehend such things as BTB misses, target addresses that have changed since the BTB was updated (called *address generation interlocks*), update cycle

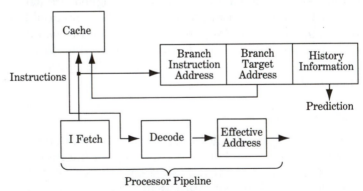

FIGURE 7.7   Branch target buffer (©IEEE [CRAG92]).

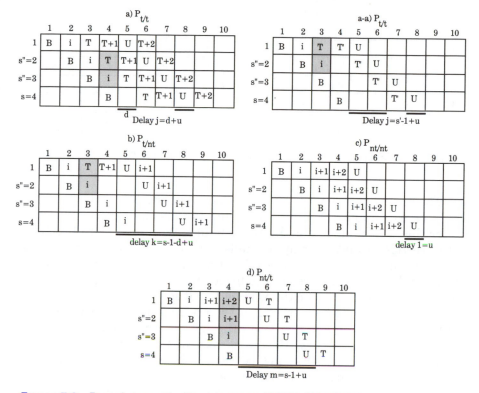

FIGURE 7.8 Branch target buffer hit cases (©IEEE [CRAG92]).

times for the BTB, and so on. The reservation tables for the BTB Hit and BTB Miss cases are shown in Figures 7.8 and 7.9.

When there is a hit on the BTB, one of five events can occur as shown in Figure 7.8. There are the usual four events of any prediction strategy. The case for an address generation interlock is shown as Case a-a) of Figure 7.8. For example, a base register value may have been changed since the last execution of the branch. The partially processed target instruction stream, because of using the wrong address, must be abandoned and the new target stream (T') fetched. This problem is discussed further in [RAO82].

Two new implementation parameters are introduced: **d** and **U**. With some designs, there will be a delay of one or more clocks, called **d** in the models, between the time that the BTB is referenced and the target stream is fetched into the pipeline from the instruction cache. However, for many designs, the time required to access the tags and data (target address) of the BTB is the same as the time required to access the tags and data of the cache. For these designs, the target can be fetched from the instruction cache on the next clock; for these designs, **d** = 0.

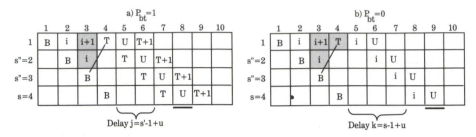

a) $P_{bt}=1$

	1	2	3	4	5	6	7	8	9	10
1	B	i	i+1	T	U	T+1				
s"=2		B	i		T	U	T+1			
s"=3			B			T	U	T+1		
s=4				B			T	U	T+1	

Delay j=s'-1+u

b) $P_{bt}=0$

	1	2	3	4	5	6	7	8	9	10
1	B	i	i+1	T	i	U				
s"=2		B	i		i	U				
s"=3			B				i	U		
s=4				B				i	U	

Delay k=s-1+u

FIGURE 7.9 Branch target buffer miss cases (©IEEE [CRAG92]).

The second parameter is **U**, the cycle(s) required to update the BTB. For Figures 7.8 and 7.9, **U** = 1. Updating can also be performed with a buffer that is similar to a cache write buffer. With an update buffer, a large fraction of updates may be made with **U** = 0. In addition, if only one bit of history is used in the BTB, the history needs updating only when the branch is incorrectly predicted. With A_p = 0.9, updating will be required only 10% of the time. Thus **U** ≈ 0.1.

The BTB miss cases, as shown in Figure 7.9, assume prediction method A. When there is a miss on the BTB, the processor executes a static predict-take strategy. However, even with the prediction to take the branch, the branch may not be taken. As a result, there are two cases for the BTB miss case: P_{bt} = 1 and P_{bt} = 0.

As with the BTB hit case, if one bit of history is used, the frequency of updating the history is low and **U** should be close to zero. The prediction methods for a BTB can be, in most cases, the same as those described above for the decode stage prediction. The one exception is for op-code prediction. Because all instruction addresses are sent to the BTB, testing the op-code of the branch is not practical.

The Intel Pentium [ALPE93, INTE93, INTE93a, INTE93b] uses a BTB that, in conjunction with prefetch queues, can supply either the in-line or target stream with zero branch delay. A simplified block diagram and reservation table of the Pentium queues are shown in Figure 7.10. The available documentation states that prediction is made, but it is not clear on the prediction strategy [INTE93b]. The best that can be deduced is that the BTB carries no history information; when there is a hit on the BTB, a prediction to take the branch is made and the target sequence is always fetched from the instruction cache into the target queue.

The address presented to the cache accesses the cache and, in parallel, is presented to the BTB. On alternate cycles, the instruction cache fills the in-line queue and, if there is a hit on the BTB, the cache is accessed to load the target queue. The processor can issue up to two instructions per clock, each instruction averaging 4 Bytes. Thus, the processor can place a demand of 8 Bytes per clock on the instruction

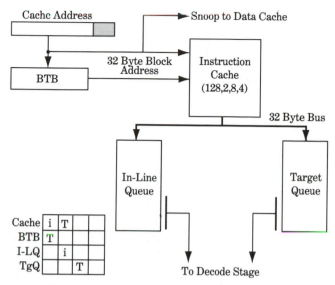

FIGURE 7.10 Pentium BTB and instruction queues.

queues and the cache can supply 32 Bytes per clock, providing four times the required bandwidth.

Even with the early prediction, it is still necessary to compute the target effective address at stage s'. The target address stored in the BTB may be incorrect due to a modification to one of the components of the effective address after the time the target address was stored in the BTB. The events and delays that follow a reference to a branch instruction are [INTE93b]:

BTB Hit. The branch is always predicted to be taken.

- Correct prediction; delay = 0.
- Incorrect prediction; flush the pipeline and refetch the branch instruction.
- Wrong target address (AGI); flush the pipeline and refetch the branch instruction.

BTB Miss. The branch is always predicted to be not-taken.

- Correct prediction; delay = 0.
- Incorrect prediction; flush pipeline and refetch the branch instruction.

Store Target Instructions

Another group of strategies can also reduce the value of s' by storing not the target address in a cache but the target instruction itself. Such

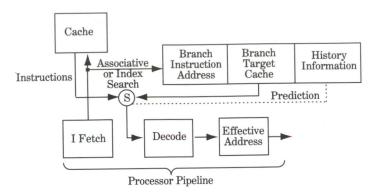

FIGURE 7.11 Branch target cache (©IEEE [CRAG92]).

a cache is called a *branch target cache* (BTC). As Figure 7.11 shows, the cache stores the target instructions that are passed directly to the decode stage of the pipeline. As with all caches, the BTC can be organized as full associative, set associative, or direct. The search of the BTC is on the address from the program counter that is accessing the next instruction. The instruction cache and the BTC are accessed in parallel, with the instruction presented to the decoder selected by the BTC prediction. If there is a miss on the BTC or the prediction is to not take the branch, the branch instruction is fetched from the cache.

The type of prediction statistics stored in the BTC is a design option. Note that only historical information is available for prediction as characteristic information has been lost in the process of accessing the BTC and cannot be used.

The Am29000 uses a BTC in conjunction with an instruction prefetch buffer [JOHN87, AMD 90]. Figure 7.12 shows a block diagram; this BTC is 2-way set associative, late select, with each block having four sequential target instructions. Note that the AU and instructions are four bytes. The most significant four bits of the six least significant bits of the instruction address index into the 2-way set associative cache consisting of sixteen sets of two sectors containing the tags, valid, and space ID bits. The 26 tag bits are compared to the 26 most significant bits of the instruction real address. A hit on either of the two sectors will gate out the first (of a group of four) selected target instruction. The other three instructions are addressed by the 2-bit displacement field.

The Am29000 BTC does not use a history field; the branch prediction is made by the processor based on checking condition codes and treats all BTC hits as take, as is done with the Pentium discussed previously. All BTC misses are predicted as not-take. There are four valid bits, one for each of the four instructions in the referenced sequence. The space

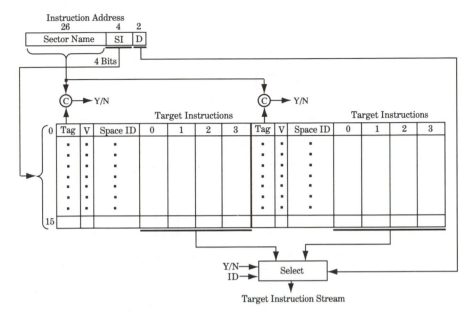

FIGURE 7.12 Am29000 branch target cache (©IEEE [CRAG92]).

ID bits are used to identify the use of the referenced instructions and are compared to corresponding bits in the processor status register. These uses are: ROM Enable, Physical Addressing Instruction, and Supervisor Mode. There is control to ensure that the four target instruction sequences do not cross cache block boundaries. The operation of the Am29000 BTC is illustrated in the reservation table of Figure 7.13.

The BTC is not referenced until a branch target address is available at stage s', resulting in a delay **d** of one clock. The delay slot can be filled by the compiler with a useful instruction as with a delayed branch strategy (discussed in Section 7.4). If the delay slot is always filled and the branch prediction is always correct, the branch delay is zero. Incorrect predictions have a delay of one. The next three target instructions are accessed by the displacement and do not require tag comparisons.

The Motorola MC88110 uses a BTC called a *target instruction cache*. This BTC is fully associative with 32 sectors and has two instructions per sector. The information that is available [DIEF91] indicates that there is a take/don't-take bit in the instruction that provides a semistatic prediction. The compiler sets this bit, which cannot be altered at run time. A BTC hit that is predicted taken and is actually taken has a zero delay.

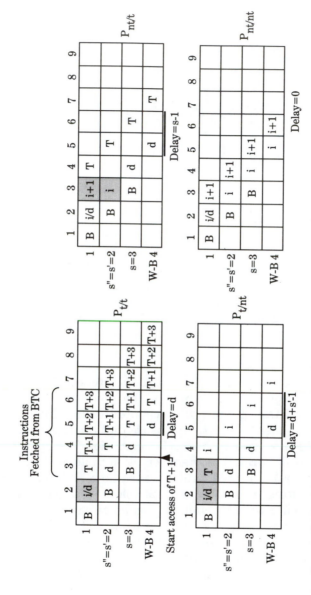

FIGURE 7.13 AM29000 BTC reservation tables (©IEEE [CRAG92]).

338

Preloaded BTC

The BTC is a cache that is loaded under hardware control. That is, when there is a miss, and after the outcome of the branch is known, hardware inserts the new information into the BTC. Another variation of the BTC is for it to be an addressable register file that can be explicitly preloaded, by the program, with the target instructions.

The compiler inserts code into the program that will compute the effective address of the branch instructions and load the addressed target instructions into the addressable BTB. If the overhead of precomputing and loading the target instructions is less than the savings in WABD, the strategy is a success. This strategy was proposed and studied for the PIPE processor [FAR90].

When a branch instruction is decoded, the addresses of these registers are in the instruction and the target can be fetched on the next clock. Thus, the branch delay is $s'' - 1$. If the branch is predicted to be not-taken, the target is not fetched. There are problems with avoiding self-modifying code and changes during execution that will invalidate the contents of this BTC.

7.4 Instruction Sequence Alteration Strategies

Other methods for reducing WABD are to alter the sequence of instruction execution so that instructions do not have to be abandoned. If no instructions are abandoned, there are no branch delay cycles. These strategies require that the compiler is knowledgeable about the structure of the pipeline and will make the necessary changes to the executable code. This is different from the prediction strategies that use hardware techniques to reduce WABD and are relatively insensitive to the compiler generated code.

7.4.1 *Delayed Branch Strategy*

Consider the reservation table of Figure 7.14(a). This code fragment of nine instructions has two branches, one of which (6/B) is taken; instructions 7, 8, and 9 must be abandoned. Nine clocks are required for this fragment, giving a CPI of 1.5.

For a delayed branch strategy, the compiler introduces a sequence of no-ops, **N**, after all branches, as shown in Figure 7.14(b); the number of clocks increases to 12 for this code fragment. A *no-op* is an instruction that produces no state change and has no side effects. Thus, it is not necessary to abandon no-ops when the branch is taken.

The compiler, after inserting the no-ops, examines the code and

	1	2	3	4	5	6	7	8	9	10	11	12	13	14
1	1	2	3/B	4	5	6/B	7	8	9	T1				
s″=2		1	2	3/B	4	5	6/B	7	8		T1			
s″=3			1	2	3/B	4	5	6/B	7			T1		
s=4				1	2	3/B	4	5	6/B				T1	

(a)

#Clocks=9 CPI=9/6=1.5

	1	2	3	4	5	6	7	8	9	10	11	12	13	14	15	16
1	1	2	3/B	N	N	N	4	5	6/B	N	N	N	T1			
s″=2		1	2	3/B	N	N	N	4	5	6/B	N	N	N	T1		
s″=3			1	2	3/B	N	N	N	4	5	6/B	N	N	N	T1	
s=4				1	2	3/B	N	N	N	4	5	6/B	N	N	N	T1

(b)

#Clocks=12 CPI=12/6=2.0

	1	2	3	4	5	6	7	8	9	10	11	12
1	3/B	1	2	N	6/B	4	5	N	T1			
s″=2		3/B	1	2	N	6/B	4	5	N	T1		
s″=3			3/B	1	2	N	6/B	4	5	N	T1	
s=4				3/B	1	2	N	6/B	4	5	N	T1

(c)

#Clocks=8 CPI=7/6=1.33

FIGURE 7.14 Delayed branch development (©IEEE [CRAG92]).

attempts to replace the no-ops in the delay slots with useful instructions. A useful instruction must be allowed to complete regardless of whether the branch is taken or not. This has been done in Figure 7.14(c). Notice that instructions 1 and 2 have been moved into two of the delay slots after instruction 3/B and instructions 4 and 5 have also been moved. By replacing no-op with useful instructions, the CPI has now been reduced from 1.5 to 1.3 for the delayed branch strategy. The number of instructions used in computing CPI is 6. The two no-ops are not counted as useful instructions even though some performance measurements of delayed branch strategies do count them.

The CPI model for the delayed branch strategy can now be generalized. The delays for this strategy are shown in Figures 7.15(a) and (b) for the prediction method A.

The term Δ is the number of no-ops replaced by useful instructions.

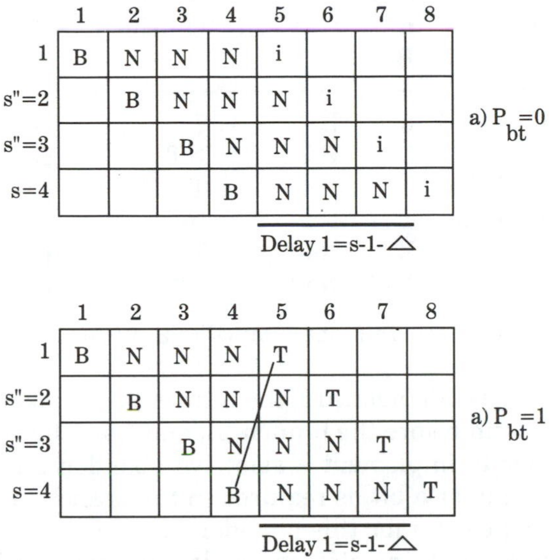

	1	2	3	4	5	6	7	8
1	B	N	N	N	i			
s"=2		B	N	N	N	i		
s"=3			B	N	N	N	i	
s=4				B	N	N	N	i

a) $P_{bt}=0$

Delay $1 = s-1-\triangle$

	1	2	3	4	5	6	7	8
1	B	N	N	N	T			
s"=2		B	N	N	N	T		
s"=3			B	N	N	N	T	
s=4				B	N	N	N	T

a) $P_{bt}=1$

Delay $1 = s-1-\triangle$

FIGURE 7.15 Delayed branch, prediction method A (©IEEE [CRAG92]).

The delays for both taken and not-taken branches are $(s-1-\triangle)$. Thus the WABD is:

$$\text{WABD} = s - 1 - \triangle.$$

If $\triangle = s - 1$, the WABD is zero.

A number of studies show that $\triangle \approx 1$ for many programs. Thus, the WABD is approximately $s - 2$. For short pipelines, such as the RISC 1 with $s = 2$, the WABD is zero. Because the CPI of this strategy is a function of s, long pipelines cannot benefit greatly from this strategy. Delayed branch strategies are most frequently used in processors with small values of s. And, as $s - 1$ no-ops need to be replaced, the shorter the pipeline, the greater the chance of success for replacing no-ops. An extensive discussion on the number of delay slots that can be filled can be found in [GARD91].

7.4.2 *Delayed Branch with Abandon*

With the delayed branch strategy, the instructions replacing no-ops *must be executed*. Because these instructions can only be taken from before the branch, this requirement significantly reduces the pool of instructions available to be moved. If instructions could be selectively executed or abandoned, the pool of candidate instructions would be greater. For example, it would be helpful if an instruction selected from the taken

Event	Strategy	**a** Bit	Slot Fill	Outcome	Slots Executed	Delay
1	DB A	0	B	T	Yes	0
2	DB A	0	B	NT	Yes	0
3	Always Take	1	F	T	Yes	0
4	Always Take	1	F	NT	No	$s-1$
5	Always Take	X	No-Op	T	Yes	$s-1$
6	Always Take	X	No-Op	NT	Yes	$s-1$

TABLE 7.2 Delayed branch with abandon (©IEEE [CRAG92]).

branch path could be abandoned if the branch is not-taken. This strategy fills delay slots from before the branch, B, and from the forward or taken path, F. In order to implement a selective abandon strategy, a control bit, called the annul or **a** bit, is required in the branch instruction. Table 7.2 shows the six events for this abandon strategy.

For Events 1 and 2 the strategy is delayed branch; *all* of the delay slots are filled from before the branch B, and the **a** bit is 0. The branch delay is zero for both the taken and the not-taken cases.

For Events 3 and 4, the implemented strategy is always take, and the **a** bit is 1. The delay slots are filled from the target stream F. If the branch is taken, Event 3, the delay is 0. However, if the branch is not-taken, Event 4, the moved instructions are abandoned with a resulting delay of $s-1$.

For Events 5 and 6 the implemented strategy is always take. However, for this case, the delay slots are filled with no-ops and the branch delay is always $s-1$.

The compiler reorders instructions in such a way that the cases with zero delay are used if at all possible. Thus there are three steps in the process:

1. The compiler attempts to fill all of the delay slots from behind the branch. If successful, Events 1 or 2 result in having zero delay.
2. If the compiler is not successful with step 1, an attempt is made to fill all of the delay slots from the taken direction. If successful, Events 3 or 4 result and the **a** bit is set.
3. If not successful, the compiler assigns no-ops to each delay slot.

The WABD model for this strategy is found in [CRAG92]. This model is

$$\text{WABD} = (s-1)(P_{no} + P_{ff}(1 - P_{bt}))$$

where P_{fb} denotes the probability that $(s-1)$ delay slots will be filled from behind the branch, P_{ff} the probability that $(s-1)$ delay slots will be filled from the target path, and $P_{no} = 1 - P_{fb} - P_{ff}$.

This strategy was implemented on the MIPS-X [CHO86]. Another version of this strategy is used in the SPARC. Experimental data from MIPS-X [CHO87] indicates that $P_{fb} = 0.25$, $P_{ff} = 0.65$, and $P_{no} = 0.1$ are reasonable values. However, for pipelines with large s, P_{no} can become large and any performance advantage of this strategy may disappear.

7.4.3 *Delayed Branch with Fast Compare*

A large fraction of conditional branches compare the contents of two registers or compare the contents of one register to zero. For this reason a special integer ALU, that gives $s = 2$, is added to the processor pipeline, giving a branch delay of one.

When fast compare is used with delayed branch, there may be only one delay slot and the probability of filling that slot is high, usually greater than 0.75. Thus the WABD for this class of branch instruction can be quite small. That is, WABD $= s - 1 - 0.75 = 0.25$.

7.4.4 *Branch Spreading with Condition Codes*

The strategies discussed above assumed that the branch is resolved at stage s. This is the stage where a compare operation is completed and the outcome of the branch is known. However, if the architecture uses condition codes, the opportunity exists for resolving the branch at an earlier time. Branch spreading is a form of instruction reordering that moves the condition code setting instruction forward into the instruction stream so that the branch instruction can be resolved at stage s' rather than at stage s.

Reservation tables for branch spreading are shown in Figure 7.16. The symbol **C** denotes the condition code setting instruction; the condition codes are set at stage s. The **C** instruction is moved forward in the basic block by inserting no-ops until the setting of the condition codes is in the same clock cycle in which the branch instruction computes its effective address (t_5 in the figure). The number of moves in clock cycles is $(s - s' - 1 - \Delta)$ where Δ is the number of useful instructions that can replace the no-ops. After the branch instruction, in-line instructions are fetched.

For the branch taken case, $P_{bt} = 1$, the in-line instructions are abandoned and the target stream is fetched starting at $t6$; the branch delay is $(s - 2 - \Delta)$. For the branch not-taken case, $P_{bt} = 0$, the delay is $(s' - s - 1 - \Delta)$. With these delays, the WABD is

	1	2	3	4	5	6	7	8	9	10	11	12	
1	C	N	B	i	i+1	T							
2		C	N	B	i		T						
s'=3			C	N	B			T					a) $P_{bt}=1$
4				C	N	•			T				
s=5					C	N	•			T			

Delay=s-s'-1 + s'-1 =s-2-Δ

	1	2	3	4	5	6	7	8	9	10	11	12	
1	C	N	B	i	i+1	i+2							
2		C	N	B	i	i+1	i+2						
s'=3			C	N	B	i	i+1	i+2					b) $P_{bt}=0$
4				C	N	B	i	i+1	i+2				
s=5					C	N	•	i	i+1	i+2			

Delay=s-s'-1-Δ

FIGURE 7.16 Branch spreading reservation table (©IEEE [CRAG92]).

$$\text{WABD} = s - s' - 1 - P_{bt}(s' - 1) - \Delta.$$

For pipelines where $s - s' - 1 - \Delta = 0$ (the case if all the no-ops are replaced with useful instructions), the WABD becomes $P_{bt}(s' - 1)$. Additionally, if $s' = 1$, a zero branch delay is achieved. This strategy is used with the Intel Pentium described in Section 7.3.3 to help achieve a zero-cycle branch. Note that if the condition code setting instruction is not moved forward, a true dependency will exist that will stall the pipeline (discussed in Section 8.4).

7.5 Fetch Multiple-Path Strategies

With a prediction strategy, a decision is made as to which path is to be fetched conditionally—the in-line or target streams. If the prediction is wrong, the predicted paths must be abandoned and the other path fetch started. Why not fetch and process *both* paths conditionally and discard the incorrect one? With this strategy, the time delay to restart the correct path will be eliminated. Riseman and Foster [RISE72] investigated the potential speedup of a processor that is limited only by branch delays. They showed, by experimentation, but without a theoretical basis, that the maximum speedup is approximately the square root of the number of branches bypassed. The models presented below suggest that this speedup is not obtainable with realizable pipelined processors.

There can be two variants of this multiple-path strategy. The first variant fetches only one additional path (the in-line and target), and the second fetches all paths (all in-line and target paths spawned by all paths).

7.5.1 *Fetch Two Paths*

This strategy fetches the in-line and the target paths of *one* branch instruction; when that branch is resolved, the unneeded path is abandoned. Four cases are possible with this strategy. Cases 1 and 2 are for isolated branches; Cases 3 and 4 are when *every* instruction is a branch. The weighted average delays of these four cases will be the WABD for the strategy.

The reservation tables for the first two cases are shown in Figure 7.17. Case 1, $P_{bt} = 1$, is shown at the left of the figure; the effective address of the branch is known at stage s' and the target path is fetched into an auxiliary pipeline. When the branch is resolved, the in-line instructions i to $i + 3$ are abandoned and the target path is transferred into the main pipeline; the delay for a taken branch is $s' - 1$. For Case 2 where the branch is not-taken, the target path is abandoned when the branch is resolved and the delay is 0. The usual caveats about abandoning instructions with side effects apply here.

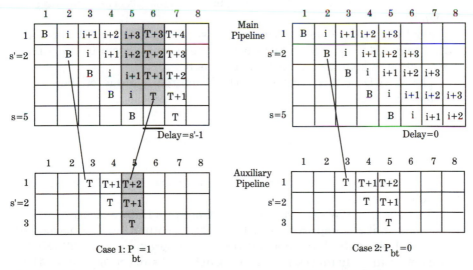

FIGURE 7.17   Reservation table, isolated branch (©IEEE [CRAG92]).

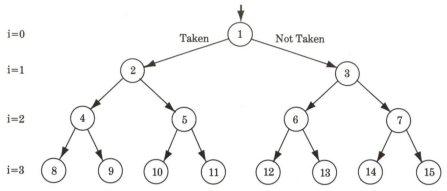

FIGURE 7.18   Every instruction is a branch (©IEEE [CRAG92]).

If every instruction is a branch, the program flow is represented as a binary tree, as in Figure 7.18. The instruction numbers in the nodes of this figure are used in the reservation tables to follow. Even numbered instructions are the taken paths, while odd numbered instructions are the not-taken in-line branch paths.

Given the flow of instruction shown in Figure 7.18, the reservation tables of Figure 7.19 show the activity in the main and auxiliary pipelines. Consider Case 3, where the branch is taken. The main pipeline fetches the in-line stream 1,3,7,15. When 1 is in stage s', its target instruction 2 and the in-line streams 5 and 11 are fetched into the auxiliary pipeline. When 1 reaches stage s, the branch is resolved and the sequence 3,7,15,31 is abandoned and replaced with the taken target sequence 2,5,11 from the auxiliary pipeline. This process continues as shown.

For Case 3, the delays alternate between $s' - 1$ and $s - 1$ and have an average of $(s + s' - 2)/2$. For Case 4, the target stream in the auxiliary pipeline is abandoned and the delay is 0.

The WABD of this strategy is the weighted average of the delays for the four cases:

$$\text{WABD} = (1 - t)P_{\text{bt}}(s' - 1) + tP_{\text{bt}}(s + s' - 2)/2$$

where t denotes the fraction of branches that are followed immediately by another branch.

Schwartz [SCHW89] gives evidence from programs executing on the Intel 8086 that t is approximately 0.25. On the other hand, MacDougall [MACD84] presents data showing that t is approximately 0.08. Histograms of branch distances for SPEC benchmarks executing on a MIPS process are given in [UNWA94].

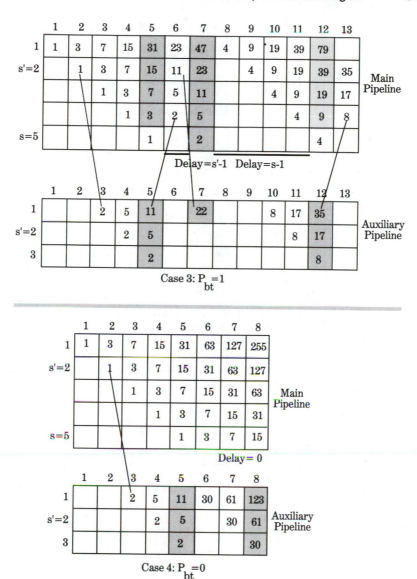

FIGURE 7.19   Reservation table, every instruction a branch (©IEEE [CRAG92]).

7.5.2 *Fetch All Paths*

This strategy requires a pool of auxiliary pipelines so that whenever a branch is decoded and its effective address is known, the in-line path and target path are fetched. This is the case for the main pipeline as

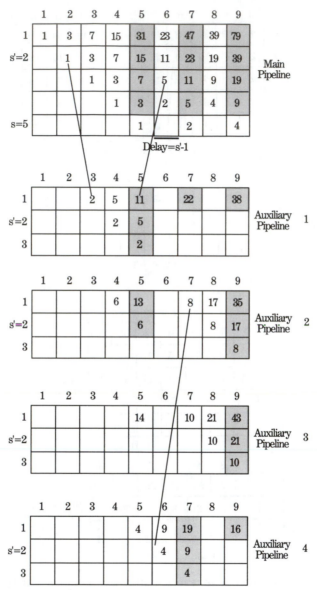

	1	2	3	4	5	6	7	8	9
1	1	3	7	15	31	23	47	39	79
s'=2		1	3	7	15	11	23	19	39
			1	3	7	5	11	9	19
				1	3	2	5	4	9
s=5					1		2		4

Main Pipeline

Delay=s'-1

	1	2	3	4	5	6	7	8	9
1			2	5	11		22		38
s'=2				2	5				
3					2				

Auxiliary Pipeline 1

	1	2	3	4	5	6	7	8	9
1				6	13		8	17	35
s'=2					6			8	17
3									8

Auxiliary Pipeline 2

	1	2	3	4	5	6	7	8	9
1					14		10	21	43
s'=2							10	21	
3							10		

Auxiliary Pipeline 3

	1	2	3	4	5	6	7	8	9
1					4	9	19		16
s'=2						4	9		
3							4		

Auxiliary Pipeline 4

FIGURE 7.20 Fetch all paths Case 3 reservation tables (©IEEE [CRAG92]).

well as for all of the auxiliary pipelines. The four cases for this strategy are

1. Isolated branch, taken;
2. Isolated branch, not-taken;
3. Every instruction a branch, taken; and
4. Every instruction a branch, not-taken.

It can be seen that Cases 1 and 2 are the same as the cases described in Figure 7.17 with delays of $s' - 1$ and 0 for the taken and not-taken cases. Case 4 is the same as the Case 4 of Figure 7.19 with a delay of 0.

The reservation table of Case 3 is shown in Figure 7.20. The instruction numbering is the same as in Figure 7.18. Notice, for example, that when the effective address of the target of instruction 1 is known at $t3$, its target (2) is fetched into auxiliary pipeline 1. When the effective address of the target of instruction 2 is known at $t4$, its target (4) is fetched into auxiliary pipeline 4.

Instruction fetching continues until the main pipeline is full and instruction 1 is resolved at $t5$. As this case is for branch taken, instructions 3,7,15,31 are abandoned and instructions 2,5,11 are transferred into the main pipeline. Because 3 is abandoned, 6 and 13 are also abandoned. Because 7 is abandoned, 14 is also abandoned. Instructions 15 and 31 have not yet initiated target fetches. Instruction 4 in auxiliary pipeline 4 is not abandoned because it is the taken path from instruction 2, which is still active. Note that instruction 4 initiates the fetch of 8 into auxiliary pipeline 2. When instruction 2 is resolved, instructions 4,9,19 are transferred from auxiliary pipeline 4 into the main pipeline. The delay for this case is $s' - 1$. Thus, the delays for the four cases are

Case 1. Delay $= s' - 1$.
Case 2. Delay $= 0$.
Case 3. Delay $= s' - 1$.
Case 4. Delay $= 0$.

$$\text{WABD} = P_{bt}(s' - 1).$$

This is an interesting result. If all paths are fetched, the WABD is the same as the theoretical WABD for prediction strategies when $A_p = 1$. And, if the effective address stage, s', is stage one, the WABD is zero. BTCs would closely approximate this performance if all paths could be fetched.

7.5.3 *Hardware Requirements*

The fetch-two-paths strategy requires one auxiliary pipeline; the number of auxiliary pipelines for the fetch-all-paths strategy is shown in Table 7.3 [CRAG92]. The number of auxiliary pipelines depends on the pipeline design parameters s and s'. Clearly, the number of auxiliary pipelines increases as the depth of the pipeline increases because more branch instructions can be conditionally processed.

While the logic cost of auxiliary pipelines can be large, a more serious problem with this strategy is that the memory system must be capable of supporting the pipelines that are fetching instructions and data. For

s'	s						
	1	2	3	4	5	6	7	8
1	0	1	3	7	15	31	63	127
2	0	0	1	2	4	7	12	20
3	0	0	0	1	2	4	5	8
4	0	0	0	0	1	2	3	4

TABLE 7.3 Number of auxiliary pipelines
(©IEEE [CRAG1992]).

the case of fetch all paths with $s = 5$ and $s' = 2$, the instruction band-width must be $5\times$ the bandwidth of a single pipeline. Additional register files may also be required, and all instructions must be conditionally processed so as to prevent state changes and side effects. For this aspect of memory bandwidth requirements, a prediction strategy is more at-tractive than the fetch-all-paths strategy. Prediction strategies fetch only the path that will be used, assuming $A_p = 1$.

As far as I know, only a few fetch-two-paths processors have been built. These processors were the IBM 370/165 [FLOR74], and the IBM S/360/195. Unless s' is small, say 1, there is only a modest increase in branch performance with a very large price in processor hardware and memory bandwidth. Processors using instruction queues have $s' = 1$ (S/360/195 and Pentium) and can have very satisfactory branch perfor-mance. VLIW architectures (discussed in Chapter 10) are based, in part, on providing multiway branch instructions. In effect, these architectures fetch a number of paths and have $s' = 1$.

8

Dependencies

8.0 Overview

The designers of the earliest overlapped computers recognized that dependencies between sequential instructions must be resolved and the logical constraints of the program must be maintained [COCK59]. In general, designers identified these dependencies and solved them by ad hoc methods. For example, all possible pairs of instructions were examined to determine if conflicts existed and then steps were devised to prevent them. The examination was frequently done at the computer console, single-stepping test cases. This process was tedious, not comprehensive, and generally error prone. These ad hoc methods were less than satisfying, and significant research has been directed to finding general solutions to the dependency problem. Three general solutions to dependence detection and resolution have emerged.

1. Halt the release of all instructions until the dependencies are resolved.
2. Halt the instruction that has the dependency but continue to release instructions without dependencies.
3. Place all control in the resolution of dependencies. Operations are released when inputs are present. This is the *data flow* paradigm and is not be covered in this book. However, data flow techniques are used for the detection and resolution of dependencies (as discussed later).

For the first and second solutions it can be seen that instruction issue is closely bound to dependency resolution. In fact, the purpose of dependency detection and resolution is to ensure the logic of the program execution by scheduling instruction issue. Another way of viewing this problem is to recall that a purely serial execution model processor—no overlap between instructions—will have no dependencies between

351

instructions. There can be dependencies at the micro-code level however, but this is a topic outside the scope of this book.

Note should be taken that the question of dependency detection and resolution is also closely related to the question of ensuring the correct execution of programs on a multiprocessor [LAMP79, GHAR91]. Also, the coherency problems, as discussed in Chapter 5, are related to this issue.

The CDC 6600 Scoreboard [THOR70] is the first known processor design that considered a general solution to the dependency problem. The design of the processor started in 1960, and the first installation took place in 1964. The IBM S/360/91 Common Data Bus [TOMA67] also solved the dependency problem, but the published description is more ad hoc than that for the Scoreboard.

Names used in the literature for dependencies include: hazards, constraints, and conflicts. In general, the terms hazard and conflict have been used by authors concentrating on hardware while the term dependencies has been used by authors concentrating on operating systems and compiler design. However, the term dependencies is now gaining favor with many authors. A list of all of the names, known to me, for dependencies as well as the known author follows.

Flow dependent	Banerjee, 1976
True dependent	
Read After Write	
Write/Read	Stone, 1990
Second-Order Conflict	Thornton, 1970
Destination-Source Conflict	Hennessy, 1982
Write to Read	
Antidependent	Banerjee, 1976
Write After Read	
Read/Write	Stone, 1990
Third-Order Conflict	Thornton, 1970
Source–Destination Conflict	Hennessy, 1982
Read to Write	
Output dependent	Banerjee, 1976
Write After Write	
Write/Write	Stone, 1990
First-Order Conflict	Thornton, 1970
Destination–Destination Conflict	Hennessy, 1982
Write to Write	

Bernstein [BERN66] published the first work, known to me, on the problems associated with dependencies. His work concerned multiprocessor execution of programs rather than parallelism within a single processor. Three conditions, *Bernstein's Conditions*, must be satisfied for correct execution of the program. These conditions are recast by Karp and Miller [KARP69] in their paper on parallel programming. Many of the problems with dependencies, addressed by the processor designers of the 1960s, are being revisited by researchers investigating scheduling of multiprocessors [BANE88].

Keller took the idea of dependencies into the field of concurrency within a single processor in his classic paper [KELL75]. He provides the necessary conditions that must be satisfied for dependencies to be resolved. In the discussion to follow, the term *resolved* is defined as the action taken to eliminate the dependency; dependencies are resolved for ranges (outputs, sinks) and domains (inputs, sources) with instructions having the ordering i, j when

$$R(i) \cap D(j) = \emptyset \quad \text{true dependence,}$$
$$R(j) \cap D(i) = \emptyset \quad \text{antidependence,}$$
$$R(i) \cap R(j) = \emptyset \quad \text{output dependence.}$$

where $\emptyset$ denotes the empty set.

Keller shows a program fragment that illustrates the occurrence of dependencies in a register-based architecture. Eight instructions have two source operand registers and a destination register. The functions performed are *F1*, *F2*, and *F3*.

Inst.	Operation
I1	$1 \leftarrow F1(2, 3)$
I2	$5 \leftarrow F3(1, 2)$
I3	$4 \leftarrow F2(2, 2)$
I4	$3 \leftarrow F1(1, 4)$
I5	$6 \leftarrow F1(5, 6)$
I6	$1 \leftarrow F1(2, 3)$
I7	$4 \leftarrow F2(2, 5)$
I8	$3 \leftarrow F1(1, 4)$
I9	$5 \leftarrow F3(5,5)$

Table 8.1 lists all of the dependencies that can be indicated when executing this program fragment. Some of the listed true dependencies are *shadowed* by a prior operation that eliminates the dependency. For example, when the true dependency on register 1 between instructions I1–I2 is resolved and the read of register 2 can proceed, the dependency on instructions I1–I4 and I1–I8 are removed but the dependency on instructions I6–I8 stands.

Shadowing of true dependencies can be more formally stated as: If

Register	True	Anti-	Output
1	I1–I2, I1–I4, I1–I8, I6–I8	I2–I6, I4–I6	I1–I6
2			
3	I4–I6	I1–I8, I6–I8	I4–I8
4	I3–I4, I7–I8	I4–I7	I3–I7
5	I2–I5, I2–I7, I2–I9	I5–I9, I7–I9	I2–I5

TABLE 8.1 Program fragment dependencies.

instruction c is dependent on instruction b, which is dependent on instruction a, then instruction c is indirectly dependent on a and will not be an actual dependency.

Dependencies operate via the domains and ranges of the instructions, which are also called *regions* [RAMA77] and *objects* [KOGG81]. In this book, the term object(s) is used. This chapter addresses three major locations of objects.

1. Data Registers or Data Path, Section 8.2.
2. Memory, Section 8.3.
3. Special Registers, Section 8.4.

Each of these three object locations presents unique problems and has unique solutions for dependency detection and resolutions. If problems exist, schemes for eliminating the problems must be implemented. Designers must make a thorough examination of all memory locations, either architected or implemented, to determine if dependencies can be a problem.

Architected registers are addressable by the instructions and are defined by a formal definition of the architecture such as ISP [BELL71].

Implemented registers support the interpretation of an instruction but do not carry information between instructions. They have been called *underground* or *temporary* registers [BELL71].

Another dependency problem has to do with data types. If the processor has more than one data type there are additional complications. For example, if a true dependency is based upon a single precision word integer, what if the output from instruction i is a byte in the left-hand end and the input to instruction j is the right-hand byte? For this case, there is no true dependency even though the same word is the range and domain. In the discussions to follow, except where noted, I assume that the data types of the domain and range are the same.

Problems associated with different data types are only discussed in the context of specific processors. However, it is important to note that the large number of data types used by processors such as the ix86, VAX, and MC680x0 significantly complicates dependency detection and resolution, especially when these processors are reimplemented using pipelining techniques.

There are two dimensions to dependencies: data dependencies and structural hazards. Data dependencies are discussed in Sections 8.1 through 8.6. Structural dependencies are discussed in Section 8.7.

8.1 Instruction Issue and Release Techniques

Before discussing data dependencies and the methods for detecting and resolving them, it is instructive to examine the various techniques for issuing instructions into the execution unit(s) of the processors. Processors have a buffer, called an *instruction window*, between the decoder and the execution units; Figure 6.8 has been modified in Figure 8.1 to show the placement of the window.

Instruction window designs for processors that decode one instruction per clock and with one execution unit are shown in Figure 8.2 and are named Type A and Type B windows. Processors that decode more than one instruction per clock, called *superscalar*, are discussed in Chapter 10. After the fetched instruction is decoded, it is issued to the window and then released to the execution unit(s). These two steps are logical and may not be implemented as two steps in the pipeline.

The notations i-o and o-o indicate in-order and out-of-order, respectively. A number of terms are used to describe window and execution unit designs in the following sections.

FIGURE 8.1 Instruction window.

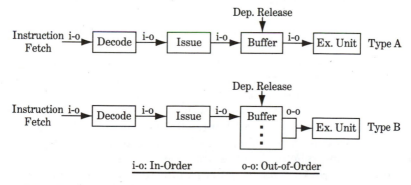

FIGURE 8.2 Single execution unit instruction window designs.

Instruction issue. An instruction is issued when it is sent from the decoder to a buffer or an execution unit.

Instruction release. After all dependencies are resolved, an instruction is released from the buffer into the execution unit.

Completion. Completion is achieved when an operation has traversed a function unit and resides in the last stage.

Retire. Retire when a result is written from a function unit into its destination and/or the process state is updated. (This definition is expanded in Chapter 9.)

Issue Latency. The time between the issue of successive operations into a pipeline is issue latency. Issue in adjacent clocks has an issue latency of 1. Issue latency is the reciprocal of the issue rate.

The signals called *Dep. Release* in Figure 8.2 are generated when all dependencies have been resolved and an instruction can be released to the execution unit. The techniques for generating data dependency release signals are discussed in Section 8.2 and structural dependencies are discussed in Section 8.7.

Window Type A. This design decodes instructions in-order and issues the instructions to a single buffer. If there is a dependency, instruction issue stalls until the dependency is resolved; then the instruction is released to the execution unit. With this design, instructions are released to the execution unit in-order. The buffer may be as simple as the output staging register of the decoder. This window design, with one execution unit, can only have true dependencies; antidependencies and output dependencies will not occur. The integer unit of the IBM S/360/91 is an example of this window design.

Window Type B. This design is similar to the Type A design except that the buffer can hold more than one instruction and instructions can be released out-of-order as their dependencies are resolved. Out-of-order release permits instructions without dependencies to be released without stalling, thereby reducing the number of stall cycles, compared to a type A, and reducing the CPI. I know no example of this window design.

When additional execution units are added to the processor, complications are added to the window design. Figure 8.3 shows three possible window designs: Types C, D, and E. A dotted line is shown at the input to the execution units; the possible order indicated at this interface means the order with respect to the instruction fetches that are always in-order. The order of retiring or writing results to the register file after execution is discussed in Chapter 9. With out-of-order release and variable-length execution units, out-of-order retirement is a possibility and must be comprehended in the processor design.

Window Type C. This design is similar to Type A except that there are multiple execution units. The window is a single register or a FIFO

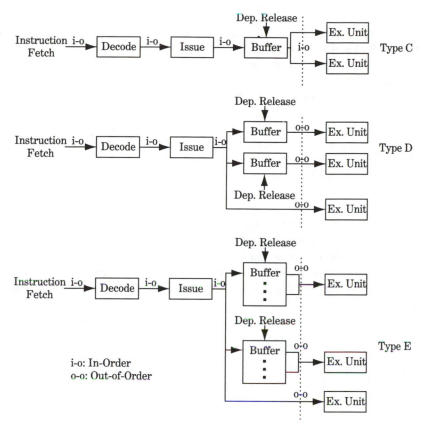

FIGURE 8.3 Multiple execution unit window designs.

queue. Instructions release in-order as dependencies are resolved. The Cray-1 is an example of this window design.

Window Type D. With this design, some of the execution units have a buffer, as with Type A, to delay release until dependencies are resolved. One execution unit is shown without a buffer because some execution or function units are not subject to a dependency delay. For example, some forms of branch instructions and loads will not be delayed due to dependencies. With this design, instructions are issued in-order and can be released out-of-order with branches and loads releasing at the earliest possible time. Concurrent release, in the same clock period, of instructions into all of the execution units is possible. Example processors using this window design are the CDC 6600 and the PowerPC 601.

Window Type E. This window design has multiple entry buffers, similar to the buffer of a Type B window, associated with each dependency-influenced execution unit. These buffers are called *reservation stations* in the IBM S/360/91. Out-of-order and concurrent instruction

358   *Dependencies*

release into the execution units is possible with this design. The buffers for the execution units can be unified into one functionally equivalent buffer, called a *dispatch stack* [ACOS86].

The size of the instruction window can influence the performance of an out-of-order release processor. If the window is too small, instruction fetching and decoding may be halted by a full buffer. If the window is too large, resources are wasted and the clock period may be increased. A distributed window has the advantage of reducing the complexity of the search logic but the disadvantage of limiting the sharing of window resources between execution units. Different window designs are used in combination with some processors. For example, the IBM S/360/91 uses a Type A window for integers and a Type E window for floating point.

Smith [SMIT89] uses other terms to describe the operation of a window: the scheduler *prefetches* instructions from the decoded trace stream, attempts to *place* these instructions in the window, and then *issues* instructions from the window to available execution units. Unfortunately, other terminology is used in the literature of various manufacturers.

As discussed in Chapter 9, for processors with more than one execution unit and out-of-order results, the order of the results may be merged in a buffer in such a way that they are placed in the register file in-order, which is a requirement for precise interrupts. This buffer has been called a *result window* [LAIR92].

8.2 Data Register or Data Path Dependencies

The discussion of dependencies has two dimensions: the object type and the dependency type. I take the approach of discussing the object type as the major topic with the dependency types as subtopics. In the following sections the register or data path dependencies are discussed: true dependencies are addressed first, then antidependencies, and finally output dependencies. The discussions to follow describe how the Dep. Release signals of Figure 8.2 and Figure 8.3 are generated.

8.2.1 *True Dependencies*

A *true dependency* exists when the output of one instruction is required as an input to a subsequent instruction. Examples of true dependencies between instructions i and j (instruction j follows i, but j is not necessarily the instruction next to i) are:

1. i loads a data register from memory;
   j uses the contents of that data register for an operation.

2. *i* sets a condition code;
   j branches based on the condition code.
3. *i* writes to memory via a write buffer;
   j loads this same value into a data register.
4. *i* writes a value into a data address register;
   j uses this value in the data register.

The critical characteristic of true dependencies is that they are artifacts of the program and an instruction cannot release until its inputs are valid. For this reason true dependencies cannot be eliminated, only detected and resolved. Reduction in performance, which is the consequence of resolving a true dependency, can only be mitigated.

The frequency of occurrence of true dependencies is influenced by the instruction set architecture. For example, a RISC load or store instruction forms the effective address by adding a displacement in the instruction to a base value. For base plus index plus displacement addressing, the base value may have been formed in a previous instruction by incrementing an index register and adding the results to the base register. Thus, there is a sequence of three arithmetic operations with true dependencies.

A CISC architecture, on the other hand, has an auto increment or decrement of the index register, and a base plus index plus displacement addressing mode has a true dependency between the side effect of the auto increment or decrement and the formation of the effective address. The three input adder needed to form the effective address may require a longer clock period than that of the two input adder of the RISC architecture.

Detecting and Resolving True Dependencies

Because of the importance that the detection and resolution of true dependencies has on the performance of a pipelined processor, these dependencies will be considered first. There are three basic techniques of detecting and resolving true dependencies:

1. Stall instruction release until the dependencies are resolved.
2. Dynamically create a directed graph that schedules instruction release.
3. Provide a process flow model of activity in the execution unit(s) that schedules instruction release.

The window designs discussed previously are used in combination with the strategies for detecting and resolving true dependencies.

Stall Instruction Release

A simple way, which requires no hardware support, to resolve true dependencies is for the compiler to insert enough no-ops into the instruction stream to delay the release of the second instruction. This is the approach taken with the first MIPS processor, except for loads [HENN82], and it is generally recognized as a rather blunt instrument. Further, because of nondeterministic delays in the pipeline, such as a cache miss, the use of no-ops for resolving true dependencies is not completely safe. For this reason, and because it imposes a severe performance penalty on the pipeline, stalling with no-ops is not employed in any known pipelined processor and is not discussed further.

There are, however, relatively simple hardware schemes that stall instruction release. These schemes are discussed in the following paragraphs and are called *simple tags* and *indicator counters*.

Simple Tag Scheme. One hardware scheme uses a single bit associated with each entry of the register file to mark a register as *reserved*. When an instruction releases, the destination register is reserved. Subsequent instructions compare their source and destination registers with the table of reservation bits and delay their release if there is a match. If a source register is reserved by a previous instruction as a destination, there is a true dependency.

This scheme is used by the MC88100 processor [MOT90]. Unfortunately, the Motorola designers chose to call their technique *scoreboarding*, but there is little comparison between the Motorola scheme and scoreboarding as it is historically known.

This scheme is also used on the Cray 1, a processor with a Type C window with in-order release. For scalar code, there are four execution units, each with a busy bit, and each register has a tag bit. For an instruction to release, the following checks must be true.

1. Source and destination registers are free.
2. Result bus will be free when needed.
3. Execution unit is free.
4. For load and store instructions, the memory bank is free.

If all of these conditions are true, then the necessary resources are reserved: registers, result bus, execution unit, and memory bank. The instruction then releases. When the instruction is complete and the result is written into the register, the control bits are reset on the registers, the execution unit, the bus, and the memory bank. Issued instructions stall until the above conditions are met; then the blocked instruction releases. Methods for reserving a future time slot on a result bus are discussed in Chapter 9.

Indicator Counters. Another method for detecting and resolving true dependencies uses *indicator counters* that are associated with each of the registers [KELL75, KOGG81]. The IBM S/360/91 [ANDE67] is an example of a processor that uses this technique for integer operations. This processor has the usual general-purpose registers and instructions for integer operations that require dependency detection and resolution.

This scheme extends the simple single one-bit tag for marking destination registers with marking the source registers as well. Associated with each register is a counter that can be in a value from the set $\{1, 0, -1, -2, \ldots, -N\}$ where N is the maximum number of concurrently executable operations [KELL75]. For the case where there is only one execution unit, $N = 1$ and the three states are: 0 is unassigned, 1 is assigned as a destination, and -1 is assigned as a source. As instructions issue into the window, the indicator counters are tested to see if the instruction can release and then are adjusted as the instruction releases. For an instruction to release, the following tag conditions must hold:

destination register $= 0$.
source register ≤ 0; that is, 0 or -1.

When an instruction completes, the destination counter is reset to 0 and the source counters are incremented by one. By using the indicator counters on the source registers, instructions can release out-of-order if there are no true or output dependencies. The indicator counter scheme permits dependency-free instructions to release out-of-order, giving a performance increase over the simple tag scheme.

Directed Graph

The directed graph method of detecting and resolving true dependencies is discussed in this section and focuses on true dependencies. This approach is accomplished through hardware control and is illustrated by the CDC 6600 Scoreboard and Tomasulo's Common Data Bus (CDB). For both of these processors, a directed graph is dynamically constructed as a program executes, and the directed graph releases operations into the function or execution units. Various tags and associative searches of tag fields synchronize this process.

[A note on terminology is in order. Function units have *input* and *output* registers. However, when a bus is the point of reference, the output register becomes a *source* and the input register is the *sink* for the transfer between function units or registers and function units.]

The flow of operands and results through pipelined execution units and registers will be discussed first. Figure 8.4 shows three execution units that can be either real or virtual. A virtual execution unit is a single execution unit with an input buffer, window Type E, that can release out-of-order. To illustrate the principle, assume that the output

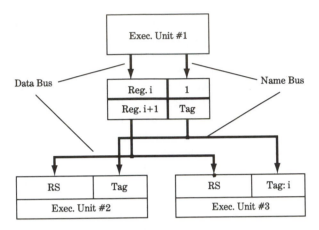

FIGURE 8.4 Instruction flow directed graph.

of EU 1 is written into a register that is then an input to the instruction to be executed in EU 3. The source execution unit name, in this case, 1, is placed in the tag field of the sink, register (*i*), and the name of the input register (*i*) is placed in the tag of the reservation station of EU 3. When EU 1 completes its operation, the result is placed on the data bus, the execution unit name is placed on the name bus, and the result is routed to the sink register. On the next clock the contents of the register are placed on the output bus and broadcast to EU 2 and EU 3. The tag on EU 3 matches the name of the register and the result is captured in EU 3's reservation station.

The transfer from the output of EU1 to the register and then to an input of EU3, consumed the time to store into and then read from the register. This extra time associated with the register is overhead that can be eliminated.

Forwarding. Forwarding is a technique commonly used to reduce the time for transferring an operand from a producer to a user by bypassing the step of placing a result into a register that will be immediately used [KELL75]. The sink registers can be loaded in parallel with the data routing to the sink execution unit, saving the clock that is needed to read the value. This process is called *forwarding*, *short-circuiting*, or *bypassing*; see Figure 8.5.

The tag field of Reg. (*i*) and EU3 are loaded with (1), the name of the source execution unit. When this execution unit completes its operation, its name and result are broadcast to all the registers and execution units. With a match between the tag values and execution unit name, the data is latched into the destinations.

The concept of forwarding was first noted by Block [BLOC59] and is a common design technique today. Note that this operation is similar to

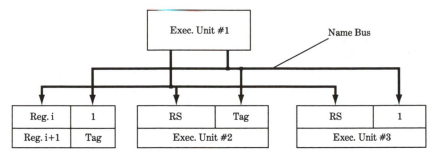

FIGURE 8.5   Forwarding.

the concept of bypassing the cache on a cache miss (discussed in Chapter 2). Forwarding cannot eliminate true dependencies; this technique can only reduce the delay of a true dependency.

   CDC 6600 Scoreboard. The CDC 6600 is a three-address, register file, load/store architecture. The processor possesses a multiplicity of resources: registers, function units, and buses [THOR70]. Function units are execution units, branch units, and load/store units. The scheduling of these resources in response to the decoded instruction stream is the responsibility of the Scoreboard that performs in-order issue but out-of-order release and, with its multiple function units, has out-of-order retirement: a Type D window. The scoreboard schedules both floating point and integer function (data and addresses) units.

   A simplified diagram of the CDC 6600 data path is shown in Figure 8.6. There are 24 CPU registers, 10 function units, and a number of busses for concurrent data movement. Five read channels and one write channel connect the memory and the CPU registers. There are forwarding paths from the output of the function units to their destination inputs. The two inputs to a function unit are gated into input registers when they are available. Upon completion of the function, the result is stored in an output register (Out F) until it can be routed to its sink register (In j or In k).

   The instruction format of the CDC 6600 is three address. Each

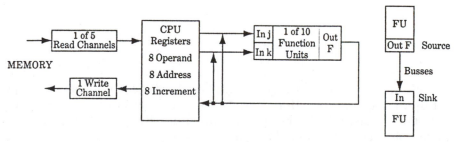

FIGURE 8.6   CDC 6600 data path.

address in the instruction is three bits, addressing one of eight registers: either operand, address, or increment depending on the instruction (a more detailed discussion of the CDC 6600 instructions is found in Chapter 11).

$$F_i \leftarrow F_j \text{ op } F_k.$$

The Scoreboard can be viewed as a unified structure that schedules issue and release of all of the execution units. However, for expository purposes, the scoreboard components of one execution unit will be described. Control of releasing operands into the function units and routing of results is performed by a version of the directed graph mechanism discussed above. Routing is vested in tags that "look up" into the stream of results to find the desired operands. That is, tags are associated with the input (sink) registers of the function units; the tags contain the names of the output (source) registers or function unit. Sources broadcast their names when a result is available, permitting the sink registers to accept the operands.

A tag in the function unit contains the name of the sink register. This tag is used to resolve output dependencies.

Each function unit has a busy bit that indicates its status to the Scoreboard. The two flags (j and k) are set when the conditions are resolved for an operand to be gated into an input register.

Tags are associated with each 24 general registers that contain the names of source execution units. These tags reserve the register to receive a source result.

Each function unit has the tags and flags listed below:

F_i Operation sink register, 3 bits.
F_j Operation source register, 3 bits.
Q_i Operation source function unit, 4 bits.
F_k Operation source register, 3 bits.
Q_k Operation source function unit, 4 bits.

Busy Bit Function unit Busy Bit

flag j Source j is ready/not ready.
flag k Source k is ready/not ready.

When an instruction reaches the decode stage, the following steps set up the tag structure that controls the release of instructions and the data flow through the buses and function units. Remember the "look up" philosophy of control. Note that these steps are not actually implemented as sequential steps but are all performed at once.

Step 1 (called SET UNIT BUSY). This step checks to see if the desired functioning is busy. If not, the busy bit is set. If busy, test again on the next cycle.

Step 2 (called SET F). This step transfers the contents of the instruction register fields (F_i, F_j, and F_k) to the corresponding tags of the selected and reserved function unit.

Step 3 (called SET Q). This step transfers the contents of tags associated with a register that was a *sink* of a previous instruction and is a *source* for the current instruction. In other words, F_j and F_k address the register tags and transfer the address tags into the Q_j and Q_k tags of the function unit. This transfer establishes the Q_j and Q_k tags in the "look up" configuration. Note that either of the two inputs to an function unit may have valid tag values in both F_j and Q_j as well as F_k and Q_k.

Step 4 (called SET XBA). This step places the selected function unit name into the register tag associated with the sink of the instruction. Note that it is this function unit name that is used on a subsequent instruction Step 3. This step is not a "look down" philosophy but merely the saving of a pointer for subsequent use in "look up" with forwarding.

When a function unit or load path has a value to place in a register, routing is determined by the sink tag as discussed above. This step is accomplished by (1) clearing the destination register and (2) setting the register tag to zero, which is the equivalent of "valid." I can best explain the resolution of true dependencies in an example. Consider the following three-instruction program fragment with instruction 3 using FU 5.

1. R7 ← memory (via Read Storage Channel 4, Code: 14).
•
2. R6 ← result from FU 4.
3. R3 ← R6 [op FU 5] R7.

This instruction sequence has a true dependency on R6 which must be detected and resolved either by forwarding around the register file or via register 6. The operation of issuing instruction 3 is described by a reservation-table-like display, as shown in Table 8.2.

Note that the tag value of 4 is transferred from the tag field of register 6 to Q_j on step 3; however, the result has not yet been transferred into R6. The tag associated with R7 has the value 14 as it is waiting for the transfer from the memory system. There is no forwarding on register 7, as it is assumed that this register was loaded well in advance of the decoding of instruction 3.

The state of Function Unit 5 at release time is shown in Figure 8.7. The input from memory to register R7 has been stored in the register and its tag cleared to zero. The F_k tag has been compared to the address of register 7, and when its tag goes to zero, flag k is set to permit the k

Function Unit 5

Function Unit 5	Initial Condition	Step 1	Step 2	Step 3	Step 4	Release
F_i sink register			3	3	3	
F_i source register			6	6	6	
Q_i source function unit				4	4	
Flag$_i$ source ready/not ready					1	
F_k source register			7	7	7	Function Unit #5
Q_k source function unit						
Flag k source ready/not ready		1	1	1	1	
Busy Bit FU busy/not busy					5	
R3 value in register tag	4	4	4	4	4	
R6 value in register tag	14	14	14	14	4	
R7 value in register tag					0	

TABLE 8.2 Scoreboard operation.

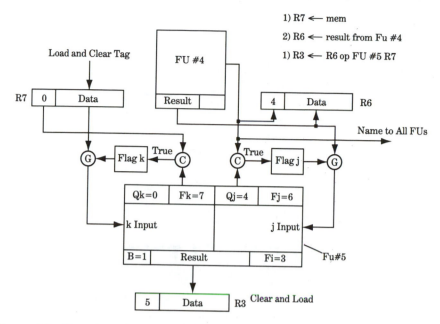

FIGURE 8.7 Scoreboard true dependency resolution.

input to be read from register 7. When the result is available from Function Unit 4, its name is broadcast over the name bus and detected by register 6 and the Q_j tag of Function Unit 5. The result is transferred to both register 6 and the J input of Function Unit 5. On the next clock execution begins.

This process resolves the true dependency on register 6 between instructions 2 and 3 while forwarding the result around register 6. Note that Figure 8.7 does not show that a comparison is made on the Function Unit Name Bus by Q_k even though such a comparison is performed. Also, the value in F_j is compared with all of the register tags to see if there is a register j input. There is an abundance of design detail of the CDC 6600 busing structure that is important from a performance point of view. However, this detail is not germane to the basic discussion of true dependency detection and resolution. Interested readers should refer to Thornton [THOR70].

Tomasulo Common Data Bus. The IBM S/360/91 floating point unit has a Type E window with in-order issue and out-of-order release. The Tomasulo common data bus (CDB) detects and resolves true dependencies only in the floating point unit [TOMA67]. As with the Scoreboard, this detection and resolution scheme creates a dynamic directed graph and employs forwarding. The tags associated with the sink registers hold the identification number (ID) of the source. Thus, like the Score-

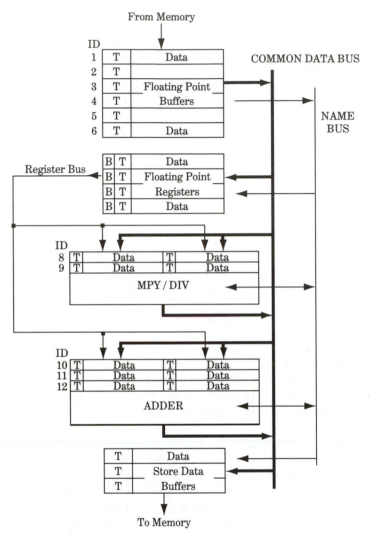

From Memory

COMMON DATA BUS

NAME BUS

Register Bus

FIGURE 8.8 IBM common data bus.

board, the CDB scheme is "look up." Fixed-point dependency detection and resolution are implemented by indicator counters.

The CDB works by increasing the register resources through the addition of buffers and resolving true dependencies by transferring results over a single result bus that provides a generalization of forwarding. The buffers, called *reservation stations*, hold the operands for the two execution units and constitute *virtual execution units*. As shown in Figure 8.8, there are three virtual floating point adders and two virtual floating point multipliers. Each of these virtual execution units is given a number (Flt. Pt. MPY/DIV 8, 9 and Flt. Pt. ADDER 10, 11, 12). There are two buses: first, the CDB routes operands between the execution units and the floating point register file; a second bus, called the *register bus*, routes operands from the floating point register to the execution units. The register bus is explicitly controlled by the decoder, and it is not controlled by the directed graph. The register bus is frequently forwarded, by the CDB, and only infrequently is it in the critical path for instruction execution.

The four addressable floating point data registers each have a tag field and a busy bit, shown as an explicit bit in the figure. However, these bits do not really exist in either the floating point registers or other sinks. The tags contain the ID of the source (numbered 1–6, 8–12); the code 0111 (7) is not allocated and is used for the busy bit. It is possible for all reservation stations to be full at one time (that is, to have one destination with a valid tag). In this case, the instruction issue is halted until a reservation station of the correct type is free and can be assigned.

When an execution unit completes an operation, the result is placed on the CDB along with its ID on the name bus. The CDB performs an associative match on the tags of the reservation stations and registers. When a match is found, the data is routed to the proper reservation station input registers and/or floating point registers and their busy bits are set (tag set to 0111).When both operands are valid in a reservation station, the virtual execution unit releases, thereby resolving true dependencies.

Register loads from memory are routed to the *floating point buffers* (FLB), which are not explicitly addressed by the instruction, and then to the *floating point registers* (FLR) via the CDB. For loads, the FLR tag field is loaded with the number of the FLB assigned at decode time. Thus, the CDB resolves load true dependencies using the same mechanism as used for arithmetic operations.

Store instructions place the number of the execution unit or register that will have the operand into the tag field of the *store data buffers* (SDB). Each transaction on the CDB does an associative search on the SDB, and if there is a hit, the value will be pushed onto the SDB.

The IBM S/360 has a multiple accumulator instruction architecture, also known as a two-address architecture. For example, an add instruction performs the operation

$$FLR0 \leftarrow FLR0 + FLR1.$$

An example of the control of a program fragment with the CDB is taken

370   *Dependencies*

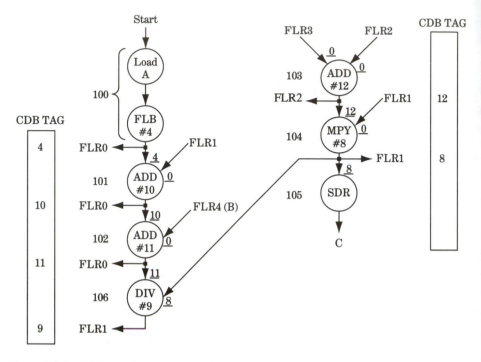

FIGURE 8.9 CDB directed graph example.

from Kogge [KOGG80]. The floating point registers are used while memory addresses are denoted as A, B, and C.

100	LOAD	FLR0, A
101	ADD	FLR0, FLR1
102	ADD	FLR0, B (FLR4)
103	ADD	FLR2, FLR3
104	MPY	FLR1, FLR2
105	STORE	FLR1, C
106	DIVIDE	FLR1, FLR0

A directed graph representation of this program fragment is shown in Figure 8.9. An instruction is represented by a circle with its assigned execution unit. Arrows entering the circle show the inputs to the operation with the tag values underlined. The initial condition assumes that FLR1, FLR2, and FLR3 contain valid precomputed data and that FLR4 has the memory variable B. Thus, these four values have been transferred into the reservation stations of three adders and one multiplier and their tags set to 0, a representation of the valid code 0111.

To illustrate the operation of the CDB, consider instruction 102 that is assigned to ADD #1. One of its inputs, FLR4, is already present; the other tag is set to 10 while it waits for the result from ADD #10. When this input value from ADD #10 is available, it is transferred to ADD #11 and to FLR0. ADD #11 releases, and when its result is available it is transmitted over the CDB and received by DIV unit #9 and sent to FLR0.

Note that the right-hand path can execute in parallel with the left-hand path. However, because instructions issue in-order, instruction 103 will issue and be assigned to ADD #12 only after instruction 102 issues. ADD #12 will release in the clock after instruction 102 issues because its inputs FLR2 and FLR3 are available in floating point registers.

The detection and resolution of true dependencies is illustrated by the true dependency on FLR2 between instructions 103 and 104 and 106. The FLR1 input to MPY #8 is already present and the other input tag is set with #12, establishing the data flow control. Only when the result is available from ADD #12 can MPY #8 receive this input via the CDB forwarding path. With both inputs valid, the multiplier will release, producing its result that is routed to FLR 1 and the DIV #9 and SDR 0.

Notice that in three cases results are transferred to FLR0 and never used because of the forwarding action of the CDB. Results are similarly transferred to FLR2 and not used. Because of forwarding, the register bus is not used in this example and, in general, has low use. The only use of this bus is if a FLR has been loaded by an instruction that preceded this program fragment. For example, the output of instruction 106 placed a result in FLR1 without routing to a reservation station. A subsequent instruction, outside this program fragment, would then need to transfer the value into its reservation station as was done for instruction 103.

Process Flow Model

Another method for detecting and resolving true dependencies uses a model of the process flow through the pipeline. Before an instruction can be released, the model is searched for instructions in process that will have true dependencies. This scheme is a generalization of the scheme used on the IBM S/360/91 for detecting and resolving true dependencies associated with main memory and condition codes [ANDE67] (discussed in Section 8.4).

The Texas Instruments ASC [ASC73, CRAG89] has a Type C window and resolves true dependencies using the process flow model technique—a hardware model called the *register stack*. This stack is in reality a shift register that follows in lock step with the operands as they pass through the execution units as shown in Figure 8.10. The register stack contains

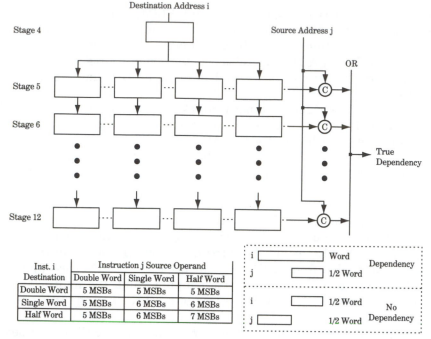

FIGURE 8.10 TI ASC register stack.

the destination register address of the instruction. As the TI ASC can be configured with four execution unit pipelines, the register stack consists of four stacks, one for each pipeline. Instructions can be released into any one of the four identical execution units.

When an instruction j is a candidate for release in Stage 4, an associative search is made of the register stack (all four shift registers) to see if a source register of the candidate instruction is the destination register of a previous instruction i. The results of these parallel probes are ORed together to signal a true dependency. It is not necessary to know which pipeline has the true dependency, only that it exists. If there is a hit, the candidate instruction does not release because a previous instruction has yet to update its destination register or make available its result via forwarding.

When instruction i, which caused the true dependency, exits the execution unit, the result is routed for storage into the register file and forwarded to the input of an execution unit. The associative search of the register stack will now show that the true dependency has been resolved and the candidate instruction j will issue.

There is a complication with the TI ASC that does not exist with either the implemented Scoreboard or the common data bus. These two systems process constrained data types: the CDB processes only double-precision floating point and the Scoreboard processes either integers or floating point but not both in the same function unit. In addition, the floating point and integer register files are disjoint. The TI ASC, on the other hand, processes a number of data types through the same execution units and has a unified register file. There are three integer forms: double word, single word, and half word plus single- and double-precision floating point. Thus, the register file is addressed to the double word, single word, and half word; the word is 32 bits. The TI ASC has six register files of eight words, each requiring a register address of 7 bits:

3 bits to select one of six files,
3 bits to select one of eight words in each file,
1 bit to select the LH/RH half word in each word.

As shown in Figure 8.10, if instruction *i* writes to a word and instruction *j* reads a half word that is contained within that word, 6 bits of both addresses must be compared in the register stack. A true dependency is present in this example. On the other hand, if instructions *i* and *j* both reference half words within the same word, all 7 bits of address must be compared. For the case shown, there is no true dependency. Figure 8.10 shows a table describing the address bits to be compared in the register stack. It can be shown that if a larger number of bits than those shown in the table are compared, an erroneous true dependency signal can be generated.

Load True Dependencies

Here I treat the case of load true dependencies. These dependencies occur because of the delay of reading an operand from memory into the register file and then using the operand on a later instruction. This delay can be two or three clocks in a short pipeline, such as the one shown in Figure 6.8. Instructions 100 and 101 of the CDB example, Figure 8.9, constitute a load true dependency on FLR0.

Load true dependencies on early pipelined computers were a potential source of significant performance degradation because of a long memory cycle time that resulted in long register load times. For these machines, it was imperative to continue processing during these long load delays. Modern processors, on the other hand, employ caches with a much shorter load delay. However, caches do not eliminate the need to detect and resolve load true dependencies. In fact, load true dependencies are still of such importance that this class of dependency is the only one that receives special hardware consideration with the IBM RS/6000. Methods of detecting and resolving load true dependencies are discussed below.

Delayed Load

Load true dependencies can be resolved using a technique similar to the delayed branching technique discussed in Chapter 7. To use this technique, the pipeline unconditionally executes the instruction in the delay slot(s) between the load instruction and the actual loading of the target register. The number of delay slots is deterministic, depending only on the design of the pipeline while assuming no cache misses that stall the pipeline.

The compiler attempts to schedule instructions that can always be executed into the delay slots; otherwise, no-ops are scheduled into the delay slots. Recall that no-ops are instructions that can always execute without modifying the state of the program or the machine. There can be a major problem with instruction reordering for delayed load. Consider the following program fragment, the memory variables of which may be in the cache:

$$
\begin{array}{lll}
i & \text{Store} & M(Rx) \leftarrow R7, \\
j & \text{Load} & R1 \leftarrow M(Rx), \\
k & \text{Add} & R9 \leftarrow R1 + R2.
\end{array}
$$

There are two true dependencies: one on $M(Rx)$ and the other on R1. Assume that the program is reordered (j releases before i) to remove the R1 load true dependency. Instruction j has been moved far enough up in the instruction stream that the dependency is hidden by the depth of the pipeline.

$$
\begin{array}{lll}
j & \text{Load} & R1 \leftarrow M(Rx), \\
\bullet & & \\
i & \text{Store} & M(Rx) \leftarrow R7, \\
k & \text{Add} & R9 \leftarrow R1 + R2.
\end{array}
$$

This reordering has accomplished three things: (1) removed the true dependency on R1, (2) created an antidependency on $M(Rx)$, and (3) placed an incorrect value in R1—clearly not a good thing to do. Removing load true dependencies by reordering code must be approached very carefully as improper reordering can destroy the logic of the program.

Hardware Solution to Load True Dependencies

Due to the unreliability of resolving true dependencies with code reordering, processors usually incorporate a hardware solution; examples are found in MIPS and the RS/6000. The approach is that of the simple tag scheme discussed in Section 8.2.1. When a load is decoded, a flag is set on the destination register of the load instruction and the pipeline stalls.

When the load is completed, the flag is reset and the blocked instruction will release. Forwarding provisions are included to eliminate the one clock delay required to load and then read the register.

8.2.2 *Resource Dependencies*

Unlike true dependencies, resource dependencies stem from sharing various hardware resources such as storage spaces that must be reused by instruction j before instruction i no longer needs the resource. With most pipelined processors, the data register resources are limited. The smaller the number of addressable registers, the greater the probability of a resource dependency. For example, the IBM S/360/91 has only four addressable floating point registers while the CDC 6600 has eight. The two types of resource dependencies are:

1. Antidependence

i R4 ← R3 × R1 • j R3 ← R7 + R8	The dependency is on R3. If instruction i is still using R3 when instruction j writes into R3, an error will occur.

2. Output dependence

i R4 ← R3 × R1 • j R4 ← R7 + R8	The dependency is on R4. If instruction j writes into R4 before instruction i, an error will occur.

Antidependencies and output dependencies are problems because of the following chain of events:

1. A processor is designed with a limited number of registers to save hardware and address bits in the instruction.
2. An optimizing compiler reorders code and assigns registers. The register assignment process copes with the limited number of registers in the processor by reusing a register as much as possible. By reuse, the number of loads and stores is reduced.
3. Because of register reuse, the limited number of registers now have the potential for causing resource dependencies.

In every solution to this problem, execution time is traded off for space, that is, the lack of resources (registers). If there is an infinite pool of resources, there would be no antidependencies or output dependencies in the data path. Two general approaches can be used to detect and resolve these resource dependencies and manage the performance loss when resources are limited.

1. *In-order retirement.* The release or execution of an instruction must be halted until the dependency is resolved. Halting ensures that instructions are retired in-order, thereby maintaining the serial execution model. Antidependencies and output dependencies cannot occur with the serial execution model. Recall that the Type A window also gives in-order retirements, thus only true dependencies are possible.

2. *Register renaming.* The executing code can be fooled into believing that there are more resources and hence, no resource dependencies. Register renaming is similar to virtual address extension of a virtual memory (discussed in Chapter 3).

The discussion above is couched in terms of registers as the limited resource. Other limited resources can be the causes of resource dependencies. For example, output dependencies can occur because of the following conditions.

1. While memory is an almost infinite resource, memory-mapped I/O is not and offers the potential for output dependencies. Memory dependencies are discussed in Section 8.3.
2. A processor usually has one set of condition code locations—a limited resource that presents the opportunity for output dependencies. Special register dependencies are discussed in Section 8.4.

Detecting and Resolving Antidependencies

Recall that an antidependency results from a potential premature write to a resource, that is, before that resource has been read. If instructions are serialized, antidependencies cannot occur. The effect of serialization can be provided by renaming the sources to an execution unit, which is a technique called buffering [KELL75] and also known as *copying* [JOHN89]. The buffers increase the number of implemented registers over the architected registers to eliminate antidependencies. Consider the following example program fragment with an antidependency on R3:

$$i \quad R4 \leftarrow R3 \times R1$$
$$\bullet$$
$$j \quad R3 \leftarrow R7 \times R8.$$

When instruction i is decoded and released, the values in R3 and R1 are transferred into buffer registers that are then the input to the execution unit. The register R3 is now free to accept the write from instruction j. That is,

$$\text{Buff } 1 \leftarrow \text{R3 and Buff } 2 \leftarrow \text{R1.}$$

The program fragment becomes

i $\text{R4} \leftarrow \text{Buff } 1 \times \text{Buff } 2$

•

j $\text{R3} \leftarrow \text{R7} + \text{R8.}$

The use of buffering to prevent antidependencies is discussed for four processors in the following paragraphs.

IBM S/360/91. The multiple accumulator architecture of the IBM S/360 eliminates antidependencies through its instruction set architecture for integers, and buffering is used for floating point operations. Recall the instruction format $\text{R}x \leftarrow \text{R}x$ op $\text{R}y$ and there is only one integer ALU with this processor. For an integer instruction to release, the value in $\text{R}x$ must be read into the ALU input buffer. In other words, the instruction cannot release until the input has been buffered. If a second instruction follows that uses the same register for its destination (and source), an antidependency cannot occur.

For floating point operations, the CDB requires in-order issue of instructions but can produce out-of-order release—a Type E window. Antidependencies are prevented in the following way. When an instruction is decoded, valid input variables present in the register file are transferred into the reserved reservation station. The buffering of inputs resolves the antidependencies and is illustrated in Figure 8.10. Consider instructions 104 (reads FLR1) and 106 (writes FLR1) that have an antidependency on FLR1. For instruction 104 to release, the value in FLR1 has been transferred into the reservation station of the MPY #8, and a write to this register (as with instruction 106) will not cause an antidependency problem.

Texas Instruments ASC. The TI ASC uses buffering to eliminate integer and floating point antidependencies. When an instruction issues, the input variables are read from the register file into buffers. The registers are then available to receive writes from another instruction.

CDC 6600 Scoreboard. The CDC 6600 is different from the cases noted above because the number of implemented registers is equal to the number of architected registers. As discussed in the section on true dependencies, there are no input buffers with the function units and the scoreboard; the window is Type D. Antidependencies, called *third-order conflicts* [THOR64], are resolved in the following way.

Instead of buffered inputs, function units can hold results at their output registers. The Scoreboard holds the result of instruction j in the execution pipeline until it is known that the inputs to instruction i (a preceding instruction) have been released into its execution unit. The result can then be written into the register file. The Scoreboard compares the destination register address with the registers. If the read flags corresponding to a destination register are set, the result waits in the execution unit until an "all clear" signal, saying that the operand has been read into the execution unit, has been sent.

There is a potential for the processor to stall with this scheme that is not present with input buffering. However, I know of no studies that compare the performance of the two techniques.

PowerPC 601. I believe—the documentation is not clear—that both the integer and floating point execution units read their inputs from the disjoint register files in the same clock that releases the instruction. Thus the buffers are found in the pipeline stage registers. In other words, careful circuit design ensures that antidependencies will not occur. Both register files must be dual ported so that both inputs can be read in one clock.

Detecting and Resolving Output Dependencies

As discussed previously, output dependencies occur if instruction j attempts to write into an object that will be written into later and out-of-order by instruction i. This dependency is resolved by (1) serialization or (2) buffering.

With serialization, a write by instruction j to an object is held up until instruction i completes its write to the same object. The design issue is how to provide the interlocks that guarantee serialization. Simple tags that, on issue, reserve the destination register will prevent a following instruction from writing out-of-order to that register.

Buffering resolves this dependency by increasing the number of implemented registers. The output of instruction i is buffered into a temporary register and serves as the input to any instructions issued before instruction j [KELL75]. Consider the example, used previously to illustrate an output dependency, that has an added instruction k with a true dependency on R4:

$$
\begin{array}{ll}
i & \text{R4} \leftarrow \text{R3} \times \text{R1} \\
\bullet & \\
j & \text{R4} \leftarrow \text{R7} + \text{R8} \\
k & \text{R9} \leftarrow \text{R4} + \text{R5}.
\end{array}
$$

If instruction i writes into R4 after instruction j, then instruction k will give an incorrect result. To solve this problem, when instruction j

executes, the result is placed into R4 as well as a buffer. Then instruction k takes its operand from the buffer:

$$i \quad \text{R4} \leftarrow \text{R3} \times \text{R1}$$
$$\bullet$$
$$j \quad \text{Buf} \leftarrow \text{R4} \leftarrow \text{R7} + \text{R8}$$
$$k \quad \text{R9} \leftarrow \text{Buf} + \text{R5}.$$

Note that the output dependency has not really been solved: R4 is still retired out-of-order. However, by using a buffer, the logic of the program is not destroyed. The use of buffers for resolving output dependencies is not completely safe. For example, memory-mapped I/O cannot use buffers, and buffering is difficult with special registers such as condition codes. Thus, serialization is the preferred design option for many processors.

IBM S/360/91. The Tomasulo CDB resolves floating point output dependencies by serialization. When an instruction issues, in-order, its destination register is reserved by loading the register tag field with the number of the source execution unit. A following instruction that uses the same register as a destination finds the register reserved and will not issue until the previous write has been completed. Thus, serialization of register operations is ensured by using the register tags. Serialization of memory writes is discussed in Section 8.3.

Texas Instruments ASC. The TI ASC is a multiple accumulator architecture with strict in-order instruction release into the execution units that process both integer and floating point operations. Consider the instruction sequence

$$i \quad \text{R3} \leftarrow \text{R3} \times \text{M(a)}$$
$$\bullet$$
$$j \quad \text{R3} \leftarrow \text{R3} + \text{M(b)}.$$

The true and antidependencies on R3 have to be resolved before instruction j can issue. Therefore, there can be no output dependency on R3. However, the following sequence will have an output dependency on R3:

$$i \quad \text{R3} \leftarrow \text{R3} \times \text{M(b)}$$
$$\bullet$$
$$j \quad \text{R3} \leftarrow \text{M(a)}.$$

This dependency is resolved by serialization. Shift registers, shown in Figure 8.10, shift the destination register addresses in the register stack described previously. There are four shift registers, one for each execution unit. Instruction j searches the shift registers to see if its destination address is present. If the address is in one of the registers, instruction j releases into the same execution unit pipeline being used by instruction i, thus serializing the writes to the same register. Because the execution units are multifunctional, a delay to flush the pipeline may be required before the instruction can release. The use of a different execution unit would not guarantee the resolution of output dependencies.

CDC 6600 Scoreboard. The Scoreboard also resolves output dependencies by serialization. Before instruction j can issue, a search is made of the F_i tags of each function unit. If there is a match, indicating that a previous instruction has the same destination register, an output dependency exists and instruction j will not issue. Not issuing is more severe, from a loss of performance point of view, than issuing with a delayed release but is easier to implement. Output dependencies are considered to be rare events, and the performance penalty can be tolerated.

8.2.3 *Other Methods*

The methods for detecting and resolving antidependencies and output dependencies discussed above are very ad hoc. That is, each case is examined and a unique solution is found. However, there are other, more general, approaches to this problem. The following section describes some of these techniques. For two of the cases discussed below, more implemented registers exist than architected registers. These two methods are called *register renaming* and *reorder buffers*. These two schemes differ in that register renaming is an early select of registers that generally increases the depth of the pipeline. In contrast, reorder buffers are late select and have more complicated implementation.

Register Renaming

Recall that the Tomasulo CDB extends the architected registers with implemented registers called reservation stations. The TI ASC has input registers for the execution unit pipelines, and the CDC 6600 holds results in the execution unit output register. These, and other, ad hoc methods for increasing the register resources to resolve antidependencies and output dependencies have been extended to a general solution called register renaming (usually just called renaming) [TJAD70, KELL75, LOGR79].

Renaming provides a pool of implemented registers—more than the architected register set—that are accessed by mapping the register ad-

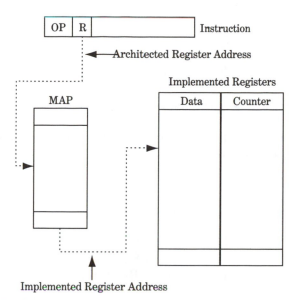

FIGURE 8.11 Register renaming.

dress of the instruction. This mapping is similar to virtual memory mapping with the difference that a small address is mapped to a larger address rather than the other way with virtual memory. As long as the pool of implemented registers is large enough, resource conflicts (anti- and output dependencies) will not occur. Moreover, the short register addresses are preserved in the instruction format. As discussed below, there can be a performance penalty associated with mapping register addresses.

Johnson [JOHN91] describes the implementation of register renaming as "To implement register renaming, the processor typically allocates a new register for every new value produced; that is, for every instruction that writes a register."

Register renaming is illustrated in Figure 8.11. An instruction register address field can have a number of unique names, for instance 32 with the IBM RS/6000 architecture; there are more implemented registers than architected registers, say 40. A map translates the register address from the instruction into the renamed address in the implemented register file. The effect is that there can be more implemented registers with a small number of register address bits. Another view of renaming is that one level of indirection is used for register addressing.

Implemented register addresses are assigned (placed in the map) for the destination or range address of an instruction from a pool of unused addresses. The map is relatively small, 16 or 32 entries, and is direct addressed. Consider the following modified example from [JOHN 91].

Register	True	Anti-	Output
3	1–3, 3–4, 5–6	4–5	3–5, 1–3
4	4–6		
5	2–3, 2–5		

TABLE 8.3 Program dependencies.

Assume that there are three instruction address bits for eight architected registers and sixteen implemented registers. The original instruction sequence is

Inst.	Operation
I1	Load R3
I2	Load R5
I3	R3 ← R3 op R5
I4	R4 ← R3 + 1
I5	R3 ← R5 + 1
I6	R7 ← R3 op R4

The dependencies of this program are shown in Table 8.3. Note that the apparent true dependency on R3 between instructions I1 and I6 does not exist because it is "shadowed" by instructions I3 and I4. In the case of R3, I6 is dependent on I5, which is dependent on I3, which is dependent on I1; thus I6 is not dependent on I1.

Because true dependencies cannot be removed, the best that can be done with renaming is to remove the antidependencies and output dependencies. Assume that none of the implemented registers are assigned when this program starts and that if a one-to-one mapping is available it is used. For these cases, the map is an identity map: $0:0$, $1:1$, and so on. The original and renamed program is shown in Table 8.4.

Instruction	Original Program	Map	Renamed Program
I1	Load R3	3:3	Load R3
I2	Load R5	5:5	Load R5
I3	R3 ← R3 op R5	3:6	R6 ← R3 op R5
I4	R4 ← R3 + 1	4:4	R4 ← R6 + 1
I5	R3 ← R5 + 1	3:7	R7 ← R5 + 1
I6	R7 ← R3 op R4	7:8	R8 ← R7 + R4

TABLE 8.4 Register renaming example.

The Map column shows the entries into the address translation map that are created for each new destination address. For example, instruction I3 has R3 as its destination, and this address is renamed to *R6*. R4 is renamed to *R4* as R4 has not been allocated previously. However, R3 is again renamed to *R7* at instruction I5. R7, having been used, is renamed to *R8* by instruction I6. With the renamed program all anti- and output dependencies have been eliminated.

Counters are maintained that erase an entry in the renaming map when the translation is no longer valid. Address translation adds the access time of the map to each register reference. However, the translation of names via the map can be pipelined, lengthening the pipeline by one stage as done with the RS/6000 pipeline and discussed in Chapter 10.

There is danger in renaming around loops. Assume that a register is expected to carry an argument into the next pass of a loop and that the register holding the argument has been renamed. At the start of the next pass of the loop, the register referenced by an instruction will be the unrenamed register, thereby destroying the ability to reference the value.

The IBM RS/6000 employs limited register renaming for floating point registers only; eight renaming registers are used in addition to the 32 architected registers for a total of 40 registers. Note that the description in [GROH90] is for a general scheme that managed all data-path and load dependencies. However, as floating point instructions are released in-order and a full renaming scheme is complicated, only load output dependencies are renamed. Load output dependencies are of the form

$$i \quad R1 \leftarrow M(\text{address } x)$$
$$\bullet$$
$$j \quad R1 \leftarrow M(\text{address } y).$$

Reorder Buffer

Another method for resolving anti- and output dependencies by renaming is by use of a *reorder buffer* [SMIT85]. The reorder buffer is used with Type C window designs to support precise interrupts, as discussed in Section 9.3.2, by delaying some writes to the register file so as to provide in-order retirement. Antidependencies and output dependencies are thus eliminated.

The reorder buffer receives out-of-order results from two or more execution units and writes in-order to the register file. When an instruction issues or releases, the destination register address is placed in-order in the associative tag field of the reorder buffer along with a unique sequential temporary identifying tag. When the result is produced by an execution unit, it is stored in the reorder buffer location found by an associative search of the destination register address and the valid bit is set. The sequential identifying tags then schedule the writes to the register file in-order or serialized.

The reorder buffer must provide a forwarding path that permits the rapid resolution of true dependencies. A following instruction consults the reorder buffer by an associative search in order to obtain the result of a previous instruction if it is available. If the result is not yet available, the identification tag is returned, indicating that a true dependency exists, and the instruction must retry on the next clock pulse. Because a sequence of instructions can write to the same register, an associative search of the reorder buffer can return more than one hit. So the most recent valid result is bypassed; thus, another tag is maintained in the reorder buffer that indicates the order of allocation. Johnson [JOHN91] points out that a simpler method would be to discard the old and write the new result to a register. However, this scheme does not permit recovery of in-order retirement for precise interrupts.

Reorder buffers can be compared to register renaming in the following way. As discussed earlier, register renaming is a form of early selection of alternative spaces and tends to increase the depth of the pipeline. Reorder buffers, on the other hand, are a form of late selection of the alternative spaces that do not increase the effective depth of the pipeline because of forwarding. However, reorder buffers are generally more difficult to implement, resulting in an increase in the clock period.

Unified Tag Unit

Sohi described a scheme based upon the Tomasulo CDB algorithm [SOHI87] that unifies the tag of the registers into a common pool of tags, resulting in possible hardware savings. A base machine is proposed that has 144 registers rather than the four registers found in the CDB system. With this large number of registers, the cost of the associative logic may be excessive. However, as only a small number of registers are waiting for a result at any one time, pooling of the associative logic could be effective. This idea is similar to the use of a map for renaming, illustrated in Figure 8.11. The major difference is that this map, called the *tag unit*, may be fully occupied and result in a delay in issue.

Sohi also suggested unifying the reservation station hardware as well as the tags. Simulations performed to assess the effectiveness of these proposals give ambiguous results. Interested readers should refer to [SOHI87] for further details.

8.3 Memory Dependencies

The preceding sections have discussed data register or data path dependencies. This section discusses memory object dependencies. This is a complicated subject because an object may be in the cache, main memory, or even in the disk. For objects in the disk, the management of dependencies is the responsibility of the operating system and is outside the scope of this book. Examples of the three dependencies on memory location with address (Rx) are

	i	M(Rx) ← R1
	•	
Output	j	M(Rx) ← R7
	i	R1 ← M(Rx)
	•	
Anti-	j	M(Rx) ← R7
	i	M(Rx) ← R1
	•	
True	j	R7 ← M(Rx)

TABLE 8.5

8.3.1 *Anti- and Output Dependencies*

The basic approach to resolving anti- and output dependencies, as with registers, is to ensure in-order retirement. That is, if i is completed before j, there will be no dependencies. Recall the Type A window design; if there is a single execution unit and with in-order release, there must be in-order retirement. As memory is viewed as equivalent to a single execution unit, in-order release results in in-order retirement.

These memory referencing instructions, however, may be issued out-of-order with respect to other instruction types. That is, if instruction i is a register operation and instruction j is a load, j can issue before i if there is no dependency between i and j. A later store instruction k cannot release ahead of instruction j. There must be provisions in the memory system that prevent a later memory reference from racing ahead of an earlier reference. Recall that this is not the case with some disk systems that employ SATF scheduling.

8.3.2 *True Dependencies*

True dependencies in memory are not as simply solved as are anti- and output dependencies. A memory operation is similar to a pipeline in

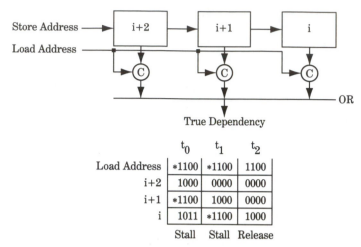

FIGURE 8.12 Memory true dependency detection.

that it requires a number of cycles to complete. With register objects, a reservation can be placed on a register, a scheme that is clearly impractical with a large memory. Thus another scheme is required to prevent or resolve true dependencies.

The IBM S/360/91 [ANDE67] and the TI ASC [ASC73] used a register model to detect and resolve true dependencies in memory. These processors do not have caches. When a store to memory is issued, the address of the store is placed in a shift register that parallels the memory equivalent pipeline that carries the data to the memory. This memory model is called the Z-Pipe Model on the TI ASC. Any subsequent load tests all stages of this address shift register to check for a true dependency, which is indicated by a match at any stage. The shift registers and a reservation table for this method of memory true dependency detection are shown in Figure 8.12. At t0, the three previous writes to memory have the addresses 1011, 1100, and 1000. The load address is 1100. This load address matches the write address of $i + 1$, and a true dependency is noted, stalling the load one clock. At t1, the store addresses have shifted down and there is another stall of the load because of a match on the load address. This stall delays the load one more clock. At t2, the 1100 write address has been shifted out of the shift registers and there is no match on the load address, permitting the load to be released to the memory system. Note that the memory system may not be a pure pipeline and an operation cannot be issued every clock.

For cache-based systems, true dependencies are handled in the cache write buffer. All reads or loads do an associative search on the write buffer to see if the desired item is there or in the cache. The special problems of true dependencies in a memory-based vector processor are discussed in Chapter 11. In general, memory vector dependencies are managed by software, not hardware as with scalar memory dependencies.

8.3.3 *Load Bypass*

As discussed above, a true dependency can occur on a load following a store. What if there is a load following a store without a true dependency? In this case, performance would improve if the loads preceded the stores even if the store has not been released or retired, a technique called *load bypass*. It is desirable to issue loads as early as possible because true dependencies can delay the issue of subsequent instructions.

There can be a problem with load bypass, however. Recall, from Chapter 2, that a write to a cache is an early select operation. Load bypass must assume that the previous store has not had a cache miss or a TLB miss, otherwise interrupts may not be guaranteed to be precise. This issue is discussed further in Chapter 9.

8.3.4 *Self-Modifying Code*: *True Dependencies*

Self-modifying code is considered bad programming practice. However, this was not the case in the past, and true dependencies must be dealt with in some processor designs. A modified instruction should not be read from memory until the modified instruction has been written into memory. As with all true dependencies, forwarding can mitigate the delay.

The design of the memory system plays a large part in the schemes for resolving instruction true dependencies. Processors without a cache have long, and usually different, load and store latencies and require a different approach than processors with caches and short, usually one clock, latencies. Self-modifying code in MS-DOS has generally precluded split caches. Examples of each memory design are discussed below.

The TI ASC is a good example of a processor without a cache having long memory latencies. Two mechanisms are required: one to check a store and the other to check the instruction fetch.

1. Consider that instruction i stores a modified instruction that will be fetched for instruction j. A dependency check is necessary because instruction i can get behind the fetch of instruction j. The old unmodified instruction will be fetched into the processor—a program logic error. To resolve this dependency, when a store instruction releases, a register map of the instruction fetch stages is searched to see if an instruction

from the store address has been fetched. If this instruction fetch has occurred, it is abandoned and refetched after the store is complete.

2. When an instruction is fetched, a search is made of the store shift register, Figure 8.12, to see if an instruction in execution will modify this instruction. If it will be modified, the instruction fetch is abandoned and restarted when the true dependency is resolved.

These checks may seem redundant, but they are not because of the design of the pipeline. Due to the delays that result from halting instruction fetching, forwarding is used to preclude the need to write the modified instruction into memory and then refetch it.

Systems with a one-level unified cache have these true dependencies resolved as any other memory true dependency. An instruction fetch, as with a data read, consults the cache tags and the write buffer to see if there is a dependency. However, if the cache is split, there are difficulties.

The Intel Pentium provides an example of a split cache design that accommodates self-modifying code. An instruction fetch reads the instruction cache tags and snoops the data cache tags and the write buffer. If there is a hit on the data cache or write buffer, the instruction is read from that source rather than the instruction cache. Modified instructions are posted to memory via the data cache and its write buffer rather than the instruction cache. Note that the data cache tags must be four-ported for the following snoops: data read reference, data write reference, instruction reference, and I/O reference.

8.3.5 *MU5 Name Store*

The discussion of dependencies in memory concludes with a mention of the MU5 [IBBE77]. This processor is a single accumulator architecture without a register file. The 16-bit address in the instruction is viewed as a displacement and is extended with 18 bits to create a 34 bit virtual address. With this architecture most dependency objects are in memory address space.

High-speed memory is provided to the processor by means of a data cache, called a *name store*, shown in Figure 8.13. The name store is an early select associatively addressed buffer, not a program-managed cache. For this reason, the name store has interesting properties for managing dependencies based upon renaming into virtual address space. Because there is an almost infinite supply of virtual addresses, anti- and output dependencies in memory can be significantly reduced, but not completely eliminated, with proper programming. This system can be viewed as the ultimate in renaming as virtual addresses have a very large name space.

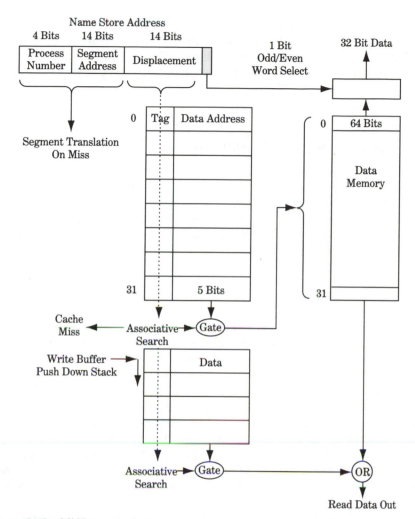

FIGURE 8.13   MU5 name store.

However, due to the finite size of the name store, dependencies can occur and must be managed. Antidependencies are managed by the simple technique of read buffering. The operand values are read from the name store as the instruction is decoded. Output dependencies are interlocked via a valid bit in the write buffer. If an output dependency is detected, the processor stalls.

True dependencies are managed by means of a write buffer associated with the name store. A write to the virtual memory goes first to the write buffer, a push down stack with the 16 LSBs of the address appended as a tag. A following read from that address will find the requested value either in the write buffer or the main memory if the write has been retired. The read results are taken either from the write buffer or the name store. As the write buffer is late select, reads from previous writes that are still in the write buffer are faster than reads that have not been modified.

8.4 Special Register Dependencies

There are a number of special registers (both architected and implemented) in any processor that can be the objects for dependencies. Some of these are address registers, index registers, and status registers. The schemes for dealing with special register dependencies can be more ad hoc than for the data path and general-purpose registers discussed above.

8.4.1 *Address Registers*

Address registers of various types are required to form the effective address of a memory reference. Two schemes for dealing with address register dependencies are discussed below.

The IBM S/360/91 has address registers (base and index) embedded in the address space of the integer general-purpose register file. The same scheme, as discussed in Section 8.2.1, for handling data dependencies in these registers suffice for address dependencies. A counter is assigned to each register that is incremented when that register will be the output of an operation. As operations are completed, the counter is decremented. An instruction that will use that register as an input can only release when the count is zero. Anderson [ANDE67] discusses this solution to address dependencies.

The CDC 6600 uses a separate set of address registers, the contents of which are operated on by the normal arithmetic instructions. Address arithmetic precedes a load or store and is performed by the instruction stream. Recall from Figure 8.6 that there are load and store function units that appear to the scoreboard as any other function unit. Thus, the scoreboard controls all address dependencies and no additional steps need to be taken to detect and resolve them.

Instruction set architectures with indirect addressing present special problems for address-dependency resolution. An address is stored in memory that will be used on a following memory access; the following instruction has a true dependency on this address in memory. For multi-level indirection, the problem is compounded. The normal memory data dependency detection and resolution schemes discussed earlier in this section should be sufficient to resolve these dependencies with a significant performance penalty.

8.4.2 *Status Registers*

Status registers and condition code bits present the possibility of true, anti-, and output dependencies. A condition code is composed of bits that retain the outcome of a test until the outcome of a subsequent test changes the bits. Some contemporary pipelined processors, such as MIPS, have branch instructions without condition codes, thereby eliminating one source of dependency problems. As discussed in Chapter 7, this form of branch instruction may have a longer clock period than branches with condition codes. True, anti-, and output dependencies on condition codes are discussed in the following paragraphs.

True Dependencies

True dependencies exist because an instruction j, which uses the condition code result of instruction i, can complete out-of-order before the dependency is resolved. The IBM S/360/91 again provides an example of a solution to condition code true dependencies [ANDE67, RAMA77, KOGG81]. An interlock scheme is used that places one bit of a shift register with each pipeline stage down stream from the decoder—a structure identical to that of Figure 8.12, except that there is only one bit involved, not an address. The condition codes are either addressed or not, thus only one bit is needed.

When an instruction that may change the condition codes is decoded, either implicitly of explicitly, the bit in the first stage of the shift register is set to a one on the next clock. As the instruction progresses down the pipeline, this bit follows the pipeline flow and disappears at the end of the pipeline. A following conditional branch instruction that tests the condition codes, while in the window, tests all of the shift register bit locations, and if any one is set, the instruction does not release. As only one of these bits can be set at a time, the instruction waits in the window until the update of the condition code is complete.

It is interesting to note that the IBM RS/6000 has eight condition fields in the condition code register [GROH90]. This is an example of increasing the resources to help eliminate resource dependencies. The additional resources are *implemented* (a term defined earlier) and are addressed by the register address that is renamed or mapped into another address. Adding resources is a fundamental design technique for eliminating resource dependencies. Another RS/6000 example is the number of general-purpose registers. The 32 registers of the IBM

RS/6000 are addressed by five bits in the instruction. However, this processor has 40 implemented registers.

The RS/6000 has eight condition code group fields, each of four bits. Each group is independently modified by instructions and is architected with no renaming or buffering. It is not known to me how true dependencies are detected and resolved. However, if the shift register scheme is applied to this processor, three bits would be required in the shift register to address the condition code fields. Branch instructions that use a condition code register that does not have a pending update would release without delay due.

There is a pure software solution to the true dependency problem. Recall from Chapter 7 the discussion on branch spreading. This technique moves the condition code setting instruction well forward in the instruction stream so that its results are available when the conditional branch is executed. The slots are filled with useful instructions or no-ops.

Antidependencies

An example of an antidependency on a condition code is shown in the following program fragment:

i Branch on overflow
•
j R1 ← R2 + R3, set condition on overflow.

If the add instruction j completes before instruction i, the condition tested by i may not be valid. With a reasonable pipeline design, this dependency should not occur. However, the designer must verify carefully that this is so and take steps if it is not. The type of window will influence the steps to be taken. For example, with a Type C window that has in-order release combined with buffering the condition code, the potential antidependency is eliminated.

Output Dependencies

Output dependencies exist if instructions that may change the condition codes, either explicitly or as side effects, can complete out of order; the condition code bits should not be overwritten until they have been used by an intermediate instruction. Consider the following program fragment:

i R1 ← R2 + R3, set condition code on overflow
j Branch on overflow
k R1 ← R2 + R3, set condition code on overflow.

If instruction k completes before instruction j, the branch will be taken based on the logically incorrect condition code result. The obvious solution to this output dependency problem is to serialize, ensuring in-order retirement—one of the schemes used with registers. With in-order release, the condition code can be buffered. Another scheme uses a reservation tag on the condition codes. When an instruction issues that may change a condition code, instruction i in this example, a reservation is placed on the condition code that is not removed until the condition code has been used. Instruction k will stall and not release until the reservation is removed by instruction j.

Instruction k will place another reservation for a subsequent branch. A problem with this scheme is that by clearing the reservation on the condition code, a number of branch instructions cannot be conditional on one setting of the condition code. Output dependencies with condition codes are similar to those of memory-mapped I/O.

8.4.3 *Program Counter*

The program counter is another special register that requires design attention for dependencies. The program counter can be read under a number of circumstances, for example, for accessing an instruction, for computing an effective branch address, and for the management of interrupts (discussed in Chapter 9). Writes into the program counter are the normal incrementing of instruction sequencing when a branch address is loaded. Thus, an examination of all dependencies is in order.

True dependencies are not a problem with the program counter because any instruction that modifies the program counter is immediately followed by an instruction that reads the program counter for the next instruction fetch; the read cannot get ahead of the write (for example, the next instruction in sequence when the program counter is incremented, and the branch target when a branch address is placed in the program counter). There is no way that the instruction that reads the program counter can execute before the instruction that modified the program counter.

Antidependencies occur in the following example. Instruction i computes a program counter relative effective load address, stored in R1, and instruction j is a branch that places a new value in the program counter.

i R1 ← M(PC + Displacement)

•

j Branch to location x; PC ← Branch Effective Address.

This dependency is resolved by buffering the program counter prior to the addition of the displacement. As I note in Chapter 9, the program counter must be shifted down the pipeline synchronously with the information associated with each instruction. This shift register meets the requirement for program counter buffering of an antidependency resolution.

Output dependencies can occur with branch instructions that change the value in the program counter. Consider the example

i Branch to location x; PC ← Branch Effective Address (x)

•

j Branch to location y; PC ← Branch Effective Address (y).

The solution to this dependency problem is to ensure that branches are serialized and retired in-order. This is a difficult problem to solve with hardware unless a reservation can be placed on a flag that will inhibit a branch from completing out-of-order.

However, if the branches can be accurately predicted, that is, $A_p = 1$, then the branches can be executed and retired in any order without destroying the logic of the program [JOHN82]. If a branch is accurately predicted, when the PC reaches instruction j, the release of instructions is in-order and the instructions on the path to j are in the pipeline; thus, the logic is not destroyed. However, as discussed in Chapter 7, complete accuracy in branch prediction cannot be obtained, thus reasserting the requirement that branches must retire in order.

8.4.4 *Global Impact Registers*

The effect of modifying some registers is so global in scope that it is difficult to provide specific dependency detection and resolution support. These registers can be (1) loaded explicitly by the program or (2) modified as side effects. For both cases these objects are stored by a context switch.

Examples of the first type are the virtual memory name translation maps and cache mode registers. The MC68040 cache can be placed in write-back or write-through mode. Program writes to global impact registers occur infrequently, and a dependency protection scheme that may degrade the performance of an infrequently occurring event is a reasonable design choice. Examples of the second type, global impact registers that are loaded only as side effects, are data caches, instruction caches, and BTC.

Designers must ensure that dependencies cannot occur on these global registers. For this discussion, however, only global impact registers that are written into by the program are considered.

A true dependency can occur under the following conditions. For example, the program releases an instruction i to load a new name translation map but the next instruction j makes name translation accesses of the map before the new values are loaded. This true dependency will cause a name translation error.

For an example of an antidependency, assume that the last instruction to use an old version of the name translation map is i and the instruction j that will load new values into the map completes before instruction i accesses the map. An antidependency error will occur.

If two instructions that load global impact registers get out-of-order, an output dependency may occur.

The most common solution to the design problem of dependencies on global impact registers is *serialization* [JOHN90]; the complexity of other schemes is too daunting. Recall that dependencies do not exist if a processor is executing the serial execution model. Serialization was first viewed as a requirement for synchronization of a multiprocessor system [CASE78]. Due to the concurrency of pipelined processors, however, serialization and synchronization have become requirements for uniprocessors as well. Serialization to enforce a memory consistency model is outside the scope of this book. A serialization instruction places the processor in a mode that is equivalent to the serial execution model, forcing the processor to complete one instruction before issuing another and thereby eliminating all dependencies. The serialization instruction halts the fetching and processing of instructions and completes all the instructions that have been issued and/or released. When the pipeline is flushed, the special instruction, and only this instruction, is issued and executed—for example, loading a virtual memory name translation map or cache mode register. After the completion of this load instruction, normal pipelined instruction fetching resumes.

RS/6000. This processor has two instructions, ics (Instruction Cache Synchronize) and dcs (Data Cache Synchronize), that permit serialization and synchronization. These instructions have been renamed **isync** and **sync**, respectively, in the PowerPC Architecture [IBM93]. A list of these instructions is found in C.2.1 of [IBM90]. The serializing operations, or semantics, of ics are:

1. Any prefetched instructions are discarded.
2. The program counter stack is emptied. The PC stack maintains a list of outstanding instructions in the fixed point unit.
3. There is a set of instructions that must complete execution and not cause an interrupt.

Other instructions, such as svc (Supervisor Call), also implement all three of the serializing operations of ics. The instruction dcs waits for all outstanding data cache operations (clf, dclst, dciz) to complete.

PowerPC 601. Another example of serialization instructions used to resolve global register dependencies is found in the PowerPC 601 [MOTO93]. This processor has a number of *special purpose registers* (SPRs) that are addressed explicitly and implicitly as side effects. These registers are loaded and stored by Move to/from instructions mtspr and mfspr and can be the object of true, anti-, and output dependencies. There is no automatic checking for dependencies on these registers; thus serialization is the only dependency preventative.

The following quotations from [MOTO93] explain the problem and solution.

> If an mtspr instruction writes a value to a SPR that changes how address translation is performed, a subsequent load instruction cannot use the new translation until the CPU is explicitly synchronized by using one of the following context synchronizing operations: isync, sc, rfi, and any exception, other than machine check and system reset.

The operation of the isync synchronization instructions is explained as:

> This instruction waits for all previous instructions to complete and then discards any fetched instruction, causing subsequent instructions to be fetched (or refetched) from memory and to execute in the context established by the previous instructions.

Thus, to ensure that dependencies do not occur, the isync instruction must precede a modification of an SPR. For example, instruction i loads a new value into a segment register that is used by the address translation of instruction j. If instruction j executes early, a true dependency of the segment register occurs:

i	mtsr (sr, rn)	Load a segment register from register n
j	Load	Use new value of segment register for translation.

The isync instruction will prevent this true dependency by serializing the load of the segment register:

h	mtsr (sr, rn)	Load a segment register from register n
i	isync	Finish execution and discard fetched instructions
j	Load	Use new value of segment register for translation (discarded)
	SYNCHRONIZED	
k	Load	Use new value of segment register for translation.

Because instructions are issued in-order, the isync instruction will, for example, discard or abandon the Load instructions. This instruction will be refetched after the isync instruction completes, thereby resolving any dependency.

The PowerPC architecture [IBM93] has an instruction eieio. This instruction will

> enforce in-order execution of I/O that ensures that all applicable loads and stores previously initiated by the processor are complete with respect to main storage before any applicable loads and stores subsequently initiated by the processor access main storage.

Intel i860. Another form of serialization, at the execution unit level, is found in the Intel i860. The pipelined execution unit has three stages and an issue latency of one clock. When dependencies will not be present, the processor is placed in the *pipeline mode* that streams the operands into the pipeline as the issue latency. However, if dependencies will be present, the processor is placed in the *scalar mode* that changes the issue latency to three clocks. In effect, the operational latency is three and the issue latency is three; thus no dependencies can occur. The mode is set by a P/S bit in the instructions that will use the pipelined execution unit.

8.5 Peformance Models

C. V. Ramamoorthy et al. [RAMA77] and P. G. Emma et al. [EMMA87] give models for determining the delays incurred while detecting and resolving dependencies. These models essentially require that the probability of a dependency and the subsequent delay be known or can be estimated.

The Emma model determines the number of delay cycles per instruction for detecting and resolving dependencies. This model is for a processor with one execution unit and true dependencies as other dependency types are not possible. The model can be simply expanded to multiple execution unit systems.

$$\text{delay cycles/inst.} = \text{Max}(0, (E - 1)P_0) + \text{Max}(0, (E - 2)P_1)$$
$$+ \cdots + \text{Max}(0, (E - n)P_{n-1})$$
$$= \sum_{d=1}^{E} (E - d)P_{d-1}$$

where E denotes the number of stages in the execution unit or the operational latency (as defined in Chapter 10) and P_d is the probability that an instruction has a dependency at distance d. For adjacent instructions, $d = 1$.

An example of a true-dependency delay is shown in the reservation tables of Figure 8.14 for a pipeline of $E = 4$. A two-instruction-code-fragment with a true dependency on R1 between i and j serves as an example.

$$
\begin{array}{ll}
i & \text{R1} \leftarrow \text{R2} + \text{R3} \\
j & \text{R4} \leftarrow \text{R1} + \text{R5.}
\end{array}
$$

Two cases of dependency distance are considered. For Case (a), the two instructions are adjacent ($d = 1$). At t0, instruction i is in the window and has not yet released. At t2, i releases and j comes into the window. Because of the true dependency between these two instructions on R1, j stalls in the window and does not release until t5, which creates a delay of $3(E - 1)$ clocks.

For Case (b), the two instructions with a true dependency on R1 are separated by one instruction, a, that is free of dependencies and $d = 2$.

$$
\begin{array}{ll}
i & \text{R1} \leftarrow \text{R2} + \text{R3} \\
a & \text{no dependencies} \\
j & \text{R4} \leftarrow \text{R1} + \text{R5.}
\end{array}
$$

	0	1	2	3	4	5	6	7	8	9	
Window	I1	I2	I2	I2	I2						
1		I1	S	S	S	I2					
2			I1	S	S	S	I2				Case a
3				I1	S	S	S	I2			
4					I1	S	S	S	I2		

(Stage labels: 1, 2, 3, 4)

	0	1	2	3	4	5	6	7	8	9	
Window	I1	I2	I3	I3	I3						
1		I1	I2	S	S	I3					
2			I1	I2	S	S	I3				Case b
3				I1	I2	S	S	I3			
4					I1	I2	S	S	I3		

(Stage labels: 1, 2, 3, 4)

Pipeline Length: E=4

FIGURE 8.14 Dependency delays.

Benchmark

P_{d-1}	gcc	eqntott	fpppp	matrix300
P_0	0.256	0.218	0.286	0.130
P_1	0.136	0.159	0.087	0.112
P_2	0.038	0.049	0.041	0.089
P_3	0.017	0.028	0.049	0.053
P_4	0.005	0.019	0.023	0.034
P_5	0.003	0.009	0.025	0.018

TABLE 8.6 True dependency probabilities.

The reservation table shows that a release after i and j is stalled for only $2(E-2)$ clocks. Combining the two delays with the probability of the dependencies gives the weighted average dependency delay cycles per instruction, confirming the Emma model:

$$\text{delay cycles/instr} = 3P_0 + 2P_1.$$

The magnitude of true-dependency probabilities has been investigated by O'Connor [OCON93, OCON93a]. Four benchmarks are compiled and executed with a SPARC instruction level simulator; the dependencies for integer and floating points are recorded. Control dependencies are not counted; that is, no instruction is counted as having a dependency on a branch instruction. The results of this study for P_0–P_5 are shown in Table 8.6.

These results are interesting because of the large absolute values and the range of P_0: 0.13 to 0.286. If E is greater than 1, a significant performance loss occurs due to true dependencies. For this reason, most RISC processor implementations have $E=1$ for integers even if the clock period is longer than necessary. For execution units having $E>2$, scheduling instructions by the compiler can reduce the dependency delay cycles.

Partitioning the execution unit pipeline can significantly influence the value of E and the clock rate. Five design options are illustrated in Figure 8.15, having values of E from 1 to 3 and with differing clock periods.

The three basic operations of an execution unit (read registers, execute, and write back) can be partitioned in a number of ways, and forwarding can be employed. The influence of execution unit partitioning on the weighted average delay per instruction is illustrated in the following examples. Assume that each of the three operations requires one time unit, and that the clock skew plus set up time is 0.1 time unit.

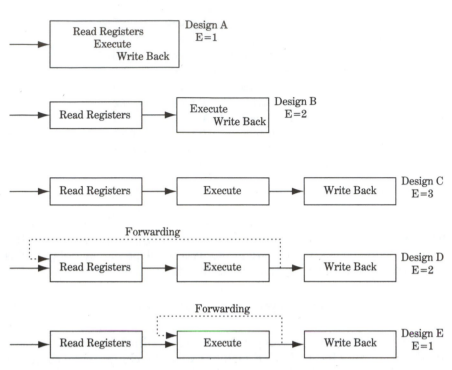

FIGURE 8.15   Execution unit partitioning.

Table 8.7 shows the clock period, delay cycles for each true-dependence distance, CPI, and time per instruction. The dependency probabilities of Table 8.6 for the gcc benchmark are used. This example considers delays due to dependencies only; other delays such as branch delays are not included.

The performance benefit of aggressive forwarding and a fast clock is shown by design D, which has the smallest time per instruction. Design A, with one stage and no true-dependency delays, has the poorest

Design	Clock Period	$P_0(E-1)$	$P_1(E-2)$	CPI	Time/Inst.
A	3.1	0	0	1	3.10
B	2.1	0.256	0	1.256	2.63
C	1.1	0.512	0.136	1.648	1.81
D	1.1	0.256	0	1.256	1.65
E	1.1	0	0	1	1.10

TABLE 8.7   Execution time with dependencies.

performance, even though its $CPI = 1$, because of the very long clock period.

8.6 Summary Comments

In summary, it is useful to review the MIPS (Microprocessor without Interlocked Pipeline) project that was envisioned to vest all dependency detection and resolution in software rather than hardware. The rationale for this design approach is that dependency detection and resolution hardware lengthened the clock period and that if this task is done in software, faster execution will result; MIPS therefore constitutes a pure RISC approach to performance in the face of dependencies.

The first version of MIPS is underpipelined, which eliminates all true dependencies in the data path; that is, $E = 1$. Load true dependencies are handled by the compiler, which inserts no-ops following loads. The second version of MIPS, MIPS-II, incorporated interlocks on loads that stalled the pipeline until the true dependency of a load is resolved [HENN90]. The use of interlocks continues with all subsequent versions of MIPS.

MIPS designers opted for a relatively larger number of processor registers: sixteen 64-bit floating point registers, which can also be addressed as thirty-two 32-bit integer registers. The relatively large number of architected registers mitigates the effect of anti- and output dependencies.

The influence of the MIPS project on other designers is mixed. Most new processors incorporate dependency detection and resolution hardware, as discussed previously. Pipelines have become longer, particularly with floating point, and register files are not large enough to make anti- and output dependency detection and resolution unnecessary. Type C and Type D windows with simple tag schemes are used in processors such as the PowerPC 601. These simple dependency systems preserve the desirable high-frequency clocks while providing positive protection.

Designers of a pipelined processor should not overlook the potential benefits of a richer instruction set that executes compound operations, thereby including true dependencies within one instruction. For example, RISC type architectures perform address arithmetic by the execution of instructions prior to the execution of a load or store instruction. These instructions have true dependencies as the effective address is formed.

The effective address operation is illustrated in the following three instruction code sequences of a RISC type processor. Instruction I1 performs an index decrement; instruction I2 adds the base to the index:

$$
\begin{aligned}
&\text{I1} && \text{R2} \leftarrow \text{R2} - 1 \\
&\text{I2} && \text{R1} \leftarrow \text{R2} + \text{R3} \\
&\text{I3} && \text{R4} \leftarrow \text{M(Disp} + \text{R1)}.
\end{aligned}
$$

There are two true dependencies: one on R2, the other on R1. If E is not equal to 1, there will be delays as the effective address is formed.

On the other hand, an architecture with a Base + Displacement + Index addressing mode will not have this problem. An architecture of this type will require only the load instruction:

$$
\text{I1} \qquad \text{R4} \leftarrow \text{M(Disp} + \text{R2} + \text{R3)}.
$$

R3 is an index register that is auto-incremented (a potential side-effect problem with branching) and added to the base and displacement as part of the load instruction. Because the architecture has a compound effective address, the three-instruction sequence becomes one instruction, eliminating two true dependencies. A three-input adder is usually only three gate delays longer than a two-input adder, thus there is a minor increase in clock period.

Another example of a compound instruction that eliminates, or hides, true dependencies is found with multiply–add (also known as *multiply cumulatively*) instructions. A number of processors have a multiply–add instruction that folds these two operations into one ALU, thereby reducing if not eliminating another instance of a true dependency, for example, the RS/6000. The effectiveness of architectures with compound operations, including effective address formation, have been studied by [MALI93] and [OCON93].

8.7 Structural Dependencies

In the preceding sections we discussed anti- and output dependencies that are the result of time-sharing storage locations such as registers, caches, TLBs, and memory. This section describes dependencies that are the result of sharing computational resources such as pipeline stages and execution units.

A structural dependency occurs if two or more requesters want to share the same resource at the same time, also known as a *collision*.

Sharing is employed by designers to reduce cost while introducing delays. The following section discusses techniques for evaluating the performance consequences of sharing. Data dependencies are assumed to have been resolved and are not considered.

The study of sharing that leads to structural dependencies is not as relevant today as it has been in the past. VLSI technology permits designers to be more concerned with performance and less concerned, within limits, with reducing the number of gates for an implementation. Nevertheless, sharing of resources and the resulting structural dependencies are still important and should be understood.

This section discusses a technique, called *collision analysis*, for the performance analysis of shared structures with structural dependencies. Techniques will also be discussed for both removing and introducing structural dependencies to change the cost-performance of a pipeline.

8.7.1 *Single-Function Pipelines*

A single-function pipeline is expected to process only one function. For example, a floating point multiplier pipeline would not be expected to perform integer division, while an integer adder could do addition and subtraction. We begin by examining the case of single-function pipelines; the specific function being performed does not matter because only scheduling and performance issues are important for this discussion. Consider the reservation table in Figure 8.16. A pipeline with five stages, the X's signify that a stage is used to perform the function [HWAN84]. The function requires 9 clock periods to transit the pipeline, which is the operational latency. Notice that all of the stages, except stage 3, are used more than once and at t8, stages 2 and 5 are both active.

A number of questions can be asked about this pipeline. For example: After one operation is issued into the pipeline, when can a second or third issue, the issue latency? How is performance measured? And, can stages be replicated in such a way that the performance can be improved?

The first question of issue latency can be answered by means of overlays to find collisions. That is, a copy of the reservation table, on transparent material, can be overlaid on the original reservation table

		1	2	3	4	5	6	7	8	9	1 0
S T A G E	1	X								X	
	2		X	X					X		
	3				X						
	4					X	X				
	5							X	X		

FIGURE 8.16 Function unit reservation table.

		1	2	3	4	5	6	7	8	9	10	11	12
S T A G E	1	X	O							X	O		
	2		X	Ñ	O				X	O			
	3				X	O							
	4					X	Ñ	O					
	5							X	Ñ	O			

Case a)

Second Initiation at t2

		1	2	3	4	5	6	7	8	9	10	11	12
S T A G E	1	X		O						X		O	
	2		X	X	O	O			X		O		
	3				X		O						
	4					X	X	O	O				
	5							X	X	O	O		

Case b)

Second Initiation at t3

FIGURE 8.17 Collisions.

and collisions can be found. One shifting of the overlay is shown in Figure 8.17. For example, Case (A) shows a second issue, indicated by 0, attempted at t2, with collisions in stages 2, 4, and 5.

Additional shifting of the overlay indicates that a second issue can start at t3, t4, t5, t8, and t10 without collisions. The issue at t3 is shown in Figure 8.17, Case (b). Note that an issue can start at any time after t10. The delays between collision-free issues are called *issue* or *initiation latencies*. The issue at t3 has an issue latency of 2, which means that the second issue can start on the second clock after the first issue.

State Transitions

Davidson [DAVI71] provides an elegant method for identifying collision-free issue latencies and determining the possible issue sequences that are collisionfree—sequences called state transitions. The process of generating state transitions is described and illustrated with the reservation table of Figure 8.16. The Davidson method consists of the following four steps:

1. Compile a list of the issue latencies that will cause collisions for each row (stage) of the reservation table. For example, row 1 will have a collision with an issue latency of 8.

Row 1: 8
Row 2: 1, 5, 6

Row 3:0
Row 4:1
Row 5:1.

2. Form the *forbidden list* for the reservation table that is the set union of the nonnull row forbidden issue latencies:

$$\text{forbidden list, } F = 1, 5, 6, 8.$$

The forbidden list tells us that new issues can be made without collisions at latencies of 2, 3, 4, 7, 9^+ or at t3, t4, t5, t8, $t10^+$. Note that the + exponent means any latency greater than the one indicated.

3. A collision vector for the initial state is constructed from the forbidden list. This vector reads from right to left (by latency) using 1 for collision and 0 otherwise. The last nonforbidden latency of 9 can be ignored in the collision vector:

$$\text{collision vector, } \mathbf{V} = [1, 0, 1, 1, 0, 0, 0, 1].$$

4. A state transition diagram is constructed from the collision vector. The initial state collision vector has an out-transition for each 0 in the collision vector. In this case the transitions are 2, 3, 4, 7, and 9^+, as shown in Figure 8.18. To find the collision vector of the next state, the collision vector of the present state is shifted right for each out-transition. The shifted collision vector is ORed with the initial state collision vector to form a new state. In this case, there are three new states and two returns to the initial state. The latency used for the new state is indicated by a number on the arrow connecting the states.

Notice that the latency of 7 returns to the original state. Any latency equal to or greater than 9 will also return to the original state—an effect that is indicated by 9^+. The shifting process continues by taking the

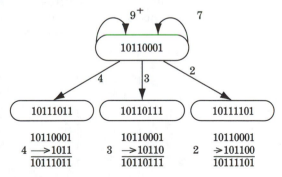

FIGURE 8.18 Initial state transitions.

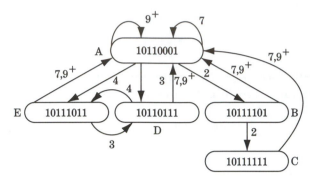

FIGURE 8.19 Complete state transition diagram.

collision vector of each new state, shifting, and ORing with the initial state collision vector. The completed state transition diagram is shown in Figure 8.19. For expository purposes, I name the states A, B, C, D, and E.

Issue Latencies

The various issue cycles can be identified from Figure 8.19. Eight paths through the state transition diagram are listed in Table 8.8 with the issue latencies for each transition, the *average latency* for each of the cycles, and the acceptance ratio. Note that all cycles start with an issue into an empty pipeline—state A.

The *minimum average latency* (MAL) is 3.5 for cycles 3 and 5. These cycles also have the highest acceptance ratios and are the highest processing rate of this pipeline. The lower bound on MAL is found by counting the number of X's in the rows of the reservation table; the

Cycle	Path	Issue Latencies	Average Latency	Acceptance Ratio
1	A, A, A, A	7, 7	7	0.14
2	A, D, A, D	3, 7, 3, 7	5	0.2
3	A, D, E, D, E	3, 4, 3, 4	3.5	0.28
4	A, D, E, A, D, E	3, 4, 7, 3, 4, 7	4.66	0.21
5	A, E, D, E, D	4, 3, 4, 3	3.5	0.28
6	A, E, A, E	4, 7, 4, 7	5.5	0.18
7	A, B, A, B	2, 7, 2, 7	4.5	0.22
8	A, B, C, A, B, C	2, 2, 7, 2, 2, 7	3.66	0.27

TABLE 8.8 Example paths, issue latencies, and acceptance ratio.

maximum number of X's is the lower bounds on MAL. For this example, the lower-bound MAL is 3.0, which is the number of X's in the second row. Note that the lower bound on MAL may not be the achieved MAL but will indicate how close the pipeline implementation is to its lower bound. The proof of this lemma is by L. E. Shar and given in [KOGG81].

Cycles that permit issues at a constant latency can have a *minimum constant latency* (MCL); the only MCLs for this pipeline are 7 and, of course, 9^+. The MCL is the smallest integer that is not a factor of any of the forbidden latencies. The smallest latency that is not a factor of 1, 5, 6, and 8 is 7. A latency of 2 will collide with 6 and 8, a latency of 3 will collide with 6, and so on. Constant latencies are of interest because the control is easier to implement than a controller that achieves the MAL of a pipeline.

Performance Improvements

The question can be asked: Are there design changes that can be made to this pipeline to improve its performance by reducing its MAL and MCL? There are two methods by which this can be done.

1. Introduce redundant stages that reduce the number of Xs in a row, thereby reducing the MAL and MCL.
2. Introducing delay stages that will break up the collision patterns and permit the MAL and MCL to be reduced.

Consider the first approach. If a redundant stage 2 is introduced (shown as 2'), the maximum number of X's in a row is two as shown in Figure 8.20. Forbidden latencies 5 and 6 are removed from the collision vector, and the forbidden list is now 1, 8. The new MAL is 2.25; as there are 2 X's in several of the rows, the lower-bound MAL of the modified pipeline is 2. By inspection we see that an MCL of 3 can now be used as 3 is not a factor of 8. An MCL of 2 will collide with 8 because it is a factor of 8.

The second approach of inserting delays lengthens the pipeline but

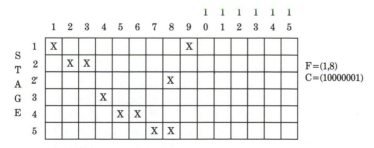

FIGURE 8.20   Redundant stage two.

STAGE	1	2	3	4	5	6	7	8	9	10	11	12	13	14	15
1	X									X					
2		X		X					X						
3					X										
4						X	X								
5								X	X						
Delay			X							X					

$F = (1,2,5,7,10)$
$C = (1001010011)$

FIGURE 8.21   Pipeline with delay stage.

breaks up the collision patterns so that a smaller MAL and MCL can be obtained. A delay is a pipeline stage that performs no function other than delay. Kogge [KOGG81] describes an algorithmic method for inserting delays. In the following example, however, a delay is selected by a heuristic.

From the original pipeline reservation table, as in Figure 8.16, we see that the theoretical MCL is 7. What delays are required to achieve an MCL of 3? Figure 8.21 shows the pipeline with the delay stage that is incorporated into the pipeline. As 3 is a factor of 6, a delay prior to t3 changes the row 2 collision with an issue latency of 6 to an issue latency of 7. However, the collision on row 1 at t9 is now a collision eliminating an MCL of 3. Thus, another delay is inserted between the original t8 and t9. The forbidden list of the modified pipeline is 1, 2, 5, 7, 10. As 3 is not a factor of any of these latencies, an MCL of 3 will work and is also the lower bound on MAL.

Notice that the pipeline length *E*, or operational latency (also known as the *result latency*), of the delay method for reducing MCL is two stages greater, 11 versus 9, than the pipeline of the redundant stage method. If short vectors are to be processed or if true dependencies are frequent, lengthening the pipeline by two stages may not be a good design choice. Also, this second method does not change the MAL because row 2 has 3 X's.

8.7.2 *Multifunction Dynamic Pipelines*

The above discussion examines pipelines that perform only one function. However, if we have a multifunction pipeline, how can it be scheduled? The execution unit pipeline of the TI ASC is an example [CRAG89] of such a pipeline and is discussed later in this section. With these pipelines it is desirable to be able to reconfigure the pipeline on-the-fly as required by the issuing instructions.

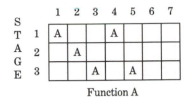
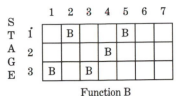

Function A   Function B

FIGURE 8.22 Two-function pipeline.

Consider the example of Figure 8.22 [HWAN84]. This three-stage pipeline can process two functions: A and B. The figure shows the state transitions and reservation table for each function. The scheduling problem is concerned with the issue latencies between the same functions and different functions. For example, a series of A or B functions can be handled as a single-function pipeline. But how do we schedule a sequence such as A, B, A, A, B, or any other sequence that might dynamically present itself to the pipeline?

As with single-function pipelines, overlays can be used to schedule multifunction pipelines. However, there is an algorithmic approach to this problem [HWAN84]. This method generates the collision vectors for the four cases

A following A	(AA),
A following B	(AB),
B following B	(BB),
B following A	(BA).

The number of these collision vectors that must be generated is 2^f where f is the number of functions that can be performed by the pipeline. Thus, this example, with only two functions, is relatively simple.

The A,A and B,B collision vectors are generated in the same way as the collision vectors for single-function pipelines; the collision vectors are

$$V_{AA} = 0110, \qquad V_{BB} = 0110.$$

The other two sequences are generated from a superposition of the two reservation tables shown in Figure 8.23. For the case of A following B, on the first row there are forbidden latencies of 1 and 4. For row 2 the forbidden latency is 2, and for row 3 there are no forbidden latencies. The forbidden list for A following B is 1, 2, 4.

For the case of B following A the forbidden list is 2, 4 and the collision vectors are

	1	2	3	4	5	6
STAGE 1	A	B		A	B	
STAGE 2		A		B		
STAGE 3	B		AB		A	

FIGURE 8.23 Dynamic scheduled pipeline.

$$V_{AB} = 1011, \qquad V_{BA} = 1010.$$

Two cross-collision matrices are constructed from the four collision vectors. These collision matrices become the starting states for the state transition diagram.

M_A	M_B
0110 (AA)	1011 (AB)
1010 (BA)	0110 (BB)

That is, if the first function to issue into an empty pipeline is A, the M_A matrix is the starting state. In order to illustrate the development of the state transitions, consider the A starting state. There are four possible transitions out of this state, as shown in Figure 8.24. These are A transition with latencies of 1 and 4^+ and B transitions with latencies of 1 and 3.

Consider the A1 transition. What is the new collision matrix after this issue? The next state can be determined from the reservation table shown in Figure 8.23 or by shifting the matrix one place to the right and ORing it with the M_A matrix.

Start State	Shift, r1	M_A	OR result
0110	0011	0110	0111
1010	0101	1010	1111

Likewise, the A4 transition creates the following collision matrix, which is also the starting collision matrix. There is an A4 transition from this new state that takes the collision matrix back to the starting point. As long as the sequence of issues is limited to A functions, the MAL is 2.5 and the MCL is 4.

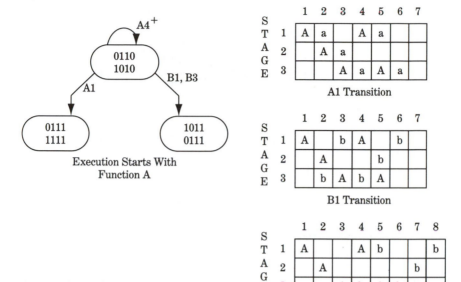

FIGURE 8.24   Start with function A.

Start State	Shift, r1	M_A	OR result
0110	0000	0110	0110
1010	0000	1010	1010

Consider now the B1 transition from the A starting collision matrix. This matrix is shifted right one place and ORed with the M_B collision matrix as shown below. The B3 transition creates the following new collision matrix.

Start State	Shift, r1	M_B	OR result
0110	0011	1011	1011
1010	0101	0110	0111

This process continues until the complete state transition diagram is generated as shown in Figure 8.25. Although it is difficult to enumerate all of the possible sequences of issues, I examine a few. For example, if the sequence starts with A and alternates A, B, A,..., with greedy scheduling, the MAL is 2.0 (B1, A3, B1, A3,...). If the sequence starts

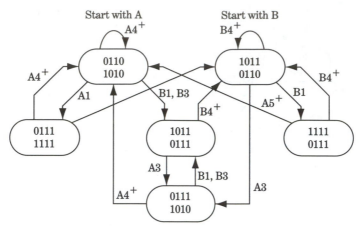

FIGURE 8.25   Complete state transition diagram.

with B and alternates with A with greedy scheduling, the MAL is also 2.0.

A controller for a multifunction pipeline would need to follow the changes in state as functions are issued. The controller would then be able to determine the latency required for a new issue that would be collisionfree.

Applications of Multifunction Pipelines

The TI ASC [CRAG89] employs multifunction arithmetic pipelines. These pipelines have eight stages that are capable of reconfiguration by microcode interpretation of the instruction operation code. Four of the functional interconnections are shown in Figure 8.26.

The designers of the TI ASC considered the control complexity of dynamic rescheduling to exceed any potential performance benefit. Thus, the pipelines are rescheduled only at the end of an operation. If consecutive instructions are of the same class, for example, an ADD followed by a SUBTRACT, these operations are pipelined with an issue latency of one. Likewise, a sequence of adds, because the pipeline does not require reconfiguration, has an issue latency of one. In these cases, MCL = 1.

8.7.3 *Arithmetic Pipelines*

As examples of a pipeline design that uses reservation tables and structural dependency analysis, we use pipelines that perform arithmetic operations. Two cases are examined: multiplication pipelines and pipe-

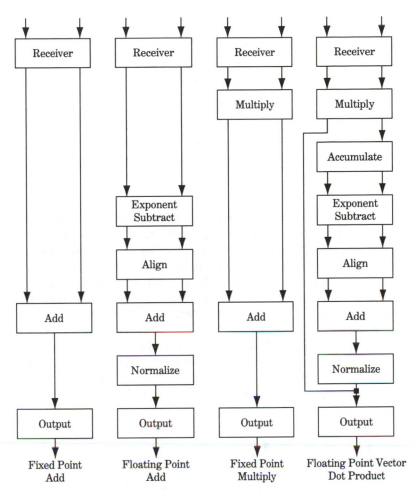

FIGURE 8.26 TI ASC arithmetic pipelines.

line configurations for performing the *multiply-add* operation, also known as the *vector dot product* when applied to data vectors.

Multiplication Pipelines

The multiplication operation is illustrated in Figure 8.27. Two 4-bit words are multiplied together to form an 8-bit product; the product bits are indicated with *sum*. As shown, there are four partial products, w_0 to w_3, that are summed to produce the product. Because addition is commutative, the order of summing is not important.

A pipelined multiplication takes advantage of the fact that the addition of the partial products produces the final product. A 4-bit multi-

				a_3	a_2	a_1	a_0	multiplicand
				b_3	b_2	b_1	b_0	multiplier
			a_3b_0	a_2b_0	a_1b_0	a_0b_0		w_0
		a_3b_1	a_2b_1	a_1b_1	a_0b_1			w_1
	a_3b_2	a_2b_2	a_1b_2	a_0b_2				w_2
a_3b_3	a_2b_3	a_1b_3	a_0b_3					w_3
carry	sum	sum	sum	sum	sum	sum	sum	product

FIGURE 8.27   Four-bit multiplication.

plier pipeline with its reservation table is shown in Figure 8.28. The first stage of the pipeline is the logic that forms the partial products. The implementation assumes *carry save adders* (CSA) with operational latency of one clock and a *carry propagate adder* (CPA) that assimilates the carries in two clock periods. In the second stage of the pipeline three of the partial products, w_0 to w_2, are added together in a three-input CSA that produces a sum (s) and a carry (c). A second CSA sums the output of the first CSA and w_3 in pipeline stage three. Finally, the CPA adds the sum and carry of the CSA to form the product (WALL64).

The second stage is a 6-bit CSA, and the third stage is a 7-bit CSA. For word lengths other than four bits, the depth of the pipeline increases as does the number of CSAs and the number of bits per CSA.

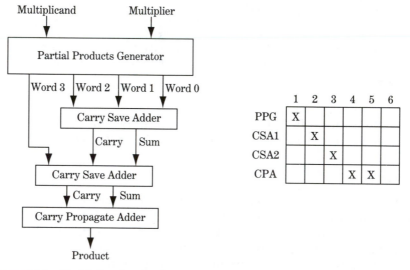

FIGURE 8.28   Multiplication implementation.

Consider the general case of a pipelined multiplier design. We can observe that the number of pipeline stages is related to the number of bits in the multiplier and multiplicand and vice versa. The number of multiplier and multiplicand bits and the number of carry save adder (CSA) pipeline levels are determined by the following recursive definition [SWAR72]:

$$N(v) = \left\lceil \frac{N(v-1)}{2} \right\rceil \times 3 + N(v-1) \, \text{Mod} \, 2$$

$$N(1) = 3$$

where $N(v)$ is the number of bits at stage v.

Applying this relationship gives

Number of Stages	Operand Bits
1	3
2	4
3	6
4	9
•	•
•	•
8	42
9	63
10	94

The number of pipeline stages and CSAs for long word-length multiplication can get large. Notice the problem with 64-bit multiplication: Nine or ten pipeline stages may be required depending on how the sign is treated.

Before the advent of VLSI technology, designers examined a number of folding strategies to reduce cost without unduly reducing performance. Folding is the controlled introduction of structural dependencies that may result in reduced performance in terms of an increase in operational latency and, in some cases, a decrease in acceptance ratios. When folding techniques were developed, performance reductions were consistent with the very high cost of logic. Today, folding is usually used to provide extended precision operations that can have lower performance than single precision.

Some folding options remove the inefficiencies implicit in the reservation table of Figure 8.28. From this reservation table, the observation is made that MCL = MAL = 2. Further, as the CSAs of stages 2 and 3 are underutilized, the pipeline can be folded as shown in Figure 8.29. In

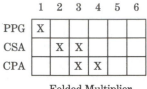

	1	2	3	4	5	6
PPG	X					
CSA		X	X			
CPA			X	X		

Folded Multiplier

	1	2	3	4	5	6	7
PPG	A	B					
CSA		A	B				
CSA			A	B			
CPA				A	A		
CPA					B	B	

Duplicate Carry Save Adders

FIGURE 8.29   Folded multiplier, duplicated CPA.

other words, only one CSA is required and the MCL and MAL have not been affected. Two notes of caution are required here. The additional routing logic to fold this short word–length multiplier may be more costly than the savings from the CSA. Also, the clock period may need to be lengthened to accommodate the longer logic path. For longer word–length multipliers, these considerations may not be as important.

The MCL and MAL can be reduced, at additional cost, to one if the CPA stage is duplicated as shown in Figure 8.29. With duplication, two successive multiplications, A and B, are shown to illustrate that MCL = MAL = 1 is achieved.

Now consider the effect of folding a relatively long-word multiplication. A 32-bit multiplier requires eight stages and can be folded by 1/2, 1/4, or 1/8. A folding of 1/2 with its reservation table is illustrated in Figure 8.30. Without folding, stage 8 produces the sum and carries into the CPA. With folding, the outputs of stage 4 are introduced into the pipeline at stage 1 and the inputs to the CPA are produced at stage 4. With a forbidden list $F = [1, 4]$, this pipeline has MCL = 3 compared to the MCL = 2 of the unfolded pipeline with $F = [1]$.

Note from Figure 8.30 that the low-cost end (smallest number of CSAs) of the pipeline has been eliminated by this type of folding. The high-cost end of the pipeline can be eliminated by another type of folding if the partial products are generated sequentially rather than in parallel.

The designers of the IBM S/360/91 multiplier examined a number of folding strategies [ADCE67a]. The design they selected used shifting, folding, and encoding of the multiplier shown in Figure 8.31. The "shifted partial products generator" generates four partial products each cycle and presents them to the pipeline. The output of stage 4 is folded back into the input of stage 2. There are eight issues of four words of partial products into the pipeline. On the last cycle, carries from the previous cycles are assimilated. The reservation table shows the flow through the pipeline.

Because the rows, except for the CPA, have eight X's the lower bound MAL of this pipeline is 8. With the forbidden list $F =$

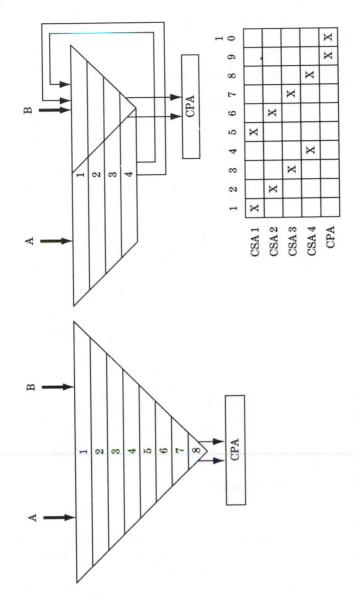

FIGURE 8.30 Folding by one-half.

417

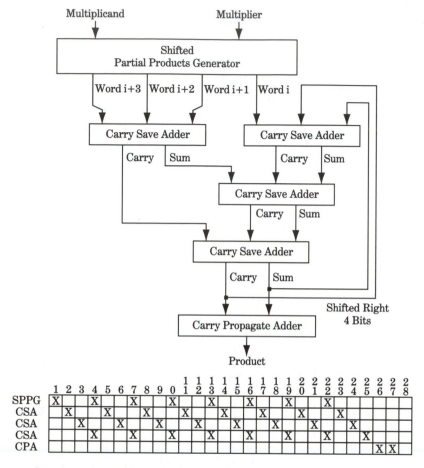

FIGURE 8.31   IBM S/360/91 multiplier.

[1,3,6,9,12,15,18,21], the MCL is 8 also. The unfolded multiplier has MAL = MCL = 2. Note that for scalar operation the latency of this pipeline is identical to the pipeline that is not folded.

Pipeline folding is used in the Intel i860 processor to implement double-precision floating point multiplications. Published information is sketchy [INTE92a, INTE92b]. The multiplier is three stages, and, in order to multiply the single-precision floating point mantissa, the pipeline has an MCL = MAL = 1, as shown in Figure 8.32.

For double precision, the output of the second stage is folded back into the input of the first stage. Twenty-three of the 52 bits are multiplied on the first pass with the remainder, 29 bits, multiplied on the second pass and MAL = MCL = 2.

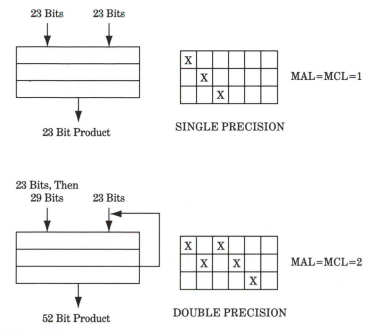

FIGURE 8.32   i860 Floating point mantissa multiplier.

The floating point adder is also a three-stage pipeline that has MAL = MCL = 1 for both single- and double-precision addition. For cases where the multiplier and adder can be operating concurrently at their streaming rate, the combined processing capability is two floating point operations per clock in single precision, $a = 0.5$. Double-precision operations have $a = 1/2 + 1/1 = 1.5$. At 40 MHz, this combined streaming rate gives 80 MFLOPS for single precision and 60 MFLOPS for double precision.

Multiply-Add Operation

A common operation for scientific computing is multiply–add. This operation needs to have low values of MCL and MAL because it is applied to relatively long vectors. Because of the feedback and the repetitive application of this operation, collision analysis as discussed previously is ineffective. Analysis by reservation table will be described.

Figure 8.33 shows the block diagram and reservation table for a multiply–add pipeline. For the purpose of this analysis, the multiply pipeline is of length 2 (no folding) and the add pipeline is also of length 2, giving $n = 4$. For analysis purposes, the first stage of the add pipeline is denoted $\tilde{n}$; for this example, $\tilde{n} = 3$. The input stream consists of the

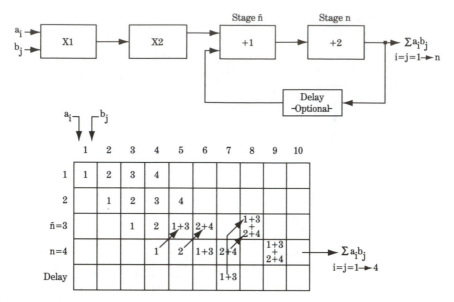

FIGURE 8.33   Multiply–add pipeline.

two vectors, $\mathbf{a}_i$ and $\mathbf{b}_j$, that enter at the left; the scalar output exits to the right. There is a delay stage in the feedback path that may or may not be scheduled. Note that for the TI ASC pipeline shown in Figure 8.26, $n = 6$ and $\tilde{n} = 4$, ignoring the receiver and output stages.

The reservation table shows the flow through the pipeline for vector length $k = 4$. The entries in the reservation table are the index values of the input vectors. Note that $\mathbf{a}_1$ and $\mathbf{b}_1$ enter at t_1 and their product plus 0 completes at t_4. This output is added to the product of $\mathbf{a}_3$ and $\mathbf{b}_3$ starting at t_5. At t_7, all of the multiplications and all of the additions, less one, are complete. Note that $1 + 3$ is delayed one clock to align with $2 + 4$ exiting the add pipeline. The final addition is complete at t_9.

The number of clocks needed to perform this operation is the sum of $(n - 1)$ clocks that are required to fill the pipeline, k clocks that are required to process all the vector elements, and $(n - \tilde{n} + 1)$ clocks that are required to perform the last additions. Thus, the total number of clocks is

$$\text{total clocks} = 2n - \tilde{n} + k$$

where k denotes the vector length and the number of multiplies.

	n	$\tilde{n}$	Clock	CPMA
TI ASC	7	4	85 ns	$1 + 10/k$
RS/6000	2	2	33 ns	$1 + 2/k$
i860 (SP)	6	4	25 ns	$1 + 8/k$

TABLE 8.9 Multiply–add performance.

The number of clocks per k multiply-add (CPMA) operations is

$$\text{CPMA} = 1 + (2n - \tilde{n})/k.$$

Table 8.9 shows the multiply–add performance of three computers that have the performance of this operation as a design goal.

For large values of k, the CPMA of these three processors is the same. However, for small values of k the RS/6000 has a considerable performance advantage as far as CPMA is concerned. The break-even value of k for the RS/6000 and i860 is 16 (for single precision). If k is greater than 16, the i860 will execute the vector operation faster than the RS/6000 due to its faster clock.

Vector Sum Pipeline

Another common operation for scientific computing is the *vector sum*: vector sum $= \Sigma_{i=1}^{n} \mathbf{a}_i$. This operation sums the elements of a vector, producing a scalar result. There are two strategies for implementing this operation in a pipelined adder. The first method, Design A, which is shown at the top of Figure 8.33, sums an eight-element vector. With this method, the elements of the vector are presented two at a time to the pipeline and the partial sums are then summed, with a greedy strategy, into the final sum. The partial sums are stored temporarily in either a delay stage or in the register file. The values shown in the reservation table are the sums of the indices.

The sum of the first two elements completes at t_3; it is buffered and introduced into the pipeline with the sum of elements 3 and 4 at t_5. Likewise, the sum of elements 5, 6, 7, and 8 is introduced into the pipeline at t_7. The sums of these operations are introduced into the pipeline at t_{10}, and the vector sum is complete at t_{12}. If the output buffering is performed in the register file it must be able to support two reads and one write in a clock cycle.

There are a number of scheduling problems with this greedy strategy. For example, if the vector length is not an even power of two or is an odd number, the rollup of the final sum is complicated and must be comprehended in the control. The bottom of Figure 8.34 shows another

GREEDY SCHEDULE

	1	2	3	4	5	6	7	8	9	10	11	12	13	14	15
1	3	7	11	15	10		26			36					
2		3	7	11	15	10		26			36				
3			3	7	11	15	10		26			36			
Delay				3		11		10	10						

(Arrows: 1,2 → col 1; 3,4 → col 2; 5,6 → col 3; 7,8 → col 4)

SEQUENTIAL SCHEDULE

	1	2	3	4	5	6	7	8	9	10	11	12	13	14	15
1	3	7	11	15			10	·26			36				
2		3	7	11	15			10	26			36			
3			3	7	11	15			10	26			36		
			$n-1+\frac{k}{2}$				$n-1+\frac{k}{4}$					$n-1+\frac{k}{8}$			

(Arrows: 1,2 → col 1; 3,4 → col 2; 5,6 → col 3; 7,8 → col 4)

FIGURE 8.34 Vector sum reservation tables, Design A.

reservation table with a simple sequential scheduling strategy. With this strategy, a phase does not start until the previous phase is completed. The number of clocks required to execute this strategy is

$$\text{number of clocks} \approx \log_2 k(n-1) + k.$$

The clocks per add (CPA) are

$$\text{CPA} = 1 + \log_2 k(n-1)/k.$$

The sequential scheduling method requires more storage than the greedy strategy. But, if the register file can sustain two reads and a write per clock, the pipeline will not be delayed due to register file references.

A second method, Design B, for performing the vector sum of an

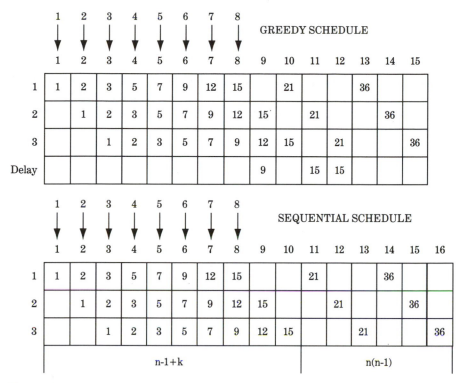

FIGURE 8.35 Vector sum reservation tables, Design B.

eight-element vector is shown in Figure 8.35. With this method, the input vector is read from the registers one element at a time—an action that does not require the higher register file bandwidth. The pipeline itself buffers the elements. Element 1 is added to element 4 starting at t_4. The partial sums are successively added to the input vector until the operation is complete at t_{15}. For very long vectors, this second method has a larger CPA than that of Design A, but it also has the benefit of reduced register file bandwidth.

The simple sequential schedule is shown at the bottom of Figure 8.35. All of the partial sums have been rolled up except the last n: 9, 12, and 15. The first two, 9 and 12, are introduced into the pipeline at t_{11}, partial sums 15 and 21 are introduced at t_{14}, and the final sum is available at t_{16}. The number of clocks required to perform this operation is

$$\text{number of clocks} = n^2 + k - 1.$$

The clocks per add (CPA) are

$$CPA = 1 + (n^2 - 1)/k.$$

For both Designs A and B, as k becomes very large, the number of clocks per add approaches one. Design B will be only slightly slower than Design A. Thus, a designer may opt for the design that is the simplest to implement.

9

Exceptions and Interrupts

9.0 Overview

Discontinuities (delays and stalls) in the pipeline flow that result from branch instructions are described in Chapter 7; dependency and structural hazard discontinuities are described in Chapter 8. Discontinuities caused by other internal and external events are addressed in this chapter. These discontinuities generally call for a *context switch* from the executing program to another program, called an *interrupt handler*.

There is no accepted nomenclature associated with interrupts; every manufacturer seems to be creative in their use of terms. Nevertheless, the following classification and nomenclature of the three interrupt types are used in this chapter.

External interrupt (*asynchronous interrupt*) events are external to the processor and are completely asynchronous with the executing program. An I/O interrupt event or a time-out are examples. After the interrupt handler completes, control is returned to the interrupted program.

Internal interrupt (*exception, trap*) events occur as a result of an event within the processor, such as a page fault, divide check, arithmetic exception, or illegal op-code. Depending upon the type of interrupt, control may or may not return to the interrupted program.

Software interrupt (*program interrupt*) events are invoked by the executing program. Examples include breakpoints, op-code traps to unimplemented instructions, and calls to the operating system. After the interrupt handler completes, control is returned to the interrupted program.

Note that software and internal interrupts will occur at exactly the same time if a program is rerun with the same data and initial conditions. In the following discussion, the term *exception* is used to identify any of

425

the three interrupt types described above. Early computers were designed based on the *serial execution model*, defined in Chapter 6, but defined again here as follows:

> A processor in which a program counter sequences through instructions one by one, finishing one instruction before starting the next (paraphrased from [HWU87]).

The serial execution model places few constraints on the design of the interrupt system. When an exception occurs, the exception interrupt event is noted and at the end of the execution cycle the program counter is saved and the interrupt handler is started. By means of the saved program counter, execution of the interrupted program can be restarted. However, providing the effect of this simple exception control with pipelined processors presents major design problems. An additional definition is needed for the following discussion.

> The *processor state* is "the amount of information that can be held at the end of one instruction to provide the processing context for the next instruction" [BELL71] and is sometimes called the *process state* [SMIT85].

The processor state can also be defined to consist of information that has to be saved and then restored for context switches. Examples of processor state are the program counter, the register file, condition codes, the general purpose register file, and some caches that can be explicitly loaded and/or stored under program control. This state is said to be *architected* as it is visible to the program.

Other processor storage units are *implemented*, such as the pipeline stage registers and memory address registers. Implemented state is not visible to the program nor is it part of the processor state in the context of supporting interrupts.

Exceptions present significant problems for pipelined processors, which do not follow the serial execution model. These problems develop because, when an exception occurs, there can be as many instructions being processed as there are pipeline stages and results may be retired out-of-order. In addition, there is internal state that may be modified as instructions flow through the pipeline. These design problems and considerations lead to the concept of a *precise interrupt* that permits a return to the interrupted program. That is,

> If an interrupt is precise, the current program can logically be suspended immediately and restarted at the next instruction when desired [KOGG81].

If the saved processor state does not meet the criterion that a restart of the interrupted program is possible, an interrupt is *imprecise*. External interrupts present design problems about the selection of the interrupted instructions—an issue discussed later in this section. Ensuring that interrupts are precise will generally have a performance impact on dependency resolution (discussed in Chapter 8), increasing the CPI. Thus, the design of systems for precise interrupts must address the problems of performance loss.

The reason for concern about whether or not an interrupt is precise is due to the requirement that program flow control must return to the interrupted program after the interrupt is serviced. If interrupts are not precise, an errorfree return is not guaranteed and the interrupted program cannot be reliably restarted. Most early pipelined processors did not provide precise interrupts and were not virtual memory machines. Note that precise interrupts are not required to support caches as cache misses only freeze the processor, not interrupt it.

Consider one example of the requirement for restarting the interrupted program: a virtual memory page fault interrupt. After servicing this interrupt, restarting the interrupted program without error is mandatory. Smith and Pleszkun [SMIT 85] provide a list of conditions under which precise interrupts are either necessary or desirable.

1. For I/O and timer interrupts a precise process state makes restarting possible.
2. For software debugging it is desirable for the saved state to be precise. This information can be helpful in isolating the exact instruction and circumstances that caused the exception condition.
3. For graceful recovery from arithmetic exceptions, software routines may be able to take steps, rescale floating point numbers for example, to allow a process to continue. Some end cases of modern floating point arithmetic systems might best be handled by software—for example, gradual under flow in the proposed IEEE floating point standard.
4. In virtual memory systems precise interrupts allow a process to be correctly restarted after a page fault has been serviced.
5. Unimplemented op-codes can be simulated by system software in a way transparent to the programmer if interrupts are precise. In this way, lower performance models of an architecture can maintain compatibility with the higher performance models using extended instructions sets.
6. Virtual machines can be implemented if privileged instruction faults cause precise interrupts. Host software can simulate these instructions and return to the guest operating system in a user-transparent way.

I believe that the first instance of an interrupt is to be found in the

ERA 1103, circa 1957. One of these machines was used for wind tunnel data reduction at NASA in Cleveland, Ohio. The processor would normally be executing a background task, but when data was to be collected in the wind tunnel, the processor changed mode by executing a context switch, recorded the incoming data stream, and then returned to the background task. The 1103 has two program counters to facilitate this context switch. Another early use of interrupts is found in the IBM Stretch [COCK59].

The IBM S/360 architecture was specified to follow the serial execution model and was not intended to be pipelined [Bell71]. Consequently, the designers did not have the problem of providing precise interrupts. However, the S/360/91 [ANDE67] is pipelined and the designers were reluctant to incur the complexity of precise interrupts; therefore, the interrupts are imprecise because of the romantic condition called the *gulf of ignorance* by [CHEN64]. This name implied that as instructions progressed down the pipeline there is complete ignorance as to their precise status. By 1967, the terms precise and imprecise interrupts were in common use.

Early supercomputers, such as the CDC 6600, CDC 7600, and the TI ASC, all have imprecise interrupts. However, the CPUs of these computers, by design, are not expected to be frequently interrupted and are supported by peripheral processors that run the operating system and service interrupts or support polling. The only interrupts that are processed in these pipelined CPUs are interrupt events such as power-going-down or major arithmetic faults. These interrupt events are so severe that ensuring precise interrupts is not required because restart is not possible.

The CDC 6600 and CDC 7600 have the ability to be switched from task to task by the peripheral processor. This action is called an *exchange jump* that saves the processor states in an orderly fashion so that restart is possible by means of another exchange jump.

The TI ASC has the ability to capture all of the CPU machine states for checkout and maintenance purposes. All registers, both architected and implemented, could be read out into a protected memory area [CRAG89] for diagnostic purposes. Because of the large number of registers, the time to save the processor state is too long to be consistent with the required latency of an interrupt.

The advent of pipelined microprocessors that are intended for solo use (without peripheral processors) revives the requirement for precise interrupts. The luxury of peripheral processors has not been available to these processors. However, this may not be true in the future. With very high density VLSI, the inclusion of an interrupt processor on the chip with the CPU may be a better solution than ensuring precise CPU interrupts, an approach suggested by Keller [KELL75].

The designers of pipelined versions of the VAX, ix86, and MC680x0 architectures have to cope with providing precise interrupts. These architectures, which are intended for solo use, were initially serial execution model machines. Pipeline implementations are required, however, to provide precise interrupts while coping with the complexity of an instruction set that make precise interrupts very difficult to provide. The solution to this design problem is discussed later.

Pipelined processors and virtual memory have significantly increased the complexity of responding to interrupts. In addition to external interrupt events and processing exceptions that must be responded to, there are interrupt events internal to the processor and memory system that must be responded to before processing of the instruction stream can continue. Examples of these interrupt events are: TLB misses, page faults, bus errors, misaligned memory accesses, and memory protection violations.

It is interesting that some early users of the Motorola 68000 wanted to design a virtual memory system and had problems. This processor executed the serial execution model and could only respond to interrupts that occurred between executed instructions (such as external interrupts). With virtual memory, a page fault interrupt can occur during the execution of an instruction, an instruction fetch for example, and cannot be handled by this processor. The MC68000 could, however, be placed in a wait state to accommodate slow memory systems. Thus, to provide virtual memory, the designers of the Apollo Work Station used two processors. One processor executes the program while the other stands by to execute the virtual memory page fault tasks. When a page fault is detected, the primary processor is placed in a wait state while the secondary processor services the interrupt. Note that the use of two processors is a variation of the scheme used on supercomputers except that the processors are homogeneous and do not run concurrently.

9.1 Precise Interrupts

The functional requirements for precise interrupts are given in the previous section. These requirements imply that there is no ambiguity between the interrupted program and the interrupt handler. Three conditions under which an interrupt is precise are given by [SMIT85]. The first two conditions apply to all types of interrupts.

1. All instructions preceding the instruction indicated by the saved program counter have been executed and have modified the process (*processor*) state correctly.
2. All instructions following the instruction indicated by the saved pro-

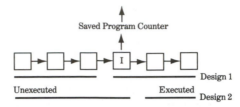

FIGURE 9.1 Handling the interrupted instruction program counter.

gram counter are unexecuted and have not modified the process (*processor*) state.

Unfortunately, these two conditions do not directly address the interrupted instruction and its saved program counter, only those instructions *preceding* and those *following* the save program counter stage. The saved program counter is the major item of processor state that must be saved correctly. This ambiguity is resolved by one of two designs, as shown in Figure 9.1. The stage of the pipeline that is the interrupted instruction is noted by the letter I, and the program counter of this stage is saved.

The program counter that is saved may or may not be the program counter value of the pipeline stage processing the interrupted instruction. For implementation reasons, the program counter value may be that value or it may be one less. The two design options show the pipeline stages that are completely executed and those that are unexecuted. If the interrupted instruction is executed and its program counter is saved, processing resumes at PC + 1 when the interrupted process is restored.

For internal and software interrupts, Smith's third requirement also holds.

3. If the interrupt is caused by an exception condition raised by an instruction in the program, the saved program counter points to the interrupted instruction. The interrupted instruction may or may not have been executed, depending on the definition of the architecture and the cause of the interrupt. Whichever is the case, the interrupted instruction has either completed or has not started execution.

Again a design choice is needed; what happens to the interrupted instruction? The answer is the same as shown in Figure 9.1; the interrupted instruction is either executed or not executed. Additional terms used in this chapter are defined as follows:

Completion is the state when an operation has traversed a function unit and resides in its last stage.

Retire is the action of writing a result to its destination and/or updating the processor state after an instruction completes without ex-

	Interrupted Instruction	Preceding Instructions	Following Instructions
External interrupt	Selection is a design option		
Software interrupt	Stage detecting the interrupt	Retire by flushing or Retire in-order or Undo out-of-order retirements	Retire or Abandon or Undo state changes or Save state
Internal interrupt	Stage causing the interrupt		

TABLE 9.1 Design options for precise interrupts.

ception and is also known as commit or finish. An instruction is being executed conditionally until it is retired.

Interrupted instructions cause an interrupt or, for an external interrupt, a designated instruction.

Preceding instructions preceded the interrupted instruction down the pipeline and have not yet been retired.

Following instructions follow the interrupted instruction in the pipeline.

Table 9.1 shows the design options for meeting the three conditions for precise interrupts for the three interrupt types. For each type, the designer has a number of design options. For example, the preceding instructions may be 1) retired by flushing, 2) retired in-order, or 3) if the results have been retired out-of-order, these retirements may be undone. These design options are discussed in later sections.

The reader should note that processor designers may use different schemes to ensure precise interrupts for the three types of interrupts. In general, each interrupt is implemented in such a way as to simplify the total design.

Two concepts are important for the following discussion, which focuses on ensuring precise interrupts.

1. *Side effects* are state changes that are not the primary purpose of the instruction. Program counter changes, posting condition codes, and auto index register changes are examples of side effects.
2. *State changes* result from retiring the results of operations to a resource object: either the architected registers or the memory.

Side effects that change the values in resource objects pose major problems in pipeline design, as I discuss later. To complicate matters further, with processors that permit out-of-order retirement, instructions following the interrupted instruction may have already been retired with the result written into the register file. Recall from Chapter 7 that instructions are abandoned when the predicted direction of a branch is incorrect. The discussion here on undoing side effects after an interrupt applies equally well to undoing side effects after a branch.

Because of the concurrency that exists in a pipeline, any analysis of exceptions and interrupts must comprehend three significant situations:

1. the possibility of concurrent interrupt events. That is, two or more instructions can have exceptions in the same clock period. An example is an illegal op-code being detected at the same time an external interrupt occurs.
2. the possibility of sequential interrupt events. That is, one or more exceptions can occur after another exception has been recognized. An example is that an illegal op-code is detected as an operation is issued to the execution unit that then has an arithmetic exception.
3. the possibility that concurrent interrupt events are followed by one or more sequential interrupt events.

In other words, the designer must not only comprehend the behavior of the pipeline with an isolated interrupt but provide for concurrent and sequential interrupts as well. All possible cases must be comprehended, either ensuring predictable behavior or indicating to the user in the processor documentation when unusual behavior will occur. For example, the MC88000 gives up on the second interrupt and takes an "error exception" [MOTO90].

The sections to follow discuss the pipeline design issues involved in satisfying the three conditions for a precise interrupt: (1) the saved program counter, (2) the correct modification of the processor state by ensuring in-order results, and (3) treatment of the following instruction (not in the same order as given previously). The basic strategy is to modify the processor state in such a way that the state is correct; that is, to coerce the pipeline to behave as if it is executing the serial execution model. Coercion can be by initial design or by the addition of interlocks and storage. Current research on exceptions with pipelined processors is reported in [SMIT85, SOHI87, VENK90, JOHN91, WALK92].

9.1.1 *Interrupted Instruction and Saved Program Counter*

Fundamental to the discussion of strategies for handling interrupts is the idea of the interrupted instruction and its *saved program counter*. Because it is possible to have as many instructions in execution as there are pipeline stages, the identification of the program counter value to save is nontrivial and is determined by (1) the type of interrupt and (2) the pipeline stage at which the interrupted instruction resides. I note the following definition.

> The *saved program counter* is "the program counter value that points to the first instruction to be loaded into the pipeline after the interrupt is serviced" [WALK92].

It should be apparent that there must be some method of associating the program counter value with each instruction in each stage of the pipeline. As shown in Figure 9.2, a shift register operating in parallel with the pipeline shifts the value of the program counter in synchronization with the instruction passing through the pipeline. Thus, each pipeline stage has its own program counter value since each stage is processing a different instruction.

In a pipelined processor, interrupts are recognized only at the clock pulses that shift the instructions down the pipeline. The interrupted instruction is, except for external interrupts, the instruction that causes the interrupt, such as an illegal op-code detected at the decode stage or a memory read stage for a virtual memory address translation error. An example of the designation of the interrupted instruction is found in the R4000 [MIRA92]. Table 9.2 shows the stage of this pipeline that is designated the interrupted instruction.

The design of the R4000 pipeline and the identification of the pipeline

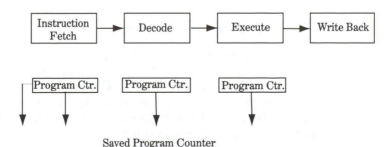

FIGURE 9.2 Interrupted instruction and saved program counter.

Pipeline Stage	External Interrupts	Software Interrupts	Internal Interrupts
IF			
IS			
RF	Bus error	Breakpoint Syscall ECC instruction Virtual coherency instruction	Illegal instruction Instruction translation Coprocessor is unusable
EX	Interrupt		
DF			
DS		Floating point	Overflow
TC			TLB modified Data translation
WB	Data Watch NMI Reset	Virtual coherency	Bus error data

TABLE 9.2   R4000 stage designation of interrupted instruction.

stages are discussed in Chapter 10. However, note that a bus error on an instruction fetch from the cache is not signaled until the RF stage. The reason for this is that the data cache is pipelined and the checks of the cache tags occur in the RF stage as shown in Figure 2.31. For concurrent interrupts, the R4000 gives priority to the interrupted instruction furthest down the pipeline. This processor illustrates the need to recognize interrupts and save the program counter value over most of the stages of the pipeline.

9.1.2 *Handling Preceding Instructions*

The methods for handling preceding instructions, described below, are for systems that issue one instruction at a time. Systems that issue more than one instruction at a time are described in Chapter 10. Preceding instructions have the potential to modify the processor state in registers and/or memory. Recall that Smith's Condition #1 states that: All instructions preceding the instruction indicated by the saved program counter have been executed and have modified the process (processor) state correctly. This *sequential execution model* condition is defined as:

A processor that satisfies the condition that "the result of an execution is the same as if the operations had been executed in the order specified by the program" [LAMP79]. Note that a processor that executes the serial execution model also executes the sequential execution model.

The sequential execution model is enforced by one of the three design options for handling preceding instructions shown in Table 9.1. The options are:

1. to flush the pipeline, retiring all issued instructions;
2. to take steps to ensure that all issued instructions retire in-order;
3. to undo the processor state changes of any instructions that have been retired out-of-order.

The design issues involved in selecting the option for handling the preceding instructions are whether or not to (1) penalize the normal performance of the pipeline, as measured by CPI, at the expense of a longer interrupt latency when there is an interrupt, or (2) have a smaller CPI and a longer latency. Cost and complexity are also design considerations.

Only a Type A instruction window (described in Chapter 8) with in-order release will always have in-order retirements. The other types of windows have the potential for out-of-order completions and out-of-order retirements. Figure 9.3 shows windows with two execution units that can produce out-of-order retirements. Multiple execution units can have a different number of stages, such as an integer unit and a floating point unit as found in many microprocessors. Multiple register files, for integer and floating points, are not shown but have the same out-of-order retirement problem. Systems with a common result bus that store integer and floating point values in the same register file can have structural hazards on the output bus and the register file.

The operation of these windows and pipelines is illustrated with two examples of a four-instruction sequence using the long and the short execution units. For the Type C window, if an interrupt occurs at the end of t_4, i2 has already been retired out-of-order by writing to the register file. In addition, even if the interrupt had not occurred, there will be a structural hazard on the result bus and register file at t_5 that must be resolved.

For the Type D or E window, the instructions issue in-order to the reservation stations. For this example, instruction i3 is delayed two clocks because of a dependency on i2 (without forwarding). If an interrupt occurs at t_5, i2 will have been retired out-of-order. Notice that the release is out-of-order; i4 releases before i3 due to the dependency. The characteristics of these two configurations follow.

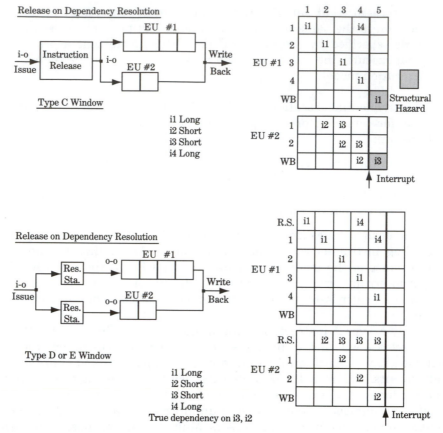

FIGURE 9.3 Multiple execution units.

Type C window (Cray-1, MIPS, Pentium integer) characteristics include

1. in-order issue,
2. dependencies resolved before release,
3. in-order release,
4. deterministic time from issue to completion.

Type D or E window (CDC 6600, IBM S/360/91 Flt. Pt., MC68110) characteristics include

1. in-order issue,
2. dependencies resolved in the reservation stations,
3. out-of-order release,
4. nondeterministic time from issue to completion.

Resolving Structural Hazards

For systems with multiple-variable length execution units, the potential exists for a structural hazard on the result bus and register file even if instructions are released in-order. There are two methods for resolving this structural hazard.

1. Deterministically schedule the issue or release of instruction to eliminate the hazard.
2. Resolve the hazard with priority logic.

Consider the first method. Structural hazards can be resolved by delaying an instruction release until the hazard is eliminated; the result bus is scheduled so that hazards will not occur. Figure 9.4 shows a result shift register [SMITH85], called a RSR(a), that schedules the result bus and writes to a common register file.

The reservation table of a shift register, shown on the right of the figure, is the same length as the longest execution unit pipeline; in this case four stages, and the stages are numbered in reverse order. This result shift register reserves a time slot for the result bus and the path to the register file but does not ensure in-order retirement. Scheduling of instructions into the execution units is illustrated by a three-instruction sequence. Instruction i1, because it uses the long pipeline, places its destination address in stage four at t_1. Then i2 releases and places its destination address into stage 2 at t_2. Instruction i3 cannot release into EU #2 at t_3 because the bus will be blocked by the result of i1. Thus, i3 is delayed one clock and releases at t_4. When a result is ready to exit the execution unit, the result bus is gated on.

The TI ASC uses a Type C window and a RSR(a) to schedule its four execution units into the result bus and register file. Because of the number of data types, the RSR required seven bits to indicate the address and type of register. For example, an operation with an upper half-

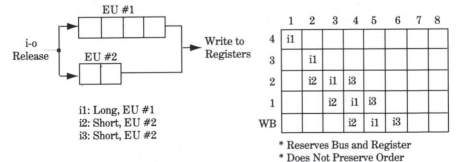

FIGURE 9.4 Result shift register (a).

word result will not have a structural hazard with a result with a lower half-word result.

The second method for resolving the structural hazard employs priority logic. Type C, D, and E windows cannot easily use a RSR(a) to schedule the result bus because of the possible release delays while waiting for dependencies to be resolved. The CDC 6600 scoreboard and CDB must resolve these structural hazards on their result bus(ses) and move the delays to the completion end of the execution units. In the case of the scoreboard, each of the busses, called *trunks*, has priority hardware to delay lower priority bus requests. I am not certain, but I believe that some form of priority scheme is used with the CDB as well. The two floating point execution units probably receive CDB access priority based on a random selection.

Retirement by Flushing

After ensuring that there are no structural hazards, the requirements for properly handling the preceding instructions must be satisfied. A common method, used in a number of processors, is a simple flush of the pipelines; that is, the issued instructions in the pipelines are run to completion and all results are retired. After flushing, the processor state is correct, the context switch can be performed, and the interrupt serviced.

Flushing is illustrated with the reservation table in Figure 9.5, which shows an instruction sequence: long, short, long, short. The window can be Type C, D, or E.

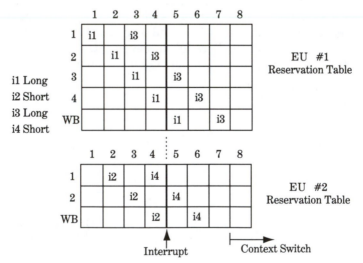

FIGURE 9.5   Flush pipelines.

If an interrupt occurs at t_4, instruction release is halted, the pipelines flush and perform their write backs to the register file out-of-order. The context switch does not occur until after the flush operation is complete and the register file is in the correct state. The flush time, in this example, is three clocks. The time to flush, or the latency of the context switch, can be long and indeterminate. For example, all dependencies must be resolved before the instructions release, and there could be a major delay if there is an address translation miss on a released load or store instruction.

The flush latency causes another problem: the instructions being flushed can themselves be interrupted. The general solution to this problem is to mask off all interrupts after the first has been recognized. Because interrupts will be masked off, unpredictable results can result and an error condition is signaled by the processor.

This strategy is useful when an internal interrupt or exception is detected prior to release and before any side effects can occur. Examples are page faults on instruction fetch or the detection of an illegal op-code. This simple flush scheme is called *interrupts prior to instruction issue* in [SMIT85].

The PowerPC 601 and the Intel Pentium both use pipeline flushing to handle preceding instructions. Both of these processors have relatively short execution unit pipelines, and released instructions are guaranteed not to produce interrupts.

With the Pentium, the processor checks for pending interrupts before each instruction is issued. If an interrupt is pending, fetching instructions is halted and the pipeline is flushed [INTE93]. It is not clear from the Pentium documentation what happens if a second interrupt occurs during the pipeline flush operation. I assume that this is prevented by control logic in the processor. Some exception conditions are not handled by interrupts with the Pentium. Internal exceptions, such as register file parity errors, indicate that the processor can no longer be trusted, and the pipeline is shutdown with no hope of recovery.

In-Order Retirement

Because of problems with flushing, it is desirable to provide a method that will ensure that the processor state will be updated in-order regardless of the order of release. Design solutions to providing in-order-retirement are discussed in the following sections and require in-order release, Type C windows, except where noted. Some of the solutions to this problem have hardware at the end of the pipelines that restore results into order before retirement; this hardware is called the *result window* by [LAIR92].

Recall that the MIPS concept is based on software managing the pipeline without interlocks; the only interlock provided in the hardware is the load true dependency. The MIPS idea completely breaks down when a second execution unit—for instance, a floating point coprocessor—is added. Sohi [SOHI87] posits, "We are unaware of any software solutions to the imprecise interrupt problem for multiple functional unit computers." To cope with the problem of out-of-order-retirement, techniques have been developed to coerce the processor to behave as if there are in-order-retirements even though completions are out-of-order.

Equal Length Execution Unit Pipelines

A simple strategy for Type C windows that ensures in-order retirement is to make all execution pipelines the same length. In other words, if the floating point pipeline is four stages, then the integer pipeline is four stages as well. As an integer pipeline can usually be one stage, three stages will simply be delays. This strategy will provide in-order retirement with in-order release and will eliminate any structural hazards on the result bus or register file.

The problem with padding out short pipelines is that other operations may be adversely affected. For example, the delays for true dependencies can be increased. In addition, as the integer pipeline is frequently used for branch calculations, branch performance may be adversely affected. The cost in execution time and hardware of implementing equal-length pipelines is excessive, and I know of no system that uses this technique.

I take issue with the proposition that there is no software solution to precise interrupts on multiple execution unit processors with a Type C window. No-ops can be used to delay instruction release to short pipelines, giving the same results as equal-length pipelines. There will be a significant performance loss. I know of no published information on no-op scheduling for in-order retirement.

Result Shift Register

Smith [SMIT85] describes another type of result shift register, RSR(b), shown in Figure 9.6, that can be used with Type C windows. For RSR(b), when instruction 1 is released to the four-stage execution unit, its destination address is placed in the stage of the result shift register along with X's in stages 3, 2, and 1. These time slots are thus blocked out or reserved. Instruction 2 would like to be released at t_2, but stage 2 has been reserved and this instruction must wait until t_4, when it can be released and its destination address placed in the result shift register. Instruction 3, because it is released in sequence, can now be released at t_5. There are no X's to block its release, as is the case with instruction 2. As we can see, the results are retired in-order.

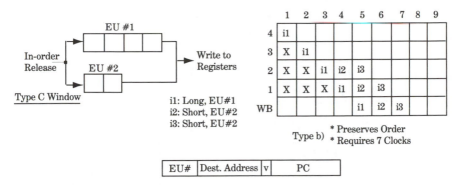

FIGURE 9.6 Result shift register (b).

In summary, when an instruction is issued, (1) a time slot is reserved on the single bus that connects the execution units to the register file and (2) the X's reserve time slots so that an instruction that uses a shorter pipeline will not get ahead of the issuing instruction. Delays are dynamically inserted, only when needed, compared to static introduction of no-ops into all slots whether or not delays are needed. As with the RSR(a), the time through the execution units must be deterministic; there can be no delays after the instruction is released.

The RSR(b) entries have a number of fields; the execution unit number and destination address provide routing information to write the result into the correct register file location. A valid field is needed to distinguish between reserved slots and the slots that are only blocked out. The program counter value associated with each entry is required so that an instruction with an exception can be uniquely identified. The field for the program counter is an extension of the program counter pipeline of Figure 9.2.

Because results are retired in-order, an interrupt at any time will find the register file processor state correct; thus, it is not necessary to flush the pipelines. Because the processor state is correct, the context switch can start immediately. The price for zero-context switch latency is that the normal processing CPI has been increased. For out-of-order results scheduled with a RSR(a), of Figure 9.4, six clocks are required for the last instruction write to the register file. For the RSR(b), seven clocks are required, a significant performance loss of 16%, to achieve in-order retirements.

In the examples to follow, two program fragments will be used to illustrate the operation of result shift registers handling preceding instructions. One program fragment has a true dependency while the other does not.

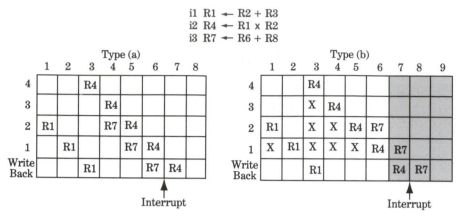

i1 R1 ← R2 + R3
i2 R4 ← R1 x R2
i3 R7 ← R6 + R8

FIGURE 9.7   Result shift register—with a true dependency.

	W True Dep.		W/O True Dep.	
i1	$R1 \leftarrow R2 + R3$	i1	$R1 \leftarrow R2 \times R3$	
i2	$R4 \leftarrow R1 \times R2$	i2	$R4 \leftarrow R5 + R8$	
i3	$R7 \leftarrow R6 + R8$	i3	$R7 \leftarrow R8 \times R9$	

The operation of a RSR(a) and (b) in the presence of an interrupt is illustrated with these two program fragments. The first example, shown in Figure 9.7, is the three-instruction program fragment with a true dependency on R1 between instructions i1 and i2, assuming forwarding around the write back stage. The add pipeline is assumed to have two stages while the multiply pipeline has four stages. The destination register address is shown in the RSRs rather than the instruction number as in Figure 9.6.

For the RSR(a), the instructions are released in-order but are retired out-of-order: i1, i3, i2. If an interrupt occurs a time t_6, the register file has been updated out-of-order. Note that if there is an i4, an add instruction for example, it could not release until t_6 because of the reservation placed on the result bus and register file. There is no structural hazard with this example.

Because of the introduced delays, the RSR(b) ensures in-order retirement of results, permitting an interrupt at any time to be properly handled. Instruction i2 will not release until t_3 because of the true dependency (bypassed around the register), and i3 will not release until t_6 because of the reservation that has been placed on the result bus by i2. Because i2 and i3 have not modified the processor state by writing into the register file, they can be abandoned. The RSR(a) required seven

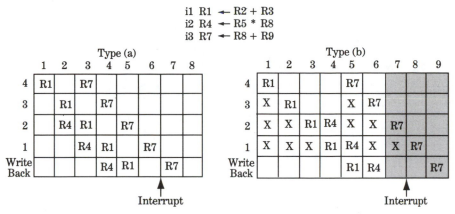

FIGURE 9.8   Result shift register—without a true dependency.

clocks to retire the sequence, while the RSR (b) required eight clocks. The time penalty is approximately 14% to ensure in-order retirement.

The second example of RSR operation is shown in Figure 9.8 for the code fragment without a true dependency. Instructions issue and release in-order. With the RSR(a), there are no delays to resolve true dependencies or structural hazards. Seven clocks are required to complete this sequence and, if an interrupt should occur at t_6, i3 can be abandoned with the register file in the correct state—purely accidental due to the sequence of instructions. Such would not be the case if the interrupt had occurred at t_4.

The RSR(b) schedules the release of instructions, i2 at t_4 and i3 at t_5, so that an interrupt at any time, not just at t_6 as shown, will find the register file in the correct state. Nine clocks are required for this same instruction sequence—a penalty of approximately 28% to ensure in-order retirement. The latency to start the context switch is zero because all of the instructions that have not been retired are abandoned.

Reorder Buffer

The reorder buffer [SMIT85] assumes a Type C window that releases instructions in-order as their dependencies are resolved and ensures in-order retirement to the register file without the performance penalty of the RSR(b). As the operations complete, the results are posted to the reorder buffet, which then retires the instructions, in-order. The reorder buffer scheme, shown in Figure 9.9, is controlled by a RSR(a) that reserves a time slot on the result bus for posting completed results to the reorder buffer.

The reorder buffer is shown, and implemented, as a circular buffer

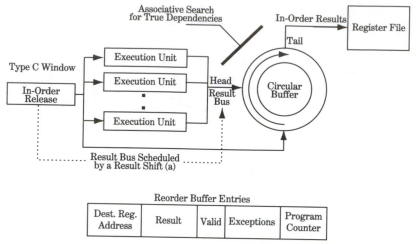

FIGURE 9.9   Reorder buffer.

with head and tail pointers into a register file. The pointers increment modulo the size of the register file. The information carried in each of the reorder buffer entries includes destination register address, the result of the operation, a valid bit that is set when the results are posted, any exceptions that occur during execution such as overflow, and the program counter value. The instructions are released into the pipelined execution units in-order with the information shown in the figure being placed in the reorder buffer location at the head pointer in-order. If the reorder buffer is full, the window stalls until there is a vacant location.

As instructions complete (perhaps out-of-order) the results are written into their reserved slot in the reorder buffer and the valid bit is set. Rotation of the reorder buffer then permits the results to be retired in-order into the register file. In other words, a series of in-order slots rotate around the reorder buffer and are posted out-of-order by the execution units and then are retired in-order into the register file.

The operation of the reorder buffer follows these steps.

RELEASE. Write the following into the reorder buffer at the head pointer location:

- Destination Register Name
- PC value
- Increment the tail pointer.

In addition, the head pointer value is written into the RSR(a).

COMPLETION. Write the following to the reorder buffer associated with the correct PC.

- Result
- Set Valid bit
- Post any exception information.

TESTS AT THE TAIL POINTER. If Valid = 1, the head pointer value is either in the last stage or is not present in the RSR(a), and there are no exceptions

Then: retire the result and increment the head pointer
Else: test on the next clock.

Because completed results are delayed to ensure in-order retirement to the register file, a subsequent instruction with a true dependency on that result would be delayed until the result is retired. However, if the reorder buffer can be associatively searched on the destination register address by the window release logic, the needed result can be forwarded into the dependent instruction execution. Handling true dependencies with a reorder buffer is discussed in Section 8.2.3 and in [SMIT85].

Notice that the reorder buffer, because it holds results waiting for in-order retirement to the register file, is another form of renaming that provides more implemented registers than architected registers.

The operation of a reorder buffer is illustrated in Figure 9.10 using the same execution pipelines and the program fragment with a true dependency on R1 used in the previous examples. The contents of the reorder buffer and the RSR are shown for each clock period. The head and tail pointers point to location 2 at Time 0. Instruction i1 releases at Time 1; the destination register address and the PC value are inserted in the reorder buffer and the head pointer value is placed in the RSR(a). The tail pointer is incremented to indicate the location to receive information from the next released instruction.

As with Figure 9.7, i2 releases at t_3, having been delayed to resolve the true dependency, and i3 releases at t_4. At t_2, the value of the head pointer (2) is found in the last stage of the RSR and the valid bit is set at the head pointer entry. Thus, i1 will write to R1 at t_3. The head pointer is incremented and the valid bit is reset because that entry is now vacant. For this example, i3 must be delayed before it is written into the register file to retire in-order. This is accomplished as R7 is set up for writing in t_7 with the write being accomplished in t_8, just as is done with the RSR(b) of Figure 9.7.

What happens if there is an interrupt, at say t_6? Even if the write to R4 is accomplished, all results will have been retired in-order to the register file. The write to R7 will not have taken place and the processor

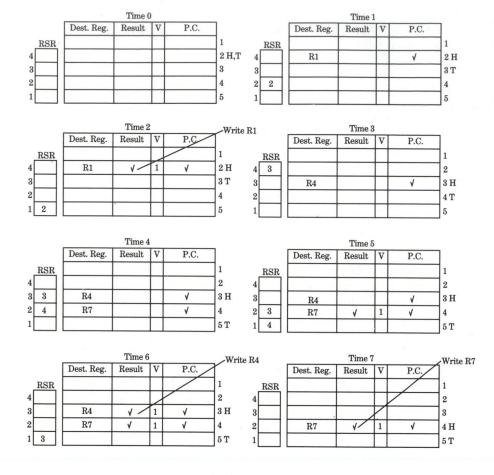

FIGURE 9.10   Reorder buffer operation—with true dependency.

state is correct. Thus, all of the instructions in execution can be abandoned and there is a zero-latency interrupt to start the context switch.

The reorder buffer provides the instruction release rate and low CPI
of an RSR(a) with the zero latency of a RSR(b).

Figure 9.11 shows the operation of the reorder buffer with the example program fragment without the true dependency.

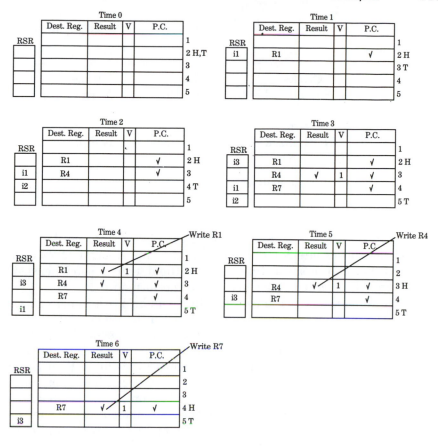

Time 0

	Dest. Reg.	Result	V	P.C.	
RSR					1
					2 H,T
					3
					4
					5

Time 1

	Dest. Reg.	Result	V	P.C.	
RSR					1
i1	R1			√	2 H
					3 T
					4
					5

Time 2

	Dest. Reg.	Result	V	P.C.	
RSR					1
	R1			√	2 H
i1	R4			√	3
i2					4 T
					5

Time 3

	Dest. Reg.	Result	V	P.C.	
RSR					1
i3	R1			√	2 H
	R4	√	1	√	3
i1	R7			√	4
i2					5 T

Time 4 — Write R1

	Dest. Reg.	Result	V	P.C.	
RSR					1
	R1	√	1	√	2 H
i3	R4	√		√	3
	R7			√	4
i1					5 T

Time 5 — Write R4

	Dest. Reg.	Result	V	P.C.	
RSR					1
					2
	R4	√	1	√	3 H
i3	R7			√	4
					5 T

Time 6 — Write R7

	Dest. Reg.	Result	V	P.C.	
RSR					1
					2
					3
	R7	√	1	√	4 H
i3					5 T

√ = value inserted

FIGURE 9.11 Reorder buffer without a true dependency.

Because there is no true dependency in this example, the reorder buffer only must restore order while using the RSR(a) for reserving time slots on the result bus. For this example without the true dependency, eight clocks are required to retire the last result into the register file—the same as that for the RSR(a).

The performance of the RSR(b) and the reorder buffer schemes for ensuring in-order retirement is compared to the RSR(a) and tabulated in Table 9.3. For the program fragment examples, the RSR(b) and the reorder buffer require the same number of clocks when there is a true

Program Fragment	RSR(a)	RSR(b)	Reorder Buffer
With true dependencies	7 Clocks Normalized = 1	8 Clocks Normalized = 0.875	8 Clocks Normalized = 0.875
Without true dependencies	7 Clocks Normalized = 1	9 clocks Normalized = 0.77	7 Clocks Normalized = 1

TABLE 9.3 Performance comparisons.

dependency. However, without a true dependency, the reorder buffer requires two fewer clocks for a performance improvement of 22% over a RSR(b). For the program fragments without true dependencies, the RSR(a) and the reorder buffer give equal performance.

These simple examples show that there can be a cost in performance for ensuring in-order retirement; speedup is in the range of 0.77 to 1.0. Fractional speedup means that the performance is reduced. Smith and Pleszkun [SMIT85] simulated a RSR(b) and a reorder buffer added to a Cray-like processor having a Type C window to evaluate their performance impact. In general, adding protection for precise interrupts to this processor degrades the performance depending on (1) the strategy used and (2) how writes and true dependencies are handled. Recall that processors such as the Cray do not provide support for precise interrupts so as not to degrade performance.

The results of the simulation are shown in Table 9.4. The work load is the Lawrence Livermore Loops, and the comparison is to the Cray-like processor. The table also shows the effect of the size of the reorder buffer.

Another evaluation of the speedup penalty of providing in-order

Number of Entries in the Buffer	Result Shift Register (b)	Reorder Buffer
3	0.81	0.75
4	0.81	0.82
5	0.81	0.84
8	0.81	0.85
10	0.81	0.85

TABLE 9.4 Result shift register and reorder buffer performance impact, Cray-1.

retirements is given by Wang and Emnett [WANG93]. Their results show that a result shift register has $S = 0.81$ while a reorder buffer has $S = 0.83$ compared to a Cray-like base machine. Their results will be discussed further in Section 9.5.

The conclusion from the simple examples given above and the simulations of [SOHI87] and [WANG93] are clear. Providing RSRs and/or reorder buffers to ensure precise interrupts, even in a processor without early side effects to undo, is an expensive (in terms of performance) design decision. The performance cost is in the range of 10% to 20% in addition to the hardware cost of reorder buffers and result shift registers. Even in the face of hardware complexity and a loss in performance, the AMD K5 [HALF94] and the Intel P6 [HALF95] processors are reported to use reorder buffers. With both processors, the reorder buffer performs the additional functions of renaming and undoing state changes for miss-predicted branches.

Register Update Unit

Sohi and Vajapeyam [SOHI87] describe a system called a *register update unit* (RUU), which overcomes some of the performance problems associated with a reorder buffer. In-order retirement is assured by using the register update unit upstream from the execution units, as the window, rather than down stream, as with the buffer functions.

The root idea of the register update unit is found in a move to consolidate the Tomasulo CDB reservation stations into a pool instead of associating them with each of the function units. The RUU is similar to a Type C window except that instructions can be released out-of-order to the execution units. The execution unit reservation tables and the register update unit reservation table are shown in Figure 9.12. The RUU is organized as a FIFO using a head and tail pointer into a register file.

An instruction issues from the decoder into a vacant RUU location indicated by the tail pointer, and the source operands or tags are placed in the RUU, as with a CDB reservation station. After an instruction is placed in the RUU, the tail pointer is incremented. For an instruction to release from the RUU, two conditions must be satisfied: the dependencies are resolved, and a time slot is available on the result bus. There is a RSR(b) associated with or a part of the RUU that reserves the result bus. Thus there are three sources of potential delay: the RUU is full, there is a true dependency, and there is a structural hazard on the result bus.

When an instruction completes, the result is written to the RUU entry indicated by its destination register address or, if in order, directly into the register file. Results are retired, in-order, from the head pointer entry with a valid result.

A simple example of the operation of the RUU is shown in Figure 9.12. The three-instruction sequence has neither a true dependency nor

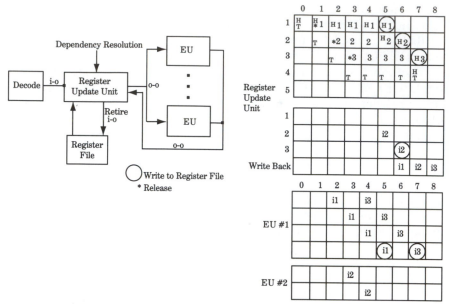

FIGURE 9.12 Register update unit.

a structural hazard on the result bus. Instruction i1 releases at t_1 into the long execution unit at t_2. Because there is no structural hazard, i2 releases into the execution unit at t_3 and i3 at t_4. Instruction i1 retires directly to the register file as does i3. However, the result of i2 is stored into the RUU and its retirement is delayed until the clock after i1 is retired.

Because results are retired in-order, an interrupt occurring at any time will find the register file in the correct processor state and the context switch can begin with zero latency. All instructions that have not been retired can be abandoned.

The RUU should show improved performance over a Cray window because it releases instructions out-of-order. However, performance can be lost if the RUU is too small because instruction issue can be blocked, true dependencies cannot be forwarded, and the result bus will have structural hazards. Sohi and Vajapeyam provide simulation results that indicate the efficacy of the register update unit technique. The simulations used the Lawrence Livermore Loops and compared the performance on a Cray-like processor; excerpted results are shown in Table 9.5. Fractional speedup indicates a loss of performance.

Note that the register update unit not only provides precise interrupts but an increase in performance over the basic Cray-like processor as well. What is most surprising is the result that adding a register

RUU Entries	Speedup
4	0.85
8	1.17
16	1.48
30	1.53
50	1.81

TABLE 9.5   Register update unit performance improvements.

update unit to a Cray will increase its performance by about 80%! This result is counterintuitive and can only be explained by an improvement due to out-of-order release; remember that the Cray has in-order release. This data suggests that a register update unit that has sixteen entries is probably the correct size for a processor with a large number of execution units.

Undo Out-of-Order Results of Preceding Instructions

A third method of handling preceding instructions, after pipeline flush and reorder, is to undo any results that have modified the processor state out-of-order. In other words, execute as fast as possible; schedule only for dependencies and hazards, and when an interrupt does occur, undo out-of-order retirements. The contents of the register files can be restored to their original values as if the out-of-order results had never been retired. This restoration can be done by either a *history buffer* or a *future file*—two techniques that are forms of checkpointing.

History Buffer

Smith and Pleszkun [SMIT85] describe the operation of a history buffer: "Primarily, these methods place computed results in a working register file but retain enough state information so a precise state can be restored if an exception occurs." This scheme works for Type C, D, or E windows with in-order or out-of-order release. When an instruction issues, the *current value*, called "old," of the destination register is saved to replace a *new value* out-of-order result if that instruction is abandoned.

The current value and other control information such as the program counter and destination register address are placed at the head of a FIFO, as shown in Figure 9.13. When an instruction reaches the tail of the FIFO without an interrupt, the entry is deleted by changing the tail pointer and changing the valid bit to zero. The result bus and register file can be scheduled by an RSR(a), which is not shown in Figure 9.13.

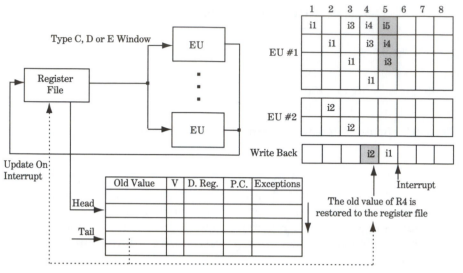

FIGURE **9.13**   History buffer.

Saving the current values of the register file preserves the previous correct processor state on a rolling basis.

Exception reports, when they occur, are recorded in the history buffer. When an exception reaches the head of the history buffer, instruction release is halted and the operations in the execution units are abandoned. The history buffer places the "old" values back into the register file. The program counter of the instruction with the exception is the saved program counter. Instructions that have been retired in-order without exception are then purged from the history buffer. True dependencies are satisfied by forwarding or by reading the register file; an associative search of the history buffer is not needed.

Figure 9.13 shows a five-instruction sequence with an interrupt at t_5. Instruction i2 has been retired out-of-order and i1 has just been retired into register file location R4. In this example, the old value in the history buffer replaces the value in R4 computed by i2, thereby restoring the state of the process. The saved program counter is either that of i1 or i2, depending on implementation details. Instructions i3, i4, and i5 are abandoned as they have not modified the processor state.

The MC88110 [ULLA93] uses a history buffer to ensure that instructions are retired in-order. This processor is superscalar (discussed in Chapter 10) and can release one or two instructions per clock in-order into ten execution units. Upon release, information concerning the instruction(s), plus the "old" value(s) of the destination register(s), is placed at the head pointer entry of the history buffer.

With this system, a result shift register is not needed to schedule the result bus. Scheduling is done by the history buffer itself. Instruction information is placed at the tail of the FIFO in-order and when an instruction reaches the head of the FIFO its results are written to the register file. A short pipeline instruction, such as an integer add, that released after a floating point operation will hold in the output of the execution unit until its identification information reaches the head of the FIFO.

Future File

A future file [SMIT85] solves the problem of results retired out-of-order without adding delay overhead by employing two register files. One is called the *architected register file,* and the other is called the *future register file.* A block diagram of this system is shown in Figure 9.14. The two register files are both the size of the architected register file and operate concurrently.

Results from the execution units are written into the future register file as completed (which may be out-of-order) and in time slots reserved by a RSR(a), not shown. Results are also retired into the architected register file after being placed in-order by a reorder buffer; hence, the architected register file contains the correct processor state, lagging behind the future file state. The future register file, with its out-of-order results, is used for normal execution, thus forwarding is of minimum complexity.

When an interrupt occurs, the contents of the architected register file are transferred into the future register file, thereby placing the

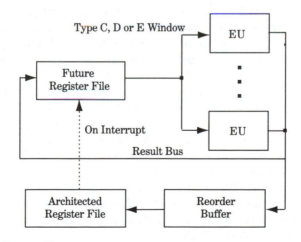

FIGURE 9.14   Future file.

processor in the correct processor state. The architected register file is then cleared to prepare it for the next sequence of instructions. This combination of two register files minimizes the cost and improves the performance of resolving true dependencies and only adds overhead time when there is an interrupt. I know of no implementation of a future file on a real processor.

Handling Writes to Memory

In-order release and completion of loads and writes are discussed in Section 8.3.1 in the context of preventing anti- and output dependencies. It is also necessary to maintain in-order retirement of memory writes in the context of the register retirements so that the correct processor state in memory is ensured. Thus, memory writes are not made until all preceding instructions have been retired in-order.

Memory can be viewed as an execution pipeline that can contribute to the out-of-order retirement problem. For example, a write to memory can be retired after a preceding instruction that uses a short execution pipeline. Also, with writes to a data cache, a write can be retired before a following instruction that uses a long execution pipeline. Even in the face of these problems, it is necessary to maintain the in-order logical consistency of the memory as well as the registers to have precise interrupts.

Memory has the added problem that the read or write access time is not deterministic due to name translation errors, bus delays, and cache misses. However, as far as program execution is concerned, writes are viewed as taking deterministic time, because of the use of write buffers. However, when an interrupt occurs, changes to the state of memory must be made in such a way as to preserve the correct processor state. For the examples used in the sections above, the assumption is made that the last stage of the pipeline writes to the register file or retires the operation. If a sequence of instructions are stores, the modification to the processor state in the memory must be in-order as well.

A simple method for ensuring precise interrupts on writes is to stall the pipeline when a store instruction is decoded and wait for the pipeline (including a result shift register if used) to empty. Then the write to memory is released and ultimately retired. Another method for scheduling writes, without the performance problem of the stall strategy, is to hold all writes until all of the preceding instructions are known to be exception-free before the writes are released. This scheme can be implemented by lengthening the result shift register to the number of clocks to accomplish a write. Writes are then placed on the result shift register as any other instruction [SMIT85].

The MC88110 provides an example of handling writes to memory that preserve the in-order consistency· of the program [DIEF92, ULLA93]. As with other instructions, write instructions are placed in the history buffer when they are released to the load/store execution unit. However, the write is not retired to memory until the write instruction has reached the head of the history buffer. Thus, writes always retire in-order and do not modify the memory until all preceding instructions have been retired. There can be a delay after the write instruction is at the head of the history buffer, but this delay will not change the order of the instruction retirement.

The PowerPC 606 is an example of a processor that uses a history buffer (called a *completion buffer*) to schedule writes to memory in order to preserve in-order retirement [BURG94]. This history buffer can schedule up to five instructions at a time and can retire up to two instructions in one clock.

The DEC Alpha provides an instruction for serialization of memory operations that is required only in multiprocessor systems. This instruction **MB** has the following operation. "Guarantee that all subsequent loads or stores will not access memory until after all previous loads and stores have accessed memory, as observed by other processors." This processor provides minimum support for precise interrupts, only retirement and serialization instructions.

9.1.3 *Handling Following Instructions*

The instructions following the saved program counter can be handled in one of four ways, as shown in Table 9.1: retire, abandon, undo, or save. The method chosen depends upon the design of the instruction set (whether or not there are early state changes), the method by which the interrupted program will be resumed, and the desired latency in responding to interrupts. Early state changes are changes to the processor state that occur before an instruction is released. An example is the pre-auto increment addressing mode of the VAX architecture. Early state changes are usually side effects to the executing instructions.

Before discussing the four methods for handling following instructions, the methods for resuming the execution of the interrupted program will be discussed. After an interrupt is serviced by the interrupt service routine or trap handler, the *return* instruction restores the processor state, and in some cases the process and the program control returns to the interrupted program. Note that some internal interrupts do not return due to the seriousness of the event causing the interrupt. The steps for returning from an interrupt are determined by the way the criteria for ensuring precise interrupts are implemented in the pipeline.

There are two methods for returning from the interrupt and resuming execution of the interrupted program: *continuation* and *restart*. One or the other of these methods can be used in conjunction with the method of handling following instructions, to be discussed in this section. Design implications of these two methods include the quantity of state that must be saved with continuation and for processors with early state changes and the amount of work required to undo the side effects.

The details of continuation and restart at the microprogrammed level for the MC68020 are thoroughly discussed in [MACG83]. Note that, because the MC68020 is a microprogrammed implementation of a serial execution model machine, an instruction can be interrupted during the execution of an instruction. Thus, the design of the micromachine must address continuation or restart of microinstructions that are interpreting macroinstructions.

Continuation implies that all of the instructions that have not been retired will be continued in execution from the point where they are interrupted. In the context of a pipelined processor, this means that the state of all partially processed instructions must be saved and then restored when these instructions are continued.

Continuation is illustrated with reservation tables at the top of Figure 9.15. Assume that an external interrupt occurs during t_3. Instruction 1 will successfully complete, and its result is written into the register file at t_4. The state associated with instructions 2 and 3 is saved and the interrupt processed. The state of these two instructions is then restored to the pipeline and processing resumes. Note that the three in-

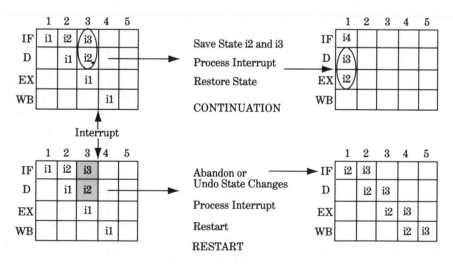

FIGURE 9.15 Continuation and restart.

structions may be restored to the pipeline one step earlier than shown in this diagram depending on implementation details.

As the state of instructions i2 and i3 are saved, the saved program counter is for i4 as this is the next instruction that will be fetched from memory. The value of the program counter is saved as part of the saved state of these instructions.

Restart implies that all of the instructions that have not been retired will be restarted, that is, refetched. In the context of a pipelined processor this means that any early state changes or side effects made by the partially-processed following instructions must be undone. If there are no state changes, the following instructions are abandoned.

With restart, shown in Figure 9.15, i2 and i3 are abandoned or, if there any early state changes or side effects, are undone before the interrupt handler is executed. As a consequence, it is as if these instructions were never fetched and partially processed. The saved program counter is for i2; to restart the interrupted process, i2 is fetched anew. The design issues associated with undoing the state for restart are directly related to the nature of the instruction set architecture.

Restart is used if the following instructions are allowed to run to completion, as discussed in the following section. For this case, the save program counter would be for i4 as that instruction is the next fetched after the interrupt handler has run.

Complete Following Instructions

The simplest method for ensuring the correct modification of the processor state is to let the complete pipeline flush after the receipt of an interrupt. The saved program counter is the program counter value $+1$ of the last instruction fetched and processed to retirement. In other words, with this saved program counter, all of the instructions in the pipeline become preceding instructions and are run to retirement as described in Section 9.1.2.

This technique for handling following instructions cannot be used for exceptions such as page faults, illegal op-codes, and internal interrupts. Instructions with these problems cannot execute correctly and run to retirement. In addition, external interrupts must be masked off so as not to interrupt the flushing process. Another problem with this technique is deciding how to handle branches that are in the pipeline when the interrupt occurs. If the branch is predicted to be taken, is the target path followed? What happens if the prediction is incorrect? Despite these problems, this technique works well for most external interrupts. For short pipelines, the latency is only a few clock cycles. However, the latency is variable and can be quite long if interrupt events such as cache misses are allowed after the flush process begins.

Abandon Following Instructions

For processors that do not have early state changes, the interrupted instruction and saved program counter can be any pipeline stage that is consistent with the type of interrupt. All of the instructions that have passed this stage will flush and be retired while those that have not passed this stage are abandoned. An example of this design is found in the MIPS R4000 with the location of the interrupted instruction shown in Table 9.2. Because there are no early state changes with this processor, regardless of the interrupt type, the following instructions can be abandoned.

Contemporary microprocessor architectures, like the R4000, are explicitly designed to eliminate early side effects in-order to simplify interrupt as well as branch handling. Specifically, if all state changes (write back, setting of condition codes and updating the program counter) are restricted to the last stage of the pipeline (in-order for multiple execution units), then all instructions, except the one retiring, become following instructions and can be abandoned [VENK90].

Undo Following Instructions

For processors designed with a complex instruction set and intended to execute in the serial execution model, early state changes and side effects are the norm. If the early state changes can be undone, the interrupted program can be restarted from the interrupted instruction. A number of techniques for undoing early state changes and side effects of following instructions have been used in real processors. These are

1. simple stage changes,
2. instruction undo.

Simple State Changes. If there is only one instance of a resource whose state can be changed only once during the execution of an instruction, it is only necessary to record that the state has been changed. Upon an interrupt, these side effects can be undone to restore the state for restart.

For example, if there is only one index register and only an auto increment address modification to that index register, then the side effect can be undone by decrementing the index register. The PDP-11 [VENK90] uses this technique to save address register changes, and the interrupt service routine has the responsibility of undoing the side effects. For this reason, the code that undoes the side effects must be executed, as a minimum, before control can revert back to the interrupted program.

VAX 8600 Instruction Undo. The problem with complex architectures such as the VAX is that the processor has more than one instance

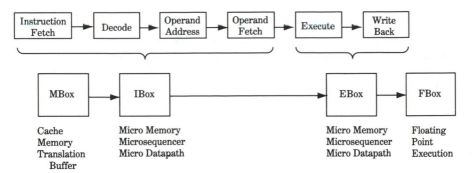

FIGURE 9.16   VAX 8600 pipeline.

of a resource class. That is, there are a number of general-purpose registers (16, 32 bits) that can be used for addressing and are subject to modification by side effects. In addition, there may be more than one side effect that impacts them during the execution of a series of instructions.

A very high level block diagram of the VAX 8600 is shown in Figure 9.16 [DERO85, FOSS85]. The processor can be viewed as a pipeline that consists of six stages as shown. The first four stages are implemented in the IBox, while the last two stages are implemented in the EBox. In addition, there are the MBox and FBox. The IBox and EBox are microprograms controlled with interlocks between the two boxes. Only in very special cases does the six-stage pipeline flow smoothly with one clock per stage; rather the micromachines interpret the instructions as required and pass on the required information to the next stage or box. Naturally, the number of clocks required for each stage of interpretation varies from instruction to instruction.

To support the undoing of the following instructions, three program counters are maintained in the processor [DERO85].

1. *CPC* contains the address of the next operand specifier or op-code in the IBuffer.
2. *ISA* contains the starting address of the macroinstruction that the operand fetch stage is currently processing.
3. *ESA* contains the starting address of the macroinstruction being processed by the EBox or FBox.

In addition, a *register log* maintains a log of register side effects that must be undone for the following instructions. When instructions in the pipeline must be undone, the micromachines execute a microprogram that performs this task at each stage. The register log and three program counters provide the information about how many instructions must have state changes undone and the exact steps to take. Consider the case of the auto increment addressing mode. The IBox may have incremented three registers or the same register three times. To undo these changes, old values of address registers are saved along with the addresses of the instructions for which the addresses were changed. When an interrupt occurs, microcode can identify the last instruction retired in-order and proceed to undo the state changes or side effects of following instructions, a very complex and time-consuming operation.

Save Following Instructions

Instead of undoing the state changes of the following instructions, the state can be saved in anticipation of restarting the interrupted program. A major design issue is the amount of state to be saved and where to save it. The state to be saved can be all or a subset of the architected and implemented registers and is not an isolated decision as the need for old state information by the interrupt handler must be considered. An extreme case is that none of the architected register state is saved. In this case, the interrupt handler must save enough register state so as to give it space for its task. After executing the body of the interrupt handler, the interrupt handler then must restore the state of the saved registers. Some implemented registers such as the register renaming map and cache mode control registers may not need to be saved automatically since these registers can be saved by the interrupt handler. On the other hand, the pipeline that contains the PC values may need to be saved, as would any tags or flags associated with dependency detection and resolution.

The complete design issue of what state to save is outside the scope of this book and is greatly complicated with pipeline processors and processors with a large amount of implemented state. However, where the state is saved is of concern to us here. Saving the architected state is usually provided by some automatic mechanism, while saving the implemented state is usually done with instructions that execute in the interrupt handler—for example, instructions that store and load the virtual memory maps. These maps may have been changed by the executing program subsequent to their being loaded into the processor; thus they must be saved. There are a number of possibilities for the locations needed to save state, as discussed below.

Memory resident stacks. It may be convenient to push the saved state onto a special stack in memory. The use of a stack permits any number of interrupts to be stacked, within the limits of allocated memory. Stacks for state changing have been used in a number of processors such as the MC68030, MC68040, and i386. If the state saved in a memory stack is voluminous, the latency of interrupt service can become quite long. Further, there can be interrupts during the saving process due to bus and/or memory errors. These errors are mitigated by using an unmapped, noncached region of memory for the stack.

A degenerate form of stack is the use of *shadow registers* [MOTO90]. Each architected and implemented register has a one-level stack that always saves the contents of the register from the last clock period. One level of state is always saved with little or no time overhead, and the chip area for the shadow registers is an acceptable price. However, with only one level of stack, only one level of interrupt can be processed. The MC88110 is an example of a processor that uses shadow registers for saving state on interrupts.

The use of an *auxiliary processor* is suggested by [KELL75]. Another type of space for state saving is found in virtual memory applications of the MC68000—a processor that does not support page faults. For these systems, two processors are used, one executing the main program, the other the page fault handler. When a page fault occurs, the processor is placed in a wait state while the other processor handles the page fault. Thus state is saved in the main processor's registers.

Saving old values. A method for saving state works by means of check pointing [HWU87]. This method stores the state of the machine at periodic intervals and, if an exception occurs, then the state of the machine can be restored to the checkpoint.

Hwu and Patt describe this method as well as specific algorithms for check pointing registers, memory, and implemented registers. As they described it, check pointing is also a useful technique for restoring the machine state on miss predicted branches. We should note that the use of shadow registers is a form of checkpoint that checkpoints on every clock.

9.2 Performance and Cost of Precise Interrupts

Some performance information on the processors that have precise interrupts is given in Section 9.1.2. In addition, Wang and Emnett [WANG93] provide information on the performance and cost of ensuring precise interrupts. In their paper, they evaluate five of the methods for handling preceding instructions discussed above. The evaluation consists of estimating the gate count, leading to the chip size and the number of cycles required to execute five programs. The base processor has an RSR(a) to schedule the result bus and register file but does not provide for precise interrupts. Table 9.6 shows the complexity estimates of the five design options for precise interrupts, while Table 9.7 shows the normalized chip size and speedup obtained by simulation.

These results closely follow the performance results presented earlier in Tables 9.3 and 9.4 except for the Sohi data of Figure 9.5 that indicate

Method	Subunits and Complexity
Base machine	RSR(a), 4 bits per entry
Result shift register (a)	RSR(b), 20 bits per entry
Reorder buffer	RSR(a), 6 bits per entry
	+ Reorder buffer, 38 bits per entry
History register file	RSR(a), 11 bits per entry
	+ History register file, 37 bits per entry
Future register file	RSR(a), 6 bits per entry
	+ Reorder buffer, 38 bits per entry
	+ Future register file, 16 bits per entry

TABLE 9.6   Description of evaluated methods for handling preceding instructions.

Method	Normalized Size	Speedup
Base machine	1	1
Result shift register (b)	1.042	0.81
Reorder buffer	1.148	0.83
History register file	1.148	0.85
Future register file	1.457	0.85

TABLE 9.7   Normalized chip size and speedup for handling preceding instructions.

the inclusion of a register update unit improves the performance of a base machine. However, Wang and Emnett [WANG93] did not evaluate a register update unit, so no conclusions on this point can be drawn.

The excessive cost, in size, of a processor with a future file may indicate why there are no implementations known to me. And, as the history file can do double duty in restoring the order of incorrectly predicted branches, its cost of around 15% does not seem excessive. The cost and performance of a reorder buffer is reasonable, and it is used on the Intel P6 and the AMD K5 processors.

9.3 Precise Interrupt Comments

There have been various taxonomies proposed for classifying instruction issue, release, and retirement policies of pipelined processors. One of these taxonomies is by [JOHN91]. This taxonomy uses the terms issue for release and completion for retire. Combinatorics gives four cases.

Case 1. In-order release, in-order retire. This case is typified by a simple processor with a Type A window design and one execution unit pipeline.

Case 2. In-order release, out-of-order retire. The requirements of this case are met by a processor with a Type C window design and two or more execution unit pipelines of unequal length.

Case 3. Out-of-order release, out-of-order retire. This case is typified by a processor with a Type B window design with one execution pipeline or a Type D or E window design with more than one execution unit of unequal length.

Case 4. Out-of-order release, in-order retire. This case is not cited by [JOHN91] but is noted here for completeness. This case is not normal because out-of-order release and nonequal length execution units guarantee that many operations will retire out-of-order.

As discussed previously, all interrupt types are not handled the same way in a particular processor design; the three requirements for a precise interrupt are implemented differently. Unfortunately, manufacturer documentation does not provide enough information to taxonomize completely the interrupt-handling technique for all interrupt types. The following paragraphs present some general discussion on the implementation issues of the three types of interrupts.

External interrupts are the most straightforward to handle and are discussed first. In essence, the designer designates a stage in the pipeline that will be the interrupted instruction and the saved program counter. By combinatorics from Table 9.1, there are twelve possible design options. However, the use of a RSR(b) to ensure in-order retirements of preceding instructions is not viewed as a viable option due to its poor performance. Thus, this option is not considered, leaving eight possible design options.

Internal interrupts are interrupt events that result from anomalous actions in the pipeline. Examples are arithmetic exceptions, illegal opcodes, and parity errors in the register files. In some processor implementations, these interrupt events will result in imprecise interrupts.

Because of the difficulty of implementing precise internal interrupts, the DEC Alpha [DEC92a] provides an instruction that will place the processor in the serial execution model mode so that these interrupt events can be isolated and diagnosed if they occur. This instruction, TRAPB, "stalls instruction issuing until all prior instructions are guaranteed to complete without incurring arithmetic traps." A discussion of serialization instructions for the RS/6000 is found in Section 8.4 and in [IBM90a]. While these instructions are not provided for the support of precise interrupts, they are illustrative of the serialization instructions that are required for highly concurrent processors.

Other processors will record the interrupt event and continue processing until a later time when the system will determine what has happened. These techniques result in either a loss of performance or imprecise interrupts or both.

Software interrupts are events that are explicitly caused by the executing program. These interrupt events are also called program interrupts, software interrupts, procedure calls, and traps. Internal interrupts call for a context switch and differ from branches in that the

Processor	Preceding Instructions	Following Instructions	Restart or Continuation
MC68020, 30, 40	To retirement	No early state changes*	C
i 80386, 486	To retirement	Saved on stack	C
i Pentium	To retirement	To retirement	R
VAX 8600	Complete memory accesses	Undo all side effects for restart	R
R4000	To retirement	No early state changes	R
DEC Alpha	To retirement	No hardware support	–
SPARC	Implementation dependent	No early state changes	R
RS/6000	To retirement	Undo with shadow stack	R
PowerPC 601	To retirement	No early state changes	R
MC88100	Shadowed (1 level), memory to retirement	Shadowed (1 level)	C
MC88110	Last to retirement, other results restored by history buffer	No early state changes	C

*Assumption, documentation is not clear.

TABLE 9.8 Instruction handling.

program counter and other state are saved so that the originating program execution can be resumed. In general, the interrupting instruction is detected at the decode stage of the pipéline.

The MC88110 provides an example of the nonuniform treatment of interrupt types. Because of the added complexity of more than one level of shadow registers, all interrupts are not precise. Data memory accesses and floating point instructions may have imprecise interrupts. Recovery and restart from these interrupts is a software task. With only one level of shadow registers, an interrupt routine cannot be interrupted.

To my knowledge, no processors are being designed today with early side effects, and microcode is not used. Thus the method of undoing early state changes used in the VAX 8600 is not employed. However, multiple EUs are common and provisions for restoring in-order retirement must be provided if precise interrupts are supported. Because of the large quantity of state found in a modern microprocessor, many recent designs use the restart method.

A summary of methods for handling the instructions before and after the interrupted instruction is provided in Table 9.8, which is taken from Walker [WALK92]. For all of the example processors, internal and software interrupted instructions do not complete; the external interrupted instruction does complete.

10

Enhanced Implementations

10.0 Overview

In the last decade, there has been intense research into improving the performance of a processor above the limit imposed by issuing one instruction per clock. Three general approaches to improving performance by enhancing the implementation are found in the notions of *superpipelining, superscalar,* and *very long instruction word* (VLIW) processors. Studies comparing these three approaches are found in [JOUP89, JOUP89a], while Johnson describes the design issues of superscalar processors in great detail [JOHN89, JOHN91]. Industrial designs of superscalar and superpipelined processors were well underway in the late 1980s with product announcements in 1991–1992. The terms used above can be informally defined as follows.

Superpipelining (SP) is a technique of dividing the major stages of a pipeline into substages [JOUP89]. Also, a superpipelined processor is one in which the clock period is set by the execution unit with the smallest simplest operational latency.

Superscalar (SS) is a technique that allows concurrent execution of instructions in the same pipeline stage as well as concurrent execution of instructions in different pipeline stages [JOHN91].

Very long instruction word (VLIW) is a technique that requires the compiler to assemble a group of sequential instructions into a single long instruction that is then released to multiple execution units.

Other terms used in this chapter include the following.

Simple operational latency (SOL) is "the time (in cycles) until the result of an instruction is available for use as an operand in a subsequent instruction" [JOUP89a]. For $SOL = 1$, a second instruction, even with a true dependency, can release in the next clock with a delay of zero cycles.

Instruction level parallelism (ILP) is the number of instructions that can be in simultaneous execution. Instruction level parallelism is determined inversely by the number of true dependencies, the number of branches, and the branch strategies [JOHN91]. See Tables 10.10 and 10.11 for examples of ILP.

In order to compare the performance gains that can be obtained from an enhanced implementation, Jouppi [JOUP89a] defines a *base machine* with the following characteristics.

1. One instruction per cycle can be released.
2. Simple operational latency is one cycle.
3. Instruction level parallelism needed to fully utilize processor is one.

The defined base machine is a four-stage pipeline ($n = 4$) that is similar to the pipeline shown in Figure 6.8 but without a memory read/write stage; thus, only register type operations are considered. The four stages are: (1) instruction fetch, (2) decode and register reads, (3) execution, and (4) write back.

The execution time of simple instructions, a register add for instance, determines the clock period of the base machine. The partition of the pipeline is similar to design E of Figure 8.15 with register reads in the decode stage and register writes in the write back stage. This pipeline is different from, for example, the MIPS I, which has the register reads, execution, and write back in the same stage [MIPS87]. The MIPS I is considered to be underpipelined because this stage could be further subdivided.

10.1 Superpipelined Processors

Jouppi [JOUP89a] expands the informal definition given above of superpipelining with the following list of characteristics, wherein the parameter π is the *degree of superpipelining*.

1. Instructions released per cycle   1.
2. Machine cycle time (clock period) $1/\pi$ of base machine cycle.
3. Simple operational latency π cycles.
4. ILP to utilize the pipeline fully π.

Superpipelining is based on subdividing the pipeline stages into a larger number of shorter stages. Thus, this design process is similar to that of finding the optimum pipeline length as described in Chapter 6 and in Figures 6.3 and 6.4. Unfortunately, superpipelining is a *relative term*. One cannot look at a processor and say it is or is not superpipelined. One can only compare two processors and say that one has a higher degree of superpipeling than the other. The definition of superscalar does not have this problem.

10.1.1 *Elementary Performance Model*

The models to be developed here assume the theoretical ability to subdivide the pipeline stages without limit. However, note that subdividing pipeline stages is not a simple task and some stages cannot be subdivided in the world of a real design. Thus, as described in Chapter 6, the stage that has the longest delay sets the clock period of the pipeline. In addition, the models assume that parallelism is limited only by branch delays; true dependencies are not considered. The influence of clock skew and setup time are not considered in this model but are addressed in Section 10.3.

This section presents the derivation of an elementary performance model that compares the performance of superpipelined processors to the base machine. The performance models will be compared to the simulation results of [JOUP89a].

Figure 10.1 shows the reservation table for the base machine and a superpipelined version of degree $\pi = 2$ that process the same run of

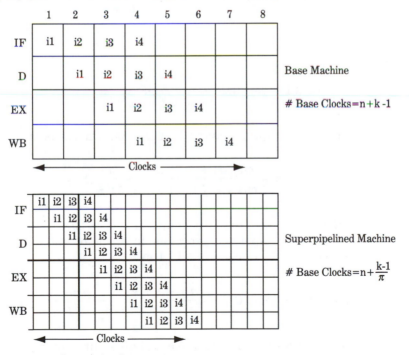

FIGURE 10.1 Superpipeline.

instructions with $k = 4$. Note that each of the four stages of the base machine are subdivided into two stages. The superpipelined machine is now eight stages long with a clock period equal to half that of the base machine. An execution takes two cycles ($SOL = 2$), which means that functions such as integer add are now pipelined.

A very simple branch strategy model is used for these models. That is, a taken branch requires that the pipeline is flushed and a not-taken branch has zero delay. The number of base clock cycles is the normalizing function for comparing the two machines. The figure of merit for making the comparisons is Instructions per Clock (IPC) in addition to the CPI measure used elsewhere in this book. As noted previously, the models do not consider true dependencies or clock distribution. From Figure 10.1, the number of base clock cycles required to execute the program on the two machines is

$$\text{for the base machine} \quad \text{base clocks } (B) = n + k - 1,$$

$$\text{for the superpipelined machine} \quad \text{base clocks } (SP) = n + \frac{k-1}{\pi}.$$

$$\text{IPC, Base, } (SP) = \frac{k}{n + (k-1)/\pi}.$$

And CPI is

$$\text{CPI, Base, } (SP) = \frac{1}{\pi} + \frac{1}{k}\left(n - \frac{1}{\pi}\right).$$

The speedup of the superpipelined over the base machine is

$$\text{speedup} = \frac{\text{clocks}(B)}{\text{clocks}(SP)} = \frac{n + k - 1}{n + (k-1)/\pi}.$$

As $k \to \infty$, speedup $\to \pi$. As $\pi \to \infty$, speedup $\to 1 + (k-1)/n$.

The CPI of the superpipelined processor in terms of its clocks, not the base clocks, is derived from Figure 10.1 as

$$\text{CPI, superpipelined, } (SP) = \frac{n\pi - 1 + k}{k} = 1 + \frac{n\pi - 1}{k}.$$

As noted above, these models assume a simple but poor branching strategy. A more reasonable model assumes that the delay at the end of a sequence of length k is d base machine cycles, where d is the delay of a taken branch with a not-taken branch having zero delay. Refer to Chapter 7 for methods for determining branch delays and the value of d. Speedup can be determined from the reservation table of Figure 10.1. The branch delay d is used rather than $n = 1$, then

$$\text{speedup} \approx \frac{d + k}{d + k/\pi}.$$

The speedup limits are as $k \to \infty$, speedup $\to \pi$; as $\pi \to \infty$, speedup $\to 1 + k/d$.

For example, if $d = 1$, $k = 6$, and $\pi = 4$, the maximum speedup of a superpipelined processor over the base machine is $S = 2.8$. The limit speedup for large values of π is $S = 7$.

10.1.2 *A Refined Model*

Simply put, the problem of determining the degree of superpipelining is that of modeling the effects of branch delays, true dependencies, clock skew, and setup time to find the optimum number of stages.

This section develops a pipeline performance model for evaluating performance as the stages of the pipeline are subdivided. The model considers not only branch and dependency delays but the clock skew and setup time as well. Recall from Chapter 6 how clock skew and setup time influence the optimum length of a pipeline. This model assumes that the number of stages in the execution unit are fractions of the length of the pipeline, not the degree of superpipelining. That is, the simple operational latency, SOL, is equal to the execution unit length, E, of Section 8.5, and is a fraction of the total pipeline length, n.

$$SOL = E = r \times n$$

where r is the fraction of the total pipeline length that is the execution unit.

The model assumes that the output of the execution unit is also the stage at which branches are resolved. The time per instruction, in gate delays, is

$$\text{time/inst.} = \text{TPI} = \text{clock period (in gate delays)} \times \text{CPI};$$

$$\text{TPI} = \left(\frac{L}{n} + t\right)(1 + P_b\text{WABD} + \text{Max}(0, P_0(E - 1)) + \text{Max}(0, P_1(E - 2))).$$

This model is used to evaluate changes in performance with an example workload and various values of n and t. The simple predict taken strategy is used for WABD; WABD $= P_{bt}(n-1)$. The parameters assumed for this example are

$$L = 128, \qquad r = 0.25,$$
$$P_b = 0.3, \qquad P_1 = 0.1,$$
$$P_{bt} = 0.6, \qquad P_0 = 0.2.$$

The result of this evaluation is shown in Table 10.1 for $t = 2, \ldots, 12$ and $n = 2, \ldots, 19$. The time per instruction is measured in gate delays. The first thing to observe from the data is how the optimum length (minimum time) of the pipeline varies for the various values of t. The optimum lengths are indicated by bold highlighting. Notice that the optimum pipeline length increases and the time per instruction decreases for smaller values of t; results are expected in light of the model developed in Chapter 6. Also note the spreading of the optimum point as t decreases. For small values of t, the optimum is very shallow, giving the designer greater latitude in selecting the design point.

Consider the design options for redesigning a base machine pipeline with $n = 4$ and $t = 10$ to a superpipelined version by lengthening the pipeline. As shown in Table 10.1, the base machine has TPI $= 65$ gate delays, distinguished by an underline. Superpipelining can, at best, decrease the TPI to 63 gate delays by increasing the number of stages to five or six. This improvement is approximately 3%, hardly worth the effort, and is probably within the estimating accuracy of the mode.

If the base machine can be reimplemented in a technology that will give $t = 2$, the TPI decreases to 52, also underlined, which is a significant improvement of approximately 20% achieved without any change in the number of pipeline stages. If superpipelining is now applied to this design, the TPI can be decreased further to 44 with $n = 8$. These two design changes, $t = 2$ and $n = 8$, give a performance improvement over the base machine of 32%.

These two examples illustrate the fact that the degree of superpipelining that will increase performance over a base machine is critically dependent upon the technology available for distributing clock pulses as well as the setup time of the registers. Another way of looking at this issue is to observe that as the number of pipeline stages increases, t becomes a larger and larger overhead for each clock pulse. This overhead represents dormant processing time and a loss of efficiency in the pipeline.

No. of Stages	$t = 2$	$t = 4$	$t = 6$	$t = 8$	$t = 10$	$t = 12$
2	78	80	83	85	87	90
3	61	63	66	69	72	74
4	52	55	59	62	65	68
5	49	52	56	59	63	67
6	47	51	55	59	63	67
7	45	50	54	59	63	68
8	44	49	54	59	64	69
9	44	49	55	60	66	71
10	44	50	56	62	68	74
11	44	50	57	63	70	76
12	44	51	58	65	72	79
13	44	52	59	67	74	82
14	44	52	60	68	76	84
15	45	53	62	70	79	87
16	45	55	63	72	81	90
17	46	56	64	74	83	93
18	46	57	66	76	86	99
19	46	57	67	78	88	102

TABLE 10.1   Superpipeline TPI (gates).

10.1.3 *Superpipeline Design Issues*

Superpipelining is a well-established concept. The CDC 7600 is a classic example of superpipelining as the execution units are pipelined, unlike its predecessor the CDC 6600. The length of the longest path through a CDC 7600 consists of the three IPU stages (plus four stages to access instructions if they are in memory) and six EU stages for a total of nine stages. The clock period of this machine is 27.5 ns, and it was first delivered in 1969.

The performance models clearly indicate that there is an optimum number of pipeline stages that, I believe, should be the definition of superpipelining. With the early development of RISC ideas, short pipelines were viewed as a virtue because of the anticipated performance loss from branch delays and dependencies with long pipelines. Precise interrupts are assured by having all state changes in the last stage. As a consequence of these design decisions, early RISC processors generally have four to five pipeline stages with a relatively long clock period.

Superpipelining advocates advance the argument that RISC pipelines are too short and clock periods are too long. Pipelines should be divided into more stages than they are in current practice. A number of papers [EMMA87, DUBE90, KUNK86] support, but do not advocate, this view. The position advanced by the advocates of longer pipelines is based, in part, upon the following arguments.

1. Branch delays can be almost eliminated by BTBs and BTCs.
2. Large register files can reduce the delays of anti- and output dependencies.
3. Short circuiting can reduce the delays of true dependencies.
4. Precise interrupts can be provided by no early state changes.

These arguments are far from convincing, and longer pipelines, except for the R4000, are almost universally used in conjunction with superscalar implementations. In other words, superpipelining is usually not used alone.

10.1.4 *Current Example of Superpipelining*

In 1991, the Hewlett-Packard Corporation announced a processor, the HP Apollo 9000 Series 700, said to provide greater performance than the IBM RS/6000 [SLAT91]. The press coverage indicated that this processor is superpipelined. However, this is not the case. The pipeline is five stages, and the operand reads and writes are separated from the execute stage. The primary contributor to its performance advantage over the RS/6000 is an increase in clock rate from 30 MHz to 50 MHz [SLAT91].

To my knowledge, there is only one example of pure superpipelining outside the supercomputer domain—the MIPS R4000. This processor, which was announced in 1991, is a superpipelined version of the R3000. The two pipeline organizations are shown in Figure 10.2. The R3000, which operates at 50 MHz, is a relatively conventional pipeline of five

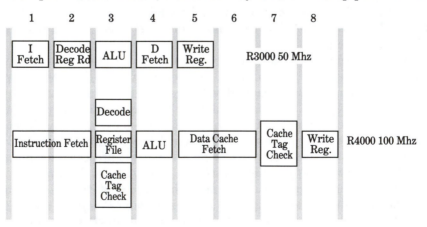

FIGURE 10.2   R3000 and R4000 pipelines.

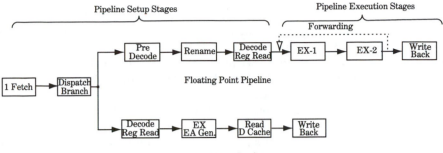

FIGURE 10.3 RS/6000 pipeline.

stages. The R4000 operates at 100 MHz, one-half the clock period of the R3000, while subdividing the instruction and data cache fetch cycles (described in Chapter 2).

For both the R3000 and R4000, the fixed point execution unit is one pipeline stage and, with short circuiting, there are no true dependency delays. Note the concurrency of decode, register file fetch, and cache tag check that give speculative register fetch and instruction decoding. If the tags do not check, the other two functions are abandoned with no ill effects because no state changes have occurred. All branches are resolved in the ALU stage.

Published performance data on these two processors indicate that there is no significant advantage in this particular superpipelined implementation [SLAT91]. The CPI of the R3000 is reported to be 1.25, while the CPI of the R4000 is 2 to 2.5. Doubling the CPI while halving the clock period (20 ns to 10 ns) yields no gain in performance. I believe that there are extended capabilities in the R4000 that justify its introduction over its raw performance.

There has been a dramatic change in direction at MIPS. The replacement for the R4000 is a superscalar processor; superpipelining has been abandoned. The topology of this new processor is noted in Table 10.4.

The IBM RS/6000 is a superpipelined implementation for floating point instructions and superscalar as well: see Figure 10.3. It is interesting to note that the IBM RS/6000 floating point pipeline is eight stages and has $SOL = E = 2$. The total length of the floating point instruction pipeline is eight stages, which is probably close to optimum. This is not the case for integer operations with pipeline lengths of six.

10.2 Superscalar Processors

Superscalar processors are receiving attention because they have the potential to improve performance without some of the high-frequency clock problems of superpipelined processors. An early reference to the possibility of issuing more than one instruction per clock is found in [ANDE67]. The designers of the IBM S/360/91 considered and rejected this idea because it "leads to a rapid expansion of hardware and complexity." Tjaden and Flynn [TJAD70] provide the first analysis of multiple instruction issue along with an analysis of dependencies and register renaming. Agerwala and Cocke revived this idea and compared dual instruction issue with a vector processor [AGER87]. It appears that they are the first to use the term *superscalar*. The benefits of a superscalar implementation seem very attractive, and a number of superscalar processors have recently been introduced: the IBM RS/6000, Motorola 88110, PowerPC 601, and Intel Pentium.

Joupi [JOUP89a] expands the informal definition of superscalar with the list of characteristics below. The *degree of superscalar, σ,* which is the number of instruction decoders in a superscalar processor, is another way of expressing the degree [JOHN90].

1. Instructions released per cycle σ.
2. Machine cycle time   1 base machine cycle.
3. Simple operational latency   1 cycle.
4. ILP to utilize the pipeline fully σ.

This definition of superscalar implies that there are σ copies of all of the stages of the base machine, a topology called *uniform superscalar*. While nonuniform superscalar implementations are more common and are discussed later, uniform superscalar ideas are useful for performance modeling purposes.

10.2.1 *Elementary Performance Model*

Figure 10.4 shows the reservation table of a uniform superscalar processor of degree 2; the reservation table of the base machine of Figure 10.1 is not repeated here. The reservation table shows the processing of the same four-instruction workload used in Figure 10.1.

Because two instructions can be issued in the same clock, the alignment of instructions can influence the performance that is actually achieved. For $\sigma = 2$, there are two cases of instruction alignment as shown in Figure 10.4 and discussed further below. Note that for any σ, there are σ alignment cases.

The alignment of the first instruction in the instruction sequence can influence the number of clocks required to process the sequence. In Figure 10.4 Case (a), the first instruction is aligned but is not aligned in Case (b).

We derive the model for the number of clocks required to process

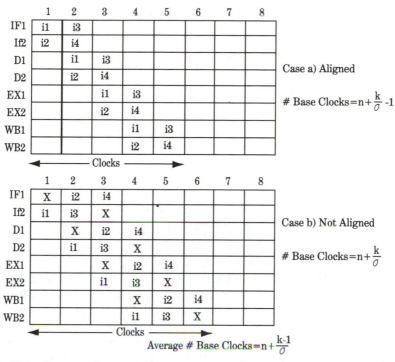

FIGURE 10.4 Superscalar processor.

the instruction sequence by enumerating all of the alignment cases for values of σ, k, and n and assuming equal probability ($1/\sigma$) for each starting alignment. In the example of Figure 10.4, the parameters $\sigma = 2$, $k = 4$, and $n = 4$ are illustrated. Note that this model does not consider the effects of clock skew and setup time because the clock period does not change with superscalar designs. The number of base cycles needed to process a sequence of instructions is

$$\text{base cycles (aligned case)} = n + \frac{k}{\sigma} - 1,$$

$$\text{base cycles (not aligned case)} = n + \frac{k-1}{\sigma},$$

$$\text{weighted average base cycles} = \frac{1}{\sigma}\left(n + \frac{k}{\sigma} - 1\right) + \left(1 - \frac{1}{\sigma}\right)\left(n + \frac{k}{\sigma}\right)$$

$$= n + \frac{k-1}{\sigma} \text{ base cycles.}$$

The number of instructions per clock, IPC(SS), is

$$\text{IPC}(SS) = \frac{k}{n + (k-1)/\sigma}$$

And the clocks per instruction, CPI(SS), is

$$\text{CPI}(SS) = \frac{1}{\sigma} + \frac{1}{k}\left(n - \frac{1}{\sigma}\right).$$

The speedup over the base machine is

$$\text{speedup} = \frac{n + k - 1}{n + (k-1)/\sigma}.$$

As $k \to \infty$, speedup $\to \sigma$. As $\sigma \to \infty$, speedup $\to 1 + (k-1)/n$.

Note that the predicted performance of this model is identical to the superpipelined model for $\sigma = \pi$. Also note that performance is improved if the first instruction in a sequence is aligned. Jouppi [JOUP89] states that "the superpipelined machine actually has less performance than the superscalar machine." This statement is true only if the first instruction of a sequence is always aligned in the superscalar machine. The effect of alignment is illustrated by the following example.

Consider the examples used above: $n = 4$, $k = 4$, and $\sigma = \pi = 2$. The probability of alignment will vary from 0 (not aligned) to 1 (aligned). Table 10.2 shows the CPIs and the ratio of the CPIs between the two processors as the probability of alignment is varied.

This data indicates approximately a $\pm 10\%$ swing in performance, depending upon alignment. We will see later that even this difference is not as great when more realistic branching assumptions are made. The later discussion of the RS/6000 cache shows how alignment has been obtained in one contemporary superscalar processor.

I now give another formulation of the speedup model for all of the alignments possible for combinations of σ, k, and d. This model is developed by enumerating all of the possible cases of the starting alignments and by assigning an equal probability of occurrence to each case.

P. Alignment	CPI(SS)	CPI(SP)	Ratio SP/SS
0.0	1.500	1.375	0.92
0.5	1.375	1.375	1.0
1.0	1.250	1.375	1.1

TABLE **10.2**   Alignment effect on performance.

The total number of clocks for all alignments, as well as the total number of instructions for all alignments, is found. This model only comprehends the blocking of the decoders due to taken branches.

Consider again the following example: $\sigma = 2$ and $k = 4$. With $\sigma = 2$, there are only two possible alignments and assume that they are equally probable. For the first case, assume that $d = 0$ as shown below.

Clock	Alignment 1	Alignment 2
1	1 2	X 1
2	3 4	2 3
3	New sequence	4 X
4		New sequence

The total number of clocks, considering both alignments, is $2 + 3 = 5$; and the total number of instructions is $4 + 4 = 8$. The weighted average CPI is $5/8 = 0.625$. Consider the same example except assume that $d = 1$. For expository purposes, the branch delay requires full clock periods. For this case, the branch delays are clock 3 for alignment 1 and clock 4 for alignment 2.

Clock	Alignment 1	Alignment 2
1	1 2	X 1
2	3 4	2 3
3	d d	4 X
4	New sequence	d d
5		New sequence

For this case with $d = 1$, the total number of clocks is $3 + 4 = 7$, and the total number of instructions is $4 + 4 = 8$. The weighted average CPI is $7/8 = 0.875$. It can be shown from these two examples and from the enumeration of other values of σ, k, and d that the total number of clocks for all possible alignments is

$$\text{total number of clocks} = \sigma + k - 1 + \sigma d$$
$$= k - 1 + \sigma(d + 1).$$

As a check, consider the pipeline in Figure 10.4. For this example, $\sigma = 2$, $k = 4$, and $d = 3$. The total number of clocks, using the above equation and from Figure 10.4, is 11. We can also see that the total number of instructions executed for all of the alignments is total number of instructions $= \sigma k$.

Therefore, the CPI for a superscalar pipeline that has an equal probability for each of the possible alignments is

$$\text{CPI}(SS) = \frac{k - 1 + \sigma(d + 1)}{\sigma k} = \frac{1}{\sigma} + \frac{1}{k}\left(d + 1 - \frac{1}{\sigma}\right).$$

This model is identical to the superpipelined model developed from Figure 10.4 for $n = d + 1$. For a check of this model, consider the case where $\sigma = 1$ and the length of the pipeline $n = d + 1$ (remember that, from Chapter 6, the WABD for a simple freeze branch strategy is $d = n - 1$). For these conditions, CPI $= 1 + (n - 1)/k$. This model is also the same model for the freeze strategy developed in Chapter 6.

Smith [SMIT89] investigated the limit of decoding instructions, called *fetch limitation*, which is the rate at which instructions can be fetched and decoded. The measure of this rate limit is *instructions issued per clock* (IPC). Simulations are conducted on two superscalar pipelines having $\sigma = 2$ and $\sigma = 4$ and for instruction sequences of varying k. The taken branch delay, d, is set at one clock. A not-taken branch is assumed to have a delay of zero.

The CPI(SS) model provides results that closely approximate the simulation results. Table 10.3 tabulates the CPI for a superscalar machine with four instruction decoders (degree of superscalar, $\sigma = 4$), $d = 1$, and various values of k. The model results are compared to the simulation results of [SMIT89, Table 8]; the maximum error is less than 4% between the model and the simulations. The error is due, in part, to the fact that the starting alignment probabilities with a real-world processor and its workload are not all equal to $1/\sigma$, which is the assumption made for the model.

	$\sigma = 2$		$\sigma = 4$	
k	CPI [SMIT89]	CPI Model	CPI [SMIT89]	CPI Model
1	2.00	2.00	2.00	2.00
2	1.29	1.25	1.10	1.12
3	1.00	1.00	0.83	0.83
4	0.86	0.87	0.64	0.69
5	0.80	0.80	0.60	0.60
6	0.71	0.75	0.52	0.54
7	0.71	0.71	0.51	0.50
∞		0.50		0.25

TABLE 10.3 Superscalar CPI, Simulation versus Model.

Smith [SMIT89] makes the comment that the *fetch limitation* of the processor limits the speedup over a simple pipeline. The efficiency of instruction fetching is the reciprocal of CPI; thus, when CPI = 2, 50% of the fetched instructions are wasted due to branches. As shown in Table 10.3, extremely large values of k are required for the CPI to approach the asymptotic values of $1/\sigma$. Furthermore, other detail design issues can impose further limits that are discussed in the next section.

10.2.2 *Superscalar Design Issues*

There are three major superscalar design issues:

1. the topology of the processor, the number and types of execution units;
2. special caches or queues to reduce the latency of instruction and data fetches;
3. special treatment of the register file to support multiple references.

Conventional pipeline design considers these three design issues in the time domain, while superscalar is in the *space domain* as well as the *time domain*. The space domain is present because there are, in essence, a multiplicity of pipelines executing in parallel with the possibility of branches, dependencies, and interrupt effects crossing between the pipelines. For example, if instruction i is in pipeline 2 and instruction $i + 1$ is in pipeline 3 and there is a true dependency between i and $i + 1$; this dependency must be resolved between the pipelines. Some superscalar processors restrict the types of instructions that can be issued in one clock so as to simplify this and other problems. For example, the MC88110 cannot issue two loads in the same clock because there is only one load execution unit. In other words, structural hazards impose limits on the instruction issue combinations.

Superscalar Topology

There are two classes of superscalar processors: uniform and nonuniform. A uniform superscalar processor has every stage replicated to degree σ. On the other hand, a nonuniform superscalar processor will replicate to degree σ only the stages up to and including the decode stage. The execution stages are provided, singularly or replicated, based upon the statistics of the anticipated workload. As a consequence, some structural hazards with a reduction in processing rate can occur due to the lack of an execution resource. The degree of replication of ports to the register file is discussed later in this section. For a number of reasons, the pure uniform superscalar processor is not used in any known commercial superscalar processor.

I now describe, in simplified terms, the topology of a nonuniform

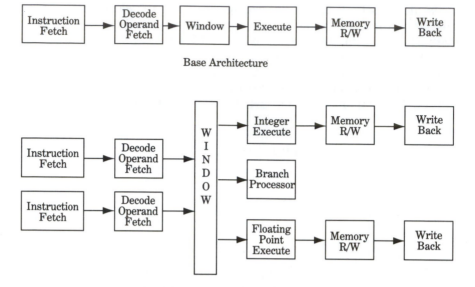

Base Architecture

Degree 2 Nonuniform Superscalar

FIGURE 10.5   Nonuniform superscalar topology.

superscalar processor, a machine that is not just σ pipelines operating in parallel. The IPU stages of the pipeline are of degree σ; downstream from the window there are enough execution units to satisfy the issue rate and the anticipated distribution of operations (for example, integer and floating point). The number and types of execution units on contemporary processors will be discussed later.

A block diagram of nonuniform topology is shown in Figure 10.5. As a point of reference, I have included the simple base machine of Figure 8.1 in this figure. The first two stages of this machine are duplicated: instructions are released through a window and distribution network to the execution units. The window designs can be variations of Type C, D, or E windows. The major difference is that σ instructions are issued, in-order, from the decoder.

As noted above, nonuniform superscalar processors are the most common with today's processors. Examples of the diversity of execution units are shown in Table 10.4.

Note that most of these processors have more execution units than the degree of superscalar. Thus there are specific instruction issue combinations that are legal. For example, the Pentium can issue two integer instructions, two floating point instructions, or one integer and one floating point instruction in one clock. The legal issue constraints help reduce the problem of structural hazards as an integer, and a floating point

Processor	σ	Execution Units
RS/6000	4	Integer, Flt. Pt. (Mpy, Add.) Branch, I/O
PowerPC 601	3	Integer, Flt. Pt. (Mpy, Add, Div.) Branch
Intel Pentium	2	2 Integer, Flt. Pt. Add, Flt. Pt. Mpy., Branch
Intel i860	2	Integer-Branch, Flt. Pt. Add, Flt. Pt. Mpy.
AMD-K5	4	Integer, Integer/shifter, Flt. Pt., Branch, Load/Store
MIPS-T5	4	2 Integer, Flt. Pt. Add, Flt. Pt. Mpy/Div/Sqrt, Load/Store
MC88110	2	2 Integer-Branch, Integer Mpy, Integer Div., Flt. Pt. Add, Load/Store, Bit Field, 2 Graphics

TABLE 10.4   Examples of superscalar topologies.

operation will not use the same result bus as the register files are disjoint.

Other design issues associated with superscalar processors are the same, although with major complications, as conventional pipelined processors. These design issues include the management of branching, dependency detection and resolution, and interrupts. Johnson [JOHN90] has an excellent treatment of all of the superscalar implementation design issues.

Instruction and Data Caches and Queues

A critical requirement for a superscalar processor is that instructions must be available with a one clock latency and a bandwidth of $1/\sigma$. This requirement can lead to significant complications in the design of the instruction cache. Instruction queues cope with the problem of multiple instruction issue quite well, as discussed in Chapter 2. There are two approaches to providing the required bandwidth in the instruction fetch stage. One approach uses a wide word cache, as with the RS/6000; the other approach is more temporal, using a high-speed queue that can be accessed from its side as with the Pentium and PowerPC 601.

Data caches must provide increased bandwidth into a register file that can be accessed by more than one execution unit. The latency of a data cache must be no more than one clock per access except when there is a cache miss. The tag memory of a data cache is multiple-ported for the number of execution unit access, I/O access, and, in some cases, instruction accesses. These instruction and data cache problems will be discussed in the context of specific processors.

IBM RS/6000. The IBM RS/6000 has a split cache: an instruction cache and a data cache. In Chapter 2, discussions on instruction caches made the implicit assumption that a processor fetches one instruction at a time. The RS/6000, however, can issue four instructions in a single clock period; thus, the instruction cache must provide a Quad Word (QW) in one clock cycle. Additionally, for performance reasons, the instructions should be aligned even though they are not aligned in the cache. The performance benefit of alignment is discussed earlier in this section.

A simple solution for the cache requirement uses four independent caches with the addresses interleaved across the caches. An access would read all four words in one cycle; the low-order address bits would be used for routing to the four pipelines. However, this approach will suffer inefficiencies due to the possible misalignments of instructions. The RS/6000 instruction cache builds on the simple approach of independent cache modules and fixes the alignment problem.

A block diagram of the RS/6000 instruction cache and the mapping of the block into the four modules of the cache is shown in Figure 10.6. This cache low-order interleaves four independent caches, and each cache is two-way set associative. Each of the four caches is organized as (256, 2, 1, 4) or 8K bytes total for the four caches [GROH90]. The cache block is 64 bytes, with 16 bytes being loaded into each of the four caches.

Because the 64-byte block is larger than four of the 4-byte blocks of each of the four caches, a block is loaded into four consecutive blocks of each cache. An example of a block allocation is shown in Figure 10.6, in which the 64-byte block is loaded into word addresses (4 Bytes) i through $i + 15$ of one set. The cache, set, and word are identified by the tuple (cache, set, word). The first instruction, i, is placed in (A, S1, 0); the second instruction, $i + 1$, is placed in (B, S1, 0); while the last instruction is placed in (D, S1, 3). This block load example assumes that the block is aligned; however, unaligned blocks can also be loaded.

Cache misses are detected when a reference into the tag directories fails, one directory for each set (not shown in Figure 10.6). However, these directories perform the usual function of comparing the block name to the entries in the tag directories and signaling a Hit or Miss as is normal for a late select cache.

A QW can be read from the cache in one cycle if the four words are aligned, that is, found in the same word locations of all four caches. However, if the QW is not aligned, two cache cycles would be required. For example, if the first three words of the QW are found in cache Word 255 and the last words of the QW are found in cache Word 256, as shown in Figure 10.6, a simple design would require two cycles to fetch the QW. This additional cycle is the price paid for nonaligned QWs.

However, for the nonaligned instructions illustrated by shading in Figure 10.6, we can assume that the index field of the cache address points to Word 255 of the caches. Alignment is provided by incrementing the index into Cache A so that the instruction in Word 256 of Cache A

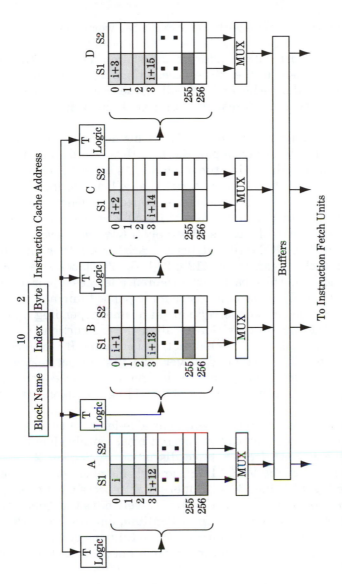

FIGURE 10.6 RS/6000 instruction cache.

485

is fetched in the same cycle with the other three words. The incrementers are indicated as "T logic" in the figure. The value of the increment added to the index is determined by address translation hardware that adds a very small increment to the cache access time. There is symmetry between accessing the cache and reloading the cache on a cache miss. The same T Logic and address mapping apply as described by Matick [MATI89].

Another situation applies if the QW spans not only two cache words but two sets as well. For example, the first three words may be held in one set with the fourth word in the other set. As a result, addresses must be processed through two tag directories that will adjust the indexes into the proper sets. The two directories are named the "Odd Directory" and "Even Directory." In this way, even if the QW spans two cache words and/or two sets, the cache can still supply a QW every cycle.

MC88110. The MC88110 instruction cache is a rather conventional late selected cache organized as (128, 2, 1, 8). The block size is 8 bytes or two instructions. Thus, each cache reference fetches a pair of instructions in one cycle. The instruction stream is pushed into a shift register that can decode one or two instructions at a time, depending upon some restrictions. There is no provision to align the instructions for normal issue as there is with the RS/6000 instruction cache. If a branch target is the right-hand instruction, however, the first target instruction is executed by itself followed by pairs of instructions. Consequently, there is a small performance penalty in not providing alignment as modeled previously.

Intel Pentium. Processors with variable-length instructions have used instruction fetch queues that permit most variable-length instructions to issue in one clock, a topic discussed in Section 2.3.2. These queues are found in the VAX 11/780 and all members of the Intel ix86 family, starting with the i8086. Superscalar processors that can issue $1, 2, \ldots$ or σ instructions in one clock effectively have the same variable-length instruction problem. The Intel Pentium, and the PowerPC 601 to be described later, use instruction queues so that one or two instructions can be issued in one clock. The instruction queue is backed up with a conventional instruction cache organized as (128, 2, 1, 32). A block diagram of the Pentium cache/queue topology is shown in Figure 10.7.

The instruction cache supplies a long 32-byte block into a queue (either the in-line or target, called buffers by Intel) from which the instructions can be extracted for parallel issue. The queue has a capacity of 64 bytes; thus, a fetch from the cache operates on a double-buffer basis and is described in Sections 2.3.2 and 7.3.3.

The Pentium data cache must support multiple accesses from the two pipelines. The cache is organized as (128, 2, 1, 32) late select, with each of the two sets in independent caches as shown in Figure 10.8. Each

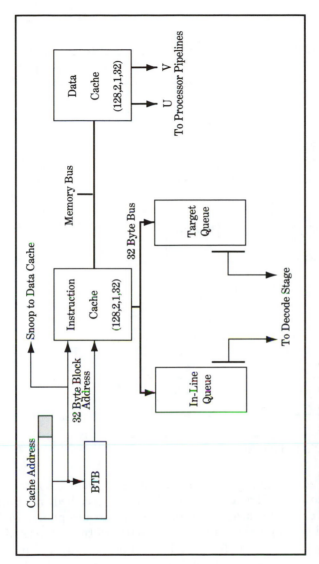

FIGURE 10.7 Pentium cache topology.

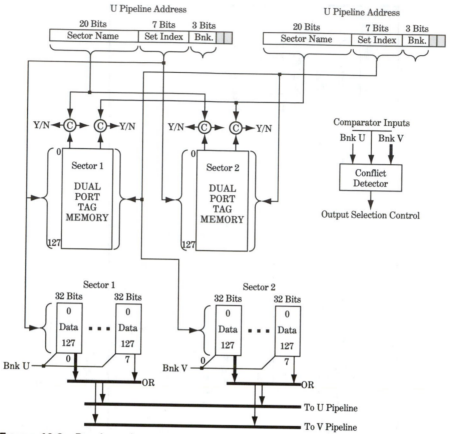

FIGURE 10.8   Pentium data cache.

cache is composed of eight data modules with low-order bit interleaving for each set (shown in Figure 5.6). Interleaving described in Chapter 5 was judged, after analysis and simulation by the designers, to be as effective as dual porting the data memory portion of the cache [ALPE93].

The cache addresses (one from each pipeline) are divided into three word-address fields: the sector name, the set index, and the bank address that provided chip enables to the interleaved modules. The set index fields address the two dual-ported tag memories. The default access path assigns the U pipeline to Sector 1 and the V pipeline to Sector 2. However, the tag memories can be dual accessed by both set indices because both pipelines may hit on the same sector. If there is a sector name conflict (that is, hits from both accesses to the same sector), only one set index is used. The results of the tag comparisons are used to select the set index fields that gate out the data memories to the two buses. As discussed above, there are a number of possible conflicts when accessing

Sector Name Conflict	Set Index Conflict	Bank Address Conflict	Action
No	No	No	Both U and V access caches
No	No	Yes	Both U and V access caches
No	Yes	No	Both U and V access caches
No	Yes	Yes	Both U and V access caches
Yes	No	No	Delay V access one clock
Yes	No	Yes	Re-access V
Yes	Yes	No	Delay V access one clock
Yes	Yes	Yes	Re-access V

TABLE 10.5 Data cache access actions.

the data cache from two pipelines. Table 10.5 lists all of the possible access cases and the action that is taken to satisfy the accesses.

The eight cases for cache access conflict illustrate that for only two cases is a re-access of the cache required by the V pipeline. In four of the cases, both U and V receive access to the cache. With two cases, the V access is delayed one clock.

Because of the need to support self-modifying code, the data cache is accessed in parallel with access of the instruction cache. Thus, there seems to be the possibility of six concurrent snoopy accesses of the data cache tag memory: two data read references, two data write references, one instruction reference, and an I/O reference. As a consequence, the tag memory of this cache should be seven-ported. I suspect that this is not the case and that the number of ports is in the range of four as seven references is an unlikely event. In fact, the discussion on dependencies in Section 10.2.4 describes restrictions on instruction issue that reduce the number of concurrent accesses to the tag memory. Published documentation does not give specific information on this issue.

PowerPC 601. The PowerPC 601 cache topology consists of a unified cache augmented with an instruction queue. The cache is organized (64, 8, 1, 64) for 32K Bytes as shown in Figure 10.9. The path from the cache to the instruction queue is 32 bytes, the path to the general purpose registers is 4 bytes, and the path to the floating point registers is 8 bytes.

The PowerPC 601 is a superscalar processor that can issue up to three instructions, one from each class, in one clock [MOTO93]. At the maximum instruction issue rate of three instructions, 12 bytes per clock, there is ample bandwidth in the path to the queue.

The path from the cache to memory is 8 bytes. Thus, 8 cache cycles are required to fill a block on a cache miss, the transfer is buffered, and there is a 16-byte bus to the cache. The cache can operate in either the

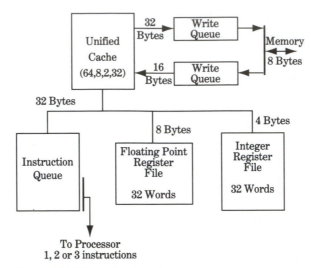

FIGURE 10.9   PowerPC 601 cache topology.

write through or write back mode. There is a 32-byte path from the cache to the write queue that permits a block to be transferred in one clock.

Registers

Designing a superscalar processor leads to the consideration of the required bandwidth of the register file. With σ instructions releasing into the execution units of a uniform superscalar processor in one clock, one might anticipate that 3σ register accesses (and 3σ register ports) would be required per clock (2σ reads for operands and σ writes for retirements). This estimate of 3σ is an obvious worst case. Johnson [JOHN91] provides data on the number of ports needed for data register accesses for four benchmarks on a processor where $\sigma = 4$. His results are shown in Table 10.6 along with the cumulative averages of the benchmarks. The data of Table 10.6 is interpreted from a bar chart in the reference and may not be the same as the author's original data.

From the data above, the weighted average number or register accesses per clock is slightly less than 2 references per decoded σ instructions, or parcel. A register file design based on this data with two ports would require 1.65 cycles for register reads and writes while a four-port register file requires 1.04 cycles. Thus we see that the required concurrency of register accesses is significantly less than the worst case estimate of $3\sigma = 3 \times 4 = 12$ accesses per clock.

This data from Johnson is for a uniform superscalar processor. The Pentium and the MC88110 are degree 2 integer superscalar and will have register access requirements less than the degree 4 superscalar of

Fraction of Accesses per decoded Parcel, $S = 4$

Register Accesses per Clock	ccom	irism	troff	yacc	Avg.	Cum. Avg.
0	0.13	0.03	0.15	0.10	0.10	0.10
1	0.32	0.17	0.32	0.28	0.27	0.37
2	0.30	0.48	0.27	0.35	0.35	0.72
3	0.15	0.15	0.20	0.23	0.18	0.90
4	0.06	0.12	0.03	0.03	0.06	0.96
5	0.02	0.02	0.02	0.01	0.02	0.98
6	0.02	0.01	0.01	0	0.01	0.99

TABLE 10.6 Fraction of register accesses per clock.

Table 10.6. The MC88110 has 32 integer and 32 floating point registers that are served with eight buses [DIEF92]. The register files are dual ported for Source 1, Source 2, and Destination. Thus, two·integer or one integer and one floating point execution units can simultaneously access the register files. There are also two history buffer ports to support precise interrupts. On the surface, the MC88110 register ports seem to be a case of some overdesign.

10.2.3 *Superscalar Branching Strategies*

Superscalar processors place unique demands on the branching strategy that can be used: a delayed branch strategy is completely unusable for most superscalar processors. Branches are handled in two ways, as shown in Table 10.4. One design type has a single branch execution unit (RS/6000, PowerPC 601, and the Pentium). The other type has multiple integer execution units that also perform the branch function (i860 and MC88110).

Consider a processor with a single branch execution unit. Because the execution unit processes only branch, it is difficult to identify other branch instructions that can be moved to fill delay slots. Thus the taken branch delay will be $s' - 1$.

On the other hand, the processors with σ integer execution units that also process branches do have the opportunity to fill the delay slots with useful instructions. The problem is that there can be $\sigma(s - 1)$ delay slots. If one delay slot can be filled, the WABD is $\sigma(s - 1) - 1$.

This problem is illustrated in Figure 10.10. The processor is $\sigma = 2$ superscalar, and the stage that resolves the branch is $s = 4$. In this example, an in-line instruction is followed by a branch. No-ops are inserted by the compiler behind each branch instruction in depth and in

		1	2	3	4	5	6	7	8	9
1		i	N	N	N	i+1				
		B	N	N	N	i+2				
s"=2			i	N	N	N	i+1			
			B	N	N	N	i+2			
s'=3				i	N	N	N	i+1		
				B	N	N	N	i+2		
s=4					i	N	N	N	i+1	
					B	N	N	N	i+2	

$$\text{Delay} = s(s-1) - \triangle$$

FIGURE 10.10   Superscalar delayed branch strategy.

width. Thus the WABD increases for both pipeline length and the degree of superscalar. The example shows that the branch is not taken and the in-line path continues at t_5.

Assume a superscalar processor $\sigma = 2$, $s = 3$, $\Delta = 1$, and a WABD of 3 clocks. With $P_{bt} = 0.3$, the CPI becomes 1.9. In other words, approximately 50% of the processing capability is lost to branches.

10.2.4 *Dependency Detection and Resolution*

Superscalar processors present unique problems in data dependency detection and resolution and structural dependencies. Data dependencies will be discussed first.

Data Dependencies

Because more than one instruction can issue in a clock, data dependencies can occur across the processor as well as down the pipeline. In other words, dependencies must be detected and resolved between the issuing instructions as well as the preceding ones. The techniques used in superscalar processors for detecting and resolving preceding instruction dependencies in the pipeline are identical to the techniques described in Chapter 8. This section describes only the unique dependency problems of superscalar processors.

The problem and solutions are illustrated by the following example. A true dependency can exist between two instructions that are issued together, as in the two instruction example

$$i \ \ R1 \leftarrow R1 - R2 \quad \text{and} \quad j \ \ R1 \leftarrow R1 + R3.$$

There are two known ways to solve this dependency problem. The first solution detects the dependency and halts the issue of instruction j until the dependency is resolved. The second solution, available when the instruction set is being designed, is to employ a three-input ALU with internal forwarding that collapses the two instructions into one to perform the operations (R1 ← R1 − R2 + R3). Invocation of this ALU can be either by software or hardware scheduling. [MALI93] has shown that this technique provides a 10% to 40% reduction in CPI.

A similar dependency occurs if a load instruction attempts to issue on the same clock as an instruction that is performing its address arithmetic. Two solutions are possible here: delay the issue of the load instruction, or bring the address arithmetic into the architecture of the load/store instructions. The IBM S/360, while not a superscalar processor, uses this second option with a base + index + displacement effective address.

An example of the first approach to dependency resolution has been taken in the Intel Pentium processor [ALPE93]. This processor is of degree $\sigma = 2$ for integers. The compiler reorganizes and schedules instructions to minimize the dependency interlocks that will stall one or more of the execution units. Only certain pairs of instructions can issue together; the following list gives the conditions that determine if instructions i and j can issue together.

i and j are "simple instructions."
i is not a jump (branch) instruction.
Destination of $i \neq$ a source of j (no true dependency).
Destination of $i \neq$ the destination of j (no output dependency).

The logic of the first decode stage determines if all of these conditions are met and if the two instructions can be issued. Simple instructions are those that are not microprogrammed and constitute 90% of the typical instructions executed. Note that antidependencies are not detected because the source operands are buffered. Information is not available on the technique used for detecting and resolving preceding instruction dependencies.

Structural Dependencies

Structural dependencies occur, for example, when there are too few execution units for the instructions available for issue together. This can be the case with nonuniform superscalar processors. These dependencies can be handled by the processor in such a way that particular pairs of instructions will not issue together. This approach transfers structural dependency detection from the domain of operand and result addresses to the domain of comparing operation codes.

An example of restricting instruction issue due to structural dependencies is found in the MC88110 processor; an excerpted list of instruction pairs that cannot issue together is shown below [DIEF92]. Recall the list of execution units of the MC88110 shown in Table 10.4.

Load, Load;
Load, Store;
Store, Load;
Store, Store;
Integer Multiply, Integer Multiply;
Integer Multiply, Floating Multiply.

Other structural dependencies, such as those on register files, are eliminated by dual porting or otherwise providing multiple resources.

10.3 Performance Comparison

Now that pipelining has become the domain of the microprocessor designer, techniques such as superpipelining and superscalar have received great attention by industrial designers and university researchers. Based upon supersymmetry, the choice between superscalar and superpipelining seems to rest principally on design and implementation issues. In this section the issues related to logic paths and clock skew are examined.

The discussions in this chapter, and Chapter 6, have pointed out the critical influence that clock skew and register setup time have on the performance achievable with superpipelining. However, there seem to be analogous logic paths between pipelines in a superscalar processor. I therefore want to discuss the relationship between these two factors that limit performance.

I use the simple performance models of Figures 10.1 and 10.4 for this analysis. Recognize that these models only comprehend branch delays: operational latencies are assumed to be one. The time per instruction, in gate delays, for superpipelined processors is modeled first; then the model for superscalar processors is presented.

$$\text{superpipelined instruction time} = \text{SPIT} = \text{base clock period} \times \text{CPI}$$
$$= \pi(\text{SP clock period}) \times \text{CPI},$$

$$\text{SPIT} = \pi\left(\frac{L}{\pi n} + t\right) \times \left(n + \frac{k-1}{\pi}\right).$$

Note that the number of logic levels is divided by the degree π as well as the number of base machine pipeline stages and there are π of these clocks required for an equivalent base machine clock; see Figure 10.1.

Likewise, for superscalar

superscalar instruction time = SSIT = base clock period × CPI,

$$\text{SSIT} = \left(\frac{L}{n} + t\right) \times \left(n + \frac{k-1}{\sigma}\right).$$

From these two models we can find the relative instruction time for the two implementations

$$\frac{\text{SPIT}}{\text{SSIT}} = \frac{\pi(L/\pi n + t) \times (n + (k-1)/\pi)}{(L/n + t) \times (n + (k-1)/\sigma)}.$$

A case of interest is to compare superpipelining and superscalar of the same degree. For this case, $\sigma = \pi$ and

$$\frac{\text{SPIT}}{\text{SSIT}} = \frac{L/n + \pi t}{L/n + t}.$$

In other words, any difference in performance is a function only of the clock periods, assuming equal alignment probabilities for superscalar. Consider the following example, which evaluates varying π and σ in the SPIT/SSIT model above; the results are given in Table 10.7. The example parameters are $L = 128$, $n = 4$, and $t = 2$.

From the results of this model we can observe that the superpipelined processor always has a longer instruction time than that of the superscalar processor of equal degree. For example, for degree 4, the superscalar advantage is in the order of 18%. The reason that the superscalar processor is faster, according to this model, than the superpipelined processor of the same degree has to do with the clock skew and setup time. The superpipelined machine incurs increasing clock overhead as the degree increases. In other words, clock skew and setup time are an ever-increasing, and logically useless, fraction of the total clock cycle.

$\pi = \sigma$	SPIT/SSIT
1	1.0
2	1.06
3	1.12
4	1.18
5	1.24

TABLE 10.7 *SP and SS performance ratio.*

These findings are not the complete story, however. The base machine logic path length must be increased when superscalar is employed. There are paths between the pipelines for alignment, dependency checking, and ensuring precise interrupts that are not present in the base machine or the superpipelined machine. The SPIT/SSIT model can be modified to account for this additional logic path length; the SPIT/SSIT relationship can be rewritten as

$$\frac{\text{SPIT}}{\text{SSIT}}\ (\text{modified}) = \frac{L/n + \pi t}{L/n + t + \gamma}$$

where γ represents the number of logic levels between pipelines with superscalar.

Consider the above example with $\gamma = 4$; the ratio of instruction time for the two implementations is shown in Table 10.8.

These are interesting results; for a low degree of σ and π, the performance of the two implementations is roughly equal. Note, however, as the degree becomes large, the instruction time of the superpipelined processor begins to become longer than that of the superscalar processor. These results reinforce the conclusion that any differences in modeled performance are within the accuracy of the model and a design decision should be made on other grounds.

However, these results lead to an interesting question: What is the value of γ for SPIT = SSIT? This question is answered by equating the two clock period models and solving for γ as

$$\frac{L}{n} + \pi t = \frac{L}{n} + t + \gamma$$

$$\gamma = t(\pi - 1).$$

If $\gamma > t(\pi - 1)$, the superpipelined processor will have better performance than the superscalar processor. Only if $\gamma < t(\pi - 1)$ will the super-

$\pi = s$	SPIT/SSIT
1	1.00
2	0.95
3	1.00
4	1.05
5	1.11

TABLE 10.8   Modified *SP* and *SS* comparison.

scalar be superior. For example, if $\pi = 4$ and $t = 2$, γ must be ≤ 6 gate delays. There is no research known to me concerning the nature and magnitude of γ based on the implementation of real processors.

There is a fine balance between the overhead of superpipelining and the overhead of superscalar. The general conclusion, I believe, is that from an implementation point of view there is very little difference between superscalar and superpipeline techniques. One must look to other considerations such as the distribution of high-frequency clocks and the ease of generating good code for differences to be significant. Diefendorff [DIEF92] presents arguments in favor of superscalar over superpipelining in the following terms: "... superscalar machines generally require more transistors, whereas superpipelined designs require faster transistors and more careful circuit design to minimize the effects of clock skew. We felt that CMOS technology generally favors replicating circuitry over increasing clock cycle rates since CMOS circuit density historically has increased at a much faster rate than circuit speed."

10.4 Superscalar Superpipelined Processor

Up to this point, superpipelining and superscalar have been discussed in the context to competing approaches to implementation. Such is not the case as illustrated by the topology of the RS/6000 as shown in Figure 10.3. This processor is superscalar as well as superpipelined. In this section I combine the two models into one model that permits the performance evaluation of these combined implementations.

The performance of a processor depends upon the parallelism of the processor and the instruction-level parallelism of the program. In practice, the performance is limited by one or the other or both of these two parameters.

10.4.1 *Processor Parallelism*

The machine parallelism is the product of the degree of superscalar and the degree of superpipeline

$$\text{machine parallelism} = \text{MP} = \sigma\pi.$$

A base machine is redesigned for superpipelining of degree π and is then redesigned for superscalar degree σ. The degree of superscalar is quantifiable as the number of instructions that can be issued in one clock. Jouppi [JOUP89a] posits a concept of the duality of latency and parallel instructions issue. The idea is that the operational latencies of the processor limit the degree of parallelism that can be exploited by multiple instruction issue. For an extreme example: if every instruction has an operational latency of two and every instruction has a true dependency on the previous instruction, the maximum processing rate is 0.5 instructions per clock. Attempting to issue more than one instruction every two clocks will not improve the performance of the processor.

The superpipeline performance model developed from Figure 10.1 assumed that all operations had an operational latency of π cycles. This symmetry is not the case in a real processor. Various function units have different operational latencies, and the net effect is determined by the *average degree of superpipelining*. (ADS), which is *the operational latencies of the function units weighted by the frequency of instruction execution that uses the functional units*.

An example of the measure of ADS for two processors, executing the same sample program, is: MultiTitan, ADS = 1.7 and Cray-1, ADS = 5.4. Table 10.9, from [JOUP89a, Table I], shows the data and the method of calculating these two values of ADS.

The Cray-1 ADS is dominated by the load latency of 11 clocks with a frequency of 0.34. The Cray-1 execution units, including the load unit, have an issue latency of one clock. However, the eleven clocks of load latency is the number of clocks required to fetch a single scalar from memory, place it in the register file, and resolve a true dependency. Likewise, the seven clocks of the floating point operations is the operational latency or the number of clocks before a true dependency can be resolved.

		Weighted Latency	
Instruction Class	Frequency	MultiTitan	Cray-1
Logical	0.06	×1 = 0.06	×1 = 0.06
Shift	0.09	×1 = 0.09	×2 = 0.18
Add/Sub	0.21	×1 = 0.21	×3 = 0.63
Load	0.34	×2 = 0.68	×11 = 3.74
Store	0.15	×2 = 0.30	×1 = 0.15
Branch	0.10	×2 = 0.20	×3 = 0.30
Flt. Pt.	0.05	×3 = 0.15	×7 = 0.35
Average degree of superpipelining		1.7	5.4

TABLE 10.9   Average degree of superpipelining.

10.4.2 *Instruction-Level Parallelism*

I turn now to the question of the ILP that can be expected from a typical program. Jouppi [JOUP89a] and Park [PARK91] supply information on the ILP that is inherent in various benchmarks. In order to determine only ILP, both Jouppi and Park assume infinite resources in the memory and processor. For example, cache hit ratios are set at 100%, branch prediction at 100%, and there is no lack of parallelism in the processor; Jouppi also assumed operational latencies of one. This ILP data, from the two sources, is shown in Tables 10.10 and 10.11. Notice that the Jouppi data shows ILP to be in the range of 1.7 to 3.2 with an average ILP of 2.2. Parks shows similar results with an average ILP of 2.5. Note that the Linpack ILP of Park is a bit more optimistic than that of Jouppi—the reason for this is unknown.

Benchmark	ILP
ccom	2.2
grr	2.0
Linpack unroll4x	3.2
Livermore	2.4
Metronome	2.0
Stanford	2.0
Whetstones	2.2
yacc	1.7
Average	2.21

TABLE 10.10   Benchmark ILPs from Jouppi.

Benchmark	ILP Op Latency = 1	ILP Op Latency = 3
Assembler	2.74	2.74
Dhrystone	2.42	2.42
Grep	3.24	3.24
Newton raphson	2.15	1.64
Sim. annealing	1.94	1.82
Linpack	4.07	3.63
Quicksort	2.21	2.21
Proc. simulator	3.01	3.01
Towers of Hanoi	3.04	3.04
Whetstone	2.12	1.19
Average	2.69	2.49

TABLE 10.11   Benchmark ILPs from Park.

As shown in Tables 10.10 and 10.11, ILP can vary widely depending on the benchmark or workload. A processor designer would like to design a processor that effectively processes all programs regardless of ILP. Thus, there is an incentive for a design to a degree of σ or π that is well up on the knee of the curve. This design will prevent the processor from saturating on high ILP programs. On the other hand, this design costs money in the form of chip area and a balance must be struck somewhere.

Recent research by Butler and Patt [BUTL91] indicates that ILP in the range of 17 to 1,165 is possible for the SPEC benchmark suit with unlimited resources. These results tend to agree with those of [RISE72]. The Butler results also show that with reasonable and implementable hardware systems, an instruction issue rate of 2–5.8 instructions per clock can be achieved.

10.4.3 *Processor Performance*

A performance model for the superscalar–superpipelined processor, called the *combined* implementation, will now be developed. Both enhancement techniques contribute to the parallelism of the processor. The average degree of machine parallelism (MP) is the product of ADS and the degree of superscalar. In the models developed below CPI is the *native* CPI, that is, the CPI of the processor, not the normalizing Base Machine CPI used previously. In order to determine actual performance from these models, CPI must be multiplied by the clock period; recall that the clock period is determined by ADS as

$$MP = ADS \; \sigma.$$

The relationship between MP and ILP determines the performance of the processor:

If ILP < MP, the performance is equal to ILP

$$\text{average CPI} = \frac{ADS}{\text{speedup over base machine}} = \frac{ADS}{ILP}.$$

If MP < ILP, the performance is equal to MP

$$\text{average CPI} = \frac{1}{\sigma}.$$

In the case that ILP < MP, the instruction-level parallelism is absorbed into the ADS and there is no limit to the number of instructions

Processor	ADS	σ	MP	ILP	CPI	Speedup
Cray-1	5.4	1	5.4	2.16	2.50	2.16
MultiTitan	1.7	1	1.7	2.16	1.00	1.7
MultiTitan	1.7	2	3.4	2.16	0.78	2.16
Base machine	1.0	1	1.0	2.16	1.00	1

TABLE 10.12 Processor CPI.

that can issue in a cycle. The ILP is the speedup over the base machine. In the second case, the window is issuing instructions at its maximum rate as there is a large pool of instructions available for issue. The combined processor CPI is

$$\text{processor average CPI} = \min\left[\frac{\text{ADS}}{\text{ILP}}, \frac{1}{\sigma}\right].$$

Jouppi provides three examples that illustrate the interrelationship between ADS, σ, and ILP. A group of eight benchmarks having an average ILP of 2.16 are used, and the results are shown in Table 10.12. The base machine and the speedup are added for expository purposes.

For the Cray-1 and MultiTitan-2, the performance is limited by the ILP; increasing either ADS or σ will not improve performance. However, when the MultiTitan σ is increased from 1 to 2, a small improvement in performance is achieved. The reason that the increase is small is due to the small ILP.

Figure 10.11 illustrates the saturating effect of ILP on speedup.

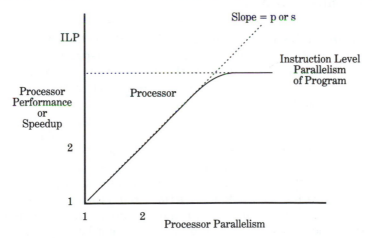

FIGURE 10.11 Speedup limit.

As the machine parallelism increases, the speedup increases proportionally until ILP is reached. At this point, further increases in machine parallelism are not beneficial.

10.5 Very Long Instruction Word (VLIW) Processors

In addition to superpipelining and superscalar processors, there are other processor configurations that have been proposed and constructed to enhance the performance of the base machine. One of these configurations is the vector processor, to be discussed in Chapter 11. In addition, processors with very long instruction words and processors that overlap loads and stores with processing have received attention.

Superpipelining provides improved performance because the basic block is processed in small time increments; superscalar provides improvement in performance due to exploitation of parallelism within the basic block. Thus, both of these techniques are limited by the characteristic of the basic block that limits speedup to a factor of 2 to 4, as discussed in Section 10.4. Any further improvements in performance must therefore come from outside one basic block, which is the philosophy of VLIW. These processors attempt to achieve spatial parallelism by issuing and releasing an instruction that can cause a number of operations that are not related in one basic block to execute in parallel.

> VLIW is "a computer architecture in which instructions are encoded with many bits and control a large number of computational facilities concurrently" [STON93].

Before examining the issue of scheduling outside the basic block, the general idea of VLSI processor performance is discussed. The performance improvement available with the VLIW technique is illustrated in Figure 10.12 for scheduling within a basic block. This figure shows the reservation table for the base machine, which is also shown in Figure 10.1. With VLIW, v instructions that can be released in parallel are collected into a single instruction, which is denoted by V. The V instructions are fetched and decoded, all components are executed, and their results are written back into the register file.

In Figure 10.12, it is assumed that k instructions of the base machine are grouped together into a V instruction that is issued and executed together. It is assumed that there are no alignment problems as with a superscalar processor, an assumption that may not be realistic.

Let v denote the number of normal instructions that can be packed

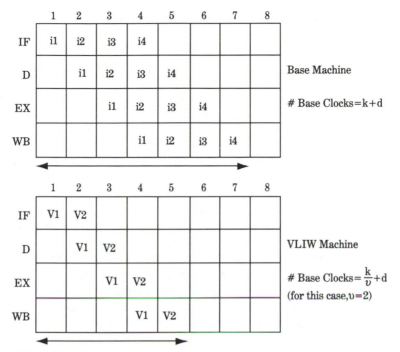

FIGURE 10.12 VLIW processor.

into a VLIW instruction; v is also the degree of VLIW. V is the number of VLIW instructions executed, $V = k/v$.

$$\text{number of base machine cycles} = k + d,$$

$$\text{number of VLSI machine clocks} = \frac{k}{v} + d,$$

$$\text{number of SS machine clocks} = \frac{k}{\sigma} + d.$$

For the case $\sigma = v$ (the degree of superscalar is equal to the degree of VLIW), the performances are equal. There is no gain in VLIW over superscalar. There are some practical considerations that may favor VLIW such as (1) the more effective use of a longer instruction word; (2) with a richer instruction set, dependencies within an instruction may be eliminated; and (3) instruction alignment can be satisfied in the compiler. These benefits are offset by the need to have a new instruction set architecture that is not compatible with a base machine architecture.

The performance of the simple VLIW described above is a result of scheduling within the basic block. Fisher [FISH81] has investigated the availability of parallelism outside a basic block with the goal of generating compact horizontal microcode. This study pointed the way to VLIW which "puts fine-grained, tightly coupled, but logically unrelated operations in a single instruction" [FISH83].

The technique he developed is called *trace scheduling*, in which long streams of instructions are scheduled without regard to basic block boundaries. In effect, every instruction is conditionally scheduled. The unproductive paths are then identified and unscheduled. The result of this process is the identification of instructions that can be executed in parallel.

Because trace scheduling combines instructions from several basic blocks into a single long instruction, the conditional branch component should be a multiway branch based on a multiplicity of conditions. With the multiway branch capability, the compiler for a VLIW processor should be able to schedule more instructions into a VLIW instruction sequence than is possible with a superscalar processor.

The block of instructions that can be executed in parallel is also increased by unrolling loops. This type of code reorganization increases the code space while reducing the number of instructions executed.

Fisher's investigations indicate that massive amounts of parallelism are available and proposed and constructed an architecture that could exploit this parallelism. The VLIW computer, named ELI, has a 512-bit instruction word and can perform the following operations in one clock cycle.

    16   ALU operations
     8   Pipeline memory references
    32   Register accesses
         Multiway conditional branch

A production version of this processor was produced by the Multiflow Computer Corporation [COLW87] and evaluated at the Supercomputing Research Center [LOPR 89]. Little information is available on this processor, however, the processor tested has 28 functional units. The benchmark used for this evaluation compared two sequences and identified the most similar subsequences. For this benchmark, the Multiflow Trace performed quite well and outperformed a single-processor Cray 2 by a factor of approximately 2. However, this benchmark is limited and conclusions about this processor's performance are difficult to draw from these results. Multiflow Computer Corporation is thought to be no longer in business. I speculate that, with the industrial experience with superscalar, VLIW processors may be under consideration by designers today. This technology could be the next major step forward in improving processor performance by enhanced implementations. The cooperative research with Intel and HP is rumored to be investigating VLSI processors.

11

Vector Processors

11.0 Overview

Pipelined processors and interleaved memories found early use in super-computers such as the CDC 6600 and IBM S/360/91. The early super-computers have evolved into the vector processor, which became the standard of all single instruction stream supercomputers. This chapter discusses the rationale for these processors and illustrates the various architectural features through a discussion of current machines.

A *vector* is a one-dimensional array of variables. The variables of the vector may be any of the usual scalar data types.

The vector processor, as found in most supercomputers, combines interleaved memory (discussed in Chapter 5) and pipelining (discussed in Chapters 6–10). Vector processors were conceived in the mid-1960s to process structured scientific problems at very high rates. Research in high-performance computer architectures was driven by problems such as geophysical data processing, weather forecasting, and nuclear weapons design, to name a few. The vector architecture contended with array processing that was being developed at the University of Illinois with the ILLIAC-IV project [CRAG89]. There were two concurrent developments in vector processors: at Texas Instruments and Control Data Corporation in the late 1960s. The designers at Texas Instruments had experience developing architectures for seismic data processing that were either stand alone processors or special-purpose processors attached to nonvector computers. The first ASC was delivered to a customer in 1971 with a vectorizing compiler. The CDC STAR, first delivered in 1974, profited from the experience of the CDC 7600, which is a highly effective pipelined processor that could execute vector macro commands that are compiled into normal instruction sequences with loops.

The first instance, as far as I know, of the use of the term *vector*

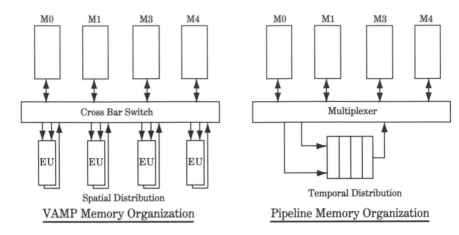

FIGURE 11.1   Contending vector processor architectures.

instruction is found in the paper by Senzig and Smith [SENZ65] describing their investigations into control mechanism for executing array problems on a SIMD architecture. Their approach (named VAMP for Vector Arithmetic MultiProcessor), shown in Figure 11.1, is to distribute the elements of a vector *spatially* across a number of multiple-clock execution units. All addressing of operands and destinations is performed in hardware that overlaps the execution in the EUs. Operands and results are routed to/from memory and the EUs via a cross bar switch.

In contrast, the control unit of a pipelined vector processor distributes the elements of a vector *temporarily* into a pipelined execution unit. The memory modules are interleaved, with operands and results routed via a multiplexer. Because elements are distributed temporally rather than spatially, vector processors do not have awkward partitioning problems, such as matrix dimensionally, that exist with array processors. As I note later, the TI ASC, Cray X-MP, and NEC SX (among others) combined both temporal and spatial element distribution approaches by using multiple pipelined execution units.

Scientific program execution drove the development of vector processors that are dominated by one, two, and three dimension matrix processing. The data structures are well ordered and can be stored and retrieved from interleaved slow memory modules (discussed in Chapter 5). Because the programs of scientific problems have a high degree of temporal locality, loops of scalar or vector instructions can be stored in an instruction buffer, eliminating most memory overhead for instruction fetches. Buffering of instruction is one of the fundamental concepts of vector computer design.

An important influence on the design of the TI ASC was the description of a vector loop described in *Planning a Computer System*

[BUCH62]. This loop, which could be expressed using FORTRAN DO loops, is implemented in hardware so that all address arithmetic and loop testing are overlapped with pipelined execution of the operation. The technique of overlapping overhead functions was well known to the designers of attached processors such as convolver for the Texas Instruments TIAC 870A [TEX65]. Four of these convolvers could be attached to a TIAC 870A, giving one 24-bit integer multiply–add operation every 56 ns: This operation results in an integer rate of 17 million integer operations per second (MIOPS). The multiply–add operation is sometimes known as *multiply cumulatively*.

The development of FORTRAN began in 1954 "to reduce by a large factor the task of preparing scientific problems for IBM's next large computer, the 704" [BACK57]. Further, "in the case of DO statements, which are designed to produce loops in the object program," we see that FORTRAN specifically supports scientific programming of structured data. Structured data lends itself to pipeline processing (discussed in Chapter 6), and the DO loops became vector instructions. With long vector operations, the processing rate through a pipeline approaches one result per clock.

The FORTRAN DO loop has properties that support the notion of vector instruction execution. Thus, the designers of the early vector processors concluded that a compiler for FORTRAN was feasible, thereby permitting vector computers to be easily programmed. Array processors, on the other hand, have major programming problems. Ideas concerning overlapped processing and pipelining were unknown at the time of the development of FORTRAN; a serial execution model was assumed and issues of dependencies between assignment statements were not considered in the design. However, dependency detection is required for DO loops that are converted to vector instructions by vector compilers [COHA73, WEDE75]. Chapter 8 discusses the problems of dependencies in the execution of scalar programs; this chapter addresses the special problems of dependency detection and resolution with vector instructions.

The confluence of four ideas: *temporal operand distribution, pipeline(s), instruction buffering*, and *FORTRAN*, combined to form the vector computer architecture that has been the design model for all supercomputers for almost three decades.

11.1 Vector Operations

There are five common forms of vector operations shown in Table 11.1. The two operands can be vectors, scalars, a mask, or nil and the result

Result	Operand1	Operand2	Example	No. of Memory References
Vector	Vector	Vector	$C(i) \leftarrow B(i) + A(i)$	$3v$
Vector	Scalar	Vector	$C(i) \leftarrow B + A(i)$	$2v + 1$
Vector	Vector	Nil	$C(i) \leftarrow \sqrt{B(i)}$	$2v$
Vector	Vector	Mask	$C(i) \leftarrow B(i) \cap \text{Mask}$	$2v$
Scalar	Vector	Nil	$C \leftarrow \Sigma\, B(i)$	$v + 1$
Scalar	Vector	Vector	$C \leftarrow \Sigma\, B(i) \times A(i)$	$2v + 1$

Note. i is the ith element of a vector of length v.

TABLE 11.1   Vector operation forms.

can be a vector or scalar. Examples of each operation are also included in the table.

The number of memory references in Table 11.1 provides insight into the memory bandwidth that must be provided to the execution unit(s). The discussion in Chapter 5 on superinterleaving discusses memory organizations that are used to provide the required data bandwidth to a vector processor.

11.2 Memory-Processor Interface

As discussed in Chapter 1, the interface between the memory and processor is an area of critical interest. With vector processors, either short loops or vector instructions are processed. The instructions can usually be buffered, leaving only the data demands to be satisfied by the memory system. The worst case, as shown in Table 11.1, is for a vector dyadic operation that produces a vector result with three references made by the processor per clock to the memory system. The flow of operands and results to/from an execution unit pipeline is shown in Figure 11.2.

Operand vectors are streamed from the memory system into the execution pipelines, and results are sent to the memory. The bandwidth

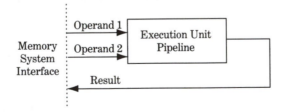

FIGURE 11.2   Memory/processor interface.

of the memory system and memory system interface is usually high enough to support dyadic operations with two vector operands and one vector result. Less than worst case designs are discussed in Section 11.2.

Unlike scalar processors where low memory latency is a critical requirement, memory bandwidth, not latency, is the critical requirement for a vector processor. As will be discussed and modeled later, memory latency is usually a small fraction of the time required to process a vector operation. Recall that vector bandwidth of almost any magnitude can be provided by interleaving. However, for a high degree of interleaving and with short vector lengths, the efficiency of interleaving diminishes. This is the so-called *short vector problem*, which will be discussed later.

Given that main memory is interleaved and has sufficient (or even excess) bandwidth, how may this bandwidth be coupled to or effectively used by the processor? In other words, how is the memory matched to the processors for the various instructions that are executed? There are two common architectural methods used to achieve memory / processor matching: Memory-to-Memory Architecture (TI ASC) and Load/Store Architecture (Cray, SX-2).

11.2.1 *Memory-to-Memory Architecture*

The TI ASC employs a memory-to-memory architecture. The vector instructions specified the starting address, the stride, and length for each of the two source operands and the destination of a dyadic vector instruction. From Table 11.1, note that the maximum demand on memory bandwidth for a single execution unit is $3v$. The TI ASC provided this bandwidth by employing an interleaved, wide-word memory system and three double buffers; one buffer for each of the two input vectors and one buffer for the result vector.

The memory is eight-way low-order interleaved with each memory word having eight computer words; 256 data bits plus ECC bits shown in Figure 11.3. One access of the memory will read or write an octet of words to/from one of the double buffers. After the latency (sometimes called *startup time* with vector processors) needed to fill the X and Y buffers, the pipeline begins execution and fills one of the Z buffers with results. Concurrently, the second half of the X and Y buffers are filled, under hardware control. When the first half of the Z buffer is filled with results, a write is initiated to main memory and the second half of the Z buffer begins receiving results from the execution unit.

Note that a cross bar switch is used for interconnection between the pipeline and memory modules, unlike the multiplexer suggested in Figure 11.1. The cross bar switch can support multiple pipelines (up to four) along with ports for I/O. The cross bar switch can be viewed as multiple

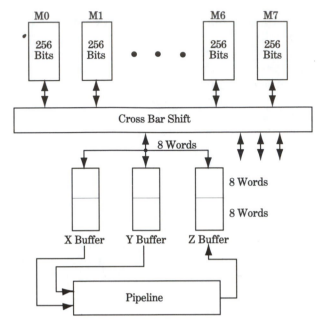

FIGURE 11.3   ASC *X*, *Y* and *Z* buffers.

multiplexers, one for each user: an execution unit pipeline, or an I/O channel.

The memory modules have a cycle time of 160 ns, providing an aggregate memory bandwidth of 400 million words per second. The CPU has a clock period of 80 ns, and, with 3 accesses per operation, require a memory bandwidth of 37.5 million words per second. As four pipelines can be attached to the memory system, the total bandwidth demand is 150 million references per second—well within the provided 400 million words per second with excess bandwidth available for I/O operations as well. With excess memory bandwidth, the small double buffers provide sufficient buffering so that the pipelines are never forced to wait for operands or to store results, except during the startup of an operation.

11.2.2 *Load/Store Architecture*

All vector processors known to me, except for the TI ASC, have been load/store architectures. These load/store architectures were pioneered with the Cray-1 and are the common architecture for all supercomputers and some high-performance microprocessors. With this architecture, the latency and bandwidth between the memory and processor are matched via a register file. All operands are explicitly loaded into this register file and processed by the execution units that can only access the register file, and the results are explicitly written into the memory. Vector instructions use *vector registers*, while the scalar instructions use *scalar registers*; these registers are usually disjoint.

We should take note of the way the literature on vector processors speaks of vector registers. These registers are not a single register in the scalar computer sense but possess a number of locations that hold elements of a vector. Furthermore, there are usually a multiplicity of vector registers, just as there are a multiplicity of scalar registers in a scalar processor. Therefore, the dimensionality of the vector registers consists of (1) the number of vector registers and (2) the number of locations in each vector register. For scalar registers, the second dimension is equal to 1. The number of locations of the registers (also known as *buffers*) is critical to achieving peak performance. The reason for this is that for vector lengths greater than the size of the register file, the vectors must be segmented into shorter vectors. This segmentation requires restarting the vector operations with the resulting cost of a number of vector startup times.

As with all load/store architectures, operand locality is critical to performance. Spatial locality within a vector register is assured by the very nature of vector operations. However, if a high degree of temporal locality exists and if the number of vector registers are limited, there can be a significant number of unnecessary transfers between the vector registers and memory. This problem is significantly reduced with chaining, which is discussed in Section 11.7.2.

11.3 Vector Performance

There are generally three methods used for assessing the performance of vector processors. These assessment methods provide insight into how the various design features of the processor impact its performance.

1. Collect all of the latency of a vector operation into one parameter. Lower latency usually implies an efficient design.
2. Measure the processor performance in MFLOPS as the vector length is varied.
3. Determine the length of a vector operation that reduces the performance to half the performance of a vector operation of infinite length.

11.3.1 *Assessment by Vector Instruction Latency*

The first assessment method measures the total latency associated with starting a vector operation. A simple model for measuring the time to execute a vector instruction [HOCK81] is

$$\text{vector time} = \text{latency} + \frac{v}{\text{streaming rate}}$$

$$= \text{LSU} + \text{startup time} + \frac{v}{\text{streaming rate}}$$

where LSU denotes the loop set-up instruction time and v is the vector length.

This model is remarkably similar to the transport time model for transfers between the main memory and the cache (discussed in Chapter 2). These processes are similar in that there is a fixed latency plus the time to perform the operation on an incremental basis. The value of LSU depends upon the number of instructions, usually scalar, that are required to initialize the processor for the upcoming vector instruction(s).

For the purposes of the following discussion, all vector operations are assumed to have their operands in memory and the results are stored in memory. The latency of a vector instruction consists of the LSU plus the startup time. In a real application, some or all of the LSU and startup time can be overlapped with scalar instruction execution and does not add directly to the execution time of the program. However, this possibility is not considered in this analysis. The compiler must be aware of the vector latency time because, in some cases of short vectors, it may be advantageous to execute a vector operation with scalar instructions rather than with a vector instruction.

The following operations comprise the LSU + startup time and include the time to store the first result into memory—in other words, all of the latency except the streaming of operations through the pipeline(s).

Loop set-up instructions
    Initialize address registers
Startup time
    Fetch and decode the vector instruction
    Transfer operand vectors to registers
    Fill the pipeline(s)
    Write the first result to memory.

Lubeck, Moore and Mendez evaluated the Cray X-MP, Fujitsu VP-200, and Hatachi S810/20 vector processors and measured their laten-

Operation	X-MP	VP-200	S810/20
1: $A(i) = B(i) + S$	47	87	152
2: $A(i) = B(i) + S$ $(i = 1, n, 23)$	84	92	154
3: $A(i) = B(i) + S$ $(i = 1, n, 8)$	83	73	170
4: $A(i) = B(i) \times C(i)$	50	97	165
5: $A(i) = B(i) \times C(i) + D(i) \times E(i)$	59	129	181
6: $S = S + A(i) \times B(i)$	392	257	346
7: $A(i) = B(j(i)) + S$	120	168	230
8: $A(j(i)) = A(i) \times B(i)$	125	160	183

TABLE 11.2 Vector latency in clocks.

cies for various elementary vector operations [LUBE85]. Their results are shown in Table 11.2.

These latencies (LSU + startup) are in clocks and must be multiplied by the clock period of the computer to obtain latency in time. The method for obtaining these results is to execute and time each of the eight operations a number of times with varying vector lengths. First order curve fitting is then applied from which the zero intercept, or latency, is determined. Notice that the latency is a function of: (1) the number of vector operands, (2) the stride, and (3) the number of levels of address indirection used. Notice also that operation 8 requires chaining three instructions and that the latency is nominal due to the overlap achieved. Chaining is discussed in Section 11.8.2. Variations in the experimental results (that are smoothed by curve fitting) for the same operation and the same vector length are due, in part, to conflicts in the memory system, which are discussed in Chapter 5.

Simple single-vector operations such as 1 and 4 have latency of approximately 50 clocks for the Cray X-MP, 90 clocks for the VP-200, and 158 clocks for the S810/20. In general, the Cray X-MP has smaller latencies than the other processors.

11.3.2 *Streaming Rate*

Before I discuss the second and third methods for assessing vector processor performance, I need to discuss the idea of streaming rate, which is the third component of the vector time model discussed previously. The *streaming rate*, or *maximum throughput*, is defined as the rate at which the execution unit(s) produce results with no interferences, delays, or stalls.

For processors with one pipelined execution unit, the streaming rate measure is the clock rate or the reciprocal of the clock period. A convention used when describing the theoretical streaming rate is to assume that the processor is executing floating point operations. Consequently, the streaming rate is frequently given as the peak mega floating point operations per second (MFLOPS) where an operation is either a multiply or an add. Note that in some cases where the multiply and add instructions can operate in parallel and are internally chained, the streaming rate is doubled. The streaming rate for the execution units (eu) is

$$\mathrm{SR(eu)} = \frac{\text{number of floating point execution units}}{\text{clock period} \times 10^6}.$$

The execution unit streaming rate should be, as a minimum design, supported by the bandwidth or streaming rate of the memory port(s) that can also be measured in peak MFLOPS. The minimum memory streaming rate, SR(mp), that can support an execution unit(s) performing dyadic operations is defined as

$$\mathrm{SR(mp)} = \frac{\text{number of memory port} * \text{AUs/port}}{3 \times \text{clock period} \times 10^6}.$$

Memory port $*$ AUs/port is a measure of memory port bandwidth as the assumption is made that there is one port transfer per clock. The port bandwidth can be provided by either multiple ports of one AU each or by one or more ports that are more than one AU wide. Jordan and Fong [JORD77] gave names to the two metrics SR(mp) and SR(eu); for SR(eu), *supervector performance*, and for SR(mp), *vector performance*.

The MFLOPS rating of several vector computers is shown in Table 11.3. Vector processors are configured with various numbers of vector execution units and memory ports. In general, if the number of these execution units and memory ports is large, then the potential streaming rate is also large.

The peak performance for these processors is the minimum for SR(eu) and SR(mp) when executing a dyadic operation, such as a vector add. Note that for all the cited processors, except the TI ASC, the execution rate is memory port limited or balanced. Chaining reduces the memory bandwidth requirement, as does executing some functions such as the matrix multiply. In these cases, the performance is limited by the execution units. As the TI ASC was designed to be memory-to-memory, excess bandwidth was a design requirement.

It is instructive to compare MFLOPS obtained by timing execution kernels to the hardware limits shown in Table 11.3. Table 11.4 shows this comparison for the Cray X-MP and the NEC SX-2. The measured performance is taken from [LUBE87]; the vector length of the measured operations is 1,000, which is long enough to amortize the latency com-

Processor	Clock Period	No. Flt. Pt. EUs	SR(eu) MFLOPS	No. Mem. Port Words	SR(mp) MFLOPS
Cray-1	12.5 ns	2	160	1	26.6
Cray X-MP (1 processor)	9.5 ns	2	210	3	105
NEC SX-2	6.0 ns	8	1,333	12	666
TI ASC	80.0 ns	4	50	$4 \times 8 = 32$*	133
Cyber 205	20.0 ns	2	400	24	400

*Note. Each of the four ports are eight words.

TABLE 11.3   Vector processor characteristics.

	From Table 11.3		Measured	
Processor	SR(eu) MFLOPS	SR(mp) MFLOPS	Dyadic MFLOPS	Chained Operation
Cray X-MP (1 processor)	210	105	68.7–77.7	115.2
NEC SX-2	1,333	666	136.6–369.5	530.8

Chained operation: $A(i) = B(i) \times C(i) + D(i) \times E(i)$.

TABLE 11.4 Measured performance.

pletely. A dyadic operation and a chained operation are compared to the performance limits.

The dyadic operations that use only one execution unit with the Cray and four execution units of the SX-2 approach the SR(mp) limit set by the memory port. On the other hand, the three operation chained instruction approaches SR(eu) of the Cray X-MP and SR(mp) of the SX-2.

11.3.3 *Assessment by MFLOPS*

The second method for assessing the performance of a vector processor and the impact of startup time is to evaluate the performance, in MFLOPS, as the vector length is varied. In general, assessment by this method ignores the LSU component of latency. As shown in Table 11.3, the Cray-1 can be starved for memory port bandwidth when performing operations that have little temporal locality. In order to hide the memory port limit, an operation that is not memory port limited is usually considered, that is, one that has significant temporal locality. For example, a square matrix multiply, of dimension n, requires approximately $2n^3$ operations and approximately $3n^2$ memory references, for a ratio of

$$\frac{\text{memory references}}{\text{operation}} = \frac{3n^2}{2n^3} = \frac{3}{2n}.$$

Thus, for even small matrix multiply operations, the memory port bandwidth is more than sufficient to support the operation. Note that algorithms for reducing the number of operations even further, to approximately $4.7n^{2.8}$, exist and are described in [BAIL90].

Because the Cray memory is limited in memory port bandwidth, small hardware-managed double buffers, such as those of the TI ASC, would not work. Instead, the Cray family of vector processors uses a set of vector registers that buffer the operands and results between the memory and the execution units. The vector registers are loaded and stored under program control by instructions that can execute concurrently with the vector operations. The effect of register size on peak MFLOPS is modeled below. Assumptions are that there is no performance degradation due to memory port limits and LSU is not considered.

$$\text{Effective MFLOPS} = \text{Peak MFLOPS} \times \text{Degradation factor}$$

$$= \text{Peak MFLOPS} \times \frac{av}{\epsilon \lceil v/b \rceil + av}.$$

where a denotes the number of clocks per operation at the streaming rate, v is the problem vector length, b is the register file size (buffer size), and ϵ denotes the vector startup time in clocks.

The factor $\lceil v/b \rceil$ accounts for the need to restart a vector operation when the vector length exceeds the size of the register file. Two limits of this model concern the degradation factor for (1) very long vectors with a fixed register file size and (2) the degradation factor with a very large register file.

For the case where $v \to \infty$,

$$\text{degradation factor} = \frac{av}{\epsilon v/b + av} = \frac{a}{\epsilon/b + a} = \frac{1}{1 + \epsilon/ab}.$$

For the case where $b \geq v$

$$\text{degradation factor} = \frac{av}{\epsilon + av} = \frac{1}{1 + \epsilon/av}.$$

These models are used to evaluate the performance of the Cray-1, which has a register file size of 512 words (8 registers of 64 words each), when performing a matrix multiplication. I assume that $\epsilon = 7$ clocks. Moreover, as the execution units are chained, a multiply–add is pipelined in one clock, which makes $a = 0.5$. With a clock period of 12.5 ns, the peak MFLOPS is 160 for this problem. With 64-word registers and very large matrix dimensions, the degradation factor is 0.82 and the upper limit on performance is 131 MFLOPS. For the other case, in which there is a very large register and a matrix size of, say, 256, the degradation factor is 0.95 and the effective performance is 152 MFLOPS.

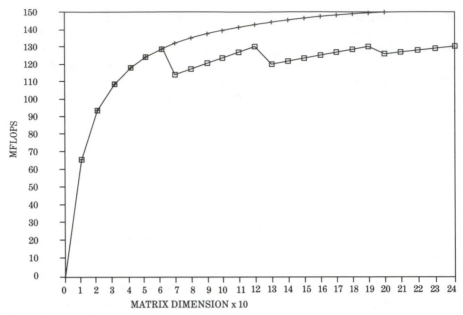

FIGURE 11.4   Cray-1 matrix multiplication.

Figure 11.4 shows a plot of the effective MFLOPS for a 64-word register file and a 512-word register file as the matrix size is increased. There is rather close agreement between the simulation from [RAMA77] and [JOHN78] and the results from the model. The two limits (131 MFLOPS and 152 MFLOPS) computed above are evident.

The dips in the plot occur at vector lengths that are multiples of the register file size and are caused by forcing a partial startup of pipeline flow. The use of $\sigma = 7$ clocks may seem strange based on the data of Table 11.2, which shows latency of 47 clocks for the Cray X-MP. The reason for this anomaly is that LSU is ignored in the model and the startup time of most of the vector operations in this matrix multiplication problem is overlapped, reducing the average startup time to a smaller effective value. Note that the matrix multiply operation is not memory port limited and this example shows only the effects of register file size and matrix dimensions.

11.3.4 *Assessment by Half Performance*

The third method frequently used to assess the performance of vector processors measures the relationship between startup time and streaming rate [HOCK81]. This measure is called *half-performance length* $v_{1/2}$, the length of a vector that will give half the performance

Computer	$v_{1/2}$
Cray-1	10–20
2-Pipe CYBER 205	100
1-Pipe TI ASC	30
CDC STAR 100	150

TABLE 11.5 $v_{1/2}$ for various computers.

of a vector of infinite length. This measure provides a feel for the short-vector performance of an architecture. The derivation of $v_{1/2}$ equates the degradation factor to 0.5 as follows.

For $b \geq v$

$$\text{degradation factor} = \frac{av_{1/2}}{\epsilon + av_{1/2}} = \frac{1}{2}$$

where $v_{1/2}$ denotes the vector length that gives half performance.

Solving the equality for $v_{1/2}$ gives

$$v_{1/2} = \frac{\epsilon}{a}.$$

In other words, the half-performance vector length is equal to the vector startup time divided by the streaming rate. Hockey gives the value of $v_{1/2}$ for a number of processors, shown in Table 11.5.

Smaller values of $v_{1/2}$ indicate improved short-vector performance. This relationship is important because of the desire to vectorize not only very long vectors but short ones as well and to know when not to vectorize. The data in this table illustrates the well-known, and valued, characteristic of the Cray processors: they have good short-vector performance.

The assumption has been made in the model for $v_{1/2}$, above, that the register file is large enough to hold the short vector without the necessity of a refill. This assumption is realistic with real processors. Thus, it is not useful to derive a $v_{1/2}$ model for the cases of smaller register files.

11.3.5 *Vector-Scalar Code Mix Problem*

To this point, the discussion has focused on the performance of individual vector instructions. In any real problem there is a mix of vector and scalar instructions that degrades the performance from what is expected with pure vector execution. The effect of scalar instructions can be evaluated with Amdahl's law; the speedup of a processor with vector instructions is

$$S = \frac{1}{1 - \alpha + \alpha\mu}$$

where α is the fraction of the scalar processor time that is vectorized and μ is the ratio of the vector instruction processing time to the scalar instruction processing time.

For example, for $\alpha = 0.9$ and $\mu = 0.1$, the speedup is 5.26 over a processor without vector instructions. Only as $\alpha \to 1$ does speedup approach 10. Now consider the possibility that the vector instructions can be overlapped with the scalar instructions. Under this condition,

$$S = \frac{1}{1 - \alpha + \alpha\mu - \delta\alpha\mu}$$

where δ is the fraction of the vector instruction time that is overlapped. With $\delta = 0$, the speedup is

$$S = \frac{1}{1 - \alpha + \alpha\mu}$$

However, with $\delta = 1$, the speedup is

$$S = \frac{1}{1 - \alpha}.$$

In other words, if all of the vector time is overlapped with the scalar instructions, the execution of the vector portion of the program seems to be infinitely fast and the speedup is limited by the degree by which the program can be vectorized. This analysis is based on [HACK86]. A significant design issue is the amount of overlap that can be achieved by vector and scalar processing. A superscalar processor with two integer units—one for vector addressing and one for scalar processing—plus a floating point pipeline is a potent implementation. One should recognize, however, that the scalar code may have true dependencies on the vector code, making complete overlap impossible.

11.4 Vector Instructions

The instruction set architecture of a vector processor is designed to move operands and results between memory and the pipeline(s) and to select or command the pipeline(s) to perform the desired operation. This section discusses the vector instruction set architecture of three representative processors: the TI ASC, the Cray-1, and the Intel i860.

TI ASC. As noted previously, the FORTRAN DO statement, to be called a DO loop, has been the functional vector instruction definition. The definition of the DO loop, shown in Table 11.6, is from [MCCR61].

Consider the multiplication of matrix A with m rows and n columns and Matrix B with n rows and 1 column, to produce a matrix C. A FORTRAN program for this operation can be

```
        DO 10, l = 1,m
        DO 10, J =  1,l
        C(l,J) = 0
        DO 10, K = 1,n
   10 C(l,J) = C(l,J) + A(l,K) * B(k,J)
```

This program consists of three loops that produce the $m \times 1$ product matrix C.

A major influence in the design of the vector instructions of the TI ASC was the publication of a procedure for performing matrix multiplication in *Planning a Computer* [BUCH62]. The program for this operation contained 12 instructions, as shown in Table 11.7. Within the loops, only one instruction performed a necessary operation: $h + 5$, multiply–add. The other 11 instructions are overhead associated with computing the effective addresses. This program assumes that the operand and product matrixes are stored row major.

$$DO \; n \; i = m_1, m_2, m_3$$

Symbol	Name	Semantics
n	Range	Statement number of the last statement in the loop
i	Index	Index value for addressing the elements of the vector
m_1	Initial Value	Value of the index
m_2	Test Value	Length of the vector: maximum value of the index
m_3	Increment	Increment value applied to the index after each execution: default = 1.

TABLE 11.6 FORTRAN DO loop.

Comment		Instruction
Preparation	$h-2$	Load k from k_0
	$h-1$	Load j_0 from j_{00}
Initial setup	h	Load i_0 from i_{00}
New product row procedure	$h+1$	Load i from i_0
New vector product procedure	$h+2$	Load j from j_0
Vector multiply, inner loop	$h+3$	Set accumulator to zero
	$h+4$	Load cumulative multiplicand from location specified by i
Operation	$h+5$	Multiply–add by operand location specified by j
	$h+6$	Increment j by p
Housekeeping, inner loop	$h+7$	Advance i, count, refill when count reaches zero, branch to $h+4$ when count does not reach zero
End of vector multiplication procedure	$h+8$	Store cumulative product at location specified by k
	$h+9$	Increment k by 1
	$h+10$	Advance j_0, count, refill when count reaches zero, and branch to $h+2$ when count does not reach zero
	$h+11$	Increment i by n
End of product row procedure	$h+12$	Reduce count of k, refill when count reaches zero, and branch to $h+1$ when count does not reach zero

TABLE 11.7 Stretch matrix multiplication program.

The designers of the TI ASC decided that this matrix multiplication algorithm would be the template for all vector instructions. Less complex operations can be programmed within this template. The matrix multiply operation requires that three index values be computed to access the two argument and the product matrices. For referencing single elements in a matrix, the effective address is formed with the address polynomial.

$$\text{Address} = (A_0 - N - 1) + J \times N + 1$$

where A_0 is the starting address, I is the row index, N is the number of columns, and J is the column index.

However, for addressing the elements of a matrix as a vector, the address polynomial is solved incrementally by addition to an index register. That is, for a matrix of m rows and n columns stored column major:

$$I = 1, J = 1 \qquad \text{Address} = A_0$$
$$I = 2, J = 1 \qquad \text{Address} = A_0 + 1$$
$$I = 3, J = 1 \qquad \text{Address} = A_0 + 1 + 1$$
$$\bullet$$
$$I = m, J = n \qquad \text{Address} = A_0 + m + n.$$

The idea behind the TI ASC is that the overhead address calculations can be executed concurrently by hardware control and the multiply–add operation can proceed at the streaming rate of the execution unit(s). The benefit of this design is a significant improvement in performance, often in excess of tenfold over a scalar processor.

The designers of the ASC needed to allocate all of the addressing parameters within a single instruction, which is not possible within the self-imposed constraint of a 32-bit instruction. The approach taken was to implement the concept of a *dope vector* in hardware [VAND89], called the *vector parameter file* (VPF), that is packed into eight words, 32 bytes. The reason for this size is that the memory word is eight computer words (as discussed in Chapter 5), which permitted the complete VPF to be transferred from memory into the CPU in one memory module cycle plus the transfer time.

Thus, a vector instruction in the instruction stream has an operation code, *VECTOR*, followed by address information for finding the VPF in memory. The operation to be performed by the vector instruction is encoded in the VPF (for example, Add, Test, and Multiply). The allocation of vector parameters in the VPF is shown in Table 11.8 [ASC73]; the eight registers that hold the VPF in the CPU are numbered 0–7. The information contained in the VPF completely defines the threefold addressing needed for a dyadic operation and, by proper use, can define all of the five operations discussed in Table 11.1.

The starting address of each of the three vectors (**A**, **B**, and **C**) is determined as base plus displacement. The hex characters XA, XB, and XC select a base register from the general-purpose register file of the CPU, and its content is added to the 16-bit starting addresses SAA, SAB, and SAC in order to create a 24-bit effective address.

The three loops of the matrix multiply program (Table 11.7) are directly supported with the general vector instruction. In addition, the A and B arguments can be immediate values. The first loop, called the *self-loop*, has length L and only increments by 1. The next loop, called the *inner loop*, has its length specified by the inner loop count. The effective address for each matrix (A, B, and C) is formed by adding a

0	Operation	ALC	SV	Vector dimension
1		$I \times A$		Starting address of A
2	HS	$I \times B$		Starting address of B
3	VI	$I \times C$		Starting address of C
4		$\pm \Delta\, Ai$, inner loop		$\pm \Delta\, Bi$, inner loop
5		$\pm \Delta\, Ci$, inner loop		Inner loop count
6		$\pm \Delta\, A0$, outer loop		$\pm \Delta\, B0$, outer loop
7		$\pm \Delta\, C0$, outer loop		Outer loop count

TABLE 11.8   TI ASC vector parameter file.

signed 15-bit integer ($\pm \Delta$) to the staring address. The length of the next loop, called the *outer loop*, is specified by the outer loop count.

Since the self-loop can only increment by one, if a problem requires a stride other than one, by two or three for instance, the self-loop is set to zero and the inner loop becomes the innermost loop. By zeroing out the self-loop, only two loop levels can be programmed.

Cray-1 and X-MP. The Cray processors are typical load/store architectures that support vector instructions. The design of the Cray-1 vector instructions eliminated the complexity of three loops found in the TI ASC. Instead of only one loop or level of indexing, the equivalent of the self-loop of the TI ASC is provided. In FORTRAN, this loop is

```
     DO 10 I = 1, N
10 C(I) = A(I) op B(I)
```

For matrix multiplication, the outer two loops are controlled by scalar instructions. This design approach does not significantly reduce the performance of the processor. Consider the example when both the A and B matrixes are of dimension $n \times n$. The approximate number of operations performed is $2n^3$, with SR(eu) = 2 results per clock. The number of turns through the two outer loops using scalar instructions is n^2. If, for example, each of these turns takes 32 clocks for the scalar code, the efficiency of the processor is

$$\text{efficiency} = 100\, \frac{n^3}{32n^2 + n^3} = 100\, \frac{n}{32 + n}.$$

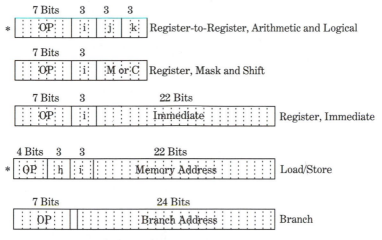

FIGURE 11.5   Cray-1 instruction formats.

For large values of n, the efficiency approaches 100%. Thus, the complexity of three hardware loops does not seem to be justified. In addition, the Cray processors, unlike the TI ASC, can execute scalar instructions in parallel with vector execution. Thus, the overhead of the outer loop turning can be further and significantly reduced.

As I noted previously, the Cray-1, and all subsequent derivative models, have a load/store register file architecture. Figure 11.5 shows the formats for the various instructions.

The register-to-register arithmetic and logical and the load/store formats serve both vector and scalar instructions; the op-codes delineate the two instruction classes. The i, j, and k fields address registers, as implied by the operation field, which can be either scalar or vector registers. Vector registers are addressed by using a scalar address register as a base address that is added to the vector length count. Table 11.9 describes the register addressing methods.

The 32 vector instructions have the operation codes 140_8 to 177_8. The register address of these instructions points to the vector register, and the length of the vector instruction (the number of elements) is provided by the *vector length register* (VL). This register is seven bits. Since only the values 001_8 to 100_8 are valid, a vector instruction cannot exceed length 64. Table 11.10 provides a map of the vector instructions along with their operation codes. The two most significant digits are the

Field	Scalar Instruction	Vector Instruction
i	Result register $S(i)$	Result register $V(i)$
j	Operand register $S(j)$	Operand register $V(j)$
k	Operand register $S(j)$	Operand register $V(j)$
h	Address index register $A(h)$	Address index register $A(h)$

TABLE 11.9   Cray-1 register addressing.

column headings; the row headings are the least significant digit of the operation code.

The vector load and store instructions have two tag fields: h specifies an address register for indexing, and i specifies the destination vector register set (1 of 8). Loading or storing to/from the vector register begins automatically at location 00 and continues upward until the vector length is exhausted. The vector-length register of seven bits must be previously loaded with the length of any vector instruction to follow.

Figure 11.6 shows the reservation table for a vector load for $v = 4$. Recall, from Chapter 4, that the Cray-1 memory is interleaved four ways. The register used to index the memory, initialized to zero, is added to the memory base address in the instruction and is then auto incremented until the vector length is achieved. Vector stores are similar except that the register is read before its contents are written into memory. The low-order six bits of the index register are also added to the vector register initial address of zero in order to provide the register word addresses.

The port between the memory and the vector registers can transfer one word per clock; therefore, the total transport time for a vector load or store is $6 + v$. If the vector is longer than 64 words, after every 70 clocks a new load or store instruction is required to transfer the next 64 words. As there is only one vector-length register, overlapping of the setup clocks is not possible.

The vector registers are not dual ported and cannot sustain concurrent reads and writes. However, as there are eight register files, reads from two vector registers and writes to two vector registers (from memory and/or the output of execution units) can be concurrent. Thus, the vector registers can support a dyadic vector operation with two inputs, vector output, and a load or store to/from memory if the addresses are disjoint and the vector lengths are the same.

A reservation table is shown in Figure 11.7 for a *vector add* instruction of length 5 with the operands in the vector registers. The first step is to load the vector length register into the VL register; then the *Add* instruction can be executed. The execution unit has six stages; the first stage reads the inputs from the register file. An additional clock is required to write a result into the vector registers. After eight clocks,

MSBs

14x	15x	16x	17x	LSBs
Log. Prod. S	Shift L	Flt. Prod. S	Flt. Sum S	x
Log. Prod. V	Shift R	Flt. Prod. V	Flt. Sum V	0
Log. Sum S	Double shift L	1/2 Rnd. Flt. Prod. S	Flt. Diff. S	1
Log. Sum V	Double shift R	1/2 Rnd. Flt. Prod. V	Flt. Diff. V	2
Log. Diff. S	Integer sum S	Rnd. Flt. Prod. S	Fl. Reciprocal and population count	3
				4
Log. Diff. V	Integer Sum V	Rnd. Flt. Prod. V	Test into Mask	5
Transmit S	Integer Diff. S	Reciprocal S	Load memory to Vect, register	6
Transmit V	Integer Diff. V	Reciprocal V	Store Vect. register in memory	7

Note. "S" indicates one scalar operand, and "V" indicates both operands are vectors. The stride of the read and store instructions can be either one or a value found in an address register.

TABLE 11.10 Cray-1 vector instructions.

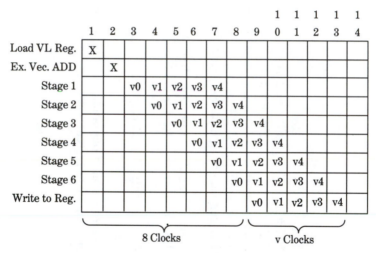

	1	2	3	4	5	6	7	8	9	10	11
Load VL Reg.	X										
Ex. Ld/St. Inst.		X									
Read Module 1			X	X	X	X					
Read Module 2				X	X	X	X				
Read Module 3					X	X	X	X			
Read Module 4						X	X	X	X		
Write to Reg.								V0	V1	V2	V3

6 Clocks   v Clocks

FIGURE 11.6 Cray-1 vector load, $v = 4$.

	1	2	3	4	5	6	7	8	9	10	11	12	13	14
Load VL Reg.	X													
Ex. Vec. ADD		X												
Stage 1			v0	v1	v2	v3	v4							
Stage 2				v0	v1	v2	v3	v4						
Stage 3					v0	v1	v2	v3	v4					
Stage 4						v0	v1	v2	v3	v4				
Stage 5							v0	v1	v2	v3	v4			
Stage 6								v0	v1	v2	v3	v4		
Write to Reg.									v0	v1	v2	v3	v4	

8 Clocks   v Clocks

FIGURE 11.7 Cray-1 vector add reservation table.

the startup latency has been paid and the results stream out of the execution unit ·and are written into the vector registers at the rate of one result per clock.

The Cray X-MP is similar to the Cray-1 in many respects. However, the major differences between them include: (1) a faster clock (9.5 ns compared to 12.5 ns), (2) a higher bandwidth memory with three ports between the register file and memory, and (3) the ability to be configured as a multiprocessor. Because the lower limit on executing any memory-limited process is the time required to transfer the operands to the processor and the results to the memory, there is a potential speedup of a single Cray X-MP processor over the Cray-1 of

$$S = \frac{\text{Cray X} = \text{MP SR(mp)}}{\text{Cray} = 1 \text{ SR(mp)}}.$$

From Tables 11.3 and 11.4

$$S = \frac{105}{26.6} = 3.9.$$

For any memory-limited benchmark, executed on these two machines, the speedup on a single processor cannot be greater than 3.9.

Intel i860. The Intel i860 has a striking correspondence to the CDC 6600. While the i860 does not have vector instruction in its instruction set, vector functions can be called by macrofunctions that are compiled into the native instruction set, as done with the CDC 6600. The i860 has one feature not found in the CDC 6600; two instructions, an integer and a floating point, can be issued in one clock. In effect it is a form of nonuniform superscalar implementation [INTE92a]. Note that the integer instructions are called the *core* instruction set in the manufacturer's literature. Another difference is that the i860 has *dual-operation* instructions that in effect chain the multiplier and adder for performing multiply–add and multiply–subtract.

There is a major difference in the memory system between the i860 and all supercomputers; the i860 memory is cache based rather than based on interleaved memory modules. However, the i860, like most supercomputers, is a load/store register file architecture. In addition, a pipelined load instruction is provided that loads a vector directly from the memory to the register file, bypassing the cache.

The floating point adder and multiplier are each three-stage pipelines (discussed in Section 8.7.3). A feature of this processor is that the pipelines can be operated in *scalar mode*, which inhibits the pipelining. What this means is that the issue latency of the pipeline is set to three, rather than one when pipelining. By operating in scalar mode, true dependencies are automatically resolved. When operating in the *pipelined mode*, there are no hardware dependencies checks; dependencies must be controlled in software. Transition from scalar to pipeline mode requires the introduction of no-ops so that results are not lost.

When operating at a 40-MHz clock rate, the SR(eu) is 80 MFLOPS in single precision and 60 MFLOPS in double precision, under the assumption that a multiply-add operation is performed each clock. All address arithmetic is overlapped by executing concurrent scalar code. Handling address arithmetic concurrently is similar to the TI ASC except that, where the TI ASC is hardwired, the i860 is programmed. Recall from Table 11.3 that the TI ASC has a streaming rate of $2 \times 50 = 100$

MFLOPS for multiply–add. The progress in producing processors in VLSI technology over the last 22 years has been truly outstanding—from a room of equipment to a chip!

11.5 Mask Operations

A number of programming situations call for the elements of a vector to be viewed as the elements of individual scalar processes. The control that makes this possible employs a *mask vector*. There are two types of mask vectors: one that is analogous to a condition code of a scalar processor called a *bit mask vector* and another that is a vector of indices called an *index mask vector*. The use of a bit mask vector to control operations is discussed below and was first, I believed, incorporated into the CDC STAR.

A bit mask vector is first generated and then applied. For example, assume we wish to load only the elements of a vector **A** that are ≥0 into contiguous locations of a vector register. A vector **B** must exist that has all of its elements equal to zero, just as many scalar processors have one register file location always equal to zero for testing purposes. The bit mask vector **M** is formed by the following operation

$$\text{if } a(i) \geq b(i), \text{ then } m(i) \leftarrow 1, \text{ otherwise } m(i) \leftarrow 0.$$

With this bit mask vector, the load can be executed by means of a *compress* operation as shown in Figure 11.8. The dual of compress is *expand*, which is also shown in the figure.

The source vector is read sequentially, and each element that corresponds to a one in the bit mask vector is placed into the register file. Think of the bits of the bit mask vector to be the condition code bits of

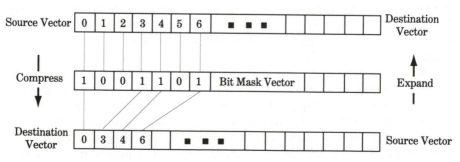

FIGURE 11.8 Compress and expand operations with a mark.

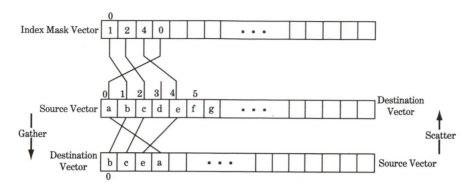

FIGURE 11.9   Scatter and gather.

a group of scalar processors. Each processor sets or resets the condition code bit depending on some operation and then uses that bit to control conditionally a load or store operation. The bit mask vector is in a reserved register, usually an architected register.

The index mask vector is used to control vector loads and stores — an operation that is the equivalent of indirect addressing applied at the vector instruction level. The *scatter* and *gather* operations use a vector of addresses in the index mask vector that address the operand or destination vector in memory; the two operations are shown in Figure 11.9.

The addresses are used to access memory and, for gather, load the gathered elements of the source vector into the processor vector register's contiguous locations. For example, the address in the index mask vector location 0 is 1; memory location 1 is addressed, finding the value *a* that is placed in vector register 0. Scatter, on the other hand, scatters the elements of a dense vector in the registers to the memory locations specified by the address in the index mask vector. In other words, this operation is a vector indirect store operation.

There are several reasons for using Compress, Expand, Scatter, and Gather. One reason is to save valuable vector register space that on early vector processors was limited. However, more recent vector processors such as the NEC SX-2 have much larger registers and saving register space is no longer important.

Another reason for gathering elements into registers is that subsequent processing is reduced because only the valid elements of a vector are processed. In other words, the vector length is reduced, which can reduce the following processing time. While the absolute processing time may be reduced, the MFLOPS measure of performance may decrease because the fixed startup time is prorated over a smaller number of operations. The effect on execution time can be found by

$$\text{speedup} = \text{S} = \frac{\text{time without compression}}{\text{time with compression}} = \frac{\epsilon + av}{\epsilon + dav}$$

where d is the ratio of the vector remaining after compression.

There can be a significant speedup or reduction in processing time for cases where d is very small, for example, if $v = 1024$, $a = 0.5$, and $\epsilon = 7$. If only 16 elements of the vector need to be processed, $d = 0.0156$ and $S = 34.6$, not counting the compress and expand time. The two speedup limits are

as $d \to 1$, $S \to 1$ (there is no speedup);
as $d \to 0$, $S \to 1 + av/\sigma$;
as $v \to \infty$, $S \to 1/d$.

For very large values of v, the speedup approaches $1/d$ for any values of ϵ and a. For example, if $d = 0.1$, the speedup is 10, not counting the compress-expand time. For the example above, if $d = 0$, the limit on speedup is 74, a speedup that must be taken with a bit of skepticism. For $d = 0$, there is nothing to process so there is no need to compress or do anything. In addition, for small values of d, it may be the best strategy to process with scalar code.

11.6 Dependencies

Vector instructions present significant problems in dependency detection and resolution compared to scalar instructions executing on pipelined processors. Two classes of vector dependencies are identified by Cohagan [COHA73] as

1. Intrastatement (recurrence relationship within a vector instruction),
2. Interstatement (dependencies between vector instructions).

The process of vectorization of a FORTRAN program, or a program in any other language, is outside the scope of this book. However, the two classes of dependency problems that are unique to pipelined vector processors are discussed below. The treatment of these dependencies is the same for either memory-to-memory or load/store architectures.

11.6.1 *Intrastatement Dependencies*

Intrastatement dependencies occur within a statement that is expressing a recurrence relationship. Note that for intrastatement dependencies, there can be no antidependencies or output dependencies. A true dependency is illustrated by the recurrence

DO 10 I = 2, 99
10 A(I) = A(I-1) + B(I)

To illustrate the problem, the first three passes through this DO loop are rewritten into a sequence of scalar instructions as

$$A2 \leftarrow A1 + B2$$
$$A3 \leftarrow A2 + B3$$
$$A4 \leftarrow A3 + B4$$

Clearly there is a true dependency on the registers holding the *A* terms. Early vectorizable compilers [COHA73] tag this DO loop as non-vectorizable and execute it as scalar code. As discussed in Chapter 8, the TI ASC hardware then scheduled this program into the execution units. Techniques for vectorizing recurrence relationships are described in [TANA90].

11.6.2 *Interstatement Dependencies*

Interstatement dependencies occur between statements within a DO loop, each of which may be compiled into vector instructions. These dependencies are handled differently by the TI ASC and the Cray. An illustration of an interstatement true dependency is

DO 10 I = 1, 1024
10 A(i) = B(i) + C(i) × D(i)

This DO loop presents a dependency that is created because of the rules of algebra; the add operation cannot begin until the multiply operation is complete. There are two ways of coping with this dependency: compiling into two instructions and chaining.

The first method is to execute two vector instructions (a multiply followed by an add). When the results of the vector multiply instruction have been stored in a temporary vector register (or in memory), the vector add instruction is executed. The two vector instructions are

Vmult: $T(i) \leftarrow C(i) \times D(i)$
Vadd: $A(i) \leftarrow T(i) + B(i)$

Note that there is a true dependency on the $T(i)$ that is resolved by delaying the vector add instruction. As with scalar processors, the temporary register is not needed if there is an overwrite of one of the input registers. This saves register or memory space if the program does not have to save that input. However, overwriting becomes an antidependency that must be guarded against. This antidependency is not likely to happen because the reads from the registers (or memory) have occurred long before the write can take place due to the buffering effect of the execution pipeline itself.

The TI ASC has interlocks that prohibit the release of a second vector instruction until a previous vector instruction completes and all state changes have been retired. The reason behind this design is found in the design of the execution units (discussed in Chapter 8). Dynamic scheduling of the multifunction pipelines was deemed too complex, ruling out the possibility of early vector instruction release. On the positive side, the possibility of intrastatement dependencies is eliminated by this design.

11.6.3 *Chaining*

Interstatement true dependencies are resolved on the Cray processors by chaining. These dependencies are created when a program with an intrastatement dependency is compiled. An example of chaining is found in the multiply–add operation needed for matrix multiplication and general signal processing. Briefly, chaining permits the first result of a vector instruction, as it becomes available out of the multiply pipeline, to become one of the inputs along with $B(i)$, which is streamed into an add pipeline. Thus, it is only necessary to wait for the first element of the vector operation to be complete for the true dependency to be resolved. The TI ASC and some contemporary microprocessors provide automatic chaining for the multiply–add operation using the Vector Dot Product instruction, shown in Figure 8.26.

Chaining is an operation that connects two or more execution units to provide a compound operation without storing intermediate results in a register or memory, that is, a form of forwarding.

Chaining with compound instructions reduces the startup time of a vector process while increasing the execution unit streaming rate. Instead of streaming at one result per clock, the chaining of two execution units gives a streaming rate of two results per clock. This is why the performance of processors is usually advertised performing multiply–add operations.

The basic control mechanism of chaining, as found in the Cray processors, is that the instruction window holds two sequential instructions. Because chaining implies a true dependency between the two chained operations, when the true dependency is resolved, the second instruction releases automatically. The operation is far simpler than the general capability of the CDC 6600 scoreboard. However, the strategy is basically the same: reservations are placed on register resources when an instruc-

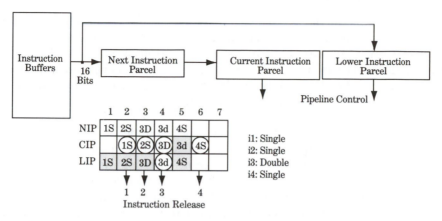

FIGURE 11.10   Cray-1 instruction issue.

tion issues. When these reservations are removed, a second instruction, which also uses these resources, can release.

Cray-1 instruction release is illustrated in Figure 11.10. The instruction buffer consists of four independent buffers, each holding sixty-four 16-bit parcels (single instructions are denoted by S in the figure). Double instructions have two 16-bit parcels denoted (D, d) in the figure. The program counter reads single parcels from the instruction buffers and shifts them, in parallel, to the *next instruction parcel* (NIP) and the *lower instruction parcel* (LIP) registers. The prior parcel in the NIP is shifted into the CIP. Single instructions are issued from the CIP, and double instructions are issued from the CIP and LIP.

When a single parcel instruction issues from the CIP, the contents of the LIP are abandoned in all cases except when holding the second parcel of a double parcel instruction such as a branch.

We can now return to the issue of chaining. Some published papers on Cray chaining imply that results from the first pipeline are written into the vector registers and then read into the next pipeline. These papers indicate that forwarding between pipelines is not used. However, this is not the case as "a result may be received by a V register and re-entered as an operand to another vector computation in the same clock period" [CRAY82].

Chaining is illustrated by the following four-vector-instruction sequence with three true dependencies:

$$
\begin{array}{ll}
i & V0(i) \leftarrow \text{Memory}(i) \\
j & V1(i) \leftarrow V0(i) \times S \\
k & V3(i) \leftarrow V1(i) + V2(i) \\
l & \text{Memory}(i) \leftarrow V3(i)
\end{array}
$$

Recall that the designated vector register consists of 64 locations for the Cray-1. The first true dependency, on $V0(i)$, is resolved when the first element of the input vector has been retired into $V0_0$. At this point the second instruction can release because its second operand is a scalar and is assumed to be already available. The second true dependency is resolved, and the third instruction is released when the first output of the multiply pipeline is retired into $V1_0$. Likewise the third and last true dependency is resolved when the output of the adder is retired into $V3_0$.

The resources required for an instruction are reserved before the instruction releases. However, with vector instructions the reservation of a resource, a destination vector register for example, reserves only the first location of an addressed vector register. When the first dependency is resolved, the chained instruction can release with full confidence that no true dependencies will exist on subsequent elements of the vector. The important point is that a second vector instruction can release when its first inputs are available, it does not have to wait until the complete vector instruction is retired.

Each time a true dependency is resolved the instruction stream is indexed by one in preparation for the next instruction to release when its true dependency is resolved. This indexing is accomplished by moving the next instruction parcel from the instruction buffer into the NIP and LIP registers.

11.7 Benchmark Performance

Previous sections discussed the various aspects of performance from the point of view of basic operations or instructions. In general, these measures are the theoretical maximum performance obtainable from a given processor. However, complete problems contain a mix of scalar and vector instruction (discussed in Section 11.3.5) and varying degrees of possible concurrent operations.

The most extensive body of published information on the benchmark performance of vector processors (and many others as well) is provided by Dongarra [DONG92]. Dongarra supplies these benchmarks to individuals interested in benchmarking a computer; he collects and adds the results to his compendium. Thus the measured performance of many computers executing the LINPACK Benchmark set are available.

Table 11.11 shows an excerpted portion of Dongarra's results for a sampling of computers. For the LINPACK benchmarks, the execution results for a problem size of 100 are converted to MFLOPS. Also tabulated are the "TPP" MFLOPS ratings that result from hand optimization for vector lengths of the order 1,000. In addition, the "Theoretical Peak" MFLOPS rating for each processor, which is the same performance measure as SR(eu) used in Table 11.3, is given.

Computer	Measured MFLOPS	TPP MFLOPS	Theoretical MFLOPS*
Cray Y-MP C90	470	9,715	16,000
NEC SX-3/12	313	4,511	5,500
IBM ES/9000-525	60	338	414
IBM 3090/180E VF	13	71	116

*SR(eu) with no memory conflicts or degradation.

TABLE 11.11   LINPACK benchmark results.

	CRAY 1-S	CRAY X-MP-1	CRAY X-MP-1
All benchmarks	8.04	9.85	15.56
Vectorized benchmarks	26.7	49.2	59.04
Max.	80.42	167.72	187.75
Min.	1.57	1.58	3.65
Compiler	CFT1.14	CFT1.14	CFT77.12

Note. Vector length = 471.

TABLE 11.12   MFLOPS for Livermore loop performance.

Observe that the measured benchmark processing rate of all vector computers is a small fraction of the theoretical performance. For short vectors, around a length of 100, the processor utilization is 3% for the Cray and 5% for the NEC SX. However, for vector lengths of around 1,000, the utilizations are 60% and 82%, respectively. The Cray processors supply higher performance with poorer utilization than the NEC processors.

Tang and Davidson [TANG88] benchmarked the Livermore FOR-TRAN Kernels with excerpted results, in MFLOPS, shown in Table 11.12. Two compilers are used that give different results for the same benchmarks.

The most startling observation is the very wide range of possible performances by the two computers and two compilers: between 50 to 1 and 100 to 1. As shown in Table 11.3, the Cray X-MP-1 has a maximum processing rate of 315 MFLOPS based on the number of execution units and 105 MFLOPS based on memory port bandwidth for dyadic operations. The maximum of 167.72 and 187.72 MFLOPS for vectorized benchmarks indicates the superior vectorization and optimization of the CFT77.12 compiler.

References

[ACOS86]   Acosta, R.D., Kjelstrup, J., Torng, H.C., "An Instruction Issuing Approach to Enhancing Performance in Multiple Function Unit Processors," *IEEE Transactions on Computers*, Vol. C-35, No. 9, September 1986, pp. 815–828.

[AGAR84]   Agarwal, R.C., Stein, D.M., "Virtual to Real Mapping for Scientific Arrays," *IBM Technical Disclosure Bulletin*, Vol. 27, No. 4A, September 1984, pg. 1931.

[AGAR87]   Agarwal, A., Cho, P., Horowitz, J., Salz, A., Hennessy, J., "On-Chip Instruction Caches for High Performance Processors," *Proceedings of the 1987 Stanford Conference on Advanced Research in VLSI*, pp. 1–24.

[AGAR88]   Agarwal, A., Hennessy, J., Horowitz, M., "Cache Performance of Operating System and Multiprogramming Workloads," *ACM Transactions on Computer Systems*, Vol. 6, No. 4, November 1988, pp. 393–431.

[AGAR89]   Agarwal, A., Horowitz, M., Hennessy, J., "An Analytical Cache Model," *ACM Transaction on Computer Systems*, Vol. 7, No. 2, May 1989, pp. 184–215.

[AGER87]   Agerwala, T., Cocke, J., *High Performance Reduced Instruction Set Processors*, IBM Technical Report, RC 12434 (#55845), January 9, 1987.

[AKEL91]   Akella, J., Siewiorek, D.P., "Modeling and Measurement of the Impact of Input/Output on System Performance," *18th Annual International Symposiwn on Computer Architecture*, 1991, pp. 390–399.

[ALEX86]   Alexander, C., Keshlear, W., Cooper, F., Briggs, F., "Cache Memory Performance in a Unix Environment," *Computer Architecture News*, Vol. 14, No. 3, June 1986, pp. 41–70.

[ALLE80]   Allen, A.O., "Queueing Models of Computer Systems," *Computer*, Vol. 13, No. 4, April 1980, pp. 13–24.

[ALPE93]   Alpert, D., Avon, D., "Architecture of the Pentium Microprocessor," *IEEE Micro*, Vol. 13, No. 3, 1993, pp. 11–21.

[AMD90]   *Am29000 User's Manual*, Advanced Micro Devices, 10620C, 1990.

[AMDA67]   Amdahl, G.M., "Validity of The Single Processor Approach to Achieving Large Scale Computing Capabilities, *AFIPS Spring Joint Computer Conference*, 1967, pp. 483–485.

[ANDE67]   Anderson, D.W., Sparacio, F.K., Tomasulo, R.M., "The IBM System/360 Model 91: Machine Philosophy and Instruction-Handling," *IBM Journal of Research and Development*, Vol. 11, No. 1, January 1967, pp. 8–24.

[ANDE67a]   Anderson, S.F., Earle, J.G., Goldschmidt, R.E., Powere, D.M., "The IBM System/360 Model 91: Floating-Point Execution Unit," *IBM Journal of Research and Development*, Vol. 11, No. 1, January 1967, pp. 34–53.

[ARCH86]   Archibald, J., Baer, J.L., "Cache Coherence Protocols: Evaluation Using a Multiprocessor Simulation Model," *ACM Transaction on Computer Systems*, Vol. 4, No. 4, November 1986, pp. 273–298.

[ARDE66]   Arden, B.W., Galleg, B.A., O'Brien, T.C., Westervelt, F.H., "Program and Addressing Structure in a Time-Sharing Environrnent," *Journal of the ACM*, Vol. 13, No. 1; January 1966, pp. 1–16.

[ASC73]   *The ASC System-Central Processor*, Texas Instruments Incorporated, Publication #929982-1, May 1973.

[BACK57]   Backus, J.W., Beeber, R.J., Best, S., Goldberg, R., Haibt, L.M., Herrick, H.L., Nelson, R.A., Sayre, D., Sheridan, R.B., Stern, H., Siller, I., Hoghes, R.A., Nutt, R., "The FORTRAN Automatic Coding System," *Western Joint Computer Proceedings*, 1957, pp. 188–198.

[BAER80]   Baer, J-L., *Computer Systems Architecture*, Computer Science Press, Rockville, Maryland, 1980.

[BAER87]   Baer, J-L., Wang, W-H., "Architectural Choices for Multilevel Cache Hierarchies," *16th International Conference on Parallel Processing*, 1987, pp. 258–261.

[BAKO90]   Bakoglu, H.B., Grohoski, G.F., Montoye, R.K., "The IBM RISC System/6000 Processor: Hardware Overview," *IBM Journal of Research and Development*, Vol. 34, No. 1, January 1990, pp. 12–22.

[BANE88]   Banerjee, U., "An Introduction to a Formal Theory of Dependence Analysis," *The Journal of Supercomputing*, Vol. 2, No. 2, October 1988, pp. 133–149.

[BARO92]   Barron, R.J., Higgbie, L., *Computer Architecture*, Addison-Wesley, Reading, Massachusetts, 1992.

[BELA66]   Belady, L.A., "A Study of Replacement Algorithms for a Virtual-Storage Computer," *IBM Systems Journal*, Vol. 5, No. 2, 1966, pp. 78–101.

[BELL71]   Bell, C.G., Newell, L., *Computer Structures: Readings and Examples*, McGraw-Hill Book Company, New York, 1971, pp. 84, 574.

[BELL74]   Bell, J., Casasent, D., Bell C.G., "An Investigation of Alternative Cache Organizations," *IEEE Transactions on Computers*, Vol. C-23, No. 4, April 1974, pp. 346–351.

[BELL76]   Bell, C.G., Strecker, W.D., "Computer Structures: What Have We

Learned from the PDP-11," *Proceedings 3rd Annual Symposium on Computer Architecture*, 1976, pp. 1–14.

[BELL78]   Bell, C.G., Mudge, J.C., McNamara, J.E., *Computer Engineering, A DEC View of Hardware Systems Design*, Digital Equipment Corporation, 1978.

[BERN66]   Bernstein, A.J., "Analysis of Programs for Parallel Processing," *IEEE Transactions on Computers*, Vol. EC-15, No. 5, October 1966, pp. 757–763.

[BERS80]   Berstis, V., "Security and Protection of Data in the IBM System/38," *Proceedings 7th Annual Symposium on Computer Architecture*, 1980, pp. 245–252.

[BLAA86]   Blaauw, G.A., Brooks, F.P., *Computer Architecture*, Fall 1986, Draft.

[BLOC59]   Block, E., "The Engineering Design of the STRETCH Computer," *Proceedings of the EJCC*, 1959, pp. 48–59.

[BLOO62]   Bloom, L., Cohen, M., Porter, S., "Considerations in the Design of a Computer With High Logic-to-Memory Speed Ratio," *AIEE Special Publication, S-136*, 1962, pp. 53–63.

[BOLA67]   Boland L.J., Granito, G.D, Marcotte, A.U., Messina, B.U., Smith, J.W., "The IBM System/360 Model 91: Storage System," *IBM Journal of Research and Development*, January 1967, pp. 54–68.

[BORR]   Borrill, P.L., "Microprocessor Bus Structures and Standards," *IEEE Micro*, Vol. 1, No. 1, February 1981, pp. 84–95.

[BRAY91]   Bray, B.K., Flynn, M.J., *Strategies for Branch Target Buffers*, Computer Systems Laboratory, Stanford University, Technical Report No. CSL-TR-91-480, July 1991.

[BROM87]   Bromley, H., Lamson, R, *LORE: A Guide to Programming The Lisp Machine*, Kluwer Academic Publishers, Boston, 1987.

[BUCH62]   Bucholz, W., *Planning a Computer System, Project Stretch*, McGraw-Hill, New York, 1959.

[BUDN71]   Budnik, P., Kuch, D.K., "The Organization and Use of Parallel Memories," *IEEE Transactions on Computers*, Vol. 20, No. 12, December 1971, pp. 1566–1570.

[BURG94]   Burgess, B., Ullah, N., Van Overen, P., Ogden, D., "The Power PC 606 Microprocessor," *Communications of the ACM*, Vol. 37, No. 6, June 1994, pp. 34–42.

[BURK46]   Burks, A.W., Goldstine, H.H., von Neumann, J., *Preliminary Discussions of the Logical Design of an Electronic Computing Instrument*, US. Army Ordnance Department Report, 1946. Reprinted in [BELL71], pp. 92–119.

[BURN70]   Burnett, G.J., Coffman, E.G., "A Study of Interleaved Memory Systems," *Proceedings of the Spring Joint Computer Conference*, Vol. 36, AFIPS Press, Montvale, New Jersey, pp. 467–474.

[BUTL91]   Butler, M., Yeh, T-Y, Patt, Y., "Single Instruction Stream Parallelism Is Greater than Two," *18th Annual International Symposium on Computer Architecture*, 1991, pp. 276–286.

[BUZE71]   Buzen, J.P., *Queueing Network Models of Multiprogramming*, PhD

Thesis, Division of Engineering and Applied Physics, Harvard University, Cambridge, Massachusetts, May 1971.

[CALA88]   Calahan, D.A., "An Analysis of Vector Startup Access Delays," *IEEE Transactions on Computers*, Vol. 37, No. 9, September 1988, pp. 1134–1137.

[CALA88a]   Calahan, D.A., "Performance Evaluation of Static and Dynamic Memory Systems on the Cray-2," *International Supercomputer Conference*, 1988, pp. 519–524.

[CALL91]   Callahan, D., Kennedy, K., Porterfield, A., "Software Prefetching," *Fourth International Conference on Architectural Support for Programming Languages and Operating Systems*, April 1991, pp. 40–52.

[CASE78]   Case, R.P., Padegs, A., "Architecture of the IBM System/370," *Communications of the ACM*, Vol. 21, No. 1, January 1978, pp. 73–96.

[CATL92]   Catlett, D.E., "Balancing Resourccs," *IEEE Spectrum*, Vol. 29, No. 9, September 1992, pp. 48–55.

[CENS78]   Censier, L.M., Feautrier, P., "A New Solution to Coherence Problems in Multicache Systems," *IEEE Transactions on Computer*, Vol. C-27, No. 12, December 1978, pp. 1112–1118.

[CHAN88]   Chang, A., Mergen, M.F., "801 Storage: Architecture and Programming," *ACM Transactions on Computer Systems*, Vol. 6, No. 1, February 1988, pp. 28–50.

[CHEN64]   Chen, T.C., "The Overlap Design of the IBM System/360 Model 92 Central Processing Unit," *Proceedings Fall Joint Computer Conference*, Vol. 26, Part 2, 1964, pp. 73–80.

[CHEN71]   Chen, T.C., "Unconventional Superspeed Computer Systems," *Spring Joint Computer Conference*, 1971, pp. 365–371.

[CHEN80]   Chen, T.C., "Overlap and Pipeline Processing," *Introduction to Computer Architecture*, Edited Harold Stone, Science Research Associates, Chicago, pp. 427–485.

[CHEN84]   Chen, S.S., "Large-Scale and High-Speed Multiprocessor System for Scientific Applications: Cray X-MP Series," Found in [KOWA84], pp. 59–67.

[CHEN89]   Cheng, U., "Vector Pipelining, Chaining, and Speed on the IBM 3090 and Cray X-MP," *Computer*, Vol. 22, No. 9, September 1989, pp. 31–46.

[CHEN90]   Chen, P.M., Patterson, D.A., "Maximizing Performance in a Striped Disk Array," *17th Annual International Symposium on Computer Architecture*, May 1990, pp. 322–331.

[CHEN91]   Chen, W-T, Sheu, J-P., "Performance Analysis of Multiple Bus Interconnection Networks with Hierarchical Requesting Model," *IEEE Transactions on Computers*, Vol. 40, No. 7, July 1991, pp. 834–842.

[CHEN92]   Chen, T-F., Baer, J-L, "Reducing Memory Latency via Non-blocking and Prefetching Caches," *Fifth International Conference on Architectural Support for Programming Languages and Operating Systems*, October 1992, pp. 51–61.

[CHEU84]   Cheung, T., Smith, J.E., "An Analysis of thc CRAY X-MP Memory System," *International Conference on Parallel Processors*, 1984, pp. 499–505.

[CHEU86]   Cheung, T., Smith, J.E., "A Simulation Study of the CRAY X-MP Memory System," *IEEE Transactions on Computers*, Vol. C-35, No. 7, July 1986, pp. 613–622.

[CHI89a]   Chi, C-H, Dietz, H., "Unified Management of Registers and Cache Using Liveness and Cache Bypass," *ACM Sigplan Notices*, Vol. 24, No. 7, July 1989, pp. 344–355.

[CHO86]   Cho, J., Smith, A.J., Sachs, H., *The Memory Architecture and the Cache and Memory Management Unit for the Fairchild CLIPPER Processor*, Report No. UCB/CSD 86/289, University of California, Berkeley, April 1986.

[CHOW86]   Chow, P., *MIPS-X Instruction Set and Programmers Manual*, Technical Report No. CSL-86-289, Computer Systems Laboratory, Stanford University, May 1986.

[CHOW87]   Chow, P., Horowitz, M., "Architectural Tradeoffs in the Design of MIPS-X," *Proceedings 14th International Symposium on Computer Architecture*, 1987, pp. 300–308.

[CHU74]   Chu, W.W., Opderbeck, H., "Performancc of Replacement Algorithms with Different Page Sizes," *Computer*, Vol. 7, No. 11, November 1974, pp. 14–21.

[CLAR81]   Clark, D.W., Lampson, B.W., Pier, K.A., "The Memory System of a High-Performance Personal Computer," *IEEE Transactions on Computers*, Vol. C-30, No. 10, October 1981, pp. 715–733.

[CLAR83]   Clark, D.W., "Cache Performance in the VAX-11/780," *ACM Transactions on Computer Systems*, Vol. 1, No. 1, February 1983, pp. 24–37.

[CLAR85]   Clark, D.W., Emer, J.S., "Performance of the VAX-11/780 Translation Buffer: Simulation and Measurement," *ACM Transactions on Computer Systems*, Vol. 3, No. 1, February 1985, pp. 31–62.

[CLAR87]   Clark, D.W., "Pipelining and Performance in the VAX 8800 Processor," *Second International Conference on Architectural Support for Programming Languages and Operating Systems*, October 1987, pp. 173–177.

[CLAR88]   Clark, D.W., Bannon, P.J., Keller J.B., "Measuring VAX 8800 Performance with a Histogram Hardware Monitor," *15th International Symposium on Computer Architecture*, 1988, pp. 176–185.

[CMEL91]   Cmelik, R.F., Kong, S.I., Ditzel, D.R, Kelly, E.J., "An Analysis of MIPS and SPARC Instruction Set Utilization on the SPEC Benchmarks," *Second International Conference on Architectural Support for Programming Languages and Operation Systems*, April 1991, pp. 290–302.

[COCK59]   Cocke, J., Kolsky, H.G., "The Virtual Memory in the STRETCH Computer," *Proceedings of the Eastern Joint Computer Conference*, 1959, pp. 82–93.

[COCK90]   Cocke, J., Markstein, V., "The Evolution of RISC Technology at

IBM," *IBM Journal of Research and Development*, Vol. 34, No. 1, January 1990, pp. 4–11.

[COFA68]   Coffman, E.G., "A Simple Probability Model Yielding Performance Bounds for Modular Memory Systems," *IEEE Transactions on Computers*, Vol. 17, No. 1, January 1968, pp. 86–89.

[COHA73]   Cohagan W.L., "Vector Optimization for the ASC," *7th Annual Princeton Conference on Information Sciences and Systems*, Princeton University Press, Princeton, New Jersey, March 1973, pp. 235–253.

[COHE81]   Cohen, J., "Garbage Collection of Linked Data Structures," *ACM Computing Surveys*, Vol. 13, No. 3, September 1981, pp. 341–367.

[COLW87]   Colwell, R.P., Nix, R.P., O'Donnell, J.J., Papworth, D.B., Rodman, P.K., "A VLIW Architecture for a Trace Scheduling Compiler," *Second International Conference on Architectural Support for Programming Languages and Operating Systems*, 1987, pp. 180–192.

[CONT68]   Conti, C.J., Gibson, D.H., Pitkowsky, S.H., "Structural Aspects of the System/360 Model 85, Part 1: General Organization," *IBM System Journal*, Vol. 7, No. 1, 1968, pp. 2–14.

[CONT69]   Conti, C.J., "Concepts for Buffer Storage," *Computer Group News*, Vol. 2, No. 8, March 1969, pp. 9–13.

[COTT65]   Cotten, L.W., "Circuit Implementation of High-Speed Pipeline Systems," *Proceedings Fall Joint Computer Conference*, AFIPS, Vol. 27, 1965, pp. 489–504.

[COTT69]   Cotton, L.W., "Maximum-rate Pipeline Systems," *Proceedings Spring Joint Computer Conference*, 1969, pp. 581–586.

[CRAG68]   Cragon, H.G., Cochran, R.G., Watson, W.J., Poe, P.H., *Multiplexing and Demultiplexing of Related Time Series Data Records*, US. Patent 3,411,145, November 12, 1968.

[CRAG80]   Cragon, H.G., "The Elements of Single-Chip Microcomputer Architecture," *Computer*, Vol. 13, No. 10, October 1980, pp. 27–41.

[CRAG89]   Cragon, H.G., Watson, W.J., "The TI Advanced Scientific Computer," *Computer*, Vol. 22, No. 1, January 1989, pp. 55–64.

[CRAG92]   Cragon, H.G., *Branch Strategy Taxonomy and Performance Models*, Computer Society Press, Los Alamitos, California, 1992.

[CRAW90]   Crawford, J.H., "The i486™ CPU: Executing Instructions in One Clock Cycle," *IEEE Micro*, Vol. 10, No. 1, February 1990, pp. 27–36.

[CRAW92]   Crawford, J.H., "The P5 Microarchitecture," *Fifth Annual Microprocessor Forum*, October 14–15, 1992, pp. 11-1 to 11-16.

[CRAY82]   *Cray-1® Computer Systems, Hardware Reference Manual*, HR-0004, Cray Research, Inc., 1982.

[DAHL80]   Dahlby, S.H., Henry, G.G., Reynolds, D.N., Taylor, P.T., *IBM System/38 Technical Developments*, G58060237, 1980, pp. 47–50.

[DASG89]   Dasgupta, S., *Computer Architecture: A Modern Synthesis*, Vol. 1, John Wiley and Sons, New York, 1989.

[DAVI87]   Davidson, J.W., Vaughan, R.A., "The Effect of Instruction Set Complexity on Program Size and Memory Performance," *Second International Conference on Architectural Support for Programming Languages and Operating Systems*, October 1987, pp. 60–64.

[DAVI71] Davidson, E.S., "The Design and Control of Pipelined Function Generators," *IEEE Conference on Systems, Networks and Computers*, Oaxtepec, Mexico, January 1971.

[DELC86] Del Corso, D., Kirrmann, H., Nicoud, J.D., *Microcomputer Busses and Links*, Academic Press, New York, 1983.

[DENN65] Dennis, J.B., "Seqmentation and the Design of Multiprogrammed Computer Systems, *Journal of the ACM*, Vol. 12, No. 4, October 1965, pp. 589–602.

[DENN67] Denning, P.J., "Effects of Scheduling on File Memory Operations," *Spring Joint Computer Conference*, 1967, pp. 9–21.

[DENN70] Denning, P.J., "Virtual Memory," *Computing Surveys*, Vol. 2, No. 3, September 1970, pp. 153–189.

[DENN72] Denning, P.J., "On Modeling Program Behavior," *AFIPS Conference Proceedings*, Vol. 40, 1972, pp. 937–944.

[DENN76] Denning, P.J. *Encyclopedia of Computer Science*, Edited by A. Ralston, Van Nostrand Reinhold Co., New York, 1977, pp. 1448–1451.

[DENN78] Denning, P.J., Buzen, J.P., "The Operational Analysis of Queueing Network Models," *Computing Surveys*, Vol. 10, No. 3, pp. 225–261.

[DERO85] DeRosa, J., Glackemeyer, R., Knight, T., "Design Implementation of the VAX 86000 Pipeline," *Computer*, Vol. 18, No. 5, May 1985, pp. 38–48.

[DERO86] DeRosa, J., "An Architectural Analysis of Branch Instructions," Technical Report No. 86-07-06, University of Washington, 1986.

[DERO87] DeRosa, J., Levy, H., "An Evaluation of Branch Architectures," *11th Annual International Symposium on Computer Architecture*, 1987, pp. 10–16.

[DIEF91] Diefendorff,K.,"The 8110: A Superscalar RISC Microprocessor with Graphics Support," *Microprocessor Forum*, November 1991.

[DIEF92] Diefendorff, K., Allen, M., "Organization of the Motorola 88110 Superscalar RISC Microprocessor," *IEEE Micro*, Vol. 12, No. 2, April 1992, pp. 40–63.

[DIGI92] *Product Brief, Digital 21064-AA Microprocessor, Preliminary*, Digital Equipment Corporation, February 1992.

[DIGI92a] *Alpha Architecture Handbook, Special Announcement Edition*, Digital Equipment Corporation, February 1992.

[DIJK68] Dijkstra, E.W., "Co-operating Sequential Processes," *Programming Languages*, F. de Genuys (Editor), Academic Press, New York, 1968, pp. 43–112.

[DIJK71] Dijkstra, E.W., "Hierarchical Ordering of Sequential Processes," *Acta Informatica*, Vol. 1, Springer-Verlag, New York, 1971, pp. 115–138.

[DONO72] Donovan, J.L., *Systems Programming*, McGraw-Hill Book Company, New York, 1972.

[DONG92]   Dongarra, J.J., "Performance of Various Computers Using Standard Linear Equation Software," *Computer Architecture News*, Vol. 20, No. 3, June 1992, pp. 22–41.

[DORA76]   Doran, R.W., "Virtual Memory," *Computer*, Vol. 9, No. 10, October 1976, pp. 27–37.

[DUBE90]   Dybey, P.K., Flynn, M.J., "Optimal Pipelining," *Journal of Parallel and Distributed Computing*, Vol. 8, 1990, pp. 10–19.

[ECKE59]   Eckert, J.P., Chu, J.C., Tonik, A.B., Schmit, W.F., "Design of UNIVAC-LARC System I," *Proceedings of the Eastern Joint Computer Conference*, 1959, pp. 53–63.

[EGGE89]   Eggers, S.J., Katz, R.H., "Evaluating the Performance of Four Snooping Cache Coherency Protocols," *16th Annual International Symposium on Computer Architecture*, June 1989, pp. 2–15.

[EICK93]   Eickemeyer, R.J., Vassiliadis, S., "A Load Instruction Unit for Pipelined Processors," *IBM Journal of Research and Development*, Vol. 37, No. 4, July 1993, pp. 547–564.

[ELAY85]   El-Ayat, Agarwal R.K., "The Intel 80386-Architecture and Implementation," *IEEE Micro*, Vol. 5, No. 6, December 1985, pp. 4–22.

[EMER84]   Emer, J.S., Clark, D.W., "A Characterization or Processor Performance in the VAX-11/780," *Proceedings 11th International Symposium on Computer Architecture*, 1984, pp. 301–310.

[EMMA87]   Emma, P.G., Davidson, E.S., "Characterization of Branch and Data Dependencies in Programs for Evaluating Pipeline Performance," *IEEE Transactions on Computers*, Vol. c-36, No. 7, July 1987, pp. 859–875.

[ESTR60]   Estrin, G., "Organization of Computer Systems—The Fixed Plus Variable Structure Computer," *Proceedings of the Western Joint Computer Conference*, May 1960.

[FAGG64]   Fagg, F., Brown, J.L., Hipp, J.A., Doody, D.T., "IBM 360 Engineering," *Proceedings of the FJCC*, 1964, pp. 205–231.

[FARR89]   Farrens, M.K., Pleszkun, A.R., "Improving Performance of Small On-Chip Caches," *16th Annual International Symposium on Computer Architecture*, June 1989, pp. 234–241.

[FAWC82]   Fawcett, B.K., *The Z8000 Microprocessor, A Design Handbook*, Prentice-Hall, Eglewood Cliffs, New Jersey, 1982.

[FERN86]   Fernbach, S., (Editor) *Supercomputers Class VI Systems, Hardware and Software*, North-Holland, New York, 1986.

[FISH81]   Fisher, J.A., "Trace Scheduling: A Technique for Global Microcode Compaction," *IEEE Transaction on Computers*, Vol. C-30, No. 7, July 1981, pp. 478–490.

[FISH83]   Fisher, J.A., "Very Long Instruction Word Architectures," *10th Annual International Symposium on Computer Architecture*, June 1983, pp. 140–150.

[FITE90]   Fite, D.B., Fossum, T., Manley, D., "Design Strategy for the VAX 9000 System," *Digital Technical Journal*, Vol. 2, No. 4, Fall 1990, pp. 13–24.

[FLOR64]   Flories, I., "Derivation of a Waiting-Time Factor for a Multiple-Bank Memory," *Journal of the Association for Computing Machinery*, Vol. 11, No. 3, July 1964, pp. 265–282.

[FLOR74]   Flores, I., "Lookahead Control in the IBM 370 Model 165," *Computer*, Vol. 7, No. 11, November 1971, pp. 24–38.

[FLYN66]   Flynn, M.J., "Very High-Speed Computing Systems," *Proceedings of the IEEE*, Vol. 54, No. 12, December 1966, pp. 1901–1909.

[FOSS85]   Fossum, T., McElroy, J.B., English, W., "An Overview of the VAX 8600 System," *Digital Technical Journal*, No. 1, August 1986, pp. 8–23.

[FOTL87]   Fotland, D.A., Shelton, J.F., Bryg, W.R., La Fetra, R.V., Boschama, S.I., Yeh, A.S., Jacobs, E.M., "Hardware Design of the First HP Precision Architecture Computers," *Hewlett-Packard Journal*, Vol. 38, No. 3, March 1987, pp. 4–17.

[FU89]   Fu, B., Saini, A., Gelsinger, P.P., "Performance and Microarchitecture of the i486™ Processor," *International Conference on Computer Design*, 1989, pp. 182–187.

[FU91]   Fu, J.W.C., Patel, J.H., "Data Prefetching in Multiprocessor Vector Cache Memories," *18th Annual International Symposium on Computer Architecture*, 1991, pp. 54–63.

[FULL75]   Fuller, S.H., Baskett, F., "An Analysis of Drum Storage Units," *Journal of the ACM*, Vol. 22, Fall 1975, pp. 83–105.

[FURH87]   Furht, B., Milutionovic, V., "A Survey of Microprocessor Architectures for Memory Management," *Computer*, Vol. 20, No. 3, March 1987, pp. 48–67.

[GALL91]   Gallant, J. "Protocols Keep Data Consistent," *EDN*, Vol. 36. No. 5, March 1991, pp. 41–50.

[GARD91]   Gardner, G.L., *The Number of Delay Slots That Can Be Filled in a Reduced Instruction Set Computer (RISC)*, Masters Thesis, The University of Texas, Austin, Texas, May 1991.

[GARN59]   Garner, H.I., "Number Systems and Arithmetic," *Introduction to Digital Computer Engineering*, The University of Michigan, 1959, pp. 14.

[GEE91]   Gee, J.D., Hill, M.D., Smith, A.J., *Cache Performance of the SPEC Benchmark Suit*, Report No. UCB/CSD 91/648, EECS, University of California, Berkeley, October 3, 1991.

[GEE93]   Gee, J.D., Hill, M., Pnevmatikatos, D.N., Smith, A.J., "Cache Performance of the SPEC92 Benchmark Suit," *IEEE Micro*, Vol 13, No. 4, August 1993, pp. 17–27.

[GEIS87]   Geist, R., Daniel, S., "A Continuum of Disk Scheduling Algorithms," *ACM Transactions on Computer Systems*, Vol. 5, No. 1, February 1987, pp. 77–92.

[GHAR91]   Gharachorloo, K., Gupta, A., Hennessy, J., "Performance Evaluation of Memory Consistency Models for Shared-Memory Multiprocessors," *Fourth International Conference on Architectural Support for Programming Languages and Operating Systems*, April 1991, pp. 245–257.

[GIBS67]   Gibson, D.H., "Consideration in Block-oriented Systems Design," *Spring Joint Computer Conference, AFIPS Conference Proceedings*, Vol. 30, Spartan Books, Washington D.C., 1967, pp. 69–80.

[GIBS89]   Gibson, G.A., Hellerstein, L., Karp, R.M., Jatz, R.H., Oattersib, D.A., "Failure Correction Tcchniques for Large Disk Arrays," *Proceedings Third International Conference on Architectural Support for Programmning Languages and Operating Systems*, April 1989, pp. 123–132.

[GOLD87]   Goldstein, S., "Storage Performance—An Eight Year Outlook," *TR 03.388-1 Second Edition*, IBM Corporation, General Products Division, San Jose, California, October 1987.

[GOOD83]   Goodman, J.R. "Using Cache Memory to Reduce Processor-Memory Traffic," *Proceedings of the 10th Annual Symposium on Computer Architecture*, Stockholm, June 1983, pp. 123–131.

[GOOD87]   Goodman, J.R., "Coherency For Multiprocessor Virtual Address Caches," *Second International Conference on Architectural Support for Programming Languages and Operating Systems*, October 1987, pp. 72–81. Also Computer Architecture News, Vol. 15, No. 5, October 1987.

[GOLB92]   Golbert, A., Farrell, Bob, MacWilliams, P., Sakran, N., Silas, I., "A Second Level Multiprocessing Cache for the i486™ DX and i860™XP Processors, *COMPCON*, Spring 1992, pp. 338–343.

[GRAH65]   Graham, R.M., "Protection in an Information Processing Utility," *Communications of the ACM*, Vol. 11, No. 5, May 1968, pp. 365–369.

[GRAH72]   Graham, G.S., Denning, P.J., "Protection-Principles and Practice," *Spring Joint Computer Conference*, 1972, pp. 417–429.

[GROC89]   Grochowski, E., Shoemaker, K., "Issues In the Implementation of the i486 Cache and Bus," *International Conference on Computer Design: VLSI in Computers & Processors*, Computer Society Press, October 1989, pp. 193–198.

[GROH82]   Grohoski, G.F., Patel, J.H., "A Performance Model for Instruction Prefetch in Pipelined Instruction Units," *11th International Conference on Parallel Processing*, 1982, pp. 248–252.

[GROH90]   Grohoski, G.F., "Machine Organization of the IBM RISC System/6000 Processor," *IBM Journal of Research and Development*, Vol. 34, No. 1, January 1990, pp. 37–58.

[GROH90a]   Grohoski, G.F., Kahle, J.A., Thatcher, L.E., Moore, C.R, "Branch and Fixed-Point Instruction Execution Units," *IBM RISC System/6000 Technology*, IBM publication SA23-2619, pp. 24–32.

[GROS53]   Grosch, H.R.J., "High Speed Arithmetic: The Digital Computer as a Research Tool," *Journal of the Optical Society of America*, Vol. 43, No. 4, April 1953, pp. 306–310.

[GUO89]   Guo, D., Cragon, H.G., "A Markovian Model For the Performance of Pipelined Processors," *Proceedings of the 1989 Southern Simulation Conference*, Pensacola, Florida, October 16–17, 1989.

[GWEN92]   Gwennap, L., "Intel Describes P5 Internal Architecture," *Micro-processor Report*, October 28, 1992, pp. 25–26.

[HACK86]   Hack, J.J., "Peak vs. Sustained Performance in Highly Concurrent Vector Machines," *Computer*, Vol. 19, No. 9, September 1986, pp. 11–19.

[HABA93]   Haban, S., personal communications, September 1993.

[HAMA90]   Hamacher, V.V., Vranesic, Z.G., Zaky, S.F., *Computer Organization*, McGraw-Hill Publishing Company, New York, 1990.

[HALF94]   Halfhill, T.R., "AMD vs. Superman," *Byte*, Vol. 19, No. 11, November 1994, pp. 95–128.

[HALF95]   Halfhill, T.R., "Intel's P6," *Byte*, Vol. 20, No. 4, April 1995, pp. 42–58.

[HAMM50]   Hamming, R.W., "Error detecting and correcting Codes," *The Bell system Technical Journal*, Vol. 26, April, 1950, pp. 147–160.

[HARA90]   Haracher, V.C., Vranesic, Z.G., Zaky, S.G., *Computer Organization*, *Third Edition*, McGraw-Hill, New York, 1990.

[HARK81]   Harker, J.M., Brede, D.W., Pattison, R.E., Santana, G.R., Taft, L.G., "A Quarter Century of Disk File Innovation," *IBM Journal of Research and Development*, Vol. 25, No. 5, September 1981, pp. 677–689.

[HARP91]   Harper, D.T., Linebarger, D.A., "Conflict-Free Vector Access Using a Dynamic Storage Scheme," *IEEE Transactions on Computers*, Vol. 40, No. 3, March 1991, pp. 276–283.

[HELL67]   Hellerman, H., *Digital Computer System Principles*, McGraw-Hill, New York, 1967.

[HENN82]   Hennessy, J.L., Gross, T.R., "Code Generation and Reorganization in the Presence of Pipeline Constraints," *9th Annual Symposium on Principles of Programming Languages*, 1982, pp. 120–127.

[HENN82a] Hennessy, J.L., Jouppi, N., Baskett, F., Gross, T., Gill, J., "Hardware/Software Tradeoffs for Increased Performance," *Symposium on Architectural Support for Programming Languages and Operating Systems*, 1982, pp. 2–11.

[HENN90]   Hennessy, J.L., Patterson, D.A., *Computer Architecture a Quantitative Approach*, Morgan Kaufmann, San Mateo, California, 1990.

[HEST86]   Hester, P.D., Simpson, R.O., Chang, A., "The IBM RT PC ROMP and Memory Management Unit Architecture," *IBM RT Personal Computer Technology*, IBM Corporation Form No. SA23-1057, 1986, pp. 48–56.

[HIGB90]   Higbie, L., "Quick and Easy Cache Performance Analysis," *Computer Architecture News*, Vol. 18, No. 2, June 1990, pp. 33–44.

[HILL84]   Hill, M.D. and Smith, A.J., "Experimental Evaluation of On-Chip Microprocessor Cache Memories," *Proceedings 11th Annual Symposium on Computer Architecture*, pp. 158–164, 1984.

[HILL86]   Hill, M.D. et al., "Design Decisions in SPUR," *Computer*, Vol. 19, No. 11, November 1986, pp. 8–22.

[HILL87]   Hill, M.D. "Aspects of Cache Memory and Instruction Buffer Performance," *Report No. UCB/CSD 87/381, Computer Science Division (EECS), University of California, Berkeley, California 94720,* November 1987.

HILL88]   Hill, M.D., "A Case for Direct-Mapped Caches," *Computer,* Vol. 21, No. 12, December 1988, pp. 25–40.

[HOCK81]   Hockney, W., Jesshope, R., *Parallel Computers,* Adam Hilger Lt., Bristol, England, 1981.

[HOLG80]   Holgate, R.W., Ibett, R.N., "An Analysis of Instruction-Fetching Strategies In Pipelined Computers," *IEEE Transactions on Computers,* Vol. C-29, No. 4, April 1980, pp. 325–329.

[HOUD79]   Houdek, M.E., Mitchell, G.R., "Hash Index Helps Manage Large Virtual Memory," *Electronics,* March 15, 1979, pp. 111–113.

[HOUD80]   Houdek, M.E., Mitchell, G.R., "Translating a Large Virtual Address," *IBM System/38 Technical Developments,* G58060237, 1980, pp. 22–24.

[HOUD81]   Houdek, M.E., Soltis, F.G., Hoffman, R.L., "IBM System/38 Support for Capability-based Addressing," *Proceedings 8th Annual Symposium on Computer Architecture,* pp 341–348, 1981.

[HSIE85]   Hsieh, J.T., Pleszkun, A.R., Vernon, M.K., "Performance Evaluation of a Pipelined VLSI Architecture Using the Graph Model of Behavior (GMB)," *IFIPS,* pp. 192–205, 1985.

[HUCK93]   Huck, J., Hays, J., "Architectural Support for Translation Tables Management in Large Address Space Machines," *Proceedings 20th Annual International Symposium on Computer Architecture,* 1993, pp. 39–50.

[HWAN84]   Hwang, K., Briggs, F.A., *Computer Architecture and Parallel Processing,* McGraw-Hill, New York, 1984.

[HWAN93]   Hwang, K., *Advanced Computer Architecture with Parallel Programming,* McGraw-Hill, New York, 1993.

[HWU87]   Hwu, W-M.W., Patt, Y.N., "Checkpoint Repair for Out-of-order Execution Machines," *IEEE Transactions on Computers,* C-36, No. 12, December 1987, pp. 1515–1522.

[HWU89]   Hwu, W.W., Chang, P.P., "Achieving High Instruction Cache Performance with an Optimizing Compiler, *Proceedings 16th Annual Internatianal Symposium on Computer Architecture,* 1989, pp. 242–251.

[IBBE77]   Ibbett, R.N., Husband, M.A., "The MU5 Name Store," *The Computer Journal,* Vol. 20, No. 3, August 1977, pp. 227–231.

[IBBE78]   Ibbett, R.N., Capon, P.C., "The Development of the MU5 Computer System," *Communications of the ACM,* Vol. 21, No. 1, January 1978, pp. 13–24.

[IBM69]   *IBM System/360 Model 195 Functional Characteristics,* IBM Corporation, Systems Reference Library, Form A22-6943-0, 1969.

[IBM76]   *IBM System/370 Principles of Operation,* GA22-7000-5, File No. S/370-01, August 1976.

[IBM90]   *POWER Processor Architecture, Version 1.52,* IBM Corporation, Austin, Texas, February 1990.

[IBM90a]   *IBM RISC System/6000^{TM} POWERstation and POWERserver Hardware Technical Reference General Information*, SA23-2643-00, 1990.

[IBM93]   *PowerPC Architecture*, IBM Corporation, SR28-5124-00, May 1993.

[IEEE90]   *International Standard ISO/IEC, 10857, ANSI/IEEE Syd. 896.I*, 1994 Edition, IEEE, New York, 1994.

[ILIF68]   Iliffe, J.K., *Basic Machine Principles*, McDonald/American Elsevier, London, 2nd edition, 1972.

[INTE84]   *Microsystems Components Handbook Vol. 1*, Intel Corporation, Order Number 230843-001, 1984.

[INTE86]   *80386 Hardware Reference Manual*, Intel Corporation, Order Number 231732-001, 1986.

[INTE86a]   *80386 Programmer's Reference Manual*, Intel Corporation, Order Number 230985-001, 1986.

[INTE90]   *i486 Microprocessor Hardware Reference Manual*, Intel Corporation, Order Number 240552-001.

[INTE92]   *Intel Microprocessors, Volume 1*, Intel Corporation, Order Number 230843, 1992.

[INTE92a]   *i860 Microprocessor Family Programmer's Reference Manual*, Intel Corporation, Order Number 240875-002, 1992.

[INTE92b]   *Intel Multimedia and Supercomputing Processors*, Intel Corporation, Order Number 272084-001, 1992.

[INTE93]   *Pentium Processor User's Manual, Volume 3: Architecture and Programming Manual*, Intel Corporation, Order Number 241428, 1993.

[INTE93a]   *Pentium Processor User's Manual, Volume 2: 82496 Cache Controller and 82491 Cache SRAM Data Book*, Intel Corporation, Order Number 241429-001, 1993.

[INTE93b]   *Pentium Processor User's Manual, Volume 1: 82496 Pentium Processor Data Book*, Intel Corporation, Order Number 241428-001, 1993.

[JENS87]   Jensen, E.H., Hagensen, G.W., Broughton, J.M., *A New Approach to Exclusive Data Access in Shared Memory Multiprocessors*, Lawrence Livermore National Laboratory #97663, November 1987.

[JOHN61]   Johnson, L.R, "Indirect Chaining Method for Addressing on Secondary Keys," *Communications of the ACM*, Vol. 4, May 1961, pp. 218–222.

JOHN78]   Johnson, P.M., "An Introduction to Vector Processing," *Computer Design*, Vol. 17, No. 2, February 1978, pp. 89–97.

[JOHN84]   Johnson, O.G., "Three-Dimensional Wave Equation Computations on Vector Computers," *Proceedings of the IEEE*, Vol. 72, No. 1, January 1984, pp. 90–95.

[JOHN87]   Johnson, M., "System Considerations in the Design of the AM29000," *IEEE Micro*, Vol. 7, No. 4, August 1987, pp. 28–41.

[JOHN89]   Johnson, M., *Super-Scalar Processor Design*, Computer Systems Laboratory, Stanford University, CSL-TR-89-383, June 1989.

[JOHN91]   Johnson, M., *Superscalar Microprocessor Design*, Prentice-Hall, Englewood Cliffs, New Jersey, 1991.

[JORD77]   Jordan, T.L., Fong, K., "Some Linear Algebraic Algorithms and Their Performance on the CRAY 1," *High Speed Computer and Algorithm Organization*, Edited, Kuck, D.J., [KUCK77] pp. 313–316.

[JOUP89]   Jouppi, N., Wall, D.W., "Available Instruction Level Parallelism for Superscalar and Superpipelined Machines," *Proceedings of the 3rd International Conference on Architectural Support for Programming Languages and Operating Systems*, April 1989, pp. 272–282.

[JOUP89a]   Jouppi, N., "The Nonuniform Distribution of Instruction-Level and Machine Parallelism and Its Effect on Performance," *IEEE Transactions on Computers*, Vol. 38, No. 12, December 1989, pp. 1645–1658.

[JOUP90]   Jouppi, N.P., "Improving Direct-Mapped Cache Performance by the Addition of a Small Fully Associative Cache and Prefetch Buffer," *17th Annual International Symposium on Computer Architecture*, May 1990, pp. 364–373.

[KAHN90]   Kahng, A., Cong, J., Robins, G., "High-Performance Clock Routing Based on Recursive Geometric Matching," *Computer Science Department Technical Report*, University of California, CSD-900046, December 1990.

[KAIN89]   Kain, R.Y., *Computer Architecture: Software and Hardware*, Vol. 2, Prentice-Hall, Englewood Cliffs, New Jersey, 1989.

[KALA91]   Kalaiber, A.C., Levy, H.M., "An Architecture for Software-Controlled Data Prefetching," *18th Annual International Symposium on Computer Architecture*, May 1991, pp. 43–53.

[KAPL73]   Kaplan, K.R., Winder, R.O., "Cache-based Computer Systems," *Computer*, Vol. 6, No. 3, March 1973, pp. 30–36.

[KARP69]   Karp, R.M., Miller, R.E., "Parallel Program Schemata," *Journal of Computer and System Sciences*, Vol. 3, No. 2, May 1969, pp. 147–195.

[KATE84]   Katevenis, M.G.H., *Reduced Instruction Set Computer Architecture for VZSI*, The MIT Press, Cambridge, Massachusctts, 1984.

[KATZ71]   Katzan, H., "Storage Hierarchy Systems," *Spring Joint Computer Conference*, 1971, pp. 325–335.

[KATZ89]   Katz, R.H., Gibson, G.A., Pattcrson, D.A., "Disk System Architectures for High Performance Computing," *Proceedings of the IEEE*, Vol. 77, No. 12, December 1989, pp. 1842–1858.

[KELL75]   Keller, R.M., "Look-Ahead Processors," *Computing Surveys*, Vol. 7, No. 4, December 1975, pp. 177–195.

[KESS89]   Kessler, R.E., Jooss, R., Lebeck, A., Hill, M.D., "Inexpensive Implementations of Set-Associativity," *16th International Symposium on Computer Architecture*, 1989, pp. 131–139.

[KILB62]   Kilburn, T., Edwards, D.B.G., Lanigan, M.J., Summer, F.H., "One-level Storage System," *IRE Transactions on Electronic Computers*, Vol. 11, No. 2, 1962, pp. 223–235.

[KIM86]   Kim, M.Y., "Synchronized Disk Interleaving," *IEEE Transactions on Computers*, Vol C-35, No. 11, November 1986, pp. 978–988.

[KIM87]   Kim, M.Y., Tantawi, A.N., "Asynchronous Disk Interleaving," *IBM Research Report* RC12497, January 30, 1987.

[KLAI91]   Klaiaber, A.C., Levey, H.M., "An Architecture for Software-Controlled Data Prefetching," *18th Annual International Symposium on Computer Architecture*, 1991, pp. 43–53.

[KLAS92]   Klass, F., *Balancing Circuits for Wave Pipelining*, CSL-TR-92-549, Stanford University, 1992.

[KNUT68]   Knuth, D.E., *The Art of Computer Programming: Volume 1: Fundamental Algorithms*, Addison-Wesley, Reading, Massachusetts, 1968.

[KOHN89]   Kohn, L., Fu, S-W., "A 1,000,000 Transistor Microprocessor," *1989 International Solid-State Circuits Conference Digest of Technical Papers*, 1989.

[KOGG81]   Kogge, P.M., *The Architecture of Pipelined Computers*, Hemisphere, New York, 1981.

[KOWA84]   Kowalik, J.S. (Editor), *High-Speed Computation*, Springer-Verlag, New York, 1984.

[KR0F81]   Kroft, D., "Lockup-free Instruction Fetch/Prefetch Cache Organization," *8th Annual Symposium on Computer Architecture*, May 1981. pp. 81–85.

[KUCK77]   Kuck, D.J., Lawrie, D.H. Sameh, A.H., *High Speed Computer and Algorithm Organization*, Academic Press, Inc., New York, 1977.

[KUCK78]   Kuck, D.J., *The Structure of Computers and Computations, Volume 1*, John Wiley and Sons, New York, 1978.

[KUGA91]   Kuga, Mo., Murakami, K., Tomita, S., "DSNS(Dynamically-hazard-resolved, Statically-code-scheduled, Nonuniform Superscalar): Yet Another Superscalar Processor Architecture," *Computer Architecture News*, Vol. 19, No. 4, June 1991, pp. 14–29.

[KUNK86]   Kunkel, S.R., Smith, J.E., "Optimal Pipelining in Supercomputers," *Proceedings of the 13th Annual Symposium on Computer Architecture*, 1986, pp. 404–411.

[KURI91]   Kurian, L., Hulina, P.T., "Classification and Performance Evaluation of Instruction Buffering Techniques," *18th Annual International Symposium on Computer Architecture*, 1991, pp. 150–159.

[LAHA88]   Laha, S., Patel, J.H., Iyer, R.K., "Accurate Low-Cost Methods for Performance Evaluation of Cache Memory Systems, *IEEE Transactions on Computers*, Vol. 37, No. 11, November 1988, pp. 1325–1336.

[LAIR92]   Laird, M., "A Comparison of Three Current Superscalar Design," *Computer Architecture News*, Vol. 20, No. 3, June 1992, pp. 14–21.

[LAM79]   Lam, C-Y., Madnick, S.E., "Properties of Storage Hierarchy Systems with Multiple Page Sizes and Redundant Data," *ACM Transactions on Database Systems*, Vol. 4, No. 3, September 1979, pp. 345–367.

[LAMP66]   Lampson, B.W., Lichtenberger, W.W, Pirtle, M.W., "A User Machine in a Time-sharing System," *Proceedings of the IEEE*, Vol. 12, No. 12, December 1966, pp. 1766–1774.

[LAMP79]   Lamport, L., "How to Make a Multiprocessor Computer That Correctly Executes Multiprocess Programs," *IEEE Transactions on Computers*, Vol. C-28, No. 9, September 1979, pp. 690–691.

[LANG79]   Lang, D.E., Agervala, T.K., Chandy, K.M., "A Modeling Approach and Design Tool for Pipelined Central Processors," *Proceedings 6th Annual Symposium on Computer Architecture*, 1979, pp. 122–129.

[LARS73]   Larson, A.G., Davidson, E.S., "Cost-Effective Design Of Special-Purpose Processors: A Fast Fourier Transform Case Study," *Proceedings Eleventh Annual Allerton Conference On Circuit and System Theory*, October, 1973, pp. 547–557.

[LAWR82]   Lawrie, D., Vora, C., "The Prime Memory System for Array Access," *IEEE Transactions on Computers*, Vol. 31, No. 5, May 1982, pp. 435–442.

[LEE69]   Lee, F.F., "Study of "Look-Aside" Memory," *IEEE Transactions on Computers*, Vol. C-18, No. 11, November 1969, pp. 1062–1064.

[LEE84]   Lee, J.K.F., Smith, A.J., "Branch Prediction Strategies and Branch Target Buffer Design," *Computer*, Vol. 21, No. 7, January 1984, pp. 6–22.

[LEE87]   Lee, R.L., "The Effectiveness of Caches and Data Prefetch Buffers in Large-Scale Shared Memory Multiprocessors," Ph.D. Thesis, University of Illinois at Urbana-Champaign, May 1987.

[LEE89]   Lee, R.B., "Precision Architecture," *Computer*, Vol. 22, No. 1, January 1989, pp. 78–91.

[LEE91]   Lee, R.L., Ywok, A.Y., Briggs, F.A., "The Floating Point Performance of a Superscalar Sparc Processor," *Fourth International Conference on Architectural Support for Programming Languages and Operating Systems*, April 1991, pp. 28–37.

[LEE91a]   Lee, E.K., Katz, R.H., *An Analytic Performance Model of Disk Arrays and its Application*, Report No. UCB/CSD 91/660, University of California, Berkeley, November 1991.

[LEON87]   Leonard, T.E., (Editor), *VAX Architecture Reference manual*, Digital Press, Bedford, Massachusetts, 1987.

LEVY78]   Levy, J.V., "Buses, The Skeleton of Computer Structures," Chapter 11 of [BELL78].

[LEVY82]   Levy, H.M., Lipman, P.H., "Virtual Memory Management in the VAX/VMS Operating System," *Computer*, Vol. No. 3, March 1982, pp. 35–41.

[LEVY84]   Levy, H.M., *Capability-Based Computer Systems*, Digital Press, Bedford, Massachusetts, 1984.

[LEVY90]   Levy, H.M., Eckhouse, R.H. Jr., *Computer Programming and Architecture The VAX-11*, Digital Press, Massachusetts, 1980.

[LEWI88]   Lewis, T.G., Cook, C.R., "Hashing for Dynamic and Static Internal Tables," *Computer*, Vol. 21, No. 10, October 1988, pp. 45–56.

[LIVN87]   Livny, M., Kohoshafian, S, Boral, H., "Multi-disk Management Algorithms," *Proceedings Sigmetrics*, May 1987.

[LIPT68]   Liptay, J.S., "Structural Aspects of the System/360 Model 85, II The Cache," *IBM Systems Journal*, Vol. 7, No 1, 1968, pp. 15–21.

[LOGR79]   Logrippo, L., "Renamings, Maximal Parallelism, and Space-Time Tradeoff in Program Schemata," *Journal of the Association for Computing Machinery*, Vol. 26, No. 4, October 1979, pp. 819–833.

[LOPR89]   Lopresti, D.P., *Sequence Comparison on Commercial Supercomputers*, Supercomputing Research Center Technical Report SRC-TR-89-010, October 1989.

[LUBE85]   Lubeck, O., Moore, J.W., Mendez, R., "A Benchmark Comparison of Three Supercomputers: Fujitsy VP-2000, Hitachi S8100/20, and Cray X-MP/2," *Computer*, Vol. 18, No. 12, December 1985, pp. 10–23.

[LUBE87]   Lubeck, O.M., Moore, J.W., Mendez, R., "The Performance of the NEC SX-2 and Cray X-MP Supercomputers," Los Alamos National Laboratory, LA-UR-87-227, 1987.

[MACC65]   McCracken, D.D., *A Guide to FORTRAN Progromming*, John Wiley and Sons, New York 1965.

[MACD84]   MacDougall, M., "Instruction-level Program and Process Modeling," *Computer*, Vol. 17, No. 7, July 1984, pp. 14–26.

[MACG83]   MacGregor, D., Mothersole, D.S., "Virtual Memory and the MC68010," *IEEE Micro*, Vol. 3, No. 3, June 1983, pp. 24–39.

[MACG84]   MacGregor, D., Mothersole, D., Moyer, B., "The Motorola MC68020," *IEEE Micro*, Vol. 4 No. 4 August 1984, pp. 101–118.

[MAHO86]   Mahon, M.J., Lee, R.B-L, Miller, T.C., Huck, W.R, Bryg, W.R., "The Hewlett-Packard Precision Architecture: The Processor," *Hewlett-Packard Journal*, Vol. 37, No. 8, August 1986, pp. 4–22.

[MALI90]   Malik, N., *A Design Methodology for Synthesis of Enhanced Support for Programming Environments*, Ph.D. Dissertation, University of Texas, Austin, May 1990.

[MALI93]   Malik, N., Eickemeyer, R.J., Vassiliadis, S., "Architectural Effects on Dual Instruction Issue with Interlock Collapsing ALUs," Submitted to: *Twelfth Annual IEEE International Phoenix Conference on Computers and Communications*, March 1993.

[MATI77]   Matick, R.E., *Computer Storage Systems and Technology*, John Wiley and Sons, New York, 1977.

[MATI80]   Matick, R.E., "Memory and Storage," *Introduction to Computer Architecture Chapter 5*, Science Research Associates, Inc., Chicago, 1980.

[MATI89]   Matick, R.E., "Functional Cache Chip for Improved System Performance," *IBM Journal of Research and Development*, Vol. 33, No. 1, January 1989, pp. 15–31.

[MATT70]   Mattson, R.E., Gecsei, J., Slutz, D.R., Traiger, I.L., "Evaluation Techniques for Storage Hierarchies," *IBM Systems Journal*, Vol. 9, No. 2, 1970, pp. 78–117.

[MCFA89]   McFarling, S., "Program Optimization for Instruction Caches," *Third International Conference on Architectural Support for Programming Languages and Operating Systems*, 1989, pp. 183–191.

[MCKE79] McKevitt, J., Bayless, J., "New Options from Big Chips," *IEEE Spectrum*, Vol. 16, No. 3, March 1979, pp. 28–34.

[MEAD70] Meade, R.M., "On Memory System Design," *Fall Joint Computer Conference*, 1970, pp. 33–43.

[MEND66] Mendelson, M.J., England, A.W., "The SDS Sigma 7: A Real-Time Time-Sharing Computer," *AFIPS Conference Proceedings*, Vol. 29, 1966, pp. 51–66.

[MILL89] Miller, J., Roberts, B., Madland, P., "High Performance Circuits for the i486 Processor," *International Conference on Computer Design*, October, 1989, pp. 188–191.

[MILE90] Milenkovic, M., "Microprocessor Memory Management Units," *IEEE Micro*, Vol. 10, No. 2, April 1990, pp. 71–85.

[MILL91] Miller, E.L., *Input/Output Behavior of Supercomputing Applications*, Report No. UCB/CSD 91/616, Computer Science Division, University of California, Berkeley, 1991.

[MIPS87] *R2000 Processor User's Guide*, MIPS Computer Systems, Inc. Order Number 02-00029(A), July, 1987.

[MIRA92] Mirapuri, S., Woodacre, M., Vassegbi, N., "The MIPS R4000 Processor," *IEEE Micro*, Vol. 12, No. 2, April 1992, pp. 10–22.

[MITC86] Mitchell, C., *Processor Architecture and Cache Performance*, Ph.D. Thesis, Stanford University, Stanford Techical Report No. CSL-TR-86-296, June 1986.

[MOGU91] Mogul, J.C., Borg, A. "The Effect of Context Switches on Cache Performance," *ASPLOS-IV*, April 1991, pp. 75–84.

[MOOR91] Moore, C.R., "*A Taxonomy of A Memory Management Structures in General Purpose Computer Systems*, Masters Report, University of Texas at Austin, May 1991.

[MONT90] Montoye, R.K., Hokenek, E., Runyon, S.L., "Design of the IBM RISC System/6000 Floating-point Execution unit," *IBM Journal of Research and Development*, Vol. 34, No. 1, January 1990, pp. 59–77.

[MORR68] Morris, R., "Scatter Storage Techniques," *Communications of the ACM*, Vol. 11, No. 1, January, 1968, pp. 38–84.

[MORR79] Morris, D., Ibben R.N., *The MU5 Computer System*, Springer-Verlag, New York, 1979.

[MORS80] Morse, S.P., Ravenel, B.W., Mazor, St., Pohlman, W.B., "Intel Microprocessors—8008 to 8086," *Computer*, Vol. 13, No. 10, October 1980, pp. 42–60.

[MOTO83] Motorola MC684511 Memory Management Unit, ADI-872-RI, Phoenix, April 1983.

[MOTO87] *Motorola MC68030 User's Manual*, Document MC68030UM/AD, Phoenix, 1987.

[MOTO89] *Motorola MC68040 User's Manual*, Document MC68040UM/AD, Phoenix 1989.

[MOTO90] *MC88100 RISC Microprocessor Users Manual*, Prentice Hall, Englewood Cliffs, New Jersey, 1990.

[MOTO90a]   *Motorola MC88200 Cache/Memory Management Unit User's Manual*, Second edition, Prentice-Hall, Englewood Cliffs, New Jersey.

[MOTO90b]   *Motorola MC68020 32-Bit Microprocessor User's Manual*, Third edition, Prentice-Hall, Englewood Cliffs, New Jersey, 1990.

[MOTO93]   *Motorola Power PC 601 RISC Microprocessor User's Manual*, Document MPC601 UM/AD, Phoenix, 1993.

[MURR90]   Murray, J.E., Hetherington, R.C., Salett, R.M., "VAX Instructions that Illustrate the Architectural Features of the VAX 9000 CPU," *Digital Technical Journal*, Vol. 2, No. 4, Fall 1990, pp. 25–42.

[NG91]   Ng, S.W., "Improving Disk Performance Via Latency Reduction," *IEEE Transactions on Computers*, Vol. 40, No. 1, January 1991, pp. 22–30.

[NOYC81]   Noyce, R.N., Hoff, M.E., "A History of Microproccssor Developmcnt at Intel," *IEEE Micro*, Vol. 1, No. 1, pp. 8–21.

[OCON93]   O'Connor, M.J., *Evaluating The Performance of Instruction Set Archiectures For Superscalar Processors*, Masters of Science Thesis, The University of Texas at Austin, August, 1993.

[OCON93a]   O'Connor, M.J., Personal Communications, 1993.

[OED85]   Oed, W., Lange, O., "On the Effective Bandwidth of Interleaved Memories in Vector Processor Systems," *IEEE Transactions on Computers*, Vol. C-34, No. 10, October 198S, pp. 949–957.

[OEHL90]   Oehler, R.R, Groves, R.D., "IBM RISC System/6000 Processor Architecture," *IBM Journal of Research and Development*, Vol. 34, No. 1, January 1990, pp. 23–36.

[ORGA72]   Organick, E.J., *The Multics System*, The MIT Press, Cambridge, Massachusetts, 1972.

[OUST85]   Ousterhour, J.K., et al., "A Trace-driven Analysis of the UNIX 4.2 BSD File System," *Proceedings of the Tenth ACM Symposium on Operating Systems Principles*, 1985, pp. 15–24.

[PARM72]   Parmelee, R.P., Peterson, T.I., Tillman, C.C., Hatfield, D.J., "Virtual Storage and Virtual Machine Concepts," *IBM Systems Journal*, Vol. 11, No. 2, 1972, pp. 99–117.

[PATT83]   Patterson, D.A., Garrison, P., Hill, M., Lipupis, C.N., Sipple, T., Van Dyke, K., "Architecture of a VLSI Instruction Cache for a RISC," *Proceedings 10th Annual Symposium on Computer Architecture*, 1983, pp. 108–116.

[PATT88]   Patterson, D.A., Gibson, G.A., Katz, H., "A Case for Redundant Arrays of Inexpensive Disks," *Proceedings ACM SIGMOD Conference*, Chicago, June 1988, pp. 109–116.

[PETE83]   Petersen, W.P., "Vector Fortran for Numerical Problems on CRAY-1," *Communications of the ACM*, Vol. 26, No. 11, pp. 1008–1021.

[PETE85]   Peterson, J.L., Silberschatz, A., *Operating System Concepts*, Addison-Wesley, Reading, Massachusetts, 1985.

[PIRT67]   Pirtle, M., "Intercommunication of Processors and Memory," *Proceedings of the FJCC*, 1967, pp. 626–633.

[POHM81]   Pohn, A.V., Smay, T.A., "Computer Memory Systems," *Computer*, Vol. 14, No. 10, October, 1981, pp. 93–110.

[POPP77]   Poppendieck, M, Desautles, D.J., "Memory Extension Techniques for Minicomputers," *Computer*, Vol. No. 5, May 1977, pp. 68–75.

[PRIC71]   Price, C.E., "Table Lookup Techniques," *ACM Computing Surveys*, Vol. 3, No. 2, June 1971, pp. 49–65.

[PRZY88]   Przybylski, S., Horowitz, M., Hennessy, J., "Performance Tradeoffs in Cache Design" *Proceedings 15th Annual International Symposium on Computer Architecture*, 1988, pp. 290–298.

[PRZY89]   Przybylski, S., Horowitz, M., Hennessy, J., "Characteristics of Performance-Optimal Multi-Level Cache Hierarchies," *16th Annual International Symposium on Computer Architecture*, 1989, pp. 114–121.

[PRZY90]   Prybylski, S. "The Performance Impact of Block Sizes and Fetch Strategies," *Proceedings 17th Annual International Symposium on Computer Architecture*, 1990, pp. 160–169.

[PRZY90a]   Przybylski, S., *Cache and Memory Hierarchy Design*, Morgan Kaufmann, San Mateo, California, 1990.

[PUZA85]   Puzak, T.R., *Analysis of Cache Replacement-Algorithms*, Ph.D. Dissertation, University of Massachusetts, 1985.

[RAMA77]   Ramamoorthy, C.V., Li, H.F., "Pipeline Architecture," *Computing Surveys*, Vol. 9, No. 1, pp. 61–102.

[RAND68]   Randell, B., Kuehner, C.J., "Dynamic Storage Allocation Systems," *Communications of the ACM*, Vol. 11, No. 5, May 1968, pp. 197–304.

[RAND69]   Randell, B., "A Note on Storage Fragmentation and Program Segmentation," *Communications of the ACM*, Vol. 12, No. 7, July 1969, pp. 365–369.

[RAO82]   Rao, G.S., "Technique for Minimizing Branch Delay Due to Incorrect Branch History Predictions," *IBM Technical Disclosure Bulletin*, Vol. 25, No. 1, June 1982, pp. 97–98.

[RASH87]   Rashid, R. Revanian, A., Young, M., Golub, D., Baron, R., Black, D. Bolosky, W., Chew, J., "Machine-Independent Virtual Memory Management for Paged Uniprocessor and Multiprocessor Architectures," *Second International Conference on Architectural Support for Programming Languages and Operating Systems*, October 1987, pp. 31–39.

[RAU91]   Rau, B.R., "Pseudo-randomly Interleaved Memory," *18th Annual International Symposium on Computer Architecture*, May 1991, pp. 74–83.

[REDD89]   Reddy, A.L.N., Banerjee, P., "An Evaluation of Multiple-Disk I/O Systems," *IEEE Transactions on Computers*, Vol. 38, No. 12, December 1989, pp. 1680–1590.

[REDD90]   Reddy, A.L.N., Banerjee, P., "A Study of I/O Behavior of Perfect Benchmarks on a Multiprocessor," *17th Annual International Symposium on Computer Architecture*, May 1990, pp. 312–321.

[RIGA84]   Riganati, J.P., Schneck, P.B., "Supercomputing," *Computer* Vol. 17, No. 10, October 1984, pp. 97–113.

[RISE72]   Riseman, E.M., Foster, C.C., "The Inhibition of Potential Parallelism by Conditional Jumps," *IEEE Transactions on Computers*, Vol. 21, No. 12, December 1972, pp. 1405–1411.

[ROBE90]   Roberts, D., Layman, T., Taylor, G., An ECL RISC Microprocessor Designed for Two Level Cache," *IEEE Compcon*, Spring 1990, pp. 228–231.

[ROSE69]   Rosen, Saul, "Electronic Computers: A Historical Survey," *Computing Surveys*, Vol., No. 1, March 1969, pp. 7–36.

[ROWL86]   Rowland, RE., "Systems Memory Cards, *IBM RT Personal Computer Technology*, IBM, Form NO. SA23-1057, 1986, pp. 18–20.

[SAAV93]   Saavedra, R.H., Smith, A.J., *Measuring Cache and TLB Performance and Their Effect on Benchmark Run Times*, Report No. UCB/CSD 93/767, University of California, Berkeley, August 1993.

[SALE86]   Salem, K., Garcia-Molina, H., "Disk Striping," *Proceedings IEEE Data Engineering Conference*, Los Angeles, February 1986.

[SARG86]   Sargent, M., Shoemaker, R.L., *The IBM Personal Computer, From the Inside Out*, Addison-Welsey, Reading, Massachusetts, 1986.

[SATY81]   Satyanarayanan, M., Bhandarkar, D., "Design Trade-offs in VAX-11 Translation Buffer Organization," *Computer*, Vol. 14, No. 12, December 1981, pp. 103–111.

[SCHW89]   Schwartz, R.J., "The Design and Development of a Dynamic Program Behavior Measurement Tool for the Intel 8086/88," *Computer Architecture News*, Vol. 17, No. 4, June 1989, pp. 82–94.

[SCHA91]   Schauser, K.E., Asonovic, K., Patterson, D. Frank, E.H., *Evaluation of a 'Stall" Cache: An Efficient Restricted On-Chip Instruction Cache*, Report No. UCB/CSD 91/#641, July 30, 1991, University of California, Berkeley.

[SCHR71]   Schroeder, M.D., "Performance of the GE-645 Associative Memory While Multics is in Operation," *ACM Workshop on System Performance Evaluation*, April 1971, pp. 227–245.

[SENZ65]   Senzig, D.N., Smith, R.V., "Computer Organization for Array Processing," *AFIPS*, Vol. 27, No. 1, 1965, pp. 117–128.

[SHI86]   Shires, G., "80386 Cache Design," *80386, A Collection of Article Reprints*, Intel Corporation, Santa Clara, California, Order Number 231737-001, 1986, pp. 44–49.

[SIEW82]   Siewiorek, D.P., Swarz, R.S., *The Theory of Practice of Reliable System Design*, Digital Press, Bedford, Massachusetts, 1982.

[SHEM66]   Shemer, J.E. Shippel, G.A., "Statistical Analysis of Paged and Segmented Computer Systems," *IEEE Transactions on Electronic Computers*, Vol. EC-15, No. 6, December 1966, pp. 855-863.

[SIMP86]   Simpson, R.O., "The IBM RT Personal Computer," *Byte*, Extra Edition, 1986, pp. 43–76.

[SITE80]   Sites, R., "Operating Systems and Computer Architecture," in [STON80], pp. 591–643.

[SLAT91]   Slater, M., "PA Workstations Set Price/Performance Records," *Microprocessor Report*, Vol. 5, No. 6, April 1991, pp. 8–12.

[SLAT91a]   Slater, M., Case B, "MIPS R4000 Sets Performance Records," *Microprocessor Report*, Vol. 5, October 2, 1991, pp. 6–13.

[SLAT92]   Slater, M. "Intel Begins Gradual P5 Unveiling," *Microprocessor Report*, Vol. 6, No. 12, September 16, 1992, pp. 1–8.

[SMIT78]   Smith, A.J., "Sequential Program Prefetching in Memory Hierarchies," *Computer,* Vol.11, No 12, December 1978, pp. 7–21.

[SMIT78a]   Smith, A.J., "A Comparative Study of Set Associative Memory Mapping Algorithms and Their Use for Cache and Main Memory," *IEEE Transactions on Software Engineering*, Vol. SE-4, No. 2, March 1978, pp. 121–130.

[SMIT79]   Smith, A.J., "Characterizing the Storage Process and its Effect on the Update of Main Memory by Write Through," *Journal of the Association for Computing Machinery*, Vol. 26, No. 1, January 1979, pp. 6–27.

[SMIT82]   Smith, A.J., "Cache Memories," *Computing Surveys*, September 1982, Vol. 14, No. 3, pp. 473–530.

[SMIT85]   Smith, A.J., "Disk Cache-Miss Ratio Analysis and Design Considerations," *ACM Transactions on Computer Systems*, Vol. 3, No. 3, August 1985, pp. 161–203.

[SMIT86]   Smith, A.J., "Bibliography and Readings on CPU Cache Memories and Related Topics," *Computer Architecture News*, Vol. 14, No. 1, January 1986, pp 22–42.

[SMIT87]   Smith, A.J., "Line (Block) Size Choice for CPU Cache Memories," *IEEE Translations on Computers*, C-36, 9, September 1987, pp. 1063–1075.

[SMIT87a]   Smith, A.J., "Cache Memory Design: An Evolving Art," *IEEE Spectrum*, December 1987, pp. 40–44.

[SMIT82]   Smith, I.E., "Decoupled Access/Execute Computer Architecture," *9th Annual Symposium on Computer Architecture*, 1982, pp. 113–119.

[SMIT83]   Smith, J.E., Goodman, J.R, "A Study on Instruction Organizations and Replacement Policies," *Proceedings 10th Annual Symposium on Computer Architecture*, Stockholm, June 1983, pp. 132–137.

[SMIT85]   Smith, J.E., Pleszlmn, A.R., "Implementation of Precise Interrupts in Pipelined Processors," *Proceedings 12th Annual International Symposium on Computer Architecture*, June 1985, pp. 36–44.

[SMIT85a]   Smith, J.E., Goodman, J.R., "Instruction Cache Replacement Policies and Organizations," *IEEE Transactions on Computers*, Vol. C-34, No. 3, March 1985, pp. 234–241.

[SMIT89]   Smith, M.D., Johnson, M., Horowitz, M.A., "Limits on Multiple Instruction Issue," *Third International Conference on Architectural Support For Programming Languages and Operating Systems*, 1989, pp. 290–302.

[SOHI87]   Sohi, G.S., Vajapeyam, S., "Instruction Issue Logic for High-performance, Interruptable Pipeline Processors," *Proceedings 14th An-*

nual International Symposium on Computer Architecture, 1987, pp. 27–34.

[SRIN83] Srini, V.P., Asenjo, J.F., "Analysis of the Cray-IS Architecture," *Proceedings 10th Annual Symposium on Computer Architecture*, June 1983, pp. 194–206.

[STEE89] Steenkiste, P., "The Impact of Code Density on Instruction Cache Performance," *Proceedings 16th Annual International Symposium on Computer Architecture*, 1989, pp. 252–259.

[STEN90] Stenström, P., "A Survey of Cache Coherence Schemes for Multiprocessors," *Computer*, Vol. 23, No. 6, June 1990, pp. 12–24.

[STEP731] Stephenson, C.M., "Control of a Variable Configuration Pipelined Arithmetic Unit," *Proceedings Eleventh Annual Allerton Conference On Circuit and System Theory*, October 1973, pp. 558–567.

[STEV81] Stevens, L.D., "The Evolution of Magnetic Storage," *IBM Journal of Research and Development*, Vol. 25, No. 5, September 1981, pp. 663–675.

[STON80] Stone, H., (Editor), *Introduction to Computer Architecture*, Second Edition, Science Research Associates, Inc. Chicago, 1980.

[STON90] Stone, H., *High Performance Computer Architecture*, Second Edition, Addison-Wesley, Reading, Massachusetts, 1990.

[STON93] Stone, H., *High-Performance Computer Architecture*, Third Edition, Addison-Wesley, Reading, Massachussets, 1993.

[STRE78] Strecker, W.D., VAX-11/780: A Virtual Address Extension to the DEC PDP-11 Family," *Proceedings of the National Computer Conference*, AFIPS Press, Montvale, New Jersey, pp. 967–980.

[STRE83] Strecker, W.D., "Transient Behavior of Cache Memories, *ACM Transactions on Computer Systems*, Vol. 1, No. 4, November 1983, pp. 281–293.

[SUN87] SPARC program reference manual, pp. 107.

[SUN88] *The SPARC Reference MMU Architecture, Revision 1.2*, Sun Microsystems, Mountain View, California, 1988.

[SWAR72] Swartzlander, E.E., *The Inner Product Computer*, Ph.D. Dissertation, The University of Southern California, June 1975.

[TANG76] Tang, C.K., "Cache System Design in the Tightly Coupled Multiprocessor System, *National Computer Conference*, AFIPS, Vol. 45, 1976, pp. 749–753.

[TANG88] Tang, Ju-ho, Davidson, E.S., "An Evaluation of Cray-1 and Cray X-MP Performance on Vectorizable Livermore Fortran Kernels, *International Supercomputer Conference*, 1988, pp. 510–518.

[TANN84] Tanenbaum, A.S., *Structured Computer Organization*, Prentice Hall, Englewood Cliffs, New Jersey, 1984.

[TEX65] Texas Instruments Incorporated, *TIAC Model 8704 Programmers Reference Manual*, 1965, pp. 11–1.

[TEX91] Texas Instruments Incorporatcd, *MOS Memory Data Book*, 1990.

[THIE87] Thiebaut, D., Stone, H.S., "Footprints in the Cache," *ACM Trans-*

actions on Computer Systems, Vol. 5, No. 4, November 1987, 305–329.

[THOR64]   Thornton, J.E., "Parallel Operation in the Control Data 6600," *AFIPS Conference Proceedings*, Vol. 26, Part II, 1964, pp. 33–40.

[THOR70]   Thornton, J.E., *Design of a Computer: The Control Data 6600*, Scott, Foresman, Glenview, Illinois, 1970.

[TJAD70]   Tjaden, G.S., Flynn, M.J., "Dectection and Parallel Execution of Independent Instructions," *IEEE Transactions on Computers*, Vol. C-l9, No. 10, October 1970, pp. 889–895.

[TOMA67]   Tomasulo, R.M., "An Efficient Algorithm for Exploiting Multiple Arith metic Units," *IBM Journal*, Vol. 11, No. 1, January 1967, pp. 25–33.

[TOPH88]   Topham, N.P., Omondi, A., Ibbett, R.N., "Conventional Pipelined Computers," *Journal of Supercomputing*, Vol. 1, No. 4, March 1977, pp. 353–393.

[TRON93]   Trong, H.C., Day, M., "Interrupt Handling for Out-of-Order Execution Processors," *IEEE Transactions on Computers*, Vol. 42, No. 1, January 1993, pp. 122–127.

[TUCK86]   Tucker, S.G., "The IBM 3090 System: An Overview," *IBM Systems Journal*, Vol. 25, No. 1, 1986, pp. 4–19.

[ULLA93]   Ullah, N., Holle, M., "The MC88110 Implementation of Precise Exceptions in a Superscalar Architecture," *Computer Architecture News*, Vol. 21, No. 1, March 1993, pp. 15–25.

[ULLM82]   Ullman, J.D., *Principles of Database Systems, Second Edition*, Computer Science Press, Rockville, Maryland, 1982.

[UNWA94]   Unwala I.H., Cragon, H.G., "A Study of MIPS Programs, *Computer Architecture News*, Vol. 22, No. 5, December 1994, pp. 30–40.

[VAND89]   van de Goor, A.J., *Computer Architecture and Design*, Addison-Wesley, Reading, Massachussetts, 1989.

[VANN8]   Van Name, M.L., "Compaq Flexes Its Muscles," *BYTE*, Vol. 13, No. 2, February 1988, pp. 117–122.

[VASU88]   Vasudeva, A., "A Case for Disk Array Storage Systems," *Proceedings of the Reliability Conference*, Santa Clara, California, 1988.

[VENK90]   Venkatramani, K., *A Semantics-Based Approach for the Design and Verification of Concurrent Processors*, Ph.D. Dissertation, The University of Texas, Austin, August 1990.

[VLOD81]   Voldman, J., Hoevel, L.W., "The Software-Cache Connection," *IBM Journal of Research and Development*, Vol. 25, No. 6, November 1981, pp. 877-893.

[VOLD83]   Voldman, J., Mandelbrot, B., Hoevel, L.W., Knight, J., Rosenfeld, P., "Fractal Nature of Software-Cache Interaction," *IBM Journal of Research and Development*, Vol. 27, No. 2, March 1983, pp. 161–170.

[WAKE89]   Wakerly, J.F., *Microcomputer Architecture and Programming The 68000 Family*, John Wiley and Sons, New York, 1989.

[WALK92]   Walker, W.A., *A Taxonomy of Interrupt Processing Strategies in*

Pipelined Microprocessors, Masters Thesis, University of Texas at Austin, Decmber 1992.

[WALL64] Wallace, C.E., "A Suggestion for a Fast Multiplier," *IEEE Transactions on Electronic Computers*, Vol. EC-13, No. 1, February 1964, pp. 14–17.

[WANG89] Wang, W-H, Baer, J-L, Levy, H., "Organization and Performance of a Two-Level Virtual-Real Cache Hierarchy," *Annual International Symposium on Computer Architecture*, 1989, pp. 140–148.

[WANG93] Wang, C-J., Emmett, F., "Implementing Precise Interrupts in Pipelined RISC Processors," *IEEE Micro*, Vol. No. 8, August 1993, pp. 36–43.

[WARD90] Ward, S.A., Halstead, R.H. Jr., *Computation Structures*, The MIT Press, Cambridge, Massachusetts, 1990.

[WEBE89] Weber, W-D., Gupta, A., "Analysis of Cache Invalidation Patterns in Multiprocessors, *Third International Conference on Architectural Support for Progamming Languages and Operating Systems*, pp. 243–256.

[WEBS63] *Webster's Dictionary, Ninth New Collegiate Dictionary*, G & C. Merriam Company, Springfield, Massachusetts, 1983.

[WEDEL75] Wedel, D., "Fortran for the Texas Instruments ASC System," *Programming Languages and Compilers for Vector and Parallel Machine*, Goddard Institute for Space Studies, New York, March 18–19, 1975, pp. 219–233.

[WEIC84] Weicker, R.P., "Dhrystone: A Synthetic Systems Programming Benchmark," *Communications of the ACM*, Vol. 27, No. 10, October 1984, pp. 1013–1030.

[WEIS84] Weiss, S., "Instruction Issue Logic for Pipelined Supercomputers," *11th Annual Symposium on Computer Architecture Conference*, 1984, pp. 110–118.

[WEIS84a] Weiss, S., Smith, J.E., "Instruction Issue Logic for Pipelined Supercomputers," *IEEE Transactions on Computers*, Vol. C-33, No. 11, November 1984, pp. 1013–1022.

[WEIS92] Weiss, R, "Superscalar SPARC Executes As Many As Three Instructions in Parallel," *EDN*, June 4, 1992, pp. 89–108.

[WEST93] Weste, N.H.E., Eshraghian, K., *Principles of CMOS VLSI Design*, Addison-Wesley, Reading, Massachusetts, 1993.

[WHEE92] Wheeler, B., Bershad, B.N., "Consistency Management for Virtually Indexed Caches," *Fifth International Conference on Architectural Support for Programming Languages and Operating Systems*, October 1992, pp. 124-136.

[WILK53] Wilkes, M.V., "The Best Way to Design an Automatic Calculating Machine," in *Report of the Manchester University Computer Inaugural Conference*, 1951. (Not published until 1953), pp. 16–18.

[WILK65] Wilkes, M.V., "Slave Memories and Dynamic Storage Allocation," *IEEE Transactions on Electronic Computers*, Vol. 14, No. 2, April 1965, pp. 270–271.

[WILK68]   Wilkes, M.V., *Time-Sharing Computer Systems*, American Elsevier, New York, 1968.

[WILS92]   Wilson, R., Lammers, D., "Rambus Lets Loose Fast DRAM Channel", *Electronic Engineering Times*, March 16, 1992, p. 1.

[WU93]   Wu, C.E., Hsu, Y., Liu, Y.-H., "A Quantitative Evaluation of Cache Types for High-Performance Computer Systems", *IEEE Transactions on Computers*, Vol. 42, No. 10, pp. 1154–1162.

[WOLM65]   Wolman, "A Fixed Optimum Cell-Size for Records of Various Lengths," *Journal of the ACM*, Vol. 12, No. 1, January 1965, pp. 53–70.

[WOOD86]   Wood, D.A., Eggers, S.J., Givson, G., Hill, M.D., Pendleton, J.M., Ritchie, S. A., Taylor, G.S., Katz, R.H., Patterson, D.A., "An In-Cache Address Translation Mechanism," *13th Annual Symposium on Computer Architecture Conference*, 1986, pp. 358–365.

[YANG93]   Yang, Q., "Introducing a New New Cache Design into Vector Computers," *IEEE Transactions on Computers*, Vol. 42, No. 12, December 1993, pp. 1411–1424.

[YEN85]   Yen, W.C., Yen, D.W.L., Fu, K-F., "Data Coherence Problem in a Multicache System," *IEEE Transactions on Computers*, Vol. C-34, No. 1, January 1985, pp. 56–85.

Subject Index

Processors Index

Trademarks

AMD2900, AND K5 are trademarks of Advanced Micro Devices.

470/v6 is a trademark of Amdahl Corporation.

UNIX is a trademark of AT&T Bell Laboratories.

CDC6600, CDC7600, and STAR are trademarks of Control Data Corporation.

Deskpro is a trademark of Compaq Computers.

Cray X-MP, Cray Y-MP. and Cray-1 are trademarks of Cray Research.

Alpha, Unibus, PDP-11, VAX, VAX 11/780, VAX 8600, VAX 8800, and VAX 9000 are trademarks of Digital Equipment Corporation.

Apollo DN100, DN300, and Precision Architecture are trademarks of Hewelett-Packard Company.

Future Bus is a trademark of the Institute of Electrical and Electronic Engineers.

IBM, 350 RAMAC, 801, 3090, 7030 Stretch, 7040, 7084, 9337, AS/400, OS/2, RT-PC, PowerPC, PowerPC 601, PowerPC 606, RS/6000, S/360, S/360/85, S/360/91, S/360/168, S/360/195, S/370, S/370/165/, S/370/168, S/370/195, S/38 are trademarks of International Business Machines Corporation.

8080, 8086, i386, i486, i860, P6, and Pentium are trademarks of Intel Corporation.

Lotus 1-2-3 is a trademark of Lotus Development Corporation.

NuBus is a trademark of Massachusetts Institute of Technology.

MS-DOS is a trademark of Microsoft Corporation.

R2000, R3000, R4000, R6000, T5 are trademarks of MIPS Computer Corporation.

MC68000, MC68020, MC68030, MC68040, MC68851, MC88200, and VMEbus are trademarks of Motorola, Inc.

Multiflow is a trademark of Multiflow Computer Corporation.

NEC-SX is a trademark of NEC Corporation.

MIPS-X is a trademark of Stanford University.

SPARC, and SPARC II are trademarks of Sun Microsystems.

Advanced Scientific Computer, and TI ASC are trademarks of Texas Instruments Corporation.

Connection Machine is a trademark of Thinking Machines Corporation.

B5000 is a trademark of Unisys Corporation.

SPUR is a trademark of the University of California, Berkeley.

ILLIAC-IV is a trademark of the University of Illinois.

Dorodo, and Sigma 7 are trademarks of Xerox Corporation.

Z800, Z8000, Z80,000 are trademarks of Zilog Corporation.

Axioms for Implementation

5 Structural dependencies are resolved by replication of resources, employing a faster resource, or by introducing delays.

> Replication of resources is similar to spatial concurrency, and examples are found in split caches and multiple execution units. Examples of a faster resource are found in a unified cache that meets the dual access requirement of a pipelined processor and the use of dedicated ALU's for effective address calculations and execution as found in a pipelined processor. Delays can be scheduled by software or hardware to eliminate, for example, issuing an operation into a execution unit that is busy.

6 True dependencies cannot be completely eliminated, they must be detected and steps taken to prevent the program from being logically incorrect with the smallest time penalty.

> Detection and resolution of true dependencies can be either static (by software) or dynamic (by hardware) in most cases. Introduction of no-ops is an example of static, while Scoreboarding is an example of dynamic. If the cause of the true dependency is not resolved in deterministic time, hardware solutions must be used.